Goodman

Property of
Mrs. Eleanore Goodman
1512 N Ricketts
Sherman Texas.

Not yours
Not yours
Either!

INTRODUCTION TO GENERAL PSYCHOLOGY

INTRODUCTION TO

ESTON JACKSON ASHER · JOSEPH TIFFIN
Purdue University

D. C. HEATH

GENERAL
PSYCHOLOGY

FREDERIC B. KNIGHT
Late of Purdue University

AND COMPANY BOSTON

Preface

THIS TEXT is designed to give the beginning student an introduction to the science of psychology. It is felt that such an introduction is basic both for students who go on to other courses in psychology and for those whose only formal contact with the subject is confined to the first course. It is the conviction of the authors that the latter group in particular should learn that psychology is a science, wherein it is a science, what the psychologist studies, how he studies psychological phenomena, and something of the facts and principles of the science. This does not preclude an application of these facts and principles to everyday problems, but it definitely recognizes that students cannot, after a one or two semester course in psychology, qualify as self-therapists, mental examiners, personnel consultants, child guidance experts, or psychological practitioners. If psychology is to contribute to a student's general cultural education or prepare him for acceptable service in business, industry, and the professions, it must do so as a scientific study, the science of human behavior and experience.

In preparing this text, which is based on our earlier *Psychology of Normal People*, we have tried not only to bring the previous book up to date and to remedy certain shortcomings in it, but to give a more comprehensive coverage of the topics of general psychology. To this end we have added three new chapters (II, III, and V) and have rewritten five others (I, IV, VII, IX, and X). Two chapters (II and XV) that appeared in the previous book have been omitted as chapters, but significant portions of each have been included elsewhere in the book. The remaining chapters have been revised by the deletion of obsolete material, the transfer of topics to other chapters, and the inclusion of new topics and recent research findings. The number of chapters has been reduced to fourteen and the chapters are presented in an order which we feel will prove to be more satisfactory both to teachers and students than the one followed in the earlier editions.

Contents

ATTENTION 267

EMOTION 297

THINKING 339

IMAGINATION 366

INTELLIGENCE 395

ABILITIES AND APTITUDES 420

PERSONALITY AND ADJUSTMENT 455

Figures

Tables

INTRODUCTION TO GENERAL PSYCHOLOGY

INTRODUCTION

1

THE SUBJECT MATTER OF PSYCHOLOGY

In the chapter titles of textbooks of psychology one finds such words as *learning*, *thinking*, *emotion*, *motivation*, *perception*, *attention*, and *intelligence*. These words have one thing in common: they all refer to kinds of human activity or behavior. Learning, for example, is a type of human activity; it is something that a person does. The list of terms could be almost indefinitely expanded by the addition of such words as *remembering*, *forgetting*, *dreaming*, *working*, *playing*, *studying*, *reading*, *sneezing*, *fighting*, *loving*, *laughing*, *crying*, *looking*, *listening*, and so on through the entire repertoire of human behavior.

Some of these activities are very specific and quite simple as compared with others, though all of them can be broken down into simpler components. Sneezing, for example, is a relatively simple kind of behavior. Perception is much more complex; it covers such activities as sensing (seeing, touching, hearing) and comprehending the world about us.

Several of these activities may occur together as parts of still larger units of behavior. Large units of behavior in which several separate acts or responses are joined or integrated are called *adjustments*. Thus the listening, reading, attending, reciting, remembering, forgetting, and the other more incidental acts in which one engages or might engage in a classroom situation may be designated as a classroom adjustment. The reader may like to list some of the separate responses that are involved in home adjustments, school adjustments, family adjustments, marital adjustments, occupational adjustments, and religious adjustments. Many other kinds of adjustments might be listed. For example, one may speak of an individual's adjustment to people, to minority groups, to the demands of society, or to life. The individual's adjustment in each case is the combination of his reactions or ways of acting in each given situation. The sum total of these adjustments and the separate activities or responses into which they may be analyzed we designate as human behavior. It is this that constitutes the subject matter of psychology.

Definitions of Psychology

Psychology has been defined as the field which deals with human nature or human activity in general (16); as the science of the activities of the individual (17); as that branch of science which studies the behavior of an organism in its environment (4); as the science of experience and behavior (11); the science that studies the responses which living individuals make to their environment (12). These definitions are different ways of saying the same thing. To study human nature is to study human behavior and experience. To study human behavior and experience is to study human adjustments (reactions of individuals to their environment) and the activities into which these adjustments can be analyzed.

All men and women have some interest in human behavior, at least in their own behavior or that of their immediate associates. This interest has led some of them to such foolish practices as the consulting of astrologers (who assert a connection between human behavior and the stars), phrenologists (who claim to analyze character from the shape and the "bumps" of the head), and fortunetellers (who claim to predict behavior by means of cards, tea leaves, or lines of the hand). But fortunately this interest has led many to more valuable efforts to gain a better understanding of themselves and others. This is indicated by the popularity of books and articles on such subjects as the development of character and personality, making a success of marriage, and the prevention of crime and delinquency. There is further evidence of it in the growing number of consulting psychologists who find occupation in our larger cities, and in the increasing demand for psychologists in our larger school systems, in hospitals, and in a rapidly growing number of industries.

Interest in psychological problems has been greatly stimulated by recent advances in psychology, but it is by no means new. From the earliest times man has felt the need of knowing more about himself. The Greeks felt this need so deeply that they wrote above the Delphic Oracle "Know thyself"; and no teachers among them were more popular than those who promised youth understanding of human nature and aid in self-improvement. The literature of other ancient peoples, also, indicates a profound interest in these matters. All language is replete with psychological concepts. If a large sample of words is taken at random from an English dictionary, nearly half will refer directly or indirectly to psychological ideas: love, hate, ambition, worry, dreams, wishes, attitudes, and emotions.

Because of the universality of the interest in human behavior, everyone gains, as a matter of course, considerable knowledge of psychological phenomena. Infants learn to interpret the responses and attitudes of others and to modify their behavior accordingly. Wider contacts add to the knowledge acquired in the nursery. Later, the reading of fiction, biography, history, and current news increases our understanding of human nature and of its problems. The beginning student of psychology, therefore, has already accumulated a fund of information about behavior.

Naïve Psychology

An examination of this information, however, reveals that while some of it is essentially correct, some of it is incorrect and should more properly be designated as misinformation. This is the conclusion to be drawn from the data in Table I, which shows the scores made by 556 students in an elementary psychology course on a true-false "Common Psychological Conceptions" test (6). The test consisted of 90 statements like the following:

T F   1. Women are equal to men in intelligence.

T F   2. Some animals are as intelligent as the average man.

T F   3. The behavior of left-handed individuals is nearly always more erratic than that of right-handed individuals.

T F   4. Psychologists are able to pick the specific job for which an individual is best suited.

T F   5. Criminologists are able to determine the likelihood of criminal behavior by an analysis of physical characteristics.

T F   6. Dishonesty is indicated by inability of a person to look another in the eye.

T F   7. Long hands indicate an artistic nature.

T F   8. Children of average intelligence can be born of parents both of whom are feeble-minded.

T F   9. One's conscience is an inborn trait of character.

T F   10. Criminals are rarely above average in intelligence.

T F   11. Red is especially exciting to cattle.

T F   12. It is possible to make a person turn around by staring at his back.

Table I

Scores of Elementary Psychology Students on a "Common Psychological Conceptions" Test

Scores	87–89	84–86	81–83	78–80	75–77	72–74	69–71	66–68
No. of Students	1	2	6	29	70	96	110	83
Scores	63–65	60–62	57–59	54–56	51–53	48–50	45–47	42–44
No. of Students	60	34	34	15	12	2	1	1

The scores ranged from 43 to 88 correct. One student answered 47 of the items incorrectly. The median score was 69.5; that is, half of the students missed 21 or more of the items. Some of the items were answered correctly by everyone. Other items were missed by as many as 70 per cent of the students.

A Comparison of Naïve and Scientific Psychology

What is the explanation of the facts in Table I? Why do we have so much misinformation about human nature? Much of this kind of information about behavior may be labeled as common-sense or naïve psychology in contrast to scientific knowledge. A description of the defects and limitations of naïve psychology will throw some light on the question asked at the beginning of this paragraph, and point up the over-all adequacy of scientific knowledge in contrast to common-sense knowledge.

(1) Naïve psychology is uncritical of its problems. One of our leading newspapers once published an article entitled "Why Men Prefer Blondes," which was an example of uncritical consideration of a problem. The writer simply assumed that men do prefer blondes. If a psychologist had undertaken a study of the subject, he would have begun by attempting to discover what percentage of men actually do prefer blondes and what percentage prefer brunettes. Undoubtedly he would have found that some men prefer blondes, others brunettes; that still others prefer at one time a blonde and at another time a brunette; and even that some men are unable to decide which they prefer. Only after gathering data about the preferences of men would he have attempted to explain them. Similarly, before attempting to explain the alleged superiority of women in making intuitive judgments, he

would first determine whether they actually are superior in this respect. In general, we need to establish facts before attempting to explain them.

(2) Naïve psychology indulges in hasty generalizations. We make a hasty generalization when, on the basis of a few instances, we make a statement regarding all instances. For example, to say that all men prefer blondes because the first few questioned indicate a preference for blondes would be a hasty generalization. A distinguishing mark of a trained thinker is the ability to restrain the tendency to rush to conclusions. Common sense, generalizing on the basis of a few cases, frequently produces two contradictory generalizations. For instance, it says, "Absence makes the heart grow fonder"; but it also says, "Out of sight, out of mind." The scientific psychologist cannot sanction attempts of this sort to offset one hasty generalization with another. Instead of jumping from dubious statement to dubious statement, he attempts to discover the kernel of truth in each of the opposing statements. This procedure leads him to seek the conditions under which the alleged situations exist. For example, he asks, "Under what conditions does absence make the heart grow fonder?" By virtue of his discoveries he modifies the original statement into a less comprehensive but more accurate one. He finds, perhaps, that absence increases affection *if* the affection already rests on some substantial foundation.

(3) Naïve psychology lacks organization. Every science seeks to organize its observed facts. It makes facts intelligible through inclusion in a system. Take, for example, the saying, "Unworthy offspring brag most of their ancestry." Assuming for the moment that this statement is true, we wish to know further why it is true. By relating it to our knowledge of the general tendency of man to seek social recognition and to compensate for feelings of inferiority, we can make it intelligible; for those who are successful do not need to bolster their self-esteem and bid for social recognition by bragging of their ancestors, since they are not likely to suffer from feelings of inferiority.

The illustration just given indicates the nature of scientific explanation. An event is explained when it is properly related to other events. The individual timbers of a building cannot stand alone; yet, joined together, they form a solid structure. In the same way, no single event in isolation is intelligible; it becomes so when related to other events. We cannot explain any event or condition until we see how it fits into our general body of knowledge and beliefs. Hence science is frequently defined as a body of organized knowledge.

(4) Naïve psychology lacks an exact terminology. The lack of an exact terminology in a science is a serious handicap. If men are to

cooperate in the development of a science, they must be able to understand each other easily. They therefore need an exact language. Unfortunately, psychologists, like other scientists, have not completely
succeeded in meeting this need. Considerable progress has been made,
however, and when scientific psychologists use terms that do not have
definite meanings, they define them as clearly as possible to avoid
ambiguity. In the rough approximations of naïve psychology, no such
need is recognized. For example, until mental diseases were studied
scientifically, the term *insanity* was a glittering generality which
covered many different kinds of mental breakdown, some as different
from others as typhoid fever from yellow fever.

(5) Naïve psychology possesses no technique of research. Science
is fundamentally an outgrowth of the effort to discover how things came
to be as they are. Such knowledge frequently enables us to remake
things as we desire them to be. In physics, for example, we attempt
to learn more about physical phenomena and to extend our control over
them. Similarly, in the field of psychology we make a systematic effort
to increase our knowledge and control of human nature. The *deliberate*
effort to do this is perhaps the sharpest distinction between naïve and
scientific psychology. As soon as we seek knowledge systematically,
we are no longer naïve; we are scientific, and aware that our present
knowledge is insecure or inadequate.

THE AIMS OF PSYCHOLOGY

The basic aim of any science is the discovery or determination of the
principles and laws that govern its subject matter. Psychology has
this aim in common with other sciences. It seeks to discover the
principles and laws that govern human behavior. It does not stop here,
however. The psychologist, as a scientist, wishes to discover the
principles and laws which govern human behavior, because, in the final
analysis, he is interested in understanding, predicting, and controlling
human behavior. While individual psychologists may concentrate
upon "fact finding" and may even deny any interest in applying the
facts that are discovered, psychologists in general are very much interested in the use of these facts in solving problems which involve human
reactions and adjustments in schools, in industries, in hospitals, and
in the myriad situations which arise in everyday living.

It must be recognized, however, that this practical aim of contributing
to the solution of the problems of human adjustment is secondary to

and depends for its ultimate success upon the attainment of the basic aim of the science, namely, the discovery of the facts and principles of human behavior. The need for answers to problems of child training, marital relations, education, occupational adjustments, and human relations in industry, regardless of how pressing it may be, does not alter the fact that the basic aim of psychology as a science is the discovery and formulation of principles and laws. To abandon this basic objective in favor of some solution to the immediate problems which does not contribute to the over-all task of understanding the dynamics of behavior is to abandon the scientific approach to the solution of these problems.

Understanding Human Behavior

Two kinds of facts are needed for understanding behavior. One must have, first, a factual description of the behavior (adjustment) itself and, second, a description of the antecedent and concomitant conditions which lead to or produce the behavior. The first is related to finding out *what* the individual does or *how* he reacts. The second is related to finding out *why* the individual acts as he does.

The first requirement is a factual description of the behavior. A factual description is not an evaluative or judgmental description. A child is observed to put his hands against another child's chest and push, so that the other child falls down. This is a factual statement of what was observed. It does not say that the behavior was bad, or that the child was bad or mean, or that he should be treated in such and such a fashion, or that his parents should be reprimanded for permitting him to push other children about. All such statements are evaluative and voice the observer's disapproval of what the child did. A factual description does not say that the child was aggressive or engaged in an aggressive act. Such a statement goes beyond the observed facts. To call the behavior of the child an aggressive act implies that the act (pushing in this case) took place because the child is aggressive, a fact which is not yet established.

The importance of a factual description of the behavior in this case becomes clear when one looks for its causes. It is one thing to look for the *why* of the "pushing down" behavior and quite a different thing to look for the *why* of an aggressive act. A search for the cause or causes of the "pushing down" behavior may reveal that the child has been observed to act in this fashion on fifteen previous occasions over a period of three months, that three other children have been the victims of these acts, and that in each case the child acted in this fashion after another child had taken something from him or had refused to let him participate in what was going on. The observer at this point may hypothesize that the first child is aggressive and he may proceed to look for other acts (biting, kicking, kissing, embracing) which fit and do not fit the hypothesis. If subsequent observations fit the hypothesis, he may at this point be said to have established the fact that the original act (pushing) was a part of a larger pattern of habitual behavior to which he may assign the label aggressive behavior. In so doing, he has given us some understanding of the original act of pushing, but has now created a new problem: namely, why the child is aggressive or why he has this pattern of behavior.

Pursuing this problem, the investigator recalls that each act of the pattern occurred or seemed to be provoked when the child had something taken from him or when he was not permitted to have something that he wanted. Further observation and study of the child's behavior may establish the fact that aggressive acts occurred when the child was "frustrated" or thwarted. This fact may suggest to the investigator that frustration leads to or produces aggressiveness in some form in people in general. In effect the investigator is willing at this point to hazard the guess (hypothesis) that what he has found to be true of one person's behavior may be true for other people; that people in general will be found to be essentially alike with respect to this kind of behavior. The student may wish to suggest what further investigations would be necessary to check this hypothesis.

These further investigations may reveal that, in general, people in our culture react to frustrations by acts of aggression; that these acts are essentially retaliatory in nature; that people perform such acts only when they are threatened, but that individuals differ from one another with respect to the conditions (people and things) which they regard as threatening and with respect to the kinds of retaliatory responses they will make to such threatening conditions. The investigator is now in a position, assuming that these facts have been verified, to formulate a general statement to the effect that "aggressive acts, essentially retaliatory in nature, occur in people in our culture when they perceive themselves to be threatened." In effect this statement asserts that people in our culture are in a general way alike with respect to a particular kind of behavior. This kind of statement is called a principle or law. It is a verbal statement of the way a certain class of events (human behavior) consistently and uniformly occur.

Predicting Human Behavior

The stated relationship between "perceived threat" and "retaliatory behavior" in this principle makes it possible to *predict* that people in general or any single person will react to perceived threats by aggressive acts which are essentially retaliatory in nature. It does not say what will be perceived by a particular individual as a threat, or what kind of retaliatory reaction any particular person will make. It was pointed out above that the investigations of this problem revealed that individuals were found to differ with regard to these points while remaining alike with respect to the general relationship between the two variables, aggression and frustration. In effect the investigations revealed the presence of another kind of variable that must be taken into account if this general principle is to be used in predicting a particular individual's behavior. In order to predict the specific form of aggression in a particular person, one would have to know how the person has acted on previous occasions, what condition he is in at the moment, what conditions he has perceived as threatening in the past, and what the circumstances are at the moment. In short, one would have to know the person and his environment.

Lewin's behavior formula (10). The problem of prediction in this example and the prediction of behavior in general will be clarified considerably if we let certain symbols stand for the variables involved and state the relationships between these variables in the form of an equation. Let E stand for the environmental conditions (persons or things) which the individual may perceive as threatening. Let P stand for the person, and B stand for the behavior (aggressive act). The relationships between these variables are given in the equation: $B = f(PE)$. In general terms this equation states that behavior (B) is a function (f) of a person (P) interacting with or responding to his environment (E). This equation lays particular emphasis upon the point that P and E are dynamically interrelated. Environmental conditions affect P or stimulate P to react in certain ways. On the other hand, P may react in such a way as to change the environmental conditions. At the same time, each reaction by P effects certain changes in P. A given stimulus provokes a response in a given person. This response has the effect of changing the person so that the same stimulus (or what appears to an outside observer to be the same stimulus) may fail to elicit the same response in this person on some subsequent occasion. This is seen in the example of a baby and a candle flame. A baby (P_1) sees a candle flame (E_1), reaches for it, and touches it. On subsequent occasions the sight of the flame does not produce a reaching response in the baby. The first reaction or experience changed the baby, so that we now have a P_2 in the equation. If B_1 (reaching) is a function of P_1E_1, and if we substitute a P_2 in the equation, we will not get B_1 (reaching).

This interrelation between a person and his environment has far-reaching consequences for the prediction of behavior. It means in effect that an act or a response cannot be attributed to an environmental condition alone, or to the person, or a particular characteristic of the person, alone. In every case the act is the result of a person interacting with his environment. A person doesn't steal in a vacuum. His stealing cannot be explained by saying that he is bad or that he has the undesirable characteristic of stealing. On the other hand, his stealing cannot be attributed entirely to bad companions, picture shows, poverty, or the like. The stealing is a function of or the result of what the person is at the moment and the circumstances in which he finds himself at the moment. Take a person with certain characteristics and place him in a certain situation and you get a given kind of behavior. The same person in another situation will not respond in the same way. A different person in the same situation will not respond in the same way. Change either the person or the situation and you change the behavior.

The S→O→R formula. Some psychologists have described the individual's reaction to his environment or some aspect of his environment by use of the formula: S→O→R, in which S refers to stimulus or stimulating condition, O refers to organism or person, and R refers to response or reaction. Relatively simple kinds of behavior may be covered very nicely by this formula, as one can see when a person touches a finger to a hot object and draws it away. But in this form, the formula is far too simple. A person may fail to eat food that is placed before him, because he is not hungry, or because he is waiting for others to be served, or because he believes the food to be poisonous. He may fail to be made angry by an insulting remark, because of his contempt for the person offering the insult, or because of the restraining presence of others, or because he realizes that the insult is his opponent's technique of combat, calculated merely to arouse his anger and to decrease his judgment. He may fail to study in spite of the best efforts of the teacher, either because he is interested in something else or because of disturbing conditions about him. The formula, therefore, should be made to represent these changing conditions within the individual and the general circumstances of which the selected stimulus is a part. It may consequently be elaborated by the inclusion of as many modifications (M_1, M_2, etc.) of the stimulus and of the organism as are necessary to represent adequately the complexity of the stimuli playing upon the organism and the changing conditions of the organism itself. So modified, the formula may be represented as follows:

$$S \rightarrow O \quad \rightarrow R$$
$$SM_1 \rightarrow OM_1 \rightarrow R_1$$
$$SM_2 \rightarrow OM_2 \rightarrow R_2$$

In this book we shall use Lewin's behavior equation.

Controlling Human Behavior

As we have seen, the prediction of behavior in the scientific sense requires a knowledge of the variables affecting or determining behavior and a knowledge of the relationships which exist between these variables and the behavior. If one knows that a certain kind of behavior is likely to occur in a certain individual or group of individuals under certain circumstances, he has the knowledge needed for doing something about it. Doing something about it involves controlling or manipulating one or both of the variables involved, the P or the E or both P and E in the behavior equation, in such a way as to bring about some desired change in behavior. Regardless of the kind of change desired or the complexity of the behavior involved, any control of human behavior is accomplished by manipulating or dealing with the variables represented by the P and E of the behavior equation.

An example of the control of behavior. This is illustrated in the following simple example. An eighteen-month-old baby is found playing in the dead ashes in an open fireplace. He is dipping the ashes with a spoon and pouring them on his head and clothing. The mother might put an end to the playing by (1) removing the environmental variables, the ashes and the spoon, or (2) doing something to the baby, such as putting him in a playpen. This would solve the immediate problem but it would not automatically eliminate the likelihood that the response would occur again. The reoccurrence of the act could be prevented by (1) seeing to it that the baby, spoon, and ashes never come together again, or (2) teaching the baby to make some other kind of response to ashes in an open fireplace. In this particular example, it may be far easier to follow the first method. In many other cases, where manipulation of the environmental variables is difficult or inadvisable, one might be forced to use the procedure of teaching the person to respond differently to the situation.

While this example is admittedly simple, it serves to illustrate the fruitfulness of thinking of behavior in terms of our behavior equation.

In simple cases, like the one above, one can see the essential variables quite easily and quickly. With more complex behavior, the variables are not readily observable. Careful experimental study may be needed to discover the essential variables and the relationships between them. The variables and relationships involved in complex behavior such as delinquency, school adjustments, etc. may be of such a degree of complexity that control of the behavior is difficult. But, no matter how complex the variables are, control involves the same basic procedure as in the simple example given above: first, discovering what variables are involved and in what way; and second, doing something with the variables in order to bring about the desired change in behavior.

Kinds of behavior to be controlled. In order to understand the ways in which behavior may be controlled, it will be helpful to think of behavior as falling into two broad classes. The first includes all of the responses which make up one's total repertoire of behavior at the moment. This class includes the responses which an individual is making at the moment and the responses which he has already acquired and can make but is not making at the moment. The second class includes all of the habits, ideas, modes of adjustment, interests, abilities, etc. which are not a part of the individual's present behavior equipment, but which, if he is properly directed, might develop or fail to develop at some future time.

It is possible to do one of four things with behavior of the first class. First, one may encourage the continuation or repetition of behavior which is in progress. "Go on," "you are doing fine," "do it again," and "stay with it" are common verbal attempts to get individuals to continue or repeat what they are doing. Second, one may, just as a temporary measure, induce an individual to stop what he is doing. There is no effort in this second kind of control to eliminate or prevent the later reoccurrence of the behavior. The traffic signal changes from "go" to "stop," but in a few seconds it will again say "go." A mother may at one moment ask her child to be quiet and at the next to say something. Third, one may induce an individual to do something which he can do but isn't doing at the moment. The salesman may persuade us to purchase and use the brand which he is selling. The production manager may manipulate workers and working conditions to get an increase in production or an improvement in morale or a decrease in accidents. Fourth, one may completely eliminate certain responses or ways of acting. Here the emphasis is upon preventing the reoccurrence of the behavior.

There are two ways of controlling behavior of the second class. The first is by preventing the appearance or development of certain kinds of behavior. The second is by teaching those skills, interests, attitudes, and modes of adjustment which an individual might not otherwise develop. In one sense the second is itself a preventive measure, perhaps the surest way of preventing the development of certain ways of acting and of avoiding the problem of having to eliminate them later on.

Everyday control of behavior. Control of behavior of the first class represents the bulk of our everyday control of our own or other people's behavior. We are eternally trying to influence people to act in one way rather than in another, or at least to stop doing what they are doing. Occasionally, we may take steps to eliminate certain ways of acting, or prevent their reoccurrence, but in general we attempt our control of present behavior with little or no thought of the problems which such control may produce at some future time. A mother may succeed in her efforts to make her child eat a certain kind of food, but may in the process give him an everlasting dislike for the food. A teacher may make a child learn the multiplication tables, but at the expense of a permanent distaste for arithmetic. A salesman may make a sale and lose a customer. With one exception, it is very unlikely that control of behavior of the first class will be attacked in any systematic or scientific fashion. Indeed, skill in such control is more an art than a science. The one exception arises in connection with the problem of eliminating certain persistent habits or modes of adjustment. Such habits as fingernail biting, enuresis, and swearing do not disappear upon verbal command or even under threat of punishment.

The psychologist's interest in controlling behavior. The problem of eliminating present ways of acting and the problems of preventing the development of such modes of adjustment in people who have not yet acquired them and of teaching or producing certain other desired modes of adjustment require for their solution more knowledge and skill and more systematic treatment than is likely to be used in the everyday control of behavior. Indeed, these are the problems that are of primary concern to psychologists. They are not only interested in these problems but are actually in the business of using the facts, principles, and methods of their science to solve problems which involve human adjustments in the home, in the nursery, in schools, in industry, on the playground, in international relations, in hospitals, in penal institutions, in government agencies, and in the armed services. They serve either as professional psychologists who handle these problems directly or as expert consultants to others who do the work. In either case the psychologist is *applying* his understanding of human nature and his knowledge of the facts and principles of behavior to the solution of problems which arise in these areas.

Psychologists have a distinct advantage over most other groups in controlling behavior. The advantage lies in the fact that, with few exceptions, they are most likely (1) to know the facts and principles of their science, a knowledge which is tantamount to understanding human nature; (2) to know the methods used in discovering these facts; (3) to have the skills and techniques needed to discover new facts; (4) to know how to use their knowledge and skill in dealing with people; and (5) to know the consequences of dealing with individuals in different ways. The training of psychologists today includes not only a thorough grounding in the basic facts, principles, and methods of the science, but practice in the application of this knowledge and skill to everyday problems of human adjustment.

Psychologists are not the only people in the business of controlling behavior. Everyone exerts some control over his own behavior and that of others. Parents, teachers, salesmen, law enforcement officers, lawyers, ministers, writers, lecturers, and entertainers, just to name a few of many groups, are specifically concerned with the problem of influencing, guiding, directing, or forcing people to act in one way rather than another. While some individuals in each of these groups are familiar with much of the science of human behavior and make use of this knowledge in their dealings with people, others are ignorant of the facts and principles of human adjustment or refuse to make use of whatever knowledge is available, preferring to use outmoded methods and mistaken notions in the face of repeated failures to produce the kinds of results which they wish to produce. These individuals rely heavily upon what we have chosen to describe as naïve psychology, and upon methods which trained psychologists have long since discarded as inadequate.

It must not be supposed, however, that those individuals who rely upon naïve psychology to control behavior are always unsuccessful, or that those who rely upon the available scientific knowledge are always successful. Apart from chance success, the former group is sometimes successful because it does not depend exclusively upon outmoded methods and inaccurate knowledge. Some facts and methods from our scientific laboratories have a way of creeping into our everyday thinking and influencing our everyday living whether we are aware of it or not. On the other hand, those who rely upon scientific knowledge in controlling behavior are not always successful because they cannot always apply the available knowledge, or because all of the necessary facts are not yet available. The latter group, however, is more likely to succeed than the former because scientific psychology is more adequate than naïve psychology, and because the scientific method is more adequate than the method of trial and error.

Factors Determining the Direction of Control

In our discussion so far we have avoided the question of what behavior is to be eliminated, prevented, continued, etc. or why behavior is to be controlled in one direction rather than another. There was an implication in some of our examples that one would want to eliminate one kind of response, teach individuals to make another, and prevent the development of still another. There was no indication, however, of how or upon what basis one would decide to do one of these things rather than another. There are a number of factors which determine the particular way in which behavior will be controlled.

One determiner is the objective or purpose of the person who is attempting to exercise control. Parents *want* their children to act in a certain way, and to develop certain habits, skills, interests, and modes of adjustment. Teachers, production managers, workers, and salesmen control individuals in such a way as to produce the kind of behavior which they *want*. Individually and collectively we want to act in certain ways and we want others to behave as we want them to behave. These wants are important determiners of the way behavior will be controlled.

A second determiner is the personality of the individual whose behavior is being controlled. Since the control of behavior involves the manipulation of an individual, the individual's personality — made up, as we shall see, of his total behavior, including desires and interests — will play a determining role in his final action. Actually, any individual has ideas of his own as to what he wants to do. What the individual does will be in part the result of the controls exerted by others, and in part the result of his control of himself, or of his reactions, at least, to the efforts made by others. The part played by the individual in the way he reacts may be great or small, depending upon his age, ability, and previous training and upon the nature of the outside controls.

A third determiner is the method or procedure used in controlling behavior. Suppose that a mother wants to eliminate her child's fear of the dark. She attempts to do so by explaining that there is nothing to be afraid of or that big boys are not afraid of the dark. This procedure does not work. The fear persists and becomes more intense. The method used is having the effect of encouraging the continuation of the response, the exact reverse of what the mother wants. The method one employs in controlling behavior has an effect upon the individual and his behavior, an effect which may not be the one desired. It is this fact that accounts for the many cases in which a person has been responsible for producing some change in behavior which he did not wish to produce.

How desires develop. We have indicated that people want to control behavior in a given way, that they want people to act in one way rather than another, and that these wants are important in determining the results obtained in controlling behavior. Where do these wants come from? Why does a mother want to rid her child of fears? Why do we want to prevent delinquency and crime? Why do we want children to learn to read? What is operating behind and through these wants to determine the direction of our efforts to control behavior?

These wants or desires are in part the result of the demands made upon us by society. The social group says in effect that there are certain forms of individual and group behavior which will further the group's welfare. Regardless of how the group defines its welfare, those ways of acting which contribute to this welfare will be regarded as socially acceptable or desirable, and those which do not will be regarded as socially unacceptable or undesirable. Thus in our society we regard literacy, voting, worship, and monogamy as desirable forms of behavior, and illiteracy, stealing, blasphemy, and polygamy as undesirable. In growing up, most individuals and groups come to accept, in whole or with some modification, these standards of what is socially acceptable, and to use them as guides in controlling themselves and others. Some few individuals do not accept these standards as their personal guide to conduct, but they do learn what the standards are. In effect they come to know what is "right" and what is "wrong," but they do not choose to guide themselves by these standards, although they may attempt to control others in terms of them.

An individual's system of values. The process of accepting social standards as one's own is one of combining or *integrating* these standards with basic impulses and motives of a more strictly personal nature. In this process the individual's impulses interact with, and are modified by, the demands of the social group, and the social standards are interpreted by the individual in terms of these basic impulses. Out of this interaction the individual develops a number of new desires, such as the desire for social approval, the desire to do the acceptable thing, and the desire for recognition. These in turn become integrated or combined in some way with the basic impulses and the social standards as accepted by the individual to form his personal standards, his system of values, the principles (if any) which he lives by, his hopes, ambitions, ideals, and aspirations.

These individual standards and values may correspond rather closely to those held by the social group, or they may differ markedly from them. In general the cases of close correspondence far outnumber the cases of little or no correspondence. This is seen in Allport's (1) study of the number of people stopping, slowing up, and disregarding a traffic stop sign. The vast majority of people either stopped or slowed down, as can be seen in Figure 1. While this study does not attempt to measure the extent to which one's desires are actually determined by social demands, it illustrates the kind of relationship which very probably obtains between individual standards and group standards.

The role of values in controlling behavior. One's attempt to control behavior in a given way is motivated by these individual standards or values. A mother wishes to rid her child of certain fears because she has certain ideas of what she wants the child to be and certain ideas of what she as a mother should be and do. She regards fear as a threat to the goals which she has set for herself and her child. She may not be able to verbalize these motives. Indeed, she may not be aware of them. But there is implicit in her attempts to eliminate fear a value

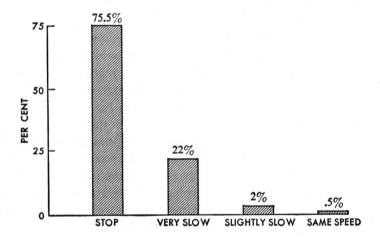

Figure 1

Per Cent of 2114 Motorists Stopping, Slowing Down, and Continuing
at Same Speed at Traffic Signal

judgment to the effect that fear is "bad" or undesirable. It may be stated that any control of behavior carries with it the desire to attain some goal or objective. The actual result may, of course, differ from the one desired or originally planned by the individual or group responsible for the control. This is inevitable, since, as we have seen, the desire to control behavior in a given way or for a given purpose is only one of the factors which determine the ultimate result. What people actually do is in part the result of their control of themselves and in part of what people do inadvertently or unintentionally in trying to satisfy their own wants and needs.

One of the pressing problems in the present-day control of human behavior arises from the conflict between the objectives which different people have in mind in trying to control behavior. On many objectives there is general agreement, but on some there is little or none. We may agree that an educated citizenry is a desirable objective, but we may disagree on the kind of education, the amount, how it is to be provided, or by whom. Difficulties in adjustment arise when an individual finds himself the center of conflicts in which different groups pull against one another in their attempts to control him or shape his destiny.

HOW THE PSYCHOLOGIST STUDIES BEHAVIOR

The methods by which psychologists study behavior can best be illustrated by a description of some actual procedures.

Virtually everyone is familiar with the general fact that much of what one learns is forgotten. This much is a matter of common observation. But how many individuals know from their everyday experience (1) that forgetting is a function of time, the relationship being one in which the amount forgotten increases with time but at a decreasing rate; (2) that the rate of forgetting is dependent upon what one does after learning; (3) that forgetting is less rapid for meaningful than for nonmeaningful material; or (4) that the rate of forgetting is affected by the method used in learning. These are some of the facts that have been discovered in experiments on learning and forgetting. Some of these experiments are described below.

Ebbinghaus's Study of Forgetting

Ebbinghaus (5), a pioneer in the study of memory, published in 1885 the results of extensive studies of forgetting. One of his findings was that forgetting is a function of time. This fact is represented in Figure 2.

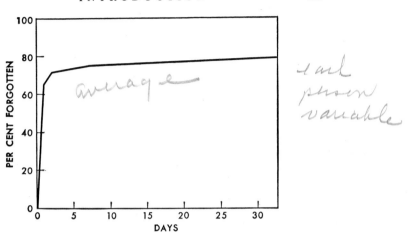

Figure 2

Curve of Forgetting (Ebbinghaus) for Nonsense Syllables
after Various Time Intervals

It will be noted that the amount forgotten is very large immediately after learning. As time continues, the amount forgotten per period of time decreases. According to this curve and the relationship between time and forgetting which it represents, one could say that more will be forgotten in 10 days than in 5 days, or in any given period of time than in any shorter period of time. This follows from the fact that the curve continues to rise with time. In one study, however, Ebbinghaus (5) discovered that three times as much forgetting occurred after a 24-hour period as after a 15-hour period. Quite obviously there is a discrepancy between this finding and the results represented in Figure 2. One could expect more forgetting 24 hours after learning than 15 hours after learning, but not three times as much. What does one do when faced with such a discrepancy or with what appear to be contradictory results? If he is a scientist or adopts a scientific point of view, he looks for an explanation of the discrepancy. This looking eventually takes the form of additional experiments to check the validity of certain suggested explanations which occur to the experimenter or others who examine the original data. Ebbinghaus himself suggested that the above discrepancy might be due to the fact that more is forgotten during a waking period than during a sleeping period of equal length. If this hypothesis is correct, it might account for the discrepancy, because sleeping would ordinarily occupy a larger part of a 15-hour period than it would of a 24-hour period following learning. But Ebbinghaus did not test this hypothesis.

The Jenkins-Dallenbach Experiment

An experiment designed to test the hypothesis was performed almost forty years later by Jenkins and Dallenbach (7). These investigators had two college seniors memorize lists of nonsense syllables. Each list contained ten such syllables as "boq," "zer," and "muc." Some of the lists were learned just before the subject went to sleep. These were recalled 1, 2, 4, or 8 hours after learning, the subject being awakened in order to recite. Other lists were learned in the forenoon and recalled 1, 2, 4, or 8 hours later, but with no sleep intervening between the learning and the recall. Both subjects recalled more after 1, 2, 4, or 8 hours of sleep than after corresponding periods of waking activity. One subject recalled an average of 5.5 syllables after 8 hours of sleep and only an average of 0.4 syllable after 8 hours of normal waking activity. The corresponding results for the other subject were 5.8 and 1.4 syllables. The results show rather clearly that the forgetting of material of the sort used in this experiment is less after a period of sleep than after a corresponding period of normal waking activity.

This finding not only provides a probable explanation of the discrepancy in the results obtained by Ebbinghaus, but it extends our knowledge of the phenomenon of forgetting by uncovering a factor which affects the rate of forgetting. We can now say that forgetting nonsense material is a function of time (Ebbinghaus, Figure 2) and that the rate of forgetting for this kind of material is less if the interval after learning is filled with sleep than if it is filled with normal waking activity (Jenkins and Dallenbach). A point that should not be overlooked is the fact that this extension of knowledge resulted from the attempt to find an explanation for an apparent contradiction in the results of two experiments. This is a common occurrence in scientific work.

Seeking an explanation of a discrepancy in the results of two or more experiments is a special case of the more general experimental procedure of trying to interpret or explain the results of an experiment. As was pointed out (page 7) in the discussion of scientific and naïve psychology, an event is explained when it is properly related to other events, when it is found to fit with other facts into an organized system. In attempting to explain the results of an experiment, one quite frequently discovers that additional facts are needed to round out the total picture and to give meaning to the present findings. Present experimental findings, therefore, serve as a take-off point for further research. From them one formulates new hypotheses, which must be tested in turn.   For example, the results of the experiment by Jenkins and Dallenbach might suggest that different kinds of waking activity have a differential effect upon the rate of forgetting.   Since this experiment and the ones by Ebbinghaus were carried on with nonsense syllables, one might wonder if the forgetting of meaningful material during sleep and waking is the same as the forgetting of nonsense materials.   Another investigator may wonder if there is any generalized forgetting curve of the sort in Figure 2, or if there are different kinds of forgetting curves for different kinds of material and for different individuals.   Experiments have been carried out to answer these questions.

Newman's Experiment

Newman (13) conducted an experiment to see if the results obtained by Jenkins and Dallenbach hold for meaningful material.   He used three short stories constructed in such a way that each contained a number of items which were essential to the plot (meaningful) and a like number of items which were not essential and therefore less meaningful. Eleven college students read each story at a different time of the day and reproduced it approximately 8 hours after reading.   The order of the stories and the relation between the story learned and the time of learning were rotated for each subject.   An equal number of the stories were recalled after 8 hours of waking activity and after 8 hours of sleeping.   Since each story contained both essential and nonessential material, it was possible to compare the amount of forgetting of essential material with the amount of forgetting of nonessential material both after waking and after sleeping.   The results showed that there was no difference in the amount of essential material forgotten after waking and after sleeping.   On the other hand, twice as much of the nonessential material was forgotten after waking as after sleeping. The per cent forgotten over the 8-hour period was very much greater for the nonessential than for the essential material.   These findings extend our knowledge still further and also suggest new problems or uncover facets of the problem which need to be investigated if we are to understand the phenomena of memory and forgetting.

THE METHODS USED BY PSYCHOLOGISTS

Without pursuing this problem further or describing the many experiments which have been done on memory and forgetting, we can see that the psychologist studies behavior by (1) asking questions about a given kind of behavior, (2) making observations designed to provide answers to these questions, (3) reporting the results of these observations carefully and accurately, and (4) interpreting the findings by pointing up the relations to other facts.   Asking questions about the findings becomes the starting point for making more observations and repeating the entire procedure.   This is the procedure which the scientist uses to solve his problems.   As Johnson (8) has pointed out, it is a procedure which an individual may well adopt in solving the problems of everyday living.   It is commonly called the scientific method, or the experimental method.   Let us examine this method more closely.

Experimental Method — Step One

One begins by asking questions.   The experiment by Jenkins and Dallenbach started with the question: Why did Ebbinghaus find three times as much forgetting after 24 hours as after 15 hours?   Such a question is examined in the light of all of the available information, and a tentative answer is formulated.   This tentative answer is sometimes called a guess, and in one sense it is, but it is more than an ordinary guess.   It is arrived at by weighing all of the available facts.   It is, therefore, supported by whatever evidence is at hand.   If few or no facts are available, it may be little more than a "stab in the dark." Technically it is known as a hypothesis.   Jenkins and Dallenbach hypothesized that people forget more while awake than asleep.   If this is true, it could be the answer or a partial answer to their question.

Experimental Method — Step Two

Once a hypothesis is formulated, the experimenter proceeds to design a set of conditions or circumstances, technically called an experimental design, in which the behavior in question can be produced and observed and its relation to one or more of the variables making up the set of conditions determined.   A hypothesis states that behavior will be affected in a certain way by a certain variable.   This variable must be part of the set of conditions under which the behavior is produced. Further, one must be able to introduce this critical variable into the set of conditions, or take it out, or change it in known ways once it is introduced while holding the remaining variables constant.   Each time this variable is introduced or changed, observations and/or measurements are made to determine the effect it is having upon the behavior.   The set of conditions which constitutes the experimental design consists of some combination of variables found in the P and E of the behavior equation. The critical variable may be some condition of P or some environmental variable. This variable, known as the *independent variable*, is manipulated in a given way while all of the other P and E variables making up the design are held constant. Observations are made to determine the effect of these manipulations on the B of the equation. The behavior under observation in an experiment is known as the *dependent variable*.

Experimental designs. The two experimental designs needed to check the hypothesis in the experiment by Jenkins and Dallenbach may be described as follows:

Design A

DEPENDENT VARIABLE

Recall
▼

Subject H recalled an average of 5.5 syllables from all of the lists learned under this design.

P AND E VARIABLES

1. Subject H
2. List of 10 nonsense syllables (list A)
3. List learned to one correct repetition
4. Each syllable exposed for 0.7 second in learning
5. 8 hours between learning and recall
6. Subject asleep during 8-hour interval
7. List learned between 11:30 p.m. and 1 a.m.

Design B

DEPENDENT VARIABLE

Recall
▼

Subject H recalled an average of 0.4 syllable from all of the lists learned under this design.

P AND E VARIABLES

1 Subject H
2. List of 10 nonsense syllables (list B, but of same difficulty as list A)
3. List learned to one correct repetition
4. Each syllable exposed 0.7 second in learning
5. 8 hours between learning and recall
6. Subject awake during 8-hour interval
7. List learned between 8 and 10 a.m.

The P and E variables listed under A are exactly the same as those listed under B with the exception of variable number 6, being awake or asleep during the 8-hour interval. The time at which the lists were learned is not the same (this difference was introduced so that the learning of list A could be followed more quickly and easily by sleep), but the difference is not regarded as a variable, since it probably affects only the number of trials needed for learning and since learning was carried in both cases to one correct repetition. The nonsense syllables in list A and list B, while not the same, are of equal difficulty. The subject is the same in both designs, and steps were taken to insure similarity of interest, attitude, etc. from one design to the next. Other miscellaneous variables, such as the place of learning, what the subject ate for breakfast or dinner, etc., are not listed, since the period of time covered by this experiment and the number of lists learned under each design very probably cancel out any effect of such variables. Designs A and B were repeated for other lists of nonsense syllables, for intervals of 1, 2, and 4 hours, and for the other subject used in the experiment. Any difference between the number of syllables recalled under these two designs can be attributed to the one variable that is different in the designs, namely, being awake or asleep following learning.

Methods of control. The important point to remember in connection with this step in the experimental procedure is to establish rigid controls, to keep all variables constant except the one under investigation, and to vary or change this one in such a way that its relation to the dependent variable (behavior) can be determined. Special instruments or laboratory equipment are necessary in some experiments to control the duration, frequency, and intensity of certain variables and to insure their constancy. This is particularly true of E variables, or those extraneous to the subject. In our example, each nonsense syllable was presented in the learning series for 0.7 second. This was accomplished by the use of an exposure apparatus which presents visual material for a controlled period of time.

A variety of methods has been developed for controlling P variables. One of these is illustrated in the above experiment. It consists in having the same subject perform under two sets of conditions. The subject is his own control. In some experiments, however, the problem under investigation is of such a nature that it is not feasible to follow this method of control. In such cases it is a common practice to use what is called the *control-group method.* In this method two groups of subjects, or two persons, are matched or equated for all characteristics which might affect the dependent variable. One group, referred to as the experimental group, performs under the same conditions as the control group except that a critical variable is added. One variation of this method of control is to use sets of identical twins, placing one of each pair in the control group and the other one of the pair in the experimental group. If only one set of twins is used, one of the pair is used as a control and the other as an experimental subject. This is the method of *co-twin control.* These and many other methods of control are used in psychological experiments to eliminate or reduce the influence of uncontrolled variables. Experiments with human beings are of such a nature, however, that in some cases it is impossible to exert control over all variables that might influence the results of an experiment. In these cases it becomes necessary, as Andrews (2) points out, to repeat the experiments and produce consistency of results under a variety of conditions before accepting the results as "facts."

Observation. The basic idea underlying control in an experiment is to provide a setting in which the dependent variable can be produced and observed or measured, and its relation to some critical variable determined. It does little good to control conditions and then fail to observe carefully and accurately the behavior produced under these conditions. Methods of observation and measurement, therefore, are crucial in any experiment. It goes without saying that the experimenter should be skilled in making observations. This skill is acquired through training which is designed to acquaint him with the kind of behavior to be observed, with behavior in general, with methods of observation, with instruments that might be used in making observations, and with the kinds of errors which human observers are likely to make. Ample practice in making observations is essential. The observer may increase the accuracy of his own observations by using instruments or mechanical devices to supplement them. An instrument like the motion picture camera not only "observes" more accurately and adequately than a human observer, but provides a relatively permanent record of what is observed. Such an instrument does not completely eliminate the experimenter, since the experimenter has to decide what will be photographed and when and under what conditions. Nor does the instrument eliminate the fact that the film record will have to be analyzed and interpreted by a human observer. It does, however, provide a more objective and a more complete record than is likely to be obtained by a human observer.

The observer as a variable. It is highly important in psychological experiments for the experimenter to be aware of the fact that the observation of a person by an experimenter or even by an instrument may affect the behavior under observation. Steps must be taken to see that the observer and the method of observing are not uncontrolled variables in the experiment. In some experiments an observer may produce and observe a given kind of behavior in an individual or even in an animal, only to discover that the behavior disappears or changes when a different observer takes over. As a safeguard it may be necessary to make the observer a critical variable in a preliminary experiment in order to find out how the observer affects the behavior under investigation. The procedure is to set up an experiment using one observer and repeat the experiment with another observer. In some studies of child behavior, the observer works with the children who are to be observed for a period of time before the observations start, so that the children will become accustomed to his presence (14).

Objective and subjective observation. In most psychological experiments the experimenter is the observer and is in the position of observing the behavior of another person. This kind of observation is called *objective observation*. There are some experiments in psychology, however, in which the behavior or experience under investigation cannot be observed directly by an outside observer. Such experiences as ideas, thoughts, daydreams, feelings, sensations, and emotions fall in this category. In experiments in which the dependent variable is an experience of this sort, it is customary for the experimenter to ask the subject to report his experiences verbally or in some other way. For example, in measuring visual acuity, the experimenter or examiner presents a visual stimulus and asks the subject to report what he sees. A variety of methods is used in experiments of this sort to present the critical stimulus a large number of times under carefully controlled conditions. Repetition serves as a check on the accuracy of the subject's report and may reduce the chance errors which affect a small number of such reports. It should be noted that the experimenter in these cases does not actually observe the subject's visual experience. He is, in a sense, taking the subject's word for the fact that he sees what he reports, but in another sense he is not, because his experimental procedure, including the critical stimuli, provides adequate checks on the reliability of the reports.

Subjective experiences may be studied in another way. It has been found that some experiences are accompanied by certain bodily changes or reactions other than verbal reports which can be observed by the experimenter directly. For example, certain changes in breathing and circulation either accompany or are a part of the emotional experiences of fear (See Chapter 9). In studying fear one may measure changes of this sort and use them as signs or indicators of the experience, thus eliminating the necessity of asking the subject to report. It must be recognized, however, that this procedure cannot be followed until it has been shown that a valid relationship exists between such bodily reactions and subjective experience. The bodily reactions can be studied in their own right even in the absence of such known relationships, but not as indicators of subjective experience.

In experiments on subjective experiences, such as the one on visual acuity, the experimenter could ask the subject to report, not what he sees, or its position, etc., but the nature of the experience itself. If the subject were to do this, he would be making the experience the object of his observation, and might make statements about the intensity or duration or other attributes of the experience. This kind of observation is called _introspection._ It was basic in psychological experiments many years ago when the subject matter of psychology was mental states or the content of consciousness. Its importance declined as the emphasis in psychology shifted from the study of consciousness to the study of behavior.

Experimental Method — Step Three

A careful, accurate record of what is observed in an experiment is no less important than careful, accurate observation. It is so important that experimenters use, whenever they can, an instrument or an observing procedure which automatically records what is observed — for example, photographic and sound equipment. In some studies the subjects make their own records, as when subjects answer questions on a test. In experiments where recording is not done by the observing equipment or by the subject as part of the response being studied, care is taken to prepare forms or special recording devices and to train the observers to record their observations as they are being made or as soon thereafter as possible. In one experiment in the infant research laboratory at Ohio State University (15), observers watched the activity of a baby continuously for a given period of time. This left them no time to record their observations on the spot. The difficulty was overcome by having each observer dictate his observations to a stenographer. A system of abbreviations for various kinds of responses was worked out as a means of speeding up and increasing the accuracy of the observing-dictating procedure.

Quantitative measures of behavior. The results of an experiment should be stated and reported in quantitative terms. This requirement can be met only if the behavior under observation is measured in quantitative terms or units. While behavior is the thing under observation, it is some quantitative measure of the behavior which is sought. How can behavior be described in quantitative terms? An examination of the more common quantitative measures will serve to answer this question and at the same time stress the importance of quantitative records and reports. In many experiments the experimenter observes and records the _number of responses_ made by the subject. This may take the form of the number of nonsense syllables recalled, the number of words written, the number of pieces of work completed in a given unit of time, the number of eye fixations per paragraph of reading material, the number of ideas reproduced after reading a story, the number

of questions answered correctly on a standard test, the number of errors
or mistakes made in performing a given task, or the number of brain
waves of a given kind which occur in a single period of time. The
amount accomplished or attained in a given amount of time is another
measure of behavior. This may be represented by the number of
responses per period of time, but it may also be represented by such
things as the distance run, the load lifted or pulled, or the amount of
pain, noise, or other obstruction an individual will endure in order to
attain or reach a certain goal. Another common measure of behavior
is the *time required to make a response* or a series of responses. Some
time measures are: the time required to run a given distance, the time
required to reach a given stage of proficiency in learning, the time one
can keep his attention fixed on a given stimulus, the time required to
solve a problem or answer a given number of questions, and the time
required to perceive a given stimulus object.

These quantitative measures are sometimes converted into ratings
or ranks to show the position of the individuals with relation to one
another. In your course in psychology, for example, you will probably
take a number of quizzes and answer a given number of test items
correctly. Your instructor will probably arrange the scores of all
members of the class on a scale from low to high and then assign
ratings such as A, B, C, D, E to the scores according to their position
on the scale and according to the number of people making each score.
This measure of an individual is a statement of where he stands in some
group and is, therefore, a relative measure of the behavior in question.

There are some kinds of behavior or characteristics of one's total
behavior which at present cannot be measured objectively and in quantitative terms. It is customary in studies of such behavior to obtain
estimates or judgments of the extent to which the characteristic or
trait is present in a particular person. Rating scales are prepared on
which the judge can indicate where he thinks a person stands in relation
to other people with respect to a particular trait. The procedure is
essentially the same as that followed in assigning letter grades except
that no quantitative measure, such as scores on quizzes, is available to
serve as a base for assigned ratings. The base is the judge's subjective
impression of the behavior of the person who is being rated. The
rating, therefore, may be as much a measure of the rater as it is of the
person rated.

One additional step can be taken to insure a reasonably exact, quantitative description of the results of an experiment. Once the behavior

under observation has been measured in quantitative units, the measurements can be tabulated or arranged systematically and analyzed by statistical procedures which are designed to simplify, clarify, and test the significance of the findings inherent in the measurements. The final report of the answer to the question under investigation in the experiment may well be some one or a few statistical values which represent or summarize the essential points of the findings.

Experimental Method — Step Four

The final step in the experimental procedure is concerned with the interpretation or explanation of the results. Do the results provide an answer to the question under investigation? Are they related to other known facts? Do they support any theoretical position? What are the implications of the results? Are the results specific to the particular groups studied and to the procedure used, or can they be generalized to other groups and conditions? To what extent can the results be used in prediction and control? These are questions which one attempts to answer in interpreting the results of an experiment.

The answers are obtained (1) by examining the results in relation to the procedure and subjects used in the experiment itself, (2) by comparing them with other experimental findings, and (3) by trying to fit them into the prevailing theoretical framework. Regardless of how much care is exercised in setting up an experiment, it is important to check or re-examine each step in the procedure after the results are obtained, especially if the results do not support the hypothesis under investigation. One may find an explanation of discrepancies or inconsistencies in his results in some unobserved error in the experimental procedure. If the results are supported by other findings and in turn support these findings by fitting with them into an organized system, and if they satisfy certain statistical criteria of significance and reliability, they can be accepted as valid with a high degree of confidence. This means that there is a high probability that the results are valid.

If the results can be accepted as valid at a reasonable level of confidence, one may then proceed to point out the implications of these findings for his science, for scientific theory, for further research, and for the practical problems of prediction and control. One might also make certain generalizations from his findings. If the results in a particular experiment are obtained from a study of a representative sample of adult, white, native-born males in federal prisons, one may legitimately generalize his findings by saying that what is true for the sample is true for all adult, white, native-born males in federal prisons. This generalization is warranted from the experimental conditions and the subjects used.   If, however, one should attempt to say from his results something about what is true of all federal prisoners, or all male citizens of the United States, he would be covering more territory than his findings warrant.   In this case he would be overgeneralizing.   This error, common in naïve psychology, is one which the scientist must be careful to guard against.

Statistical Methods

As pointed out above, the results of an experiment are ordinarily stated in quantitative terms.   This means that in most experiments the experimenter has, at the conclusion of Step Three of the experimental procedure, a set of numbers each of which represents a different person's behavior, or a different example of one person's behavior.   In either event, the experimenter is confronted with the task of handling or treating these numbers in order to find the facts which may otherwise remain buried in the data.   The methods used in analyzing such numerical data are called statistical methods.

Tables and graphs.   Some of these methods are used for the purpose of arranging and classifying data in an orderly and systematic form. Table I on page 6 is one kind of orderly arrangement of measures of behavior.   It is known as a frequency table.   The scores (number of correct answers) are arranged from high to low and grouped into intervals or groups of three.   The number of students making the scores in each interval is shown in the second and fourth rows of the table.   The grouping of scores into intervals does not harm the data or change the facts that may be obtained by subsequent statistical methods.   It is done for the purpose of presenting the data in a more compact and manageable form.   Another kind of orderly arrangement of data is shown in Figure 1.   Here a graph is constructed to show the percentage of people making each of four degrees of a response to a traffic stop signal.   All of the possible degrees of stopping are grouped into four classes.   The number of individuals making each response is represented by a vertical column, the height of which is proportionate to the number of individuals making the response.   Another kind of graph is shown in Figure 2.   Arranging numbers in an orderly fashion as in Table I or in Figures 1 and 2 not only allows one to answer certain questions about the data rather quickly and easily, but makes possible further analyses that would be difficult or impossible if the data were assembled in some haphazard order.

Measures of central tendency. These methods are designed to reduce the complexity of data by obtaining some single figure from the total number of measurements which will adequately represent the entire group. For example, one may obtain 100 visual reaction times from a given subject as shown in Table II. Since one is likely to be interested in a single measure of a person's visual reaction time, he will not want tó read off a list of 100 numbers each time a question regarding the individual's visual reaction time is raised. It would be far more convenient to have a single number represent the individual's reaction time. This can be obtained by calculating the mean (the arithmetic average) of the 100 reaction times. The mean reaction time in Table II is .155 second. This single figure is calculated in such a way that each of the 100 measures is involved in the calculation. The mean is, therefore, what it is because the 100 measures are what they are. In short, the mean represents the entire group of 100 measures. One may raise the question of why the experimenter obtained 100 reaction times in the first place if only one figure is to be used. The answer to this question is found in the fact that a single measure or observation is not very reliable because certain chance errors affect it. Since the chance errors do not operate for each successive individual measure in the same way, it is possible to obtain a reasonably stable measure of reaction time by making a large number of observations. Calculating the mean reduces the large number to a single measure. The mean is only one of a group of similar statistical measures each of which is called a *measure of central tendency.* Two other widely used measures of this kind are the median and the mode. In a series of measurements the median is the middlemost and the mode is the one which appears most frequently. These measures are called measures of central tendency because they fall at or near the middle or center of the group of measurements in which they are calculated. Each one is used to represent the entire group, and is therefore an indication of the extent to which the measurements in a group are alike.

Table II

One Hundred Visual Reaction Times

Reaction time in hundredths of a second	.23	.22	.21	.20	.19	.18	.17	.16	.15	.14	.13	.12	.11	.10	.09
Number of reaction times	1	1	4	6	6	7	8	13	15	14	10	7	4	2	2 = 100 *Total*

Measures of variability. Everyone is familiar with the fact that an individual cannot perform in exactly the same way or with the same degree of proficiency each time he is called upon to make a given response. One's reaction time to a visual stimulus, or to any other stimulus, will vary or fluctuate from trial to trial, as shown in Table II. A worker doesn't do exactly the same amount of work each hour or each day. A runner doesn't run the 100-yard dash in exactly the same time each trial. One doesn't recall the same number of items from previously learned lists even if the items are of the same difficulty. But this is not all. The amount of variability is not the same from one kind of behavior to another. Two responses such as visual and auditory reaction time differ in two ways. The mean of one, visual, is larger than the mean of the other. They also differ in the degree or amount by which the individual measures of each vary or scatter about the mean. It is this fact of variation of performance that is represented by a *measure of variability.* A measure of variability is a number whose size indicates the degree to which the individual measurements scatter around a measure of central tendency. If the number is small, it indicates that the individual measurements are relatively close together, or that they do not deviate by very large amounts from their mean. If the number is large, the measurements deviate by relatively large amounts from the mean. The measure of variability may be regarded as a measure of the homogeneity-heterogeneity of the measurements. If a large number of different individuals are measured with respect to some kind of behavior as in Table I, a measure of variability is an indication of how the individuals differ from one another, or the extent of the differences between the individuals.

Correlation. Still another statistical procedure is designed to determine the degree of relationship which exists between two sets of measurements both of which are obtained on the same population. Suppose, for example, that 100 male college students are selected at random and arranged in a row from tallest to shortest. A number representing each individual's height could then be recorded. Now, suppose each man is weighed and a number representing each man's weight is set down opposite his height. An examination of these two columns of figures will very probably reveal a marked tendency for the taller individuals to weigh the most and a tendency for the shorter men to weigh the least. This correspondence between height and weight can be calculated by a method known as the *method of correlation.* One obtains by this method a number which is called a *coefficient* of correlation. This coefficient is a measure of the degree of correspondence or co-relation between two sets of measurements of a single population. The statistical symbol for this coefficient is the small letter r. The methods of correlation are such that the different degrees of relationship are represented by numbers between zero and one. Zero represents a complete lack of relationship. Perfect relationship is represented by the figure 1.00. The intermediate degrees are represented by decimal fractions such as .10, .35, .63, etc. Since relationships may be positive or negative (inverse), it is customary to place a plus or minus sign in front of the coefficient to indicate the kind of relationship represented. The relationship between height and weight is positive because high values for height tend to be accompanied by high values for weight. If one measures the intelligence of college freshmen and correlates these measurements with the ages of the freshmen, he will probably obtain a negative correlation of some amount. This negative correlation indicates that the younger freshmen tend to make the higher scores on the intelligence test while the older freshmen tend to make the lower scores.

The importance of correlation in studies of behavior is found in the fact that once a degree of relationship is established between two variables it is possible when the amount of one variable is given to predict the amount of the other. For example, the relationship between freshman psychological test scores and grades earned during the first semester in college provides a basis at the beginning of the semester for predicting the grades students are likely to make during the semester. The accuracy of prediction is dependent upon the degree of relationship and this is indicated by the size of the coefficient. The degree of relationship ordinarily found to exist between group intelligence test scores and grades is about .60. How accurately can one predict with a coefficient of .60? A glance at Figure 3 shows that the per cent better than chance prediction (the per cent of one's prediction which would be correct if he simply guessed) for a coefficient of .60 is 20. The coefficient of .60 is more than half way between zero and 1.00, but it increases one's accuracy of prediction by only 20 per cent. It can be seen from Figure 3 that a coefficient of .80 is not twice as good as a coefficient of .40. As the size of the coefficient increases, the degree of relationship increases but not in direct proportion to the increase in the size of the coefficient.

While we can make predictions on the basis of the established relationships represented by coefficients of correlation, it must be recognized that such relationships are not necessarily causal relationships. A coefficient of correlation does not prove that the two correlated variables are causally related. One does not necessarily cause the other.

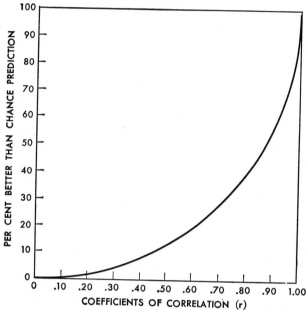

Figure 3

The Relationship between Coefficients of Correlation
and Their Predictive Value (9)

The coefficient of correlation is a measure of a kind of relationship that is known as *concomitant* relationship. If two sets of measurements vary together, or if a given amount of change in one is accompanied by some amount of change in the other, they are concomitantly related, and the amount of this relationship is represented by a coefficient of correlation. In contrast a *causal* relationship indicates that two variables are related in such a way that one (variable A) is the cause of the other (variable B). When any factor (variable) is known to be an invariable antecedent of some event, and it is also known that this event does not occur in the absence of this factor, it is called a cause.

Many other statistical procedures are available for analyzing the many and varied problems which arise in psychological research. Some of these are concerned with the problem of testing the significance or the reliability of the results obtained in an experiment, especially in those cases where the results are expressed as measures of central tendency, variability, correlation, etc. Others are concerned with special kinds of relationships between two sets of measurements or with the relationships between three or more sets of measurements. Special techniques are available for determining the influence of variables in experimental designs in which it is impossible or impractical to hold such variables constant. Some of these techniques are particularly valuable in setting up experimental designs in which complex behavior problems are to be investigated. As one moves from an investigation of relatively simple segments of behavior, the problem of adequately controlling all pertinent variables in the experimental designs, or of analyzing the results of such studies, increases. Such problems cannot be handled without using a variety of special statistical techniques.

Clinical Methods

The term *clinical* is applied to a large number of methods and techniques which are used in the diagnosis and treatment of the behavior problems or difficulties of a particular individual. As Brown points out, "any device, scheme, procedure or instrument which a trained psychologist can use and which will give him a better understanding of human behavior or assist in its modification may be rightfully regarded as falling within the scope of clinical methods." (3) The distinction, therefore, between clinical methods and nonclinical methods is to be found in the purpose for which the methods are used, not in the methods themselves. In a broad sense all methods, instruments, and techniques are used to further our understanding of human behavior and provide facts and principles for the prediction and control of behavior. Any of these methods are referred to as clinical methods when they are used in dealing with the adjustment problems of a single individual, although such an objective is only a special instance of the general aim of understanding, predicting, and controlling behavior.

While any method may be used as a clinical method, some methods are so used more commonly and widely than others. These include (1) the case history method, (2) the personal interview method (sometimes called the clinical interview method to distinguish it from the same method as used for other purposes), (3) the testing method, and (4) the autobiographical method. Other methods and many of the tests used in clinical studies are described in the chapter on personality and adjustment (Chapter 14). These methods are used primarily for the purpose of obtaining information from an individual which may lead to a better understanding of him and his problem. With the exception of the testing method which is described in Chapters 12, 13, and 14, these methods are highly subjective and individually of low reliability. This means that different clinicians, or others who use these methods, will not necessarily obtain exactly the same information from a patient, or come to the same conclusions about the case even if they have the same information at hand. Used together, however, the various methods tend to corroborate each other and thereby yield reliable data. In general, clinical methods lack the rigid objectivity of the experimental method, not because they are clinical methods, but because individually they yield results which are not readily repeatable. They are just as unreliable when used as nonclinical methods. Nevertheless, in any field in which they are used they provide information that at present is not obtained by rigidly controlled experimental procedures — information that does throw some light on the problems of human adjustment.

SUMMARY

All students begin the study of psychology with a fund of knowledge regarding human nature, which may be called naïve psychology. Though this knowledge is of value, it is unscientific in five respects: (1) it is uncritical of the problems it raises; (2) it is guilty of hasty generalization; (3) it lacks organization; (4) it lacks an exact terminology; and (5) it has no technique of research. The aims of psychology are to understand, predict, and control human behavior. The attainment of these objectives is dependent upon a knowledge of what people do, how they act, and why they act. This knowledge is gained primarily by experimentation. The four steps in experimentation are: (1) the formulation of a hypothesis, (2) the production and observation of behavior under controlled conditions, (3) the recording of the results of the observations, and (4) the interpretation of the results. In experimenting one asks questions, makes observations designed to provide answers to the questions, reports the results of his observations, and analyzes the results to see if his questions have been answered. The crux of the experimental method is step two. The variables are so controlled in setting up the experiment that all variables save one, the independent one, are controlled or held constant.

Statistical methods are used in summarizing and analyzing the results of experiments. Some of the more commonly used statistical measures are: measures of central tendency, measures of variability, and measures of correlation. All methods, instruments, and techniques used in psychology are used to further our understanding of human behavior and provide facts and principles for the prediction and control of behavior. Any of these methods are referred to as clinical methods when they are used in dealing with the adjustment problems of the individual.

QUESTIONS

on the Chapter

1. Give a general definition of psychology which includes the major points brought out in this chapter.
2. What are the differences between scientific psychology and naïve psychology?
3. Show the difference between objective and subjective observation.
4. What factors determine the way in which behavior will be controlled?
5. Explain the formula: $B = f(PE)$.
6. Describe the steps involved in the experimental method.
7. What were the results of the experiment by Jenkins and Dallenbach?
8. In what way are the results of Newman's experiment related to those obtained by Jenkins and Dallenbach?
9. Define: mean, measure of variability, coefficient of correlation, dependent variable.
10. Describe the control-group method.

for Discussion

1. Does the control of behavior always imply value judgments regarding the outcome of the behavior?
2. If two variables are correlated, is one necessarily the cause of the other?
3. Is it possible for one to use the experimental procedure in solving personal problems?
4. Is the experimental method a clinical method?
5. Is a hypothesis anything more than a guess?
6. Do the results of an experiment *prove* that a hypothesis is correct (or incorrect)?
7. Is it most important to understand behavior, predict it, or control it?

REFERENCES

1 ALLPORT, F. H., "The J–Curve Hypothesis of Conforming Behavior," *J. Soc. Psychol.*, 1934, 5, 141–183.
2 ANDREWS, T. G., "An Introduction to Psychological Methodology." In Andrews, T. G., ed., *Methods of Psychology.* New York: John Wiley and Sons, 1948.
3 BROWN, ANDREW W., "Methods and Techniques in Clinical Psychology." In Andrews, T. G., ed., *Methods of Psychology.* New York: John Wiley and Sons, 1948, p. 574.
4 DOCKERAY, FLOYD C., *Psychology.* New York: Prentice-Hall, 1942.
5 EBBINGHAUS, H., *Memory: A Contribution to Experimental Psychology* (translated by H. A. Ruger and Clara E. Bussenius). New York: Teachers College, Columbia University, 1913.
6 FRANDSEN, ARDEN, *A Common Psychological Conceptions Test.* Unpub-

lished. Utah State College, Ogden, Utah. Results reported here were obtained from students at Purdue University.

7 JENKINS, J. G., and DALLENBACH, K. M., "Obliviscence during Sleep and Waking," *Amer. J. Psychol.*, 1924, 35, 605–612.

8 JOHNSON, WENDELL, *People in Quandaries*. New York: Harper and Brothers, 1946.

9 LAIRD, DONALD A., *The Psychology of Selecting Men*, 2nd edition. New York: McGraw-Hill, 1927.

10 LEWIN, KURT, "Environmental Forces in Child Behavior and Development." In Murchison, Carl, ed., *Handbook of Child Psychology*, 2nd edition. Worcester: Clark University Press, 1933.

11 MUNN, NORMAN L., *Psychology*. Boston: Houghton Mifflin Company, 1946.

12 MURPHY, GARDNER, *An Introduction to Psychology*. New York: Harper and Brothers, 1951.

13 NEWMAN, EDWIN B., "Forgetting of Meaningful Material during Sleep and Waking." *Amer. J. Psychol.*, 1939, 52, 65–71.

14 OLSON, W. C., *A Study of Nervous Habits in Normal Children*. University of Minnesota Institute of Child Welfare Monographs, 1929, No. 3.

15 PRATT, K. C., NELSON, A. K., and SUN, K. H., *The Behavior of the Newborn Infant*. Columbus: Ohio State University Press, Contr. Psychol., 1930, No. 10.

16 RUCH, FLOYD L., *Psychology and Life*, 3rd edition. Chicago: Scott Foresman and Company, 1948.

17 WOODWORTH, R. S., and MARQUIS, DONALD G., *Psychology*, 5th edition. New York: Henry Holt and Company, 1947.

DEVELOPMENT OF THE INDIVIDUAL

2

In the preceding chapter it was pointed out that behavior is a function of a person interacting with his environment. The person and the environment are the variables which one must know if he is to predict and control behavior. Moreover, both the person and the environment are to be regarded, not as single variables, but as complex combinations of variables. A person at a single instant of time is a complex of forces or processes. He is a living organism, an animal, a man. He has certain body structures. Certain physiological processes are in progress. Certain kinds of behavior are in progress. To this must be added the very important fact that this complex of forces changes from moment to moment. Within a life span a single individual is a succession of persons. In a similar fashion environmental variables too must be regarded as changing or, at least, as different from moment to moment, because the environment represented in the behavior equation is the operative or effective environment, the one the organism is responding to at the moment. It is necessary, therefore, to write a new equation, with new values for P and E, for every response at every level of development and for every instant in an individual's life span that is significantly different (for the behavior in question) from a previous instant. It is an error, as Carmichael (7, pp. 43–44) points out, to assume "that later performance is somehow implicit or hidden in earlier types of response." As an illustration of this point, he goes on to say, "One who wishes to describe the linguistic performance of a five year old child must describe that performance as it appears at five. It is not possible to infer the full character of that performance in any given individual from any study of linguistic performance, for example, in the first year of life. The five year old performance is not implicit in the two year old performance. The environment of the third and fourth years is all important in determining, for example, whether the child at five will speak Spanish or English."

While behavior is a function of a person as a whole, it is recognized that some feature, characteristic, or part of the person may be more intimately involved in a given response than some other. For example, a verbal response is more dependent upon the speech and hearing mechanisms than it is upon those involved in walking or smelling. It is important, therefore, to know: (1) what the person is at a given instant of time, and at each level of development; (2) the separate features or parts of the organism which combine to make the person what he is at a given point in his development; and (3) the particular environmental forces present at each of these points. This chapter is concerned primarily with the first two of these problems, or in general terms, with the development of the individual.

HEREDITY (24)

While a study of an individual's development might logically begin with the individual at his first stage of development, as a single-celled organism, it is necessary to inquire into the origin of this single cell if one is to understand the individual at this or subsequent stages of his development. This inquiry into the origin of the individual takes us back into a study of the development of the germ cells in the parents and parents' parents, and the processes by which the individual comes to be what he is at his first stage of development. In other words, it involves a study of the individual's heredity.

Definitions of Heredity

For some individuals the term *heredity* has come to stand for the visible resemblances between the offspring and his parents or their progenitors and for the influence of ancestry on the development of the individual thus demonstrated. In the face of present knowledge this definition of heredity has only a limited utility even in practical life and has been abandoned by most students of genetics. The essential reason is that the influence of ancestry can show up in the individual either as a resemblance or as a difference between him and his parents or more remote ancestors. Your eyes may be blue rather than brown as a consequence of your parentage although both of your parents had brown eyes. In this case, there is a practical certainty that some of your ancestors had blue eyes. On the other hand, it is theoretically possible, most probable in certain rare diseases, for you to have, as a result of your parentage, a disease which none of your ancestry ever exhibited. The reason is that your traits, whether they are structural or psychological, are the consequences not of some trait in your ancestry but of the biological material which your parents contributed to your development.

This biological material includes the reproductive cells, the spermatozoon from the father and the ovum from the mother. At conception these two cells merge in a process known as fertilization. The result is, first, a single-celled organism, called the *zygote*, which is the individual at his first stage of development. In modern genetics the term *heredity* refers to these biological materials. Psychologically, we shall find it advantageous to restrict the term to the zygote, which in the present discussion will be regarded as the heredity of the individual. Thus heredity is the individual at the first stage of his development.

The Zygote

Since the zygote is formed of a union of the reproductive cells of the parents, the nature of these parent cells determines the nature of the zygote or heredity. It is, therefore, important to see how variations in the reproductive cells can produce differences between various zygotes; that is, between the heredities of various individuals. The zygote in its organization as a single cell fundamentally resembles other single cells in having an outer covering or cell membrane, a mass of viscous material called cytoplasm, and within this a globular body called a nucleus (see Figure 4). Although other variations may have importance, those which have attracted the most notice occur in the nucleus. Here may be visible at certain times under the microscope long threadlike structures which are named *chromosomes* (see Figure 4).

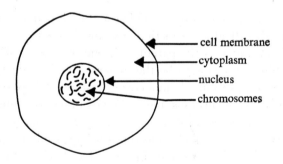

Figure 4

Diagram of a Cell

Cells have many different shapes, but each cell, of whatever shape, contains cytoplasm, a nucleus, and chromosomes.

Reduction division of germ cells. The zygote of man contains 48 of these chromosomes. These are organized into 24 pairs. What makes the chromosomes particularly significant is (1) that the development of the individual depends upon the nature of the particular chromosomes in the zygote, and (2) that half of the chromosomes, one from each pair, come from one parent while the other half come from the other parent. Thus half of the individual chromosome inheritance is contributed by each parent. This is brought about by the fact that the germ cells of each parent, while originally containing 48 chromosomes arranged in pairs (24 pairs), mature in such a way that the number of chromosomes is reduced by half. Each mature germ cell, therefore, contains only 24 chromosomes, one from each of the original 24 pairs. One step in this process, known as reduction division, is illustrated in Figure 5 with a cell which has four pairs of chromosomes. Each

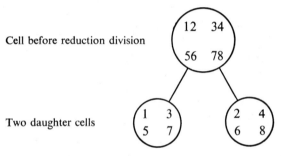

Cell before reduction division

Two daughter cells

Figure 5

Diagram Illustrating Reduction Division of Germ Cells

chromosome is represented by a number and each pair by two numbers together. Each cell after reduction division has taken place has half as many chromosomes as the parent cell, one from each of the original four pairs. Since it seems to be the general rule in reduction division for the chromosomes to divide in a chance fashion, it is possible to have other combinations of chromosomes. For example, one might get two cells with chromosomes 1467 and 2358, or 2357 and 1468, or 2457 and 1368. With 4 pairs of chromosomes it is possible to get 16 different combinations of chromosomes in the reduced cells. Stated another way, the chance of getting two cells exactly alike from the reduction division of a large number of original cells is 1 in 16. With 24 pairs of chromosomes in human germ cells the number of possible arrangements in the daughter cells would be 2 to the 24th power, or 16,777,216.

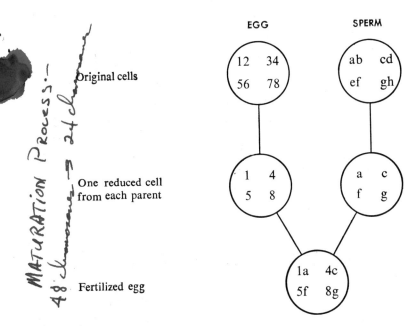

Handwritten margin notes:
MATURATION PROCESS.—
48 chromosomes → 24 chromosomes

Figure 6

Diagram Illustrating the Pairing of Chromosomes

This illustrates the pairing of chromosomes in fertilization and the restoration of the number of chromosomes characteristic of the species.

Fertilization. In the process of fertilization the material of the male germ cell merges or unites with the material of the female germ cell. The chromosomes of the one cell pair up with the chromosomes of the other. Thus the human zygote has 24 pairs of chromosomes. This process of pairing of chromosomes in the zygote is illustrated in Figure 6, using a cell with 4 pairs of chromosomes as before and adding another parent with chromosomes represented by letters to indicate different germ material.

Interaction of Chromosome Materials

In this pairing of the chromosomes of the two parents in the zygote, the chromosomes interact or affect each other in a variety of ways to produce similarities and differences between parents and offspring. The possible interactions are greatly complicated by the fact that each chromosome is made up of a very large number of very minute particles called *genes.* These act as factors or determiners singly or (in most cases) in combinations or teams. The determination of even a simple characteristic in an offspring may involve the interaction of a number of factors. There is also the possibility that some hereditary factors may be qualities of the totality of the gene and chromosome arrangements.

Mendel's laws. Some of the facts underlying these interactions were discovered many years ago by Mendel and were formulated into what are now referred to as Mendel's laws. One of the simple principles was discovered by Mendel in working with plants. In crossing certain varieties of peas which were characteristically tall and short, he observed that all of the peas of the next or filial generations (F_1) were tall. On crossing these second-generation peas, he got in the third generation (F_2) tall and short peas in the ratio of 3 tall to 1 short.

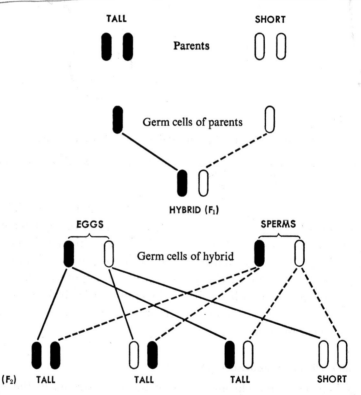

Figure 7

Diagram Illustrating How a Pair of Chromosomes Behaves
in the Cross between a Tall and a Short Pea

(From T. H. Morgan, "The Mechanism and Laws of Heredity," in *The Foundations of Experimental Psychology*, edited by Carl Murchison, 1929, p. 19. By permission of the Clark University Press, Worcester, Mass.)

This is illustrated in Figure 7, in which a pair of black rods carrying the gene for tall represents the tall peas of the first generation, and a pair of white rods carrying the gene for short represents the short peas. After reduction division of the two parent cells, one black and one white rod come together at fertilization to produce an offspring. Each offspring has one gene for tall and one for short, but, as Mendel observed, the offspring are all tall. This result is explained by saying that the gene for tall is *dominant* over the gene for short, and that whenever the genes for these two characteristics are paired, the result of the pairing will be determined by the gene for tall. The other gene is ineffective or nonoperative in this pairing. The possible results of crossing two second-generation peas are shown in the lower part of Figure 7. After reduction division each germ cell will be represented by a black or a white rod. Fertilization will bring a rod from each cell together as in the F_1 generation. It will be noted that the possible pairings in the F_2 generation include one pair of black rods like the original tall pea, one pair of white rods like the original short pea, and two pairs each with one black and one white rod like the F_1 generation peas. Since three of the four carry a dominant gene, three of the four peas are tall. The fourth pea with the pair of white rods has no gene for tall but two genes for short and it is, therefore, short. The gene for short which is ineffective when paired with one for tall is effective when paired with another gene for short. A trait which acts as shortness does in this example is said to be *recessive.* In instances of the kind under discussion it is a trait which, present in a parent of one generation, disappears in the second generation, and appears in one fourth (on the average) of the offspring of the third generation.

Heredity and Environment

When one attempts to make predictions about the characteristics which will result from certain combinations or interactions of chromosome materials in a zygote, he is assuming, of course, that the zygote will develop and that the conditions which are essential for the development of the characteristic will be present. Heredity alone is insufficient to produce the individual or any of his characteristics at any stage of development subsequent to the first or zygote stage. For development beyond this level, it is essential to have not only heredity but a developmental environment which will provide the materials and conditions necessary for growth. These include nourishment, protection, and opportunities for stimulation. Without these the individual would no more grow than he would if he had no heredity. The basic fact of development is that both heredity and environment are essential to it. This applies to every trait of the individual — anatomical, physiological, or psychological — beyond the single-celled stage. It is impossible to separate traits into those which are hereditary and those which are environmental, because every trait is both hereditary and environmental (24). In short, the individual, the P of our equation, is what he is at every stage of his development because of the joint operation of both heredity and environment.

Are traits hereditary? In spite of this fact it is still a common practice to speak of certain traits as being hereditary, of others as being acquired, i.e. dependent upon environment. In stating that a characteristic is hereditary it is assumed that the hereditary material will develop under those conditions which are essential or have been essential for the development of the characteristic in the parent stock. If these conditions are constant, differences in the characteristic in different organisms will be due to differences in heredity. This does not mean that the trait is due to heredity alone. If on the other hand these conditions are not constant, i.e. not like those under which the hereditary material ordinarily develops, one may obtain results which differ from those which are normally obtained. Experimenters have obtained results indicating that a particular heredity which would produce a given trait under one set of environmental conditions may not do so under another. For example, Stockard (30) has shown that the embryo of a marine fish, Fundulus, which normally becomes a fish with two eyes, will develop but one eye when its environment is changed by the introduction of sea-water solutions of magnesium chloride. Other studies have shown that alterations in the structure of certain lower organisms can be produced experimentally by environmental changes brought about by the use of x-rays, chemicals, insufficient oxygen, and temperature changes. While these alterations are in the nature of exceptions and are not necessarily desirable ones, the fact that such variations have been produced by environmental means shows that environment does more than simply unfold the characteristics inherent in the germ material.

Are traits due to environment? In a similar fashion, to say that a particular trait is due to environment is correct only if it is recognized that there would be no trait if there were no heredity, and no trait (of the sort under discussion) if the heredity were essentially different from that which is now interacting with the environment. A particular environment which produces a given trait with one heredity will not produce the same trait with another heredity. The problem, therefore, is basically not one of what traits are hereditary or environmental, but one of finding out what changes in human traits can be produced by varying heredity while keeping environment constant, or by varying environment while keeping heredity constant.   It should be noted that the problem as stated says nothing about determining the relative importance of heredity and environment.   One may discover that greater changes in a given trait can be produced by varying heredity than by varying environment.   This does not mean that heredity is more important than environment.   One would have no trait at all without both.   The situation is somewhat analogous, as someone has said, to the question of deciding which is more important in producing a wave, wind or water.

Importance of heredity and environment.   Even though studies which attempt to determine the effect of variations in heredity or environment fail to show that the one variable is relatively more important than the other, their results may be highly important.   If studies show, for example, that differences between the intelligence of individuals of like heredity can be produced by varying the developmental environment of these individuals, one has a fact that may be utilized in predicting and controlling behavior regardless of whether the study shows that environment is more important than heredity.   The latter information, even if it were established, would add nothing to the value of the observed fact in predicting and controlling behavior.   If another study should show that differences in behavior of the same magnitude can be produced by holding environment constant and making heredity the variable factor, it would in no way change the usefulness of the first finding.   On the contrary, it would merely show that there are two ways of producing the same result.

Difficulties in experimenting on heredity and environment.   In examining the results of experiments on heredity and environment, one point should be kept in mind.   These experiments do not exercise the degree of control of the variables involved which one strives to attain in well-designed experiments.   Heredity and environment are complex variables, and apparently they are dynamically interrelated in determining an individual's behavior.   They operate continuously from the first stage of development.   If one separates identical twins at birth or at an early age and places them in what appear on the surface to be dissimilar environments, he is not varying environment in any measurable way because he has no way of knowing what elements in the dissimilar environments the twins will respond to.   In the face of these facts it is more reasonable to say that certain studies have been performed in which an experimenter has done thus and so with hereditary and environmental variables and that under these conditions certain results have been obtained.   This makes it unnecessary, and perhaps it is incorrect, to say that environment is held constant or that heredity is held constant.

Experiments with Heredity as the Independent Variable

Since it is impossible to arrange an experiment with human beings in which heredity is varied at will, one resorts to the procedure of studying individuals who are known to differ in heredity.   These individuals are studied under conditions in which environment is reasonably uniform or in which differences in environment are regarded as of little consequence for the behavior under observation.   Thus, members of a family, who are known to have similar heredity, are compared with individuals who are unrelated to one another.   A comparison of siblings (children of the same parents), fraternal twins (twins who have developed from different zygotes), identical twins (twins who have developed from a single zygote), and unrelated individuals in two physical traits and one mental trait (I.Q., or intelligence quotient) is shown in Table III.

Table III

Correlations Showing the Increase of Similarity in Mental and Physical Traits with Increase of Relationship (33)

	IDENTICAL TWINS	FRATERNAL TWINS	SIBLINGS	UNRELATED INDIVIDUALS
Standing height	.93–.95	.50–.65	.50	.00
Head length	.91	.58	.50	.00
I.Q.	.90	.63–.70	.50–.60	.00

Since it is known that identical twins are identical in heredity and that members of the same family are more alike than unrelated individuals, the results may be interpreted as indicating that the greater the similarity in heredity, the greater the similarity in physical and mental traits.   It is interesting to note, however, that though fraternal twins are no more similar in heredity than siblings, they are slightly more alike in the three traits in question.   This very probably means that the environments of fraternal twins are more alike than those of siblings.   Some of the differences between the two groups, and perhaps between all four groups, are not to be attributed to differences in heredity alone.

Holzinger's study of identical and fraternal twins. A somewhat similar study is reported by Holzinger, who studied 50 pairs of fraternal and 50 pairs of identical twins. He found that the intelligence of fraternal twins correlated .63 while that of identical twins correlated .88 (14). This difference between fraternal and identical twins is in accordance with the presumed difference in heredity of fraternal and identical twins. Whether this difference between the two coefficients of correlation is indicative of the real difference in heredity cannot be determined from a study of this sort. It merely indicates that the more similar individuals are in heredity, the more they will be found to resemble one another in intelligence under the developmental conditions which generally exist for fraternal and identical twins.

Brain-wave patterns of identical and fraternal twins. The fact that identical twins are very much more alike in a given trait than fraternal twins has been used as an indication that the trait in question is hereditary. For example, Lennox, Gibbs, and Gibbs (19) present data from a study of brain-wave patterns of identical and fraternal twins which they interpret to mean that brain-wave patterns are hereditary. They obtained electroencephalographic tracings from 55 pairs of monozygotic (identical) twins and 19 pairs of dizygotic (fraternal) twins. The tracings of the monozygotic twins were judged to be identical in 85 per cent, not identical in 4 per cent, and in doubt in 11 per cent of the records. The tracings for the dizygotic twins were judged to be unlike in 95 per cent of the cases and alike in 5 per cent. Apart from the authors' interpretations, it appears that the greater similarity of brain-wave patterns of identical twins in contrast to fraternal twins is in the direction of the known similarity in heredity.

Studies of siblings reared in different homes. Another kind of study bearing on this problem is one in which siblings are separated and placed in homes of different social levels. Since siblings are children of the same parents, they are somewhat similar in heredity. When siblings are reared in the homes of their parents, the resemblance in developed traits, as shown in Table III, is represented by a coefficient of .50. When they are separated and placed in other homes, but homes of similar cultural advantages, the degree of resemblance falls to .35. When they are separated and placed in dissimilar homes, the correlation for 63 pairs of siblings is represented by a coefficient of .24 (10). Were heredity of no significance, the relationship for siblings living in unlike homes should be approximately zero. The fact that the correlation between siblings in dissimilar homes was found to be .24 is interpreted, therefore, to mean that similarity of heredity is of some significance.

Were environment of no importance, siblings should show the same degree of resemblance whether reared together or apart. The fact that the correlation between siblings dropped to .24 instead of remaining near .50 indicates that environment is of importance, at least in this study.

Tryon's experiment. In general it seems that as the similarity in heredity between individuals increases or decreases, the similarity in intelligence of these individuals increases or decreases, not directly but in some degree. A further test of this conclusion could be obtained by artificially increasing or decreasing the hereditary similarity between animals and measuring the increase or decrease in the similarity with respect to some trait, keeping environment as constant as possible. This in effect was done by Tryon with a group of white rats (32).

A group of 142 white rats were tested for their ability to run a maze (a picture of a maze is shown on page 186). The number of times the rats entered a blind alley (error) in 19 trials is shown in Figure 8. It will be noted that there are very few rats with high error scores and very few with low error scores. Most of the rats fall in the middle of the range. Two groups of rats were selected from this total group. The rats with the very lowest error scores were designated as the "bright" group, and those with the highest scores were designated as the "dull" group. The rats of the bright group were mated with one another, as were those of the dull group. The offspring of the bright and dull groups were tested, and the brightest and dullest ones from this group were selected. Again bright rats were mated with bright rats, and dull rats were mated with dull rats. This procedure was

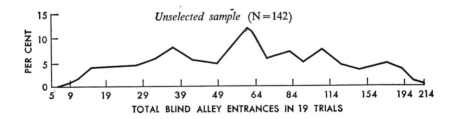

Figure 8

The Performance of an Unselected Group of White Rats in Learning
to Run a Maze

(From Robert C. Tryon, "Individual Differences," in *Comparative Psychology*, Revised, edited by F. A. Moss, p. 344. Copyright, 1934, 1942, by Prentice-Hall, Inc. Reprinted by permission of the publisher.)

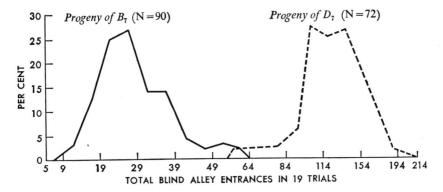

Figure 9

The Performance of Bright and Dull Rats in Learning to Run a Maze

These rats were obtained by the selective breeding of the bright and dull rats of each of seven successive generations beginning with the unselected rats whose performances are shown in Figure 8. (From Robert C. Tryon, "Individual Differences," in *Comparative Psychology*, Revised, edited by F. A. Moss, p. 345. Copyright, 1934, 1942, by Prentice-Hall, Inc. Reprinted by permission of the publisher.)

continued for eight generations. The bright and dull rats of the eighth generation were tested with the results shown in Figure 9.

It will be noted that the procedure of selective breeding has produced two groups of rats that are distinctly different in their ability to run a maze. The test results for the intermediate generations show that this separation is gradual. As the two groups become less and less alike by selection and inbreeding, they become less and less alike in their ability to run the maze. As a further check on this relationship Tryon crossed the bright and dull rats and the brightest and dullest of their offspring. The offspring of these matings were found to be quite similar to the original parents in their ability to run the maze. A distribution of their error scores resembles the one shown in Figure 8. The variation in heredity is accompanied by a variation in ability to run a maze under conditions in which external environmental conditions were held as constant as possible.

Whether the change in ability to run the maze is directly proportional to the change in heredity cannot be determined from this study because the elements in the environments to which the two groups were reacting were not necessarily the same. One trial run on a maze to a dull rat is not equal to one trial for a bright rat. Munn's (23, p. 77) suggestion that "no two human beings live in the same environment or react in the same way to the same aspects of their surroundings" is just as true for rats as it is for human beings.

Experiments with Environment as the Independent Variable

The studies of siblings who were separated and placed in different homes (described above) indicate that environment has an effect upon differences in intelligence. Studies of identical twins separated at an early age and reared in different environments also indicate that environment is a factor in intelligence test performance. Newman, Freeman, and Holzinger reported a study of 19 pairs of identical twins separated in infancy and reared apart. Among the tests used in this study was the Stanford-Binet individual intelligence test (see Chapter 12). The results of the study showed that the correlation between the Binet I.Q.'s of these identical twins was about .67 in contrast to a correlation of .91 reported for another group of identical twins reared together (25).

Studies of foster children. The influence of environment is further indicated in a study of foster children by Freeman, Holzinger, and their associates. A correlation of .37 between the intelligence of children and that of their foster parents was obtained. The expected correlation for adults and children paired at random is zero. The correlation between unrelated children reared in the same home ranged from .25 to .37 (10). The expected correlation between unrelated children paired at random is zero. In contrast to these findings, Burks found that the foster home had little effect upon the intelligence of a group of foster children adopted before the age of twelve months. She estimated the effect of heredity to be as high as 75 to 80 per cent (4). Another investigator matched 194 foster children with a like number of children reared by their own parents. The intelligence of the foster children and their foster parents correlated about .25 in contrast to a correlation of about .50 between the other groups of children and their true parents (18). The figures of all these studies seem to indicate rather definitely that part of the high correlation of intelligence between parents and children and between siblings reared together is due to similarity in environments.

A word of caution. The results of these experiments, dealing in one case with learning and in the others with intelligence, a complex kind of human performance measured by intelligence tests, can hardly be taken as representative of what is likely to be true of physical traits or other mental traits. The amount of variation that may be produced in a trait by varying either environment or heredity may be large or small, depending upon the stage of development at which variations are undertaken and upon the degree to which heredity and environment can be manipulated or controlled. A variation in environment, for example, may produce a considerable amount of variation in a trait if introduced early in the growth process, yet fail to do so at a later stage of development. Then, too, the failure to produce a marked variation in such a trait by varying the environment may simply mean that the essential environmental variables are unknown or not controlled by the experimenter.

PRENATAL DEVELOPMENT

The period from conception to birth in man is one of extremely rapid development. During this period the zygote develops into a very complex organism with highly differentiated structures capable of functioning in many specialized ways; and into a human infant about 20 inches long and weighing 7 to $7\frac{1}{2}$ pounds. This period of development, approximately nine months, is customarily divided into three stages.

Stages of Prenatal Development

The first stage is known as the *period of the ovum* or the germinal period. It begins at the moment of fertilization and extends to the end of the second week. The zygote or single-celled organism divides into two cells, these into four, and so on until a cluster of many cells is formed. Some differentiation of the cells begins to occur, with the result that an outer and an inner cluster of cells appear. The outer layer eventually develops into accessory tissue which provides protection and nourishment. During the second week the ovum becomes implanted in the uterus and begins to receive nourishment from the mother.

The second period is described as the *embryonic period*. It extends from the end of the second week to the end of the eighth week. This is a period of rapid change characterized by marked differentiation of development, i.e., development of parts of the embryo in different directions to form different body parts. By the end of the fourth week a head, mouth, trunk, and various internal organs are discernible. By the end of the eighth week the embryo is unmistakably human in appearance. The head is very large, being almost as long as the rest of the body (see Figure 10). Arms and legs have started to develop. The muscles of the body are formed, and spontaneous movements can be observed in operatively removed embryos (7, p. 113). The entire period is one in which the parts of the body are established or their formation is started.

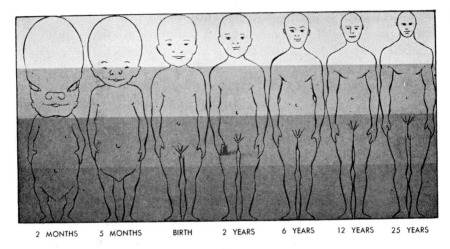

2 MONTHS   5 MONTHS   BIRTH   2 YEARS   6 YEARS   12 YEARS   25 YEARS

Figure 10

Changes in Bodily Proportions from Fetal Stages to Adulthood

(From R. E. Scammon, "Developmental Anatomy," in H. Morris, *Human Anatomy*, 9th edition, Fig. 24. Copyright, 1933, The Blakiston Company, publishers.)

The third stage of prenatal development, covering the period from the end of the eighth week to birth, is called the *fetal period*. It is a period of rapid development characterized by an increase in size of the parts which first appeared in the embryonic period, by a change in body proportions (see Figure 10), and by the appearance and rapid development of behavior. Activity or behavior occurring in response to nerve stimulation appears at about 16 weeks. The spontaneous movements reported above as appearing at about 8 weeks now involve the arms and legs, are more pronounced, and may be felt by the mother. The first signs of reflex activity appear about this time. A reflex is a very simple, involuntary, unlearned response elicited immediately by the application of a stimulus to a sense organ. One such reflex in the fetus or newborn is the *plantar reflex* — an extension of the big toe and a flexion of the other toes in response to stroking the sole of the foot. As development progresses during this period, more and more responses appear or can be elicited by stimulation. The body structures which are directly involved in behavior — the sense organs, the nervous system, muscles, and glands — mature to the point where activity near the end of the prenatal period cannot be distinguished from that of full-term infants. There are some responses, of course, which depend upon outside stimulation and do not appear until such stimulation is provided after birth.

Learning before Birth

One problem of considerable psychological significance has to do with
the question of learning before birth. Learning is discussed in detail
in Chapter 6. It is sufficient at this point to regard learning as activity
which produces or results in some change or modification of behavior.
Behavior appears before birth. It develops or changes as a consequence
of the growth of the body structures. But does it change as a consequence of practice, experience, or activity?

Spelt's experiment. A recent experiment by Spelt (29) indicates
that learning can occur before birth. In this experiment human fetuses,
during the last two months of the fetal period, learned to make a response to a vibrotactile stimulus, a stimulus which did not produce the
response before the experiment started.

This learning occurred by means of a process called *conditioning* (see
pages 180–184). In this process the vibrotactile stimulus (a vibrator
placed perpendicularly to the mother's abdomen), which at first did
not produce a response in the fetus, was presented along with a loud
noise, a stimulus which did produce a response. The response produced
by the loud noise was a movement, generally of the head or limbs,
which was vigorous enough to be recorded by an instrument attached
to the mother's abdomen and/or to be felt and reported by the mother.
The two stimuli were presented together several times. After some
15 to 20 paired presentations, the vibrotactile stimulus alone produced
fetal movements. While this experiment was concerned with the
reactions of fetuses to sound stimuli, there is no claim that the fetuses
could hear in the sense in which hearing occurs after birth. Strong
sounds may affect the hearing mechanism of the fetus, but it is unnecessary to suppose that this is true in Spelt's experiment. The important
point is that the loud noise produced a measurable response and that
this response was eventually aroused by a stimulus which did not at
the outset produce it.

Methods of Studying Prenatal Development

Information about human fetal development has been obtained by three
principal methods. These are (1) mother's reports of fetal movements,
(2) instrumental detection of movement, and (3) observation and study
of operatively removed fetuses. In the previously cited study by Spelt
and in studies by Sontag and Wallace (28) and Sontag and Richards
(27), fetal movements were recorded by the first two of these methods.
To increase the accuracy of the mother's reports of fetal movements,

a recording device is set up whereby the mother presses a button each time she feels a movement. The button activates a recording mechanism which records the number of times the button is pressed. Movements are also recorded by placing diaphragms on the mother's abdomen and connecting these by means of rubber tubes to a recording device. Any vigorous movement of the fetus against the abdomen will push on the rubber diaphragm and change the air pressure in the tubes and in the cuplike instrument holding the diaphragm; this in turn activates the recording mechanism, so that an objective record is made of the movements of the fetus. In addition to this instrumental procedure, heartbeats may be detected by the use of a stethoscope.

Fetal electroencephalograms. One investigator, Lindsley (21), has developed a method for obtaining fetal electrocardiograms and fetal electroencephalograms. The latter are records of so-called brain waves and represent the electrical potentials set up by activity of the brain. Electroencephalography is a technique in which electrodes are attached to the head (in Lindsley's study the electrodes were attached to the mother's abdominal wall over the head of the fetus) and connected to an exceedingly delicate measuring apparatus which amplifies electrical discharges as much as half a million times or more. Rhythms of electrical discharge have been detected which differ in frequency or number of waves per second, amplitude, and regularity. Some of these rhythms have been shown to change when a subject goes to sleep or when he is stimulated or emotionally aroused. It appears also that these waves are of significance in the diagnosis of certain brain diseases and behavior disorders (20). The significance of brain waves for understanding fetal development or the subsequent behavior of the fetus is not known. This is a problem for future study. It is significant, however, that a technique which has revealed some interesting relationships between a measurable phenomenon in the individual and his behavior is now available for the study of the human fetus.

Observations of operatively removed fetuses. Many of the facts about human fetal development cited above and many additional facts regarding the onset of behavior, spontaneous activity, reactions to stimulation, reflexes, and instinctual processes have been obtained from observations of fetuses operatively removed at some stage prior to the normal birth time because some condition of the mother necessitated the artificial termination of pregnancy. The most complete and systematic studies of such fetuses have been made by Minkowski (22) and Hooker (15, 16). The fetus is removed by means of a Caesarean section under a local anaesthetic, and is placed in a bath of physiological salt solution at normal blood temperature. Since its oxygen supply is cut off, any activity observed is the activity of an increasingly asphyxiated organism. Asphyxiation has the effect of increasing activity and then decreasing it (7, p. 108). While studies of prematurely born fetuses provide some information about fetal development, it is felt that such studies are not exactly comparable to the kind described above, because the prematurely born fetus can and does live outside the mother in an environment that differs so much from the uterine environment that comparisons with the latter are probably not justified.

Studies of Animal Fetuses

Our most exact information about prenatal development in general has been obtained from studies of animal fetuses. Lower animals such as amphibians and birds are favorite subjects for such studies because they develop outside a mother from an egg which can be observed quite readily throughout the period of growth, and because they have a relatively short developmental period. Though mammals are more difficult to study, many important studies have been done on guinea pigs, cats, rats, and opossums. The mammalian fetuses are operatively removed and kept alive for a time by being left attached to the mother by means of the umbilical cord. In these studies the fetuses are observed and stimulated, and records are made of the responses which appear. In this way it has been possible to obtain a fairly complete picture of the entire period of prenatal development of the animals under investigation.

Processes of development. A number of investigators have found in these pictures of prenatal development indications of certain orderly sequences which they have designated as general principles or generalized descriptions of behavior development. For example, Coghill (8), working with the salamander *Amblystoma*, Angulo y González (1), working with white rats, and Coronis (9), working with cats, suggest that behavior in the fetal period starts as a mass reaction or as a total pattern of activity and that the development of behavior consists of a breakdown of this mass activity into separate or individualized movements. The process by which separate responses develop out of the original mass action of the whole organism is called *individuation.* Individuation as a process of development is to be contrasted with another process, *integration*, in which behavior develops through the combination of simple movements into larger movements, and of these into still larger movements. Both of these processes seem to be involved in the development of finger and hand movements after birth.

At birth the baby uses his hand as if the four fingers were fastened together. This mass activity eventually breaks down (individuation) into separate finger movements. Later the separate finger movements become combined or integrated into many patterns of activity, such as picking up objects with the forefinger and thumb, threading a needle, writing, playing a piano, and typewriting.

Developmental sequences. The investigators mentioned above and others have described the development of fetal behavior as starting in the head region and progressing toward the tail. The first responses appear as movements of the head and upper part of the trunk. As development proceeds, other parts of the body become involved in a definite head-to-tail sequence, technically known as the *cephalo-caudal sequence.* Development of activity in the limbs seems also to follow a definite sequence. Coronis (9, p. 378) describes this development by saying, "The entire limb is first involved in the response and then gradually the more distal points become, as it were, independent of the total movement." This course of development is called the *proximo-distal sequence.* All experimenters have not obtained clear-cut evidence to support these generalizations. For example, Carmichael (5) feels that his study of guinea pig fetuses does not confirm the cephalo-caudal or proximo-distal sequences of development and that it does not give unqualified support to either the individuation or the integration theory of development.

It should be recognized, of course, that these descriptions of fetal development hold, strictly speaking, for the organism studied, and that it is premature, as Carmichael points out (7, p. 89), to regard such generalizations as specific formulas that can be applied to other non-human mammals or to man in advance of observation. But the value of such generalized formulations as hypotheses to be tested in studies of postnatal as well as prenatal development in man must be recognized. It may well be that such hypotheses will prove to be the most important contribution from studies of behavior development in infrahuman and human fetuses. Therefore, the generalizations as well as the facts regarding prenatal development may contribute to our understanding of individual development.

BEHAVIOR OF THE NEWBORN INFANT

During the fetal period the developing child is dependent upon the mother for food, oxygen, temperature regulation, protection, and in fact for all the things necessary for maintaining life. At birth this parasitic relationship is severed. The child enters into an environment in which he must get his own oxygen, take food and digest it, excrete waste products, and maintain a relatively constant body temperature, and which provides new stimulations and opportunities for development. As was indicated in the discussion of prenatal growth above, near the end of the fetal period the child has reached a stage of development where the appearance of many responses only awaits the application of the proper stimulations and the greater freedom of movement present in this new environment.

The vital functions of breathing, eating, and elimination which the newborn takes over must begin immediately after birth or within a few hours. Breathing is initiated almost immediately, as is the change in circulation which is necessary to carry the blood to the lungs for aeration. The other vital functions needed for carrying on an independent existence — eating, digestion, assimilation, elimination, and sleeping — appear within a few minutes to a few hours. The appearance of new responses is not due to any sudden upsurge in the child's development or any miraculous change resulting from birth. Development is a continuous process, and birth is to be regarded as a stage in this process. An inventory of the behavior of the newborn will provide us with a picture of the child at this stage of his development and so contribute to a fuller understanding of the developmental process.

Mass Activity

The newborn does much more than breathe, eat, and sleep. Anyone who has watched an infant while he is crying has noted that he is virtually moving all over. His body, arms, legs, head, face, eyes, mouth, and vocal mechanisms all seem to be going at the same time. Essentially the same picture is found when the child is not crying but is lying awake with no specific external stimulations present. This is essentially the picture obtained by Irwin (17) in a carefully controlled study in which newborn infants were observed continuously during the first ten days of life except for short periods taken out for feeding, bathing, and changing clothes. In this study each infant was placed in an experimental cabinet upon a small platform set on ball bearings. The platform, described as a stabilimeter, was attached by means of a system of wires and pulleys to a recording device located outside the cabinet. The cabinet, which was closed once the baby was inside, was equipped in such a way that external conditions could be kept constant or uniform. The stabilimeter made it possible for the movements of the infant to be recorded automatically and objectively. In addition to the stabilimeter record, observers were stationed at windows around the cabinet to observe and report specific movements. Observations of movements were dictated to stenographers (see page 29) in order to permit uninterrupted observations. This study revealed in an objective way and in precise figures what we indicated above. The infants were exceedingly active, making on the average almost one response per second. Responses occurred at such a rate and in so many parts of the body at the same time that it was difficult or impossible for the observers to record all of the separate movements. Irwin used the term *mass activity* to describe this kind of behavior. It is the kind of behavior in which virtually all parts of the body are involved, and the kind which occurs when external stimulations remain relatively stable.

Reactions to Specific Stimulations

Studies (26) of the reactions of the newborn infant to specific stimulations indicate that he is sensitive to visual, auditory, pain, temperature, pressure, taste, smell, and other kinds of stimuli. However, the reactions to these stimulations reveal in general that the newborn is not as sensitive as adults or older children, i.e., these stimulations do not produce observable reactions as frequently or as consistently as they do in later life. Nor do they produce the same kinds of reactions. Furthermore, ability to discriminate between stimuli of different qualities or intensities is either absent or very poorly developed. For example, the newborn reacts to light, but it is questionable whether he can respond differently to different colors or to different intensities of a given light stimulus. An example in the field of audition is provided in a study by Stubbs (31). Using the stabilimeter for recording the infant's movements, she found that there were no differences in amount of activity in response to sound stimuli of four different frequencies, 128, 256, 1024, and 4096 cycles. While the newborn responds to taste stimuli, it is uncertain whether he differentiates between salt, sour, bitter, and sweet, the four primary taste qualities.

A great variety of reactions are aroused by the stimulation of a given sense organ or of different sense organs. For example, visual stimuli of sufficient intensity produce eyelid responses, respiratory and circulatory changes, a change in general body activity, "startle" responses, and certain reflex movements such as the change in the size of the pupil of the eye to changes in the intensity of illumination. Similarly, smell stimuli produce a variety of responses. These include "throwing-back or turning-away of the head, wrinkling or grimacing of the face, squirming of the trunk, movements of the extremities, and frequently sneezing and crying" (26, p. 215). Gross muscular responses or general body activity which resembles mass activity seems to be produced by a variety of specific stimuli. In some cases it appears that this general activity starts in the area stimulated and then spreads until other parts of the body are involved. For example, a needle prick on the big toe may produce general body activity which starts as a leg movement; or a similar prick on the hand may arouse a mass of activity in which arm movements are more prominent than the movements of other parts of the body.

Reflex Activity

In contrast to this picture of mass activity or generalized activity in which almost any kind of stimulus produces a response in almost any part of the body, there seem to be some fairly specific, localized responses which are called out by simple, specific stimuli. One such response is the grasping reflex, or the involuntary closure of the fingers over a rod or pencil placed in contact with the palm. This reflex is so strong that an infant may be lifted from his bed as he holds the rod. Another, but somewhat more complex, response of this sort is the Moro or embrace reflex. The infant throws his arms out and brings them together as if in an embrace. The legs are extended and then flexed. These reactions are ordinarily called out by a sharp or jarring sound, but may be produced by other stimuli. Some investigators seem to regard this response as a kind of fear reaction. Earlier it was thought to be a kind of defensive response (26, p. 233). The plantar reflex has already been mentioned (see page 56). A very large number of responses have been identified as reflexes. When these are examined, however, in the light of the definition of a reflex — namely, a specific, localized, involuntary, unlearned reaction to a simple, specific stimulus — it is questionable whether many of them should be called reflexes. There are very few specific local reactions which are invariably aroused by a single, specific stimulus. The grasping reflex comes quite close to being one such response. The plantar response, on the other hand, is not so specific. It involves an extension of the big toe, a flexion and fanning downward of the other toes, and a retraction of the foot, leg, and thigh. The response is elicited ordinarily by stroking the sole of the foot, but it may be called out by other stimuli. This indicates a lack of a fixed connection between one stimulus area and one response area. Essentially the same statement can be made in regard to the Moro reflex and to such responses as sneezing, sucking, and yawning.

In summary, it appears that the view which held that the infant's behavior consists of a large number of unorganized reflexes which later combine to form complex patterns of behavior is not borne out by the facts. Most of the infant's behavior lacks the degree of specificity and the definite and fixed connections between stimuli and responses which such a view suggests or demands. On the other hand, it would be a mistake to characterize the infant's behavior as consisting entirely of mass activity. Neither formulation fits the facts completely. There are some relatively simple, specific reactions; some more complex ones, some more fully developed than others; some loosely organized; and some organized and coordinated to the extent that the infant is able to carry on his independent existence from the moment he is born. These are the responses present at this stage in the child's development, the responses out of which subsequent behavior and behavioral character- istics develop.

MATURATION — *Becoming Mature — Growth*

Con refer to bodror behavior.

An individual begins his existence as a single-celled organism. Through cell division and cell differentiation, this single cell develops to the point where organs and structures begin to appear. These parts develop or mature to the point where behavior begins. As body struc- tures develop still further, more activity appears and earlier activity develops. The appearance and growth of body structures continues throughout the prenatal period and after birth until maturity is reached. Along with this development, and as a consequence of it, behavior appears and develops. This process of development is called *matura- tion*. Increases in size, height, and weight, changes in body proportions (see Figure 10), changes in the nature of body tissues, and the appear- ance of new structures are said to be due to maturation. This simply means that these changes occur in the normal course of growth as a consequence of the interaction of the hereditary material of the zygote with intracellular, intercellular, and external environmental stimula- tions. Likewise, any behavior whose initial appearance or subsequent development is dependent upon the development of body structures is said to be due to maturation. For example, breathing as an activity in the newborn is due to maturation because it appears as a consequence of the development of the lungs, and without any previous training or exercise. While the subsequent development of breathing is dependent in part upon the exercise or activity involved in breathing, it also depends upon the growth or maturational changes of the breathing mechanisms. Thus the initial appearance of the act and some of its subsequent developments are to be attributed to maturation.

Measures of Maturation

Everyone is familiar with many of the changes which occur in the maturation of structure or physical characteristics. Measures of height, weight, arm length, waist girth, chest girth, leg length, and many others are indicators of size. Successive measures of any one of these provide a measure of growth, as seen in Figure 11. Other measures have been used as indicators of the degree of physical maturity. These include the extent to which bones have been ossified, the number of permanent teeth which have erupted, height-weight ratio, and age at onset of puberty. Using the latter as an index of maturity level, it appears that girls mature earlier than boys, as seen in Figure 12. Measures of specific parts of the body indicate that different parts mature or grow at different rates and reach their maximum degree of maturity at different times. This is illustrated in Figure 13 for four kinds of bodily tissues. It is significant to note that lymphoid tissue

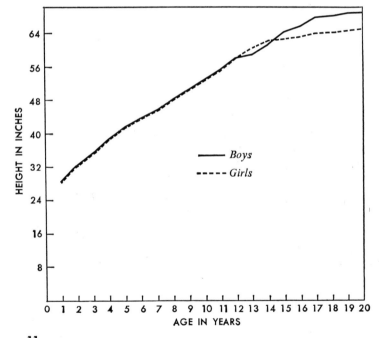

Figure 11

Age Changes in Height of Boys and Girls from Birth to Maturity

(Plotted from data in A. R. Gilliland, *Genetic Psychology*. Copyright 1933, by the Ronald Press Company. By permission of the publishers.)

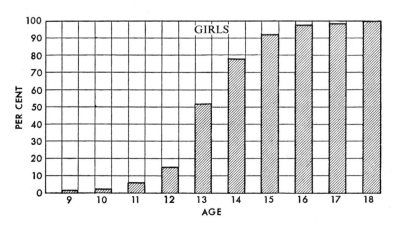

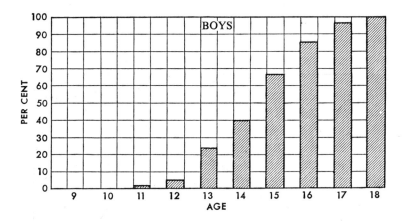

Figure 12

Differences in the Age of Boys and Girls at the Onset of Puberty —
Evidence that Girls Mature Earlier than Boys

(From Luella Cole, *Psychology of Adolescence*, p. 36. Copyright 1936. Reprinted by permission of the publishers, Farrar and Rinehart, Inc. Original data by Crampton, Baldwin, Boas, and Atkinson.)

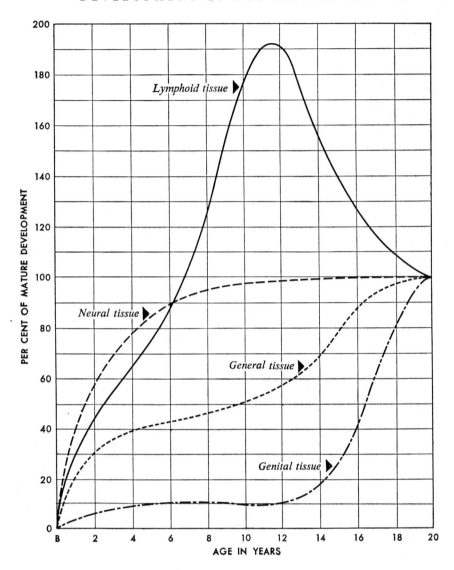

Figure 13

The Development of Different Parts of the Body at
Different Ages from Birth (B) to Twenty Years

(From R. W. Scammon, "The Growth of the Body in Childhood," in J. A. Harris and
others, *The Measurement of Man*, 1930, p. 193. By permission of the publisher, the
University of Minnesota Press, Minneapolis, Minnesota.)

actually develops beyond its adult level by about 8 years, reaches its peak development between 10 and 12, and then declines to the adult level at age 20. In contrast, the reproductive system (genital tissues) develops very slowly to about 12 years and then very rapidly to maturity. The nervous system, which is of particular interest to psychologists because of its role in behavior, develops very rapidly during the early years. According to the data in Figure 13, neural tissues reach at 6 years a stage of maturity which is 90 per cent of the adult maturity level. This rapid maturation of neural tissue is also indicated by the fact that at birth the brain accounts, on the average, for about one tenth of an infant's weight. During the first year after birth the brain increases in size 115 per cent; in the following year, 25 per cent; and in the next, 10 per cent (12). This growth in size and weight is accompanied by a remarkable increase in complexity of nervous organization and function. Figure 14 shows the increasing complexity of certain cells in the brain. Figure 15 shows the increasing conductivity, one of the activities or functions of neural tissues, of the cerebrum and the cerebellum (main parts of the brain) from just before birth to the age of $2\frac{1}{2}$ months.

Maturation and Learning

But maturation is not the only way by which development takes place. The development of both structure and behavior is dependent upon exercise, practice, experience, or activity. It has been shown that the size of a muscle is dependent upon the exercise of the muscle (34). This confirms our common observation that exercise or practice develops muscles. It is probable that the exercise of the lungs and accessory apparatus in breathing is a factor in the development of the breathing mechanisms. Thus the maturation of structures is essential for activity, and activity, once it is initiated, is a factor in the subsequent development of the structures as well as in the further development of the activity itself.

This further development of behavior through exercise or practice is said to be due to *learning*, which, as we noted earlier (page 57) and shall see in more detail in Chapter 6, is defined as the modification or change of behavior through experience or practice. Beginning with his early vocalizations, the child learns to talk. He learns a language, the particular one depending upon the environmental opportunities which are provided. While fingers and hands and their initial movements are largely the result of maturation, it is through learning that

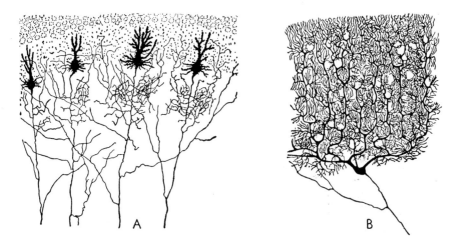

Figure 14

Difference in Complexity of Certain Brain Cells (Purkinje Cells)
in a Newborn Child (A) and an Adult (B)

(From G. W. Crile, *The Phenomena of Life*, Norton, 1936, p. 110; after Cajal.)

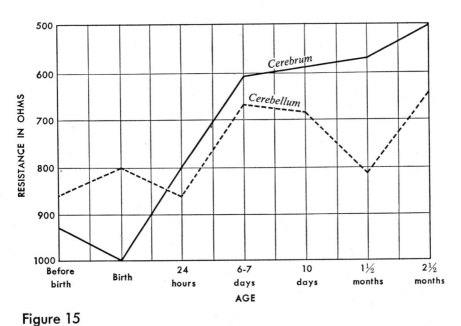

Figure 15

Changes in Conductivity of the Cerebrum and the Cerebellum from
Birth to the Age of Two and a Half Months

This graph is plotted in terms of resistance per cubic centimeter of tissue to a thousand-cycle current. (Modified from G. W. Crile, *The Phenomena of Life*, Norton, 1936, p. 111.)

these finger and hand movements develop into such skills as typing and playing the piano.

It is obvious, of course, that both maturation and learning are involved in the development of behavior. They operate together. An organism learns as he matures. How much of the change in a given kind of behavior is due to learning and how much to maturation can be determined only by arranging conditions experimentally in such a way that only one of the two is operating at a given time.

Bird's and Carmichael's experiments. Several investigations, dealing with both animals and human beings, show the role and importance of maturation in the development of certain kinds of behavior. At the animal level, Bird has studied the pecking of newly hatched chicks. He divided chicks into groups, allowing some to try their skill at pecking immediately after hatching, while others were kept in the dark and fed artificially for varying intervals of time before being allowed to peck. He found that a chick kept in the dark for hours before being allowed to peck will learn the skill in a fraction of the time required by a chick just out of the shell (2). The curve of maturation (without learning) for chicks is shown in Figure 16. Bird also reports that certain errors, such as missing the grain completely, seem to be practically eliminated by general physiological development, even in the absence of any practice (3).

Carmichael (6) reports work on frogs pointing in the same direction. He allowed a number of frogs' eggs to hatch in water containing an anaesthetic, which prevented the developing organisms from moving, though it in no way affected their physical development. At the same time, he allowed a number to hatch in plain water. After the latter group had turned into tadpoles and were swimming well, he placed the anaesthetized tadpoles in water containing no drug. In a few minutes these swam as well as those that had practiced swimming for some time. Evidently tadpoles do not learn to swim. They need only sufficient maturity.

Gesell and Thompson's experiment. Studies of a similar nature have also been conducted with children. Gesell and Thompson (11) separated a pair of identical twins when they were about a year old. One twin was regularly given ten minutes' practice playing with small blocks and ten minutes' practice climbing a short flight of stairs. The other twin was kept away from stairs and articles of furniture which could be used to climb upon, and was denied small blocks to play with. At the end of six weeks the performances of the infants were compared. There was no difference in their ability to play with blocks. The infant

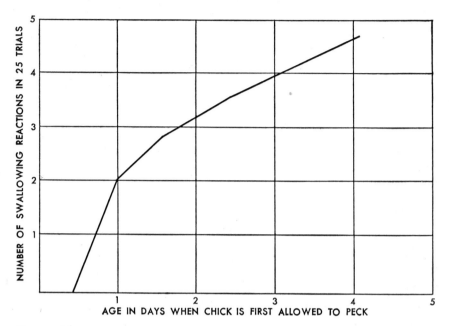

Figure 16

A Typical Curve of Maturation

This shows how ability to peck more accurately increases with age even without practice. (From Charles Bird, "The Relative Importance of Maturation and Instinct in the Development of a Habit," *Ped. Sem.*, 1925, 32, 68–91.)

who had practiced climbing stairs, however, was decidedly superior in climbing. This superiority, however, was overcome by her sister in two weeks of practice. From the experiment Gesell and Thompson conclude that the child who had six weeks of practice was no further ahead at the end of eight weeks than she would have been without her preliminary practice. This conclusion has been substantiated by Hilgard's (13) experiments involving groups of preschool children. In the acquisition of skill in later childhood, practice plays a more important part.

Maturation in mental activities. In more purely mental activities, the role of maturation is equally clear. No one tries to teach an infant a few weeks old to talk, a child of three years to read, nor a child of five to remember the multiplication table. Nor do we expect young children to be able to reason logically, or to show depth, richness, or control in their emotional states. For these things there must be a sufficient degree of maturation, as truly as there must be to walk or to suckle.

The proper "grade-placement" of curricular materials is an important psychological problem. To recognize maturation as a necessary condition of learning is vitally important for teachers, parents, and all others directing the development of children. Learning, at each level, must wait for maturation. Attempting to instruct a child before he has achieved the necessary maturation is not only fruitless; it is likely to awaken feelings of defeat and despair which will persist and render the task difficult even after sufficient maturation has taken place. What is more, if one waits for maturation, a great deal of learning will not have to take place at all. A more detailed discussion of learning is reserved for Chapter 6.

SUMMARY

Male and female germ cells merge in a process known as fertilization to form a single-celled organism, called the *zygote*. The zygote is the individual at his first stage of development. The chromosomes and genes in the nucleus of the male and female germ cells interact at fertilization in various ways. Some of the facts underlying these interactions were discovered by Mendel and formulated into what are now referred to as Mendel's laws.

The materials in the zygote interact with environmental conditions to determine the characteristics of the individual at all stages in his growth beyond the zygote stage. Thus, every trait of the individual is dependent upon both heredity and environment. Attempts have been made to determine the relative importance of heredity and environment in determining such traits as intelligence and learning ability.

The period of prenatal development in human beings has been divided into three stages: (1) the period of the ovum (first two weeks), (2) the embryonic period (third to eighth week), and (3) the fetal period (ninth week to birth). Human fetal behavior has been studied by (1) mother's reports of fetal movements, (2) instrumental detection of movement and (3) observation of operatively removed fetuses. Studies of human and animal fetuses indicate that behavior develops through the two processes of individuation and integration.

The majority of the behavior of the newborn is characterized as mass activity. However, many specific reactions to specific stimulations, known as reflexes, are found at birth or shortly thereafter. The newborn is sensitive to visual, auditory, pain, temperature, pressure, taste, smell, and other kinds of stimulations.

Development is dependent upon two processes: maturation and

learning.   Maturation is identified with the growth of body structures; learning is identified specifically with the acitvity of the organism.   It appears that changes through learning are dependent upon the prior maturation of body structures.   Maturation and learning go hand in hand, and the effects produced by one can only be determined in experiments in which one is held constant while the other is operative.

QUESTIONS

on the Chapter

1. Define: heredity, zygote, reduction division, fertilization, dominant characteristic, recessive characteristic.
2. Why is it difficult to experiment on heredity and environment?
3. Summarize the results of studies in which heredity was the independent variable.
4. Do the same for studies in which environment was the independent variable.
5. What are the principal developmental changes of each of the periods of prenatal development?
6. Define: plantar reflex, conditioning, electroencephalogram, individuation, integration, cephalo-caudal sequence, proximo-distal sequence, mass activity, maturation.
7. Describe Spelt's experiment on learning before birth.
8. What measurements have been used as indicators of the degree of physical maturity?
9. Name three methods of studying prenatal development.

for Discussion

1. Are some traits hereditary and others acquired? Explain.
2. What does Tryon's experiment indicate regarding the importance of heredity?
3. What is the relative importance of maturation and learning in an individual's development?
4. Do all parts of the body develop at the same rate and reach their maxima at the same time?
5. Is selective breeding the only method of producing a superior strain?
6. Are individuation and integration separate processes or phases of the same process?
7. Why do psychologists study prenatal development?

REFERENCES

1 ANGULO Y GONZÁLEZ, A. W., "The Prenatal Development of Behavior in the Albino Rat," *J. Comp. Neurol.*, 1932, *55*, 395–442.

2 BIRD, CHARLES, "The Effect of Maturation upon the Pecking Instinct of Chicks," *Ped. Sem.*, 1926, 33, 212–234.

3 BIRD, CHARLES, "The Relative Importance of Maturation and Instinct in the Development of a Habit," *Ped. Sem.*, 1925, 32, 68–91.

4 BURKS, B. S., "The Relative Influence of Nature and Nurture upon Mental Development," *Twenty-seventh Yearbook of the National Society for the Study of Education*, 1928, Part I, 219–316.

5 CARMICHAEL, L., "An Experimental Study in the Prenatal Guinea-Pig of the Origin and Development of Reflexes and Patterns of Behavior in Relation to the Stimulation of Specific Receptor Areas during the Period of Active Fetal Life," *Genet. Psychol. Monogr.*, 1934, 16, 337–491.

6 CARMICHAEL, L., "The Development of Behavior in Vertebrates Experimentally Removed from the Influence of External Stimulation," *Psychol. Rev.*, 1926, 33, 51–58.

7 CARMICHAEL, L., "The Onset and Early Development of Behavior." In Carmichael, L., ed., *Manual of Child Psychology.* New York: John Wiley and Sons, 1946. Quotation by permission of the publishers.

8 COGHILL, G. E., *Anatomy and the Problem of Behavior.* New York: The Macmillan Company, 1929.

9 CORONIS, J. D., "Development of Behavior in the Fetal Cat," *Genet. Psychol. Monogr.*, 1933, 14, 283–386.

10 FREEMAN, F. N., and others, "The Influence of Environment on the Intelligence, School Achievement, and Conduct of Foster Children," *Twenty-seventh Yearbook of the National Society for the Study of Education*, 1928, Part I, 103–217.

11 GESELL, A., and THOMPSON, H., "Learning and Growth in Identical Infant Twins," *Genet. Psychol. Monogr.*, 1929, 6, 1–123.

12 GOODENOUGH, FLORENCE L., *Developmental Psychology.* New York: Appleton Century Company, 1934, pp. 71, 162.

13 HILGARD, J. R., "Learning and Maturation in Pre-School Children," *J. Genet. Psychol.*, 1932, 41, 35–56.

14 HOLZINGER, K. J., "The Relative Effect of Nature and Nurture Influences on Twin Differences," *J. Educ. Psychol.*, 1929, 20, 241–248.

15 HOOKER, D., "Fetal Behavior," *Res. Publ. Ass. Nerv. Ment. Dis.*, 1939, 19, 237–243.

16 HOOKER, D., "Fetal Reflexes and Instinctual Processes," *Psychosomatic Med.*, 1942, 4, 199–205.

17 IRWIN, O. C., "The Amount and Nature of Activities of Newborn Infants under Constant External Stimulating Conditions during the First Ten Days of Life," *Genet. Psychol. Monogr.*, 1930, 8, 1–92.

18 LEAHY, A. M., "Nature-Nurture and Intelligence," *Genet. Psychol. Monogr.*, 1935, 17, 236–308.

19 LENNOX, W. G., GIBBS, E. L., and GIBBS, F. A., "The Brain Wave Pattern, an Hereditary Trait; Evidence from 74 'Normal' Pairs of Twins," *J. Hered.*, 1945, 36, 233–243.

20 LINDSLEY, D. B., "Electroencephalography." In Hunt, J. McV., ed., *Personality and the Behavior Disorders*, Vol. II. New York: Ronald Press, 1944.

21 LINDSLEY, D. B., "Heart and Brain Potentials of Human Fetuses in Utero," *Amer. J. Psychol.*, 1942, 55, 412–416.

22 MINKOWSKI, M., "Über frühzeitige Bewegungen. Reflexe und muskulare Reaktionen beim menschlichen Fötus und ihre Beziehungen zum fötalen Nerven- und Muskelsystem," *Schweiz. Med. Wschr.*, 1922, 52, 721–724, 751–755.

23 MUNN, NORMAN L., *Psychology*. Boston: Houghton Mifflin Company, 1946.

24 NEWBURY, EDWARD, *Heredity in Behavior*. Unpublished paper prepared for class use at the University of Kentucky. Paragraphs 2, 3, and 4 are taken from this paper by permission of the author.

25 NEWMAN, H. H., FREEMAN, F. N., and HOLZINGER, K. J., *Twins: A Study of Heredity and Environment*. Chicago: University of Chicago Press, 1937.

26 PRATT, KARL C., "The Neonate." In Carmichael, L., ed., *Manual of Child Psychology*. New York: John Wiley and Sons, 1946.

27 SONTAG, L. W., and RICHARDS, T. W., "Fetal Heart Rate as a Behavioral Indicator," *Monogr. Soc. Res. Child Development*, 1938, 3, No. 17.

28 SONTAG, L. W., and WALLACE, R. F., "An Apparatus for Recording Fetal Movement," *Amer. J. Psychol.*, 1933, 45, 517–519.

29 SPELT, DAVID K., "The Conditioning of the Human Fetus in Utero," *J. Exp. Psychol.*, 1948, 38, 338–346.

30 STOCKARD, C. R., "The Artificial Production of a Single Median Eye in the Fish Embryo by Means of Sea-Water Solutions of Magnesium Chloride," *J. Comp. Neur. and Psychol.*, 1909, 17, 191–192.

31 STUBBS, E. M., "The Effect of the Factors of Duration, Intensity, and Pitch of Sound Stimuli on the Responses of Newborn Infants," *Univ. Iowa Stud. Child Welfare*, 1934, 9, No. 4.

32 TRYON, R. C., "Genetic Differences in Maze-Learning Ability in Rats," *Thirty-ninth Yearbook of the National Society for the Study of Education*, 1940, Part I, pp. 111–119.

33 WOODWORTH, R. S., *Psychology*, 3rd edition. New York: Henry Holt and Company, 1934, p. 144.

34 WOODWORTH, R. S., and MARQUIS, D. G., *Psychology*, 5th edition. New York: Henry Holt and Company, 1947, p. 282.

BODY STRUCTURES AND BEHAVIOR

3

It should be amply clear from what was said about the development of the individual in the preceding chapter that an individual's behavior is intimately related to body structures; that behavior is the activity of the organism as a whole; and that particular responses involve the functioning of particular body structures. This dependence of behavior upon body structures is implied in the words which we use to describe different kinds of behavior. The following pairs of words, one denoting an activity, the other a body structure, illustrate the point:

> walking — legs
> seeing — eyes
> hearing — ears
> throwing — arms and hands
> talking — vocal cords
> writing — fingers

The student may wish to see how far he can extend this list.

Some responses, however, involve body structures which are not so readily identified from the names of the responses. This is true for such activities as intelligence, memory, thinking, imagination, emotion, and feeling. Some of these we identify with the head or brain; others with the body as a whole. In any event, all responses are dependent upon or involve the functioning or activity of body structures. At the same time these structures set certain limits within which activity must occur. The sense organs, for example, are constructed in such a way that they are sensitive to a rather limited range of stimulation (see p. 106). The reacting mechanisms impose certain restrictions upon the kinds of responses which can occur. A gland can secrete only a limited amount at a given time. A muscle because of its size and its attachments to bones can only pull a certain load, or contract at a certain rate. Behavior is limited still further by the characteristics of the nervous system. For example, for a fraction of a second after a nerve has transmitted an impulse it is inexcitable and nonconductive. Regardless of the amount of stimulation present or the frequency of the successive stimulations, the nerve cannot be aroused more often or transmit impulses more frequently than prescribed by this characteristic. A knowledge of these body structures will help us to understand particular kinds of responses, such as fear or seeing, and at the same time provide us with a more thorough knowledge of the individual, the P of our behavior equation.

A response of a human organism ordinarily involves or is dependent upon the functioning of three kinds of body structures. These three kinds of structures are (1) the *receiving mechanisms* or sensory apparatus (commonly called the *sense organs*), (2) the *connecting mechanisms* or nervous system, and (3) the *reacting mechanisms*, the muscles and glands. The involvement of a receiving mechanism, nerve pathways, and a reacting mechanism in a simple response such as a reflex is illustrated in Figure 17. A skin sense organ is stimulated. A nerve impulse is aroused in this organ and is then conducted over a *sensory nerve* (also known as an afferent nerve) to the nerve center, the spinal cord. In the spinal cord the impulse is relayed to an outgoing nerve, known as

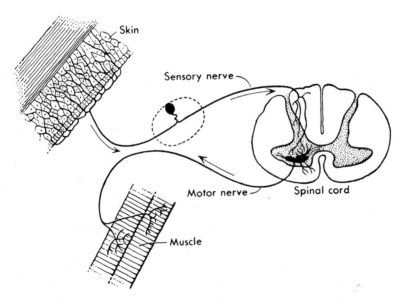

Figure 17

The Pathway of a Simple Reflex Arc

(Adapted from C. J. Herrick, *Introduction to Neurology*, Saunders, 1921, p. 26; after Van Gehuchten.)

a *motor* or *efferent nerve*, and it is then conducted along this nerve to a muscle. The whole process takes place in approximately .019 of a second (4). The discharge of the nerve impulse in the muscle results in a muscle contraction and a response. The pathway from a sense organ through a nerve center to a muscle is called a reflex arc. It should be recognized that this illustration oversimplifies the actual situation. It is doubtful whether any such simple response, in isolation from what is going on in the body as a whole, ever occurs or can occur. The actual structural involvement in even the simplest response is probably much more complex than Figure 17 indicates.

THE RECEIVING MECHANISMS

As we have said above, the receiving mechanisms are commonly called the sense organs. A sense organ is made up of one or more *receptors* and in most cases a variety of accessory apparatus. The receptor either is a nerve ending or is in contact with a nerve and is therefore the part of the sense organ which is sensitive to stimulation and in which nerve impulses are aroused. Accessory apparatus, such as the outer ear or the lens in the eye, is involved in bringing the stimulus in contact with the receptor.

Table IV

A Classification of Receptors

CLASS OF SENSES AND RECEPTORS	SENSE	LOCATION OF RECEPTORS
1. Exteroceptors		
a. Teleoceptors	Sight	In eye
	Hearing	In ear
	Smell	In nose
b. Proximoceptors	Taste	In tongue
	Touch	In skin
	Warmth	In skin
	Cold	In skin
	Pain	In skin and in membranes within the body
2. Interoceptors	Organic	In internal organs
3. Proprioceptors	Kinaesthetic	In muscles, tendons, joints
	Static	In semicircular canals

Nature and Location of the Receptors

A list of the senses, the receptors for each, and a classification of the senses are shown in Table IV. Popular psychology speaks of five senses — sight, hearing, smell, taste, and touch. Table IV shows that there are several more. If the organic were subdivided, as it might well be, the list would be still longer. The sense organs are classified as exteroceptors, interoceptors, and proprioceptors, according to whether they are stimulated by external conditions (exteroceptors), by internal conditions (interoceptors), or by movements or contractions of muscles (proprioceptors). The two subdivisions of the exteroceptors, the teleoceptors and proximoceptors, are so named because the stimuli affect the receptors from a distance (teleoceptors) or are in contact with the receptors (proximoceptors). Let us now examine each of the sense organs in more detail in order to obtain some idea of the nature and location of the receptor mechanisms. It may be repeated that the receptors are the structures in the sense organs which are sensitive to stimulation and in which nerve impulses are initiated.

The receptors for vision. The receptors for vision are located in the inside back part of the eyeball in a layer of nerve cells known as the *retina.* As can be seen in Figure 18, there are two kinds of receptor endings in the retina. These are known as *rods* and *cones.* It appears that the cones are the receptors for color vision, the rods for light-dark vision or vision under dim illumination. The cones are thickest at the center of the retinal field, the concentration decreasing as one moves from the center toward the periphery. On the other hand, the rods are more numerous at the periphery of the retina and apparently fewer in number toward the center. This means that the retina is not uniformly sensitive to color stimulation or to twilight, night, and daylight illumination. In daylight illumination, objects are seen most clearly when the light from the objects is focused upon the center of the retina. In twilight or at night, objects can be seen most clearly if the light waves are focused on the retina at a point away from the center. At the point in the retina where the nerve fibers leave the retina — that is, at the point of entry of the optic nerve — there are no rods or cones and, therefore, no vision. This point is called the *blind spot.* Other parts of the eye — the cornea, the iris, the lens, the outer layers of the eyeball, the muscles of the eye, and even the liquids inside the eyeball — serve as accessory apparatus and are involved in one way or another in bringing visual stimuli to a focus on the retina.

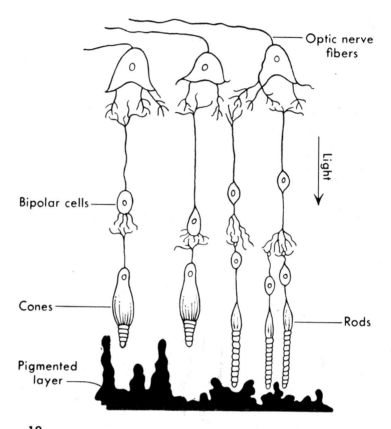

Figure 18

An Enlarged Diagram of the Sensory Cells and Connected Nerve Cells in the Retina

Light passes through the nearly transparent substance of the retina, in the direction indicated by the arrow on the right, and is stopped by the pigmented layer beneath. Just above this layer are shown the "rods" and "cones" in which are aroused the nerve impulses which are transmitted to the optic nerve fibers. (From Arthur I. Gates, *General Psychology*, Revised edition, p. 46. Copyright, The Macmillan Company, 1929. By permission of the publishers.)

The receptors for hearing. In the cross-section view of the ear shown in Figure 19 it will be noted that the inner ear consists of a cavity of several parts: the *cochlea*, the *semicircular canals*, and the *vestibule*. The cochlea contains the receptors for hearing. The three semicircular canals, one in each plane of the body, and the vestibule are not involved in hearing; they contain the receptors for the static sense.

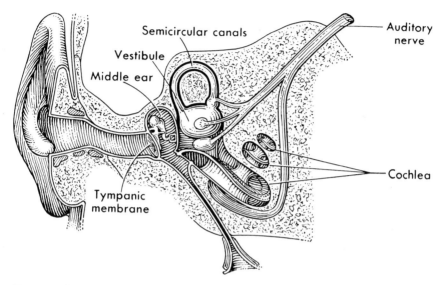

Figure 19

Cross Section of the Ear, Showing the Cochlea
and the Semicircular Canals

(Modified from T. Hough and W. T. Sedgwick, *The Human Mechanism*, p. 259. Copyright, Ginn and Company, 1906. By permission of the publishers.)

Figure 20 shows a diagram of a cross section of the cochlea with a single row of sense cells (hair cells). There are about 5000 such rows standing on the basilar membrane (8). Air vibrations are picked up by the outer ear and directed into the ear canal to the tympanic membrane, or eardrum. Vibrations of the eardrum set the three small bones of the middle ear in motion. One of these, the stirrup bone, fits into a small opening in the cochlea. Movements of this bone set up motions in the liquid in the cochlea. This motion arouses or stimulates the hair cells, setting up nerve impulses which are transmitted from the ear over the nerve fibers (axons in Figure 20) to the brain.

The receptors for smell. These receptors are located in the olfactory epithelium, a small area in the upper part of the right and left nasal passages. The receptors are spindle-shaped cells connected with the olfactory nerve. Fine hairlike projections from these cells extend into the nasal passage, where they may be stimulated by gaseous particles in the air which pass through the nose. The nose itself is not a sense organ, but a part of the breathing apparatus.

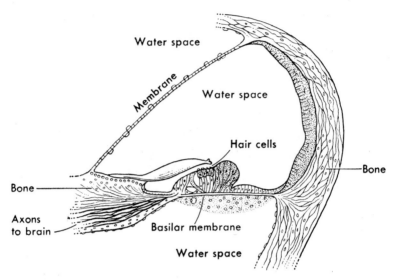

Figure 20

Cross Section of a Cochlea, Showing a Single Row of Hair Cells

(From R. S. Woodworth and Donald G. Marquis, *Psychology*, 5th edition, p. 479. Copyright, Henry Holt and Company, 1947. By permission of the publishers.)

The receptors for taste. The taste receptors are hair cells located in the "taste buds," which are embedded in the sides of the protuberances, or papillae, on the tongue (see Figure 21). The hair cells in each taste bud are connected with an afferent nerve. The tips of the hair cells are activated by chemicals in the liquids which penetrate the pits in the tongue. Taste buds in different parts of the tongue are sensitive to different taste substances. For example, sensitivity to bitter substances is greatest near the back of the tongue and to sweet near the tip of the tongue. Other taste buds are sensitive to substances which taste sour, while others are sensitive to salt. Other taste experiences are combinations of these elementary tastes together with experiences of warmth, cold, and smell.

Cutaneous receptors. When a small area of the skin is stimulated systematically with a variety of stimuli, warm and cold metal points, needle pricks, and objects that touch a hair or press lightly on the skin, four kinds of experiences are aroused. These experiences are described as touch or pressure, warmth, cold, and pain. Taken together they are called *cutaneous* experiences. The spots which mediate each of these experiences are scattered irregularly over the entire body surface and

SURFACE OF TONGUE
Papillae

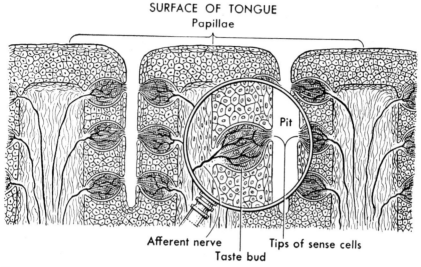

Figure 21

A Drawing of a Taste Bud, Showing Its Location in a Papilla
(highly schematic)

(From J. F. Dashiell, *Fundamentals of General Psychology*, 3rd edition, p. 238. Copyright, Houghton-Mifflin Company, 1950. By permission of the publishers.)

in some instances (pain in particular) are found in the membranes within the body. Pain spots are most numerous and are followed in order of decreasing frequency by the touch, cold, and warmth spots. It is thought that there is a different kind of receptor mechanism in the skin for each experience. It is known that there are different kinds of nerve endings in the skin, but it is not clear just which ones are the receptors for warmth, cold, pain, and pressure.

Organic receptors. Several kinds of sensory experience go to make up what is called in Table IV the organic sense. There are sensory cells (receptors) for hunger in the stomach, for thirst in the back of the throat, and for nausea in the digestive tract. In addition it is probable that there are sensory cells in the respiratory, circulatory, and reproductive systems which give rise to a number of experiences or feelings which we associate in a vague way with the parts of the body from which they arise.

The kinaesthetic receptors. The kinaesthetic sense may be thought of as the sense of movement. Through it we are able to judge the difference in the weight of objects by sensing the difference in muscular effort or pull required to lift the weights. We sense the vigor of a blow or the distance moved or the speed of movement primarily through the kinaesthetic sense. The receptors for this sense are located in the muscles, tendons, and joint surfaces. They are platelike expansions of finely divided nerve fibers which scatter and wind through the muscle fibers and among the spindles of tendons at the point of attachment to the muscles (3, p. 243). It is clear that a muscular contraction and the resulting pull on tendons and movement of bones will stimulate the kinaesthetic receptors. Thus the muscle is not only a reacting mechanism but a receiving mechanism in the sense that receptors in the muscles are stimulated by muscular contractions and bodily movements. This arrangement means in effect that a response to a stimulus may itself become a stimulus for some other response.

Receptors for the static sense. It was pointed out above in describing the ear that the receptors for the static sense are located in the semi-circular canals and the vestibule of the inner ear (see Figure 19). These cavities, like the cochlea, are filled with a liquid which can be set in motion by movements of the head. Fine hairlike projections from nerve cells extend from the walls of the canals into the liquid. A sudden displacement of the liquid in a canal by the starting or stopping of the body results in a pressure against these hairlike projections, thus setting up nerve impulses. These impulses are involved in the maintenance of muscular tension and of body equilibrium or orientation in space (3, p. 247). The commonly known difficulty in maintaining one's balance after rapid rotation is due primarily to static stimulation. The familiar motion sickness resulting from riding in elevators or trains or airplanes results from a disturbance of the coordinated relationship which is customarily maintained between visual, kinaesthetic, and static stimulations.

THE NERVOUS SYSTEM

Between these receiving mechanisms, which are sensitive to environmental stimulations, and the reacting mechanisms, which respond to stimulation and produce changes in the environment, there is a tremendously complex system which enables any receptor mechanism to become connected with any reacting mechanism. In addition, this system coordinates and integrates the activities of the various parts of the body, thus enabling the organism to act as a unit or a whole, to direct its over-all activity toward a goal while at the same time disposing of relatively isolated stimuli which do not contribute to the main stream of activity.   These functions are carried out by the nervous system.

Divisions of the Nervous System

The nervous system has two main divisions: the *cerebro-spinal* and the *autonomic*.   The cerebro-spinal system has two subdivisions: the *central* and *peripheral* divisions.   The central division is made up of a great mass of nerve tissue in the head and spinal column, making up the cerebrum, the cerebellum, the medulla, and the spinal cord (see Figure 22).   The peripheral division includes all of the nerve tracts which go out from the central division (with the exception of the autonomic system) to all parts of the body.

The autonomic system is in a sense a system within a system.   It enjoys such a high degree of independence in the performance of its

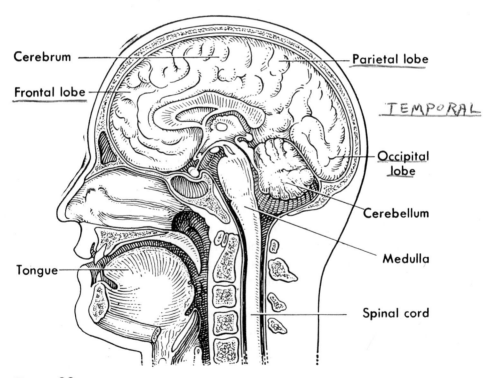

Cerebrum — Parietal lobe
Frontal lobe — TEMPORAL
Occipital lobe
Cerebellum
Medulla
Tongue — Spinal cord

Figure 22

The Location of the Cerebrum, Cerebellum, Medulla, and Spinal Cord

(From R. S. Woodworth and Donald G. Marquis, *Psychology*, 5th edition, p. 248.   Copyright, Henry Holt and Company, 1947.   By permission of the publishers.)

duties that the name autonomic (self-governing) is quite appropriate. It consists in part of a series of *ganglia* (small nerve centers found at various places in the body outside the brain and spinal cord) located along the length of the spinal column just inside the body cavity. The remainder of the autonomic system consists of the nerve pathways which go out from the ganglia to the vital organs and certain other parts of the body. This system is divided into three subdivisions (shown schematically in Figure 23): the cranial, sympathetic, and sacral. It has charge of the vital processes, such as digestion, circulation, and breathing. The upper part promotes the building up of the body and the storing up of energy; the lower controls elimination and the sex organs; the middle controls the rapid discharge of energy. The sympathetic division is therefore antagonistic to the other two parts. It is given right of way when there is an emergency, since in an emergency there is no time to store up energy. Instead, all energy must be mobilized to meet the crisis.

The independence of the autonomic system is, however, by no means complete. Like a subordinate official in a corporation, it is unmolested only as long as things run smoothly. When difficulties arise — when, for instance, a person restrains the expression of fear or anger — the organism as a whole gives it new orders.

Nerve Cells

The entire nervous system contains billions of structural units, the nerve cells, called neurones. Taken in bundles these neurones form nerve tracts which connect parts of the nervous system with one another and receptors with muscles and glands. The primary function of a nerve cell or of bundles of cells is to conduct nerve impulses from one part of the body to another. This job of conducting impulses is divided among the nerve cells. Some of them only conduct impulses from receptors to nerve centers; these are sensory or afferent neurones (see Figure 17). Others only carry impulses from nerve centers to response mechanisms; these are called motor or efferent neurones. A third kind of neurone conducts the impulses through the nerve center to the place where the motor neurone leaves the center; this neurone is called a connecting neurone. In most cases a series of connecting neurones may be needed to get an impulse from a given receptor to the point of exit from the nerve center of the appropriate motor neurone.

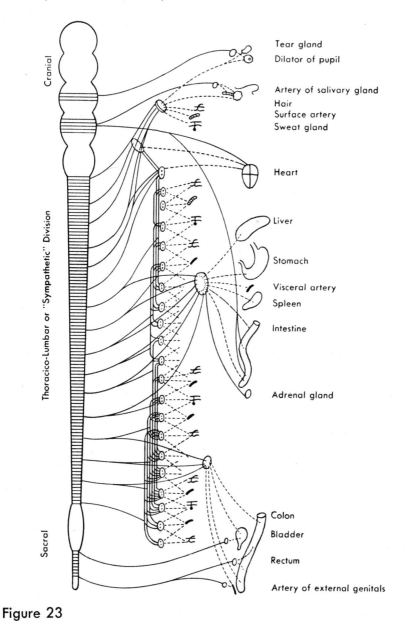

Cranial

Thoracico-Lumbar or "Sympathetic" Division

Sacral

Tear gland
Dilator of pupil

Artery of salivary gland
Hair
Surface artery
Sweat gland

Heart

Liver

Stomach

Visceral artery
Spleen

Intestine

Adrenal gland

Colon
Bladder

Rectum

Artery of external genitals

Figure 23

General Schematic Drawing of the Autonomic Nervous System,
Showing the "Automatic" or "Semi-Automatic" Bodily Functions
Which It Serves

(From W. B. Cannon, *Bodily Changes in Pain, Hunger, Fear, and Rage*, Appleton-Century,
1929, p. 23.)

Nerve Centers

While the nervous system functions as a highly organized and integrated unit, each part and division performs certain specific tasks. It was pointed out above that the autonomic system and its subdivisions control the vital processes, each subdivision having its own special task. The same division of labor is found throughout the nervous system. The spinal cord, the medulla, the cerebellum, the cerebrum, and other parts of the brain have specialized functions.

The *spinal cord* serves as a connecting center for simple adjustive acts which involve the lower parts of the body. Perhaps more important, it relays impulses from the point of entry in the cord to higher levels in the cord or brain, and from the brain down the cord to the point of exit of the appropriate motor nerves.

The *medulla* serves as a connecting center for the control of such vital processes as breathing, heart action, blood pressure, and digestion. Being an expansion of the spinal cord where it enters the skull, it also acts as a pathway between the brain and the spinal cord.

The *cerebellum*, the second largest part of the brain, lies at the back of the head and somewhat beneath the cerebrum (see Figure 22). It plays a major role in the coordination of muscular activity and maintenance of equilibrium. Destruction of portions or all of the cerebellum in animals results in a marked reduction or loss of the ability to coordinate the movements involved in locomotion.

The *cerebrum* (see Figure 22) is the largest, the most complex, and the most highly specialized part of the nervous system. It has reached its highest development in man, as can be seen in Figure 24. It is the cerebrum that we are talking about in our everyday references to the brain. It is composed of two hemispheres or halves, the left half being connected with the right side of the body and the right half with the left side of the body. A section through the cerebrum reveals that it is composed of a surface layer of gray matter, known as the cortex (bark), and a deeper mass of fibers which appear as white matter. The surface shows many convolutions separated by fissures. Fissures mark off areas which are called lobes. The frontal, parietal, and occipital lobes are shown in Figure 22.

The cerebrum is the center for the highest mental processes: thinking, perceiving, recognizing, abstracting, learning, concept formation, voluntary action, and consciousness. These processes involve many parts of the body, many receptors, many response mechanisms, and an elaborate system of connections in the nervous system whereby the

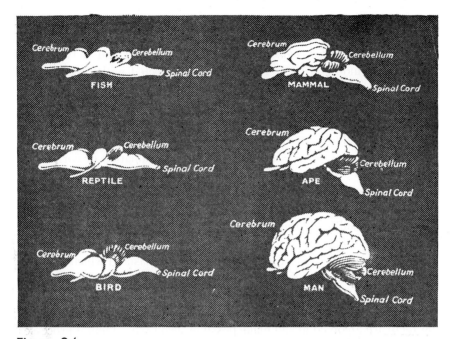

Figure 24

Relative Complexity of Brains of Different Forms of Life

In general, the more complex the brain and nervous system, the more complex the behavior. The brain of man is far more complex than that of any other organism. (From J. A. Thomson, *Outline of Science*, Putnam's, 1922, I, 73.)

separate receptor and response processes may be coordinated and integrated. This process of coordination and integration is the function of the cerebral cortex. The receiving and reacting mechanisms are connected with the cerebral cortex in such a way that impulses from a particular sense organ go to a particular portion of the cortex. For example, impulses from the eyes go to the occipital lobe, those from the ears to the temporal area, and those from the cutaneous receptors to the parietal area. These areas are called *sensory areas*. An area just back of the frontal lobes and just forward of the parietal lobe is connected with response mechanisms. It is known as the *motor area*. Destruction of portions of this area results in loss of ability to move the response mechanisms which are connected with the destroyed tissues. It was thought at one time that such loss of function was permanent, but experiments with animals and work with human subjects indicate that the lost function can be restored, apparently because some other part of the cortex takes over the functions of the part destroyed (5).

Association areas. In addition to the sensory and motor areas, which take up a relatively small part of the total cortex, there are a number of *association areas.* These lie adjacent to and between the sensory and motor areas. They are not connected with specific parts of the body but serve as centers for integrating or organizing incoming and outgoing impulses. For example, the occipital area receives impulses from the eyes. The area adjacent to the visual area combines and correlates these impulses to the end that the facts presented to the eyes have meaning for the individual. Such coordination or correlation of functions is seen in the *auditory speech* area which is adjacent to the auditory area in the temporal region of the cortex, and in the *motor speech* area which is adjacent to the motor area. Injury to the auditory speech area results in an inability to understand words without any loss of ability to speak or hear words, a condition known as *auditory* or *sensory aphasia.* There is also a motor type of aphasia in which a person understands words but finds it difficult or impossible to say words, or pronounce them, or put them together.

While the functions of receiving and initiating impulses and integrating them are involved in and make possible such higher mental processes as learning, thinking, and imagination, it should be recognized that there is no specialized area in the cortex for any of these processes. There is no special area for thinking. Nor are there special areas in the brain, as phrenologists claim, for such general character traits as self-esteem, firmness, benevolence, and cautiousness. The higher mental processes are dependent upon the organizing activity of the brain as a whole. That this is true for learning in rats has been demonstrated in a series of experiments by Lashley (6). He destroyed varying amounts of the cortical tissue in white rats and then tested their ability to learn a maze or open a latched door, comparing the amount of cortical tissue destroyed and the portion of the cortex destroyed with the performance of the rats in the learning trials. The results showed that (1) the greater the amount of tissue destroyed, the greater was the loss in ability to learn, either simple or more complex tasks, and (2) the loss in ability to learn was no greater from the destruction of one area than from the destruction of another so long as the size of the area destroyed remained the same.

THE REACTING MECHANISMS

The reacting mechanisms consist of two kinds of body structures, *muscles* and *glands.* These are the structures into which nerve impulses are discharged and in which the effects of stimulation are observable.

Striped Muscles

The muscles of the body are divided into two classes: *striped* and *smooth*. The striped muscles are the ones involved in such bodily movements as walking, running, jumping, skipping, hopping, crawling, throwing, reaching, pulling, lifting, maintenance of body posture, and the hundreds of skills which involve the use of the arms, hands, fingers, legs, feet, head, eyes, and trunk, singly or in combination. Because of the importance of such skilled movements in many occupations and jobs, tests have been developed for measuring many of them. These will be described in Chapter 13.

The striped muscles are attached by means of tendons to the skeleton, which serves as a framework for the body and as a system of levers. Movements of the body or parts thereof are effected by pulls on bones, exerted by contraction of the muscles. For example, the biceps and triceps muscles of the upper arm are attached to the bones of the lower arm and operate it as a lever with the elbow serving as a fulcrum (7). The biceps pulls the lower arm up; the triceps pulls it down. The two work in a coordinated fashion, the triceps tending to relax as the biceps contracts, and vice versa. Most of the striped muscles are found in this paired and antagonistic arrangement.

Muscles are always in a state of contraction of some degree. Even when no movement is outwardly observable the muscles are in a state of *tension*. This tension is due in large measure to the kinaesthetic impulses set up by muscle contractions or by the tension itself. Being a mild form of muscular contraction, it stimulates the kinaesthetic receptors and thus reproduces itself. Other striped muscle activity, such as throwing, "takes off," as it were, from the tension already present in the muscles.

Smooth Muscles

These muscles are found in the walls of the internal organs of the body. The intestines, stomach, esophagus, blood vessels, urinary tract, ducts and passages of the respiratory and reproductive system are composed of smooth muscles. These are the organs and parts of the body involved in what are called the vegetative processes, or those functions which are essential to the maintenance of life. These muscles contract more slowly and recover from contraction more slowly than striped muscles. They are likewise more susceptible than striped muscles to certain drugs and to ductless gland secretions such as adrenalin and thyroxin (2).

Glands as Reacting Mechanisms

As indicated above, the glands of the body are reacting mechanisms. Their special function is the secretion of certain chemical solutions, and their primary importance is found in the effects which their secretions have upon other body processes. For example, glandular secretions are largely responsible for the digestion of food and the regulation of body temperature. They are also involved in or affect such processes as heart action, circulation, elimination, sexual activity, and body growth. They have profound effects upon specific kinds of behavior and the over-all adjustment of the individual. The secretions of the ductless glands in particular appear to play an important role in personality.

The glands are of two types: *duct* and *ductless* or *endocrine*. The duct glands are so called because they discharge their secretions through ducts into body cavities or onto the surface of the body. The salivary glands, the gastric glands, the pancreas, and the liver are duct glands which are directly involved in digestion. The direct functions of such glands as the kidneys, sweat glands, and tear glands are obvious. In addition, the secretions of these glands are indirectly involved in such psychological processes as emotion and motivation. Everyone is familiar with cold sweat and tears in relation to the emotions of fear and grief. Prolonged emotional stress likewise affects digestive processes, particularly the secretions of the liver (see p. 302). The distended condition of the sex glands resulting from the accumulation of the secretions of the glands is an important source of internal stimulation and the instigator of other bodily activity.

Figure 25 gives the names and shows the general location within the body of the ductless or endocrine glands. These glands throw their secretions directly into the blood stream without the aid of ducts. These secretions are called *hormones*. Since they are thrown into the blood stream and are carried to all parts of the body, they serve to integrate all reacting mechanisms, and cause them to act in an organized pattern. This regulation of muscles and glands by hormones is referred to as *chemical* integration; it is in addition to but closely related to the unification of body processes by the nervous system. Besides their function in the general chemical integration of the body, these glands are involved in or play a part in body growth, mental growth, emotional behavior, body metabolism, the development of personality, and other more specific body functions. Some of the specific functions of the endocrines are given below.

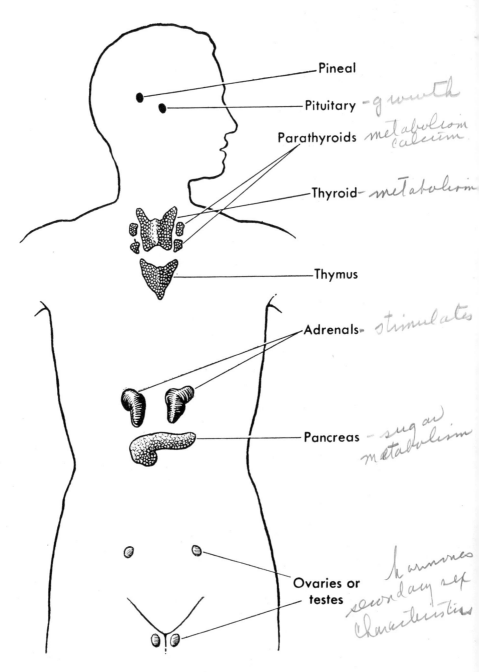

Pineal

Pituitary —growth

Parathyroids metabolism calcium

Thyroid— metabolism

Thymus

Adrenals- stimulates

Pancreas — sugar metabolism

Ovaries or testes — hormones secondary sex characteristics

Figure 25

Location of the Endocrine Glands

(From E. T. Prothro and P. T. Teska, *Psychology*, p. 314. Copyright, Ginn and Company, 1950. By permission of the publishers.)

93

The thyroid gland. This gland, located in the neck on either side of the windpipe (see Figure 25), secretes a chemical known as *thyroxin.* This secretion plays an important role in general body metabolism. A marked undersecretion of this gland from birth or very early infancy results in a condition of arrested mental and physical growth known as *cretinism.* Cretinism is remedied by giving thyroxin, which supplies the chemical needed for normal development. A striking example of the remedial effect of thyroxin in cases of thyroid deficiencies existing from birth is seen in the case history which follows.

At birth, Sam Curtis seemed a normal baby. His mother did notice that he slept more than other babies and that he did not awake and start crying for food, but she told herself only that "Sam is a good boy; he's going to be the kind of child that doesn't give much trouble."

But after nine months, the family noted that Sam hadn't developed like most babies. For one thing, he hadn't any teeth — only a thickening of the gums. His tongue seemed to be too large, and it interfered with his breathing because it stuck out of his mouth at all times. His skin was yellow and dry and scaly; his eyes watered; he showed no interest in his surroundings; he was pugnosed and thick-nostriled. His hair was thin and brittle, and his eyebrows were scanty. He did not get his first tooth until he was more than a year old, and then it decayed quickly. He was all trunk, with tiny arms and legs; he was as pot-bellied as an alderman and had a fat, padded bull neck. Nor could Sam recognize either of his parents. And he would indicate his desire for food or water by grunting or by a scream. He never smiled or laughed; in fact, he seemed not to live, but to *vegetate.*

His parents became alarmed and began to look at each other with suspicion. Was their child to be a hopeless idiot? And whose fault was it? Each began a hasty search of his family tree, and at last they breathed a sigh of relief when they could recollect no insane or mentally abnormal ancestors. But they finally became impatient with their family physician who kept assuring them that "Sam will outgrow it." They became convinced that the physician was behind the times and unable to diagnose the condition. So they took their child to a specialist in a large city.

The specialist needed but a glance to see that the child was a cretin, due to a lack of thyroid secretion. Both parents, he noticed, had enlargements of the neck that suggested a tendency to goiter. In addition, they had lived all their lives in the "goiter belt," which comprises the states of the Great Lakes section.

So Sam was fed small doses of thyroid substance. And within several months a miracle seemed to have happened. His skin became warm and moist, several teeth were cut, he grew several inches; and, best of all, the cranky and irritable child disappeared; in its place there was a new

Sam. His dull eyes became bright, and his vacant expression gave way to a cheerful face. He became active and seemed to discover suddenly all the possibilities for play in this new world. He learned to talk and became interested in everything that went on around him. Of course, the Curtises were overjoyed at the miracle which had converted an apparently irritable imbecile into a normal child, and they marvelled at the wonders of science.

But a few months later they became tired of continuing the thyroid feeding and stopped it. Why not? "Sam is getting along fine now: no need for medicine." And they were right — for a week.

Within ten days, Sam became listless, dull, lost interest in things; his skin began to take on a dry, bloated appearance, and he became again the hopeless and helpless thing he had once been.

Frightened, the Curtises returned to the specialist and confessed their neglect. He advised them to begin the feeding of thyroxin again and never to discontinue it for even one day of Sam's life. Within a week, Sam became normal again. He has developed into a normal boy. At present he attends school and shows average intelligence. No one would ever suspect that he had been a cretin (1).

A marked undersecretion of thyroxin occurring in later life produces a condition known as *myxedema*. This condition is very much like cretinism except that something approximating normal body stature is attained before the thyroid deficiency develops. The physical characteristics — loss of hair, thick and puffy skin, low metabolism, and obesity — are accompanied by such behavior characteristics as loss of interest, emotional depression, and sluggishness in physical and mental activities. Figure 26 illustrates the results of treatment for myxedema.

A marked oversecretion of thyroxin likewise produces certain deviations from what is regarded as normal body functioning and behavior. The effects upon bodily processes include rapid pulse, high blood pressure, increased metabolic rate, and loss of weight. The effects on behavior include nervousness, overactivity, irritability, and insomnia.

The pituitary gland. This gland, located near the middle of the head and at the base of the brain, is composed of two main bodies known as the posterior and anterior lobes. One hormone from the anterior lobe (this lobe secretes other hormones as well) controls body growth. An oversecretion of this hormone beginning in early life produces *gigantism.* This condition is characterized by abnormal height, up to eight or nine feet, and extreme growth of the long bones, hands, and feet. An excessive amount of this hormone occurring after maturity has been reached results in marked changes in the shape of the face, (heavier jaws, separated teeth, bulging nose), overdevelopment of the

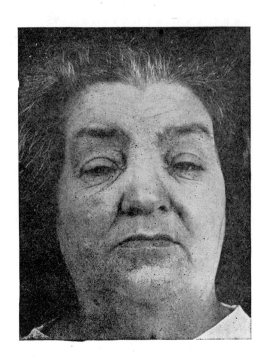

Figure 26

Patient with Myxedema and After Treatment with Thyroxin

(Photos from Massachusetts General Hospital)

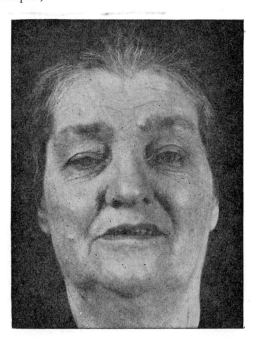

hands and feet, and some change in the shape of the chest. These may be accompanied by such mental characteristics as listlessness, loss of memory, loss of sex drive, and irritability. An undersecretion of this hormone in early life may produce *dwarfism*. In this condition all parts of the body are subnormal in size, though the body proportions remain normal. Mental characteristics are apparently unaffected by this deficiency.

One hormone of the posterior lobe of the pituitary gland affects the smooth muscles, increasing the activity of the intestines, the bladder, and the uterus. This hormone (the extract pituitrin) is commonly used at childbirth because of its tonic effect upon the uterine muscle.

The adrenal glands. Figure 25 shows that there are two adrenal glands; one lies on top of each kidney. Each gland is composed of two parts, an internal core known as the *medulla* and an outer layer called the *cortex*. Each part produces its own hormone. The secretion of the cortex is called *cortin*. This secretion is essential to life. A marked undersecretion of cortin is characterized by low blood pressure, muscular weakness, digestive disorders, excessive fatigue, and lowered resistance. These symptoms are removed by supplying the hormone artificially. The hormone also plays a part in sex development. Overactivity of the cortex in early life appears to produce a tendency toward masculinity in both boys and girls, the effect in girls being an inhibition of the female functions.

The adrenal medulla manufactures a hormone known as *adrenalin*. The synthetically produced form of this hormone is called *adrenin*. This hormone is of particular importance in psychology because of its relation to emotion. While some amount of the hormone is normally present in the blood, large quantities are released during emotional excitement or under conditions of stress. The effects upon bodily processes are profound. The heart beats faster, blood pressure rises, the blood coagulates more rapidly, the liver releases stored sugar, digestive processes are inhibited or checked, the air passages in the lungs are dilated, and in general bodily processes are mustered for vigorous activity. The relation of these effects to emotion will be discussed more fully in Chapter 9.

The sex glands. In their primary function of producing reproductive cells, the sex glands — the testes in the male and the ovaries in the female — may be regarded as duct glands. Certain cells in the sex glands, however, serve as endocrine glands. The hormones of these glands in the male are responsible for such secondary sex characteristics as the growth of a beard, change of voice, and the growth of hair in the

armpits and in the pubic area. If the endocrine function is lost by removal of the testes or by injury or disease prior to puberty, these
secondary sex characteristics will not appear. The difference in appearance and behavior of a normally sexed animal and a castrated animal,
such as an ox, a capon, or a gelding, can be attributed in large measure
to the absence of the hormones of the sex glands.

The endocrine functions of the female sex glands are considerably
more complex than those in the male. In general, the hormones of the
reproductive system in the female are responsible for or are involved
in the development of the secondary sex characteristics and in the
preparation of the ovaries, uterus, and mammary glands for their
respective roles in the reproductive process.

Other endocrine glands. The *pineal* gland functions during childhood, deteriorating rapidly after puberty. It is thought that the gland
is associated with sexual development, acting to delay sexual maturity
until puberty is reached. The *pancreas*, in addition to its duct-gland
function in digestion, secretes a hormone known as *insulin*, which is
involved in the sugar metabolism of the body. The specific function
of the *thymus* gland and the exact nature of the gland are not known.
It reaches its maximum size at puberty and then gradually deteriorates.
The liver and other internal organs are known to have endocrine functions, but exact knowledge regarding the secretions of these organs
and their effects on bodily functions and behavior is lacking.

The endocrine system. It must be kept in mind that the endocrine
glands function as interdependent mechanisms. These glands are
interrelated in such a way that they affect one another, stimulating and
inhibiting one another and in some cases compensating for one another.
These interrelations are of such an order that the malfunctioning of a
single gland may throw the entire system out of balance. We have
described very briefly the more general functions of the individual
glands. Perhaps this will suffice to indicate that in the endocrine glands
we find a tremendously important kind of reacting mechanism and one
which has far-reaching effects upon all other reacting mechanisms, upon
such specific forms of behavior as emotion and motivation, and upon
behavior in general.

We have elected to describe the body structures which are directly
involved in behavior in the order: receiving, connecting, and reacting
mechanisms. It is recognized that, from the standpoint of an observer,
it is the reaction or behavior and the reacting mechanisms that are the
objects of first concern. In most cases we are concerned directly with

an individual's response, with what he does; only secondarily do we look for the exciting condition. We trace back, as it were, from the response to the stimulating condition, and forward again through receptors and connectors to the response mechanisms. It should be emphasized, however, that from the standpoint of function the three kinds of structures operate together as a unit. The three can be separated as different kinds of structures, and their respective roles in an individual's behavior can be differentiated, but the contraction of muscles in a response like walking is more than muscle contraction. It is a receptor-connector-effector process. There would be no effect or activity without receptor and connector activity.

SUMMARY

All behavior is dependent upon or involves the functioning of body structures. Three kinds of body structures are directly involved in behavior: (1) the receiving mechanisms, or sense organs, (2) the connecting mechanisms, or nervous system, and (3) the reacting mechanisms, or muscles and glands.

The sense organs with their receptor mechanisms are classified as exteroceptors, interoceptors, and proprioceptors. The senses of sight, hearing, smell, taste, touch, warmth, cold, and pain are classified as exteroceptors. The organic sense is classified as an interoceptor. The kinaesthetic and static senses are classified as proprioceptors.

The nervous system serves as a connecting link between the sense organs and the muscles and glands to conduct nerve impulses from one part of the body to another. It is composed of two main divisions: the cerebro-spinal system and the autonomic system. The structural unit of the nervous system is the nerve cell or neurone. The spinal cord, medulla, cerebellum, and cerebrum are nerve centers which serve as connecting and relay centers for impulses from various parts of the body. The cerebrum in particular serves as a coordinating and integrating center for the highest mental processes: thinking, perceiving, recognizing, learning, and consciousness.

The reacting mechanisms consist of two kinds of body structures, muscles and glands. There are two kinds of muscles, striped and smooth; and two kinds of glands, duct and ductless or endocrine. The principal characteristic of the muscles is contractility. The work of the body is carried on through the contractions of the striped muscles. The endocrine glands throw their secretions directly into the blood stream without the aid of ducts.   The secretions are carried to all parts of the body, and serve to integrate and regulate all of the reacting mechanisms.   The principal endocrine glands are the thyroid, pitui-tary, adrenals, sex glands or gonads, pineal, and the pancreas.

QUESTIONS

on the Chapter

1. What is the functional unit of the nervous system?
2. Name and give the specific function of each part of this functional unit.
3. Locate and give the function of (a) rods and cones, (b) cochlea, (c) semi-circular canals, (d) taste buds, (e) medulla, (f) cerebellum, (g) autonomic nervous system.
4. What were the results of Lashley's experiments on the relation of learning ability in rats to the destruction of cortical tissue?
5. Distinguish between smooth and striped muscles.
6. Locate and describe the functions of each of the endocrine glands.
7. What is cretinism?   Myxedema?   Aphasia?

for Discussion

1. How do you account for the fact that people in general still speak of five senses when it is known that there are more than five?
2. It has been a common practice to compare the nervous system to the tele-phone system of a large city.   Is this a good comparison?   Why?
3. Why aren't we more aware of the static and kinaesthetic senses?
4. Does the destruction of a part of the brain result in the loss of a specific function or in a general reduction of efficiency?   Discuss.
5. Why is a knowledge of body structures of value in studying human behavior?

REFERENCES

1 BERG, LEWIS, *The Human Personality.*   New York: Prentice-Hall, 1933, pp. 54–56.   Reprinted by permission.
2 CRUZE, WENDELL W., *General Psychology for College Students.*   New York: Prentice-Hall, 1951.
3 DASHIELL, J. F., *Fundamentals of General Psychology*, 3rd edition.   Boston: Houghton Mifflin Company, 1949.
4 DYSINGER, D. W.: "An Action Current and Reflex Time Study of Psychiatric and Neurological Cases," *Psychol. Monogr.*, 1932, 43, 31–52.
5 LASHLEY, K. S., *Brain Mechanisms and Intelligence.*   Chicago: University of Chicago Press, 1929.
6 LASHLEY, K. S., "Studies of Cerebral Function in Learning. XI," *Comp. Psychol. Monogr.*, 1935, 11, No. 52.
7 MORGAN, JOHN J. B., *Psychology.*   New York: Farrar and Rinehart, 1941.
8 WOODWORTH, R. S., and MARQUIS, D. G., *Psychology*, 5th edition.   New York: Henry Holt and Company, 1947.

ENVIRONMENT

4

While we have pointed out repeatedly that an individual's behavior is dependent upon environment, we have not attempted, except somewhat incidentally, to describe what we mean by environment, or in what respects behavior is dependent upon it. It is the purpose of this chapter to examine the E of our behavior equation in order to indicate more exactly what it refers to and in what way environmental variables are involved in behavior.

WHAT IS MEANT BY ENVIRONMENT?

We have suggested from time to time that the term *environment* is used to refer to all of the variables or conditions with which an organism interacts. At various times these variables have been described as stimulating conditions or simply as stimuli. In this sense, environment includes all of the conditions within the organism and external to it which affect its development or its behavior either directly or indirectly. The internal conditions include glandular secretions, muscular contractions, intercellular and intracellular processes, and bodily processes such as circulation, digestion, elimination, and nerve functioning. The external conditions include all of the objects, forces, situations, and relations of the physical world to which an individual is sensitive or which produce changes in him. These include, quite obviously, such forces as light, sound, pressures, heat radiations, and a variety of chemical, mechanical, and electrical stimulations. The external environment also includes a vast array of *social* conditions: the behavior of other individuals; the relations which exist between people, such as parent-child, husband-wife, employee-employer, and teacher-pupil relationships; social institutions; social standards; the many physical objects and situations produced by people; and in short all of the things falling under the headings of society and culture which affect an individual's behavior or his adjustment.

Psychological Environment

One point needs to be emphasized. An individual's environment is made up of those conditions which affect him, those to which he responds or with which he interacts. An external condition is not part of an individual's environment unless it produces some effect upon or in the individual himself. An external object may be physically present but psychologically absent. One may appear to be staring fixedly at another person's face yet not see it nor be affected by it. The face is physically present but it is not producing an effect upon the apparent observer and is not at that instant an environmental condition. On the other hand, some external object may be a part of the psychological environment of each of several individuals, i.e., it is producing some effect in each one, yet a close examination of the effects of this common external object may reveal that it is having different effects and is, therefore, a different environmental object to each individual. For example, a chicken to be carved and eaten at dinner seems, at first sight, to be an element of environment common to all the diners. But to father it presents a struggle between being generous and saving his favorite piece for himself; to mother it is a product of her cooking; to the guests it raises the interesting question of who will be selected for the first serving; to the older children it is merely food; to the youngest child, if he is served last, it is a reminder of his position in the family.

All of this adds up to the point that environment, as it is used in psychology, refers to those conditions with which the individual interacts. It cannot be described in terms of any set of characteristics or properties inherent in the conditions themselves; rather, it is to be defined in terms of its effect upon the individual or upon people in general. For example, one may determine by investigation the range of light waves to which individuals in general are sensitive. Waves above and below certain frequencies do not produce reactions in any individual. We can speak of the light waves within this range as the adequate stimuli for vision. But a particular person may be blind to stimuli within this range. The adequate stimuli for this person would have to be defined in terms of the effects of such stimuli upon the person himself. Environment in the above sense may be thought of as the effective or *psychological environment*. It is a common practice to use the term environment to refer to all of the external conditions which *might* affect an individual and which presumably exist when no organism is present. We may distinguish environment in this sense from the psychological environment by calling it the *geographic environment*.

Environment in the Behavior Equation

It should now be clear that the E of our behavior equation is the psychological environment and that it refers to the conditions, situations, variables, or stimuli with which the person is interacting at the moment. It is equally clear that the effect of the interaction is to be found in the behavior (B) of the equation. But E affects behavior in another way. It will be recalled from our discussion in Chapter 2 that the person (P) of our equation is what he is at any given time because of the joint operation of hereditary and environmental variables. In short, previous environmental effects are represented in the P of the behavior equation. A child's reaction to the command "Come here" is dependent in part upon the immediate environmental stimulus and in part upon previous environmental stimulations which were involved in his learning the meaning of such verbal commands. This means in effect that behavior at any given time is a function of the accumulated effects of the interaction of heredity with a long series of environmental variables (the P of the equation) interacting with an immediate stimulating situation. The behavior equation might be rewritten as follows: $B = f(HEd)(E)$, in which H refers to heredity and Ed refers to the developmental environment which, interacting with heredity, has produced the person as he is at the moment of his interaction with some immediate stimulating situation (E).

PRENATAL ENVIRONMENT

The environmental conditions which are known to affect the development of the organism from fertilization to birth are: *intracellular* conditions, *intercellular* conditions, and *external* conditions (29).

Intracellular conditions are processes within a cell which affect the development of the cell itself. It appears that the genes and the cytoplasm (see Figure 4, p. 43) of the zygote interact to produce the structures characteristic of the organism, this interaction being, of course, only one of the conditions essential for development (35, p. 183).

Intercellular conditions are the stimulating effects of one cell on adjacent cells. The zygote divides into two cells, these into four, and so on until many cells are formed. As the number of cells increases, the location of the cells with respect to each other changes. Thus, one cell is adjacent to and is influenced by one group of cells, while another cell is adjacent to and is influenced by a different group of cells. Experiments indicate that the position of the cells with respect to one another is a factor in the development of the organism. When cells from the region that produces skin are removed, during early development, and are transplanted to the region that is to produce the brain, they become part of the brain instead of part of the skin. Similarly, if cells from the region that produces the brain are transplanted to the region that produces the skin, the cells become part of the skin. "What the cells become depends on their surroundings; on what the cells about them are becoming." (25, p. 94)

External conditions are stimulations which arise outside the developing organism. As previously indicated (see page 55), the embryo lives as a parasite grafted upon the uterus of the mother. Through the placental tissues oxygen and food pass from the mother to the fetus and various waste products pass in the opposite direction from the fetus. At the same time it is possible for the fetus to be affected by various harmful substances which might enter the mother's blood stream. Toxins, bacteria, and certain drugs may pass from the mother to the fetus. In fact, disturbances of the mother's metabolism brought about by glandular imbalances or in other ways may affect the development of the fetus. The fetus is surrounded by membranes, and although it is subject to outside pressures and changes in position, it is well protected from extreme pressures, injury, and changes in temperature. Most stimulations outside the mother, such as light, sound, social conditions, and the like, can have no influence on the fetus except in so far as they affect the mother's metabolism and the food supply of the fetus.

POSTNATAL ENVIRONMENT

It is obvious that most of the physical and social conditions which affect an individual's development and to which he must adjust himself are postnatal phenomena. These conditions are of little or no consequence during the prenatal development, since there is no direct interaction between the fetus and the outside world. At birth, however, a great change occurs. The child moves from one kind of environment into another, into one in which he must be active instead of passive, self-supporting instead of parasitic. External conditions, which were of little consequence during prenatal development, now become of primary importance. Internal processes will continue to affect the child's development and behavior and they must be regarded as aspects of the postnatal environment, but with birth they become relatively less significant because the individual from birth on must maintain himself in his new surroundings. He must be sensitive to these surroundings and, more important, he must react or learn to react to them in certain ways if he is to survive.

The child at birth is equipped to do just this. Most of the sensory mechanisms are developed to a point such that within a very short time they are sensitive to external stimulations. Some of the response mechanisms — for example, breathing — are ready to function at once. The child is able to maintain himself on an elementary level, but he has a long way to go. Many of the external conditions, especially those constituting the social world, will have little or no effect upon him immediately, and will only come to do so slowly and gradually. Sensitivity to physical stimulations, while it is present at birth, is of a relatively low order. Considerable development must take place before the child can sense small differences between stimuli or make finely graded responses to stimuli of different intensities.

The external conditions with which the individual interacts may be divided into two groups: *physical conditions* and *social conditions*. Quite obviously these two groups are interrelated. Some aspects of our physical world have been created by people; and some social customs and practices, such as heated and air-conditioned homes and the wearing of clothes, are dictated in large part by physical conditions. Nevertheless there are certain distinguishing characteristics. For example, physical conditions, while variable, are less so than social ones. A rock is more likely to stay put than is a social custom or an institution. Individuals as objects differ from inanimate objects, the characteristic of primary concern for human behavior being the ability of a person to initiate activity in himself and to respond, not only to things and people, but to his own activity.

Every human reaction is the result of the stimulation of a receptor mechanism, and all knowledge of external conditions, whether physical or social, is gained through such stimulation. External objects, situations, or relationships arouse receptor mechanisms through direct contact with the receptors or through some intermediary condition or energy transmission from the external object or situation to the receptors. (We have seen already, in Table IV, that the exteroceptors are classified as teleoceptors or proximoceptors depending upon whether the stimulus object is in contact with the sense organ or affects it from a distance through some medium.) This situation holds whether the external condition is a social situation, the activity of other people, or a physical object. In any event we come to know the physical and social worlds, including ourselves, and we are affected by conditions in these worlds through such physical media as sound waves, light waves, and chemical, mechanical, and electrical stimulations. While the exteroceptors are specifically designed for external stimulations, it must be recognized that both the interoceptors and proprioceptors are affected, at least indirectly, by external conditions.   In the case of the proprioceptors, muscle contractions and bodily movements serve as the media between external stimulations and subsequent behavior.   External conditions may also produce internal bodily disturbances through exteroceptive or proprioceptive stimulations.   Such a disturbance becomes a cue to external conditions.   Thus the entire receptor system may be involved in our interactions with our external environment.

Adequate Stimuli

As was pointed out in the previous chapter, the sense organs are special body structures which are sensitive to particular kinds and ranges of stimulation.   The stimuli for which a sense organ is structurally adapted are called *adequate stimuli*.   Thus light or, more correctly, ether vibrations are the adequate stimuli for vision.   The visual receptors may be activated by other stimulations, such as a blow on the head or pressure on the eyeball, but they are especially designed to be activated by ether vibrations.   The adequate stimuli for the various senses are given in Table V.

Table V

The Senses and the Adequate Stimuli for Each

SENSES	ADEQUATE STIMULI
1. Vision	Ether vibrations ranging in length between 400 and 760 millimicrons
2. Hearing	Air vibrations ranging ordinarily between 20 and 20,000 vibrations per second
3. Smell	Gaseous particles in the air
4. Taste	Chemicals in solution
5. Touch	Objects that press, touch, wrinkle, or pull the skin, or touch a hair
6. Warmth	Heat radiations above 30° C
7. Cold	Heat radiations below 30° C
8. Pain	Objects that cut, prick, burn, or tear the tissues
9. Kinaesthetic	Muscle contractions or movements of body parts which result in pulls on muscles, tendons, or joint surfaces
10. Static	Movements of the head

Limited range of stimuli.   Table V indicates that the sensitivity of each sense organ is limited to a particular kind of stimulation, and, further, to a limited range of that kind of stimulation. For example, the ether vibrations to which the human eye is ordinarily sensitive range in length between 400 and 760 millimicrons (1/1,000,000 mm.). There are many longer and shorter vibrations. The shorter ones include the ultraviolet rays and x-rays; the longer ones include the infrared rays, heat rays, and the waves used in radio broadcasting (12). Such vibrations are outside the visible range. Similarly, the ear is sensitive to a limited range of air vibrations, the effective range being between 20 and 20,000 vibrations per second. Vibration rates above and below these limits are outside the audible range. Many chemicals and gases arouse no taste or odor experiences. Heat radiations above or below a certain temperature do not arouse experiences of warmth or cold but may activate pain sense organs.

Characteristics of stimuli. The adequate stimuli for a given receptor have certain characteristics and may differ from one another in one or more of these characteristics. For example, the adequate stimuli in any sense field may differ in *intensity* or strength. Each stimulus must be of a certain minimum intensity in order to arouse a receptor. This minimum intensity is used as a measure of the *lower threshold* of stimulation. Intensities below this threshold will not activate the sense organ. Likewise at the upper end of the intensity scale a point is reached where additional increases in intensity will not be sensed by the person. Stimuli within a given range for a given sense organ may also differ from one another in *length* or *frequency* or *rate of transmission*. For example, ether vibrations differ from one another in length. Vibrations of one length give rise to one color experience, while those of another length give rise to a different color experience. Though the vibrations are all within the field of vision, they are qualitatively different in that they produce qualitatively different results, almost as if they were arising in different sense fields. Air vibrations differ in frequency or in the number of vibrations per second, and produce sounds that differ in pitch. Likewise, in the field of taste different chemicals produce different taste experiences.

Stimuli within a sense field also differ in *complexity* or *composition*. A light wave may be made up of a number of components, i.e., a number of vibrations of different lengths. If the components are of about the same length, the resulting color is said to be *saturated* or pure. If a wave of a given length is mixed with many other waves of quite different lengths the resulting experience will tend to be gray or white. Sound waves also differ in complexity. An auditory stimulus composed of a single vibration rate gives rise to a pure tone. If higher frequencies are added, the pitch of the tone produced will remain the same but the tone will now have a characteristic quality or *timbre*, the particular quality depending upon the number of higher frequencies.

While the characteristic of complexity or composition has to do with the number and nature of the components in a stimulus within a given sense field, something quite analogous to this is found between sense fields. For example, a given taste stimulus may be a compound of two or more chemicals in solution, one or more kinds of cutaneous stimuli, such as touch and warmth or cold, and one or more odor stimuli. Similarly, many cutaneous stimuli are combinations or patterns of different cutaneous stimuli of different intensities. In fact it is extremely difficult to arouse a warmth or cold receptor with the appropriate stimuli without arousing touch receptors as well.

THE SOCIAL ENVIRONMENT

The external stimulations which arise out of man's reactions to his fellow man, out of the relationships which exist between individuals and groups, out of social institutions, and out of social and cultural phenomena in general, are of such importance in an individual's behavior that we will examine these conditions in some detail. While these conditions affect an individual through his sense organs, it is not light waves or sound waves as such which cause a child to hate his parents. A complex set of relationships involving the child and his parents is interpreted or perceived by the child in such a way that hate is the result. Sight, hearing, touch, and even smell may provide the sensory data out of which the child's perceptions are formed; but a knowledge of the social relationships giving rise to the sensory data and the child's perception is the significant cue to an understanding of the child's behavior.

Influence of the Home

Of all the conditions in the social environment that influence the development and behavior of an individual, the home is the most potent. This is true largely because the home is the first and, for some time, the only social situation affecting the child. It affects the child during his most formative years, beginning even before birth, and before he has been shaped or affected by other social conditions. Most of a child's basic habits and attitudes have their beginnings in the home, some of them actually becoming firmly established before influences from outside the home begin to be of much significance. A glance at some of these habits and attitudes will serve to indicate the importance of home influence. A partial list includes such habits as eating, handedness, talking, walking, habitual ways of dealing with people, and such attitudes as those toward sex, other people's property, other people's rights, male-female relationships, parent-child relationships, supervision, and one's role in the home. Let us consider some of the factors which enable the home to exercise this profound influence on behavior.

Prestige of parents. The young child obviously has little knowledge of, or opinion about, the world or his place in it. At first, behavior patterns or ideals of conduct presented to him do not have to pass the criticism of ideals and beliefs already accepted, as they must a few years later. Hence the child, lacking a basis of criticism, readily accepts the ideals and conduct of his parents. His tendency to do this is strengthened by his own helplessness and by the prestige of his parents, who seem to have unlimited power to punish and to reward. Furthermore, the tendency of children to identify themselves with their parents also strengthens the tendency to imitate them. The home is, for the child, a closely knit unit. It is *our* home; the things connected with it are *ours* — *our* car, *our* way of doing things, *our* position. These considerations, apart from any question of hereditary behavior patterns, are sufficient to explain why children act as their parents do.

One can readily understand, in the light of the foregoing discussion, why it is important that nothing should happen to impair the prestige of parents in the eyes of their children. Since children identify themselves with their parents, a blow to their regard for their parents is a blow to their own self-respect and confidence. Furthermore, children need someone to imitate and someone to discipline them. If the prestige of the parent suffers, he can no longer provide a pattern for his children to imitate, and the difficulty of imposing wise discipline increases. In a culture changing as rapidly as ours, many parents lose much of their prestige when their children reach adolescence, sometimes with disastrous consequences. The loss is most frequent and most serious in families where parents are foreign-born. The children in such families, on accepting American ideals and standards, begin to look down upon their old-fashioned parents. Needless to say, both parents and children suffer.

Economic status. The economic level of the home influences even the prenatal development of the child. During pregnancy a well-to-do mother has medical care. Her diet is carefully regulated for the good of the child as well as for her own good. This care is important; for, though nature has done much to insure the fetus against changes in the mother's health, it has not succeeded in giving complete protection. This is shown by the effect of lead poisoning, which produces abortions, deaf-mutism, imbecility, and macrocephaly (a condition characterized by an excessively large head and caused by too much fluid). It is claimed that the fetus is injured 92 times out of 100 when the mother suffers lead poisoning (32, p. 16). What is true of lead poisoning is probably true, though to a less noticeable degree, of malaria, toxins in the body, and alcoholism. At the time of the child's birth, the well-to-do mother and the child are given the best care that medical science offers, whereas the infants of the poor are frequently not even fed in accordance with the best practice. If the child of well-to-do parents is thought to need sea breezes or mountain air, he is taken to the sea or the mountains. He is at all times provided with the medical care and supervision necessary to insure his best development. He enjoys a proper diet, the importance of which for normal development is becoming more and more evident. The omission of a certain vitamin is a cause of defective eyes; the omission of another, of defective bones; of another, of emotional instability. Deficiency of secretion of one endocrine gland may cause idiocy; the excess of another, prolonged childhood. Fortunately, these conditions can be detected by experts and, in many instances, corrected. Obviously it is difficult for families of insufficient means to give these advantages to their children.

The economic conditions of the home may influence the personality of children in more direct ways. The fear of hunger and the denial of many legitimate wants deeply influence the outlook of those who are unable to have necessary food, clothing, and shelter. Children who have experienced hunger and who have been compelled to spend much of the day in bed to keep warm dream of warm shelter and plenty of food, while more fortunate children dream of a life of leadership and social recognition (9, p. 33; 20, p. 173). Children of the poor look forward to a life of toil and seem to expect nothing more than the necessities of living; while those of the well-to-do anticipate college, travel, and adventure. The former are expected to curtail their desires, the latter to pursue a vigorous program of self-realization.

We should not wonder that the attitudes of children are influenced by the economic status of their parents. Children whose early life is spent in want feel that they are insecure and that they are a burden to their parents, especially if they hear their parents discuss financial difficulties. Children whose early life is a "bed of roses" are spared these fears and negative self-feelings. To belong to a wealthy home practically insures the child a satisfactory standing in society; to belong to a poor one means a decidedly lower social standing. The fortunate child is surrounded with beautiful things and is spared an early introduction to disease and filth, or an intimate acquaintance with birth and death. Children of the poor frequently acquire an early familiarity with these sobering conditions and events.

The consequences of poverty and extreme wealth are intensified in a democratic society where all children go to the same schools. Two boys may go through high school side by side; one goes out to security, social position, and luxury, and is given every opportunity to develop all that is in him; the other goes out to get a job with no assurance that he will find one, or that the job offered him will be suitable. It is not surprising that such underprivileged boys often become resentful and embittered, or that many of them follow a life of crime or become parasites on society.

The influence of poverty on respect for property rights has been clearly shown by a study of the effect of the depression on moral ideas. In 1924 and again in 1933, after three years of depression, Schatz (31) asked a large number of high-school boys and girls the question, "Is it ever right to steal?" The high-school boys and girls of 1924, with few exceptions, answered, "No." More than half of the high-school group of 1933 answered, "Yes." Many justified their answer by saying, "Everyone is doing it — the rich on a large scale; why shouldn't the poor steal too, if they can?" This study corroborates the conclusion reached by Hartshorne and May (21), who found that children from homes economically and culturally superior are more honest than children from homes that are inferior in these respects.

Though it is clear that superior economic status provides a favorable background for the development of desirable personality traits, yet it by no means insures the development of a fine character or personality. If wealthy parents lack wisdom, their children are apt to become arrogant, extravagant, dissipated, insensitive to social obligations, and contemptuous of the opinions and rights of others. On the other hand, an economically underprivileged home does not always crush the spirit or make a child resentful. Instead, it may inspire a boy with a spirit of courage and thrift and with the determination to work hard in order not to remain poor; it may teach him to be cheerful in the face of want, and to appreciate possessions which do not depend on money; it may instruct him in the value of mutual love, helpfulness, and respect for others. Economic status is only one condition, though an important one, that affects behavior.

A problem investigated by Baker and Traphagen (3) is interesting in this connection. They rated, on a scale of five points, the economic status of the homes of 189 problem children and 181 non-problem children. The highest rating was 5. This rating was given families who owned the houses they lived in and were in fair circumstances. The rating 4 was given to homes where wealth had been acquired suddenly, and where false standards had resulted. Families that were paying for an average house or renting a good one but that were practicing strict economy were rated 3. Those who were renting fair quarters and had an irregular income were rated 2. Chronic charity cases living in very poor quarters and families that assumed no responsibility were rated 1. The average rating of the economic status of the non-problem children was 3.63; that of the problem children, 2.86.

The children were also rated on 65 other items, such as their general behavior, attitude toward school, discipline at home, scholarship, attitude toward home, etc., and the total score was computed. The median, or score of the middle child, of the non-problem group was 285; that of the problem group, 220. Only two children of the non-problem group fell below the median of the problem children. The total score measures what Baker and Traphagen call excellence of "behavior motivation." (3, p. 345)

The most significant results regarding the importance of economic status were obtained when the relation was determined between the economic-status score and the total score. The question to be answered was: Does a high score on economic conditions indicate a high score on behavior excellence? In order to answer this question, Baker and Traphagen determined the relation between economic status of homes and the quality of behavior motivation as revealed by the total scores on their ratings, using the correlation technique (see p. 34). They found a correlation of $+.53$ for the group of problem children, $+.22$ for the non-problem children, and $+.49$ when both groups were combined (3, p. 355). While these correlations leave no doubt regarding the importance of economic status as a factor influencing behavior, they are still far below $+1.00$. They indicate, therefore, two facts: first, that economic status does matter; and second, that other factors are also of importance.

This conclusion is supported by the results of the recent work of Glueck and Glueck (19). These investigators made a careful and detailed study of 500 delinquent and 500 non-delinquent boys. The two groups were carefully matched for age, general intelligence, national origin, and residence in underprivileged neighborhoods. An exhaustive study of the two groups covering many specific measurements of physique, temperament, attitudes, behavior characteristics, and socio-cultural conditions revealed that

> the delinquents as a group are distinguishable from the non-delinquents: (1) physically, in being essentially mesomorphic in constitution (solid, closely knit, muscular); (2) temperamentally, in being restlessly energetic, impulsive, extroverted, aggressive, destructive (often sadistic) — traits which may be related more or less to the erratic growth pattern and its physiologic correlates or consequences; (3) in attitude, by being hostile, defiant, resentful, suspicious, stubborn, socially assertive, adventurous, unconventional, non-submissive to authority; (4) psychologically, in tending to direct and concrete, rather than symbolic, intellectual expression, and in being less methodical in their approach to problems; (5) socio-culturally, in having been reared to a far greater extent than the control group in homes of little understanding, affection, stability, or moral fibre by parents usually unfit to be effective guides and protectors or, according to psychoanalytic theory, desirable sources for emulation and the construction of a consistent, well-balanced, and socially normal superego during the early stages of character development. While in individual cases the stresses contributed by any one of the above pressure-areas of dissocial-behavior tendency may adequately account for persistence in delinquency, in general the high probability of delinquency is dependent upon the interplay of the conditions and forces from all these areas (19, pp. 281, 282).

An examination of the socio-cultural conditions reveals that the familial background of the delinquents was less adequate than that of the non-delinquents. A higher proportion of the parents of the delinquents than of the parents of the non-delinquents had no more than a grade-school education at the time of their marriage. More of the homes of the delinquents were broken by divorce, desertion, separation, or death. The parents of the delinquents attempted to meet disciplinary problems with either more laxity or more harshness than did the parents of the non-delinquents. A higher proportion of the families of the delinquents were disorganized. This lack of cohesiveness is interpreted as a lack of warmth and of respect for the integrity of each member of the family. Sporadic or chronic dependency was more prevalent among the families of the delinquents.

Thus here, as in the study by Baker and Traphagen, economic status is a factor in delinquency, but it appears that the problem is more deep-rooted. Glueck and Glueck (19, p. 280) suggest that the greater prevalence of dependency among the families of the delinquents is to be attributed in part at least to the "poorer work habits of the fathers, and in part to less planful management of the family income." They go on to say: "These differences between the families of the delinquents and the families of the non-delinquents do not so much pertain to the obvious issue of the relationship of dependency or poverty to crime (the vast majority of both groups of families are of the underprivileged class); they are important, rather, as reflecting the differences in the quality of the adults in the families and therefore the variance in influence on the children."

Attitudes of parents. All of us have had the experience of going into a home that depressed us. The parents may have been filled with fears. They may have felt that their investments were insecure, that a dependent old age stared them in the face; or they may have been unduly anxious concerning political developments; or they may have felt that God was about to inflict some dire calamity on society. Any topic mentioned was sure to bring forth an expression of fear and anxiety. Even adults, after a visit in such a home, feel that their cares have been increased. How much more depressed must a child become who for years is subjected to its atmosphere!

Wickes (40) has reported how such home conditions led to the actual nervous breakdown of a girl of nine. This little girl, through identifying herself with her father, who was finding it difficult to pull himself together and assume his duties, bore a burden too heavy for her. When the father finally met his problem, the nervous disorder of the child disappeared. In this case, the father was able to change his attitude. Unfortunately, the anxieties of many parents are so deep-seated that they are beyond the powers of the parents to change. In such cases, the damage to sensitive children is apt to be more permanent.

Excessive anxiety over the children themselves is usually a focus for anxiety in general. Who has not observed a home in which the parents' eyes, thoughts, and interests are unduly concentrated on the children? A spirit of tension, almost an expectation of impending catastrophe, pervades the home life. Common experience tells us (and child-guidance clinics confirm it) that many children suffer from "too much parents." Dunbar (15) goes so far as to suggest that exposure of children to intense adult emotions is traumatic to their personality development. The situation is easier to detect in the homes of others than in our own. In contrast with the gloomy home, an environment of cheer and good feeling is more healthful. Homes take on a general atmosphere. Minute by minute, day by day, the general emotional tone of the home is an environmental factor which has a deep as well as a superficial effect on members of the family.

Specific attitudes and values of parents are also reflected in their children. If the parents are rabid pleasure-seekers, the adolescent youth will be influenced — either to follow their example or to avoid what seems to him an empty life. If the parents look upon work as drudgery and are quickly fatigued by it, the child will in all probability develop the same attitude. If the parents are snobs, the child will in all likelihood become one. If the parents are critical of the school and of teachers, the child will become so. If the parents usually escape the disagreeable by becoming ill, the child is likely to develop the same neurotic trait.

That specific attitudes and opinions of parents are reflected in their children was shown in a recent study of Weltman and Remmers (37). The Purdue Opinion Poll for Young People was given to 207 high school pupils and their parents. The poll items had to do with political and educational issues. The results indicated a degree of similarity between the opinions of the pupils and their parents of such magnitude that the authors felt justified in considering that "measurement of high-school pupils gives a fairly accurate measure of adult public opinion."

Friction between parents. Constant nagging, bickering, and criticism between parents leave a mark, and a bad mark, upon the children. Careful studies of problem children show that the parents, not the child, are often the real problem. Adults know how they feel when two persons they esteem highly are constantly quarreling. Sympathizing with both, they are pulled in opposite directions by their loyalties. For children this state is probably intensified by the feeling that their security depends upon the love between parents. Regarding this Brown (5, p. 88) writes:

> If the parents are at enmity with one another, however hard they may try to conceal it, the fact becomes apparent and exerts a baneful influence upon the child. The child sympathizes with both parents, and so internalizes in itself the outer conflict — the conflict becomes implanted in the child's mind, and is a source of weakness later on.

The same thought has been vividly expressed by another writer: "The house divided against itself often becomes the battle ground on which a child's future is sacrificed." (16) This is illustrated by the case of a little girl of nine who ran a temperature for three months and was unable to attend school. She had no other physical symptoms of trouble except loss of appetite and languor. The physician could find no cause for the condition. Both parents felt that they had the child's confidence, and that she was not unhappy or worried about anything. Finally, the mother admitted that she was not happily married, and that she wished a divorce but could not make up her mind to accept the changes that would be involved. Though the matter of a divorce was an open question with the parents, she felt sure that the child knew nothing of this. The mother was finally made to see that she was not helping her daughter by allowing the present state to continue, and it was made clear to her that she and her husband should either adjust their difficulties or decide to separate. Though the mother felt sure that a separation would be a hardship for the child, they decided to try it. They therefore explained the situation to the child and separated. The child immediately began to improve. Her relief at being no longer the victim of her vague fears was so great that she soon returned to normal health and to a real enjoyment of her school and play (40, pp. 46, 47).

Friction between parents may lead also to the undoing of discipline and to the division of the family into two hostile camps. The following case will serve as an illustration. The parents of two boys were at odds with each other. One of the brothers sided with the father, the other with the mother. Since the father was away most of the day, one of the boys was without a defender. As a result, he was constantly treated unjustly by the other, who always had the support of the mother. This, as might be expected, caused him to feel bitter, and from time to time he gave violent expression to his anger. Under such conditions the other boy became extremely arrogant and domineering. Both boys were thus injured by the favoritism and injustice of the mother, which was caused ultimately by the friction between her and her husband.

In yet another way friction between parents has an injurious effect on the child. Children need to have someone to admire and to love. Parents usually meet this need; but if there is jealousy and friction between them, they are apt in many ways, sometimes consciously but more frequently unconsciously, to undermine each other's influence and prestige. When this happens, the child not only is deprived of a valuable example, but often develops feelings of insecurity which result in actual suffering. A boy who identifies himself with his father under such circumstances may develop an unhealthy attitude toward members of the opposite sex and toward marriage. Girls may, of course, be similarly injured.

Strained relations between parents may also injure the child by making him a substitute object of affection for the husband or wife. There is general agreement that lavishing on a child love that should be directed toward an adult is undesirable, and yet this substitution is by no means infrequent. When parents are unable to find in marital relations the love and sympathy they crave, or when they feel that their partner is unworthy of their love, they are likely to seek an outlet by showering affection upon their child. Under these conditions, discipline is apt to be undermined and emotional bonds developed between parent and child that are hard for the latter to break even when he becomes an adult. A child so treated is apt to go through life unable to assume adult responsibilities or to take an adult attitude toward life; he remains emotionally undeveloped (39).

In this connection it is interesting to note that the death of one parent, separation of parents, divorce, or commitment of one parent to an institution brings about a condition — broken home — which looms large as a factor in juvenile delinquency. Healy and Bronner (22) found that defective family relationships were involved in a little over 50 per cent of their 4000 cases of delinquency. Other investigators have found similar high relationships between home conditions and the children's behavior. In a recent study by Torrance (34), boarding students in a military school who came from broken homes were found to have more behavior, emotional, social, and health problems than the boys of a control group with whom they were paired. All of the dismissals from the school because of serious behavior problems were of boys from the broken-homes group.

Lack of real interest in the child. It is not difficult to find among clinical cases histories of children who have been injured by a real, though often unrecognized, lack of interest in their welfare. Children need more than good food, warm clothes, toys, and sunshine. They need to know that they are wanted, that they are loved, that they "belong." Some parents seem to think that any display of love would be a weakness. Hence they assume a cold attitude, and, as a result, their children are, at least in one important respect, emotionally starved. Some parents actually do not love their children. They feel that their children stand in the way of the attainment of their ambitions. Children sometimes sense the situation and, in their efforts to hold their parents, regress to an infantile attitude. The following case illustrates this. A little girl who had a strong love for her parents was regarded by them as a handicap in attaining their social and professional ambitions. The child had been sent to a summer camp at six; and when she was nine, her parents prepared to send her to a boarding school. At this point she suddenly began to be willful and to make all sorts of arbitrary demands for attention. Then certain regressions to infantile behavior, such as sucking her thumb, made their appearance. Commenting on the case, Wickes (40, pp. 253, 254) writes:

> No one with any psychological insight could talk long to the mother without seeing the personal ambition peering from behind her ardour for a "larger life" and for being of use to her husband. It was this un-admitted and unrecognized personal ambition that was the corroding influence in the relationship, and that had destroyed the child's feeling of security in love. Therefore, she tried in these pathetic little power ways to gain control of her parents.

Discipline. However heatedly psychologists may argue among themselves about the truth of the old maxim, "Spare the rod and spoil the child," they are well agreed that the wisest use of discipline is a moderate use. Too harsh and too rigid rules make it difficult for the child to learn the reason for the rules. Parents who make the life of a child little more than following a set of commands usually succeed in teaching only that "rules are made to be broken," or in making the child believe that complete subservience and repression of initiative are the correct guides to social adjustment in later life.

Other parents seem to feel that in order not to crush the initiative of the child they should respect his every whim and fancy, regardless of the rights of others. Such training makes it hard for the child to make any social adjustments except by dominating his companions. Some parents encourage their children to be aggressive and to act without consideration for others, apparently believing that will power and determination are thus developed. In this they are poorly advised, since respect for, not disregard of, the rights and opinions of others is the best ally of persistent and determined conduct.

People sometimes allow their emotional states rather than the needs of the child to determine their disciplinary measures. Such a procedure, by its lack of consistency and rationality, not only fails to help the child develop self-control, initiative, perseverance, and consideration for others, but actually creates chaos in the child's whole conception of morality and social obligation. The importance of wise discipline is indicated by the fact that the control exercised over the non-problem children studied by Baker and Traphagen (3) was rated 1.9 times as high as that exercised over the problem children.

Frequently parents injure their children by being unwilling to accept them as they are. They wish to make them over in the light of their own desires, and to choose vocations for them. To such parents the advice of Angelo Patri is commended: "If you prayed for a fig and the

Fates decreed you a thistle, reflect upon the truth that a thistle full-grown and blossoming is a heartsome sight, but a thistle upon which a misguided soul has tried to graft a fig is a sorry, not to say a ridiculous sight." (30, p. 262)

Many parents make their children feel that if they do not achieve a certain goal, the family will be disgraced. The parents may do this because of pride, or in an effort to bolster up their feelings of personal worth. They may even do it out of sincere love for their children. Unfortunately, the sincerity of the love does not prevent the consequences from being disastrous, especially if the child returns that love and fears above all things that he may disappoint his parents. Under such circumstances, the child may drive himself so hard that his health, both mental and physical, is adversely affected.

Some parents make the opposite mistake of not expecting enough of their children. They ought to gauge the child's capacity carefully, and require him to live up to his capacity. Instead of doing this they make excuses for their children and treat them as babies. Such parents might study with profit *The Home Life of a Golden Eagle* by MacPherson (27). When the golden eaglet is young and helpless, the parents care for it with utmost devotion, but they do not neglect the important task of teaching it how to care for itself; when finally the eaglet has reached the point where he can take care of himself, the old eagles, who were formerly so devoted, forcibly drive him away (17). Human parents must be willing to face separation from their children. More than this, they must realize that it is one of the highest duties of parents to help their children become adults in every sense of the word.

Many parents, by suggesting undesirable patterns of conduct, make it hard for their children to develop normally. If a child has been noisy and has caused some confusion and disorder, they call him "a little devil" or "a bad boy," instead of reflecting that they would not really desire their child to sit quietly throughout the day and show no interest in investigating and manipulating things. Perhaps, in his presence and before others, they say that they "cannot do anything with him"; and the child, thus given the center of the stage, finds his vanity and love of attention satisfied. As a consequence of both of these kinds of treatment the child attempts to live up to the type set for him.

Children are frequently made bashful, shy, and cowardly in a similar manner. If, for example, a child is a bit shy, thoughtless parents, friends, and teachers speak of it before him. In this way they direct the attention of the child to himself instead of to what he is doing, and they heighten his self-consciousness and make it harder for him to overcome his weakness. Furthermore, since the child is extremely suggestible to begin with, these remarks serve to remind him of his undesirable reaction pattern and so to aggravate it.

Parents at times ridicule their children. By so doing they erect an impassable barrier between the children and themselves. They laugh at the children's fears, make light of their dreams, and show no interest in the products of their imagination. Yet later they wonder why their children do not come to them with their problems. The child, as a matter of course, opens the door to his inner life. If those who are invited to enter are callous or ruthless, they should not be surprised or grieved when he bars the door and becomes indifferent to their desire to gain his confidence.

Size of family. It has been discovered that the size of the family and the order of birth of the children are related to certain aspects of character and personality. According to Crane (10), men who are only children (who had no brothers or sisters) show 5.72 times the average in the number of their divorces, whereas men who are in the middle in order of birth show only .58 of the average number. The corresponding figures for women are 4.18 and .65.

Data published by Lentz (26) show that the average intelligence of persons from large families is lower than that of persons from small families. Other investigators have verified this finding. In a study of how family size, position in the family, sex and age of siblings affect intelligence and adjustment, Damrin (11) found that size of family was negatively correlated with intelligence, i.e., the larger the family the lower the intelligence tended to be. There are two possible explanations of this finding: either persons of low intelligence tend to raise larger families than do persons of higher intelligence (the action of heredity), or children in large families do not receive as much attention and hence are not stimulated in their intellectual growth as much as are children in smaller families (the action of environment). Judging from several recent investigations of the relative strength of heredity and environment (see page 47), we may safely say that these causes are jointly responsible for the facts.

Influence of the School

Next to the home and the interpersonal relationships connected with it, the school is the most important source of influence in the development of the individual, at least in our society. From the standpoint of time alone, the school plays an important role in an individual's life.

At the normal rate of progress an individual finishing high school will have spent eleven or twelve years in school. Four additional years are normally required for college. Sixteen years is approximately one fourth of a normal lifetime. Granted that one is not in school all of the time during these school years, he is still spending a fairly large portion of his life in school.

An even better estimate of the importance of the school in an individual's development is obtained if one makes an inventory of what one learns in school and then examines the ways in which this learning is used during the remainder of one's lifetime. It is only necessary to point to the almost indispensable skill of reading, with its widespread use in every walk of life, to illustrate the way in which the school influences one's behavior. This does not mean that learning is confined to school situations. Learning occurs in any life situation, and what is learned in these situations becomes a part of one's ability to adjust himself to his environment. But the school is especially designed to provide learning situations which might not arise in everyday living or which, if they did, would be less likely to result in the desired learning. Let us examine some of the ways in which the school influences human behavior.

Educational and mental development. The most obvious purpose of the school is, of course, the stimulation of educational and mental development. Everyone recognizes that without a system of universal education many of our citizens would be illiterate. It is hardly necessary to dwell upon the increased possibilities for individual development and understanding which arise through the sheer ability to read and write. Over and above these routine duties of the school, however, are a number of more subtle effects which it can exercise upon personality development. Formerly psychologists were generally agreed that an individual's intelligence or general mental ability was relatively fixed. One was either "smart" or "average" or "stupid," as the case might be; while education could give one more knowledge or facts, it was thought to have practically no effect upon general intelligence. This philosophy resulted in a fatalistic attitude on the part of teachers toward their pupils. After all, if a stupid child is destined always to remain stupid, why waste time trying to change him? Recently some very thorough experiments investigating the effect on intelligence of changing the environment have shown that a shift to a good home or a good school may actually increase some children's intelligence (as measured by the best intelligence tests) (36). There are, of course, limits to the amount of change in intelligence that will occur, even under the best environmental stimulation; but the fact that *some* change may reasonably be expected greatly increases the importance of schools.

Socializing influence. An important effect of the schools, particularly upon children between five and ten years old, is the socializing influence which results from bringing a large number of children together under the control of trained teachers. Schools make for social adaptability; they give the child an opportunity to play under supervision; they teach ideals; they stimulate the child's aesthetic interest and broaden his horizon; they equip him with the tools necessary for entering into and enjoying the accumulated insight and knowledge of his group. Not to have attended school is to suffer social disinheritance. Unfortunately, however, the school does not succeed in socializing all of its pupils. Frequently it fails to inspire its brightest pupils to do their best, while many of the duller ones are injured by being required to study subjects beyond their capacity or foreign to their interests. Happily, we are awakening to the fact that compulsory attendance imposes upon school authorities the duty of making the school such that every child who goes to it shall be helped.

To make the school a help to every pupil, more attention must be paid to differences in ability to learn. If the same amount of work is required of a very dull boy and a very bright one, the latter will find nothing in the requirements to test his powers, while the former will find that no matter how hard he works, he is unable to perform the required tasks. The bright one, therefore, assuming an attitude of superiority, develops habits of laziness and of working at low efficiency; the dull one becomes discouraged, and may attempt to save his self-respect by being disorderly or completely indifferent. He finally leaves school, beaten before he ever begins the life of an adult.

Emotional development. Schools should also pay more attention to the emotional differences of children. If a child is a leader and good "mixer," the school becomes an arena for the development of his capacities. He is called on to recite in public, to take a leading part in school plays, and to be a leader in many other activities. But what of the shy, timid, reflective child, who is a poor mixer? Though he is the one who particularly needs to take part in social activities, he is frequently neglected, or placed in a situation in which he is forced to compare his performance with that of those who are not similarly handicapped. Perhaps on the playground he is made sport of by the more aggressive children, with the result that he is driven more and more to live the life of an introvert. A little help on the part of the school authorities might be sufficient to check his tendency toward this extreme maladjustment. Children of this type usually do well under teachers who are sympathetic and who help them to make proper adjustments, but they do poorly if their teachers are insensitive to their inner conflicts. If the school is to fulfill its obligations to the children who are compelled by law to attend, the instruction must be adapted to the needs of the child; the school must cease trying to compel every child to conform to a rigid program designed to meet the needs of the majority (23).

Attitudes. Attitudes, also, are much affected by the school (4). It has been shown that men's attitudes toward such matters as capital punishment, labor unions, and government control of farming can be greatly modified by education or propaganda. The effect of education upon attitudes is seen in a study of 144 freshman students at the University of Louisville. These students were given interest and belief tests before and after they had taken a social science survey course. The results showed that the students became more liberal in their attitudes toward war, Negroes, and democracy (38). That attitude changes so induced are as permanent as the retention of material learned in a course in geometry or history is indicated in a study by Bugelski and Lester (6). Attitudes of university students which had changed in the direction of greater liberality between their freshman and senior years showed no indication to shift away from the position held in the senior year even two and three years after graduation.

Influence of Motion Pictures

Of the many features of twentieth-century environment, perhaps few are as important in their effect upon us as the motion picture. A series of studies recently published has shown experimentally that the motion pictures teach facts, influence attitudes, stimulate emotions, affect sleep, and influence conduct. The information taught by them is, at least in some cases, more permanent than material learned in other ways. "At all ages, including the adults, the slow drop of the curve of forgetting is striking. . . . 'The curves of forgetting are considerably higher than those obtained by previous investigators'" (using other materials) (7).

Attitudes as well as information are related to motion-picture attendance. Children who attend motion pictures to excess have "lower deportment records and do poorer work in school subjects." That desirable attitudes may also result, however, is shown by the fact that a single showing of a picture favorable to the Chinese resulted in a definitely more favorable attitude toward this race among the children who saw it.   After pupils had seen *Journey's End* or *All Quiet on the Western Front*, their attitudes toward war were much less favorable than before.

A study by Thurstone (33) showed that the attitude of children toward gambling was affected by seeing a motion picture about gambling. The children regarded gambling as a more serious offense after seeing the picture than before. Figure 27 shows the positions in which the students placed gambling on a "crime thermometer" before and after seeing the picture. It will be noted that the position of "Gambler" shifted toward the most serious end of the scale after the motion picture was shown. The positions of the other offenders on the before-and-after scales are essentially the same.

Experiments (7) upon the emotions of children show that "scenes of danger, conflict, or tragedy produce the greatest effect . . . upon children . . . from six to twelve years old." They also show that love scenes and romantic scenes generally have very little effect upon this group but a marked effect on persons from twelve to eighteen years of age. More important than these general trends are the striking individual differences discovered to exist between one child and another. Apparently, the same advice concerning motion-picture attendance should not be given to all children. One must first know the child before he can tell what or how many pictures will be genuinely stimulating experiences and not an "overdose" of emotion.

Another part of the study of the effects of motion pictures dealt with sleep. How is a child's sleep affected by motion-picture attendance? An ingenious technique was devised for measuring the restlessness of a child while asleep or while trying to sleep. The experiments showed, among other things, that a picture "is about as disturbing to sleep patterns as sitting up till midnight, [and] that the influence of some pictures . . . is as great on some children as drinking two cups of coffee in the evening."

The effect of motion pictures on the behavior of children was also clearly shown by these studies. Charters concludes that motion pictures "stir powerful ambitions, good and bad; develop permanent ideals, high and low; and crystallize the framework of life careers." These investigations prove quite clearly that the "movies" are an important factor in our emotional and intellectual development.

Influence of the Community

The habits, beliefs, customs, attitudes, and occupations of the people who make up the community in which we live constitute another im-

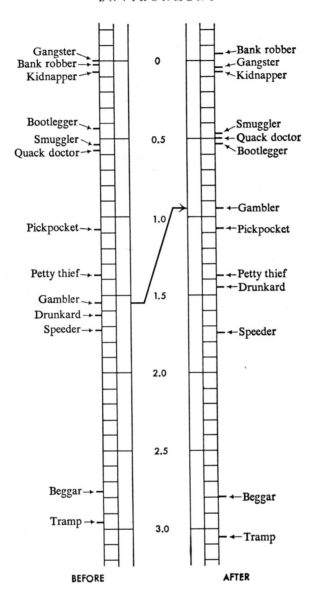

Figure 27

The Influence of Seeing a Motion Picture (William Powell in "Street of Chance") on the Attitude of Children toward Gambling

Notice the shift in the gambler's position. (From L. L. Thurstone, "Influence of Motion Pictures on Children's Attitudes," *J. Soc. Psychol.*, 1931, 2, 291–305.)

portant set of influences in our social environment. Just as a child's interests, attitudes, and even his vocabulary reflect the interests, attitudes, and ability level of his parents, so the individual reflects the interests, attitudes, religious beliefs, superstitions, and intellectual level of the community in which he lives. That our respective communities have given us different beliefs, different standards of conduct, different habits of speech, and different value systems becomes obvious when we are thrown together in a new social environment such as a college community. Marked differences between communities in material goods and in opportunities for social intercourse and for education may result in marked differences, not only in the habits, attitudes, and customs of the individuals growing up in the community, but also in their measured intelligence (2).

The interests, problems, and required activities of an urban community are different from those of a rural one. Even greater are the differences between the attitudes generated in a pioneer community and those of an old, established one. There is a story of a newcomer in a mining community, who, for privacy, hung his shirt before the door. It was not long before he was surprised by a man walking in unannounced. He asked the intruder what he wanted, and the latter replied, "I just wanted to see what was going on in here that requires so d—— much privacy." In many respects the manners and attitudes of those living in an established community appear finicky to people from a pioneer community; on the other hand, outsiders consider the manners of a pioneer community crude and lacking in the niceties of cultured society.

An interesting study of the relation of values and interests to the environment has been made by Davis (13). He gave a list of forty-five occupations to American and Russian boys and girls with the request that they rate the occupations in order of preference. The Americans rated banker first; then came, in order, college professor, doctor, and clergyman; ditch-digger was given the lowest rating. The Russians gave high ratings to the following: peasant, aviator, government official, physician, and party worker. They placed the following occupations near the bottom: clergyman (lowest), banker, prosperous businessman, manager of a small factory, owner of a store, and small storekeeper.

Communities also differ in their dominant values, and boys and girls absorb as a matter of course the dominant interests and values of the group in which they are reared. If the advancement of science is an important interest of a city, the youth of that community will share that interest. If the predominant interest of a community is political power, or industrial development, or evangelizing the world, or living a life of sensuous ease, the youth will be influenced accordingly. To understand the personality and behavior of another we should keep in mind the influence of the group in which he was reared. Though one may in some respects outgrow his early environment, the traces of it can never be wholly eradicated from his personality.

Perhaps the clearest evidence of the effect of the community on personality and behavior has been unearthed in the study of crime. A study of 911 delinquents showed that 86 per cent came from neighborhoods which were (1) business districts; (2) manufacturing districts; and (3) districts in which the population was changing, that is, in which the racial or national homogeneity of the community was being disturbed by the moving in of people of a different race or nationality. Commenting on such neighborhoods, Cole (8, p. 266) writes:

> Perhaps the outstanding characteristics of all these "bad" districts is that they offer no social cohesion, little protection, and only warped outlets for childish activities. The "good" district presents the opposite picture. It is one in which there are social traditions, excellent protection (in the form of observant adults), and adequate outlets for the restlessness and emotional drives of childhood and adolescence. In all investigations "bad" neighborhoods or "bad" companions are found to be important elements contributing to delinquency in the great majority of cases.

This study and the one by Wellman cited on page 121, as well as a number of others, prove the importance of the environment in affecting, if not determining, one's development. Even genius, born in communities which for one cause or another desire little beyond the satisfaction of physical wants and appetites, is often crushed under a load of indifference. A talented boy will find it difficult to rise above the intellectual level of such a community. He will be forced to spend a considerable portion of his time seeking or trying to create conditions which are intellectually stimulating. He will reach his highest level of accomplishment in such circumstances only at the cost of much suffering, caused by a lack of appreciation of his objectives and of encouragement to do his best. Everyone needs companionship, and appreciation of his cherished values and efforts. When these are denied, scars are left that time and success cannot wholly eradicate.

The Presence of Others

One is influenced in his behavior by the mere presence of others. The psychological situation is not exactly the same when someone is watching as it is when we are alone. To typewrite, for example, with someone looking over your shoulder requires more effort and consumes more energy than it would otherwise do. This is doubly true if you are composing as you write. Curious people sometimes do not understand the unwillingness of workers to be watched. The onlooker cannot understand that a worker must expend more energy when he is watched (24).

The effect upon output of working in groups is indicated by numerous studies. Allport (1) investigated this by means of a *free association* test. Testing his subjects both in groups and alone, he had them write as rapidly as possible the words which came to mind after a stimulus word was given. The results are shown in Table VI. In every case, the majority of persons wrote more words when working in a group than when working alone. Similar experiments with various other types of behavior have shown that working with a group tends to increase speed. At the same time, group activity frequently results in poorer quality.

To be observed may also cause us to exercise a little more restraint, or to make a little more display than we otherwise should. If, for example, in driving a nail you should hit your finger, you would probably express yourself more freely if you were alone than if another was present. The expression of fear is similarly affected. If others are present, we are more apt to try to inhibit its expression. In public disputes we are apt to be more polite than we are in domestic ones. The way in which the presence of others makes for display is frequently seen in the play of children. If alone, they may play contentedly; but if someone else is present, they are apt to begin "playing to the gallery." Adults also play to the gallery, but in ways which themselves are often the last to recognize.

Allport summarizes a number of researches on the effect of the group as follows:

> The social stimulations present in the co-acting group bring about an increase in the speed and quantity of work produced by individuals. This increase is more pronounced in work involving overt, physical movements than in purely intellectual tasks. In adults the group produces no improvement in the constancy of attention or the quality of work performed. Some individuals, in fact, do inferior work in the presence of

co-workers. There is a lowering of the logical value of reasoning carried out in the group, but an increase in the number of words by which such reasoning is expressed (1, p. 271).

Table VI

Influence of the Co-working Group upon Speed of Association (1)

Experiment number		1	2	3	4
Number of subjects		3	15	14	8
Number of tests ▶	Alone	9	11	5	8
	Together	12	13	6	11
Method		*Every word written*	*Every word written*	*Every 4th word written*	*Every 3rd word written*
Number of subjects writing more words alone		1	1	4	2
Number of subjects writing more words together		2	14	8	6
Number of subjects writing an equal number of words alone and together		0	0	2	0

(By permission, from F. H. Allport, *Social Psychology*, Houghton Mifflin.)

After summarizing the results of experiments dealing with this problem, including the one by Allport which we have just mentioned, Dashiell (12, p. 484) states that two trends are discernible in these experiments. First, working in groups is likely to result in an increase in speed but a decrease in quality and accuracy. Second, there is in most cases a leveling effect; the poorer workers do better while the superior ones do less well.

Other Environmental Influences

The numerous social institutions and practices which comprise our modern society obviously have an important and continuous effect upon us. Studies have been made of the effects of the church, of the Boy Scouts, of clubs, gangs, and summer camps. From the psychological viewpoint, such organizations may be thought of as agencies of education or development. What they will teach, how they will teach it, what effects upon personality they will have, and how permanent these effects will be — these things differ from one situation to another. But that social institutions are important factors is proved by studies such as the one by Dimock and Hendry (14), which showed how a summer camp increases self-reliance and courtesy, and the one by Glueck and Glueck (18), which showed that delinquents come from families having few religious contacts much more frequently than from families associated with a church.

Membership in groups. The desire to be accepted or to belong is one of our strongest social motives. This motive is unquestionably one of the major factors in the formation of social groups. Membership in these social groups is an important determiner of one's personality and modes of adjustment. The group exerts certain pressures upon the individual members. If it is a highly organized group, it will have rules and regulations which are designed to regulate or control the conduct of its members. If it is not formally organized, there will be unwritten rules, such as the generally accepted dictum in criminal or delinquent groups against "squealing."

Let us contrast for a moment the groups to which two adult males may belong. Let us suppose that Mr. X and Mr. Y live in an urban community of 50,000 population. Mr. X is a stone-cutter and Mr. Y is a building contractor. Mr. X is a Catholic, a member of the local Skeet Club, a bowler with the "Stone-Cutters" in the Classic Bowling League, of which he is vice-president, a member of the stone-cutters' union, and the Democratic committeeman from his voting precinct. Mr. Y, on the other hand, is a Protestant, a Republican, a member of the country club and chairman of its membership committee, a bowler with the "Contractors" in the Classic Bowling League, a member of the Elks, and a member of the American Legion. Apart from many other factors which affect or have affected the behavior and personalities of Mr. X and Mr. Y, it is clear that marked differences in behavior are forced upon these men by virtue of the fact that they are members of different groups. Some of these differences existed prior to membership and were in part responsible for the membership in the first place, but it must be recognized that once membership is established, it becomes an important determiner of subsequent behavior and adjustment. Membership in one group automatically excludes one from membership in certain other groups. This situation reduces one's contacts with certain people in the community, and this in turn has a directional influence on one's development.

Another factor that must be considered in this connection is the status of the individual in the group. One may be a member of a group yet not belong in the sense of being accepted by other members of the group. Moreno (28) has developed a sociographic technique for showing the interpersonal relationships within a group. When this procedure is used in a classroom group, each child is asked: "Which boy or boys or girl or girls would you like to work with, or not like to work with?" A tabulation of results shows the number of times each child is chosen or rejected. A child who is not accepted by anyone or who may be rejected by members of the group is in effect socially isolated in the midst of people. It will be recalled that Glueck and Glueck (19) found that the homes of delinquent boys showed a lack of cohesiveness as compared with those of non-delinquent boys. It is the degree of group cohesiveness and its effect upon the behavior of the individuals composing the group that can be investigated by Moreno's sociographic technique.

Since so many things influence the development and behavior of an individual, it is difficult to say what factor is chiefly responsible for a given personality trait or for a given act. For example, is the bad temper of a particular man due to his having been too much humored as a child, or to a feeling of insecurity and of "not-belonging," or to frequent disappointments in the past, or to jealousy? Is the overaggressiveness of another due to an inferiority complex against which he is fighting, or to self-assertion overstimulated by constant success? Is another's lack of ambition due to an organic disorder, or to the community life of his boyhood, or to conditions within his family? Is the antisocial attitude of another a protest against the injustices he has suffered, or does it come from a lack of ability to comprehend social obligations or from faulty discipline within the home?

The attempt to select a single factor as the cause of an act or personality trait is always inadvisable. Behavior is an outgrowth of the whole situation in which it occurs. To understand anyone's behavior or personality we must have before us a complete case history of the person. This should include, on the one hand, an account of his intelligence, complexes, mood, temperament, and organic condition; and on the other, an account of his home and school life, the community in which he was reared, the gangs to which he belonged, his religious instruction, and all other situations or events that may have influenced his life. When this knowledge has been obtained, the act under consideration will become intelligible.

SUMMARY

Environment includes all of the conditions within an organism and external to it which affect its development and behavior either directly or indirectly. Environmental conditions are classified as prenatal and postnatal. The prenatal environment includes the intracellular and intercellular processes within the developing organism and the conditions external to it, such as the food supply of the mother. The postnatal environment includes the physical and social conditions or stimulations which affect the individual after birth. Human beings are equipped with bodily mechanisms which are sensitive to particular kinds of physical stimulations, such as sound waves and ether vibrations. The social environment is composed of those stimulations which arise out of the relationships which exist between individuals and groups, out of social institutions, and out of social and cultural phenomena in general.

One of the most important social conditions is the home. The elements of the home that are of most significance are: its economic level; the prestige, attitudes, and intelligence of the parents; the amount of friction between the parents; the degree of real interest in the child; discipline; and the size of the family. Next in importance is the school, which not only determines educational and mental development but also has its effect upon intelligence, attitudes, and social behavior. In addition, schools can do a great deal toward solving problems of emotional adjustment. Motion pictures are a third effective agency of education and of general influence upon our attitudes and emotional life. Other environmental factors of consequence are: the community in which we live, the people with whom we work and associate, our church, and the other organizations with which we have some contact. In no case can a single factor — either within the individual or in his external environment — be singled out as the sole cause operating in the individual's development. We must always look at the whole environment and the whole individual in our attempt to understand and explain behavior.

QUESTIONS
on the Chapter

1. Distinguish between psychological and geographic environments.
2. What are some of the conditions external to the developing embryo which affect its development?
3. What is meant by adequate stimuli?
4. What are the characteristics of stimuli?
5. In what ways will the economic level of a home exercise an effect upon the individuals living in it?
6. How do the dreams of children reflect the economic status of the home?

7. What is the status of home discipline among problem children?
8. What effect does the size of the family in which children are reared have upon later personality and behavior?
9. In what ways does the school supplement the home as an environmental influence?
10. What is the effect of a group of co-workers upon speed and accuracy of the work of the individual?
11. What are some of the other important environmental influences?

for Discussion

1. What is your reaction to the statement: One's morals must be evaluated in the light of one's home conditions?
2. In what way might social conditions affect the development of an organism before it is born?
3. Can delinquency and crime be attributed to any one environmental condition?
4. Can an environment be evaluated as good or bad apart from its effects upon people?
5. What do you think will be the influence of television on children's (a) education, (b) attitudes, (c) morals?
6. Suggest some ways by which a child who is now rejected by a group might be brought into the group or accepted by the group.

REFERENCES

1 ALLPORT, F. H., *Social Psychology*. Boston: Houghton Mifflin Company, 1924.
2 ASHER, E. J., "The Inadequacy of Current Intelligence Tests for Testing Kentucky Mountain Children," *J. Genet. Psychol.*, 1935, 46, 480–486.
3 BAKER, HARRY J., and TRAPHAGEN, VIRGINIA, *Diagnosis and Treatment of Behavior-Problem Children*. New York: The Macmillan Company, 1935.
4 BOEDT, W. J., and STROUD, B. J., "Changes in the Attitudes of College Students," *J. Educ. Psychol.*, 1934, 25, 611–619.
5 BROWN, WILLIAM, *Mind and Personality*. New York: G. P. Putnam's Sons, 1927.
6 BUGELSKI, R., and LESTER, P. P., "Changes in Attitude in a Group of College Students during Their College Course and after Graduation," *J. Soc. Psychol.*, 1940, 12, 319–322.
7 CHARTERS, W. W., *Motion Pictures and Youth, a Summary of the Payne Fund Studies*. New York: The Macmillan Company, 1933. Quotations by permission of the publisher.
8 COLE, LUELLA, *Psychology of Adolescence*. New York: Farrar and Rinehart, Inc., 1936. Reprinted by permission of the publisher.
9 CONKLIN, E. S., *Principles of Abnormal Psychology*. New York: Henry Holt and Company, 1927.
10 CRANE, G. W., *Psychology Applied*. Evanston: Northwestern University Press, 1932.

11 DAMRIN, DORA E., "Family Size and Sibling Age, Sex, and Position as Related to Certain Aspects of Adjustment," *J. Soc. Psychol.*, 1949, 29, 93–102.

12 DASHIELL, J. F., *Fundamentals of General Psychology*, 3rd edition. Boston: Houghton Mifflin Company, 1949.

13 DAVIS, JEROME, "Testing the Social Attitudes of Children in the Government Schools in Russia," *Amer. J. Soc.*, 1927, 32, 947–952.

14 DIMOCK, H. S., and HENDRY, C. E., *Camping and Character*. New York: The Association Press, 1929.

15 DUNBAR, F., "Effect of the Mother's Emotional Attitude on the Infant," *Psychosomatic Med.*, 1944, 6, 156–159.

16 FOSTER, SYBIL, "Personality Deviations and Their Relation to the Home," *Mental Hygiene*, 1925, 9, 735–742.

17 GESELL, ARNOLD, *Infancy and Human Growth*. New York: The Macmillan Company, 1928, p. 339.

18 GLUECK, S., and GLUECK, E. T., *One Thousand Juvenile Delinquents*. Cambridge: Harvard University Press, 1934.

19 GLUECK, S., and GLUECK, E. T., *Unraveling Juvenile Delinquency*. New York: The Commonwealth Fund, 1950. Quotation by permission of the authors and publisher.

20 GRUENBERG, SIDONIE M., *Your Child Today and Tomorrow*, 3rd edition. Philadelphia: J. B. Lippincott Company, 1928.

21 HARTSHORNE, H., and MAY, M. A., *Studies in Deceit*, Vol. I. New York: The Macmillan Company, 1928.

22 HEALY, W. A., and BRONNER, A. F., *Delinquents and Criminals*. New York: The Macmillan Company, 1926.

23 IRWIN, E. A., and MARKS, L. A., *Fitting the School to the Child*. New York: The Macmillan Company, 1924.

24 JANET, PIERRE, *The Major Symptoms of Hysteria*, 2nd edition. New York: The Macmillan Company, 1920.

25 JENNINGS, H. S., *The Biological Basis of Human Behavior*. New York: W. W. Norton and Company, 1930.

26 LENTZ, T., "Relation of I.Q. to Size of Family," *J. Educ. Psychol.*, 1927, 18, 486–496.

27 MACPHERSON, H. B., *The Home Life of a Golden Eagle*, 2nd edition. New York: Charles Scribner's Sons, 1910.

28 MORENO, S. L., *Who Shall Survive*. Washington, D.C.: Nervous and Mental Disease Publishing Company, 1934.

29 MUNN, NORMAN L., *Psychological Development*. Boston: Houghton Mifflin Company, 1938.

30 SAYLES, M. B., *The Problem Child at Home*. New York: Commonwealth Fund, Division of Publications, 1928.

31 SCHATZ, A. H., "The Effect of the Depression on the Moral Ideas of Boys and Girls of Sioux City High Schools." Unpublished paper, 1934.

32 SCHEIDEMANN, N. V., *The Psychology of Exceptional Children*. Boston: Houghton Mifflin Company, 1931.

33 THURSTONE, L. L., "Influence of Motion Pictures on Children's Attitudes," *J. Soc. Psychol.*, 1931, 2, 291–305.

34 TORRANCE, P., "The Influence of the Broken Home on Adolescent Adjustment," *J. Educ. Soc.*, 1945, 18, 359–364.

35 WEISS, PAUL, *Principles of Development.* New York: Henry Holt and Company, 1939.

36 WELLMAN, B. L., "Our Changing Concept of Intelligence," *J. Consult. Psychol.*, 1938, 2, 97–107.

37 WELTMAN, N., and REMMERS, H. H., "Pupils', Parents', and Teachers' Attitude-Similarities and Differences," *Purdue Univ. Studies, Higher Educ.*, 1946, 56, 1–52.

38 WHISLER, L., "Changes in Attitudes toward Social Issues Accompanying a One-Year Freshman Social Science Course," *J. Psychol.*, 1940, 10, 387–396.

39 WHITE, WILLIAM, *The Mental Hygiene of Childhood.* Boston: Little, Brown and Company, 1919.

40 WICKES, F. G., *The Inner World of Childhood.* New York: Appleton-Century Company, 1927.

MOTIVATION

5

WHAT IS MOTIVATION?

The topic of motivation in psychology is concerned with the general question of why individuals act as they do. Why are you reading this chapter? Why are you taking a course in psychology? Why are you attending college? Why does a man who has been noted for his honesty for years embezzle money? Why does one child in a family turn to criminal pursuits while other children in the family do not? Why are some people embarrassed and awkward in the presence of strangers while others are poised and self-possessed? Why does one student make high grades in school while another student with the same ability makes poor grades? These are the kinds of questions one asks if he is trying to discover the motives which determine an individual's behavior. In asking why a man who has been noted for his honesty for years embezzles money, we suppose that the behavior is motivated, i.e., that there are certain reasons, causes, or motives which are responsible for the behavior. We suppose further that a knowledge of these motives will provide us with an explanation of the behavior, and will make it possible for us to predict and control future behavior. A knowledge of motivation, therefore, is basic to the achievement of the aims of psychology.

The Problem of Motivation

The problem of motivation may be thought of as involving two basic issues. One is concerned with the arousing or initiation of activity. The other is concerned with the direction the activity takes and the ends toward which it is directed. On the one hand, there is some condition which initiates activity. On the other hand, there is some goal toward which the activity, once it is aroused, is directed. In seeking an answer to the question, why does John Doe go to college, we may look in his home, in his community, or in John Doe himself for the conditions which prompted him to go to college. A knowledge of these conditions may throw some light on why he decided to go to college rather than into the army or elsewhere, but it does not tell the whole story. We must know in addition what goals he has in mind, what he hopes to accomplish by going to college that he cannot accomplish in any other way. It should be noted in this example that "going to college" is not regarded as a goal, but as a means to an end. This raises a very important point in the psychology of motivation. In one sense, going to college is a goal, an aim, something that one may want to do for its own sake, but it is much more likely to be the means by which an individual reaches some other goal. Let us suppose that John Doe wishes to become an engineer. Engineering becomes the goal and going to college becomes a means. But let us push our questioning one step further. Why does John Doe wish to become an engineer? Whatever his reasons, engineering as a profession is regarded as a means of attaining these ends. Without pushing the matter further we can see that we have a series of goals, each one of which is a means of reaching the next one in the series. Each one is a goal, but all except the final or ultimate one must be regarded as intermediate goals.

Goals. The word *goal* as it is used here means the object, condition, or state of affairs toward which the initiated activity is directed, which ultimately reduces the activity or brings it to a conclusion, and which satisfies the conditions that gave rise to the activity in the first place. Some initiating conditions can be satisfied only by bringing to the body certain things, such as food; others can be satisfied only by getting rid of or avoiding certain things, such as pain-producing stimuli. The word *goal* includes both types. If a college degree is John Doe's goal, graduation from college brings the "going-to-college activity" to a conclusion and satisfies the conditions which initiated it. If a college degree is regarded as an intermediate goal, it has the effect of bringing one phase of a long series of adjustments to a conclusion, and makes possible the initiation of the next phase of the sequence. It should be recognized that the attainment of a goal brings with it new sources of stimulation and the initiation of new activities which become directed toward new goals. This means, of course, that one's efforts to reach a given goal, even though the goal is never reached, may change the nature of the original stimulating conditions to such an extent that the search for the original goal is terminated.

It should be recognized that the initiating conditions, the aroused behavior, and the goals toward which the behavior is directed are all parts of one process.   One may assign different labels to the parts, may describe the parts separately, and may, in talking about motivation, emphasize one part rather than another, but the arousal of behavior presupposes an initiating condition and an end toward which the behavior is directed.   An organism does not respond without responding in some direction and toward some end that eventually brings the activity to a conclusion.

Motivating Conditions

Any condition which arouses an organism to action, which reinforces activity in progress, or which changes or modifies the direction of the activity in progress is called a *motivating condition* (49).   All kinds of stimulations, both internal and external, are to be regarded as motivating conditions.   All of the activities and processes going on in the organism serve to stimulate or produce other activities.   The internal motivating conditions include muscular contractions; the secretions of glands; the activities of the digestive, circulatory, respiratory, and reproductive systems; ideas, attitudes, conflicts, tensions, feelings, intentions, internalized social demands, and any kind of experience to the extent to which it is represented by activities of the nervous system and/or other bodily mechanisms; and, in short, all interoceptive and proprioceptive stimuli.   To these must be added all of the external stimulations, including the conditions of the social environment.   If environment is conceived broadly to include the internal and external conditions described in Chapter 4, motivating conditions and environmental conditions may be regarded as synonymous.   Motivating conditions, therefore, are to be identified with the E of our behavior equation.

Some terms defined.   One or another or all of these motivating conditions are variously referred to as drives, motives, urges, needs, demands, wants, desires, wishes, likes, dislikes, incentives, aversions, rewards, punishments, purposes, cravings, interests, and instincts.   The student may be able to extend this list still further.   It is obvious, of course, that all of these words do not mean exactly the same thing. Most of the words refer to stimulating conditions which initiate activity. Some of them refer to the objects toward which activity is directed; and others refer to an entire motivated sequence, namely, the initiating condition, the behavior, and the goal object.

In our discussion the word *motive* will be used as a general term to denote any motivating condition.   Thus a craving, or a wish, or a desire, or anything that arouses, sustains, or directs activity will be regarded as a motive.   The word *drive* will be used to denote any motivating condition which is *internal,* that is, which arises out of internal bodily processes. Some writers (9, 29, 36) limit the use of the word *drive* to those internal conditions which arouse activity, or which propel or push an organism into action. They contend that physiological conditions such as hunger arouse activity but do not determine the form or direction of the activity. The aroused activity is regarded as random, aimless, or blind. This concept of drive may be descriptive of the behavior of immature, inexperienced organisms, but not of all behavior. In general, as we pointed out above, an organism does not respond without responding in some direction and toward some end. Hunger in a newborn may arouse what appears to be random, aimless activity, but once the newborn has learned what to do to get food the hunger persists and stimulations produce a particular kind of activity. There is evidence in animals that physiological conditions such as hunger not only arouse behavior but also determine its direction even in the absence of specific training. This is illustrated in a study by Richter (35). The removal of the adrenal glands from white rats results in the excretion of salt in large amounts through the kidneys. Adrenalectomized rats placed in cages with two water bottles, one filled with salt water and the other with tap water, drank up to twenty times as much of the salt water as they did just prior to the operation. Here it appears that a salt hunger is operative. The rat is not only hungry, he is hungry for a specific substance. Organisms deprived of particular foods or food elements develop cravings for these elements (28). Something analogous to this is found in human behavior. Individuals whose diets are deficient in some food element frequently develop a craving for foods which contain this element. Here, however, the food-seeking behavior may be complicated by many non-physiological factors.

Other words like *want, desire,* and *aversion* imply both an initiating condition and an object toward which the activity will be directed. In a statement such as "I want a cracker," the emphasis is placed upon the object or condition, generally an outside stimulus, that will satisfy an implied internal condition. Perhaps the word *need* should not be included in the above list because it is not itself a stimulus but an underlying organic condition of lack or insufficiency which presumably gives rise to stimulations. Thus, an organism is said to "need" food. Depletion of food in the body brings about in some way the stimulation of the interoceptors in the stomach. This stimulation initiates food-seeking. At least this is the ordinary state of affairs, as we shall see subsequently in discussing the hunger drive.

Internal vs. external stimuli. It appears that internal stimulations are more important in motivating behavior than external ones. Some psychologists go so far as to restrict the use of the term *motivation* to internal stimulating conditions. For example, Symonds (42, p. 11) states that the argument of his book on Dynamic Psychology "is based on the hypothesis that all behavior originates in response to urges within an individual." On the other hand, many psychologists, while emphasizing the importance of internal conditions in arousing behavior, recognize that external stimulations are to be included as motivating conditions. Dashiell (9, p. 156) points out that external stimuli serve to arouse activity and become, through learning, increasingly potent in doing so. A child may eat a particular article of food for the first time because he is hungry. The food as such has no special motivating qualities, being, we shall say, the only food available. The food-seeking and eating are aroused primarily by the internal conditions of hunger. Later, however, the child may select this food from several foods which are available and eat it even when he is not hungry. In this case the behavior is aroused primarily by the external stimulus, food. One may hypothesize, of course, that the food is motivating because of some other condition (not hunger) in the child, such as his memory of how good the food tasted on previous occasions. To be sure, previous experiences (learning) are responsible for the change in the attractiveness of the food, but such experiences change the person (P). The arousal of behavior is at all times a function of the interaction of P and E variables.

Other conditions as motives. A review of the psychological literature reveals that some psychologists have postulated the existence of forces or tensions which drive the organism or arouse it to action. For example, Lewin's (21) concept of motive is that a state of tension is said to exist within the individual. This state of tension is analogous to a disequilibrium and has the property of changing or tending to change in the direction of a state of equilibrium. Tension is a "psychological construct" and as such has no basis in physiological processes such as those found for most physiological drives. McDougall (23) and Freud (12) attribute the arousal of behavior to forces within the individual which they call instincts. To McDougall instinct, or propensity as he later called it, involves a predisposition on the part of the organism to perceive certain stimuli and to strive toward certain goals. It is not clear whether this predisposition is to be identified with internal stimulations or with some characteristic inherent in the body structures. If the former, McDougall's instinct is practically synonymous with the word *drive*.

Unfortunately for psychology, it was fashionable for a time to create instincts to account for any and every kind of activity. If a man went to church, he did so because he had an instinct to worship. If he collected things, he did so because he had a hoarding instinct. If he played, he did so because he had an instinct to play. In this sense, instinct was regarded as a little godlike agent in a person that made him act in a given way. Because of this unscientific use of the term, it fell for a time into disrepute. In recent years it has again gained favor, but it is now used to designate unlearned patterns of activity. It is particularly applicable to certain patterns of activity in lower animals. It is no longer used in connection with motivation except possibly by some psychoanalysts who follow Freud's formulations of instincts as motivating forces.

Motivation a Function of P and E Variables

In the formula $B = f(PE)$, behavior is a function of, and is therefore aroused by, the interaction of a person and an environmental situation. It is perfectly clear that the motivation of behavior, both in the sense of its initiation and in the sense of the determination of its form or direction, is dependent upon both P and E variables. Environmental conditions act upon a living organism. This organism, by the very nature of the fact that it is living, is in a state of activity at the moment when environmental stimulations are presented. The organism is at this moment, as we have seen in Chapter 2, what it is because of the hereditary materials out of which it has developed and because of the effects of developmental conditions upon these materials. It has reached a certain maturity level. It has had certain experiences. The effects produced by the stimulation of this organism will, quite obviously, depend upon its body structures and their organization, the degree of maturity it has reached, its body posture, and what it is doing at the moment, including the functioning of all of the body structures. The fact that the effect of a motivating condition depends upon what an individual is doing at the moment must be kept in mind at all times in considering the problems of motivation. When we talk about arousing an individual to action, we must not assume that the individual is an inert mass to be prodded into action. Since the individual is always in a state of activity, he is always motivated. Introducing new motivating conditions merely changes the nature of the total pattern of motivation. Changes in this pattern may have the effect of facilitating the activity in progress or changing it in some other way — for example, by reducing or eliminating one kind of activity and introducing another kind.

It is clear that the arousal of behavior in an organism is dependent partly upon the motivating conditions and partly upon the organism. We can investigate the relative importance of any motivating factor by holding constant (1) all P variables, such as maturity, organization of body structures, and experience, and (2) all forms of motivation except the one which is being investigated.

Classification of Motives

Motivating conditions or motives can be classified in a number of ways. We have already indicated that some motivating conditions arise primarily within the organism, while others arise outside the organism. In addition to this possible classification, motives may be classified as primary or secondary; inborn or acquired; physiological (arising out of bodily processes) or social (arising out of contacts with people); positive or negative (according as the motive initiates behavior toward an object or away from it); viscerogenic or psychogenic. According to Murray (30), viscerogenic motives depend upon bodily needs and include such drive conditions as hunger, thirst, and sex; psychogenic motives are derived from viscerogenic motives and include tendencies to aggression, social approval, and achievement. With the exception of the positive-negative classification, these classes are essentially different ways of saying the same thing. Motives that are classified as internal may also be classified as primary, inborn, physiological, and viscerogenic. Those that are classified as external could also, with few exceptions, be classified as secondary, acquired, social, and psychogenic. In general the secondary, social, acquired, psychogenic, and to some extent the external conditions can be thought of as arising out of or developing through training from the primary, inborn, physiological, internal, and viscerogenic motives.

Adient and abient drives. The classification of motives as positive or negative, or as *adient* or *abient* (14), cuts across the other classifications. A physiological motive such as hunger would be classified as adient (positive) since it initiates activity toward food objects; whereas a physiological motive such as the temperature condition of the skin would be classified as abient (negative) because it leads to an avoidance of heat and cold. Similarly, a social motive may be classified as either positive or negative. Actually, however, every motive is both adient and abient or, as Strong (40) has suggested, every motive has both a positive and a negative aspect. In hunger, for example, the internal, persistent stimuli are annoying. The behavior initiated by these stimuli may be regarded as the organism's effort to get away from this annoyance (the negative aspect of the motive), but it may also be regarded as the organism's effort to go toward the food objects (positive aspect of the motive). Even here the organism avoids or reacts negatively to non-food objects and positively to objects which will satisfy the hunger. The organism is trying to get away from one stimulus, but is necessarily going toward another stimulus. Similarly, in the case of the pain produced by a burn an organism is trying to get away from the pain. In doing so he goes toward some objects, a pail of water or a tube of ointment, and away from hot or other harmful objects. In our earlier example of John Doe's going to college we indicated that there were positive and negative aspects to the motivations involved. In trying to understand an individual's behavior it is important to look for both the positive and negative aspects of his motives. Some advertisements, for example, are purposely designed to appeal to the negative aspects of the prospective buyer's wants by pointing up the frightful predicament of the person who does not use the advertised product. Another advertisement may play up the positive good or satisfaction that is at the end of the road for the person who buys the product.

Maslow's classification of motives. A more comprehensive classification of motives has been formulated by Maslow (24). He has proposed a theory of motivation in which motives are classified according to the basic needs underlying the motives. Needs are classified into five groups or levels and arranged in a hierarchy of pre-potency. This arrangement means that "the appearance of one need usually rests on the prior satisfaction of another, more pre-potent need." (24, p. 370) The five groups of needs, listed in descending order of their pre-potency, are as follows:

1. PHYSIOLOGICAL NEEDS. This group includes the need for food, for water, for oxygen, for constant temperature, etc.

2. SAFETY NEEDS. These needs are concerned with seeking safety and avoiding pain, threats, and danger.

3. LOVE NEEDS. These needs give rise to the desire to belong, to be wanted, to be loved by friends, relatives, and family.

4. ESTEEM NEEDS. These needs give rise to the desire for self-respect, strength, achievement, adequacy, prestige, attention, and appreciation.

5. SELF-ACTUALIZATION NEEDS. This group is characterized by saying that one must do what he can do.

The important feature of this classification is the fact that the operation of any need at any level above the first is predicated upon the satisfaction of the lower-order needs. Safety needs, in general, do not dominate one's behavior or become important to the individual until the physiological needs are satisfied. In a similar way, the safety needs take precedence over the love needs, the love needs over the esteem needs, etc. The needs at one level are regarded as stronger than those of the next higher level because the lower-level ones dominate the organism when both needs are frustrated (25). Some evidence to support this contention is found in a study of human behavior in experimental semistarvation and rehabilitation (11). Under semistarvation conditions, young men exhibited symptoms of depression and nervousness, and became increasingly ineffective in daily living. There was a narrowing of interests and an obliteration of the sex drive. Food and eating became the dominant concern. This loss of interest in everything except food is reported by men who have spent long periods of time in concentration camps or in prisoner-of-war camps under starvation or near-starvation conditions. The obsessive interest in food has been reported as taking many forms, such as dreaming about food or collecting and inventing recipes. It appears that under such circumstances virtually all motivations disappear except the most basic physiological ones.

This concept of motivation is particularly helpful in understanding behavior in relation to individual differences in ability and in relation to cultural determinants of behavior. Individuals who are low in ability, who lack high-level skills, and who live in submarginal environments or under primitive conditions spend virtually all of their waking hours trying to satisfy the physiological and, to some extent, the safety needs. They have little or no time and no surplus earning capacity to devote to the satisfaction of higher-order needs, even if such needs appear. Such individuals live pretty much on a physiological or subsistence level. On the other hand, some individuals, through a variety of circumstances, are able to satisfy the lower-level needs with a minimum expenditure of time and effort. Higher-order needs appear and, what is even more important, time is available to work at the job of satisfying these needs. An interesting feature of this situation is the lack of understanding and lack of communication between the individuals at one level and those at another level of motivation.

DRIVES

The fundamental source of human and animal motivation is to be found in the internal bodily processes by which an organism maintains itself as a living, functioning unit. The processes of respiration, circulation, digestion, assimilation, and elimination and the activities of the glands, especially the endocrines, represent a basic activity level in the individual which serves as a sort of foundation on which all other behavior is built and out of which most behavior springs. The importance of these processes as instigators of behavior can be seen if one pauses for a moment to make note of the human activities that can be traced directly or indirectly to the fact that an individual, in order to live and maintain himself in an environment, must have such things as oxygen, food, water, shelter, rest, and sleep. Think, for example, of all of the activities connected with the production, transportation, distribution, and consumption of food, or of the business enterprises that are connected solely with the production of food, or of the number of people engaged directly or indirectly in the food business.

Homeostasis

The internal bodily processes are coordinated in such a way that the organism maintains or attempts to maintain a constant internal environment. If the intricate balance between these processes, or within any one of the processes, is disturbed, the body attempts to readjust itself in order to bring the processes back into a harmonious balance. This process of maintaining a constant internal environment is called *homeostasis* (6). In order to function and maintain its integrity, an organism must have water, oxygen, salt, fat, sugar, a constant internal temperature, etc. Body temperature cannot vary from 98.6 degrees Fahrenheit more than a few degrees without endangering the life of the organism. Similarly, life is endangered if the blood sugar is too high or too low; if the oxygen supply is deficient; if the protein content of the body is too low; and so on. Equilibrium is maintained within limits by automatic adjustments within the body. If these adjustments are not sufficient to restore the equilibrium, the continued imbalance "motivates" the organism to react to its external environment in an effort to find the things needed to replace the deficiencies and restore the equilibrium.

If, for example, the amount of thyroxin produced by the thyroid gland is not sufficient to maintain the "steady state" within the body, the gland becomes enlarged in an effort to produce more thyroxin and thereby compensate for the thyroid deficiency. If the body lacks some chemical, the organism tends to develop a hunger for that food element (28). This is seen in the experiment by Richter (35) cited on page 139, in which adrenalectomized rats consumed up to twenty times as much salt water as they did prior to the creation of the salt deficiency by removal of the adrenal glands. Sontag (38) cites some interesting studies which have shown that this process of maintaining a constant internal environment operates during pregnancy between the mother and the fetus. The endocrine systems of the mother and the fetus function in a complementary fashion. For example, deficiencies in the insulin (secretion of the pancreas) supply of the mother seem to be compensated for by the fetus. Sontag reports a study by Weiner in which it was found that infants of diabetic mothers had much more insulin in their pancreases than did those of nondiabetic mothers. He cites other studies which reported an improvement in diabetic mothers during pregnancy, presumably due to the passage of fetal insulin to the mother.

The Hunger Drive

Hunger has been more widely investigated than any of the other drives which have their origin in the homeostatic needs. Not only is hunger typical of these drives, but the facts which have been discovered in studying it have tended to shape the pattern of thinking about motivation in general and about drives in particular. A number of investigators (7, 8, 45) have shown that the conscious pangs of hunger are accompanied by or occur in conjunction with rhythmic contractions of the stomach, contractions which can be distinguished quite easily from digestive contractions. These contractions are measured by the apparatus shown in Figure 28. A subject swallows a small rubber balloon with a tube leading from it out of the mouth. The balloon is inflated with air until it fills the stomach cavity. The tube is connected with the recording apparatus. Contractions of the stomach compress the balloon and increase the air pressure in the tube; this in turn activates the marker on the kymograph (recording drum). Subjects in Cannon's (5) study were asked to press a key whenever they experienced hunger sensations. In all cases it was found that hunger contractions occurred just before the subject reported that he was experiencing hunger sensations. Carlson and Johnson (8) report that the hunger contractions are greater when the subject reports sharp hunger pangs than when he reports mild hunger pangs.

The relation of hunger contractions to behavior has been investigated by Wada (45). This investigator used the balloon technique, but placed the subject on a bed which was arranged in such a fashion that general body movements could be recorded simultaneously and on the same kymograph with the hunger contractions. In addition some subjects were tested at intervals with a hand dynamometer (an instrument testing strength of hand grip) and with intelligence tests. Hunger

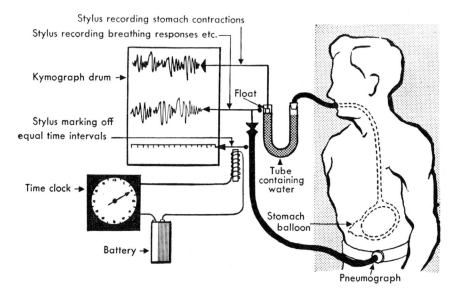

Stylus recording stomach contractions
Stylus recording breathing responses etc.
Kymograph drum →
Float
Stylus marking off
equal time intervals
Tube containing water
Time clock →
Stomach balloon
Battery →
Pneumograph

Figure 28

Schematic Representation of Apparatus Used for Recording
Changes in the Tonus of Stomach Muscles

(By permission from *Recent Experiments in Psychology*, p. 86, by L. W. Crafts, et al. Copyright, 1938, by McGraw-Hill Book Company, Inc.)

contractions were found to be accompanied by an increase in general body activity during waking and sleeping periods, by an increase in strength of hand grip, by higher scores on intelligence tests, and by a greater tendency to dream during sleeping periods. Similar results have been obtained in studies of lower animals. For example, Elliott and Treat (10) found that seven rats who had no hunger contractions required from thirty to seventy-five trials to learn to avoid an electric shock when a signal was given. Seven rats who had hunger contractions required from eighteen to thirty trials. The slowest learner in the hungry group learned as fast as the fastest in the well-fed group.

It appears from these studies that (1) the conscious pangs of hunger occur as a result of hunger contractions in the stomach, and (2) the hunger contractions are accompanied by a heightened activity level. While this latter finding is frequently interpreted to mean that hunger produces restlessness and random activity, it should be noted, at least in Wada's study, that the hunger contractions seemed to facilitate the behavior already in progress. Hunger did not cause the subject to pull on the hand dynamometer, or to take an intelligence test. Nor did it produce restlessness in the form of general bodily activity. Such activity was in progress in some degree when the hunger occurred. The hunger merely increased the amount of this general activity. If the subject had not been attached to the apparatus and required to do what he was doing, the hunger might have initiated food-seeking activity, the kind depending upon the existing circumstances and the age and experience of the subject.

One might conclude from these studies that hunger as a motivating condition is directly traceable to, or that it originates in, the contractions in the stomach, and that an organism would not show hunger if these contractions did not occur. Studies have shown, however, that this is not the case. One investigator has shown that the hunger drive was not eliminated in animals when their stomachs were removed (44). Nor was the hunger drive impaired when the afferent nerves from the stomach were cut so that impulses from the stomach could not reach the nerve centers (3). One investigator injected blood from a starved dog into a normal dog. He found that this injection produced hunger contractions in the normal dog (22). These and other findings seem to indicate that back of the hunger contractions and conscious pangs of hunger is some more general bodily condition which arises out of, or is associated with, a food deficit in the body. This more general condition is undoubtedly created by the lack of essential body material. Just how this condition sets up stomach contractions is not known, but it is reasonably clear, as Cannon (5) points out, that under ordinary conditions the hunger sensations serve as the signal to the organism that a food deficit exists.

This general description also applies to thirst. The immediate stimulating condition in thirst is the sensation arising from a dryness in the mouth and throat. But as in hunger, the underlying condition is a general bodily state — in this case a lack of water in the body. Is thirst to be regarded as the condition of dryness in the mouth and throat with the accompanying experience of thirst, or is thirst the lack of water in the body? In connection with this question, Cannon (5, p. 307) says:

> That even the early stages of a need for water may be accompanied by increased irritability, and a vague sense of weakness, is not denied. But the thirsty man does not complain of these general conditions. He is tormented by a parched and burning throat, and any explanation of the physiological mechanism for maintaining the water content of the body must take into account this prominent fact.

It would appear that although the basic condition is lack of water, it is the sensation of thirst that is the primary motivating condition.

The Sex Drive

In addition to the physiological motives or drives which are rooted in homeostasis, there are other physiological motives such as the sex drive, the maternal drive, drives toward obtaining sensory and motor pleasure (tastes, smells, sheer love of activity), drives toward obtaining rest and sleep, and the drive to avoid injury. It is not clear, or has not been demonstrated, that these drives arise out of the homeostatic needs. Moreover, although they are commonly classified as physiological, the exact nature of the underlying physiological condition for some of them is unknown. In other instances, however, the relation of a physiological process to the behavior has been demonstrated. The sex drive in animals is in the latter group. Sex aggressiveness and other characteristics in animals have been shown to be due to secretions of the gonads. Removal of the gonads results in marked changes in the appearance and activity of an animal. Compare, for example, the behavior of a castrated male animal such as an ox or a capon with that of a bull or a rooster (see p. 98).

That changes in the reproductive system act as instigators of behavior has been demonstrated by Wang (46). This experimenter found that a female white rat on the days in which she was in heat made as many as 23,000 revolutions per day in a revolving drum in comparison with a low of 9,000 to 15,000 per day when she was not in heat. In the rat these periods of heat occur about every four days. Changes in the reproductive tract were found to correspond to the periods of heat and in turn to the periods of heightened activity. It appears that the heightened activity is motivated either by the changes which occur in the reproductive system or by endocrine secretions from the ovaries or by both. Richter (34) has shown that removal of the ovaries reduces the activity level markedly. Prior to removal of the ovaries, rats made from about 7,000 to 17,000 revolutions per day in a revolving drum. After the ovaries were removed, the number of revolutions per day dropped to around 1,000 to 2,000 per day and remained at this low level thereafter. When the ovaries were replaced by grafting, the original activity level was restored. The relation of sexual behavior in the male rat to endocrine secretions has been studied by Beach and Holz (4). In this study fifty white rats were castrated at ages ranging from 1 to 350 days. After an interval of several months, the rats showed either no response to receptive females or an incomplete form of the copulatory reaction. The administration of androgen (the male gonadal hormone) resulted in the appearance of the copulatory response in all of the castrated males.

One must exercise caution in generalizing from these animal studies to the motivating effects of the sex drive in man. Sexual behavior in man does not parallel that in lower animals. Sex as a motivating condition in man is complicated by many additional factors, some of which are culturally determined. It becomes attached to various objects and situations which serve to arouse sexual behavior. It is clear enough that many of man's activities and much of his interest are directly related to or concerned with sex. To what extent his behavior can be attributed to changes in the reproductive system or to the fact that he has a reproductive system is difficult to determine. As Irwin (16, p. 216) points out, "it is scientifically interesting to demonstrate that an inexperienced male rat will pursue and copulate efficiently with a female in heat, but this by itself tells us little about what is necessary to arouse, maintain, and abolish this behavior in the male rat, and tells us nothing at all about the nature of the motivation of the human male."

Other Drives

There are a number of physiological needs, such as the need for oxygen, the need for a constant body temperature, and the elimination needs, which are customarily satisfied by automatic adjustments within the body. Only when these adjustments prove to be inadequate (or when they become subject to social controls, as in the case of elimination) is an individual likely to become aware of them and to be motivated to react to his external environment in an effort to accomplish what the automatic adjustments fail to accomplish. This is illustrated in the case of body temperature. The body can adjust to increases in temperature by sweating, a process that is carried out automatically. If this automatic adjustment is not sufficient to maintain a constant body temperature, the individual is "motivated" to reduce his activity level, seek a cooler place, equip his home with an air-conditioning system, or perhaps move to a cooler climate.

As Maslow (24, p. 372) has pointed out, a list of "physiological needs can come to almost any number one might wish, depending upon the degree of specificity of description." Thus one can speak of the existence of a sensory drive and an underlying need for sensory pleasure, or he can assume the existence of a need for each separate kind of sensory pleasure, such as a need for taste experiences, a need for visual experiences, and so on through a very long list. In these cases there is a tendency to infer the existence of a drive to explain the observed behavior. For example, one might infer that animals have an "exploratory drive" from the fact that they engage in what appears to be exploratory behavior, a kind of behavior which seems not to be the result of any other known motivating conditions.

THE ACQUISITION OF MOTIVES

Most human motives are learned. This can be seen if one compares the motives which are operative in an infant's behavior with those which are present in an adult's behavior. The newborn's motivations arise primarily out of his physiological processes. He needs food, water, oxygen, and protection from injury, but he has no wants or desires. He is motivated by hunger, and his hunger is satisfied by drinking milk; but he does not want milk, or crackers, or oatmeal, or orange juice, or any one of the scores of food objects which he will eventually *learn* to want. Similarly, he may get satisfaction from being touched, rocked, patted, and talked to, but he does not want to be loved, or to be the center of attention, or to belong, or to be played with, all of which he may eventually learn to want. After a few weeks of bottle feeding, a baby will, on seeing his bottle, respond by making mouthing responses, by reaching, and by showing excitement. No such responses are aroused in the newborn when a bottle of milk is held in his line of regard. The reactions to the sight of the bottle indicate that the hunger need has become more specific as a consequence of being satisfied in a specific way. The baby is hungry, to be sure, but the aroused activity is being channeled, so to speak, toward the specific object that has been involved in the previous satisfactions of hunger. In time the baby learns to want milk, and he may, when he is old enough to talk, ask for his bottle or for milk. In this way, and in others to be described shortly, wants, desires, and interests develop until, in adult life, (1) the number of conditions, objects, and situations which arouse, sustain, and direct behavior is very large indeed, and (2) most human behavior is motivated by acquired or secondary motives.

Methods of Acquiring Motives

Conditioning. Motives may be acquired by the process of conditioning (see pp. 180 and 181). The process of conditioning is one in which an individual learns to make a response to a stimulus or some element in a situation which did not at first arouse the response. A response that is aroused by one stimulating condition becomes connected or associated with other stimuli. Eventually the response is aroused by any of the associated stimuli even when the original stimulating condition is not present. This process is illustrated in the example given above of the baby learning to make feeding responses to the sight of his bottle. Through this process of learning, eating may be aroused in the absence of hunger by many objects and situations and even words. The word "milk" or "candy" eventually comes to arouse the same response as the food object which it represents.

Hull (15) describes this process as the principle of secondary reinforcement. A response or a mode of behavior aroused by a drive is strengthened or reinforced when it leads to the reduction of the need that gave rise to the drive, and any stimulus that is closely associated with the need reduction is also reinforced to some degree. This is illustrated in an experiment by Williams (48), in which rats who had learned to go to a box for food continued to go to the box for a time even though there was no food in it. Going to the empty food box was due presumably to the fact that the box as a stimulus had acquired some secondary power by being associated with food and the reduction of hunger. In this case, however, it is unlikely that the rats would continue to go to the box if they always found it empty. The effect of the box as a secondary stimulating condition would eventually be lost unless it were reinforced by a renewed association with food. It is even more unlikely that the rats would continue to go to the box if they were not hungry. If this principle is correct, the fact that many food objects and even ideas continue to arouse feeding responses (eating, salivation, etc.) in older children and adults would be accounted for by the fact that they continue to reoccur in connection with food and the reduction of hunger. While an individual will eat candy even when he isn't hungry, it is doubtful if he would continue to do so if candy were never associated with the satisfaction of hunger — unless, indeed, it became associated with the satisfaction of some other motive.

Functional autonomy of motives. Allport (2) takes the position that a secondary motive may become functionally independent of the motive out of which it developed. According to this view, a desire for money, while it may have developed out of the satisfaction of basic needs, becomes an independent motive capable of arousing behavior on its own account without further association with the original motivating conditions. As pointed out in the previous paragraph, it is doubtful if a desire for candy would function independently for any length of time if it were not reinforced by association with its parent motive, hunger. A desire for money, however, is somewhat more complex and develops through more stages out of the satisfactions of not one but several needs. It appears to function autonomously in many individuals and at many times. Its reinforcement by association with the satisfactions of basic needs may not be immediately apparent, but again it is easy to imagine what would happen to the desire if money should suddenly lose its value as a means of satisfying any of our needs. The connection between basic need reduction and other acquired motives, such as the desire to be famous, or the motives of the research scientist toward the discovery of new facts, or of the artist toward a new creation, is more difficult to see. To trace such motives back through several stages of conditioning to some pattern of physiological drives, assuming that such a pattern is basic to these motives, may add little to the understanding to be gained from an analysis of the immediate motivations themselves.

Trial and error learning. An inexperienced organism is aroused to action by some motivating condition. Apart from the fact that this motivating condition (e.g., hunger) can only be satisfied by a given class of objects (food), the organism does not know what will or will not satisfy the motivating condition. The activity aroused by the drive is consequently directed first here and then there. One line of activity results in satisfaction, another does not. One goal object, by actual test, proves to be more satisfying than another. In this trial and error fashion, the drive toward one goal object becomes stronger, while the drive toward another becomes weaker or disappears. It is obvious, of course, that need reduction is involved in this learning, but it is the trial and error nature of the aroused activity that brings the organism into contact with a variety of goal objects and affords him a chance to learn that some objects are more satisfying than others. This may be illustrated quite simply. Carrots will satisfy hunger and reduce the need for food, but an individual will never learn that this is so and will never learn to like carrots if his behavior is not varied enough to include this food among the possible satisfiers of hunger.

It should be noted also that the satisfaction of one motive may occur at the same time that another motive is being satisfied. The satisfaction of the first motive is reinforced by the satisfaction of the second and vice versa. For example, a child may be given a certain kind of food for the first time. On eating it, he finds that it tastes good. At the same time, however, his desire for social approval is satisfied by the way his parents react to his willingness to try a new food. This satisfaction serves to reinforce the satisfaction derived from the food itself. On future occasions the child may eat the food as a means of obtaining approval even if the food itself is not particularly satisfying. It is clear that trial and error behavior increases the likelihood that such contiguous experiences will occur.

The Acquisition of Social Motives

Such motives as the desire for attention and recognition, the desire to belong, the desire to be loved and to be wanted, and the desire for social approval are referred to as social motives. These motives develop through conditioning and trial and error learning out of an individual's contact with people and with the customs and conventions which come into play in the course of satisfying physiological needs. As pointed out in Chapter 4, a child is born into an organized social environment. Not only is this environment a source of outside stimulation, but it begins to shape and direct the child's development even before he is born. While he is motivated by internal conditions, he will find his path to certain goal objects blocked. He will be encouraged and trained to satisfy his needs in certain prescribed ways. He will learn with few exceptions to want to satisfy his needs in these prescribed ways. He will receive approval from his parents and other people for doing so. He will probably receive disapproval and even punishment if he fails to do so. If a mother fondles and talks to her child while the child is eating, fondling and talking become associated, through conditioning, with the satisfaction of hunger. Since the mother is a part of the total stimulating situation, she becomes associated with the need reduction. Eventually the child learns to want his mother, to want to be fondled, to be loved, to be played with, to be recognized, and to be with people.

In this fashion any demands or requirements of the social group may become accepted. The individual learns to do what society demands, and, what is more important, he learns to want to do it. A child not only learns to eat certain foods, prepared and served in certain ways, but he learns to want these foods prepared and served in these ways. Eventually he may reach the point where hunger is not adequately satisfied if these secondary requirements are not met. Eating from dirty dishes with one's fingers is likely to be disgusting and even nauseating to the person who has learned to want to eat his food from clean dishes with a fork or other implement. The satisfaction of any of our basic drives or acquired motives is circumscribed by the conditions which exist in our culture and by the wishes and demands of the people with whom we associate.

Drives like hunger and sex are so overlaid by social considerations that it is difficult to determine to what extent the hunger and sex motivations of an adult are due to basic physiological needs and to what extent they are dependent upon such desires as the desire for

social approval and the desire to avoid social disapproval or punishment.

The Id, the Ego, and the Superego.   There has been some tendency
in psychology to regard the internal motivating conditions, especially
the physiological drives, as giving rise to behavior which is naturally in
conflict with the demands of the social group.   Freud (12) has dramatized this notion in his psychoanalytic formulation of the concepts which
he named the Id, the Ego, and the Superego.   The Id is the striving
aspect of one's personality.   It is composed of primitive, instinctual,
unconscious impulses which operate on what Freud calls the "pleasure
principle."   This means that the primary concern of the Id is the gratification of impulses and the avoidance of pain.   The Ego may be thought
of as corresponding roughly to the self.   It is partly conscious and partly
unconscious, and is in contact with reality.   Since the Id impulses are
gratified through the Ego, the Ego acts somewhat as a censor that turns
back or *represses* certain impulses and lets others through to find gratification.   The Superego concept corresponds roughly to what we commonly refer to as conscience.   It consists of the moral views and ideals
which the individual has accepted as his own personal standards of
conduct.   These standards are supposedly in conflict with the Id impulses.   The argument here is that a drive like the sex drive initiates
behavior which is frowned upon by society and which must be suppressed
and replaced by a kind of behavior which society deems acceptable.   To
some extent this is true not only of sex but of other motives as well.
A hungry baby grabs food with his fingers, or he may even stick his
face into a dish and attempt to lap his food like a dog.   His mode of
satisfying hunger is dependent upon his maturity and experience.   It
will change as he matures, even in the absence of social training.   In a
similar way, one's mode of reacting to the sex urge varies with age and
experience.   There is nothing about the sex urge which dictates that
it cannot be satisfied quite adequately in a way that is acceptable to
society.   Here, however, we encounter a number of complicating training conditions which vary all the way from a complete denial of the sex
motive to an insistence that there should be an unhampered, undirected
expression of the urge.   The latter position would be analogous to
saying that children should be allowed to eat with their fingers or lap
food like a dog because at a certain stage in their development they
have an impulse to do so.

In this connection it should be remembered that a physiological
motive directs behavior or determines the form of the aroused behavior
only within very broad limits.   A hungry animal must have specific

food elements, but these elements may be obtained in many ways and in many forms. Environmental conditions and social training will determine the specific manner in which urges will be satisfied. An individual can learn to satisfy a need of any kind in a great many ways. He can learn to satisfy his needs in socially acceptable ways. He can learn to want to satisfy these needs in socially acceptable ways. If he fails to do so, the reason is usually not so much a matter of some basic conflict between the impulses of the individual and the demands of society as it is a failure on the part of parents, teachers, and society to provide the necessary training conditions.

THE RELATIVE STRENGTH OF MOTIVES

Everyone knows that a given motive is stronger at one time than at another, that at a given time motive A is stronger than motive B, and that some motives are in general stronger than other motives. Any number of illustrations of these facts come to mind. We are hungrier at one time than at another, or we work harder to please people at one time than at another. At a given time, hunger is stronger than thirst or vice versa, or the desire to go to the movies is stronger than the desire to study or, conceivably, vice versa. Hunger is in general a stronger motive than love of parents or the desire to be with people, although all of us recognize that on some occasions a weaker motive may be stronger than one of the stronger motives. In connection with this point it will be recalled (see p. 143) that Maslow (24) arranged the basic needs in a hierarchy of pre-potency in which the first-order needs were regarded as stronger than the second-order needs, the second stronger than the third, and so on. While these general facts regarding the strength of motives are a matter of common knowledge, any of us would be hard pressed to answer such questions as the following: How much stronger is motive A than motive B? Is motive A present more frequently than motive B? How intense is motive A when it is operative? If two antagonistic motives are operative at the same time and on many different occasions, which one usually has the right of way, and how often? To answer these and other questions regarding the relative strength of motives we must have the kind of exact knowledge provided by carefully controlled experiments.

Methods of Measuring the Relative Strength of Motives

The obstruction method. This method has been used in studying the relative strength of drives in lower animals. It is based upon the assumption that the strength of a drive can be measured in terms of the amount of resistance or opposition that an animal will overcome in order to satisfy the drive.   This method makes use of an obstruction box, the basic floor plan of which is shown in Figure 29.   A motivated

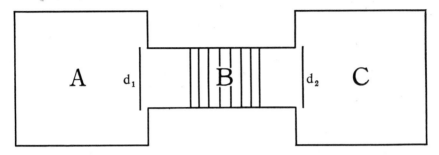

Figure 29

Basic Floor Plan for an Obstruction Box Used in Measuring
the Strength of Drives in Animals

The animal is released from compartment A and must cross the electric grid in compartment B in order to reach the incentive in compartment C; d_1 and d_2 are doors leading from A and into C respectively.   After Warden (47).

animal is placed in compartment A.   Food, mate, water, or other incentive is placed in compartment C.   The floor of compartment B is covered with an electric grid which can be charged with varying amounts of electricity.   In order to get to the incentive, the animal must cross the electric grid.   The amount of punishment, measured in terms of the number of volts of electricity he will take, or the number of times he will cross the grid when the voltage in the grid is constant, is a measure of the strength of the drive.

In a study (47) of the relative strength of the maternal, hunger, thirst, sex, and exploratory drives in rats, using the obstruction method, it was found that the maternal drive was the strongest.   Thirst was second, hunger third, sex fourth, and the exploratory drive last.   The strength of each drive was measured by taking the average number of times the animal crossed the electric grid to reach the goal object.   Care was taken to see that all drives were satiated except the one being tested.   Each animal was given preliminary training to acquaint it with the apparatus and the location of the incentive.   In testing the hunger drive, one group of animals was deprived of food for zero hours and tested; another group was deprived for twelve hours and tested; another for twenty-four hours and tested; and so on up to six days.   The same deprivations and testings were followed for thirst and for sex in the male. Since the sex drive in the female is virtually nonexistent except during periods of heat, the sex drive in the female was tested after a four-day or five-day period. The maternal drive was tested immediately after the mother was separated from her young. The exploratory drive was also measured without a period of delay between training in the exploration box and the test in the obstruction box. The average number of crossings of the electric grid made by a large number of rats under each drive condition was as follows:

	Maternal	22.4
	Thirst	20.4
DRIVE ◀	Hunger	18.2	▶ AV. NO. OF CROSSINGS
	Sex (both sexes)	13.8
	Exploratory	6.0

When no drive or a drive and no incentive was present, the average number of crossings was 3.5. A further scrutiny of the results indicates that thirst was strongest after about twenty-four hours without water. Hunger was strongest after about four days without food. The sex drive in males was greatest after twenty-four hours of deprivation.

The free-choice method. This method consists in placing an animal in a situation in which he can select with equal ease one of two goals, or one of several. A T-maze, so called because it is built in the shape of a T, is a device which permits an animal to choose between two goal objects or incentives. An animal in a T-maze may choose between water (on the right) and food (on the left) or between a mate and freedom from the maze, and so on. With food and water as the incentives, tests may be run to determine the relative strength of various amounts of water and food deprivations, such as twelve hours without water vs. twelve hours without food, or twelve hours without one vs. twenty-four hours without the other, and so on. In this connection it has been found that white rats can distinguish between different degrees of hunger and can learn to make one response (turn left in a T-maze) to the degree of hunger represented by 11.5 hours without food and another response (turn right in a T-maze) to 47.5 hours of hunger (17).

The free-choice method can be used to study the strength of motives of children and adults. Objects of almost any kind, including words or verbal descriptions of situations, are presented in pairs and the subject is asked to pick the one he prefers. By pairing every object with every other one as in the method of paired comparison, it is possible to obtain a measure of the relative drawing power, appeal value, or attractiveness of various incentives or goal objects. From these measures one can draw inferences regarding the strength of the motives which give rise to these preferences.

Another form of the free-choice method, the rating method, was used some years ago by Starch (39) in measuring the strength of human motives. He gave subjects a list of 44 motives, with the following instructions:

> Consider the strength or importance of these motives or incentives to action from the standpoint of your own personal life and behavior as a whole. Ask yourself in connection with each one how important it is in determining your own actions from day to day. Write 10 after the very strongest motives, and a number between 0 and 10 after the others, according to their relative strength or importance.

A portion of Starch's list was given to 280 college students in elementary psychology at Purdue University. The list of motives used and the average rating of each is shown in Table VII. While this method of rating is subject to the tendency on the part of individuals to rate themselves high in those traits which are regarded as desirable and low in those which society regards as undesirable, it is interesting to note (1) that the motives receiving the highest ratings are the ones which our knowledge about motives in general would cause us to expect to be highest, and (2) that no motive is rated as having no strength.

Table VII

The Relative Strength of Motives of 280 College Students

MOTIVE	AVERAGE RATING	MOTIVE	AVERAGE RATING
Appetite — hunger	9.2	Competition	4.9
Health	8.5	Hospitality	5.4
Parental affection	8.2	Sex attraction	7.1
Pleasure	8.0	Ambition	8.1
Bodily comfort	8.2	Respect for Deity	7.9
Approval by others	7.2	Possession	3.7
Personal appearance	8.4	Sympathy for others	6.2
Cleanliness	9.0	Safety	7.6
Home comfort	7.9	Rest — sleep	8.0
Social distinction	5.8	Devotion to others	6.2
Efficiency	3.4	Cooperation	4.1

Other measures of the strength of motives. In the foregoing methods the strength of motives is indicated (1) by the amount of resistance an

organism will overcome to reach a goal (obstruction method), and
(2) by the organism's preference for one of several incentives (free-
choice method). Other criteria of the strength of motives are: (1) the
general activity level of the organism as measured by activity cages,
revolving drums, or bed movements (see p. 146); (2) rate of locomotion;
(3) rate of learning under different motivations; and (4) the discrepancy between ability and achievement or the difference between what
one is capable of doing and what one actually does.

Simmons (37) used rate of learning as a method of measuring the
strength of various incentives. She had groups of white rats learn two
mazes, an easy one and a difficult one, under varying incentives. Bread
and milk, sunflower seeds, mate, escape from the maze, and returning
to the home cage were used as rewards. The bread and milk incentive
was the most effective one for learning both the easy and hard mazes.
The relative effectiveness of the various incentives was the same for
both mazes.

The discrepancy between ability and achievement as a measure of
strength of motivation rests on the argument that an individual whose
achievement level in various school subjects, for example, is above
what would be expected from a measure of his ability to learn has been
highly motivated, whereas the individual whose achievement level is
below his ability level has been poorly motivated. The same argument
may be applied to animals. If a thirsty rat does not run toward water
as fast as he can run, the discrepancy between his possible performance
and his actual performance would be a measure of the strength of his
thirst. Since it is difficult to determine how fast an animal can run
except under some kind of motivation, one resorts to the procedure of
comparing the animal's speed under one degree or kind of motivation
with his speed under other degrees or kinds of motivation.

ATTITUDES AND INTERESTS

Attitudes

One of the important consequences of learning that some goal objects are
more satisfying than others and that some ways of satisfying motives
are more acceptable than others is the development of predispositions
to act in a given way to objects and situations. Such a predisposition to act in a particular way to an object, person, group of people, or
situation is called an *attitude*. Attitudes as motivating conditions act
primarily to determine the direction of an individual's activity. The
directionality of attitudes is seen in the fact that attitudes manifest them-

selves as favorable or unfavorable reactions toward objects and situations and as tendencies to agree or disagree with statements which
are made about these situations. This directionality is evident in such
terms as approach-withdrawal, adient-abient, and likes-dislikes. In
many instances attitudes are manifested by strongly expressed feelings
for or against something. In such cases the attitude is linked with or
colored by some emotion, such as love or hate or fear. This is seen in
the favorable reactions we make to the American flag, or in the strong
negative or unfavorable reactions which we make toward such crimes
as kidnapping and rape. In other cases attitudes are associated with
feelings of pleasantness or unpleasantness and are expressed as likes
or dislikes. Some writers (33) regard feeling as the basic characteristic
of attitudes and argue from this fact that attitudes are relatively independent of rational or intellectual activity. Those attitudes in which
the predisposition to act in a given way is a cluster or system of emotional dispositions may be regarded, according to McDougall (23), as
sentiments. McDougall defined *sentiment* as "a relatively permanent
system of emotional dispositions toward some object, person, or idea."

Emotion as a motivating condition. Since emotions are involved
in attitudes and play a role in the motivating effects of attitudes, one
may properly raise the question: Are emotions as such to be regarded
as motivating conditions? In general the answer to this question is yes.
More specifically, however, the answer depends upon our definition of
emotion. As we shall see in Chapter 9, emotion is a complex unit of
behavior composed of a number of distinguishable components. These
components are: (1) the perception of an emotive situation, (2) internal
bodily changes, (3) immediate overt behavior, (4) feeling, and (5) an
adjustment to the emotive situation. According to this view the first
component initiates internal bodily changes, overt behavior, and feelings
(see Figure 57, p. 299). Components 2 and 3 may give rise to the
feeling component, and all of the first four components are involved in
the emotional adjustment. Our original question can now be answered
by saying that certain components of an emotion act as motivating conditions. When one speaks of the motivating effects of love, hate, anger,
and jealousy in man's everyday affairs, he is most likely to have the
"feeling" component of these emotions in mind. Some psychologists
have emphasized the motivating effects of the internal bodily changes
which occur in an emotion. It should be clear from our earlier discussion
of psychological motives that changes in the respiratory, circulatory,
and digestive systems, whether they occur in hunger or emotion, will
give rise to internal stimulations and thus act as motivating conditions.

Aspirations. A number of concepts such as *determining set, mental set, intention,* and *aspiration* are closely related to attitudes. These terms refer to mental states or ideas, or occasionally, as in the case of set, to physiological or anatomical conditions, which direct behavior toward specific goal objects. The concept of aspiration has received a considerable amount of attention in recent years under the heading of *level of aspiration.* In the process of adjusting to an environment an individual meets with varying amounts of success and failure. Over a period of time he builds up expectations of success and failure in relation to his demonstrated abilities. He may discover his limitations and learn to accept them. He may learn to adjust his expectations to his demonstrated abilities. On the other hand, he may develop a habit of setting his sights too high or too low in relation to his ability to achieve or perform. On the one hand he aspires to goals that are in varying degrees beyond his reach, and on the other, he fails to aspire to goals that are within his reach.

In the experimental investigations of an individual's level of aspiration he is given some task to perform, such as throwing darts at a target, sorting cards, typing, or multiplying numbers. He is given a number of trials and is given his score after each trial. At the end of a trial he is asked to state what score he expects to get on the next trial. If he fails to make the expected score, will he lower his estimate for the next trial? How many times will he have to fail to attain an expected score before he will change his estimate? What will be the effect on his estimates of being told that his older brother, or his closest friend, or an enemy, or a member of a certain race or nationality has made higher or lower scores than the one he has just made? These and other questions can be investigated and may reveal significant facts regarding one's evaluation of himself, defensiveness, feelings of security, or other personality characteristics.

Development of attitudes. Attitudes develop out of an individual's interactions with his environment. It is clear that two sets of factors are involved in these interactions: the biological and the social, or, more broadly and in terms of our behavior equation, P and E factors. Since many of our attitudes develop out of our contacts with the society in which we live, there has been a tendency to emphasize the cultural determinants of attitudes. Attitudes which are largely determined by cultural factors and which are directed toward people or conditions in society are frequently referred to as social attitudes. These and all other attitudes, however, grow out of one's internal motivations and his trial and error experiences in attempting to satisfy these motivations.

The processes of conditioning and trial and error learning by which motives are acquired operate here as they do in the acquisition of any other motives. Allport (1) describes four ways in which these processes operate in the development of attitudes. First, an attitude may develop through the accumulation and integration of experiences of a given kind over a period of time, as when an unfavorable attitude toward mathematics results from repeated failures in the subject over a long period. Second, an attitude may develop by splitting off from a more general one or as a by-product of a more general one, as seen in a favorable attitude toward golf as a result of a generally favorable attitude toward all sports. Third, an attitude may be due to an unusual or painful experience. A child may develop an unfavorable attitude toward physicians because of an extremely painful episode in a physician's office. Fourth, an attitude may be picked up by imitation or it may be adopted from parents, teachers, or other associates.

Measurement of attitudes. Attitudes are commonly measured by attitude scales. Such a scale consists of a number of statements which express varying degrees of favorableness or unfavorableness toward the attitude object in question. Part of a scale to measure attitude toward the church is given below:

NUMBER OF STATEMENT

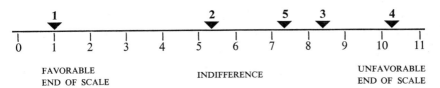

FAVORABLE INDIFFERENCE UNFAVORABLE
END OF SCALE END OF SCALE

1. I think the church is a divine institution, and it commands my highest loyalty and respect.
2. I am neither for nor against the church, but I do not believe that church-going will do anyone any harm.
3. I feel the good done by the church is not worth the money and energy spent on it.
4. I regard the church as a monument to human ignorance.
5. I believe that the church is losing ground as education advances. (43)

The complete test contains forty-five statements distributed over the whole range between the favorable and the unfavorable ends of the scale. The person whose attitude is being measured is asked to read the items carefully and check each one with which he agrees. Now, it is obvious that a person who checks a number of statements similar to the first one (the scale value of which is .8) is very favorable toward the church.   Equally clear is it that if statements like 3 and 4 (scale values of which are 8.1 and 10.2, respectively) are checked, the person is unfavorable.   In like manner, a person checking only statements falling in the center of the scale would be neutral in his attitude toward the church.   That is, small personal scores indicate favor; large, disfavor; middle, a middle attitude.

Some interesting results have been obtained with this scale.   Table VIII summarizes some of the findings, as reported by Thurstone and

Table VIII

Average Scale Value of Attitude toward the Church of Different Groups (43)

GROUPS	SCALE VALUE	GROUPS		SCALE VALUE
Roman Catholics	2.9	Those who do not attend church		5.9
Protestants	4.0	Active members of a church		3.1
Jews	5.4	Not active members of a church		5.7
Men	4.5		Freshmen	4.4
Women	4.2	University of Chicago	Sophomores	5.0
Those who attend church	3.05	students	Juniors	4.6
			Seniors	4.8

(The smaller the value the more favorable the attitude.)

Chave.   These data show, among other things, that the four college classes do not differ appreciably in their attitude toward the church, contrary to the popular belief that the longer one has been in college the more irreligious he is.

Attitude scales of this type have been developed by Remmers and his co-workers and have been used to measure attitudes produced or changed by motion pictures, lectures, education, and propaganda (32).

Interests

The term *interest* is used in two ways in psychology.   It is defined, first, as an attitude or condition which is characterized by focusing attention upon certain problems or activities, or as a tendency to become absorbed in an experience and to continue it.   Thus an interest in baseball or chemistry or psychology would be manifested by attention to and participation in these activities.   In this sense an interest is for all practical purposes the same as a favorable attitude.   The second definition characterizes interest as a feeling of pleasure resulting from giving special attention to something or from participating in some activity.

In the first definition interest is regarded as a motivating condition, i.e., the condition which sustains and directs one's activity. In the second definition interest is regarded as an effect of one's participation in some activity. On close examination the two definitions are seen to be closely related. If satisfaction results from participation in an activity, it may serve as a motive for the repetition of the activity. Eventually, if the satisfaction is repeated, an interest (predisposition) will develop, and will manifest itself as a tendency on the part of the individual to become absorbed in an activity and to continue it.

This relationship between interest as the result of activity and interest as the motive for activity is important in connection with educational and vocational guidance, where one is confronted with the problem of development of interests. How can one teach a child to be interested in something that he is not interested in? The answer is simple enough: see to it that satisfaction accompanies participation in the activity. Admittedly, this is more easily said than done. Strong external stimulations can be used; even strong-arm methods of inducing the child to engage in the activity will be effective if the satisfaction resulting from the activity itself more than makes up for the initial unpleasantness. It is in this situation that ability plays an important role in the development of interest. Some activities must be performed with a certain degree of excellence if they are to result in satisfaction. The ability to perform well, therefore, is a factor in the ultimate satisfaction. Interests thrive on successful performances. Suppose, for example, that a teacher wants a pupil to develop an interest in arithmetic. She resorts to the most acceptable techniques of getting him to study arithmetic and participate with the other children in solving problems. But suppose that his calculations and answers are always wrong because of his lack of ability to comprehend or understand what he is doing. It is then obvious that he is not likely to develop any interest in arithmetic. Continued prodding will not help. What the child needs is a taste of success, an experience which he may still get from arithmetic if he goes back to simpler tasks commensurate with his ability.

Methods of measuring interest. Precise, objective information regarding interests is no less necessary for understanding or controlling human behavior than similar information regarding abilities, intelligence, and temperament. A knowledge of the reading interests, play interests, occupational interests, and entertainment interests of children and adults is needed by teachers, salesmen, advertisers, movie directors, writers, and vocational counselors, as well as by the individuals themselves. Such knowledge is needed for the intelligent direction or control of the behavior of other people and particularly for directing one's own behavior in choosing a vocation, a course of training, a place to live, or even a mate.

A knowledge of interests can be obtained by a variety of methods, such as the personal interview, self-estimates, the questionnaire, check lists, and tests. One of the widely used methods in the case of children's reading interests and their interests in games is to make a list of the books most frequently read and the games most frequently played. These lists will show what kinds of books and stories are preferred, what games and toys are most popular, and they may reveal trends away from or toward particular kinds of interests. Since interests are indicated by the focus of attention, it is fairly safe to assume that such lists will provide information which will enable teachers and parents to prepare more adequately for controlling and directing children's activities.

Many methods have been used to obtain self-estimates of interests. Lehman and Witty (20) had a group of high school boys and girls pick from a long list of occupations the three which they preferred. As might be expected, vocational choices were found to change with age. Older boys and girls showed a shift toward the professions. In another study in which high school pupils were asked to express their occupational preferences it was found that about 60 per cent named professional work, while less than 10 per cent named mechanical work, industrial arts, and agriculture (31). That such choices may not be reliable is indicated in a study by Moffie (27). N.Y.A. students whose mean age was approximately nineteen rated their interests on a verbal graphic rating scale for the occupations listed in the Strong Vocational Interest Blank (see below). A comparison of the results with the interests as actually measured by the Strong blank revealed low positive correlations for twenty separate occupations. Moffie suggests that the lack of consistency between the estimated and measured interests is probably due to lack of maturity on the part of the student. This would indicate that self-estimates of adolescents regarding vocational choices cannot be regarded as reliable.

One of the first attempts at a systematic analysis of work interests by a printed schedule was made by Miner (26). He developed an analysis-of-work-interests blank, the purpose of which was to provide an individual with a means of discovering his special interests and abilities by observing his own likes and dislikes. The blank asks the subject to indicate two groups of school subjects which have been most interesting, to underline seven of his strongest traits, to indicate three kinds of activity with which he would be content to work permanently, and to check one of each of several pairs of interests. The blank enables the subject to come face to face with his own likes and dislikes and working interests and with the problem of making a vocational choice. It does not provide any numerical score which can be used for making comparisons with other people.

One of the oldest inventories for measuring vocational interests and perhaps the most widely used is the Strong Vocational Interest Blank (41). The blank lists names of occupations, types of people, school subjects, activities, and amusements among which the subject indicates his preferences by marking each item with an L, I, or D for like, indifference, and dislike. Different interest patterns have been worked out for men who have succeeded in various occupations. The form of the test for men can be scored for over thirty different occupations. The subject filling out the blank receives a rating of A, B, or C for various occupations. In general, if a score on the test falls within the highest 75 per cent of the scores of the men in a particular occupation, the rating for that occupation is A. If it falls within the lowest 25 per cent, it is B. An A rating indicates that an individual's interests are quite similar to those of persons successfully engaged in an occupation. The B rating indicates a slight similarity and the C rating no similarity. The test has been shown to be useful in vocational counseling, in hiring men, and in the admission of students to college.

Since the test is scored for several different occupations, each of which requires a separate key, and since the items have different numerical weights, such as 3, −2, and −1 for different occupations, the scoring is time-consuming and costly. A simplified scoring procedure, which makes possible a great saving in scoring time, has been developed by Harper and Dunlap (13). Their scoring keys were made up for several of the occupations of the Strong Vocational Interest Blank and were used in scoring the tests for 551 women at the University of Rochester. A comparison of the scores obtained from Strong's keys and the new keys seems to indicate that the new keys are valid for all practical purposes. A further validation of the simplified method was made by Kogan and Gehlmann (18). These investigators scored 208 test blanks with both Strong's and Dunlap's keys. The correlation between the scores obtained ranged from .957 to .989 for fourteen occupations. A comparison of the letter grades earned by the two scoring procedures revealed that 74.2 per cent of the letter grades did not shift, 24.76 per cent shifted only half a letter grade, and only .97 per cent shifted a whole letter grade.

A rather ingenious self-scoring interest test has been developed by Kuder (19). This test, known as the Kuder Preference Record, consists of a booklet composed of a long list of activities arranged in groups of three. In each group the subject is to pick out the activity which he likes most and the one which he likes least. He indicates his preference by punching a hole with a pin in the appropriate place in an answer sheet. After the test is completed, the subject removes the answer sheet, turns it over, and counts the number of pinholes in a series of circles drawn on the back of each of the several pages which, fastened together, form the answer sheet. Scores are obtained for nine general areas of interests as follows: mechanical, computational, scientific, persuasive, artistic, literary, musical, social service, and clerical. The score for each of the areas is plotted on a separate profile sheet, which makes it possible for the subject to determine his percentile rating for each area, and to see how he compares with other individuals. There is no attempt to give the subject a rating in a specific occupation. A number of specific occupations or jobs is listed for each area of interest merely to call attention to vocations which involve interests of the type for which the testee has expressed preference. Kuder suggests that this preference record can be used for pointing out vocations with which the student may not be familiar but which involve activities of a type for which he has expressed preference, and for indicating whether a person's choice of an occupation is consistent with the type of thing he ordinarily prefers to do. Separate percentile norms are available for high school boys and girls for each of the areas of interest.

SUMMARY

Any condition which arouses, sustains, or changes the direction of activity is called a motivating condition. The word *motive* is used to refer to any such condition; the word *drive* is used to refer to those motives which arise out of internal physiological processes. The motivation of behavior involves an initiating condition, the aroused behavior, and a goal toward which the behavior is directed. A goal is the object or state of affairs toward which the aroused behavior is directed. It satisfies the condition (motive) which initiated the behavior.

Motives are classified as internal and external, primary and secondary, adient and abient, physiological and social; they have also been classified according to their relative strengths. The internal or physiological drives are regarded as the fundamental source of human and animal motivation. Drives like hunger and thirst arise out of the organism's attempt to maintain a constant internal environment. These drives arouse behavior through the stimulations of sense organs within the body. Experiments show that the conscious pangs of hunger are accompanied by hunger contractions in the stomach and in turn by an increase in the general activity level of the organism.

Most human motives are acquired. They are acquired by the processes of conditioning and trial and error learning. Important among the acquired motives are those which develop out of an individual's contacts with people and social institutions. These motives are commonly called social motives; they include the desire for recognition, the desire to belong, the desire for social approval, and the desire to be loved.

The relative strength of motives has been measured in animals by the obstruction method, by the free-choice method, and by comparing an organism's rate of learning, rate of locomotion, or amount of general activity under different degrees or kinds of motivation. The second of these methods has been used in measuring the strength of motives in human beings.

Attitudes and interests, and such related mental states as intentions, mental sets, expectations, and aspirations, are an important group of motivating conditions in human behavior. Attitudes are predispositions to act in a given way, generally favorably or unfavorably toward certain objects, persons, groups, or situations. Attitudes are measured by means of attitude scales. Interests are measured by tests in which the individual indicates his preference for or like-dislike of certain situations, objects, or people.

QUESTIONS
on the Chapter

1. What is the problem of motivation?
2. Define: goal, motive, drive, need, motivating condition, instinct.
3. In what way is motivation dependent both upon the organism and upon environmental stimulations?
4. Give an example to show that motives are both adient and abient.
5. Describe Maslow's classification of motives.
6. What is homeostasis and what is its relation to motivation?
7. What is the balloon technique and how has it been used in studying the hunger drive?
8. Cite evidence to show that sex motivations in animals are related to physiological processes.

9. How are motives acquired?

10. What is Hull's principle of secondary reinforcement?

11. What is meant by functional autonomy of motives?

12. Describe the obstruction method of measuring the relative strength of drives.

13. What is the method of paired comparisons?

14. Define: attitude, sentiment, level of aspiration, interest.

15. In what way is emotion a motivating condition?

for Discussion

1. Is all behavior motivated?

2. Is aroused behavior always directed toward some goal or the attainment of some purpose?

3. Can you suggest a method of testing Maslow's idea that lower-level needs will dominate the behavior of an organism when both the lower-level and next-higher-level needs are frustrated?

4. List a number of questions that one might attempt to answer by studying one's levels of aspiration.

5. Why is it unwise to make generalizations about the sex drive in man from studies of the sex drive in animals?

6. Is a human being always aware of his motives?

REFERENCES

1 ALLPORT, G. W., "Attitudes." In Murchison, C., ed., *Handbook of Social Psychology.* Worcester: Clark University Press, 1935.

2 ALLPORT, G. W., *Personality. A Psychological Interpretation.* New York: Henry Holt and Company, 1937.

3 BASH, K. W., "An Investigation into a Possible Organic Basis for the Hunger Drive," *J. Comp. Psychol.,* 1939, 28, 109–136.

4 BEACH, F. A., and HOLZ, A. M., "Mating Behavior in Male Rats Castrated at Various Ages and Injected with Androgen," *J. Exp. Zool.,* 1946, 101, 91–142.

5 CANNON, W. B., *Bodily Changes in Pain, Hunger, Fear and Rage,* 2nd edition. New York: Appleton-Century Company, 1929.

6 CANNON, W. B., *The Wisdom of the Body.* New York: W. W. Norton and Company, 1932.

7 CANNON, W. B., and WASHBURN, A. L., "An Explanation of Hunger," *Amer. J. Physiol.,* 1912, 29, 441–454.

8 CARLSON, A. J., and JOHNSON V., *The Machinery of the Body.* Chicago: University of Chicago Press, 1941.

9 DASHIELL, J. F., *Fundamentals of General Psychology,* 3rd edition. Boston: Houghton Mifflin Company, 1949.

10 ELLIOTT, H. M., and TREAT, W. C., "Hunger Contractions and Rate of Conditioning," *Proc. Nat. Acad. Sci.,* 1935, 21, 514–516.

11 FRANKLIN, J., SCHIELE, B. C., BROZEK, J., and KEYS, A., "Observations of Human Behavior in Experimental Semistarvation and Rehabilitation," *J. Clin. Psychol.*, 1948, 4, 28–45.

12 FREUD, S., *The Ego and the Id.* London: Hogarth Press, 1927.

13 HARPER, B. P., and DUNLAP, J. W., "Derivation and Application of a Unit Scoring System for the Strong Vocational Interest Blank for Women," *Psychometrika*, 1942, 7, 289–295.

14 HOLT, E. B., *Animal Drive and the Learning Process.* New York: Henry Holt and Company, 1931.

15 HULL, C. L., *Principles of Behavior: An Introduction to Behavior Theory.* New York: Appleton-Century Company, 1943.

16 IRWIN, FRANCIS W., "Motivation." In Helson, Harry, *Theoretical Foundations of Psychology.* New York: D. Van Nostrand Company, 1951.

17 JENKINS, J. J., and HANRATTY, J. A., "Drive Intensity Discrimination in the Albino Rat," *J. Comp. Physiol. Psychol.*, 1949, 42, 228–232.

18 KOGAN, L., and GEHLMANN, F., "Validation of the Simplified Method for Scoring the Strong Vocational Interest Blank for Men," *J. Educ. Psychol.*, 1942, 33, 317–320.

19 KUDER, F. G., *Kuder Preference Record, Form BB*, revised edition. Chicago: Science Research Associates, 1942.

20 LEHMAN, H. C., and WITTY, P. A., *The Psychology of Play Activities.* New York: A. S. Barnes and Company, 1927.

21 LEWIN, K., "The Conceptual Representation and the Measurement of Psychological Forces," *Contr. Psychol. Theory*, 1938, 1, No. 4.

22 LUCKHARDT, A. B., and CARLSON, A. J., "Contributions to the Physiology of the Stomach. XVII. On the Chemical Control of the Gastric Hunger Mechanism," *Amer. J. Physiol.*, 1915, 36, 37–46.

23 MCDOUGALL, WILLIAM, *An Introduction to Social Psychology.* Boston: Luce and Company, 1926.

24 MASLOW, A. H., "A Theory of Human Motivation," *Psychol. Rev.*, 1943, 50, 370–396.

25 MASLOW, A. H., "Higher and Lower Needs," *J. Psychol.*, 1948, 25, 433–436.

26 MINER, J. B., *Analysis of Work Interests.* Chicago: C. H. Stoelting Company, 1921.

27 MOFFIE, F. J., "The Validity of Self-Estimated Interests," *J. Appl. Psychol.*, 1942, 26, 606–613.

28 MORGAN, C. T., *Physiological Psychology.* New York: McGraw-Hill Book Company, 1943.

29 MUNN, NORMAN L., *Psychology.* Boston: Houghton Mifflin Company, 1946.

30 MURRAY, H. A., and others, *Explorations in Personality.* New York: Oxford University Press, 1938.

31 PROCTOR, W. M., "Psychology Tests and Guidance of High School Pupils," *J. Educ. Research*, Monograph No. 1, 1923, p. 125.

32 REMMERS, H. H., and others, "Studies in Attitudes; A Contribution to Social-Psychological Research Methods," *Studies in Higher Education*, Bulletin Purdue University, 1934, No. 26.

33 REMMERS, H. H., and GAGE, N. L., *Educational Measurement and Evaluation.* New York: Harper and Brothers, 1943.

34 RICHTER, C. P., "Animal Behavior and Internal Drives," *Quar. Rev. Biol.,* 1927, 2, No. 3.

35 RICHTER, C. P., "Total Self-regulatory Functions in Animals and Human Beings," *Harvey Lectures,* 1942–43, 38, 63–103.

36 SHAFFER, L. F., *The Psychology of Adjustment.* Boston: Houghton Mifflin Company, 1936.

37 SIMMONS, R., "The Relative Effectiveness of Certain Incentives in Animal Learning," *Comp. Psychol. Monogr.,* 1924, 2, No. 7.

38 SONTAG, L. W., "The Significance of Fetal Environmental Differences," *Amer. J. Obst. Gynec.,* 1941, 42, 996–1003.

39 STARCH, D., *Principles of Advertising.* New York: McGraw-Hill Book Company, 1923.

40 STRONG, E. K., *Psychology of Selling and Advertising.* New York: McGraw-Hill Book Company, 1925.

41 STRONG, E. K., JR., *Vocational Interests of Men and Women.* Stanford: Stanford University Press, 1943.

42 SYMONDS, P. M., *Dynamic Psychology.* New York: Appleton-Century-Crofts, 1949.

43 THURSTONE, L. L., and CHAVE, E. J., *The Measurement of Attitude.* Chicago: University of Chicago Press, 1929.

44 TSANG, N. C., "Hunger Motivation in Gastrectomized Rats," *J. Comp. Psychol.,* 1938, 26, 1–17.

45 WADA, T., "An Experimental Study of Hunger in Relation to Activity," *Arch. Psychol.,* 1922, No. 57.

46 WANG, G. H., "The Relation between 'Spontaneous' Activity and Oestrous Cycle in the White Rat," *Comp. Psychol. Monogr.,* 1923, No. 6.

47 WARDEN, C. J., *Animal Motivation Studies.* New York: Columbia University Press, 1931.

48 WILLIAMS, K. A., "The Reward Value of a Conditioned Stimulus," *Univ. Calif. Publ. Psychol.,* 1929, 4, 31–35.

49 YOUNG, P. T., *Emotion in Man and Animal.* New York: John Wiley and Sons, 1943.

LEARNING AND MEMORY
6

LEARNING — *understanding*

It is indicative of the importance of learning that it has been necessary to refer to it a number of times in the preceding chapters: first, as a phenomenon which occurs before birth; second, as one of the processes of development; and third, as the process of acquiring motives. Together with maturation, learning is responsible for the development of the human infant from a stage of almost complete helplessness at birth to an adult state characterized by complex skills, abilities, interests, and modes of adjustment. In the span of a few years the young human being must learn thousands upon thousands of things and weave together into smooth working wholes innumerable items which were learned in relative isolation. No other form of life learns anything like so much, so fast, or so well as man.

The chief industry of modern civilization is learning. In order to carry on any specialized work, we must first "learn how." Learning literally *makes a man into* a professional of one kind or another. Having learned his "trade," the ballplayer, for example, responds to situations with special actions that are quite as quick, quite as vigorous, as any unlearned reactions. In every respect of his constitution the man *is* a ballplayer, and he has become so largely, if not entirely, by learning. But no group of examples of learning can begin to indicate the importance which learning has for us, or the constant dependence we place upon it. Scarcely an hour passes that does not have some effect upon us, in which we do not learn something. From birth to death, most of what we do or can do depends upon what we have learned.

WHAT IS LEARNING?

John, in the first grade, is asked by his teacher on Monday morning: "Seven plus four equals what?" This question is a problem, or a situation, or a *stimulus* to which a proper response must be attached. But John does not know the correct answer; that is, he has not *learned* it. So to this stimulus he makes whatever response he has learned to make in the face of an embarrassing situation — a worried, downcast look; a wiggle or two; a whimper; a pretense that someone else was asked the question; or a very fine response which he has learned, namely, "I do not know."

On Friday of the same week the teacher again asks John: "Seven plus four equals what?" This time John replies, "Eleven," with promptness, assurance, and a general feeling of well-being. Somehow or other during the week John has learned that seven plus four equals eleven. This means, of course, that John can do something on Friday that he could not do on Monday, namely, give the correct answer to the problem. John's way of responding to the problem has changed. What was responsible for this change? What happened between Monday and Friday to bring it about? All of us know from our own elementary school experience approximately what happened. The teacher told John the answer to the problem. She had him repeat the answer a number of times. John heard other children give the correct answer. In short, John *did* something and this something resulted in his learning the correct answer. In this example we see that two things are involved in learning: activity on the part of the learner, and a change in the learner's behavior. An analysis of any instance of learning, be it simple or complex, reveals (1) that learning always involves some change or modification of an individual's behavior, and (2) that this change is always brought about by what the individual does, i.e., by his own activity. Learning may be defined, therefore, as the change or modification of an organism's behavior that results from the organism's own activity. *or experience*

Learning and Activity

The fact that all learning involves activity on the part of the learner needs to be emphasized. Uneducated people and children sometimes say, "She learned me all I know about reading." If learning were a passive process, we could perhaps "learn" another. Since learning, however, is an active process, we can only teach another; and our problem is to get the person we are trying to teach to perform the acts necessary for learning. One learns only if, and to the extent that, he himself participates in or responds to the conditions which make up the learning situation. The more one responds and the more intense his motives for responding, the more he learns, other things being equal.

If an individual is motivated by hunger and knows what to do to satisfy hunger, the motive merely sets off the appropriate response mechanism. The individual responds but there is no learning. If, however, the individual finds that his habitual way of satisfying hunger does not work, he is faced with the necessity of learning how to satisfy the motive in some other way. If learning is to occur, the motivations must be of such a nature that they cannot be satisfied by any of the skills, knowledge, or response mechanisms now at the individual's disposal. Under these conditions the learner is faced with the problem of acquiring a new mode of behavior or of reorganizing his present ways of acting in order to resolve the motive forces. At first glance it might appear that incidental or nonintentional learning, so called, does not fit this description; that its very name (nonintentional) indicates that it is not motivated. This, however, is not the case. Any learning situation, unless it is rigidly controlled with the deliberate purpose of reducing the organism's range and variety of activity, produces a wide variety of responses. There are many facets to the learning situation. All of the organism's responses to all aspects of the situation are involved in its learning. Some of these may appear to an outside observer or to the learner himself to be incidental to the main problem, but to the extent that any of these are learned, to that extent the learning is a part of the total problem situation and therefore motivated by it.

The Changes That Occur When We Learn

Coordination and integration. Many of the changes that occur when learning takes place are easily observable. A person does not need to be an especially keen observer to note the differences between a poor and an expert skater. Conspicuous among them are the superior coordination and integration of movements of the expert. In addition to knowing, as perhaps the novice knows too, what is the correct position, the expert also knows how to assume it. His legs work coordinately with his arms and body; and his superior integration is seen in the smoothness of his movements, one movement fading into the next as he moves over the ice. There is little unnecessary activity, whereas the beginner not only makes many unnecessary movements but, much worse, makes many that conflict with the necessary ones. As a result, he is quickly exhausted. The experienced person also shows his mastery of an art by setting a pace he can maintain, whereas the novice at any task is apt to set too rapid a pace for himself.

Organization of material into wholes. Similar changes occur at a somewhat higher level of learning, as in typing and telegraphy. The

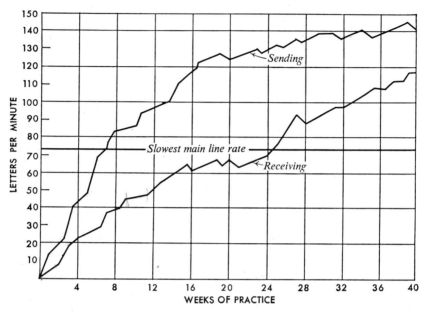

Figure 30

Learning Curves in Telegraphy

This graph is the product of one of the earliest and most influential experiments in learning. (From W. L. Bryan and N. Harter, "Studies in the Physiology and Psychology of the Telegraphic Language," *Psychol. Rev.*, 1897, 4, 27–53.)

inexpert typist or telegrapher responds to each letter or click, as the case may be, whereas the expert responds to larger groups of elementary units. The expert typist reads her material and organizes it into larger units, thus insuring smooth and highly coordinated movements. Most of us who have had practice chiefly in writing letters on a typewriter approximate this level of expertness only when we write "yours very truly." Even more remarkable is the performance of the expert telegrapher, who keeps in mind a great number of sounds so as to perceive their structural pattern and, at the same time, writes rapidly on his machine. If this were not so, improvement to the point shown in Figure 30 would not be possible. Figure 30 has historical as well as practical significance. Though it comes from one of the earliest quantitative studies of learning, it is still considered an example of the best type of scientific study in this field (8). Skill in telegraphy involves not only highly skilled muscular responses but also much training of auditory perception. The telegrapher learns to respond with his ears to large units of meaningful material in much the same way as we respond with our eyes in reading.

Negative adaptation.   Improved coordination and integration, with the consequent elimination of unnecessary and antagonistic movements, constitute the basis of all motor skills.   Many skills, however, require more than this.   They demand that we become negatively adapted to unimportant features of the situation and that we learn what is important.   We speak of the skill of a woodsman or of a hunter. By this we mean more than ease in walking, or ability to withstand exposure, or expertness in shooting.   We mean that these experts have learned to ignore many things that would be attended to by the novice and have learned to respond to many things that the novice would ignore.   Furthermore, they have learned to respond in a more satisfactory way to those features of the situation to which they do pay attention.

These characteristics of learning extend to the lowest animals.   If water is dropped upon an amoeba, it will, for a short time, make withdrawal movements.   In time, however, it will cease to do so.   It becomes negatively adapted to the harmless stimulation.   In the same way, spiders will make a protective reaction when a tuning fork is sounded; but after the stimulation has been experienced a few times and nothing of consequence has followed, they become indifferent, or negatively adapted, to it.

Animals also learn to single out and respond to the important features of a situation.   Thus, a cat placed in a cage may at first make random movements, strongly motivated by an impulse to get out.   But after a number of trials, it ceases to act at random and concentrates its efforts on those parts of the cage that offer a real possibility of escape.   Or a rat may be taught to respond positively to yellow and negatively to blue by rewards and punishment.   In a similar manner, fish can be taught to react to the brightest of three lamps, or to the least bright, or to the one of intermediate brightness (51).

The changes that occur when we master intellectual subject matter, such as economics or psychology, are also readily observable.   These correspond in general to those involved in becoming skillful.   The beginning student of a science is apt to flounder.   He gets, at first, only vague and unorganized meanings regarding the subject.   As he progresses, however, bewilderment gives place to definite organization of facts, and he is able to present what he knows in a clear manner, neglecting many irrelevant bypaths that once attracted him.

Learning frequently leads to a closed mind — closed not only to irrelevant bypaths, but to important possibilities in one's field of study. This occurs even among well-trained scientists. For example, when Einstein first presented his theory of relativity, only a few physicists gave it serious consideration. Similarly, classical economists are apt to become negatively adapted to arguments for state control of economic activities. Financiers learn that certain types of investment are unsafe and, accordingly, avoid them, as the rat avoids the door which he has learned means punishment. The tendency to develop a closed mind should be recognized and guarded against. In mastering a subject, one should seek to maintain a balance between wasting one's time on irrelevancies and closing the mind to possibilities not congenial to one's initial assumptions.

The subjective changes that occur as a person learns are also easily observable. The feeling of uncertainty and bewilderment gives place to one of confidence and assurance. There is no longer the strained attention involved in looking for meaning and clues to action. The significant elements and their implications have been discovered and are dealt with easily and efficiently. Confidence born of insight takes the place of uncertainty and of exploratory trial and error procedures.

Additive and integrative changes. The changes or modifications of behavior that occur in learning may be catalogued under two principal headings. One kind of change is mere increase in the amount that one knows or can do. Each new item of information and each new habit increases the total in an additive fashion. There is no revision or reorganization of what has been learned in the light of what is being learned. The sum total of what one has learned increases in much the same way that a snow-ball increases in size. All of us know individuals who seem to learn in this way. They acquire one item of information after another and one skill after another, but the increase in knowledge and skill does not give them any fresh insight or understanding or bring about any change in basic personality structure. Such an individual seems to feel no difficulty when he learns something that is contrary to what he has learned earlier; he makes no effort to integrate present learning with previous learning. Such an individual can go through several years of schooling, acquire a vast amount of information, and yet come out at the end without having reorganized his thinking, his philosophy of life, or his personality structure.

The other kind of change of behavior consists in incorporating what is being learned into what has been learned to effect a new whole. The new material may disagree with some of the things previously learned. These things may have to be discarded or revised, and the entire body of previously learned material may have to be reorganized before the new material can be incorporated into it. One important feature of this kind of learning is the fact that what has been learned serves as a criterion for evaluating what is being learned and may actually determine whether or not it will be learned. At the same time, what has been learned is not so rigidly organized that it cannot be reorganized or reconstructed so that new knowledge can be incorporated into it. When one recognizes that one's learning includes attitudes, motives, interests, abilities, personality traits, and ways of acting and thinking, the importance of incorporating what is being learned into what has been learned takes on added significance. To the extent that one can and does incorporate and integrate present with previous learning, to that extent he becomes a new individual, or, in a manner of speaking, a remodeled personality.

It is obvious, of course, that these two kinds of change are not mutually exclusive. They may be thought of as the extremes of a continuum. Between these extremes there are many mixtures of the additive and integrative changes. Integrative changes are not likely to characterize all of an individual's learning. They may be characteristic of particular areas of learning, but not of learning as a whole. For example, in learning psychology the student may succeed in organizing and integrating what he is learning about psychology, but he may fail to integrate this knowledge with anything else that he has learned or is learning. If the same tendency characterizes his learning in other fields, he will accumulate a considerable amount of well-organized knowledge and skill in a number of different areas, but these areas, except for being the property of one individual, will tend to be as unrelated as a haphazard collection of stones. It might be pointed out that the poor student is not very adept at organizing material even in a particular area. He learns each item as if it had no relation to the previous ones; his learning, such as it is, is strictly of the additive variety.

METHODS OF LEARNING

The above changes in behavior are produced, as we have stated, by the organism's own activity. But how does activity produce changes in behavior? Under what conditions and circumstances will an organism's responding result in learning? Why does some activity result in learning while other activity does not? How do we learn? Let us examine the methods of learning to see what light they throw on these questions.

Conditioning

It was pointed out in Chapter 2 (see p. 57) and in Chapter 5 (see p. 151) that conditioning is one method of learning. It consists essentially in the attachment of a response to a new stimulus. This is illustrated when one's mouth "waters" at the sight of food or when a horse stops in response to the word "whoa." The originally effective stimulus for the reflex action of the salivary glands is food in the mouth. Eventually, this response becomes attached to new stimuli such as the sight of food, the smell of food, and even the thought of food. In a similar way the horse learns to make the response to "whoa" that he originally made to a pull on the bit. This kind of learning is called *conditioning*.

The procedure of conditioning is illustrated in the classic experiment of the Russian physiologist Pavlov (39) on the conditioned salivary reflex in the dog. In this experiment a dog was trained to stand quietly in an experimental set-up which permitted an experimenter to measure the number of drops of saliva secreted and to control the stimuli used in conditioning the animal. The *unconditioned* or naturally effective stimulus for the salivary response was food. The new stimulus — new only in the sense that it did not at the outset of the experiment arouse a salivary secretion — was the sound of a bell. The bell did arouse other such responses as pricking up the ears or tension in the neck and leg muscles. With the dog in position and awaiting food, the bell was sounded slightly before the food appeared. The bell and food were presented in this way a number of times, after which it was discovered that the sound of the bell alone produced the salivary secretion. The stimulus-response connections present before and after the conditioning are represented as follows:

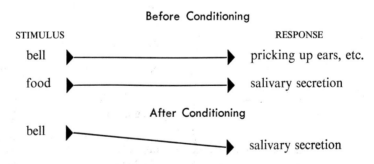

Before Conditioning

STIMULUS   RESPONSE

bell ▶——————————————————▶ pricking up ears, etc.

food ▶——————————————————▶ salivary secretion

After Conditioning

bell ▶——————————————————▶ salivary secretion

It will be noted that whereas before conditioning there was no connection between bell and salivary secretion, after conditioning there was a sufficient connection for the bell to arouse the salivary response

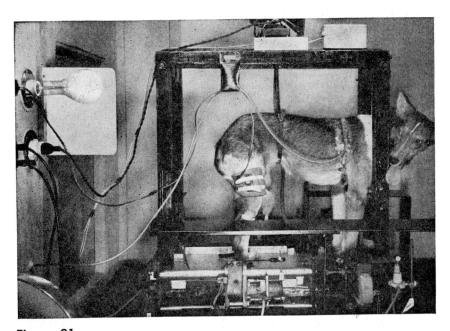

Figure 31

Experimental Set-up for Conditioning the Foot-Withdrawal
Reflex in a Dog to the Sound of a Tone

(From W. N. Kellogg, R. C. Davis, and V. B. Scott, "Refinements in Technique for the
Conditioning of Motor Reflexes in Dogs," *J. Exp. Psychol.*, 1939, 24, 318–331.)

without the appearance of food. The bell is now called a *conditioned
stimulus*, and the response to it is a *conditioned response*. Thus a conditioned response is one which is aroused by a stimulus which was
originally inadequate to produce it.

The conditioning of a very wide variety of human and animal responses has been demonstrated in psychological experiments. An
experimental set-up for conditioning the foot-withdrawal response in
a dog to the sound of a tone is shown in Figure 31. A similar set-up
was used by Liddell and Anderson (29) in studying certain characteristics of a conditioned leg-withdrawal response in sheep. Human responses which have been conditioned experimentally include the wink
reflex, the salivary reflex, finger-withdrawal to pain, breathing reactions, psychogalvanic reflex, sucking response in infants, and emotional
reactions. These responses have been conditioned to a wide variety of
extraneous stimuli.

Many examples of conditioning can be found in everyday life. A youngster learns to dislike orange juice after a few doses of a mixture of castor oil and orange juice.   In one case the emotional shock of a severe arm burn from hot coffee became attached to water and other liquids.   One three-year-old boy displayed intense fear of his barber after a very painful session in a physician's office with a man dressed in white and wielding shiny instruments.   If a child hears someone say "no-no" just as he touches something hot, he may become conditioned by that one presentation of the unconditioned stimulus (pain) and the conditioned stimulus ("no-no") to make a withdrawing response to the sound "no-no."   A teacher displays a card with the word "boy" printed on it and says to her first-grade pupils, "Say 'boy'." Obediently, the children say "boy."   After a number of repetitions, the children (the brighter ones, at least) will say "boy" at the sight of the card alone.

In order to establish a conditioned response it is necessary (1) that the conditioned and unconditioned stimuli be presented together or in close succession, (2) that the stimuli be repeated a number of times (in rare instances a single presentation may be sufficient), (3) that the subject be alert and attentive, and (4) that the conditioning situation be free of distractions.   Learning occurs if the conditioned and unconditioned stimuli are presented simultaneously, but it appears that the best learning occurs if the conditioned stimulus precedes the unconditioned by a short interval.   In one experiment the optimal interval was .5 second (52).   The number of repetitions of the conditioned and unconditioned stimuli necessary for learning depends upon the age and intelligence of the subject, the nature of the response, and the degree of freedom from distracting influences.   Mateer (34) found in conditioning children to make a swallowing response to a blindfold that some children required as many as eighteen and some as few as three trials. The younger children and the mentally defective children in the group required more trials on the average than the older and normal children.

Generalization. Much of the experimental work on conditioning has been concerned with specific aspects of the conditioning process. One of these is the phenomenon of generalization.   In its early stages, the conditioned response, commonly abbreviated as CR, is aroused by any one of a number of stimuli in the same sense field.   For example, if a dog is conditioned to make a salivary response to a bell, he will tend to make the response to any bell, not just the one used in the conditioning process.   This phenomenon has been demonstrated experimentally by a number of investigators.   Bass and Hull (1) conditioned the psychogalvanic reflex (see p. 329) to a vibrotactile stimulus applied to the shoulder.   After the CR was established, it was found that application of the stimulus to the back, the legs, or other parts of the body would elicit the psychogalvanic reflex.   There was, however, a decrease in the strength of the reflex with an increase in the distance of the point of stimulation from the shoulder.   In everyday terms this phenomenon may be described as the tendency for a response to spread to stimuli that are somewhat like the one to which the response is being established.   A baby, for example, learns to say "daddy" on seeing his father.   For a time thereafter he calls any man "daddy."   Or a child who has been frightened by a dog will be afraid of any dog.

Differential conditioning.   In differential conditioning an animal is conditioned to make a response to a certain stimulus — tone of a certain pitch, for example.   In the early stages, the CR, as indicated above, is elicited by other tones.   If, however, the conditioning is carried further, and other tones are presented without the unconditioned stimulus being present, the animal will stop responding to the other tones.   Since the animal has learned to make the CR to one tone and not to the others, it is assumed that he perceives this tone to be different from the others (36).   Differential conditioning is a convenient technique for investigating certain behavior in animals and young children that cannot be investigated by the verbal report method.   It is possible by this method to determine an animal's or a child's ability to discriminate between sounds, colors, or other stimuli.

Experimental extinction.   Some of the experiments on conditioning have revealed that the continued application of the conditioned stimulus without the unconditioned stimulus (bell without food), after the conditioned response has been established, results in the disappearance of the conditioned response (salivary response to the bell).   The animal learns not to salivate to the sound of the bell, and he does so as a consequence of hearing the bell over and over when no food is present.   This phenomenon in conditioning is known as *experimental extinction.*   The extinction is not permanent, however;   after a rest period of a day or so, or even a year, the CR reappears, although with less strength.   That it is not completely eliminated can also be demonstrated by again presenting the conditioned and unconditioned stimuli together;   it will be found that fewer trials are needed for reestablishing the extinguished CR than were needed in the original conditioning.   That extinction is due to inhibition is suggested by the fact that the extinguished CR may be reinstated by introducing a new conditioned stimulus.   Such a stimulus appears to inhibit the inhibition which is responsible for the extinction of the CR, thus permitting it to reappear.   This phenomenon is referred to as *disinhibition.*

Reconditioning. A number of experimenters have shown that it is possible to eliminate a CR by conditioning the organism to make a new or substitute response to the conditioned stimulus. For example, in an experiment by Jones (22) a small boy was conditioned to make a fear response to a rabbit. He was then conditioned to make a positive or approach reaction to the rabbit. To do this it was necessary to find a stimulus situation which would arouse a positive response. Food and eating were selected for this purpose. While the child was eating, the rabbit was brought just inside the room where the child could see it. On subsequent occasions the rabbit was brought closer and closer until it was placed beside the food. The boy showed no signs of the original fear. Instead he made the same generally positive reaction to the rabbit that he had been making to the food. In this case the fear reaction was eliminated by building up a positive response to the fear-provoking stimulus. Since the two responses, fear and approach, are antagonistic, they cannot both be elicited by the same stimulus. This process is called *reconditioning*. The role of conditioning and reconditioning in emotional development will be discussed further in Chapter 9.

Secondary conditioning. After a CR has been established it is possible to condition it again, this time to still another neutral stimulus. For example, a human subject is conditioned to withdraw the hand to the sound of a bell. Shock is used as the originally effective stimulus. The bell is the conditioned stimulus. After the CR is established, a light is presented with the bell but without the shock. After a number of times, the light will evoke the withdrawing response. In the original conditioning the bell became substituted for or associated with the shock. In the secondary conditioning the light became substituted for the bell. This substitution of one stimulus for a previously conditioned one can go on and on until a whole series of conditioned responses is built up, each one upon the preceding one. The student may wish to cite some examples of this kind of learning from everyday life.

Hull's principle of secondary reinforcement. One explanation of why a neutral stimulus comes to elicit a response which it did not at first elicit is offered by Hull (19) in his principle of secondary reinforcement. This principle was described in the preceding chapter in connection with the problem of acquiring motives (see p. 152). According to Hull, a response or mode of behavior aroused by a drive is strengthened or reinforced when it leads to the reduction of the need that gave rise to the drive, and any stimulus which is closely associated with the need reduction is also reinforced to some degree. Thus in Pavlov's experiment the fact that the bell elicited the salivary response would

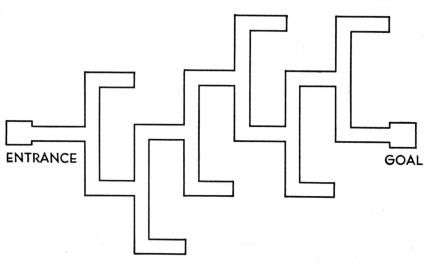

Figure 32

Floor Plan of a Maze Used in Studying Learning in White Rats

be due to the secondary reinforcement it had gained in its earlier association with food and the need reduction resulting from eating. Its eventual extinction on being presented alone would be due to its continued lack of reinforcement by food.

Trial and Error Learning

In conditioned learning a subject (human or animal) is placed in a controlled situation which does not permit him to respond in any other than a certain prescribed way. In experimental conditioning, the subject is harnessed into place with recording apparatus attached. Distractions are removed, and all stimuli except the conditioned and the unconditioned are held constant so far as possible. The experimenter knows that the unconditioned stimulus will elicit the one response that is to be conditioned. In contrast to this kind of set-up let us suppose that a hungry rat is placed at the entrance of a maze like the one diagramed in Figure 32. Since he hasn't been in this situation before, he doesn't know how to get to the food box at the opposite end of the maze. Since there are a great many pathways in the maze, some of which are blind, he can make a number of responses, some of which take him toward the goal, while others do not. His behavior is controlled in that it is confined to the maze, but not so rigidly controlled as it would be in conditioning.

What does a rat do in a situation of this sort? He runs here and there, into a blind alley and out again and in again, into another blind alley and out again, back to the entrance; and finally, after stopping many times and making many mistakes, he reaches the food box. He has made a large number of errors and has taken several minutes to reach a goal that is seconds away to an animal that knows the correct pathway. On subsequent trials, however, the rat will make fewer and fewer errors and take less and less time, until, after a large number of trials, he is able to take the correct pathway to the food box without error and in a matter of a few seconds. Figure 33 shows the time required on each of fifteen trials by a white rat in learning a maze like the one diagramed in Figure 32.

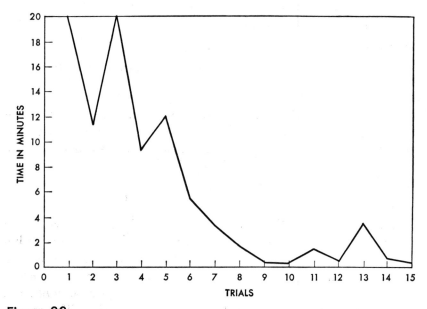

Figure 33

A Curve Showing the Time Required per Trial by a White Rat
in Learning to Run a Maze

When a rat reaches the point in his learning where no errors occur and where there is no further reduction in the time required to run the maze, it can be said that he has learned the maze. He has done so by the method of trial and error, so called because his behavior, as an observer views it, is characterized by trying and erring. This, however, is not a complete or an adequate description of the learning. A closer examination of the behavior involved in this kind of learning reveals that a number of factors are operative.

(1) The animal is motivated. This may be inferred from the fact that the animal persists in making responses, or from the fact that he has been deprived of food for a period of time.

(2) The animal is placed in a new situation, one that does not permit him to utilize any of his usual methods of satisfying hunger. He is faced with the *problem* of acquiring a new mode of adjustment.

(3) The animal makes a variety of responses, some correct and some incorrect. The criterion of correctness is whether or not the responses take the animal to the goal. This is the characteristic that gives the learning its name, trial and error. In this connection it should be noted that the animal's behavior, while consisting of a variety of responses, is not purely random or aimless. The maze does not permit the animal to make just any kind of response. In addition the animal's motivation determines in some degree the kinds of responses it will make (see p. 139).

(4) On subsequent trials in the maze, incorrect responses decrease and eventually disappear. Correct responses are eventually established. This is the vital aspect of trial and error learning. The animal learns that some responses are incorrect and unnecessary and that other responses take him to the food box. Just exactly how this is accomplished is still a matter of conjecture. Various theories of learning have proposed different explanations of why some responses are learned while others are eliminated. For example, it has been suggested that responses or modes of behavior aroused by a drive are strengthened or reinforced when they lead to need reduction. This is Hull's (19) principle of reinforcement. Since the correct response leads to the satisfaction of hunger, it is reinforced. Responses which do not lead to reward are weakened or extinguished. Stated another way, responses are learned or eliminated depending upon the effects produced by the responses.

(5) With additional practice the correct responses, represented by the several segments of the correct pathway, become integrated into a single, efficient reaction which thereafter is set off when the animal is placed at the entrance to the maze. This integration of responses is one explanation of the continued decrease in time which frequently occurs after all of the errors have been eliminated.

A very great amount of human and animal learning is of this trial and error variety. For example, a blindfolded human subject learns a pencil maze like the one shown in Figure 34 in much the same manner

as an animal learns a maze.   Figure 35 shows the time required per
trial by a college student in learning the pencil maze shown in Figure
34.   Note the general similarity between this learning curve and the
one shown in Figure 33.   Many other instances of human learning show
the same general characteristics.   This is seen in the learning curves
for telegraph sending and receiving shown in Figure 30.   It is seen in
learning curves for learning to recite the alphabet backward, for mirror
drawing, for learning to typewrite, and for learning almost any motor
skill, such as skating, dancing, swimming, or bowling.   Whenever an
organism is motivated in a situation that does not permit the immediate
satisfaction of the motive by any previously established modes of
adjustment, he engages in trial and error behavior to the extent permitted by the situation in which he finds himself (maze, problem box,
or other problem situation).

Vicarious learning.   Almost everyone is familiar with the expression "profiting from the other fellow's experience."   The idea behind
this expression is that we can observe the trying and erring of other
people, that we can see the consequences of such behavior in others, and
that we can in this way get some ideas about what to do or what not to

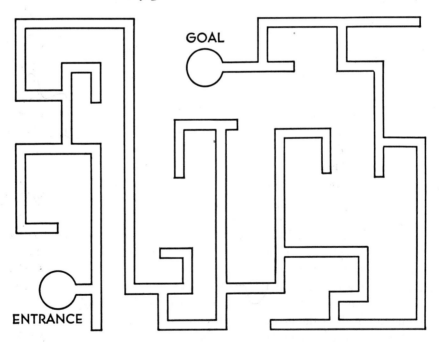

Figure 34

   Diagram of a Pencil Maze Used in Studying Human Learning

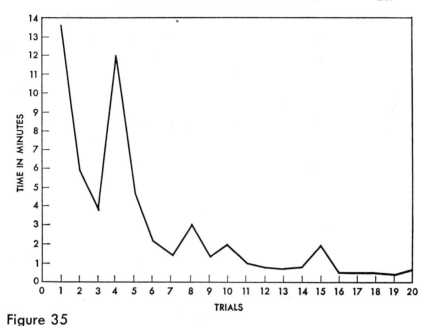

Figure 35

A Curve Showing the Time Required per Trial by a College
Student in Learning a Pencil Maze

do in our own learning. To the extent that we can learn from other
people's experience, either by observing it directly or hearing about
it or reading about it, to that extent we are learning indirectly, as it
were. We are circumventing some of the trial and error that might
otherwise be necessary. Such learning is called *vicarious learning*.
This kind of learning is possible because we develop a system of symbols, language symbols primarily, which stand for or represent the
reactions, experiences, and consequences of behavior. When we are
being taught to swim, we can "remember" what was said or what was
demonstrated long enough to attempt to reproduce it. Such imitating
is in the nature of a delayed reaction. A delayed reaction is possible
because some response, a body set, muscular tension, or verbal response,
is made to the present stimulus situation. This response becomes a
substitute stimulus for the situation so that, at a later time, one can
respond to the original stimulus although it is no longer present (see
p. 344). The most important substitute stimuli for vicarious learning
are language symbols. A child can learn that a given object is a fish,
and he can learn many things about fish without having to take one
in his hands or smell one, and without having to do over all of the
things which man has done in accumulating his knowledge of fish. The

child can do this because he understands the meaning of symbols which stand for many of these direct, manipulative experiences. If all of our learning had to come through direct, manipulative experiences, we would be in a sorry plight indeed.

Insight in Learning

Some learning problems, while permitting a certain amount of trial and error behavior, are of such a nature that some subjects can see relationships in the situation that permit them to solve the problem with little or no trying and erring. For example, Köhler (25), working with chimpanzees, set up a learning problem in which fruit was placed beyond the animal's reach outside the cage. In one case two sticks which could be fitted together were placed inside the cage, but neither stick by itself was long enough to reach the food. One of the animals attacked the problem without success by using one stick, then the other, pushing one stick with the other toward the fruit, and so on. Some time later while playing with the sticks and holding one in each hand he pushed the thinner one into the thicker one. He jumped up immediately, ran to the side of the cage, and used the longer stick to reach the fruit. It appears that the animal on joining the sticks saw the relation between the longer stick and the solution to his problem. This kind of sudden solution of a problem is known as *insight*.

Mechanical puzzles provide a learning problem for human subjects in which this phenomenon has been observed and contrasted with trial and error learning. In an experiment which will be discussed more fully in Chapter 10, Ruger (45) found that human subjects attacked the problems of taking mechanical puzzles apart in a trial and error fashion. However, after a number of trials in which the solutions seemed to be accidental, the subjects would quite suddenly "see" the solution. After this point there was virtually no further trial and error. Figure 36 shows a learning curve for solving a bent nail puzzle. During trials 11 and 12 the subject "got the idea." His performances after trial 12 were fast and uniform in comparison with his performances during the first twelve trials. In some learning problems, the sudden solution of the problem results in a more dramatic drop in the time curve than that shown in Figure 36. The amount of trial and error preceding insight may be large or small, and it may produce a marked improvement or no improvement, depending upon the nature of the learning problem and the age, experience, and intelligence of the learner. The relation of trial and error to insight learning is complicated by the fact that many of the problems which can be solved by

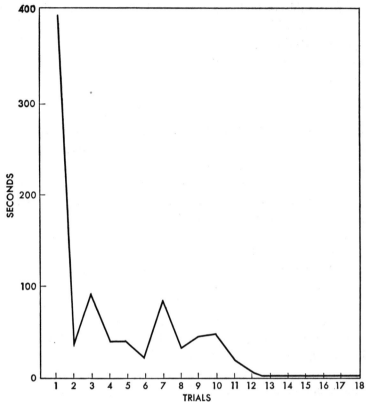

Figure 36

The Learning Curve for Solving a Bent Nail Puzzle

(From John J. B. Morgan, *Psychology*, p. 230. By permission of Rinehart and Company, Inc.)

insight are problems which involve reasoning. This means that the trial and error behavior involved in solving the problem goes on mentally and does not show up as observable trial and error behavior. A further discussion of problem-solving behavior will be found in Chapter 10.

It is entirely logical to suppose that seeing the relationships in a situation, or seeing the principle involved in a learning problem, is a conscious process; that the learner could not learn a principle and act upon it without knowing that he is doing so. In many cases, perhaps in most cases, subjects "get the idea" and know what it is and its relation to the solution to the problem. In some cases, however, subjects appear to act upon a certain principle even though they do not try to learn it and are unaware of its existence. This has been demonstrated in an ingenious experiment by Thorndike and Rock (48). They showed that subjects taking a free-association test and stimulated by a money bonus will learn to give responses which follow a certain principle of selection, even though the subjects do not try to learn the principle in question and are unaware of its existence after it has been acted upon.

HABITS

Many of the ways of acting which one learns by the methods described above become so well established that they tend to be carried out more or less automatically under the appropriate stimulating conditions. Such well-established ways of acting are called habits.   Much of our daily activity is habitual.   Such acts as walking, talking, dressing, eating, and even ways of thinking and feeling are so well established that they require little or no conscious direction or control.   If we did not relegate such activities to a more or less automatic level, we should be so lost in the details of living that there would be little opportunity for further growth and development.

Usually we think of habits as specific and stereotyped responses, but these characteristics are not necessary.   For example, a person who constantly meets the suggestions of his friends with countersuggestions acts in accordance with a habit, though his countersuggestions, in the very nature of the case, cannot be stereotyped.   Another person may have the habit of doing what others advise.   Obviously, this again cannot be a stereotyped response except in a most abstract sense.

Popular thought — and much psychological writing too — has over-emphasized the importance of repetition in habit formation.   Repetition is only one factor, and usually a minor one, in the formation of habits. Unless some satisfaction is found in acting in a certain way, repetition will not make a habit.   On the contrary, repetition may cause a counter-habit.   Some adults, for example, dislike music because as children they were forced to practice on the piano.   A little girl does not necessarily develop a habit of keeping her playthings neatly arranged, even though her mother requires her day after day to set them in order. To develop the habit, the child must get some satisfaction from the action.   Perhaps parental approval will give her this satisfaction; perhaps a love of order may be awakened in her.   With proper motivation the habit is acquired quickly, but not without.

Some people habitually jerk their heads, pucker their foreheads, make their nostrils tremble, or pull their mouths sideways.   Such activities are called *tics*.   When they are not caused by structural defects, they may properly be called habits.   They are ways the individual has found of relieving some tension.   If such spasmodic movements are prevented by bandages, similar twitchings are apt to break out in other muscles. Though these twitchings occur without conscious direction, they are of mental origin.   Usually they are brought about by some repression or anxiety;   they are ways of escaping from something disagreeable. Psychopathologists, in dealing with such cases, seek to unearth the repression and thereby help the sufferer to find a more satisfactory way of relieving the tension.

Sometimes tics and nervous habits may persist after the tension that gave rise to them has been relieved.   This has been demonstrated in the case of rabbits.   The ear of a rabbit was blistered by means of a chemical, and the rabbit began to scratch the sore ear.   The rabbit continued to scratch the ear, however, after the sore had completely healed (37).   A similar sequence has been observed in children.   They may develop the habit of moistening chapped lips with the tongue and continue the practice after the lips are well.

LEARNING CURVES

A learning curve is a graphic representation of the changes in behavior that occur during successive periods of activity.   To be called learning, the changes in behavior must be in the direction of an improvement in one's performance or an increase in the amount that one knows or can do.   These changes may be indicated in three ways.   First, improvement in performance may be shown by a decrease in the time required to do a specific task, such as reciting the alphabet backward, adding columns of figures, running a pencil maze, and so on.   In these cases the task, whatever it is, represents one trial or practice period. Second, improvement may be indicated by a decrease in the number of errors made in performing a given task, such as running a maze, typing a certain number of pages, or adding a set of numbers on an adding machine.   Third, improvement may be indicated by an increase in the amount accomplished per trial or practice period.   For example, in learning typewriting, improvement would be indicated by the fact that the number of words typed correctly per practice period increased.

A learning curve which represents changes in performance during successive periods of practice expressed in terms of the time required to do a certain task is called a *time curve*.   One that expresses changes in terms of errors is called an *error curve*.   One that expresses changes in terms of the amount accomplished per trial is called an *attainment curve*.   The curves in Figures 33, 35, and 36 are time curves.   The curve in Figure 30 is an attainment curve.   Error curves have the same general characteristics as time curves. It will be noted that the numerical values for time, errors, and accomplishment are plotted on the vertical axis of each graph, while trials or practice periods are plotted on the horizontal axis. A trial or a practice period may be a fixed amount of time or a fixed amount of work. For example, the practice period may be a thirty-minute period of practice per day, or it may be a task, such as typing one hundred lines or shooting twenty-five arrows.

Characteristics of Learning Curves

Since learning is a function of such P and E variables as age, experience, physical condition, maturation, ability, motivation, the method of learning, the difficulty of the task, and the nature of the learning situation, the curves which are used to depict this learning show a wide variety of characteristics. Some curves are characterized by the fact that the rate of learning decreases as additional trials are given. In other curves the rate of change may increase, or it may remain relatively constant throughout the learning period. Some curves are characterized by periods during which no improvement takes place. Most curves show fluctuations in performance from trial to trial, a fact that is evident in Figures 33 and 35. Let us examine some of these characteristics.

Negative and positive acceleration. An examination of the learning curves shown in Figures 33 and 35 reveals that there is a rapid decrease in time during the first few trials. As additional trials are made, however, the decrease in time from trial to trial becomes less and less until there is no further improvement. A curve in which the increments of change are relatively large in the early trials and become smaller and smaller as practice continues is described as a *negatively accelerated* curve.

Many of the learning curves obtained in studies of human learning are negatively accelerated, but there are some curves in which the rate of learning increases as additional practice periods are given, at least for a limited number of trials. A curve of this sort in which the increments of change are small during the early trials and become larger as practice continues is described as a *positively accelerated* curve. It has been suggested that a complete learning curve, one that would be obtained if the learning problem were so new that the learner could not bring any previous experience to bear on it, would be an S-shaped curve (50). An S-shaped curve (see Figure 37) is one in which the increments of change are small at the outset, become larger and larger, and then shift and become smaller and smaller. The first half of such a curve is positively accelerated while the last half is negatively acceler-

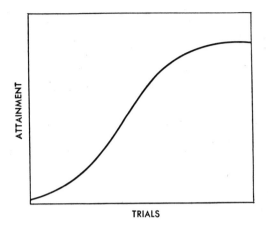

TRIALS

Figure 37

An S-shaped Curve

It has been suggested that a complete learning curve would
be an S-shaped curve.

ated.   If a complete learning curve is S-shaped, the fact that many
learning curves are negatively accelerated would be due to the fact
that the learning depicted in these curves starts at an advanced stage.
For example, in learning typewriting one starts somewhere above zero
because he has already learned to read and to make coordinated finger,
hand, and eye movements.

Plateaus.   An examination of the learning curve for telegraph
receiving in Figure 30 shows that there was a period in the learning
during which there was very little or no improvement.   This period
of no progress shows up in the learning curve as a relatively level place
between the sixteenth and twenty-fourth week of practice.   That this
is a temporary halt in the progress of learning is indicated by the fact
that the curve continues to rise after the twenty-fourth week.   Such a
temporary halt in the progress of learning is known as a *plateau,* so
named because it shows up as a level place in a learning curve.   Plateaus
occur in some learning curves and not in others.   It is interesting to
note, for example, that the telegraph-sending curve in Figure 30 has
no plateau, while the telegraph-receiving curve has one.

Many theories have been advanced to explain the plateau and to
eliminate it.   When the plateau appears, it causes still further retardation; for whatever may have been its original cause, its effect is to
discourage the learner by necessitating humdrum repetition and preventing steady advance.   Thus it stimulates factors which prolong it.

Discouragement may be responsible for the plateau in the first place. This is very likely to be true when one embarks upon a learning task, such as learning to play a musical instrument, with a high degree of enthusiasm that is due to such temporary conditions as the novelty of the task and the expectation of quick rewards. As the novelty wears off and as it becomes increasingly clear that the expected rewards are not immediately forthcoming, the learner loses his high enthusiasm and relaxes his efforts.

One important characteristic of the plateau is that it is found much more frequently in complex than in simple skills. Batson (2) has reported experiments which tend to show that in complex skill, where improvement cannot be observed until several specific skills are mastered, the plateau appears while these component skills are being mastered. Thus in telegraphy one will show improvement while he is learning the individual letters; but having learned them, he must practice a long time without apparent improvement while he learns the word and phrase units. If one is aware of this fact, he is not so likely to "let down" when a plateau in his learning is reached; for he will realize that improvement is still taking place, even though it does not show in the objective performance.

Plateaus frequently occur at the place in learning where the learner finds that further improvement is limited with the method or methods he is now using. His progress is halted while he is changing methods or developing a new mode of attack on the problem. The older method tends to interfere with the efforts to develop a new method. If one tries to shift from the habit of throwing a straight ball in bowling to the development of a habit of throwing a hook or a curve, he will go through a period during which he will not only fail to show any improvement, but may actually revert to a lower level of proficiency while the new method is being perfected.

Physiological limits. With some kinds of learning problems and under conditions of high motivation a learner may reach a point in his learning where no further improvement is possible regardless of how long he continues to practice. This point in one's learning is known as a *physiological limit.* If it is reached in learning a given task, it will show up as a level place in the curve during the last part of the learning period. The level place in the curve in Figure 36 which starts after trial twelve very probably represents the learner's physiological limit. It is a limit which is imposed upon one's performance by the characteristics of the bodily mechanisms which are involved in the learning activity. No amount of practice will enable an individual to run a distance of one hundred yards in five seconds, or throw a baseball three hundred yards, or type five hundred words a minute, or run a pencil maze in a tenth of a second, or recite the alphabet in a hundredth of a second. A certain amount of time is required to arouse a receptor. Still more time is necessary for the transmission of nerve impulses through the nervous system to the reacting mechanisms. The degree of one's muscular strength and neuromuscular maturity imposes further limits.

Most of us rarely reach or even approach our physiological limits in most of the things we learn. We learned to add many years ago but our level of performance at the moment is far below the limits imposed by neuromuscular equipment. Our explanation of this fact is that improvement becomes increasingly difficult in time and effort as we approach the physiological limit. This in turn affects motivation. In addition we reach a level of proficiency which, though it may be far short of a physiological limit, is entirely adequate for all ordinary purposes. Further improvement, while it is still possible, is in many cases impractical.

ECONOMICAL LEARNING

How can skills, like dancing or tennis, or an understanding of a subject, like a knowledge of economics, be acquired with the least expenditure of time and energy? Though the methods of acquiring a skill are, in some respects, different from those employed in acquiring mastery of a subject, they have much in common. In considering the methods of economical learning, we shall consider first the principles that are common to both kinds of learning.

Motivation

That the person who is motivated works at a higher level of intensity and learns more rapidly than the indifferent one has been well shown by Book and Norvell (5). They directed two groups, one experimental and one control, to learn a code, to multiply figures mentally, and to perform other simple tasks. The members of the experimental group were asked to watch the records of their progress and to attempt, at each practice period, to make a high score. The members of the control group, on the other hand, were not informed of their progress. The experimental group showed greater improvement than the control group in accuracy and speed. When the conditions were reversed, however, the control group being given the incentive and the experimental group deprived of it, the former suddenly spurted ahead, while

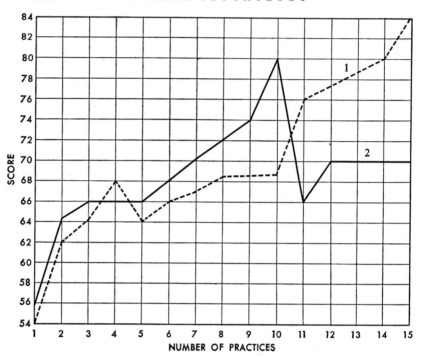

Figure 38

How Knowledge of Results Affects Performance in
Mental Multiplication

Until the tenth practice the group represented by the solid line was kept informed of results, the dotted-line group working in the dark. On the eleventh practice the conditions were reversed. Note the immediate change in accomplishment. (From W. F. Book and L. Norvell, "The Will to Learn," *Ped. Sem.*, 1922, 29, 305–62.)

the latter's gain declined rapidly. The results of this study are shown graphically in Figure 38.

Similar results were reported by Panlasigui and Knight (38), who found that sixth-grade children studying arithmetic over a period of weeks showed definitely greater progress when told of their achievement than when not told. It was also observed that knowledge of results was a more powerful motivating factor with good than with poor pupils. The maxim "Nothing succeeds like success" is sound pedagogy. Adults also improve when they are stimulated to put forth more effort, as when given a bonus for excellent or rapid work (24).

Experiments on animals show similar results. A motivated rat or dog learns faster than one not motivated. The hungry rat, as we have already seen (p. 147), learns faster than the well-fed one. When punished for false moves and rewarded for successful ones, rats learn faster than when one motive only is used.

Maturation

Effective and economical learning is dependent upon the organism's having attained an optimal degree of maturity. Experiments have shown (see p. 70) that a relatively small amount of practice at a later stage of maturity is as effective in acquiring such habits as walking and stair-climbing as a much longer period of practice at an earlier age. A baby, if encouraged by its parents, may learn to walk a little earlier than otherwise; but were the parents to wait a week, the baby would walk by itself. Similarly, a child of seven may memorize the multiplication table, but it will be easier for him at eight. We mature gradually, and not until we are in our late teens do we attain full capacity to learn.

Physical Condition

An appropriate physical condition facilitates learning. It is a mistake to make oneself too comfortable when studying, for complete physical relaxation is more favorable for sleeping than for learning. This is shown by the experiment of Elliott and Treat, proving that hungry rats learn more readily than those that are not hungry, and the experiment of Wada, indicating that human subjects when hungry do better on intelligence tests than when not hungry (see p. 147). Further evidence of this fact is provided by an investigation by Bills (3), who found that subjects who toned up their muscles by mildly squeezing some object learned more rapidly than those who did not. Too much pressure was, of course, found undesirable. In general, a certain amount of physical tension rather than complete bodily relaxation is recommended for efficient learning.

Spaced vs. Unspaced Practice

Spaced periods of practice are more economical than unspaced periods. This means that if you have to learn an assignment, it will be better to study it a short time on several days than to attempt to learn it at one sitting. The advantage of distributed periods of study is shown in Figure 39. Though the children in this experiment had the same actual amounts of practice, those who distributed their learning surpassed in achievement the ones whose learning was more concentrated.

The explanation of the advantage of distributed periods of study over undistributed periods is that a mental process, once started, continues

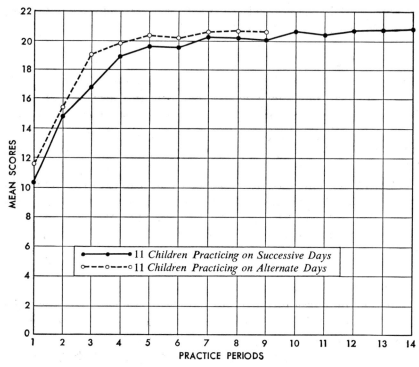

Figure 39

The Effect upon Learning of Spaced Practice Periods

Spaced practices are in general more economical than unspaced practices. (After Kirkwood, from Joseph Peterson, "Learning in Children," in *Handbook of Child Psychology*, edited by Carl Murchison, Clark University Press, 1931, p. 351.)

even though our attention is directed to other things. This is especially true if the final goal has not been attained. This has been made clear by an experiment of Lewin (28). Lewin gave a group of learners various tasks. Some he interrupted before they had finished; others were permitted to complete the work. Those who were interrupted remembered a great deal more than those who were permitted to finish. These results show that once we accept a task, there persists a state of mental tension until it is finished; whereas when a task is finished, we mark it "finished" and proceed to forget it. When periods of study are distributed, mental tension persists between them; we learn not only during the periods of study, but also during the intervals. Moreover, the interval between study periods gives an opportunity for growth. By approaching a task after an interval, we approach it with a new mental background and thus can increase the number of associations we make between the new and what we already know. In this way, the process of assimilation is hastened. Finally, a period of rest between periods of learning prevents fatigue.

Though it is well known that short study or practice periods are more efficient than long periods, there is a period for optimum efficiency, and there is just as much danger in making study periods too short as in making them too long. The student who puts aside his studies when the first discomfort or fatigue appears does little to develop mental stamina, or even to get his second wind. Experiments show that we learn more readily by distributing our periods of study; they do not show that a person interested in improving his efficiency should never work when fatigued.

As might be expected, different skills have different optimum periods of practice. In general, the less fatiguing the task and the greater the interest in it, the longer may be the period of practice or learning without loss of efficiency. For drill in adding numbers, Reed (42) states that for average subjects the optimum period is from ten to twenty minutes, and that either of these periods gives more efficient results than work periods of one hour. Obviously, however, it would not be wise to study assignments in history for such short periods.

Duration of Rest Periods

The optimum duration for the rest between work periods has also been studied experimentally. McClatchy (30) found that the optimum varies with the amount of learning which has already taken place. Shorter rest periods are advised early in the learning process and longer periods later.

Plateaus in learning can be greatly reduced by a proper distribution of work and rest periods. The chief value of the rest periods, according to Wheeler (51), is that they give the subject time to assimilate thoroughly what has been learned. They also prevent fatigue and lack of interest. An important part of the science of teaching is to determine the optimum work period for various subjects and various pupils, so as to have all work done under the conditions of greatest efficiency.

The foregoing methods of economical learning apply to acquiring both skill and understanding; the two following methods are especially applicable to acquiring understanding and information.

Whole vs. Part Learning

Organize the material to be learned into large units and study it as a whole. By so doing you reduce the material to a few meaningful units, each one of which is as easily learned as its component parts would be if taken separately.   For instance, it is as easy to learn the names of half a dozen familiar cities as it is six letters taken at random, though each of the names may contain six or more letters.

The reader may readily discover for himself the value of grouping material into meaningful wholes by memorizing the following lists of words:

niv	fox	sun
feb	book	warm
paz	sour	sand
yoz	kin	wave
lak	hat	boy
zig	glove	call
muc	paper	beach
boc	more	water
qib	list	dive

The first list of words (nonsense syllables) cannot be grasped as a meaningful whole.   The second has much more meaning.   The third creates a meaningful picture which can be comprehended as a whole and is, therefore, still more readily memorized.

By learning things as wholes, we better understand the meaning of the material and, in consequence, see how the different parts fit into a general plan.   We also avoid the labor of fitting together, in a separate operation, parts which have been learned independently of one another.

A disturbing factor in learning an assignment as a whole is the possible loss of confidence.   This can be guarded against, however, if the learner realizes that he should not expect to recall the material perfectly with the first few readings.   In practice, a modification of this method is usually advisable.   No long assignment is equally difficult throughout for everyone.   Since some parts are easier than others, it is a waste of time to study all parts equally.   The sections which are most difficult should be given extra study with each reading.   Moreover, the student should keep in mind that by wholes we mean logical wholes.   A whole is not necessarily a whole assignment.   There may be in one lesson two or more logically complete systems of ideas.   Each of these constitutes a whole.   Also, in applying this method, the student should recognize that what one person may grasp as a whole, or comprehend as a meaningful unit, may be beyond the comprehension of another.   The size of the wholes that can be grasped varies with intelligence and experience.   Our principle therefore should be: Organize as much material as possible into a logical whole.

Recitation vs. Reading

Active recitation makes for economical learning. This means that more can be learned in a given study period if part of the time is spent in reciting, or in trying to recite, than if all the time is used in reading. The amount of time that should be devoted to reciting varies with the material. If it is easy and meaningful, little time need be so spent; but if the material is difficult and has little meaning, more time should be given to recitation. This has been demonstrated by Gates (16), who gave to a group of subjects some easy biographical material and a list of nonsense syllables to study for nine minutes. Table IX gives the results.

Table IX

How Learning Is Improved by Devoting Part of Study Time to Recitation (16)

DIVISION OF STUDY TIME	SIXTEEN NONSENSE SYLLABLES ★ % Remembered		FIVE SHORT BIOGRAPHIES (totaling about 170 words) ★ % Remembered	
	Immediately	After 4 hrs.	Immediately	After 4 hrs.
All time devoted to reading	35	15	35	16
$\frac{1}{5}$ of time devoted to recitation	50	26	37	19
$\frac{2}{5}$ of time devoted to recitation	54	28	41	25
$\frac{3}{5}$ of time devoted to recitation	57	37	42	26
$\frac{4}{5}$ of time devoted to recitation	74	48	42	26

The greater efficiency of active recitation over more or less passive reading is probably due, in part, to making the study more stimulating and strenuous. To know that one is going to recite does much to prevent passive reading. We are apt to acquire the habit of holding our books before our eyes as if our minds were photographic plates. Anything that can prevent such an attitude is helpful. Furthermore, active recitation makes the study more satisfying. We like to see what we have accomplished. As we discover that we are mastering the assignment, our interest grows; with each sign of progress, we experience a feeling of satisfaction. In this private active recitation we also are practicing what we are preparing to do, since we study our lessons with the idea of eventually reciting them. Finally, active recitation encourages us to look at the material from various angles, and hence we make many associations which will help us to recall the material when it is asked for. Many students after practically committing an assignment to memory have failed to recite well because they did not make the right associations between the material and the questions of the instructor.

The importance of sound habits and methods of studying has been clearly shown by Wrenn and McKeown (53). At Stanford University these men found that of 220 students who were equal on intelligence tests and who were paired in their major studies, 110 were in the highest 10 per cent of the university with respect to scholarship and 110 were in the lowest 20 per cent. Since the difference in scholastic standing was not caused by differences in intelligence or in major subjects, it seemed probable that the two groups employed different methods of studying. When questionnaires were submitted to them, it was found, as expected, that their habits of studying, their methods of taking notes, and their attitudes on examinations differed significantly. The results of this investigation have been embodied in a convenient test which makes it possible for a student to learn whether he is studying as the best or as the poorest students do.

THE TRANSFER OF TRAINING

Does acquiring one skill make it easier to learn another? Does knowing how to swim help one in learning to shoot baskets? Or does a knowledge of Latin help in learning bookkeeping? Fifty years ago, the theory of transfer of training from one skill or mental operation to another was widely accepted. Students were universally required to study Latin, Greek, and mathematics on the ground that training in these subjects improved memory and reasoning. The practice was called formal discipline. It was believed that if a student of Latin later became an insurance salesman, he would be able to memorize premium rates and scales more easily because of his training in memorizing conjugations and declensions, and that in business generally he would be able to exercise better commercial judgment because his "power of reasoning" had been improved by higher mathematics.

Thorndike's Experiments

It is now known that little, if any, of this kind of transfer occurs. The first doubt arose from an extended and important series of experiments conducted by Thorndike and Woodworth (49) about fifty years ago. They trained subjects in a number of simple mental tasks, such as estimating areas and lengths, and they measured the improvement which such training produced in the performance of other simple tasks which had not been practiced. Their experiments showed little, if any, improvement in the unpracticed tasks. Thorndike later investigated, in another series of experiments, the effect of subjects actually studied in school. In this work he measured the general transfer effect of a number of studies. He considered not only those which were traditionally supposed to have great transfer effects, such as Latin and mathematics, but also those which were commonly thought to have little general value, such as typewriting and bookkeeping. These experiments were epoch-making. Quoting from Garrett's (15, p. 140) summary of this work:

> Mathematics, including bookkeeping and arithmetic, proved to have the greatest training effect, with general science, physics, and chemistry close seconds. Latin was inferior to mathematics and science, about equal to French, and superior to economics, sewing, stenography, manual training, and dramatic art. In general, these last-named subjects showed negative transfer — a loss in final score rather than a gain. The traditional view that Latin is the subject *par excellence* for training one to reason or think is hardly borne out by these findings.

Thorndike (47, p. 98) writes as follows in summary of his own work:

> The expectation of any large difference in general improvement of the mind from one study rather than another seems doomed to disappointment. The chief reason why good thinkers seem superficially to have been made such by having taken certain school studies is that good thinkers have taken such studies, becoming better by the inherent tendency of the good to gain more than the poor from any study. When the good thinkers studied Greek and Latin, these studies seemed to make good thinking. . . . If the abler pupils should all study Physical Education and Dramatic Art, these subjects would seem to make good thinkers.

Scores of experimental studies have been carried on in this field since the pioneer work of Thorndike. Examples which may be cited are the studies of Gates and Van Alstyne (17), which showed that there is little transfer from one type of reading to another, and of Rice (43), which showed practically no transfer in eye-hand coordination from one task to another. A conclusion somewhat opposed to the view of Thorndike is that of Brooks (7), who found only a slight relation between amount of transfer and general intelligence.

The Concept of Identical Elements

These studies, although largely negative in their results, nevertheless indicate that in some cases there is a real, though usually a small, transfer of training from one subject to another. The explanation of such transfer, when it exists, may be found in the elements or methods of study which are common to both subjects. If one acquires certain multiplication facts while learning long division, these facts will be available when needed later in the study of square roots. A transfer of ability from long division to finding square roots will take place because of the element common to both subjects. We speak of this type of transfer as due to *identical elements*. In a similar manner, if while studying Latin one learns certain methods of committing conjugations to memory, he will no doubt find the same methods helpful in learning French and Spanish. Methods of study often have transfer value, particularly in relation to subjects of a similar nature, such as the various foreign languages. We conclude from these studies that transfer between two subjects takes place to the extent that the subjects either contain identical elements or are susceptible of efficient learning by common methods of study.

These two general principles — identical elements and identical methods — account for the cumulative effect of learning, for the fact that the more we know, the easier it is to learn related things (33). Knowing how to play five hundred is a help in learning to play contract bridge. The knowledge of mathematics makes easier the mastery of chemistry and physics. After a person has taken a few courses in a subject, he finds others in the same subject easier. The information and understanding already acquired serve as grappling hooks to seize the new and to make it intelligible. Similarly, in motor skills, the muscular control acquired in one field is extended to new ones.

Since what we know aids us in acquiring additional knowledge, it should be possible to control the order of one's experience so that learning can proceed with the minimum of effort. To do this should be a guiding principle in arranging the school curriculum. Presenting a subject so that one division of its study paves the way for another has been called *pacing*. The value of such pacing rests upon the transfer of identical elements in what is learned, as well as upon the maturation of the individual. Pacing is described by Wheeler (51, p. 115) as follows:

> We shall think of pacing as gradually giving the child more and more complex tasks to perform as he grows and matures. The increase in difficulty of problems should not at any time be faster than the child's rate of maturation, otherwise repeated failures lead the child to develop undesirable habits of work and unhealthy emotional attitudes. Once he masters a task of a given difficulty he should not be presented with an-

other and more difficult task until a recess period has elapsed during which he may have a time to grow to the more difficult situation.

Another type of transfer of training that is found in certain cases is *negative transfer*. This occurs when practice in one skill diminishes one's ability in another. After extensive practice in crossing out each letter *e* which appears on a printed page, one will be less skillful in crossing out some other letter than if he had had no practice at all. In general, skills which may interfere with each other involve negative transfer.

MEMORY

Memory and learning are closely akin. There can be no learning without memory. That learning takes place at all is due to the fact that some of the changes produced in one practice period are retained or remembered until the next one. If this were not the case one would forever do over in one practice period what he had done during the previous one. The fact that there is continued improvement in learning is evidence of retention. Even if there is only one period or one experience, there is no learning unless some impression or effect remains after the experience has passed. At the same time, learning is the first step in memory. Changes in behavior could not be retained if they were not produced in the first place. Memory is identified with the processes of learning (including memorizing), retention, recall, and recognition. The essential characteristic of memory, however, is retention. To recall or to recognize past experiences is evidence of memory, in fact the most commonly used evidence, but neither is essential to it. Learning may occur and impressions may be retained, but not recalled or recognized. Such impressions may affect our behavior without our being aware of the fact that they are doing so. The emphasis in memory, therefore, is placed on the retention of experience.

RETENTION AND FORGETTING

The final and acid test of any learning is its permanence. Most learning, to be of value, must be available at any time in the future when a situation arises which calls for what has been learned. There would be little point to learning about retention and forgetting if what is learned doesn't last at least until the next quiz is given. To be of maximum value it should last much longer. If it does, it will be available for use in many situations that cannot now be anticipated. But all of us know that much of what we learn is forgotten. We know this general fact so well that we quite habitually take steps to counteract it.

We restore what has been forgotten by reviewing or relearning, or we sometimes wait to do the learning until the last minute before the learning is needed. It should be clear, however, that our control of forgetting could be far more effective if we knew more of the facts about forgetting.

As pointed out in Chapter 1, Ebbinghaus (13) found that the forgetting of nonsense syllables followed a definite pattern. Forgetting occurred very rapidly immediately after the learning, but became less and less rapid as time went on. This fact is evident in his curve of forgetting shown on page 20. This forgetting curve is negatively accelerated, i.e., the rate of forgetting decreases with time. But are we to conclude that forgetting is merely a "fading out" of what has been learned and that this fading is entirely a function of time? The answer is an emphatic no. The Jenkins-Dallenbach (21) experiment cited in Chapter 1 clearly indicates that forgetting is due in part at least to what one does immediately after learning. These investigators showed that forgetting was greater after a period of waking activity than after a period of sleep. The waking activity interfered with the retention of the learned material to a greater extent than did the sleeping activity. Forgetting, therefore, is a function of what goes on between learning and recall.

This is further demonstrated in experiments on retroactive inhibition. In these experiments subjects learn material A and follow this with the learning of material B. They are then asked to recall material A. In an experiment by McGeoch and McDonald (32) subjects learned adjectives as material A. Material B varied in different tests: synonyms of these adjectives, antonyms, unrelated adjectives, nonsense syllables, and three-place numbers. The results showed that more forgetting occurred when the original learning was followed by the learning of material which was similar to the original material. The greatest amount of retroactive inhibition resulted when synonyms were used as the interpolated material (material B); the least when the numbers were used.

That forgetting is influenced by the kind of material learned was demonstrated in the experiment by Newman cited in Chapter 1. Forgetting is slower for meaningful than for nonmeaningful material. This finding has been verified by other investigators. For example, English and Jones (14) found little relationship between memory for meaningful and for nonmeaningful material, the former remaining with the learner much longer than the latter.

Other factors which influence the rate of forgetting are the degree of learning and the method of learning. Something has already been said of the latter in the preceding section.

It should be pointed out that different methods of measuring forgetting yield somewhat different results. The results obtained when recall is used as a measure of retention are not exactly the same as those obtained by the *savings method*. In the savings method, an individual is given the task of relearning the original material. If the material can be relearned in less time or in fewer trials than were required originally, it is inferred that some of the originally learned material has been retained. The saving in time or trials is used as a measure of retention. Measures of forgetting by the recall method are affected by the fact that memories are sometimes distorted in the process of recalling them (see p. 221).

Do We Completely Forget Anything?

It is well known that we retain much that we cannot recall. Frequently students are able to recognize but not to recall answers to questions. This shows that something has been retained. In some cases it can be shown that something has been retained even though it cannot be recalled or recognized. This can be demonstrated by the savings method. For example, if, after a period of time, certain material can be relearned in only 90 per cent as much time as was necessary at first, it is assumed that 10 per cent of the original impression has been retained or remembered, even though one could not consciously recall any of the material before the relearning period.

The relearning method of testing retention, however, cannot be applied to everything that has been learned. If the nature and origin of the original learning are not known, one cannot be given the task of relearning it. For example, a person may have a fear of running water because of some painful childhood experience, the nature and origin of which are unknown. If the experience cannot be recalled and cannot be tested by the relearning method, how can one prove that it has not been completely forgotten? A number of procedures have been developed that show that such experiences have not been completely forgotten. These procedures are based upon the assumption that the recall of some experiences is inhibited or blocked by other activities, by moral restraints, by practical considerations, and the like, and that recall would be possible if one were freed of these inhibitions. Supposedly forgotten incidents may be recalled in exceptional circumstances: in dreams, in the delirium of fever, in somnambulism, in automatic writing, in crystal gazing, in hypnotic states, and in psychoanalysis.

In *automatic writing* a subject is given a pencil and paper. He is then placed so that he can write with ease, but is distracted from the writing when he has once begun. The subject continues, however, unconsciously; and he may write accounts of forgotten experiences, as well as answers to questions which are put to him (44). As an illustration of the use of this method to regain lost memories, we cite the case of a woman who had a great fear of cats, which she was unable to explain. When automatic writing was resorted to, the hand wrote, according to Prince (41, pp. 16, 18):

> I think I know about cats — I can remember myself, a little child, playing on the floor with a kitten, and it began to run about the room and had a fit, I think, and it jumped on me and I was alone, and I screamed and cried and called my mother, but no one came, and I was very much frightened. I do not believe I ever told anyone. It was a white kitten. It ran out of the room and after a bit I went on playing.
>
> There were two windows on the side of the room. The shades were gray, I think, with a border of grapes, or something of that color. The carpet was green or gray, with green figures. There was an old-fashioned sofa between one window and the door which led into the dining-room. A book-case and desk combination, you know. There was a mantel, I think, between the windows. It was the ground floor.

Crystal gazing is another technique used for bringing to mind forgotten experiences. In this method, the subject gazes at a crystal until he objectifies his own mental processes and reports seeing events in the crystal which are really dreamlike occurrences in his own mind. In one case of recall through crystal gazing, also reported by Prince, a young woman was surprised and shocked to see herself smoking a cigarette. The smoking had occurred at a former time, and she had no conscious memory of it (40). This same patient on another occasion lost some money which she was able to find by gazing into the crystal (40).

Hypnosis is a trancelike condition produced by suggestion. It is sometimes spoken of as a form of sleep, and the hypnotizer may so speak of it to his subject, but it is very different from normal sleep. For one thing, the physiological changes, as detected by the methods discussed in Chapter 9, indicate increased tension, the very opposite of normal sleep. Moreover, during hypnosis the patient is extremely suggestible to whatever the hypnotizer may say. If the hypnotizer tells the subject that a cap he is holding is a cat, he will treat it as a cat. If the subject is told that a boil is developing where a piece of paper has been stuck, inflammation may be produced at that spot. Anaesthetic conditions have been produced by hypnosis.   Before the discovery of drugs to produce anaesthesia, surgeons were looking forward to hypnosis as a means of saving their subjects pain.   Hypnosis has been employed in two ways to induce the recall of apparently forgotten experiences.   It may be suggested to a hypnotized person that when he awakes he will be able to recall events that occurred during a certain period.   Or a person, while hypnotized, may be asked to live over certain experiences.   The latter method is used when the physician does not wish the patient to remember the forgotten experiences after returning to his normal state.

An illustration of the second method is found in Morgan's (35, p. 204) account of a young woman suffering severe depression.   Morgan describes as follows what happened when the young woman was hypnotized:

> We suggested to her that she was a girl again, just beginning school, then going through later and later stages.   In all these periods she lived over varying incidents, one after another.   Finally she came to the scene when she was about eleven over which she became very much disturbed.   She was on her way home alone one dark night when she was attacked by a burly man.   She went through the whole scene of fighting off this ruffian, calling wildly for help and finally dropped down on the floor in a stupor.   When she recovered from this stupor she awoke from the hypnosis and had absolutely no memory of having portrayed this scene.   It took much painful endeavor to get her to recall this scene consciously even after we knew of its existence.

Psychoanalysis is one of the best methods of bringing into consciousness forgotten experiences.   This method consists essentially in getting the patient to throw off all moral, practical, and rational inhibitions, and then to talk perfectly freely.   It assumes that just as a man in ordinary conversation will talk of his favorite interests if he is given a chance, so the patient, when encouraged, will talk of such matters of vital interest to him as his fear of a painful event that he has driven from consciousness.   The probable explanation of such revelation is that our mental processes are ordinarily brought to a focus by the requirements of action, and that only relevant elements are admitted into consciousness.   When, however, we free ourselves of all logical, utilitarian, and moral considerations and assume a generally uncritical attitude, many forgotten memories are permitted to come into consciousness.   Psychoanalysis requires much time and patience.   Often one must talk to the analyst daily for weeks or even months before the "censor" is escaped and forgotten memories come into consciousness,

We shall discuss these matters further in our section on dreams (see Chapter 11).

The theory that freeing ourselves of practical considerations enables us to tap forgotten memories applies to automatic writing, crystal gazing, and hypnotism as well as to psychoanalysis. In each case the individual becomes less critical and less well organized. In automatic writing and in crystal gazing, disintegration is clearly induced, and this permits particular bits of the personality to find unimpeded expression. In hypnotism the hypnotizer assumes the control usually exercised by the organized interests and habits of the individual. Under his guidance the subject is directed to the forgotten memories.

Do the foregoing facts warrant the claim that we never completely forget anything? Most psychologists believe they do not, holding it unreasonable to assume that we remember all experiences. They think that if an event cannot be recalled under any of the conditions described, we should consider it completely forgotten. Just as we lose muscular skill through disuse and nervous deterioration, so, for various reasons, we may lose the ability to recall past events or the knowledge which we once had of a subject. There are times when this clearly seems to be the case. When, for example, the brain has suffered from an injury or a disease, a complete loss of memory seems to result. Instances of such amnesia, involving the loss of all knowledge of a language with which the patient had previously been familiar, are reported to have followed severe fever. Regarding such cases Conklin (11, p. 46) writes: "As the material so lost can never by any means be restored to voluntary recall, and as it is never reproducible in dreams, hypnotism, or crystal gazing, the conclusion is inevitable that the impression made in the nervous system has been obliterated."

RECALL

Common sense thinks of memory as the recalling of past experiences. It is the principal way of remembering and a measure of retention. While impressions may be retained and may affect our behavior even though they cannot be recalled, the value of most of our learning depends upon our ability to reinstate what has been learned when it is needed in making adjustments to the environment. Recall refers to the process of reinstating or reproducing what has been learned. It is, therefore, an activity and as such is a response to a stimulating situation. A situation, or some element of it, sets off the response which was established in the original learning trials. Placing a white rat at the entrance to the maze which he has previously learned to run sets

off the learned response. One recalls the names of the months of the
year in response to the stimulus, "Name the months of the year." The
stimulus for recall may be a part, large or small, of the situation in
which the learning occurred; or it may be some part of what was
learned; or it may be quite incidentally related to the original learning.
One's mood, feeling, or posture at the time the learning occurred may
serve at a later time as a stimulus to recall. Any part of the surroundings in which the learning occurred may also serve as a cue to recall.

But any such stimulus may be connected with several previous experiences. The word "day," for example, may be connected with several
past experiences and may, therefore, arouse any one of several associations, "night," "light," "hot," "cold," and so on. Which one of the
several possible responses is most likely to be reinstated? A partial
answer at least is found in a set of laws known as the *secondary laws of
association*.

The Secondary Laws of Association

The four secondary laws of association, *primacy, intensity, frequency,*
and *recency*, may be demonstrated in a class exercise in which a list of
twenty words is read aloud by the instructor. The list is read once,
but the eighth word is pronounced very much louder than the others,
and the twelfth word is repeated five times. After the list has been
read, the students are asked to write the words which they can recall.
Lawshe and Dawson (27) used this exercise in a number of college
classes and tabulated the results for 600 students. The percentage of
students recalling each word in a list of twenty is shown in Table X.

It will be noted that the first three words, the eighth word (pronounced loudly), the twelfth word (repeated five times), and the last
word were recalled most frequently. These results are in accord with
the secondary laws of association, which state that, other things being
equal, the first, the most intense, the most frequent, and the most
recent experience tends to be reinstated most successfully.

The Principle of Association

The secondary laws of association are special instances of the more
general principle of association. This principle is concerned with the
question of why two things or ideas become associated or connected
with each other in the first place. Why do we think of the American
Revolution when we think of Washington? Our first answer, that they
have been frequently thought of together, is correct to a certain extent,
but it is not complete. Why does experiencing two things together

Table X

Per Cent of Students Recalling Each of Twenty Words after One Reading

WORDS	%	WORDS	%
1. jewel	97	11. river	39
2. color	88	12. house	98 *repeate*
3. field	90	13. value	33
4. charm	49	14. watch	48
5. world	45	15. study	61
6. lover	72	16. cheat	58
7. water	74	17. paper	60
8. enemy	97 *emphasis*	18. think	78
9. great	22	19. queen	54
10. spoon	25	20. clear	90

(Table constructed from data in C. H. Lawshe, Jr., and R. I. Dawson, "A Procedure for Demonstrating the Secondary Laws of Association," *J. Educ. Psychol.*, 1947, 37, 248–250.)

cause us to think of one when the other is presented? The explanation is that the two things experienced together constitute a whole, and that when one is subsequently presented to us, we perceive it as a part of the original whole. Washington was first presented to us as a part of the American Revolution; when we think of him, we think of him in this established connection, and consequently we think also of the American Revolution.

There are two ways in which diverse things may be associated so that recalling one leads to the recall of the other. In the first place, the things may, in some way, be similar to each other; in the second place, they may be experienced together in time or space. We commonly group together similar things as members of a single class which itself constitutes a whole. For example, if we are asked to name various kinds of building material, we form in our minds a group or class, *building material*. If someone at some later time mentions a member of this class, we may think of the other members. Sometimes, however, we make associations between opposites — excessive heat may cause us to think of cold; sorrow, of former joys; black, of white — and association between opposites is due, not to similarity in nature, but to contiguity in experience. We have frequently asked whether it is hot or cold, wet or dry, clear or cloudy. The members of each pair have occurred together in our verbal experience many times, and the association has been formed between them in this way.

Subjective Factors Which Influence Recall

In addition to the factors which are inherent in the material to be learned, the methods of learning, and the external learning conditions, all of which may be classified as external factors, there are a number of subjective conditions which influence recall. Some of these conditions may aid recall or may interfere with it. Everyone is familiar with the inhibitory effect of fear upon the recall of well-learned materials. Let us examine the effects of some of these conditions on recall.

Desire to avoid the disagreeable. Common sense recognizes the effect of desire on recall. Lovers know better than to admit forgetfulness as an excuse for not keeping their appointments; they realize that it is unpleasant engagements that are easily forgotten. In general, we are apt to forget experiences that cause pain when remembered. If, for example, recalling a social blunder lowers our self-esteem, we tend to forget it. We thus free ourselves from unpleasant tension. For the same reason, we are apt to forget acts contrary to our moral code, such as being party to a questionable business transaction. The forgetting of unpleasant experiences, however, seems to be a protective device that is made use of as a last resort. According to Henderson (18), we first try to remove the unpleasant character of a disagreeable experience by dwelling upon aspects of the experience which tend to change its nature. Thus, if we have been uncivil to a friend, the memory of our behavior will not be unpleasant if we can convince ourselves that he deserved the kind of treatment we showed him. However, if we fail in our attempt to make a pleasant out of an unpleasant memory, there is a marked tendency to banish from our minds the whole experience.

An excellent, though extreme, illustration of the latter procedure is given by Janet (20) in his description of one of his patients, a young woman of twenty, named Irene. Irene lived in extreme poverty with her mother, who was slowly dying of tuberculosis. For sixty days and nights she attended her mother, at the same time sewing in order to provide them both with food. To make matters worse, her father, who visited them from time to time, quarreled with her because she would not give him money. When at last her mother died, Irene was completely distraught. In an effort to reanimate her mother's body, she tried to make it sit up; but it fell on the floor, and she had to undergo the strain of putting it back on the bed. In her grief she contemplated suicide, and discussed it with the corpse.

A few weeks later, it seemed to Irene that her mother, instead of being dead, was on a journey and would soon return. Irene had no recollection of her extreme suffering in trying to nurse her mother and to provide herself and her mother with food. But the experiences were by no means obliterated; for, from time to time, she would re-enact in detail and with considerable dramatic ability the death scene of her mother and many of the events that preceded it. Yet, on regaining normal consciousness, she would have no recollection of the scenes just enacted.

Shaffer (46) has suggested an interesting theory of repression. Suppose, he says, that a small boy after fleeing from two of his playmates has been caught and beaten. If one of the playmates were named Bishop, this name would subsequently revive a memory of the painful and disgraceful episode. Therefore, the recall of the name "Bishop" would be inhibited in the same way as a person inhibits any painful response, or as a dog that has been conditioned to secrete saliva inhibits the response after a few disappointments. The memory of the disagreeable incident, according to Shaffer's theory, is not driven into the unconscious or into any other region; the recall is simply not made at all.

Emotional states or moods. Our emotional states tend to cause us to recall events or facts in harmony with them. When we have a tender emotion for another, our recalls are different from what they are when we are angry. When a quarrel occurs between friends, the recollections of each regarding the other change. Other moods besides love and anger similarly influence our recollections.

The need of the moment. The need of the moment seems to attract and pull into consciousness memories in line with it. Our recalls are largely determined by the problem that confronts us. This is indicated by the fact that what we remember when taking an examination on psychology is different from what is remembered for a history examination. Our recalls will not be the same when we are confronted with a problem of social relations as they are in the study of a problem in farming. The problem confronting us seems to place in tune with it those memories that are relevant. The related facts seem to be drawn into consciousness as by a magnet.

To put the matter in this way seems to overlook the fact that we are frequently not able to make a desired recall. Students on examinations, for instance, find themselves unable to recall facts that they need and that they are sure they know; speakers forget some of their best illustrations when they are most needed; a person may forget the most familiar name. How can we account for such lapses of memory if the need of the moment draws into consciousness the relevant facts? The fact that memory often lapses goes to show that the determinants of recall are numerous. While the need of the moment is an important, perhaps the most important, cause of recalling one thing rather than another, yet it is not the only one. Emotional states, distraction, lack of proper connections between the confronting problem and the relevant facts — all these may make impossible the recalling of what we really know and need to recall.

Suggestions for Improving Recall

In showing that retention is much broader and more inclusive than recollection, we described various methods (such as hypnosis, automatic writing, crystal gazing, and psychoanalysis) of aiding a person to recall what he seemed unable to bring to consciousness. But these methods are too cumbersome for ordinary problems, though they sometimes accidentally help in the solution of them. A woman, for example, who had lost her key was surprised to discover in writing to her son that she absentmindedly wrote where she had placed it (35). However, to use these methods ordinarily for common matters would be like bringing up a steam shovel to dig a small ditch. As aids in everyday affairs, we make the following suggestions.

(1) Make sure of the initial learning. Inability to recall is frequently due to poor original learning. If, upon being introduced to a stranger, we concentrate our attention on such things as his manner of dress, or perhaps on our own feelings of self-consciousness, it is small wonder that we later find ourselves unable to recall his name. The investigations of Boswell and Foster (6) and of many others confirm the common-sense observation that memory and recall are improved by the intention to retain.

(2) Make numerous associations around the fact to be recalled. Many times we are unable to make the needed recall because there is no connection between the present situation and the material that would be of help to us. In other words, we have the facts, in a sense, but they do not seem relevant, and hence they are not at our command. Thus a student, on being told the answer to a question, is surprised to find that he knew it all the time, but did not know what was wanted. He failed because he had not looked at the facts in the needed way. Our mastery of facts or of a subject consists essentially in viewing them from more and more angles, or in seeing how they may apply to more

and more situations. When we wish to fixate an impression so that we shall be able to recall it, we should consciously seek to relate it to previously learned facts. The importance of this is indicated by an investigation made by Key (23), which showed that material presented in commonplace relations is more easily recalled than material presented in unusual or unique relations. Rote memory, that is, memory of things without reference to their meaning, is one of the least permanent forms of retention.

(3) Cultivate an attitude of confidence. If, for example, you become anxious on approaching a person whose name you know and wish to use, your anxiety tends to block the recall. On the other hand, if you approach a person with confidence, the confidence serves as a helpful suggestion, not wholly unlike the suggestion of a hypnotist, and increases the likelihood of making the recall. Likewise, if a student goes to an examination excessively anxious about the outcome and, instead of suggesting to himself that he can do well, says to himself, "I can't do it," he thus places himself under a handicap.

(4) If you find you are unable to make a desired recall, let the matter drop for the time being. It may come without effort later. As we sometimes find it impossible to solve a problem after getting on the wrong track and therefore put the problem aside in the hope that with a fresh start we shall do better, so, in trying to make a recall, it is sometimes helpful to cease trying for a while and later to make another attempt. When we do so, we are frequently surprised and delighted to find the needed recall flashing into consciousness. Perhaps this is the result of the tension which is produced by an unfinished task and which, as we have previously noted, improves retention and makes learning more efficient.

Errors in Recall

Knowledge of some of the more common sources of error in recall is of considerable value in the improvement of memory.

Pleasant vs. unpleasant experiences. In recalling a given experience, we tend to suppress unpleasant details and to recall pleasant ones. Darwin (12), in order to guard against the tendency to forget objections to his theory, and facts that were difficult to explain in terms of it, made a practice of writing down every suggestion or fact that seemed incompatible with it. As a result, he was able not only to call attention to the weaknesses of his theory and the objections to it, but to answer them in a way that did much to make him famous as a painstaking as well as a brilliant scientist. Knowing his weakness, which is common to everyone, he took effective steps to offset it. The relation of memory to emotional experiences will be discussed more fully in the chapter on emotion (page 333).

Simplification. A second source of error in recall is the tendency to simplify our recollection of the past by making it conform to the commonplace and typical. This has been demonstrated by the work of Wulf and Koffka (54), in which subjects were shown geometrical figures of complex patterns and were asked to reproduce them at stated intervals. It was found that the subjects tended to leave out the distinguishing and difficult features of the figures and to make their drawings symmetrical and more and more like familiar figures.

Carmichael, Hogan, and Walter (10) have shown that this tendency is influenced by giving names to the original figures. In this case the reproduced figures tended to resemble the objects designated by the names. These investigators used a list of geometrical figures (the stimulus figures shown in Figure 40) no one of which was a complete or accurate representation of any object. Each figure was given two names, each of which was the name of an object that resembled the figure. The two names of each figure are given in Figure 40. Each figure was shown to three groups of subjects. As each figure was presented to the subjects in group A, the experimenter pronounced the name of the object which appears in Word List 1 of Figure 40. To the subjects of group B he pronounced the name of the object which appears in Word List 2. To the subjects of group C the stimulus figures were presented without any names. Upon completion of one presentation of the series, the subjects were asked to draw all of the figures which they had seen. If a subject failed to make a recognizable drawing, the series was shown a second time. After the second presentation, he was again asked to draw the figures which he had seen. This procedure was repeated until every subject was able to make a recognizable drawing of each figure.

When the drawings were compared with the original figures it was found that 74 per cent of the drawings of the subjects in group A resembled the objects named in Word List 1 more than the stimulus figures did, and that 73 per cent of the drawings of the subjects in group B resembled the objects named in Word List 2 more than the stimulus figures did (see the sample reproductions in Figure 40). In short, there is a tendency for subjects in drawing the stimulus figures from memory to make them like the objects named by the experimenter at the time the figures were originally presented.

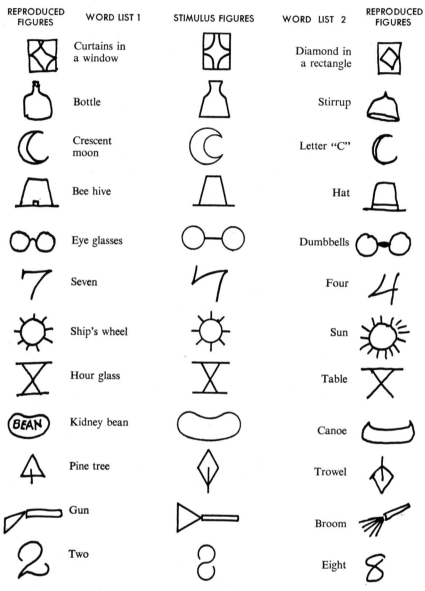

REPRODUCED FIGURES	WORD LIST 1	STIMULUS FIGURES	WORD LIST 2	REPRODUCED FIGURES
	Curtains in a window		Diamond in a rectangle	
	Bottle		Stirrup	
	Crescent moon		Letter "C"	
	Bee hive		Hat	
	Eye glasses		Dumbbells	
	Seven		Four	
	Ship's wheel		Sun	
	Hour glass		Table	
	Kidney bean		Canoe	
	Pine tree		Trowel	
	Gun		Broom	
	Two		Eight	

Figure 40

The Stimulus Figures and Examples of Reproductions Which
Conformed to the Visual Representations of the
Objects Named in Word Lists 1 and 2

(From L. Carmichael, H. P. Hogan, and A. A. Walter, "An Experimental Study of the
Effect of Language on the Reproduction of Visually Perceived Form." *J. Exp. Psychol.*,
1932, 15, 73–86. By permission of the American Psychological Association.)

Self-deception. A third source of error in recall is the tendency to supply details so as to make something reasonable and intelligible, or to make a good story. Someone has said that we have to change the truth a little to make it interesting enough to tell. Whether or not this is so, many of us certainly act as though we believed it.

Over and above the foregoing tendencies to error in recalling experiences, there are two broad classes of more serious distortion which may be described as disorders of recall. One group is of functional origin; the other is due to organic or structural defect. In the first class should be placed defective recalls due to excitement, to emotional inhibition or repression, and to exhaustion. The case of Irene given above (p. 215) and those illustrating the use of automatic writing, crystal gazing, and hypnosis are instances of functional disorders. Memories in all those cases were repressed because they were unpleasant. The following account of an experience of a seventeen-year-old girl illustrates the influence of fatigue on recall:

> In the spring of last year while attending the University I became exhausted through overwork. One afternoon when returning home something seemed to snap in my head and it went whirling. This itself is clear in memory, but how I got home and what happened the next three days or in the whole preceding month are forgotten. Of course from what has been told me I know now about what did happen but it is still impersonal as a story. I have no memory of the lessons we studied, and though during the time I was sick and before it, I wrote verses constantly, I do not know them now or recognize them as my own work (9, p. 384).

It will be noticed that the girl forgot events that occurred not only at the moment of her crisis and in the three following days, but also during the previous month. The forgetting of events that precede a crisis is called *retroactive amnesia*. This disorder of recall may be produced by a physical shock, such as a blow on the head. Football players, for example, have been known to forget events which occurred hours before the game in which they received a severe blow on the head.

In many instances the exhaustion or physical shock combines with general dissatisfaction to produce the amnesia. This was the usual combination among the soldiers in World War I. Exhaustion and worry weakened their self-control. All that was needed to produce a radical break in the stream of consciousness was a physical shock. Frequently a relatively slight one was sufficient (31).

The second kind of disorder of recall is due to organic defect. We shall merely mention two common examples.   One is the forgetfulness of old age.   This is due to actual degeneration of the brain, which is consequently no longer able to operate as successfully as it formerly did.   The other example is also a case of degeneration of the brain, but degeneration due to disease and not to mere age.   Paresis and high blood pressure are two disease conditions that affect the memory.

RECOGNITION

To *recall* is to think of an absent object previously experienced.   To *recognize* is to identify a present object and to place it in one's system of memories or of logical relations.   If I look out of my window and see a moving object, I may recognize it as an automobile.   I may not have seen the particular car before, but still I realize that it is a member of a familiar class.   In addition to recognizing it as an automobile, I may also recognize it as the car of a friend.   Recognition in both cases is essentially the same.   In one case the content is more specific and involves a more definite placing of the recognized object than in the other.   We recognize an object as a member of a class when we are able to classify it; we recognize an object as an individual thing when we can place it in our past experience.

The basis of recognition is the feeling of familiarity that results from partial re-arousal of responses that occurred when the particular object or objects of the same class were previously experienced.   Suppose a group of objects, automobiles, for example, gives rise to a certain response; any member of the same class, whether new or old, will then be able to re-arouse this response and thus awaken the feeling of familiarity.   Sometimes our responses are more definitely related to a single object.   For example, if you were unable to tell by looking at them which of two pens was yours, you would try them out.   Usually you would be able to tell yours by "the feel."   Rats show a similar tendency when placed in a new position in a familiar maze.   At first, a rat so placed is bewildered, but he soon discovers a clue and runs with assurance down the proper alleys.   Similarly, when the appearance of a person seems familiar to us, it is because we are making the same inner adjustments that we formerly made when we saw the person or one very much like him.   Without these inner changes we should not have any feeling of familiarity.   In the hope of reawakening the memory of an old man who was suffering amnesia, his favorite daughter was brought into his presence.   On being told that his daughter stood by him, he replied, "Oh no, she is not my daughter!   If she were my daughter, I should feel joy within."   Failing to experience any of the organic changes he had formerly experienced in the presence of his daughter, he thought her a stranger.

Though the feeling of familiarity plays an essential part in all acts of recognition, it is not in itself sufficient to justify our saying that we recognize an object. A second step is necessary: namely, the placing of the object definitely in our past experience. When we have done this, the act of recognition is complete.

Disorders of Recognition

Feeling of strangeness in a familiar environment. One morning a professional man who had for months been suffering from overwork, and probably from a nervous disease, went to the place where he usually boarded the street-car to go to the city. Suddenly he felt that he was in a strange environment. He made an attempt to recall the houses that surrounded the place where he took the car in order to compare them with the houses that he now saw, but this he was unable to do. However, he decided to wait for a car. When it came, he was able to read the sign correctly and, boarding the correct car, to make a safe journey to the city. Conklin (11), who reports this case from Burnham, attributes the disorder to emotional excitement of a profound and depressing nature, combined with fatigue. These may well have caused a state of temporary disintegration, involving the repression of bodily sensations. Because the bodily sensations no longer made their contribution to the stream of consciousness, however, everything seemed strange. Hence the sufferer knew that he was in a familiar place, but felt as if he were in a strange one.

Feeling of familiarity in a strange place. This disorder is much commoner than the feeling of strangeness in a familiar environment. Perhaps the reader, when entering a room for the first time or while watching the sunset for the first time in a strange place, has experienced a feeling of familiarity and yet of strangeness. The feeling of familiarity in a strange place may be due to one of several causes. One cause is incomplete recall. The following experience reported by Morgan (35) is an illustration.

One day a clergyman went with a party of friends to visit a castle. As the party approached the gateway, the clergyman became conscious of a very vivid impression of having seen it before; and he "seemed to himself to see" not only the gateway itself, but donkeys beneath the arch, and people on the top of it. Upon asking his mother if she could throw any light on this experience, he was told that when eighteen months old he had been taken by his mother with a large party to the castle, and that while the ladies and gentlemen ate their lunch on the top of the wall, he had been left with the servants below. In this instance the feeling of familiarity was undoubtedly due to incomplete recall. Had complete recall taken place, the clergyman would, on his second visit to the castle, have thought of his previous one, and there would have been no haunting feeling of familiarity. As it was, he had the feeling of familiarity, based upon bodily sensations, yet was unable to recall the previous experience.

The feeling of familiarity may also be caused by a present situation which closely resembles one that has been experienced but that is not recalled. If the earlier situation were recalled, there would result only an association of the usual type, and the similarity would be noted. But if the similarity between the two situations provokes only the bodily changes that underlie the feeling of familiarity, the haunting feeling of recognition arises, because the individual is making the same adjustments to the new situation as he once made to the old one.

A break in the continuity of an act may also produce the feeling of familiarity. If your attention is momentarily distracted by an unusual noise or by a picture when you are "set" to enter a room, you are apt to feel, as you enter the room, that you have done so before. The explanation is that when preparing to enter the room, you surveyed it, but that because of the distraction, the survey was forgotten. It persists sufficiently, however, to give rise to the feeling of familiarity when the act is resumed. Because of the break, the final action does not seem to be a continuation of an act just begun, but a repetition of an act previously performed at some unknown time. Such experiences are more apt to take place when a person has been somewhat disoriented by fatigue or depression.

Confusing one's inferences with what actually happened. This is a third disorder of recognition. If someone has witnessed an interesting event and is telling his friends about it, there will, more than likely, be breaks in what he actually recalls. Instead of telling only what he can remember, he is apt to supply substitutes for the missing parts. So readily do we do this that we ourselves cannot separate what we remember from what we supply. Our unconscious inferences are taken for parts of our experience. Particularly is this the case after we have repeated a story a few times. This is one of the reasons for taking with a grain of salt the reports of even our most trustworthy friends about their summer's vacation. With the best intentions in the world, it is hard to overcome the urge to make our accounts intelligible (that is, connected) and interesting by dressing them up and by supplying missing links. This is very likely to be done by old people whose memories are deteriorating. The procedure is called *retrospective falsification*. We tend to falsify our account of things in ways that will be flattering to us or that will enhance our feeling of importance.

Confusion of ideational experiences with actual events. Dreams — daydreams or regular dreams — and information got from others are sometimes confused with our overt acts. This disorder is called *retroactive paramnesia*. When someone asserts that he can remember what happened when he was a few months old, we are justified in believing that he is confusing what he has been told with his own first-hand memories. The confusion of fantasy with memories of real events may, on occasion, have important consequences. Morgan (35) tells of an apparently normal woman who told her husband that an uncle, with whom she wrote poetry when a child, had died and left her a large estate in England. "The gullible husband, elated at his wife's good fortune, resigned his position and made all preparations for the wonderful journey, when he was brought to the earth with a jolt upon learning that the whole story was the sheerest fabrication. Investigation showed that from early childhood this girl had been accustomed to weave such fairy tales and to act them out as though they were the truth."

CAN MEMORY BE IMPROVED?

A person has a good memory if he is able to recall those experiences that are of help to him. Can this capacity be improved? It is a common belief that native retentiveness, whatever that may be, cannot be improved. But retentiveness, in the sense of the ability to fixate information for recall when needed, can be improved. Certain correspondence schools offer courses which they claim will improve memory, so that if one is introduced to fifty strangers before dinner, he will be able to call them all by name during and after the dinner. Though a skeptical attitude is reasonable regarding this claim, there is no doubt that a person can improve his ability to fixate important facts and impressions so that they can be recalled more readily. The superiority of the blind students of Perkins Institute over the students of Harvard and Radcliffe and over a group of technical-high-school students in remembering logical material presented orally indicates that few of us have made full use of our ability to fixate and retain important experiences (4).

Observance of the following suggestions will lead to improvement: (a) Discriminate in what you attempt to remember. In studying a lesson, pick out the important facts and memorize them. Some things are of little importance; memorizing them will not be worth the time and effort it costs. (b) Memorize thoroughly important facts and principles. If material is learned so that it can be barely repeated, it will be forgotten far more quickly than if it has been studied beyond the point of immediate recitation. A little overlearning pays handsome dividends in prolonged retention. (c) Plunge into the subject you desire to master. The more you know of any field the easier it becomes to assimilate additional facts in it. (d) Stimulate your interest in the subject to be learned. This will make the fixating process more intense. (e) Practice frequent repetition. (f) Learn logically; that is, note as many relations or meanings as possible. To the extent that you organize the facts you wish to remember, you make for yourself a logical system in which one fact suggests another.

SUMMARY

Learning always involves some change or modification of an individual's behavior. Such changes are the results of the individual's activity. The changes that occur when we learn include: the coordination and integration of responses into complex habits, the organization of material into wholes, and negative adaptation. Changes in behavior may be in the nature of an over-all increase of knowledge and skill or of an integration of present and past learning.

Learning may take place through conditioning, trial and error activity, or insight. The particular method used in learning is a function of the learning situation, the nature of the problem, the kind of organism, and such characteristics of the organism as age, motivation, ability, and previous experience.

Learning curves are graphic representations of the changes which occur during successive periods of practice. Most learning curves represent improvement in terms of the time required to learn, the number of errors made, or the amount accomplished per practice period. Some of the characteristics of learning curves are: a certain kind of acceleration, plateaus, physiological limits, and fluctuations in performance.

Some of the factors which favor economical learning are: motivation, optimum degree of maturation, spaced practice, active recitation, and organization of material into meaningful wholes.

Memory has to do with the processes of learning, retention, recall, and recognition, but its essential characteristic is retention. Recall and recognition are measures of retention and learning. Forgetting is a function of what one does immediately after learning; it is more rapid for nonmeaningful than for meaningful material, and it is affected by one's method of learning and by the degree of learning. Different methods for measuring the amount forgotten produce different results.

It can be demonstrated that many experiences which cannot be recalled or recognized are not completely forgotten. This can be done by the savings method or by removing the conditions which inhibit or interfere with recall. The recall of experiences is determined by several factors: secondary laws of association, external surroundings, desire to avoid the disagreeable, present emotional state, and need of the moment. Recall may be aided by: (1) adequate initial learning, (2) numerous associations involving the material, (3) an attitude of confidence, and (4) returning to the matter later.

Recognition is the awareness that we have had an experience before, combined with the ability to place the experience logically in our past. Disorders of recognition are of four types: (1) feeling of strangeness in a familiar environment, (2) feeling of familiarity in a strange environment, (3) mistaking inferences for recollections, and (4) confusing ideational and perceptual experiences.

QUESTIONS
on the Chapter

1. What is learning? Can you think of any changes in behavior which would not be classified as learning?
2. Distinguish between additive and integrative changes in learning.
3. Give some examples of negative adaptation from everyday life.
4. Define: conditioning, generalization, experimental extinction, disinhibition, reconditioning, differential conditioning, secondary reinforcement.
5. Compare trial and error with insightful learning.
6. Distinguish between negative and positive acceleration.
7. What are the differences between "time," "error," and "attainment" curves?
8. What is a plateau? What are some of the causes of plateaus?
9. What is meant by transfer of training? What is shown by the experiments on this subject?
10. What is memory? What is its relation to learning? Recall?
11. What factors influence forgetting?
12. How can one show that experiences which cannot be recalled or recognized are not completely forgotten?
13. Define each of the secondary laws of association.
14. What factors tend to produce errors in recall?
15. Distinguish between recall and recognition.

for Discussion

1. What makes a habit "good" or "bad"?
2. Can insight occur without any trial and error?
3. Should one always strive to reach his physiological limit in learning?
4. Defend the statement: The essential characteristic of memory is retention.
5. Do we completely forget anything?
6. Design a procedure for reconditioning a student who is afraid to take quizzes.
7. Can memory be improved? How?

REFERENCES

1 BASS, M. I., and HULL, C. L., "The Irradiation of a Tactile Conditioned Reflex in Man," *J. Comp. Psychol.*, 1934, 17, 47–66.
2 BATSON, W. H., "Acquisition of Skill," *Psychol. Monogr.*, 1916, 21, 1–92.
3 BILLS, A. G., "The Influence of Muscular Tension on the Efficiency of Mental Work," *Amer. J. Psychol.*, 1927, 38, 227–251.
4 BOND, N. J., and DEARBORN, W. F., "A Comparison of the Auditory Memory and Tactual Sensibility of the Blind with Those of Persons Who Have Normal Vision," *J. Educ. Psychol.*, 1917, 8, 21–26.
5 BOOK, W. F., and NORVELL, L., "The Will to Learn," *Ped. Sem.*, 1922, 29, 305–362.
6 BOSWELL, F. P., and FOSTER, W. S., "On Memorizing with the Intention Permanently to Retain," *Amer. J. Psychol.*, 1916, 27, 420.
7 BROOKS, F. D., "The Transfer of Training in Relation to Intelligence," *J. Educ. Psychol.*, 1924, 15, 413.
8 BRYAN, W. L., and HARTER, N., "Studies in the Physiology and Psychology of the Telegraphic Language," *Psychol. Rev.*, 1897, 4, 27–53.
9 BURNHAM, W. H., "Retroactive Amnesia," *Amer. J. Psychol.*, 1903, 14, 382–386. Quoted by permission.
10 CARMICHAEL, L., HOGAN, H. P., and WALTER, A. A., "An Experimental Study of the Effect of Language on the Reproduction of Visually Perceived Form," *J. Exp. Psychol.*, 1932, 15, 73–86.
11 CONKLIN, E. S., *Principles of Abnormal Psychology*. New York: Henry Holt and Company, 1927.
12 DARWIN, CHARLES, *The Expression of the Emotions· in Man and Animals*. New York: D. Appleton and Company, 1873.
13 EBBINGHAUS, H., *Memory: A Contribution to Experimental Psychology* (translated by H. A. Ruger and Clara E. Bussenius). New York: Teachers College, Columbia University, 1913.
14 ENGLISH, H. B., and JONES, M. G., "Notional vs. Rote Memory," *Amer. J. Psychol.*, 1926, 37, 602–603.
15 GARRETT, H. E., *Great Experiments in Psychology*. New York: The Century Company, 1930, Chapter 14.
16 GATES, A. I., "Recitation as a Factor in Memorizing," *Arch. Psychol.*, 1917, 6, No. 40, 104.

17 GATES, A. I., and VAN ALSTYNE, DOROTHY, "The General and Specific Effects of Training in Reading with Observations on the Experimental Technique," *Teachers College Record*, 1924, 25, 98–123.

18 HENDERSON, E. N., "Do We Forget the Disagreeable?" *J. Phil. Psychol. Sci. Meth.*, 1911, 8, 432.

19 HULL, C. L., *Principles of Behavior: An Introduction to Behavior Theory.* New York: Appleton-Century Company, 1943.

20 JANET, PIERRE, *Psychological Healing.* New York: The Macmillan Company, 1925.

21 JENKINS, J. G., and DALLENBACH, K. M., "Obliviscence during Sleep and Waking," *Amer. J. Psychol.*, 1924, 35, 605–612.

22 JONES, M. C., "The Elimination of Children's Fears," *J. Exp. Psychol.*, 1924, 7, 382–390.

23 KEY, C. B., "Recall as a Function of Perceived Relations," *Arch. Psychol.*, 1926, 13, 1–106.

24 KITSON, H. D., "A Study of the Output of Workers under a Particular Wage Incentive," *Univ. J. of Bus.*, 1922, 1, 54–68.

25 KÖHLER, W., *The Mentality of Apes.* New York: Harcourt, Brace and Company, 1926.

26 LASHLEY, K. S., "Nervous Mechanisms in Learning." In Murchison, C., ed., *Foundations of Experimental Psychology.* Worcester: Clark University Press, 1929, pp. 524–563.

27 LAWSHE, C. H., JR., and DAWSON, R. I., "A Procedure for Demonstrating the Secondary Laws of Association," *J. Educ. Psychol.*, 1947, 37, 248–250.

28 LEWIN, K., "Untersuchungen zur Handlungs und Affekt Psychologie," *Psychol. Forsch.*, 1927, 9, 1–85.

29 LIDDELL, H. S., and ANDERSON, O. D., "A Comparative Study of the Conditioned Motor Reflex in the Rabbit, Sheep, Goat, and Pig," *Amer. J. Physiol.*, 1931, 67, 539.

30 MCCLATCHY, VIVIENNE R., "The Optimal Position of a Rest Period in Learning," *J. Exp. Psychol.*, 1925, 8, 251–277.

31 MCDOUGALL, WILLIAM, *Outline of Abnormal Psychology.* New York: Charles Scribner's Sons, 1926.

32 MCGEOCH, J. A., and MCDONALD, W. T., "Meaningful Relation and Retroactive Inhibition," *Amer. J. Psychol.*, 1931, 43, 579–588.

33 MARTIN, M. A., "The Transfer Effects of Practice in Cancellation Tests," *Arch. Psychol.*, 1915, 4, 1–68.

34 MATEER, F., *Child Behavior, a Critical and Experimental Study of Young Children by the Method of Conditioned Reflex.* Boston: Badger, 1918.

35 MORGAN, J. J. B., *The Psychology of Abnormal People*, 2nd edition. New York: Longmans, Green and Company, 1936.

36 MORGULIS, S., "The Auditory Reactions of the Dog Studied by the Pavlov Method," *J. Animal Behavior*, 1914, 4, 142–145.

37 OLSON, W. C., *The Measurement of Nervous Habits in Normal Children.* Minneapolis: University of Minnesota Press, 1929.

38 PANLASIGUI, I., and KNIGHT, F. B., "The Effect of Awareness of Success or Failure," *Twenty-ninth Yearbook of the National Society for the Study of Education*, Part II, 1930, 611–619.

39 PAVLOV, I. P., *Conditioned Reflexes; An Investigation of the Physiological Activity of the Cerebral Cortex.* London: Oxford University Press, 1927.

40 PRINCE, MORTON, *Dissociation of a Personality: A Biographical Study in Abnormal Psychology,* 2nd edition. New York: Longmans, Green and Company, 1936.

41 PRINCE, MORTON, *The Unconscious: The Fundamentals of Human Personality, Normal and Abnormal,* 2nd edition. New York: The Macmillan Company, 1921.

42 REED, H. B., "Distributed Practice in Addition," *J. Educ. Psychol.,* 1924, 15, 248–249.

43 RICE, CHARLOTTE, "Eye and Hand Movements in the Training of Perception," *Child Development,* 1931, 2, 30–48.

44 RITTER, S. M., "Automatic Writing by a Blind Subject," *J. Abnor. Soc. Psychol.,* 1928, 23, 383–392.

45 RUGER, H. A., "The Psychology of Efficiency," *Arch. Psychol.,* 1910, No. 15.

46 SHAFFER, L. F., *The Psychology of Adjustment.* Boston: Houghton Mifflin Company, 1936.

47 THORNDIKE, E. L., "Mental Discipline in High School Studies," *J. Educ. Psychol.,* 1924, 15, 83–98.

48 THORNDIKE, E. L., and ROCK, R. T., JR., "Learning without Awareness of What Is Being Learned or Intent to Learn It," *J. Exp. Psychol.,* 1934, 17, 1–19.

49 THORNDIKE, E. L., and WOODWORTH, R. S., "The Influence of Improvement in One Mental Function upon Efficiency of Other Functions," *Psychol. Rev.,* 1901, 8, 247–261, 384–395, 553–564.

50 THURSTONE, L. L., "The Learning Function," *J. Gener. Psychol.,* 1930, 3, 469–491.

51 WHEELER, R. H., *The Science of Psychology.* Philadelphia: Thomas Y. Crowell Company, 1929.

52 WOLFLE, H. M., "Time Factors in Conditioning Finger-Withdrawal," *J. Gener. Psychol.,* 1930, 4, 372–378.

53 WRENN, C. G., assisted by R. B. MCKEOWN, *Study-Habits Inventory.* Stanford: Stanford University Press, 1933.

54 WULF, F., and KOFFKA, K., "Über die Veränderung von Vorstellungen (Gedächtnis und Gestalt)," *Psychol. Forsch.,* 1922, 1, 333–373.

PERCEPTION

7

How much of your present experience is the result of your ability to see or hear or smell? Would you rather be blind or deaf? In what way would learning be affected by the loss of vision, or hearing, or touch? Could one learn if he were deprived of all three? What effect would the loss of any one of the senses have upon one's adjustment to his environment? These questions call attention to the fact that *sensory experiences* are basic to all of our reactions and adjustments. These experiences are our first reactions to internal and external stimulation. Our subsequent reactions to and interpretation of these reactions constitute our knowledge of our bodies, ourselves, and the world in which we live. Every kind of behavior — learning, perception, emotion, attending, thinking — and every kind of adjustment involves sensory stimulations and sensory experiences. What kinds of experiences do we get through the sense organs? What are the characteristics of these experiences? In what way are they related to perception? What is perception?

These and related questions have been prominent in the thinking and research activities of psychologists since Wundt established the first psychological laboratory in 1879. The field of perception is one of the most important research areas in psychology today. It is significant in this connection to note that eleven of the thirty-six chapters in Stevens's *Handbook of Experimental Psychology* (26) are concerned specifically with sensory experiences and perception. This is not difficult to understand when one remembers that perception is involved in virtually every human adjustment. One's very life may depend upon his ability to *perceive* the signal at a railroad crossing or the silhouette of a stalled automobile in the dark, or upon a pilot's ability to perceive and make quick and accurate adjustment to the instruments on a complex instrument panel.

SENSORY EXPERIENCES

Earlier, in Chapters 3 and 4, we listed and described the various sense organs and the adequate stimuli for each. We are now ready to list and describe the kinds of experiences which are mediated by these sense organs. Such sensory experiences as colors, odors, tones, noises, and the like are called sensations. Each separate color or tone or taste is a sensation. Instead, however, of trying to list all of the separate sensations in each sense field, it is customary to classify the sensations and list either the classes or the elementary sensations, those out of which all other sensations can be compounded.

Table XI

Kinds of Sensory Experiences

CLASS OF SENSES AND RECEPTORS	SENSE	SENSORY EXPERIENCES (Sensations)
1. Exteroceptors		
a. Teleoceptors	Sight	Colors and brightness
	Hearing	Tones and noises
	Smell	Odors
b. Proximoceptors	Taste	Tastes (sweet, sour, salt, bitter)
	Touch	Touch
	Warmth	Warmth
	Cold	Cold
	Pain	Pain
2. Interoceptors	Organic	Hunger, thirst, nausea
3. Proprioceptors	Kinaesthetic	Sensation of movement and muscular strain
	Static	Sensation of position and imbalance

Characteristics of Sensory Experience

Table XI shows a list of the sense organs and the kind or class of sensation mediated by each. It should be noted that some sensations have the same name as their sense organs. Thus we speak of the sensations mediated by the touch, warmth, cold, and pain receptors as touch, warmth, cold, and pain. It should be noted also that, technically speaking, light, color, odor, and sound are sensations, not stimuli.

The corresponding stimuli (see p. 106) are ether vibrations, gaseous particles, and air vibrations. In spite of this fact it is a common practice to use the name of the sensation as a means of identifying the stimulus. An extension of this practice is seen in references to the stimuli for vision and hearing as light waves and sound waves because these waves customarily arouse sensations of light and sound.

Sensations differ in quality. Each different sense organ mediates a different kind of sensory experience. Light is qualitatively different from sound, sound from odor, and odor from warmth or pain. Furthermore, various sensations aroused within a single sense field may be qualitatively different. In the field of vision, red, blue, and green are qualitatively different. Color sensations differ from the sensations of white, gray, and black. In the taste field, sweet, sour, salt, and bitter differ in quality, and, as we have seen (p. 82), are aroused by the stimulation of taste buds located in different parts of the tongue.

In some sense fields these differences in quality arise from the fact that adequate stimuli for the sense organ differ in length or frequency (see p. 107). In the field of vision, the experience of red is produced by ether vibrations (light waves, if you will) of a given length, 760 millimicrons. Waves of a length of 500 millimicrons produce blue. A mixture of all wave lengths in the visible spectrum gives rise to a sensation of white. In the auditory field, air vibrations of different frequencies give rise to tones that differ in pitch. In the taste field, different chemicals produce different taste experiences.

Sensations differ in intensity. A color experience, such as blue, may vary in brightness from a very bright blue to a very dull blue. This variation in brightness is determined primarily by the *intensity* or strength of the light wave. A tone of a given pitch may, in a similar manner, vary in loudness, from just audible at one extreme to very loud at the other extreme. This variation in loudness is determined by the intensity or amplitude of the sound wave. In these cases the basic quality of the sensation as determined by the frequency or length of the light or sound wave remains the same. A sensation of a given quality — for example, a color of a given hue, or a tone of a given pitch — may occur in many degrees of intensity. We may say then, by way of review of the above points, that sensations differ in kind or quality from one sense field to another, they may differ in quality within any sense field, and a sensation of a given quality may exist in many degrees of intensity, from very weak to very strong.

Sensations differ in purity. The stimuli within a given sense field differ in complexity or composition (see p. 107). A visual stimulus may be composed of a number of light waves of different lengths, or of waves of a single length. If it is composed of the latter, the resulting color experience is said to be saturated or pure. A saturated red is pure with respect to red. It is as red as it can be. If the wave length which produces it is mixed with other wave lengths, some degree of redness is lost, the exact degree of desaturation depending upon the number and length of the waves in the mixture. Similarly, an auditory stimulus of a single frequency gives rise to a pure tone. If other higher frequencies are added, the pitch of the tone will not change but the purity of the tone will be reduced. In the case of tones this reduction in purity gives the tone a characteristic *timbre*. The resulting tone in this case is a mixture of the fundamental tone with the overtones which are produced by the higher frequencies. This characteristic of tones is responsible for the fact that middle C on the piano sounds different from middle C on the violin, although each has the same pitch and may be of the same loudness. The differences in this case are differences in the purity or timbre of the tones.

While our illustrations of the characteristics of sensations have been taken chiefly from the fields of vision and hearing, it should be recognized that sensations in other sense fields have the same characteristics. Warmth is qualitatively different from cold or touch or pain. Any of these sensations may vary in intensity, a fact which is illustrated by words such as tepid, lukewarm, hot, and scalding hot. Stimuli in any of these fields differ in complexity or composition. The differences here, however, arise from the nature of the stimulus and the number of end organs in the skin which are stimulated. A warm object placed on the skin will come into contact with a number of warmth, touch, and even cold spots. The resulting sensation of warmth is not as pure with respect to warmth as the sensation which would result from stimulating a single warm spot.

Vision

Visual sensations differ in kind or quality (hue), in brightness or intensity, and in saturation or purity. As indicated above, hue is determined primarily by the length of the light wave, brightness primarily by the energy of the wave, and saturation by the degree of complexity or composition of the stimulus. Related to these characteristics of visual sensations are a number of facts about vision which have an important bearing upon how we see and what we see, and upon the efficiency of any adjustments which involve or depend upon vision.

Elementary visual sensations. A careful examination of all color experiences and all brightnesses (blacks, whites, and grays) indicates that some of these are elemental, i.e., they cannot be regarded as compounds and cannot be reduced to any simpler elements. It appears that all color experiences can be reduced to four elementary sensations — red, blue, yellow, and green; and that all brightness can be reduced to white and black. Some theories of color vision hold that there are three elementary color sensations: red, green, and blue. In either case all visual experiences other than elementary ones are regarded as combinations or compounds of two or more of these elementary sensations. Thus, orange is a mixture of red and yellow; violet a mixture of red and blue. Mixtures of certain colors (blue and yellow, for example) in approximately equal proportions produce a gray. Such colors are said to be *complementary.* A mixture of all colors will produce white. Mixture of colors with black or white reduces the saturation of the colors and produces shades and tints. The mixtures here referred to are mixtures of wave lengths of lights, not mixtures of pigments.

Visual after-images. The removal of an effective stimulus does not cause the corresponding sensation to cease immediately. Instead, the sensation continues in much the same way that a wheel keeps moving after the application of force has ceased. The continuation of the conscious process after the stimulus has been removed is called an *after-image.* The flaming circle caused by swinging a burning torch is a simple instance. The lag in the sensory process is such that, instead of distinguishing the position of the torch at any one time, we see a whole circle of fire. The image focused by the lens of the eye upon the retina apparently sets up a nervous process which outlasts the stimulus. This persistence is known as *retinal lag.* Motion pictures furnish another instance of the same phenomenon. A great number of still pictures are flashed before us so rapidly that an illusion of motion is created. In this instance, however, the motion which we see depends not only on retinal lag but also upon a peculiar characteristic of vision, known as the *phi-phenomenon*, which causes us to see movement when different, but stationary, views of an object are presented in the proper sequence. (See page 256.) Lags in the sensory process which cause a continuation of what we have just sensed are called *positive after-images*; those that give rise to a contrast effect are called *negative after-images.* If you watch the rays of a powerful light moving about at night, you will notice that the path remains clearly defined when the rays have left it, and that it is defined by its standing out as an intensely dark streak. In other words, there is a contrast effect.

Some interesting contrast effects can be observed with colors. If a person gazes intently for a few seconds at a gray background with a green card against it, he will experience, when the green card is removed, an after-image of red. If the original card is red, the after-image will be green. If the original color is yellow, the after-image will be blue, and vice versa. The negative after-image is in all cases the complement of the original stimulus.

Color zones. The width of the visual field differs from one person to another. A normal eye sees objects in an area 70 to 80 degrees on all sides beyond the point fixated. The width of the visual field for blue-yellow vision is smaller than the total visual field, and the field for red-green vision is smaller than the blue-yellow field. The visual fields of two persons are shown in Figure 41. Plots of this kind are obtained with an instrument known as a perimeter (see Figure 42). Three areas are indicated in each diagram. The largest white area represents the total visual field; the next largest area represents the blue-yellow field; and the smallest area represents the red-green field. Everyone is red-green blind outside the area designated as the red-green field. One can distinguish blues and yellows in both the red-green and the blue-yellow areas, but is totally color-blind outside the area

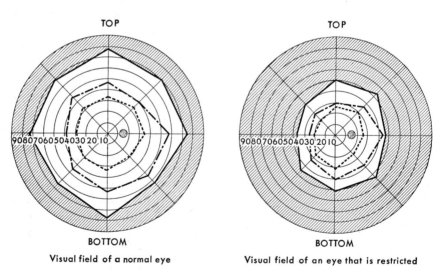

Visual field of a normal eye   Visual field of an eye that is restricted

Figure 41

A Normal and a Restricted Visual Field

The solid line indicates the limit of the visual field, the broken line the yellow-blue field, the dotted line the red-green field. The figures along the radius represent degrees from the point of fixation.

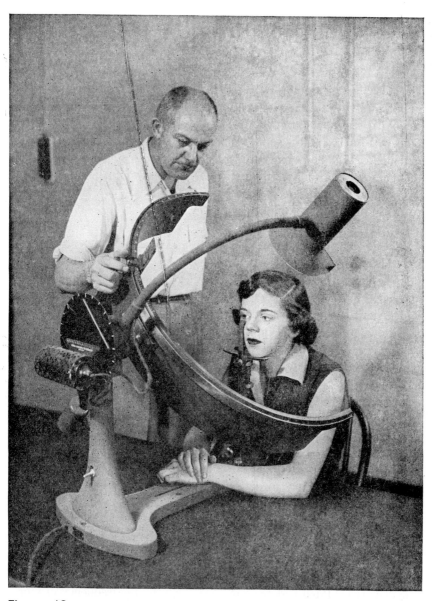

Figure 42

Measuring and Plotting the Visual Field

designated as the blue-yellow field. The small dot near the center of each plot is the "blind spot," an area in the visual field which falls on the spot in the back of the eye where the optic nerve enters the eyeball. We are blind to objects which come to a focus on this spot. Can you explain why we are not aware of this blind spot in ordinary vision?

The drawing on the right in Figure 41 indicates so narrow a visual field that the term "tunnel vision" may aptly be used to describe it. One with such a defect sees things as though he were looking through a tunnel. Tunnel vision is obviously a severe handicap to the driver of an automobile and greatly increases his chances of having an accident.

Measuring differences in vision. Individuals differ in their ability to distinguish one color from another, in visual acuity or keenness of vision for near objects and for distant objects, in ability to perceive depth, in binocular vision, and in other visual characteristics. An individual may possess different degrees of each of these skills. One degree of a given skill may be a handicap in one situation and not in another. For example, poor distance acuity is not a handicap on a job which demands good near acuity, although it may be in some other situation (28). Obviously, a color-blind person is quite unsuited for certain types of work where discrimination between colors is an important part of the job; yet this deficiency may not be a handicap in every situation. Tests have been devised for measuring many of these characteristics of vision. Some of these tests are used in eye examinations and provide information needed for the correction of visual defects. A recently developed instrument known as the Ortho-Rater for measuring such visual skills as near and far acuity, depth perception, and color blindness is illustrated in Figure 43. This instrument is being used extensively in industry to determine the particular visual skills which are needed in different kinds of work (2).

Audition

Sounds may vary in pitch, loudness, timbre, volume, and brightness (or density). Pitch is determined primarily by the frequency of vibration of the sound wave and refers to the position of a tone or sound on the musical scale. Loudness is determined by the intensity of the sound wave. Timbre, or tone quality, is determined by the complexity of the sound wave — the number and frequencies of the overtones which it contains. That the timbre of a sound should be considered as a separate attribute, and not simply as a perceptual interpretation of a combination of various component partials or overtones, is shown by such studies as

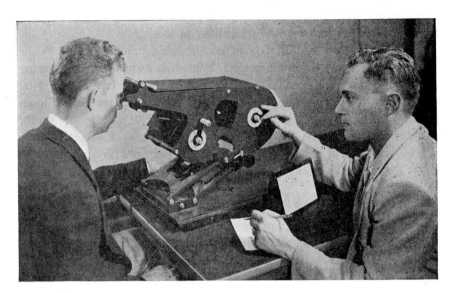

Figure 43

The Ortho-Rater

A device for the visual classification and placement of industrial employees. (Distributed by the Bausch and Lomb Optical Co., Rochester, New York.)

the one by Lewis and Lichte (12). These investigators found that "a listener might perceive two complex tones as being different in timbre and yet be unable to designate the exact nature of the difference in terms of (say) saliency of specific partials." Volume, which has been defined as the "largeness" of a tone, "increases with intensity and decreases with frequency." (27) Brightness, or density, has also been considered a separate attribute of tones, though it is possible that this characteristic is only a specific type of tone quality, or timbre (1).

Measuring differences in hearing. All persons cannot hear the various attributes of sound with the same precision or accuracy. A keen ear can detect a difference in pitch as small as one fiftieth of a tone, whereas a poor ear may require seventy-five times as much change before a difference is noted. The same is true in the hearing of loudness and timbre. The Seashore Measures of Musical Talent, which will be described in a later chapter (see page 442), measure one's ability to hear differences in several attributes of sound. They are of considerable value in determining whether one's ear is sufficiently keen to justify certain kinds of musical training. The value of the tests for this purpose rests upon Smith's (24) important experimental work showing that training does not improve the sensitivity of the ear.

Another hearing test that is of considerable practical value is the Western Electric 4–B Audiometer. With this instrument the hearing acuity of forty persons can be tested at the same time. In the measuring of deafness, or hearing loss, the *decibel* (db) is used as the unit of loudness. If silence is represented by zero, the roar of an airplane motor close at hand would be about 110 db. The loudness of other common sounds is shown in Figure 44. Obviously, a person with a hearing loss of 60 db cannot hear any of the sounds below that point on the scale.

The Relation between Stimuli and Sensations

Our ability to perceive differences between two stimuli is strictly limited. If an ounce is added to ten pounds, scales of ordinary delicacy will respond, but we should not notice the addition were we attempting to gauge the weight with our hands. We are unable to perceive differences in weight less than $2\frac{1}{2}$ per cent. In sound, we cannot detect the difference in loudness when one drum is added to five drums already beating; if one drum is added to four drums, the per cent of increase will be just sufficient for us to perceive a difference. The amount of stimulus for all of our senses must vary by a rather large per cent in order for us to perceive differences.

The fact that addition to or subtraction from a stimulus cannot be perceived unless the change is a certain per cent of the original stimulus is known as *Weber's law.* Individuals differ, of course, in their ability to detect differences, as they do in their ability to sense individual objects. The amount of difference required on the average and the individual differences for each mode of sensation have been set forth by Warren (29) in Table XII. "Each fraction denotes the *proportion of the original stimulus* which must be added to it in order that the sensation may be just noticeably greater." This fraction is called the difference threshold or the least perceptible difference and is indicated by the abbreviation L.P.D.

Weber's law holds for only the middle ranges of sensations. If this were not so, and it held true at all ranges of vision, for example, we should be able to read on into twilight and pay no attention to the increasing darkness. The values given in Table XII are rough approximations. We shall make no effort to discuss here the extensive experimental literature on quantifying the relation between stimulus and sensation nor the many factors which affect this relationship. The specialized branch of psychology which is concerned with these prob-

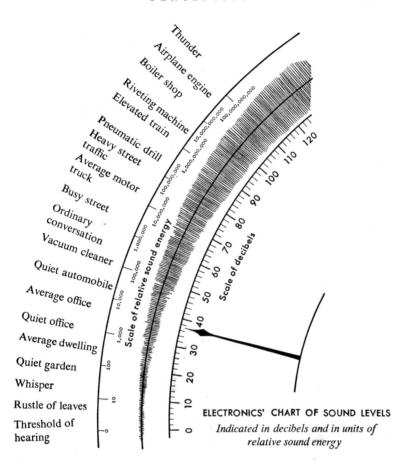

ELECTRONICS' CHART OF SOUND LEVELS
*Indicated in decibels and in units of
relative sound energy*

Figure 44

Loudness of Common Sounds on a Decibel Scale

The decibel as a measuring unit will soon be used as commonly as the degree or the pound. (By courtesy of *Electronics*.)

lems is known as *psychophysics*. It is the most thoroughly quantified — though by no means the most significant — branch of modern experimental psychology.

Table XII

Values of the Weber Constant (29)

SENSATION	L.P.D. INTENSITY	INDIVIDUAL RANGE
Visual	0.01	0.015 to 0.005
Auditory (noises)	0.333	
Auditory (tones)	0.15	0.20 to 0.125
Olfactory	0.25	0.33 to 0.25
Gustatory	0.25	0.33 to 0.25
Tactile	0.05	0.10 to 0.033
Warmth	0.036	
Cold	0.036	
Kinaesthetic	0.025	0.05 to 0.013

(By permission, from H. C. Warren, *Elements of Human Psychology*, Houghton Mifflin.)

Synaesthesia

The mistaking of the stimulation of one sensory organ as the stimulation of another is called *synaesthesia*. The most common form of this is the perception of tones as colors. "Sensations of color have also been reported to accompany sensations of taste, smell, pain, pressure, or temperature. There have been rare instances where subjects have reported the experience of a sound sensation when presented with a light stimulus; others have reported smells and tastes when presented with a sensation from another field. Quite commonly an elementary sensation results from hearing a spoken word" (15, p. 81).

Synaesthesia is probably due to incomplete differentiation of function of the various sense organs. Any response of an infant to a stimulus involves practically the whole individual. With maturity, muscular responses involve chiefly the muscles needed, the rest of the body remaining relatively at ease. Very possibly a similar development of differentiation takes place on the sensory side of experience. During infancy, sensory stimulation probably involves the whole of the sensory areas in the brain. As we develop, different parts of the sensory area take the lead in different sensory experiences, the other parts of the cortex remaining relatively passive. In the case of those who experience colored tones or other forms of synaesthesia, there has probably been an arrest of the usual differentiation of sensory areas, and sensory stimulation, therefore, is responded to by more than one mode of sensation, as was probably the case with all of us during infancy (31).

Sensory Adaptation

A sense organ becomes relatively insensitive when called upon to respond to the same kind of stimulus for any length of time. The result is, of course, that there is no sensory experience although a stimulus is impinging upon the sense organ. Perhaps the sense of smell is most easily adapted. Evidence of this is found in the quickness with which we become accustomed to obnoxious odors or cease to enjoy fragrant ones. Persons working in a tannery soon become quite unconscious of its odor. Vision also adapts readily to continuous stimulation. Wear a pair of colored glasses for half an hour and you will become totally unaware of the color. The eye adapts so completely that the color can actually no longer be perceived. Hearing is the least adaptable of the senses, though experiments show that prolonged stimulation by a constant tone somewhat reduces the sensitivity of the ear (17). Adaptation to one stimulus, while rendering us less sensitive to the same kind of stimulus, may increase or decrease sensitivity to stimuli of other kinds. For example, one investigator reported that bitter adaptation increased the sensitivity of three subjects to sour and salt, and that two bitter-adapted subjects reported increased sensitivity to sweet (6).

When there is variation in the stimuli, there is less adaptation. This is partly accounted for by the fact that in such instances different parts of the sense organ are activated, whereas, when the stimulus remains the same, the same part of the sensory organ is used continually. For example, we may quickly become insensitive to one odor, but remain responsive to all others. Our sensory organs, like our muscles, quickly tire of doing one thing. If we are called upon to bend a finger repeatedly, we soon tire; but if the same movement is part of a larger whole and there is variation and time for rest, fatigue does not set in so quickly.

Apart from the factor of adaptation, some stimuli have the capacity of rendering us insensitive to others. Ruch (22) tells of an unscrupulous lawyer who took advantage of this fact to win an acquittal for a client who had been indicted on a charge of arson. The case for the state rested largely on the testimony of the firemen that they detected the odor of kerosene in the burning building. The defense lawyer claimed that the firemen had been "smelling things"; and, to prove they were not competent witnesses, he passed them several bottles and

asked that they tell the court what they smelled in each.   The first
bottle which each fireman received contained kerosene and the remainder of the bottles perfume.   After the overwhelming odor of the kerosene, the men's nostrils were insensitive to the delicate perfume, and
they reported kerosene in all the bottles.   The lawyer then passed the
bottles to the jurors, but this time he presented the kerosene bottle
last.   The jurors were convinced that the firemen were really "smelling
things," and acquitted the client.

Reaction Time to Sensory Stimulation

The biological value of our reactions to sensory stimulation depends in
a measure on how quickly they occur.   In this respect, the reactions to
stimuli in the different sense fields differ widely.   It takes about .22
of a second for us to respond to a visual stimulus.   Our response to
sound takes about .18 of a second.   Our response to tactual sensation
is still faster, approximately .12 of a second.   The time needed for
reacting varies with the intensity of the stimulus applied.   Generally
speaking, the reaction time becomes less as the intensity of the stimulus
increases.   The reaction time is also decreased when a person is "set"
to respond.   And it is also slightly decreased by practice.   It increases
with the complexity of the situation to which the response is made.
More time is required in making a choice reaction than in making a
simple reaction.

The reaction time of a person decreases as he approaches maturity,
and then increases as he grows older.   The reaction time of a man of
70 is about equal to that of a child of 10; that of a man of 45 is slower
than that of a boy of 15.

The bearing of these facts on safety in automobile driving is evident.
Quick reaction time is obviously an asset in avoiding accidents.   Because
the reaction time of the old is too slow for modern traffic, many states
require that they pass special examinations to demonstrate their fitness
to drive.   The average man in his prime requires about .40 of a second
to apply the brakes in an emergency.   If he is traveling at 50 miles an
hour, he will go 29 feet before applying his brakes.   Some people
require as much as a second to apply the brakes.   Lauer has devised
tests for determining driving ability (10).   If the obtaining of a license
to drive were contingent upon passing these tests, the number of accidents on the highway would no doubt take a sharp drop.   It should be
recognized, however, that lack of driving skill is not the only cause of
highway accidents.   Even skilled drivers are subject to internal and
external conditions which may interfere with driving proficiency.

PERCEPTION   · *Identifying*

The most important characteristic of a sensory experience is that it is always an experience of something. One doesn't just see, or hear, or taste, or smell. He sees something, a book, a man, a patch of blue. He hears something, a melody, an automobile horn, a man's voice, his own name spoken. One identifies a taste as sour, or bitter, or sweet; an odor as turpentine, or perfume, or tar, or lemon. When stimuli excite receptors, activity is set up in the nervous system and in reacting mechanisms. The end product of this activity is the interpretation of what it is that is exciting the sense organ. We identify this something. We know what it is. It has meaning for us. We give it a name or respond to it in a way that reveals the nature of our interpretation. This process of interpreting and identifying excitations is called *perception*. It is a process that quite obviously involves the arousal of a sense organ by a stimulus, but it is more than mere sensitivity to stimulation. Something is added, as it were, by the perceiver. This something is the perceiver's interpretation of the stimulus.

Perception Is a Function of P and E Variables

We are saying in effect that perception is a function of the interaction of an individual with his environment. What an individual perceives is determined in part by the environmental stimulations and in part by what the individual is at the moment. A person brings to a perceptual situation certain attitudes, experiences, feelings, moods, values, memories, and ideas. These characteristics, themselves the products of previous interactions between an individual and his environment, interact in various ways with present excitations to determine one's perception. Bruner and Postman (4) have emphasized the point that these characteristics are the products of one's interaction with his *social* environment, and that all perception is, therefore, to some degree social perception. This would follow from the facts that (1) perception is a function of the interaction between an individual and his environment and (2) the individual is a product of his previous interactions with his social environment.

A present excitation, then, interacts with P variables in various ways to determine one's perceptions. Let us examine some of these interactions.

(1) The present excitation may arouse a previously acquired perception. In this case the present stimulus does nothing more than act as a cue or a trigger to release a previously established response. The

perception is, in a manner of speaking, already present in the individual. It is a learned response which is retained like any other learned response. Most of the words on this page serve merely to arouse meanings which have been established for some time. A word may be perceived when only a part of the word is actually exciting the receptor. Letters may be omitted from words, or only a vague outline of portions of the letters may be shown, or only the top halves of the letters may be shown, without disturbing one's perception of the words. Here it is clear that what is perceived is not in the stimulus. It is a previously learned response which is reinstated by the stimulus. While it may be influenced to some extent by aspects of the individual's total experience, and by his set to perceive, it is a relatively exact reproduction of the previously acquired perception.

(2) The activity initiated by a new stimulus may arouse impressions made by previous stimulations of the same or a similar kind, and the present activity may combine in various ways with these re-aroused activities to determine one's perception. The perception in this case is not the mere arousal of a previously established perception, but the result of the interaction of previous impressions with the present excitation. The impression produced by the present excitation may be integrated with the previous impressions to produce a new perception. This is one way in which perceptions develop. It is important to recognize that previous impressions do not exist as isolated units within the individual. They are a part of an entire integrated system of experiences, memories, attitudes, interests, moods, and so on. While a present excitation may arouse impressions produced by previous excitations of the same or a similar kind, it is extremely unlikely that the present and previous impressions can interact or become integrated without being influenced by other aspects of the perceiver's total personality. Moods, feelings, attitudes (all ingredients of the set which one brings to a perceptual situation), and other activities which are in progress influence the interaction of present and past experiences. They may facilitate the interaction or color it in various ways. For example, a child's present experience with an orange calls up previous experiences with oranges. The interaction of the present and past experiences to form a new percept may occur at a moment when the child is frightened, or angry, or happy, or unhappy. These and other experiences that may be a part of the child's social environment may be woven into the pattern of experiences which are building up around oranges in such a way that the child's perception of an orange is something more than the sum of his experiences with oranges as such.

That social values and individual needs influence perception or are woven into one's perceptions is shown in an experiment by Bruner and Goodman (3). These investigators had children estimate the size of coins, a penny, a nickel, a dime, a quarter, and a half-dollar, by adjusting a disk of light until it appeared to them to be the size of each of the actual coins. These estimates were compared with estimates of paper disks identical in size to the coins. The size of the coins was overestimated from about 15 to 35 per cent whereas the estimates of the paper disks did not differ from their actual size by more than 5 per cent. The important finding was that the amount of the overestimation of the coins increased with the value of the coin except for the fifty-cent piece. A comparison of the overestimations by ten children of poor parents with the overestimations by ten children of well-to-do parents showed that with every coin the overestimation of the poor children was greater than it was for the well-to-do children. It is quite clear that the value of the coins and the individual need for them are factors in the perception of the size of the coins.

The influence of set. The perceiver's set, determined by prevailing feelings, desires, and intentions, and by activity which is in progress, influences one's perception in other ways. It may, for example, act as a barrier that keeps a present excitation from calling up the experiences produced by similar excitations in the past. In this case the perception of the present excitation is likely to be determined entirely by the perceiver's set. If a man is lying awake thinking about burglars breaking into his house, he is likely to perceive the creaking of the porch swing as a burglar trying to open a window. In this example we can suppose that the man has experienced the creaking of the porch swing on many previous occasions. Tonight, however, the same creaking noise does not set off these previous experiences and a recognition of the source of the noise. Instead, the man is *set* to perceive a burglar. The set not only acts as a barrier to the recall of the previous experiences with creaking swings, but actually determines that the present noise will be interpreted as a burglar.

The influence of set upon perception is easily demonstrated when the stimulus is relatively unstructured, indistinct, new, or ambiguous. Since such stimuli will be less likely to set off established perceptions, their perception will be determined more largely by the individual's set. The effect of a food set on the perception of such stimuli has been demonstrated in an experiment by Levine, Chein, and Murphy (11). Eighty different objects were presented, one at a time, behind a ground-glass screen to subjects who had been deprived of food for various intervals of time.   The objects as seen through the ground-glass screen were hazy and indistinct.   The subjects were asked to identify or name the objects.   The average number of objects which were perceived as food objects increased as the time without food increased up to six hours.   That other kinds of sets act as selective factors in perception to determine or influence one's perceptions has been demonstrated by other investigators (5, 19).

Sherif (23) has shown that being a member of a group and knowing what other members of the group do affect one's perception.   He had subjects look at a point of light in a completely dark room and indicate or estimate how far it moved before it disappeared.   It is known that a fixed point of light shown in complete darkness will appear to move. This phenomenon is called the *autokinetic* effect.   The subjects were tested individually and in groups of three or four.   Individual averages in terms of the number of inches that the light appeared to move were established in the individual sessions.   The subjects then worked in groups, each individual calling out his estimate of how far the light moved.   Here it was observed that each individual was influenced by the group in such a way that all of the subjects moved toward the group average.   The subjects who had small averages on the individual trials moved up toward the group average and those who had large averages on the individual trials moved down toward the group average.   This tendency can be observed in many everyday situations.   In general people want to be like other people.   We do not like to be so different that other people regard us as queer.

Structural Factors in Perception

In discussing perception as a function of P and E variables we have stressed the importance of what Kretch and Crutchfield (9) call *functional* factors in perception, namely, those variables which derive primarily from the needs, past experiences, feelings, interests, and attitudes of the individual.   All through this discussion, however, it has been made clear that perception is also dependent in part upon environmental stimulation.   Those factors in perception which arise out of the nature of the environmental stimulations, the effects which they produce in the body, and the structure of the body itself may be regarded as *structural* variables.   The very design of the body becomes a factor in one's perception; for example, the view one gets of an object with the left eye is slightly different from the view one gets with the right eye because the eyes are in different places in the head.   One's visual perception of distance provides an excellent illustration of the operation of structural factors in perception.

Visual perception of distance. The retina, on which the visual image in the eye is focused, is a spherical surface and lacks depth; yet we are able to judge the distance of objects away from us with great accuracy. Why are processes that take place on the retina of the eye and in the brain interpreted as indicating objects external to us, and what are the clues that enable us to estimate their distance? Several factors make distance perception possible.

(1) *Angle of convergence.* When we look at an object two feet away, the angle of convergence (formed by the two lines of vision, one from each eye to the object) is much greater than when an object is ten feet away. The pulling in or out of the eyes so that they will focus upon the perceived object involves muscular activity and, consequently, kinaesthetic sensations. The importance of these sensations as clues for estimating the distance of the object is indicated by the fact that when the muscles involved are anaesthetized, all objects seem far away. Another indication of their importance is that the impression of distance can be obtained by means of a stereoscope, which causes the light rays to come to our eyes in parallel lines.

(2) *Disparity of retinal images.* When a distant object is viewed, the images focused on the retinas of the two eyes are practically identical; when the object is near, there is considerable disparity. The reader may verify this by looking at a ball first fifty feet away and then only a foot away. When it is only a foot away the left eye will see some distance around the left side and the right eye an equal distance around the right side of the ball. The varying disparity of the views obtained by the two eyes serves as a clue for the perception of distance.

(3) *Accommodation of the lenses.* When we look at a near-by object, the lenses of our eyes bulge; when we look at a distant object, they flatten. The accompanying sensations are aids in judging the distance of the object.

(4) *Angle of elevation.* The movements of the eyes upward or downward also serve as clues for estimating distance. Ordinarily, we walk with our eyes fixed on the sidewalk so that we see the walk fifteen to twenty-five feet ahead of us. As we lower the eyes, we see the walk nearer to us. As we raise them, we see more distant objects. The kinaesthetic sensations involved in raising or lowering our eyes are interpreted in terms of distance. The apparent nearness of distant objects when looked at over a cliff shows the importance of angle of elevation (25). Artists recognize this principle by placing

at the top of a picture objects which they wish to make appear far away.

(5) *Size of the retinal image.* When we see an object in the distance, the retinal image is smaller than when the object is near. For example, the retinal image of a man five hundred feet away is smaller than when he is only fifty feet away. We do not interpret the difference in the size of retinal images, however, as meaning that the man is varying in size, but that his distance from the observer is changing. Accordingly, knowledge of the size of an object is a clue for judging its distance. Artists make use of this principle in painting. Near-by objects loom up; distant ones are made small.

(6) *Clearness of outline or form.* Objects which are far off cannot be seen in detail and are more or less blurred and indistinct. Hence, when we are able to see little if any detail of an object, we infer that it is far off. Again, artists make use of this principle by washing out all detail of objects that are supposed to be in the background, and by painting in the detail and the brighter colors of objects close at hand. The tendencies to consider blurred objects as distant and those making large retinal images as near are responsible for the illusions of distance and largeness that we experience in a fog.

(7) *Interposition.* Our view of objects in the distance is often partly obstructed by other objects. We know that those which obstruct our view are nearer than the ones that are partly obscured. This provides us with some insight into relative distances, and it accounts for the greater ease of judging distances when we are looking over a field covered with various objects than when we are looking over an open prairie.

(8) *Parallax.* Focus your eyes upon an object; then move your head to the right or left. Objects that are nearer than the point of fixation will seem to move in the opposite direction from your head, while those that are farther away will seem to move in the same direction. Objects that are very near the point on which your eyes are focused will appear to move only a little. The farther objects are from the point of reference, the more they will seem to shift when your head is moved.

The Development of Perception

Try to imagine what a newborn sees when he first opens his eyes, or what a two-month-old child sees when a doll is held in front of him for the first time, or what the same child at twelve months of age sees when the same doll is presented to him. Regardless of what the newborn sees, we can be sure of one thing: it is not what an older child or an adult sees. We can be sure that the baby's perception of a doll at two months is not the same as his perception of the doll at twelve months. We may hazard the guess with William James that the world to the newborn is a "blooming, buzzing confusion." But what is the nature of the child's first impression of a doll, or a human face, or other object? It appears that these first impressions are vague, blurred, and undifferentiated. This tends to be true in some degree of first impressions at any age, as indicated by our own experiences in new and unfamiliar situations. The child reacts to an object as a whole, not to the separate parts. Even at four years of age, for example, a child can look at a drawing of a human face without seeing that the eyes or mouth or nose are missing. The child sees a square as a single, unitary object, not as a collection of four separate lines. His first perception may not be one of squareness, but it will be of the object as a whole. The method of teaching reading in which the child learns to recognize a word as a single, unitary object is based upon the assumption that this tendency to perceive objects as wholes is still present in six-year-old children.

With additional experience and through trial and error learning the child's perception of an object becomes increasingly clear, better differentiated, richer in detail, more accurate, and more complete. There is an increasing tendency to be analytical in reacting to stimulation, to differentiate one object from another, and to discriminate between the separate parts or features of an object. One consequence of this development is that the perceived object is differentiated from the background of impressions which arise from concomitant stimulations. The object stands out from its surroundings by being perceived as different from them. The object is perceived as a *figure* on a *ground*. As a figure, it has form, limits, and meaning; and it stands out from the ground. In an ambiguous design like the one shown in Figure 45 the *figure* shifts so that one sees the figure as the upper side of a staircase at one instant and as the lower side at another instant.

As a result of experience, we learn to supply more detail and to distinguish the nature of objects when only a slight clue is given. For example, we may perceive an apple by its smell alone, or recognize a friend by his walk or by his voice. We "see" a wet street or a heavy piece of iron or a hard stone. In all such instances limited sensory data provide sufficient clues for us to understand the presented object. This is what happens as a person becomes a rapid reader, though his improvement is due also, in part, to his developing a broader eye span; that is, to his learning to see more words at a time. Likewise, in looking at

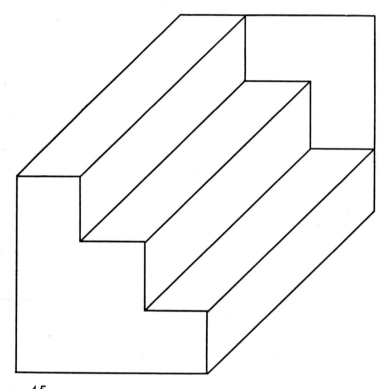

Figure 45

Do You See the Staircase from Above or Below?

complex objects we may supply missing parts. For example, in reading we frequently supply missing words unconsciously, and are apt to pass mistakes in spelling without noticing them.

A further step in the development of perception is the tendency for successive experiences to become integrated into organized and meaningful patterns, and for new impressions to be incorporated into this organized system in such a way as to produce a new organized pattern and a new perception. We have called attention to the fact that this is one of the ways in which perceptions develop (see p. 246). The new pattern that emerges in this process of reorganization tends always to be as stable, as well organized, or as good as possible under the existing circumstances. This tendency for a perception to be as good as possible or for memories to organize themselves into a stable, dynamic system is known as the *law of pregnance* (8). The significance of the term *pregnance* in this connection is roughly analogous to "goodness."

Everyone passes through three levels in the development of perception: the undifferentiated, the differentiated, and the integrated (16, p. 150), but the progress from one level to another is gradual and continuous. This progress is primarily the result of the individual's trial and error experiences in reacting to objects, and it may be rapid or slow depending upon the opportunities for learning and the favorableness of the learning conditions. For example, Postman and Bruner (18) have shown that subjects who were frustrated in their efforts to learn the meaning of words failed to make any progress in the learning trials. The experimental group was frustrated by having the learning material exposed for too short an interval to be perceived and by being criticized for what they did. A control group learned under favorable conditions. The experimental subjects not only failed to learn, but their perceptions of the poorly exposed materials reflected aggression and the need to escape from the learning situation.

But all percepts do not develop in the step-by-step fashion that is characteristic of trial and error learning. Some percepts seem to appear quite suddenly and in the manner which is characteristic of insight. One day a child does not perceive the difference between a circle and a square. When asked to copy a square, model shown, he succeeds not at all or turns up with a drawing that is more circular than square. The next day or a week later he "gets the idea." He sees the difference. To be sure, he has had many trial and error experiences with square and circular objects, and he has had many other kinds of experiences which he can bring to bear on the situation; but his perception of the difference between a circle and a square seems to emerge quite suddenly.

Errors of Perception

Since perceptions, instead of being mere photographs of physical events, are largely made up of the interpretations of the observer, we should expect to find many errors in them. "Seeing is believing" is not a particularly convincing statement to one who understands the imperfections of our sensory organs and the influence of bias and emotions on our interpretation of what is seen. Everyone has noticed that mothers find it hard to perceive the imperfections of their children. The thick-skinned and the thin-skinned find it hard to evaluate social situations correctly. The strong partisan finds it hard to perceive political realities. The lover is not the most reliable judge of the beloved. Desires have a profound influence on our perceptions.

Excitement. That excitement increases errors of perception is shown by the following account of a "planted" assault (21, p. 286):

Into a hall in which a congress of psychologists were holding a meeting, a clown rushed madly pursued by a Negro, revolver in hand. They stopped in the middle of the room, fighting; the clown fell, the Negro leapt upon him, fired, and then both rushed out of the hall. . . . The president asked those present to write a report immediately, since there was sure to be a judicial inquiry. Forty reports were sent in. Only one made less than 20 per cent of mistakes in regard to the principal facts; fourteen had 20 per cent to 40 per cent of mistakes; twelve from 40 per cent to 50 per cent; thirteen more than 50 per cent. Moreover, in twenty-four accounts, 10 per cent of the details were pure inventions, and this proportion was exceeded in ten accounts and diminished in six. Briefly, a quarter of the accounts were false.

Suggestion. Suggestion is another source of error in perception. One of the authors once uncorked a bottle in his class after telling his students that there was a very delicate perfume in it, and requested that the members of the class raise their hands as soon as they detected the odor. Although the contents of the bottle were odorless, every hand was soon raised. Sleight-of-hand performers take full advantage of our suggestibility in causing us to see what they wish us to see. It is reported that the yogis of India are able to cause the gaping and admiring crowds to see a tree grow fifty feet in a few minutes from a seed. Seasickness seems frequently to be produced by the mere expectation of it. Even where physical conditions give less encouragement, the repeated suggestion that he is sick may cause even the strongest to feel ill.

Normal illusions. Some errors of perception are made by everyone and are in a constant direction. Everyone is inclined to see a vertical line as longer than a horizontal line of the same length. It is a general error for a person coming out of the cold into a heated room to overestimate the temperature of the room. Perceptions like these that fail to give the true character of the object presented are called *illusions* or false interpretations. Because they are experienced by everyone, they are often called "normal" illusions. Illusions may be divided into three groups: (a) those that are due to the nature of the stimulus; (b) those that are due to subjective conditions; and (c) those that are due to the nature of the sensory organs.

(a) Illusions due to the nature of the stimulus. Vision furnishes the best examples of illusions of this type. Several normal visual illusions are shown in Figures 46 and 47. Visual illusions have been subjected to extensive study, and many laws concerning them have been discovered (13). These findings are of particular interest to artists,

Figure 46

Examples of the Terminal Illusion

The vertical lines in this figure are all of equal length.

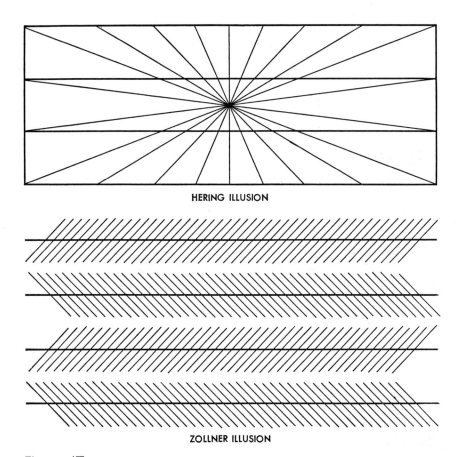

HERING ILLUSION

ZOLLNER ILLUSION

Figure 47

The Horizontal Lines in These Figures Are All Straight and Parallel

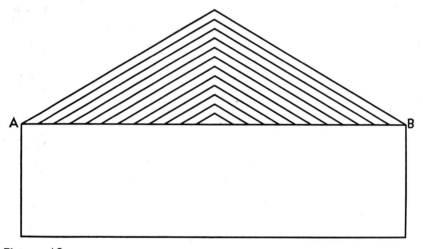

Figure 48

If the End of a Building Is Built like This the Line AB Will Seem to Sag

Figure 49

In Each Pair, Which Is Larger — the Upper or Lower Figure?
Measure Them

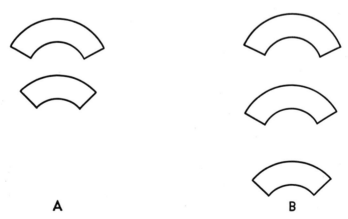

A   **B**

Figure 50

Even Chickens Experience Optical Illusions

Révész demonstrated this with figures like those shown above.

256

painters, decorators, printers, and architects.   If the lines of a finished
building are to "look" straight and square, it is often necessary to
construct them with slight bends and curvatures, in order to overcome
certain tendencies to see things as different from what they are.   For
example, if the end of a building is like the drawing in Figure 48, we
see the line AB as dropping slightly in the center.   To overcome this,
the Greeks raised the center of such a line, thus giving the final construction the desired appearance.

It is interesting that chickens and men make the same mistake in
judging the size of such figures as those shown in Figure 49.   Révész
(20) taught a hen to peck corn always from the smaller of two figures.
Sometimes circles, sometimes squares, sometimes triangles were used.
In every case, one of the figures was smaller than the other.   After
the hen had been taught to peck the corn lying in the smaller figure,
Révész put corn in the figures shown in A, Figure 50.   The hen pecked
from the smaller figure.   Finally Révész placed corn in the figures
shown in B.   The upper two figures are objectively the same size, but
the top one seems smaller.   The hen, as a rule, upon seeing corn in the
three figures, would eat first from the bottom figure and then pass by
the middle one and eat from the top one.   In the majority of instances
the corn in the middle figure was left untouched.

A very common illustration of illusions due to the nature of the
stimulus may be found in motion pictures.   Though we speak of "moving" pictures, actually the movement is in our perception, not on the
screen.   A series of stationary pictures, each slightly different from the
preceding one, is flashed on the screen at the rapid rate of twenty-four
pictures per second.   We "see" these still pictures as moving; that is,
we supply the movement as an illusion.   The illusion of movement
found under these conditions is called, as we have mentioned before,
the *phi-phenomenon*.   The laws of the phi-phenomenon have been carefully studied, beginning with the work of Wertheimer (30).

(b) Illusions caused by subjective factors.   Illusions caused by
subjective factors are those which are brought about by our expectations, interests, and habits.   A famous simple example is known as
Aristotle's illusion.   Cross your index finger with the finger next to
it.   Now, with your eyes closed, have someone place within the V
formed by your fingers some object such as a pencil.   You will have the
feeling of two objects rather than one.   The reason for this is that
ordinarily whenever the opposite surfaces of two fingers are stimulated
two objects are involved.   Mistaking a piece of paper or a dandelion
head for a lost golf ball illustrates the importance of expectancy and

desire.   Earlier in this chapter we cited an example of a man mistaking the creaking of a swing as a burglar trying to open a window.

(c) Illusions due to the nature of our sensory organs.   For an example of illusions caused by the nature of our sensory organs, run the points of a pair of compasses over the lips.   The points will seem farther apart when just under the nose than at any other point.   An individual may report that a sound is heard directly in front of him when in reality it is directly behind him, because the ears are incapable of providing correct perceptions in this plane.   A vertical line seems longer than a horizontal line of the same length.   The seemingly great size of a cavity in a tooth when the tongue is inserted in it is another illusion of this type.

Disorders of Perception

The illusions just discussed are in no sense abnormal or pathological. There are, however, pathological disorders of perception. They may be caused by a diseased condition of the sensory apparatus, as when an infection of the eye causes blindness or disordered vision.   Such conditions are called *organic* disorders.   Or they may be caused by a person's not using his sensory equipment, as when a man becomes blind even though his visual organs are intact.   The latter conditions are called *functional* disorders, and they are of more interest to the psychologist than those due to organic conditions.

Certain functional disorders are classified as *functional anaesthesias*. Those who have read the history of witchcraft will recall that the presence on a person's body of areas insensitive to pin pricks was regarded as conclusive evidence of witchcraft.   Perhaps many readers have doubted the existence of such areas and suspected that the poor old women on whom they were found were not given a fair test.   We now know that such disorders do sometimes occur.   Before physicians were careful not to make suggestions regarding such areas, they were frequently found in hysterical patients.

The following is a case of functional anaesthesia which McDougall (14, p. 245) reports that he treated by suggestion:

> A youth of flabby moral texture was sent home from the Mediterranean with lower limbs paralyzed and anaesthetic; a diagnosis of post-diphtheritic paralysis had been made. However, the signs were all in favour of a functional paralysis; and it appeared that, though he had suffered from a sore throat, the paralysis had set in just about the time that the transport on which he was going to the Gallipoli front had come within

sound of the guns on that tragic grave of so many brave men. I tried
hypnotic suggestion; but, though he passed into hypnosis, I could not
fully control him; when he was forced to move his legs, he fell into weep-
ing and moaning. I therefore decided to proceed more slowly by waking
suggestion. Following an explanation that the anaesthesia would recede
day by day and that, when it was gone, he would have full use of his legs,
I ostentatiously mapped the upper limit of the anaesthesia on both limbs
each morning, and in this way drew off the anaesthesia like a pair of
stockings, drawing it two or three inches lower each day.

Other senses may also become functionally upset. An individual may
become insensitive to certain odors, not because of organic defect but
because of some emotional disturbance. The same is true of the sense
of taste and of organic sensations. Janet (7) tells of a man who, as
the result of being struck in the face by a greasy rag, became blind and
remained so for four years. In another case, a woman was struck in
the face by scalding water while working in a laundry. Her face was
slightly burned, but none of the water penetrated her eyes. Nevertheless, she became completely blind for two years.

Functional anaesthesias have several peculiarities. They conform
to the popular conception of functional units. That is to say, instead
of the anaesthesia affecting an area that would be involved if a nerve
trunk were destroyed, it may affect part of an area which includes several
nerve trunks. The anaesthesia may be produced by suggestion, and
is frequently so caused among hysterics. It is variable in character.
Hysteric episodes or fits may aggravate the disorders or eliminate them.
During sleep the disorders may disappear. Drugs, such as alcohol,
chloroform, morphine, and hashish, may cause them to vanish, and
suggestion may modify them. For example, a physician may merely
pretend to be treating his patient with electricity, but if the patient believes that he is being so treated, there will be contractions of the muscles
similar to those caused by electricity. Finally, functional anaesthesias
are not consistent in their appearance. Janet proposed to one of his
patients that she say "yes" when she felt herself touched with an instrument and "no" when she did not feel it. (Her vision was obstructed
so that she could not see when she was touched.) Whenever Janet
touched the normal areas of her body, she would say "yes"; when he
touched the supposedly anaesthetic parts, she would naïvely answer
"no."

Recovery from functional disorders frequently seems mysterious.
The whole personality must be understood. Regarding such recoveries
Morgan (15, p. 51) makes the following comment:

When a cure is effected, it is not of a definite organic lesion, but of something deeper in the psychological mechanism of the victim. We must understand that seeing is not simply the function of the eye with its nerves to the cortex. *It is a function of the whole personality, using the optic nerves and visual apparatus in a complete integration.* [Italics ours.] It is obvious when one becomes blind with no disturbance of the optic apparatus or its connections, and when the vision returns as abruptly, that one must look to the rest of the personality for the explanation.

Ways of Making Perception More Reliable

There are several ways of determining whether we are seeing accurately or are experiencing an illusion. In the first place, we may seek the confirmation of different senses. A stick that appears bent in the water may be found to be straight by running our hands up and down it. In the second place, we may simplify the conditions under which the observation is made. In the case of the stick, we could do this by removing it from the water. In the case of the Hering illusion (Figure 47), we can simplify the conditions of observation by laying a ruler over the confusing lines. In the third place, we should check our experiences with those of other people. Of course, in the case of illusions due to the nature of the stimulus or to the nature of our sense organs, everyone is "fooled," and confirmation by others is simply evidence that they too are experiencing the illusion. But in illusions due to our subjective conditions, it is very helpful to check with others. The creaking stairs which bother you probably sound not at all like a burglar to your roommate.

The importance of simplifying the conditions and isolating the object to be observed is recognized by all scientists. It is illustrated in the accompanying figures. Find the K in Figure 51*A* and the 4 in Figure 51*B*. To hide a thing to be seen in a mass of irrelevant material makes an interesting puzzle, but should be avoided where accurate observation is desired.

To increase the reliability of our observations, we should also correct all sensory defects, maintain alertness, avoid emotional disturbance, preserve open minds, remember what to look for, and make allowances for ill health, moods, and attitudes. Above all, we should realize that accurate observations are hard to make, and we should be on the lookout for errors and ways of eliminating them. In this connection it will be recalled that one of the essentials of the experimental method (see Chapter 1) is accurate observation. In this method observations are made under controlled conditions by observers who use instruments, wherever possible, to supplement their own observations.

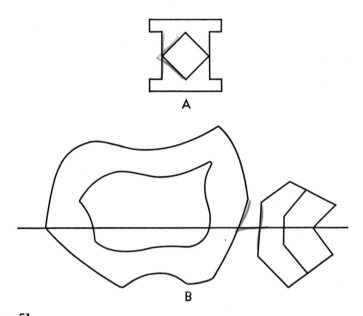

A

B

Figure 51

Find the K in *A* and the 4 in *B*

Things hidden among irrelevant material are difficult to see.

The Influence of Perceptual Defects upon Personality

Such sensory defects as deafness and blindness not only deprive an individual of important sources of sensory experience but pose many difficult adjustment problems, the solutions of which will bear directly upon the development of his personality. The blind, in addition to being deprived of valuable information, are apt to become excessively timid and cautious. The deaf and the hard of hearing, being deprived of social contacts, are likely to be suspicious. Noticing that people are talking, but rarely able to understand what is said, they are more inclined than normal people to believe that they are being talked about.

The deaf child in school is inclined to do his best to hide his defect. He taxes himself to the utmost in an effort to understand his teacher. Yet no matter how hard he tries, he makes mistakes. The teacher who regards these mistakes as indications of disobedience or carelessness is apt to scold the child for them. If this happens, the child, already suffering anxious tension and trying to do his best, is filled with the sense of injustice. He grows resentful, and lives more and more within himself. Deprived, in large measure, of the instruction of the teacher and the stimulation of hearing other pupils talk and recite, he becomes a "retarded pupil." The retardation of the deaf, however, is not wholly due to lack of hearing; for, at least in many cases, the conditions which lead to deafness may also injure the central nervous system and thereby impair the general intelligence.

To guard against aggravating the effects of blindness and deafness, children with these handicaps should very early be given special training. Every effort should be made to stimulate them to use their other senses to the fullest degree, and they should be helped to develop self-reliance and confidence. Solicitude should be avoided, for it may prevent them from putting forth the effort necessary to make the most of their lives; it may cause them to cease trying to take care of themselves and make them expect others to provide for them.

Perceptual defects that are functional in origin indicate that something is radically wrong with the personality. When a person gives up the use of his eyes, for example, something is badly amiss. That something must be found and, if possible, corrected. If the functional disorder continues, the individual, besides depriving himself of many experiences that would be helpful, develops the habit of shirking; and his personality becomes more and more abnormal.

The ability to ignore sensory stimulation, as when we become negatively adapted to sounds and voices and even to visual stimulation, throws considerable light on the nature of perceptual processes. It shows that perception, instead of being a passive mirroring of the world about us, is an integral part of the process of adjustment. If the sensory intake brings us only tension and trouble, we have ways of shutting it off. In thus protecting ourselves from prolonged tension, we act as we do regarding unpleasant memories. Just as we modify memories that are unpleasant to recall and, if we are unable to do this, repress them (see pp. 215–216), so we seek to interpret unpleasant sensory intake in a way that is congenial to us, and, if we fail, we repress this also. Such repression occurs only in seriously maladjusted individuals, and is pathological. Yet the abnormal is only an accentuation of the normal. Because the abnormal is the running wild of a normal process, it frequently throws light on the latter. The function of perception is to help the organism to make adjustments. If, instead of doing so, it makes adjustments more difficult, the personality may discard some of its perceptual ability. To what extent this is voluntary it is difficult to say. A person certainly does not stutter because he consciously wishes to do so. Yet he may regard the stuttering as an explanation of his social ineffectiveness. This may cause continued stuttering, because he would rather attribute his ineffective personality to stuttering than to some cause more basic but also more unpleasant for him to contemplate. A person who develops a severe headache when something distasteful is to be done does not consciously desire the pain, but it is significant that it nonetheless resolves a tension, and is less *undesirable* than the task which is escaped. Similarly, one does not consciously desire blindness, but blindness may be the easiest way out of some difficulties, especially if they have been accompanied by prolonged worry and fatigue.

SUMMARY

The experience aroused by the stimulation of a sense organ is known as a sensory experience or a sensation. These experiences are basic to all of our adjustments. Sensations differ in kind or quality from one sense field to another and within certain sense fields. An experience of a given quality may vary in intensity, a fact which is at the basis of our measures of visual and auditory acuity, and in purity.

Visual sensations are characterized by having a certain quality (hue), a certain brightness or intensity, and a certain degree of purity. All visual sensations can be reduced to six elementary sensations: red, blue, yellow, green, black, and white. After-images are experiences which are due to a continued activity of a sensory organ after a stimulus has been removed. In vision, after-images may be positive (the same color and brightness as the stimulus) or negative (opposite in brightness and complementary in color). Maps of the visual field reveal that the area in the retina which is sensitive to reds and greens is smaller than the area which is sensitive to blues and yellows; the latter in turn is smaller than the total visual field. Instruments are available for measuring various characteristics of vision and audition.

Perception is a process of interpreting sensory stimulation. It is dependent upon a number of factors which may be classified as functional and structural. Functional factors in perception are those which arise out of the needs, past experiences, feelings, interests, and attitudes of the individual. Structural factors arise out of the nature of the stimulus, the nature of the body structures, and the nature of the neural activity set up by stimulation. In perception, a sensory stimulation interacts in various ways with previous experiences to set off previously acquired perceptions, or to produce new perceptions. Structural factors are important in the visual perception of distance.

Perceptions are distorted by (1) excitement and (2) suggestion. Illusions are of three types: (a) those due to the nature of the stimulus, (b) those due to subjective factors, and (c) those due to the nature of our sensory end organs. To make our perceptions more reliable, we should seek confirmation by the other senses, simplify the conditions of observation, check our experiences with those of other people, and be sure our sense organs, emotional state, and attitude are not influencing or biasing us.

While most illusions are normal and therefore have no serious effect upon personality, certain other disorders of perception, known as functional anaesthesias, are indicative of profound and deep-seated maladjustment. Perceptual defects often have a marked effect upon personality — for instance, when they cause the blind and deaf to become suspicious.

QUESTIONS
on the Chapter

1. What is a sensory experience?
2. What are the three characteristics of sensations?
3. Do all sensations have these characteristics?
4. Define: elementary sensation, complementary colors, negative after-image, tunnel vision, decibel, Weber's law, sensory adaptation, synaesthesia.
5. What is a perimeter? An audiometer?
6. Give an example of an after-image from a nonvisual sense field.
7. What is perception?
8. In what three ways may one's previous experiences interact with present stimulations to determine perception?
9. Describe the three stages in the development of perception.
10. What are "functional" factors in perception?
11. What are "structural" factors in perception?
12. What is the significance of the results of Sherif's experiment?
13. List the factors which enable us to see distance.
14. What are the three types of normal illusions?
15. In what ways may sensory defects influence one's personality?
16. What is functional anaesthesia?
17. How can we make our perceptions more reliable?

for Discussion

1. Could one learn if he were deprived of vision, hearing, taste, smell, and touch?
2. Do the skin sensations differ in "purity"?
3. Why are we not aware of the blind-spot in ordinary vision?

4. Is color blindness always a handicap?
5. In the light of Sherif's findings, what can you say about the popular notion that there is "safety in numbers"?
6. Cite some examples to show how one's perceptual set may interfere with normal perception.
7. Are all illusions normal illusions?
8. In view of the fact that perception is subject to many errors, what can you say regarding the reliability of testimony?
9. Is perceptual set a more important determiner of perception than external stimulating conditions?

REFERENCES

1 ABRAHAM, O., "Zur physiologischen Akustik von Wellenlänge und Schwingungszahl," *Zeitschrift für Sinnesphysiologie,* 1920, 51, 121–152.
2 BAUSCH and LOMB OPTICAL COMPANY, Rochester, New York.
3 BRUNER, J. S., and GOODMAN, C. G., "Need and Value as Organizing Factors in Perception," *J. Abnor. Soc. Psychol.,* 1947, 42, 33–44.
4 BRUNER, J. S., and POSTMAN, L., "An Approach to Social Perception." In DENNIS, W., *Current Trends in Social Psychology.* Pittsburgh: University of Pittsburgh Press, 1945.
5 BRUNER, J. S., and POSTMAN, L., "Emotional Selectivity in Perception and Reaction," *J. Personal.,* 1947, 16, 69–77.
6 DALLENBACH, J. W., and DALLENBACH, K. M., "The Effects of Bitter-Adaptation on Sensitivity to the Other Taste Qualities," *Amer. J. Psychol.,* 1943, 56, 21–31.
7 JANET, PIERRE, *The Major Symptoms of Hysteria,* 2nd edition. New York: The Macmillan Company, 1920.
8 KOFFKA, K., *Principles of Gestalt Psychology.* New York: Harcourt, Brace and Company, 1935.
9 KRETCH, R., and CRUTCHFIELD, J., *Theory and Problems of Social Psychology.* New York: McGraw-Hill Book Company, 1948.
10 LAUER, A. H., *Manual of Tests for Automotive Operators.* Iowa State College, 1934.
11 LEVINE, R., CHEIN, I., and MURPHY, G., "The Relation of the Intensity of a Need to the Amount of Perceptual Distortion," *J. Psychol.,* 1942, 13, 283–293.
12 LEWIS, D., and LICHTE, W. H., "Analysis of a Perceptible Series of Partials in a Vocal Sound," *J. Exp. Psychol.,* 1939, 24, 254–267.
13 LUCKEISH, M., *Visual Illusions and Their Applications.* New York: D. Van Nostrand Company, 1926.
14 MCDOUGALL, WILLIAM, *Outline of Abnormal Psychology.* New York: Charles Scribner's Sons, 1926. Quoted by permission.
15 MORGAN, J. J. B., *The Psychology of Abnormal People,* 2nd edition. New York: Longmans, Green and Company, 1936. Quoted by permission.
16 MURPHY, G., *An Introduction to Psychology.* New York: Harper and Brothers, 1951.

17 PATTIE, F. A., "An Experimental Study of Fatigue in the Auditory Mechanism," *Amer. J. Psychol.*, 1927, 38, 39–58.

18 POSTMAN, L., and BRUNER, J. S., "Perception under Stress," *Psychol. Rev.*, 1948, 55, 314–323.

19 POSTMAN, L., BRUNER, J. S., and MCGINNIES, E., "Personal Values as Selective Factors in Perception," *J. Abnor. Soc. Psychol.*, 1948, 43, 142–154.

20 RÉVÉSZ, G., "Experiments on Animal Space Perception. I. Why Do Hens Not Peck in the Dark? II. Investigation of Illusory Spatial Perception," *British J. Psychol.*, 1924, 14, 287–414.

21 ROBINSON, E. S., *Practical Psychology.* New York: The Macmillan Company, 1926. Quoted by permission.

22 RUCH, F. L., *Psychology and Life.* Chicago: Scott, Foresman and Company, 1937.

23 SHERIF, M., *The Psychology of Social Norms.* New York: Harper and Brothers, 1936.

24 SMITH, F. O., "The Effect of Training in Pitch Discrimination," *Psychol. Monogr.*, 1914, 16, 67–103.

25 STEVENS, E. M., *The Psychology of Space Perception.* Northfield: Carleton College, 1915.

26 STEVENS, S. S., ed., *Handbook of Experimental Psychology.* New York: John Wiley and Sons, 1951.

27 STEVENS, S. S., and DAVIS, H., *Hearing: Its Psychology and Physiology.* New York: John Wiley and Sons, 1938.

28 TIFFIN, J., and LONG, W. F., "Visual Requirements and Job Requirements," *Amer. J. Optom.*, 1946, 23, 463–476.

29 WARREN, H. C., *Elements of Human Psychology.* Boston: Houghton Mifflin Company, 1922.

30 WERTHEIMER, M., "Experimentelle Studien über das Sehen von Bewegung," *Zeitschrift für Psychologie*, 1912, 61, 161–265.

31 WHEELER, R. H., and PERKINS, F. T., *Principles of Mental Development.* Philadelphia: Thomas Y. Crowell Company, 1923.

ATTENTION

8

As a dozen people sit around the table after dinner, a dozen minds are occupied with a dozen *different* things. Jones is thinking of the business deal he is trying to make with Smith. Smith is thinking of his stomach-ache, wondering if it is really appendicitis. The doctor is wondering what fee he can reasonably charge Smith if Smith decides to have an operation. Mrs. Jones is thinking of the new dress she saw in the afternoon and wondering whether she can squeeze the money out of the budget to buy it. Mrs. Smith is listening to the radio which is playing softly in the next room. And the minds of all the others are similarly occupied with their own thoughts. At times, all center their attention on the same thing — if someone tells a particularly funny story or if the maid drops a dish. But for the most part the consciousness of each person is occupied with his own thoughts. He is unaware of most of the things in the minds of those about him.

It is often of momentous importance to an individual whether he attends carefully to a particular thing or not. The effect may seem — indeed, may *be* — out of all proportion to the cause. A slight lapse of attention when one is driving a car may result in a fatal accident, yet the inattention may be so slight as to be scarcely noticeable. It is worth remembering that in ways less tangible than this the results of inattention may be just as great and that they may affect our lives just as critically.

As you now read, you are unaware of many things in your immediate environment. You are not conscious of your chair — until now that it has been mentioned. You do not hear certain sounds — until now that your attention has been called to them. All these things and many more have been excluded from your consciousness in order that *one* thing — the book and the ideas it contains — may be given your full mental powers. You are *attending* to the book. *Attention* is a way of responding that is familiar to everyone but is difficult to define.

Everyone realizes that of all the thousands and thousands of things which *might* be in consciousness — the many items of our immediate environment plus the memories that have been accumulating since childhood — only a very few things *are* in consciousness at any one time. Our consciousness may alternate rapidly between different things, but we cannot attend to several things at once. It is, indeed, as if our minds were a broad field which we examine at night with a small searchlight. We are located at the top of a tower in the center of the field. We may focus our spotlight where we will; but the farther from the base of the tower we focus it, the less distinctly do we see. Around the base of the tower is an area which may be seen very distinctly as the spotlight falls upon the different parts. This area comprises our present experiences and those which have happened recently or, if more remotely, have been very well learned. Around the edges of the field are immense areas which can be seen, at best, only very indistinctly. These comprise more remote experiences, those which, because of passing time or of unimportance, have nearly faded from memory. Still farther out are areas of unknown size which cannot be seen at all. These correspond to experiences which can no longer be brought into consciousness at all, which cannot be made the focus of our "attentive spotlight" — although there is much evidence that these outlying districts exercise a profound influence upon the more accessible parts of the field. As an invisible hill or mountain on one side of a real field may determine the waterways and wind currents in the closer parts, so experiences which have been lost to consciousness may have an effect upon us which is very difficult to understand without some special means of learning about these past experiences.

THE IMPORTANCE OF ATTENTION

Imagine a frightened deer listening for an approaching danger and you will have a picture of the bodily adjustments which accompany and assist the attentive process. He holds his body tense and almost motionless: consciousness of his own movements must not be allowed to compete with the danger signals for the deer's attention. But he moves his ears to hear better and sniffs the air. Experiments show that there is also an unconscious tendency to move toward the object of attention. This tendency can be observed in man. If a person attached to an automatograph (a device which records very slight movements of the body) stands in the middle of a room and listens attentively to a metronome which is moved around the four sides of the room, he will "follow" the

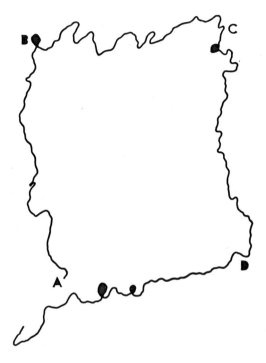

Figure 52

The Effect of Attention on Movement

Automatographic record of a person's unconscious movements as he listens to a metronome that is moved around the room. (From J. Jastrow, *Fact and Fable in Psychology*, Houghton Mifflin, 1900, p. 326.)

metronome around by leaning toward it (see Figure 52). In short, attention involves important physical adjustments. These bodily or motor adjustments in the process of attention serve several purposes.

Relation to Sensory Discrimination

By attending we are better able to isolate the parts of a complex whole. For example, in hearing, we can discriminate fine tones of the various instruments of an orchestra by attending carefully. In the second place, by attending we are able to perceive a stimulus that would otherwise pass entirely unnoticed. While listening for danger, the deer will hear a footstep that he would not ordinarily hear. If we attend to the clock on the mantel, we shall hear it ticking, though a moment ago, while attending to something else, we did not hear the clock at all. During hypnosis (which is a heightened state of attention toward certain things) the ability to detect slight differences becomes so great that a person can distinguish between sheets of paper that are ordinarily indistinguishable. Similarly, the blind and deaf notice differences that are normally unperceived, not because their sensory organs have become more acute, but because they pay more attention to the impressions received through them. In the third place, by attending we receive clearer impressions. Anyone can confirm this for himself. Look at the printed page without attending; nothing stands out distinctly. Or eat dinner while thinking of something else, and the chances are that you will be unable to tell offhand whether you are eating pumpkin or carrot pie. As focusing the eyes causes visual impressions to stand out clearly, so does attending make all sensory impressions more distinct.

Attention involves a heightened state of motor readiness. The startled deer not only listens and sniffs the air, but he is also ready to respond immediately. The runner on the mark is ready to jump as soon as the gun is fired. There is need to respond and to respond quickly. The state of attention is a preparatory adjustment to do what is needed. A person can respond to a signal more quickly if he is given a preparatory or "get-ready" signal which rivets his attention.

Attention and Memory

We can recall with most assurance and accuracy those things to which we have attended most carefully. For example, if one is shown a series of colors and attends carefully with the purpose of being able to name them afterwards, he can usually do so. But if an experimenter shows a number of colored cards while he is fixing the attention of his audience on something else, many people will not notice the cards at all; and even those who do will probably be unable to name the colors later.

Münsterberg (7) reports a very simple experiment which clearly illustrates this principle. He instructed his students to watch and describe everything he did between one signal and another. As soon as the first signal had been given, he lifted in his right hand a little revolving color wheel and made it run and change its color. While he held the instrument in his right hand at the height of his head, he took a pencil from his vest pocket with his left hand and wrote something on the desk. Next he took out his watch and laid it on the table. Then he took a cigarette case from his pocket, opened it, removed a cigarette, and closed the case with a loud click and returned it to his pocket. Then came the ending signal. Eighteen out of a hundred students had failed to notice anything of all that had been done with his left hand. Pencil, watch, and cigarettes had simply not existed for them, in spite of the fact that they had been told to observe and report everything that the instructor did. Our memory for things which do not attract our attention is likely to be very short if not nonexistent.

But attention increases the accuracy of memory only when the total situation is relatively undisturbed by personal concern. The impartial observer or the disinterested witness may, by paying keen attention, remember with reasonable accuracy. But if one's own personal fortune is involved, even intense attention does not save him from amazing inaccuracies. When one's attention is keyed up by unusual self-interest, it is easy for one to "hear" what a dictaphone would never have recorded and to "see" what a camera would not have photographed, to perceive, in short, a curious mixture of what really happens and of a very private vision of what he *wants* to happen. It is good psychology as well as common law not to force a person to testify against himself or his mate. Through the ages we have learned that attention is distorted by our desires. But inaccurate reports from interested persons do not necessarily imply dishonesty; they may well be the normal distortions of attention. A man awaiting a crucial long-distance telephone call can easily "hear" a bell which no one else near the telephone hears and which the operator reports she did not ring. Experience has led to our insistence on written contracts, because, in spite of our best intentions, attention under pressure tricks us all. Ordinarily, attention will increase the accuracy of observations in direct proportion to our freedom from personal concern.

Attention and Efficiency

The effect of attention on the higher mental processes is to make us more responsive to relevant and less responsive to irrelevant matters. A person engaged in collecting material for a debate is quick to attend to any idea or fact that will help him. When he is actually thinking through what he is going to say, he finds that ideas come to him in a more or less logical order. To be attentive is to head one's efforts in a certain direction; the ideas that come are then, for the most part, relevant. Attention may be thought of as a kind of sieve or filter which allows certain stimuli to pass through freely and easily and prevents the passage of those which are not wanted for the purpose in hand. It should be noted, however, that man is no magician in solving his problems. There is no guarantee that only the relevant stimuli will come to mind and that the irrelevant will all conveniently stay away. But the skillful problem-solver is the one who does learn to be something of a magician in this respect, and the intellectual flounderer is the one who never acquires control over the topics which flit in and out of the spotlight of his attention.

From the foregoing discussion it is easy to understand why attention greatly increases learning efficiency. Clear perception, clear analysis, fixation and retention, imagination, and logical association are all stimulated by focusing effort on the task at hand, and all of these are essential to efficient learning or study. Even in conditioning the flow of saliva to the sound of a bell, Pavlov found it necessary that the dogs be alert.

Though attention in general increases efficiency, it does not always do so. One does not increase the efficiency of his digestive, respiratory, or circulatory processes by attending to them. Indeed he is more likely to lower their efficiency. Likewise, too much attention to the emotional content of a situation may liberate excessive emotional energy and cause difficulties in executing a task. This is particularly true of anxiety when we attend to the wrong feature of a situation. Similarly, a golf player who is overanxious to make a good shot and who attends directly to this desire lowers his efficiency. Too much attention to spelling may give poorer results than comparative neglect of spelling. A person may reduce his power of conversing by paying too much attention to his words. Many students, by an excess of effort at an examination — not before — do less well than they might, had they been a little less concerned.

But in all these instances in which attention seems to lower efficiency, close inspection will reveal that attention is fixed in the wrong direction or on the wrong thing. For this reason the control of attention is a matter of great importance. The control of attention can be effective only in so far as definite principles are followed. Attention does not vary willy-nilly, nor can one by some mysterious power force himself to pay attention against the trend of the determining factors in the situation. Everyone has had the experience of "reading" a page or two of an uninteresting book only to find that he has been thinking of something else all the time. Attention had unconsciously and automatically left the book, though the eyes continued to go through the movements of reading. All of us know that calling the roll in a college class does not reveal those who are really there and those who are present in body only. Experimental studies indicate that all instances of attention or inattention are dependent upon the existence of certain internal and external conditions. The ways in which these conditions determine attention are described below under the heading of laws of attention. These laws enable us to explain the things we have been discussing.

LAWS OF ATTENTION

External Conditions

Attention, like all other responses, must be explained in terms of the whole situation in which it occurs. Because we have changing needs and interests and are in a continually changing environment, we necessarily experience periods of stress and strain as well as periods of easy effort and recesses of relaxation and relief. If we want to know why we attend to a particular object, we must therefore look to the conditions both outside ourselves (objective conditions) and inside ourselves (subjective conditions). We shall describe first the most important external, or objective, conditions of attention.

Change. The hunter, if he keeps stock-still, may not be observed; but let him move but a fraction of an inch, and his prey will be off. A slight change in the total visual pattern is very effective to the interested eye. A slight movement of the right foot of the halfback may be unnoticed by the crowd — but not by the alert defensive end. Coaches have to impress upon the beginning player the fact that movements so slight they "couldn't possibly matter" often make just the difference between the team's staying where it is and getting down into pay dirt. It might be added that some football players never learn to pay attention to this fact.

We are more likely to observe flickering lights than those that are steady, more likely to attend to a siren than to a whistle blowing a steady blast. Other things being equal, we are almost always more likely to notice a changing stimulus than an unchanging one. Advertisers recognize this in constructing electric signs and in writing magazine and newspaper advertisements. And it is hard to imagine anything more difficult to attend to than a voice that is monotonous and droning.

Strength and intensity of the impression. Other things being equal, the stronger or more intense an impression is, the more likely it is to command attention. A faint noise may not disturb the reader, when a loud one will. A flash of lightning in the distance may pass unnoticed, while one near at hand compels attention. Talking in the next room may be quite unnoticed, when a shout would immediately attract attention. But while this is true, in general, do not forget that sheer intensity of stimulus is only one external condition of attention. Even in the roar of Forty-second Street after the theater a very slight round pressure in the back and a very soft whisper in the ear, "Walk right along toward that taxi," would be quite effective in securing attention. Meaningful weak stimuli may overpower meaningless strong stimuli.

Size. Other things being equal, the larger a thing is the more likely one is to notice it. For this reason advertisers prefer large magazine space and large billboards. However, other things are often not equal. Recent experiments by the authors have shown that a small cartoon in the middle of a printed page will usually attract a reader and hold him longer than a full-page, gaudily colored advertisement on the opposite page. Notice what attracts your attention as you thumb through the next issue of the *Saturday Evening Post.*

Repetition. Other things being equal, the more often a thing is repeated, the more likely one is to notice it. This would, of course, be true by the law of chance, but it is due also to the *summation of impressions.* Each sensory impression, whether we are conscious of it or not, persists for a time. The weight of a second impression, therefore, is added to the weight of a first one. As an example consider the striking of a clock. We may not notice the first stroke, nor the second, nor possibly the third. But when the clock strikes the fourth time, let us say, we may suddenly notice it and realize immediately that it has been striking, and perhaps even be able to tell how many times it has struck before we attended to it. The first sounds, therefore, must have made impressions, though not sufficiently strong ones to arouse attention. The summation of impressions, however, finally made the fourth one so. Take another example on a higher level. We may not notice the first slight of a friend; but when his same act or attitude is repeated a few times and we begin to pay attention, we then recall the previous incidents. Much of the power of propaganda lies in the potency of repetition. Constant dripping will wear away a stone.

Novelty. Other things being equal, the more striking the quality of an object, the more likely it is to attract attention. We are more likely to notice a bright red or yellow object than one of a softer color. In listening to music, we are more apt to attend to those parts that have a definite pattern than to those which are nebulous or lacking in form. A false note, one that does not belong in the score, is still more certain to command attention. In looking at a picture, we are more likely to observe the clear-cut foreground than the background. Strictly speaking, novelty or unusualness is a relation between the observer and the object observed. It depends as much upon the individual as upon external conditions. Other things being equal, it means simply that one is more apt to attend to something that is new to him than to an object that is familiar to him. Skillful public speakers search for surprising and unusual ways of expressing their ideas. This may be done by using old words in new settings, or by challenging accustomed ways of thinking. It would challenge a good deal of popular belief to begin a speech by saying: "I have only one minor and trivial objection to the statement that 'All men are created equal,' and that is that it is an obvious and barefaced lie." Challenging popular belief, such a sentence would arrest attention. It must be remembered, however, that the pricks of novelty soon lose their sharpness. The sophomore may well "psychologize" the greenness of the freshman, since the former has become negatively adapted to the novelties of a college campus. A man in the city for the first time attends alertly to the variety of noises and sights, but the country gawk soon becomes the city sophisticate.

Nearness to point of fixation. Other things being equal, the closer an object is, the more apt it is to attract our attention (4). Persons who make up window displays recognize this principle and put the objects which they wish to emphasize fairly close to each other in the center of the display. Rumor has it that near the end of the term the front seats in a college lecture room are more frequently occupied than they are at the beginning of the term when the semester's grade is still far away.

Importance of problems. When a problem arises that must be solved, we are likely to focus our attention upon it. Attention enables us to concentrate our energies upon the problem in hand and, for the time being, to exclude from consciousness other things of lesser importance. Our resources are assembled by attention in proportion to the importance of the problem. In short, we pay attention to that which is of concern to us. The human mind does not do something for nothing, and a high level of attention costs energy. The normal person is not prodigal or spendthrift of his energy, and long-continued, highly concentrated attention is granted most surely to problems of vital interest to us.

To sum up the situation, attention can be more or less controlled by manipulating the environment, and we can do much in controlling and directing the attention of others by manipulating their environment. Were this chapter written three times as well as it is, with more skillful *changes* in rhetorical pace, more *repetition* of ideas, more *powerful* adjectives, more *intense* illustrations, with the use here and there of type of *larger size* and perhaps of some *novel* features such as occasional red ink, the attention given to the discussion would no doubt have been greater. We do not attend willy-nilly to the items in our environment, but are more or less *drawn* to those items which possess the characteristics described above.

Internal Conditions

The foregoing paragraphs indicate how attention is more or less affected by environmental factors. An adequate account of attention must give corresponding emphasis to factors within the person. It is well known that one person is heedful and another heedless of the same object, and that what may be of very high attention value at one time may have practically no attention-drawing power at another. We need to consider the personal aspects of attention, for they are of special importance in this connection.

Native desires and urges. Man has a kind of organization that tends to select for attention certain things instead of certain others because some things directly or indirectly satisfy his native desires while others have only a tenuous connection with them. Just as a chicken is attentive to grain and a dog to a bone, so man finds it far easier to give attention to that which promises fulfillment of his basic desires. Persons in danger, as in war or fire or other disaster, attend quickly and definitely to those features of the environment which seem to promise escape and self-preservation. Advertisers recognize that people notice an advertisement which appeals to native likes. Crane (3) reports that "six hundred copies of *True Story Magazine* were sold to Yale students in contrast to one copy of the *Century Magazine.*" Observe the next dozen advertisements that have enough power in them to attract your attention at all and decide for yourself whether the basic appeals are to you as a philosopher, a logician, an analyst, or a rather "human" person. The terrific power of propaganda may be found in its appeal, not to reason or to objective data, but rather to unanalyzed feelings based on native desires. To catch and keep the attention of any but a superintellectual, long experience teaches us (novelists, playwrights, and politicians included) to appeal, however guardedly, to such native desires as are embodied in the love of mastery, the need of protection against one kind of danger or another, envy, jealousy, and interest in the opposite sex.

Sentiments and complexes. The person who has the sentiment of patriotism is likely to attend to what he thinks will affect the welfare of his group. One suffering from feelings of inferiority or burdened with a sense of inadequacy is likely to attend to anything that may bolster up his self-regard. He will observe the mistakes of others, the slight evidences of weakness in his friends or acquaintances, and he will fail to attend to their accomplishments or strengths. To know a person, watch what attracts (or distracts) his attention from the main drift of the current scene. Little, and often unnoticed, movements of attention to this, that, and the other thing are brush strokes that paint an amazingly accurate picture of a person for the keen observer. Keep in mind that it is not only what one *does* pay attention to but also what he does *not* pay attention to that fills in the perspective of the portrait. A professor learns far more about you than merely your knowledge of his particular subject as he watches the fluctuations of your attention in the classroom — unless, as is sometimes the case, he is dividing his *own* attention between his duties in the classroom and other interests that flit in and out of his mind. The faraway look of the football player as he mentally rehearses formation C, the thirty times that the young lady on the left rearranges her hair, the honest yawn with which Mr. Smith to the right "attends to" any difficult idea, the starry-eyed expression of the girl who is wearing a new and sparkling diamond, the much-envied peaceful slumber of that boy in the back row, the various overt responses to an unannounced quiz, the almost universal brightening of the class when the bell rings — all these things tell the professor many things that he could never learn from examination papers. And do *you* not learn more about *him* than the subject he is teaching?

Mood. If one is despondent and downcast, he is likely to attend to things that deepen his depression. He is impressed with the ugliness and drabness of his surroundings. If elated, one will attend to the features of the environment that justify and enhance that mood. When in a "worrying mood," one goes out of his way to find something to worry about. If one has been anxious about his grade in a course and suddenly finds that he got a high one, instead of ceasing to worry he is apt to start fretting about something else which has been entirely out of mind. Mood helps to determine what we attend to and how we evaluate the object of our attention. There is a great deal of psychological insight in the statement that "unto every one that hath shall be given, and he shall have abundance."

Attitude. We attend to those things that *confirm* our attitudes. The cynic attends to things that confirm his cynicism; the person who has confidence in men, to things that confirm his optimism. In a sense, we filter out what we want to see and want to hear rather than accept an impartial sampling of what is there. The embarrassment of Mr. Jones seems greater to those who want to see him embarrassed. A decision is very unfair if you suspect the honesty of the judge. People at dinner may get very divergent ideas of the temperature of the soup. The hostess thinks it a little cool. Mrs. Smith, delighted to be invited to the party, thinks it just right. Professor Phillips does not remember the next day that soup was served at all. Mrs. Jones, a social rival of the hostess, pretends to shiver as she tastes it. To a psychologist, more than food is served at a dinner party.

Education and training. A bootblack will notice the shoes of a passer-by; a barber, his hair; a haberdasher, his suit; and a manicurist, his nails. We attend to objects we have been trained to observe. The musician notices features in the symphony that the untutored listener does not; the artist sees things in a picture that the untrained layman misses; the student of literature will notice faults of composition that the unread person will not. The eyes of specialists have been opened, as it were, to things which the ordinary person does not observe.

Purpose of the moment. A hunter and a surveyor will notice different things, even though they walk across the same field. When preparing for a debate, we may turn the pages of a book or magazine hurriedly, merely glancing at the pages, until our eyes fall on something pertaining to the debate. Then we immediately become alert and read attentively.

Purpose of the future. We often attend to things, not because they are interesting at the time, but because it is necessary that we attend in order to reach a certain goal. A student may attend to his studies when other things are much more inviting, because he is striving for the goal of graduation or parental approval. A professional man may work hard to safeguard the interests of his client when he would rather be playing golf, because the goal of professional success or monetary reward cannot be attained without attention to these immediate details.

In short, what man attends to is determined by the outside world, but it is also influenced by his own inner mental world. In the affairs of ordinary life, the nearest one usually gets to a stimulus is his own interpretation of it. Man edits his world in the service of his needs and at the demand of his tensions. We are our own editors and our own "yes men."

INVOLUNTARY VS. VOLUNTARY ATTENTION

No motion picture ever began with the statement: "This is going to be a very interesting picture, so please pay close attention!" And if a picture did begin in this way, we should surely tell ourselves that it could not be very good; for we pay attention to a good picture without being told. The most efficient form of attention is entirely involuntary — when we attend without realizing it. Involuntary attention occurs when we witness an absorbing play or motion picture, when we read a captivating novel, when we are engaged in interesting conversation, or when we become "lost" in our work. In fact, the free giving of ourselves to the task in hand is a necessary element in efficient mental habits. The capable worker, like the child in his play, attends to his work quite involuntarily and unconsciously.

In contrast to involuntary attention is the kind we experience when we find our minds "wandering" and bring ourselves back to the matter in hand with some such statement as, "I *must* pay attention to this book," or "Why did my attention drift away from this problem when it *must* be solved before tomorrow?" Mind-wandering or difficulty in attending to what in the long run is really important to us is not a trivial matter. Its significance is far greater than the lost time or the superficial discomfort would imply. Inability to attend often implies an emotional blocking the foundations of which may lie far deeper and further afield than one would suspect. Commonly we say that the inattentive man fails. It would be more correct to say that inattention is a symptom of a failure already made but perhaps not recognized. In the last analysis, man attends to what he wants to attend to, to what serves his purposes, and he is inattentive to that which does not serve his purposes. If one is indifferent to what in the long run is really important to him, it is high time for him to take a close inventory of his interests and either to rearrange them so that attention becomes natural or to accommodate himself to his real interests. One foundation of sound vocational guidance is the discovery of what the person really wants to do, the things to which his whole-hearted attention is given naturally and freely.

All attention, whether it be involuntary or voluntary, is determined by the objective and subjective factors we have discussed. But often — indeed in most cases — these several influences do not all operate together to keep a specific subject in our attention. Our interests may be so divided that, though we realize the necessity of attending to our lessons, we find it hard to exclude an approaching party from our minds. Our attention fluctuates between these two alternatives. In cases like this we speak of our attention to the matter that is difficult to concentrate upon as voluntary, and of our attention to the matter that is easy to concentrate upon as involuntary. Fortunately, after concentrating upon something for a brief time, even though only a small measure of satisfaction or success crowns our efforts, we usually become interested, and involuntary or effortless attention replaces voluntary or effortful attention.

The teacher, the lecturer, and the advertiser do well to know the general laws of attention, the importance of subjective and objective factors, and the role which each plays in developing involuntary attention. The lecturer who continually finds it necessary to pound on the table or wave his arms in order to hold attention is openly admitting that what he has to say does not appeal to his audience. The teacher who finds it necessary to say "Pay attention" is admitting that he cannot present his material in a way that appeals to the real interests of his students. Objective conditions (loud sounds, unusual behavior, large signs) are excellent devices for *attracting* attention, but poor indeed for *holding* it. One's attention is seldom held by anything unless it in some way appeals to his needs, interests, wishes, or desires. One of the most important things which every successful teacher, or anyone else who succeeds in affecting others, does is to present his material so that involuntary, effortless attention is developed. The sales talk appears in many different guises — in proposing, lecturing, reciting, examination writing, and writing to Dad for more money, as well as in selling groceries, automobiles, or what not. The sales talk may be spoken or written or communicated by a complex succession of gestures; but whatever its purpose and whatever its content, its inner purpose is to get and hold the attention of the person to whom it is addressed.

CONTROL OF ATTENTION

Prevention of Distraction

Distractions may be defined as stimuli which attract a person's attention from a task in hand to something else. The conditions which may prove distracting are varied. We usually think of distraction as being caused by a noise or some such unsettled condition. However, unusual quiet may have the same effect. A person in the habit of studying in a library or in a building on a noisy street may think that if he could only get away from all noise and confusion, he would be able to work more efficiently. Accordingly, he welcomes the first opportunity to take his books and seek quiet in the country. Perhaps he gets a canoe and drifts out on a lake, fondly imagining that under the moss-laden cypress trees he will overcome all difficulties — only to find that he is quite unable to concentrate. The novelty of the situation proves too much for him. He discovers that familiar surroundings, even though noisy, are more conducive to concentration of effort than unfamiliar surroundings, however ideal they may appear. More commonly, however, we are distracted by the stimuli of a busy scene such as noises, people moving about, the click of typewriters, or the hum of machinery. Everyone recognizes the importance of overcoming distractions of this kind.

Compare two individuals hurriedly making preparations for a trip. One moves about swiftly and smoothly, he takes no unnecessary steps. The other runs about wildly; he retraces his steps many times and responds to many irrelevant things. The former, we say, is proceeding attentively and efficiently to perform the necessary task; the latter is distracted by the emergency. He does not attend to the proper things or restrain impulsive action.

It should be remembered, however, that outside distractions are often an *excuse* rather than a *reason* for inability to attend, and that the one who always blames outside distractions for his inability to work is apt to be indulging in a little self-deception. The student who really wants to study soon learns to do so, even under circumstances that are not the most favorable. Our friend who cannot get his bag packed may simply be expressing the fact that he does not want to take a trip. Many professors who are too busy with their students and classes to take a speaking trip for the good of a cause easily arrange matters so that they can leave the campus if a fifty-dollar fee is the inducement. The freshman who finds it too noisy to read his psychology assignment in the fraternity house does not hear a sound when he is reading a letter from home.

Between normal and abnormal behavior in this matter of attention and distraction there is no sharp line of demarcation. Extreme distraction gives rise to manic forms of insanity. The manic is unable to keep any idea in mind more than an instant. He is unable to carry out any consistent line of action. Since every passing thought must be embodied in action, he flies from one thing to another. As a consequence, nothing constructive is accomplished. The opposite extreme is found among those suffering from schizophrenia, some of whom seem utterly indifferent to all outside stimulation. So absorbed are they in their own mental processes that, if their arms are raised over their heads, they leave them there until someone pulls them down. The normal person falls between these extremes. He is responsive to some of his ideas and to some of the objects in his environment, not to everything.

Though the ability to withstand distraction is an outgrowth of one's total personality, yet knowledge of some of the methods of overcoming distraction may be of help. The obvious way is to flee from the distracting influence, but this is not always possible or sure of working. Another way is to make the distracting impression or action a part of the activity one is engaged in. A person who has learned to run the scale on the piano with his right hand may find the use of his left hand a source of distraction.   But if he persists, he will soon find it easier to perform the action with both hands than with one.

Another way of overcoming distraction is to become accustomed to it. In such cases we speak of becoming *negatively adapted* to the object. This happens usually when we do not have to respond to the distracting stimulus or when it proves to be a false one.   The principle of negative adaptation is of great use when the stimuli are only bothersome.   We are ordinarily functionally deaf to the tick of a clock, or to the buzzing of a taximeter when we are riding as a guest of someone else.   In some circumstances, however, negative adaptation is extremely dangerous. Thus we must not teach others that we are joking when we cry for help. The story of the lad who cried "Wolf!" illustrates this point.   It is foolhardy to be so "tough" that one becomes negatively adapted to a sore throat, or to a stomach-ache that might be appendicitis.   One can well give his best thought to the question: To what can I afford to become negatively adapted and to what must I not allow myself or others to become chronically indifferent?

Often the speed with which one becomes negatively adapted to irrelevant stimuli indicates his fitness for the work in question.   A person beginning work in a busy office often is distracted by the noise and seeming confusion.   Since he does not have to respond to the noise, however, he ignores it and in a short time performs his work undisturbed by what is going on about him; but his companion worker who does not like his job never learns to ignore the noise.

There is some experimental evidence which indicates that conditions at first a distraction actually make for greater attention after the worker becomes accustomed to them.   Morgan (6) found that though "a seemingly unfavorable condition influenced the subject to a very slight extent . . . after a slight retardation he exceeded the speed made under normal conditions, doing as accurate work under both conditions."   Probably in situations of this type the distraction serves the purpose of shutting out new distractions, while it itself loses the power to distract as the subject becomes habituated to it.   We are constantly becoming negatively adapted to all sorts of stimuli — noises, sights, odors, uncomfortable clothes, and so on.   In general, we learn to ignore things that are of no consequence.   Though the process of becoming negatively adapted is largely passive and unconscious, yet an attitude of indifference facilitates it, while an attitude of annoyance prevents it.

Distraction may also be overcome by extra effort.   To become negatively adapted to distracting impressions, we may need to use our determination. When something distracts us, our self-assertiveness may be aroused. We *resolve* not to let it interfere with our work, or we make the experiment of seeing if we can overcome it, or we simply grit our teeth and go ahead with full speed. Under the impetus of extra effort our efficiency is not infrequently increased in spite of the distraction. That a distraction may actually cause one to put forth extra effort is shown in an experiment by Laird. By comparing the amount of carbon dioxide breathed out by girls typing in a noisy room with the amount breathed out while typing in a quiet room, Laird (5) has shown that typing in a noisy room requires more energy than typing in a quiet room. To maintain efficiency under adverse conditions, the reserves of the organism are mustered and used. This is obviously taxing to the organism's energy, and one should seek working conditions that will make this drain unnecessary.

An alert attitude against the wavering of attention is helpful. If a person knows that his attention is apt to waver, he may assume a watchful attitude. By so doing he will be able to detect quickly any fluctuation of attention and bring himself back to the job he has set for himself. It is especially desirable to keep this in mind while one is studying uninteresting assignments, though the advice is easier to read than to follow. Working with our hands in a laboratory helps to prevent distraction, but reading goes on so automatically that the reader is apt to let his thoughts wander. This is especially true if the material is difficult. If we read an abstruse passage without understanding it, the continuity of our thought is broken; and in place of the author's thoughts we are apt to substitute some of our own fancies. One good practical rule for every student is to be on the alert for the wavering of attention and to understand each thought of the author as he presents it. Another good rule is to assume the physical attitude of attention. When we attend, there is motor readiness for quick response; the runner on the mark is ready for a quick get-off; the soldier at attention is ready to respond to the officer's command. Though we cannot directly exercise control over our train of thoughts, as is shown by the tendency to daydream when we should like to study, yet an active posture of attention does much to prevent such mind-wandering and to keep us on the job we are trying to finish. Most of us find that lying in bed is a poor posture for reading any material other than a very exciting detective story. An attentive attitude may not guarantee attention, but it is helpful. Those who wish to learn to concentrate should cultivate it.

Attending to Uninteresting Things

How it is possible to attend to uninteresting things has already been stated. We attend to them because we know that, in the long run, to attend will be more in accord with our interests than not to attend. The experience of a twelve-year-old schoolboy illustrates the point. The boy had been doing so poorly in school that his teacher decided she would talk to his mother about his work. When she had told the mother the purpose of her visit, the mother said, "Tommy is a fine boy, isn't he? I was sure you would like him." And she then went on to tell how hard Tommy had worked since his father's death trying to help her support and care for the younger children. With that knowledge the teacher was able to approach Tommy differently. She convinced him that by doing his schoolwork well, he would be in a position to be of greater help to the family. So motivated, Tommy became a satisfactory pupil.

At other times we attend because of our ideals of discipline and strength. Not to attend when we feel we should, we regard as a weakness. Or we may be led to attend through less praiseworthy motives. For example, in the days of the little red schoolhouse the bunch of switches behind the teacher's chair was a powerful stimulus. It was less disagreeable to attend than to pay the fine of inattention, though the quality of the attention so stimulated was not the best. Today, rewards and punishment, though of a less tangible sort, continue to occupy an important place in helping pupils attend to uninteresting things. The desire to excel others is often an important motive in attention. Sometimes competition between groups is made good use of to provoke greater effort. Especially effective is the competition in lower schools between boys and girls. A more healthful motive is the desire to excel one's own record, or to master difficulties.

In general, the importance of attending to uninteresting things can be easily overestimated. One should not, indeed cannot and will not, pay long-continued attention to that which for him utterly lacks luster. It is often stupid to be too tolerant of that which is boring. Educators should not become negatively adapted to absence of interest among schoolchildren and make too heavy demands on the heroism of youngsters. It is far easier and it is better psychology to change the school in such a way that a normal child has at least a gambler's chance of liking it. A growing number of children go to truly fascinating schools. Problems of tardiness and truancy are largely matters of history, not of current concern. Great ingenuity should always be used to reduce essentially boring tasks to an absolute minimum. There is no virtue in the disagreeable *per se,* though rationalizations for it infest our literature.

The Proper Direction of Attention

The proper direction of attention is essential to highest efficiency. When attention does not increase efficiency, it is improperly directed. The golfer who attends to the consequences of his shot instead of to the ball should not be surprised if he plays poorly. The conversationalist who attends to his words and his manner of speaking, instead of to the people about him and to what others are saying, is not an interesting companion. The business executive who is so anxious to talk that he cannot listen should not, but would, be surprised on failing as an executive. Just as the typist must cease attending to spelling and attend to typing, so managers and speakers should cease attending to manners and concentrate on directing their men or on influencing their audiences. To attempt to do consciously what should be done unconsciously is always inefficient. As Smith (10) says, "The over-anxious person is always ineffective, and the harder he tries the worse it makes him." If attention is to make us more efficient, we must attend to the right things.

In learning a complicated activity, we must shift our attention from one phase or part of the task to another. The child who is learning to write must first attend to making his letters legible; later he should try to write rapidly. In reading, the child must attend to one thing at a time. The beginner cannot attend to calling the words accurately, to expression, and to meaning at the same time. He must first learn the words; afterwards he should try to master expression and meaning. Similarly, in learning to play billiards, we must first learn to make our shot; after we have become somewhat proficient in doing that, our further progress depends on attending to the position of the balls for our next shot. In becoming a public speaker, we must first concentrate on what we are going to say, but later we may profitably attend to our audience and to the effect of what we are saying.

The value of instruction is to be found largely in the proper direction of attention. The person who is learning penmanship needs to have someone to direct his attention to his good strokes. The same is true in acquiring skill in sports and games, such as swimming and tennis. By undirected effort we may in time master these arts, but we do so at a great waste of time and labor. To have someone set for us a good example and call our attention to good form when we attain it reduces the labor of the learning process. This also applies to logical learning. To have someone help us with the organization of the facts we have learned and point out what is significant will prevent us from wasting time with masses of unorganized and irrelevant facts. In reading a book, the student himself can do much to prevent waste, by first reading carefully the table of contents and the introduction; then he may hurriedly skim through the book so as to become acquainted with the essential position of the author and with the way he develops his subject. By so doing he gets a perspective which should enable him to pick out the essential and the important, and to see all facts in their relation to the whole.

THE MEASUREMENT OF ATTENTION

Measurements of the strength and vividness of attention often have to be made indirectly. Except in rare instances the measurements are affected by other aspects of mental life so that we are seldom sure that we are measuring attention and nothing else. Attention is not a mental process operating all by itself in such a way that it can be measured independently of other phases of the total personality. Approximate measures, however, of what is predominantly attention are of great practical use. Samples of such measurement follow.

Attention Power of a Stimulus

We have already seen that some stimuli attract attention more readily than others. For example, some advertisements attract the attention of a reader more readily than others, or one part of an advertisement attracts attention before others and holds the attention longer. Measurements of the attention value of advertisements or parts thereof may be obtained by means of an eye camera like the one shown in Figure 53. This apparatus measures the time spent by a reader on different pages of a magazine and also the time spent on parts of each page. Using this eye camera, Asher and Kahn (1) measured the length of time that subjects looked at the illustration and the text of each of twelve full-page magazine advertisements under two sets of instructions. One group of subjects was instructed to look at the advertisements just as they would if they were leafing through a magazine while waiting in a dentist's office. Another group of subjects was asked to read each advertisement just as they would if they were in their rooms without anything to do but read the magazine. Figure 54 shows the average number of seconds spent on the illustrations under the "look" and "read" direc-

Figure 53

Eye Camera with Half-silvered Mirror

A camera located above the head records where the reader looks as her eyes strike successive portions of the newspaper page. Note the reflection of the subject's eyes in the lower left corner of the mirror. A similar apparatus is used in studying eye movements in reading magazine advertisements.

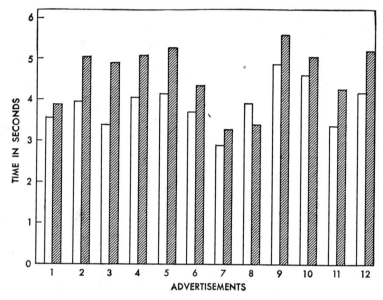

Figure 54

Average Time Spent on Illustrations under "Look" (solid bars)
and "Read" (shaded bars) Directions

(After E. J. Asher and David B. Kahn, "The Effect of 'Look' and 'Read' Directions
upon the Attention Value of Illustrations and Texts in Magazine Advertisements," *J. Appl.
Psychol.*, 1947, 31, 431–436. By permission of the American Psychological Association.)

tions. It will be noted that the illustrations in these twelve advertisements differ in attention-holding power, the illustration in advertisement 9 having the greatest holding power and the one in advertisement
7 the smallest. The texts in the twelve advertisements were found to
differ in attention-holding power also, but a comparison of the holding
power of the illustrations and texts indicated that the latter had from
$2\frac{1}{2}$ to 3 times as much holding power as the former under both the
"read" and "look" directions.

Another measure of the attention value of the illustrations and texts
in this study was obtained by counting the number of times the subjects
looked at the illustrations first and the number of times they looked at
the texts first under each set of instructions. The per cent of first
fixations on the illustrations proved to be 77.78 and 76.91 for the "read"
and "look" directions respectively. The per cent of first fixations on
the texts was 22.22 for the "read" directions and 23.09 for the "look"
directions. The illustrations have more than three times as much

initial attracting power as do the texts regardless of whether the instruction is to "read" or "look at" the advertisements.

The length of time one attends to a thing varies with the complexity of the object attended to and with one's own inner condition. Billings (2) reports that the duration of attention to very simple things, such as dots on paper and small parts of a picture, is about two seconds. He also finds that the more complex the stimulating situation, the longer the duration of attention. We can, therefore, attend to a scientific problem or to a book or to a picture for a long time. If, on the other hand, the object is very simple, such as a punctuation mark, we can attend to it for only a short time. If the reader will try to focus his consciousness on such a mark and hold it there, he will find that his attention wavers. It will come back to the object at very brief intervals, but he cannot keep it there. The mark becomes more like a basic point of operations. Attention centers upon it, but is perpetually making excursions to other items.

What happens when we attend to a complex thing is quite different. We notice its various features one after another; we associate it first with one thing and then with another. The value of attention is greatly increased by its mobility. We need to attend in order to get a clear perception or understanding of the thing to which we attend. But if we were to continue to concentrate on an object or a situation which no longer presented a problem, we should waste time and energy. In a world of great variety and constant flux we need to throw the spotlight of consciousness on various features one after another. To hold it on an object after our adjustment has been mapped out is a luxury of contemplation that we can seldom afford. A curious exception to the tendency to rove is the trancelike condition of the half-hypnotized crystal gazer, but this abnormality sets in clear relief the continuous restlessness of the attention of normal persons.

The length of time that a complex subject will be attended to varies also with the person attending. A manic person, distracted by every passing suggestion, can attend for only a very short time. A person of divided interests, torn with internal conflicts, cannot attend to anything long. A person who knows little about the object of attention cannot attend to it as long as one who knows a great deal about it. For example, a complicated problem of administration can be attended to for a long time by a trained administrator who understands the complexity of the problem and who is able to foresee the various difficulties that may arise if any of the suggested solutions is followed. On the other hand, a person of little administrative experience is unable to anticipate the difficulties that may arise. He therefore can attend to the problem profitably for only a short time. Similarly, an artist can spend hours to advantage in studying a single picture. It would be a waste of time for the ordinary person to do so, since he lacks the experience, training, and knowledge of art necessary for a rational analysis of pictures. It is the same in every field: the more we know about anything, the longer we can attend to it.

Another factor which influences the duration of attention is continued stimulation. If one drives an automobile several hundred miles, he is likely to continue "attending to the road" for some time after the trip is finished. His dreams that night may be a continuation of this state of consciousness. It is as if the mind, once in action, finds difficulty in slowing down and finally stopping. If a card game is carried on into the small hours of the night, one may continue to pay attention to the cards long after he tries to sleep. Though attention shifts from one object to another, a long-continued state of attention cannot be quickly and permanently turned off as if by an electric switch. It takes a more exciting or important rival to crowd it out of our minds.

Span of Attention

How many things can be attended to at a time? This question really contains two questions: How many things can we perceive at a glance? And how many activities can we carry on attentively at one time? The answer to the first question depends upon what we mean by a single thing. If we mean by a single thing each letter of a word, we can attend to many things at a glance. If each grouping of letters into words is regarded as a single thing, then the number of things that can be taken in at a glance is much less. What is true of words is true in other fields. The architect, the business expert, the artist, and the physician can take in a great deal in their respective fields at a glance. They are able to do so because they have learned through experience that one thing implies another, and it is difficult for them to separate sharply the implications of things observed from what is actually seen.

We can see about five unorganized or ungrouped things at a time. This number, however, is not fixed. It varies, according to Oberly (8), from about two and a half for complex things to eight for more simple things. Investigations on the range of attention are usually made with a *tachistoscope*, an instrument with which it is possible to expose to view for a short period, perhaps a small fraction of a second, a given number of unorganized things, such as letters, digits, or geometrical figures. As the number of objects presented is increased above five or six, the number perceived actually becomes smaller. This is shown both in laboratory experiments and in studies of the effect of magazine advertisement headlines of various sizes. If several cards, some containing four disconnected letters, others five, six, seven, and eight are presented tachistoscopically to a group of subjects, the number of letters recognized increases at first and then decreases after the optimum number for the range of attention is passed.

This limitation of the range of attention is particularly important in advertising. As Starch has shown, one remembers a commodity advertised with a short headline better than one with a long headline. The results of one of his experiments are shown in Table XIII. Simpler experiments, in which unrelated letters are shown tachistoscopically in groups of from four to eight, show that five letters result in more correct judgments than a larger or smaller number. This is shown in Figure 55.

To the question of how many activities can be carried on attentively at one time, psychologists in general answer One. It is recognized, of course, that any complicated act is made up of simple elements. For example, in writing an essay we think of what we are going to say; we seek appropriate words; we spell the words; and we make the necessary movements of our arms and hands. All of these activities are really one activity, namely, writing the essay. Many parts of that activity are relegated to the level of habit.

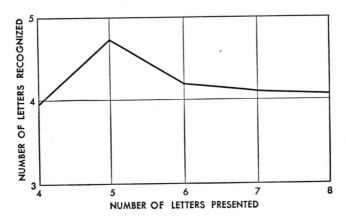

Figure 55

Relation between Number of Random Letters Presented
and Number Identified

Five is the best number for maximum identification.

Table XIII

Relation between Length of Headlines of Full-Page Advertisements
and Number of Times Advertisement Is Mentioned (11)

	HEADLINE	
	Five words or less	*Six words or more*
Number of advertisements	5	5
Number of mentions	33.6	13

There are apparent exceptions to the statement that we can perform attentively only one act at a time. At times we carry on two unrelated activities at once, as when we talk while walking. In such cases, however, the conversation is the only object of attention; walking is performed automatically. When there are difficulties in our path, and walking requires attention, we find conversation tiresome and difficult. Likewise, pianists may play familiar compositions and carry on a conversation, but they cannot do this when they are learning a difficult piece. Caesar is said to have been able to dictate several letters at a time; but, when we remember that his scribes wrote in longhand, we can readily understand that this feat may have been the result of an accurate memory and a rapid shift of attention, rather than of attending to several things at once. When the motion pictures show four or five telephones on the businessman's desk, there is some reason to suspect either exhibitionism or an approaching nervous breakdown.

A more serious objection to the view that we can attend to only one thing at a time grows out of the performance of stage magicians who seem to collect all sorts of information and at the same time perform complicated mathematical problems which have been formulated with the help of the audience. They apparently attend to two or more things at the same time. This type of performer is really taking advantage of the inability of his audience to attend to many things at once. The experiment of Münsterberg, cited on page 270, shows that we do not observe numerous things which happen right before our eyes.

Equally remarkable appears to be the case of a typesetter of the old school who, according to Phillips (9), used one eye to read the copy and the other to set the type without head rotation. Likewise, some telegraphers apparently receive at great speed and at the same time keep in contact with what is going on about them. Ripley in his *Believe It or Not* claims that a certain William W. Lord of Philadelphia can write two long letters on unrelated subjects (one with each hand), conduct

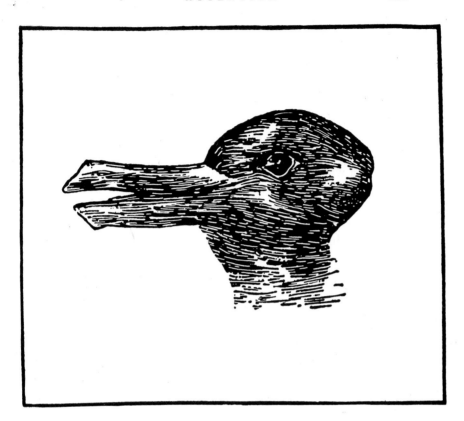

Figure 56

When It's a Duck, It's a Duck — When It's a Rabbit, It's a Rabbit!

Normally we attend to only one thing at a time. (From J. Jastrow, *Fact and Fable in Psychology*, Houghton Mifflin, 1900, p. 295.)

a conversation, and mentally solve a mathematical problem at the same time.

Psychologists are, in general, skeptical of such claims and are inclined to believe that such performances are due to a rapid shift of attention from one thing to another, or to an abnormal condition, analogous to dissociation of personality, in which one activity goes on automatically. In either case, these feats cannot be developed by most persons and should not be considered as possible goals of achievement. That one may confuse *dual* attention with rapidly *shifting* attention is shown in Jastrow's famous illusion, illustrated in Figure 56. When asked for the first time whether this picture is a rabbit or a duck, most students will immediately reply, "Both!" Upon closer examination, they will find that at one time they see it as a duck, then as a rabbit, but that however rapidly it shifts from one to the other, it is never seen as both at the same time. When it's a duck, it's a duck; when it's a rabbit, it's a rabbit! This illustrates a major trait of the attentive process and strongly suggests that normally we attend to only one thing at a time.

SUMMARY

Attention is a way of responding; a way of bringing experiences into the "spotlight" of consciousness. We attend to a succession of things. Though a number of people may be in the same room, their attention is usually on different things. Attention increases efficiency in several ways. (1) It improves our sensory discrimination by isolating the parts of a complex whole, by making us aware of stimuli that would otherwise pass unnoticed, and by making our impressions clearer. (2) It involves a heightened state of motor readiness. (3) It helps us remember experiences more accurately and fully. (4) It makes us responsive to relevant matters. Attention may decrease our efficiency if we attend to skills or habits which are better relegated to an automatic or unconscious level of performance.

Attention is determined by objective and subjective laws. The objective conditions (or the factors in the stimulus) which favor attention are: (1) change, (2) intensity, (3) size, (4) repetitions, (5) novelty or uniqueness, (6) nearness to point of fixation, and (7) importance. The main subjective determinants of attention are: (1) native desires, (2) sentiments and complexes, (3) mood, (4) attitude, (5) education and training, (6) purpose of the moment, and (7) purpose of the future.

Involuntary attention occurs when we become "lost" in an activity without conscious effort; voluntary attention, when our minds "wander" and only with effort are kept upon a given task. Both types of attention are subject to the same laws. Involuntary attention is more efficient than voluntary because it does not involve so much wavering and fluctuation.

From their study of attention psychologists have evolved numerous valuable principles of controlling it. Some of these apply to the elimination of distraction, others to the direction of attention to things that are at first uninteresting, and others to the direction of attention to the proper aspects of its object. (1) Distraction of attention may be reduced by eliminating or going away from the distracting influence, by incorporating the distraction in the major activity, by becoming negatively adapted to the distraction, by putting forth more effort, by being alert for wavering of attention, and by assuming a posture of attention. (2) Attention to uninteresting things may be stimulated by rewards and punishments, by a desire to excel others, by competition between groups, and by a desire to excel one's own record. (3) In learning any skill it is important to recognize what parts should be attended to and what parts should become habitual, automatic, and unconscious. One of the main values of instruction is to point out the proper direction of attention.

Some of the aspects of attention that have been measured are: (1) the attention-drawing power of competing stimuli, (2) the duration of attention, and (3) the span or range of attention.

QUESTIONS
on the Chapter

1. Define in your own words the concept of attention as explained in this chapter.
2. How does attention increase the efficiency of our activities?
3. Under what conditions will attention decrease the efficiency of our responses?
4. List and discuss the objective determinants of attention.
5. List and discuss the subjective determinants of attention.
6. Distinguish between voluntary and involuntary attention.
7. What is the function of the physiological changes that occur when we attend? - *increase efficiency - facilitate response*
8. What are the possible methods of overcoming or reducing distraction?
9. How may attention to uninteresting things be stimulated?
10. Describe how the attention-drawing power of advertisements may be measured.
11. What is meant by (a) the duration of attention, and (b) the span of attention?

for Discussion

1. Who pays more attention to driving an automobile, the beginner or the experienced driver? Cite similar instances.
2. Cite instances where you and a friend have attended to different things because of different backgrounds or interests.
3. Give examples where attention to the wrong thing has decreased your efficiency.
4. What situations have you been in where an effort was made to attract and hold your attention by objective conditions? Was it successful?

5. How might a teacher utilize the principles of attention in increasing his efficiency?
6. Suppose you were employed by an advertising agency to measure the attention value of advertisements before they were published. How should you go about it?
7. Cite cases where shifting attention has passed for dual attention.
8. What principles of attention are utilized by a magician?

REFERENCES

1 ASHER, E. J., and KAHN, DAVID B., "The Effect of 'Look' and 'Read' Directions upon the Attention Value of Illustrations and Texts in Magazine Advertisements," *J. Appl. Psychol.*, 1947, 31, 431–436.
2 BILLINGS, M. L., "The Duration of Attention," *Psychol. Rev.*, 1914, 19, 121–135.
3 CRANE, G. W., *Psychology Applied*. Evanston: Northwestern University Press, 1941, p. 59.
4 FRIEDLINE, C. L., and DALLENBACH, K. M., "Distance from Point of Fixation vs. Intensity as a Determinant of Attention," *Amer. J. Psychol.*, 1929, 41, 464.
5 LAIRD, D. A., "Experiments on the Physiological Cost of Noise," *J. Nat. Instit. Indust. Psychol.*, 1928, 4, 251–258.
6 MORGAN, J. J. B., "The Overcoming of Distraction and Other Resistances," *Arch. Psychol.*, 1916, 5, No. 35.
7 MÜNSTERBERG, HUGO, *On the Witness Stand*. Boston: Clark Boardman Company, 1933.
8 OBERLY, H. S., "A Comparison of the Spans of 'Attention' and Memory," *Amer. J. Psychol.*, 1928, 295.
9 PHILLIPS, W. L., "A Man Having Ocular Movements Similar to Those Found Normally in the Ungulates," *Amer. Med.*, 1906, 11, 428–431.
10 SMITH, E. D., *Psychology for Executives: A Study of Human Nature in Industry*. New York: Harper and Brothers, 1928.
11 STARCH, DANIEL, *Advertising: Its Principles, Practice and Technique*. Chicago: Scott, Foresman and Company, 1914, p. 66.

EMOTION

9

No one need study psychology to know that at times he is angry; that it is easy to be afraid or even panic-stricken; that to love and to be loved are of great value; that both remorse and pleasure "happen" to most of us; that envy, jealousy, generosity, and pride are natural to human beings, whether they are black or white, male or female, bright or stupid, rich or poor. We know through experience a great deal about feelings and emotions. What a study of psychology can do is to systematize our present knowledge of emotions; increase our sense of their importance; and, by contributing insight into their nature, give us more understanding of the feeling fraction of our total selves.

When things begin to matter to us, we have feelings about them. When they matter very much, we experience strong emotional reactions. The feelings, or emotional aspects, of life lie pretty close to the value and significance of life itself. The emotional phases of a total experience are what make the whole thing worth fighting for, or worth loving or hating; they make it absolutely necessary, despicable, or fearful, as the case may be. In discussing the role of emotion in daily life, Watson (32, p. 246), after making some comments about the biological serviceableness of emotion in keeping the race alive, goes on to say:

> Even though they were mere luxuries, so far as biological fitness is concerned, they keep the individual from existing as a machine that runs the same way every day. They give him his ups and downs, make the exact prediction of his acts more difficult (troubling the psychologist and psychiatrist thereby), and in general make him a more delightful personality with whom to work, fight and play. The world would be a sorry place indeed, from an artistic and human standpoint, if the distress of the child, of the weak and downtrodden, moved no eye to tears. Fame and ambition would be sorry crowns if the multitude were not moved to acclaim. If all hearts were calm, the great artists would have lived in-

vain.   In a sense society hangs together because of the possibility of emotional rapprochement.

WHAT IS AN EMOTION?

One can obtain a general idea of what the word *emotion* refers to by making a list of the words which are commonly used to describe the experiences we call emotional.   Virtually everyone is familiar with, and has some knowledge of the experience which we identify with, each of the following words: excitement, fear, rage, love, hate, joy, sorrow, grief, horror, anxiety, terror, distress, delight, disgust, remorse, jealousy, and elation.   What is the nature of the experiences which are the referents of these words?   Why can all of these experiences be collected under one heading, emotion?

An Example of an Emotion

A specific example will help to answer these questions.   A fourteen-year-old boy is picking blackberries in the country some distance from his home.   He is picking berries from a clump of briers when he suddenly sees a snake coiled near the center of the clump.   The perception of the snake sets up a number of processes inside the body and a number of outwardly observable responses.   These changes occur so very quickly that the boy would experience difficulty in recalling all of them or in telling the order of their occurrence.   He would undoubtedly report later that he was frightened or scared stiff.   If questioned in some detail, he might recall that he seemed to stop breathing for a brief instant, and that he tried to yell but found that the sound stuck in his throat.   He might recall that he had an impulse to jump back, but found that he was trembling and that his heart was pounding.   His next impulse was to get away and stay away from the clump of briers. Another person in the immediate vicinity who might have been observing the boy would probably report that the boy suddenly stopped picking berries, seemed to stand as if transfixed for a brief instant staring fixedly into the clump of briers, stepped backward a pace or two, and then walked or ran hurriedly away looking back over his shoulder.

If, in addition to the boy's report and the outsider's report, one could have obtained an accurate record of what went on inside the boy's body immediately upon his perception of the snake, he would have discovered in all probability an increase in blood pressure, a change in breathing rate, an increase in the amount of adrenalin in the blood, a cessation of digestive processes, a change in the electrical resistance of the skin, a dilation of the pupils of the eyes, and an increase in the amount of sugar

in the blood stream.   All of these internal and external changes, including the feeling of fear, which is the most pronounced aspect of the entire
series of events as far as the boy is concerned, constitute what we call
a fear reaction.   It is a complex reaction involving several components.
These are (1) the perception of the emotive situation, (2) internal
muscular and glandular responses, (3) immediate and involuntary overt
activity aroused directly by the emotive situation, (4) the individual's
feeling or emotional experience, and (5) the person's adjustment to
or reaction to the emotional situation.*

THE COMPONENTS OF AN EMOTION

The interrelationships of these five components are shown in the
diagram in Figure 57.   In this diagram the horizontal line 2–3 represents the immediate effects (reactions) in the individual of his percep-

* For a discussion of the components of an emotion see English, H. B., "What
is emotion?"   *Ohio J. Sci.*, 1947, 47, 62–66.

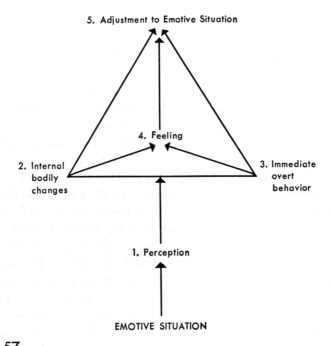

Figure 57

Diagram Representing the Interrelationships of the Components
of an Emotion

tion of the emotive situation. It is assumed in this description that internal muscular and glandular changes and overt changes occur simultaneously or in very close succession, and that these give rise immediately to the feeling. This relationship is represented by the arrows pointing from the ends of the horizontal line to point 4, the feeling. The arrows pointing upward from points 2, 3, and 4 indicate that the internal changes, the overt changes, and the feeling serve as instigators of other behavior which is directed toward the emotive situation and which become the organism's *adjustment* (of whatever degree of adequacy) to the emotive situation. It should be recognized that this adjustment includes not only the behavior aroused secondarily by the internal changes, the overt changes, and the feeling, but also these components themselves. It is this entire sequence of events, beginning with the perception of an emotive situation and culminating in some reaction or adjustment to the situation, that we call an emotion. It is a single, unitary process, although a complex one, in which the components are regarded as aspects of one and the same phenomenon. Let us examine these components in more detail.

Perception of the Emotive Situation

This component has to do with the stimulus object or the situation which sets off the subsequent reactions. While the snake in our example might be thought of as the emotional stimulus, it must be recognized that it is not the snake alone that aroused the emotion. It is the boy's perception of the snake under a particular set of circumstances. In a zoo or in a laboratory the same snake might be perceived by the same boy in a different way. What were the circumstances contributing to the boy's perception? The boy sees a snake in a clump of briers. He is not expecting to see a snake. He is alone some miles from home. We can suppose that he is not familiar with the kinds of snakes found in his community and that he has been frightened by snakes before. Quite obviously some of these conditions are in the external environment and can be regarded as E variables. Others are characteristic of the boy himself and may be regarded as P variables. The boy's perception of the snake and his subsequent reactions to it are, therefore, the result of the interaction of these P and E variables. A change in any of these variables may be expected to produce a change in the boy's perception. For example, the same snake in a glass case in a zoo would not, in all probability, be perceived as an emotional stimulus even if such variables as age, previous experiences, and expectations remained the same.

The role of internal conditions. In this example, as in any case of emotional behavior, previous experience and maturity are important determiners of how one will perceive and react to external stimulations. While the role of these variables in emotional development will be discussed in a subsequent section of this chapter (p. 314), it is significant to note that there are other internal conditions (P variables) which affect emotions. An example of the part played by internal conditions in arousing emotions may be found in the severe depressions which follow toxic diseases such as influenza, the manic excitement which accompanies intoxication, and the delusory sense of well-being caused by opiates. Everyone is familiar with the effect of fatigue and loss of sleep upon emotion. These conditions act to increase one's susceptibility to emotional stimulation, as is seen in the irritability of small children who have been kept awake past their bedtime or who have been fatigued by being taken about too much. A further example of the effect of internal conditions upon emotion is seen in a recent study of thirty patients suffering with peptic ulcers. All of these patients showed intense reactions of anxiety, insecurity, resentment, guilt, and frustration (24). The effect of internal glandular secretions upon emotion is seen in the fact that adrenalin, when injected into the blood stream, will induce many of the organic changes characteristic of emotional excitement.

Expectations. Another factor which looms large in determining what one perceives as an emotional situation, and how he responds to it, is *expectations*. As a consequence of previous experiences one comes to expect certain things from his environment and the people in it. He learns to want certain things and to expect certain results from his efforts to get these things. A baseball player may, because of previous successes, expect to maintain a batting average of .350. Failure to live up to this expectation may very well result in emotional tension and frustration. Anger, irritation, disappointment, and feelings of inferiority are quite frequently due to one's failure to get what he wants, or to live up to his expectations. The answer to such emotional problems is not the control of the emotions as such, but a correction, through realistic experiences, of one's hopes, ideals, aspirations, and expectations.

Internal Muscular and Glandular Responses

The internal changes listed above in describing the boy's fear reaction fall under this heading. They follow immediately upon perception of the emotive situation. These changes are regarded by some psychologists as adaptive in nature, i.e., as the organism's technique for adjusting itself, or of mustering its resources for handling the emotive situation.   Cannon (4) regards the entire emotion as an emergency reaction or the kind of response one makes when confronted with a crisis or a situation which demands more than the usual expenditure of energy. This picture of emotion is illustrated in Cannon's study of emotion in cats.   If a friendly cat is fed and strapped to a table, and a tube is inserted into its digestive organs, a plentiful amount of clear gastric juice will be found to be secreted.   The churning movements of the stomach characteristic of the digestive process will proceed smoothly. But if a dog enters the room while the cat is thus peacefully digesting its food, many changes occur.   The churning movements of the stomach cease abruptly;   the pancreas, instead of secreting clear gastric juice, secretes only a few drops of thick mucous matter.   The liver releases its sugar, thus providing the muscles with an abundance of food.   The adrenal gland secretes into the blood its fatigue-resisting and generally stimulating fluid.   The heart, by beating faster, sends food more rapidly to the places where it is needed, and at the same time eliminates waste products more readily.   The lungs, by working at a greater rate, provide the angry and frightened cat with more oxygen and dispel the carbon dioxide more rapidly.

These effects are made possible through the action of the autonomic nervous system (shown schematically in Figure 23, page 87).   It can be seen from this diagram that most of the vital organs are supplied by two sets of nerve fibers, one from the cranial or sacral segment and one from the sympathetic segment.   Under normal conditions the cranial and sacral segments play the dominant role in the activity of the vital organs.   Upon emotional stimulation, the sympathetic segment is thrown into gear, so to speak.   The result is an inhibition of digestion, an increased secretion of adrenalin, increased heart rate, more rapid breathing — in short, the entire group of changes described above.

The importance of these changes made in preparation for violent exertion is apparent.   An organism, to survive, must carry on processes of assimilation, and it is important that it should build up reserves of energy.   But there are times when it should cease storing up energy in order to act vigorously.   The cessation of digestion and the other organic changes that occur in fear and anger are ways of rapidly mobilizing reserves to meet the emergency.

This description of emotion fits rather nicely into the diagram of an emotion in Figure 57, where adjustive behavior is represented as the consequence of internal and external muscular and glandular changes and feelings. It is not necessary to suppose, however, that vigorous and violent exertion is always needed in dealing with an emotive situation. In some cases this is most certainly true, but the process which we designate as an emotion does not always conform to Cannon's emergency notion. Depending upon the individual's perception of the emotive situation, the immediate effects may vary in intensity and these in turn may give rise to vigorous and violent exertion, as in fighting or escape, or to much less vigorous and violent exertion, as seen in delight, remorse, or surprise.

The Immediate, Involuntary Overt Activity

The behavior under consideration here includes any overt activity which occurs immediately, more or less involuntarily, and directly upon the perception of the emotive situation. It may include any of the responses which the person is able to make. The specific reactions will depend upon (1) such variables as age, experience, fatigue, and motivation (these operate also in the perception of the emotive situation), (2) what the person is doing and the position he is in at the moment, (3) the nature of the emotive situation as perceived by the individual. In our example, the boy stopped picking berries. He stood motionless for an instant. He seemed to be staring fixedly into the clump of briers. Another individual stimulated in a similar way might have acted differently. The same boy confronted at a later time by a snake in a clump of briers would probably act differently. These conclusions would seem to be warranted from the results of an experiment by Landis (18). This investigator placed subjects in a laboratory situation and stimulated them with strong emotional stimuli. These included such stimuli as picking up a live rat with bare hands and cutting its head off, electric shock, pictures of loathsome diseases, and reading aloud bits of embarrassing personal history. The facial reactions of the subjects to these stimuli were photographed. The results of the study indicated that subjects showed some tendency to respond in the same way to all of the stimuli. Furthermore, the facial expressions which were present when the subjects reported that they were experiencing a given feeling varied greatly from subject to subject.

The immediate overt activity of component three, while it may be quite similar to and actually merge with the adjustive reactions of the fifth component, can be distinguished from the latter in two ways. First, it is predominantly involuntary. Even those types of response which are ordinarily controlled by an individual may, upon the perception of an emotive situation, occur involuntarily. This is seen in involuntary jumping, starting, screaming, laughing, and crying. Such responses appear before one has time to think or make any decision regarding what responses are appropriate. The sight of a mouse may bring forth an involuntary scream even though, because of the presence of other people, it results in ridicule or embarrassment, states which the person would prefer to avoid. Second, these responses can be distinguished, in some degree at least, from those of the final adjustment on the basis of the time of their occurrence. In our example of the boy and the snake it was stated that the boy stopped picking berries, that he stood motionless as if transfixed, that he finally stepped back and ran away. Stopping and standing occurred immediately. Stepping back and running away were acts which definitely followed the first two and should be regarded as behavior belonging to the adjustive component, behavior which was initiated by the immediate internal and external changes, and by the perception of the snake. Quite obviously there is no marked gap between the changes which occur immediately upon stimulation and those which are initiated by them. Some of the immediate changes persist and become a part of any subsequent adjustive behavior. Others may arise more slowly and overlap those which are initiated by the first reactions produced by the perception of the emotive situation. It is possible, however, to see in most emotions that an individual's eventual adjustive reactions to the emotive situation, the end point of the emotion, are removed in time from the initial reactions to the emotive situation. They are not only removed in time from the initial changes, they are qualitatively different, being aroused, as shown in Figure 57, by the initial overt changes, the internal changes, and the feeling component of the emotion.

The Feeling or Emotional Experience

To the person who is reacting to an emotive situation, the feeling of fear or anger or jealousy, as the case may be, is the most pronounced aspect of the emotion. In fact, it is likely to be regarded by most people as all there is to an emotion. According to this common-sense view the sight of a snake causes fear (meaning a feeling of fear) and the fear causes one to run or to do something else. This common-sense view is in part correct. As seen in Figure 57, the feeling is in part responsible for the ultimate adjustive reactions, but only in part, because the adjustive reactions are actually the results of the processes represented by all of the first four components.

It is the feeling component of the emotion that is our primary means of differentiating one emotion from another. It is difficult or impossible to differentiate one emotion from another, or to identify an emotion correctly, from an observation of overt behavior, internal changes, or adjustive reactions. Even if one knows the emotive situation in which the changes occur, he will still have difficulty in deciding whether there is an emotion, and, if there is, just what emotion it is. Component two is in some respects similar for all emotions. Changes in respiration, circulation, sweat gland activity, and the like occur in some degree in all emotions. It has been impossible to identify any combination of these changes which will clearly differentiate fear from anger, or love from hate, or any emotion from any other emotion. Similarly, the same immediate overt acts may occur in a variety of emotional experiences. Two different emotive situations may produce the same internal and overt changes (as far as we can tell from our observation), but in one case the subject reports that he is experiencing anger; in the other, fear. It is possible to identify an emotion with some degree of accuracy from a knowledge of the emotive situation and from the kind of adjustive reactions made to the situation. For example, the adjustment to a fear situation involves escape or withdrawing reactions whereas the adjustment to an anger situation involves attack responses. But we identify these adjustive responses and situations as fear or anger primarily because people in general report feelings of fear or anger when these situations and responses occur. We call a situation emotive because in responding to it people in general experience emotion. We call the adjustment one makes to a fear situation a fear response because we experience what we call fear when we make these adjustive responses in a given situation.

If this be true, why should we bother with a description of the internal, external, and adjustive changes which we identify as components of the emotion? Why not be content to describe emotion as one's verbal report of his feeling? One answer to these questions is that it is important to obtain information about the emotions of animals, small children, and abnormal people. These subjects either cannot report their feelings or cannot give adequate reports. Another answer is that adults and older children are frequently in situations in which they do not want other people to know how they feel. Their verbal reports of their feelings in such situations are incorrect or purposely misleading. Still another answer is to be found in the fact that in dealing with people in everyday situations where we want to know their feelings we are not always in a position to ask them what emotion they are experiencing. It wouldn't be polite if we could. In all of these cases one needs, or it would be convenient to have, some objectively observable indicator of emotion, some behavior signs that would reveal the nature of the subject's feeling.

How does one go about discovering these objectively observable indicators? We observe our own behavior when we experience some feeling in a given situation. We likewise observe the reactions of other people in situations in which they report certain feelings. We have many chances to check and recheck these observations against the reported feelings. We eventually discover that some of these behavior manifestations are not good indicators of emotion, because they can be controlled by an individual in such a way as to mislead us. We learn to rely on other manifestations which we discover are less likely to be distorted. Depending upon our ability to learn, we become more or less proficient in judging the feelings of other people from the way they behave.

The psychologist in his endeavor to obtain objectively observable indicators of reported feelings, or the concomitant processes, proceeds systematically by setting up experimental situations in which he can discover and measure the reactions which bear a consistent relationship to the emotive situation and to the person's report of his feelings in the situation. His methods of observing, measuring, and recording reactions make it possible to investigate a wider range of manifestations, and to do so more accurately than we can in our everyday observations. As a consequence he has discovered indicators which are far more reliable than those which we use in dealing with each other in everyday situations. These experiments have established the facts (1) that internal glandular and muscular changes occur upon the perception of an emotive situation in which a subject experiences a feeling; (2) that at the same time certain overt changes occur directly and immediately; and (3) that these lead eventually to some type of adjustment to the emotive situation. In short, these experiments indicate the existence of a complex unit of behavior consisting of a number of components, one of which is feeling. The feeling component is the core of this unit of behavior and gives to the unit its distinctive character. This unit of behavior is called an emotion.

The Emotional Adjustment

What one does to, in, with, or as a consequence of the emotive situation is his emotional adjustment. As in the case of the behavior of the third component, any behavior of which the individual is capable may be involved in this adjustment. The specific reactions will depend upon (1) the nature of the emotive situation, (2) the individual's perception

of it, (3) such P variables as age, sex, experience, fatigue, and motivation, and (4) the nature of the experiences and changes aroused directly
by the perception of the emotive situation. These adjustive reactions
are regarded as following upon and as being instigated by the experience, the internal changes, and the external changes aroused by the
emotive situation.

Delayed adjustments. In point of time, the ultimate adjustment
to an emotive situation may occur long after the emotive situation as
such has disappeared, as seen in the oft-quoted example of the man who
bawls out his wife, kicks the dog, and bangs through the house because
his boss made him angry earlier in the day. In this case the feeling of
anger and certain internal and external tensions have persisted from
the earlier emotive situation. Some of these may be reinstated by the
thought of the earlier episode. There is a carry-over of effect from the
earlier emotive situation because the feeling of resentment toward the
boss was not carried to a satisfactory conclusion. In a sense the primary
task of getting even with the boss is unfinished. What one does eventually to an emotive situation or as a consequence of it may occur after
a lapse of many days, or weeks, or even years. Most of us have probably
said at one time or another following an anger-provoking situation,
"I'll get even with that guy if it takes me a lifetime." It is not uncommon to find people acting as a consequence of grudges or hates which
were aroused years before.

Immediate adjustments. On the other hand, many adjustments to
emotive situations occur almost immediately. In some cases the immediate overt reactions of component three may be the only ones
actually needed in making an adjustment. A man is walking along a
path in the woods. He sees a snake in the path at the very spot where
he is about to place his uplifted foot. His immediate response may be
a longer step or jump. This response takes him past the snake and out
of danger. If, after making one jump, the man resumed his normal
walking, we would have to say that the immediate overt response (component three) was the man's adjustment (component five) to the snake.
But the man is not likely to act in this way if he perceives the snake as
a source of danger. His perception of the snake and the immediate
internal and overt changes which are set up are likely to produce a
series of secondary responses such as running. His actual adjustment,
therefore, does not stop with his first jump, but includes all of the
responses which occur from the time he perceived the snake until days
later when he is able to carry on a conversation without having to relate
his experience with the snake. All of these later responses must be

regarded as parts of his adjustment. Thus we can see that what one does as a consequence of an emotive situation (component five) is an integral part of the emotion. It does not occur by itself but as a component in the total process.

Positive and negative adjustments. In a general way emotional adjustments can be classified as being positive or negative. Negative adjustments are characterized by efforts to get away from the emotive situation, stay away from it, alter it, or destroy it. Positive adjustments are characterized by approach responses, and by efforts to hold on to, continue, or reinstate the situation. It is customary to classify the emotions of which these reactions are a part as positive or negative. Thus fear, rage or anger, distress, and jealousy are classified as negative emotions, while love, joy, delight, and elation are positive emotions. It should be recognized that while one's adjustment to a fear situation is characterized by withdrawing, there is a variety of ways in which a person may withdraw. He may jump back, cringe, turn his head, stay away from, run away from, avoid thinking about, or even become paralyzed in and insensitive to the fear situation. Anger adjustments are characterized by attacks upon the anger situation or by efforts to remove or destroy it. These attacks may be direct, as in kicking or striking a person who arouses anger, or they may be more subtle, as in talking about the person behind his back, destroying something that belongs to him, insulting his relatives or friends, or even returning good for evil. In a similar manner one may use a wide variety of specific responses in adjusting to any emotive situation. A given end result may be attained by different individuals in markedly different ways, or a given individual may adjust to a given kind of emotive situation in a number of different ways on different occasions. The specific reactions to a fear situation, an anger situation, or indeed any emotive situation change with age and experience, and depend at all times upon the factors listed in the first paragraph in this section.

OTHER VIEWS OF EMOTION

The James-Lange View

One or another of the above components has been emphasized in various views and definitions of emotion. According to James (16), a leading American philosopher and psychologist (died 1910), and Carl Lange, a Danish physiologist (died 1900), an emotion is the *awareness* of the various bodily changes which follow upon the perception of the emotive situation. These bodily changes include the internal muscular and

[handwritten annotation at top: emotion is a result of the bodily changes that take place — feeling is result of body changes & behavior]

glandular changes and the immediate overt responses which we have designated as components two and three. But these changes were not regarded as the emotion, or as part of it. The emotion was the awareness or consciousness of these changes. The order of events according to James and Lange was: stimulus — perception — bodily changes (internal and external) — awareness of these changes (the emotion). If we regard awareness as equivalent to the feeling component in our diagram in Figure 57, this view takes account of (1) the perception of the emotive situation, (2) the internal muscular and glandular changes, (3) the overt changes, and (4) the feeling. Only the latter, however, was regarded as the emotion. This view takes no account of adjustive responses except in so far as some of these responses might contribute to one's experienced feeling.

The Behavioristic View

[handwritten annotation: Emotion is body change behavior]

Some psychologists object to the James-Lange view, or any view which regards emotion as a conscious experience, on the ground that such a view automatically limits the study of emotion to those individuals who can give adequate verbal reports of their experience. To avoid this limitation to the psychology of emotion, Watson (32, p. 215) proposed that the term *emotion* be used to refer to the internal (muscular and glandular) and overt responses which occur directly upon emotional stimulation. In his own words: "An emotion is an hereditary 'pattern-reaction' involving profound changes of the bodily mechanism as a whole, but particularly of the visceral and glandular systems."

This definition makes emotion practically synonymous with components two and three in Figure 57. While it might conceivably include some of the behavior which we designate as adjustive in component five, it most certainly disregards both the perceptual and the feeling components. While it is necessary to resort to the observation and measurement of the internal and overt components of an emotion in studying the emotions of animals, babies, and abnormal people, and while it may be highly desirable to do so in studying adults, it must be recognized that this can be done only after it is established that such behavior is a component of an emotion.

Emotion as Disorganized Behavior

One view of emotion that appears rather frequently in the psychological literature is that emotion is a disorganized response. Related to this is the notion that an emotion leads to or produces disorganized behavior.

As Leeper (20) points out, both ideas are sometimes included in the same statement, so that it is difficult to determine whether the writers (7, 26) hold to the first or the second view. The notion that emotion produces disorganized behavior appears to be the more widely accepted view. According to this notion, the emotion disrupts normal activity, interferes with what one is doing, reduces efficiency, and in general is in conflict with logical, intelligent self-management. Most of us can cite instances from daily life in which our adjustive responses in a given emotive situation seemed to be illogical, immature, inefficient, and decidedly unlike what we might have done if we had not been afraid, or angry, or in love. Interestingly enough — and this is an important point — we can say essentially the same thing about some of our adjustive responses in nonemotive situations. After the conversation is over we can think of bright remarks which we might have made. After the game has been played, we recall mistakes which might have been avoided, or dozens of "ifs" which would have altered the outcome of the game. The fact is that what we do in any situation, emotive or otherwise, is the best that we can do under the circumstances. But we do not like to admit that this is true. Instead we will insist that we could have performed more effectively if so and so had not happened. In emotive situations it is a common practice to excuse ourselves, or explain our failures to adjust as we think we might have adjusted, by saying that we were afraid, or excited, or angry. But such an explanation is not a good rationalization of one's failure to respond as he wishes he had responded unless emotion is regarded as necessarily leading to or as producing a disorganized and disruptive response. To so regard it is to use a man-in-the-street rationalization as a psychological description of emotion. It is not necessary to say that emotion leads to disorganized behavior or that the emotion itself is disorganized in order to account for the fact that one's emotional behavior is not, at a given time, what he thinks later it might have been. It should be recognized that the emotional adjustment is an integrated pattern of activity which, as a unit, is as good as it can be in light of the facts that a person is what he is at the moment and that the circumstances are what they are at that moment.

THE LANGUAGE OF EMOTION

Everyone has had the experience of trying to "look" sad when he wasn't sad; of forcing a laugh when he wasn't happy; of trying to appear surprised when he wasn't surprised; of pretending to bristle with anger when he wasn't angry. On the other hand, who hasn't had the experience of trying to cover up a feeling of fear, or anger, or disappointment, or chagrin by acting or trying to act as if such a feeling did not exist? In all of these cases we attempt by word, gesture, facial expression, tone of voice, and body movements to convey to other people *ideas* about our feelings. Here the problem is not one of emotional adjustment as such, because in many cases no emotion is present, and even when one is present an attempt is made to keep others from guessing what it is. In either case the essential problem is to convey ideas which have to do with feelings but which themselves are not feelings. We call the responses (gestures, facial expressions, etc.) by which the ideas are conveyed *the language of emotion*. These responses are sometimes designated as *social expressions of the emotions* because they are used to influence other people.

Social Expressions vs. Emotional Responses

Social expressions of emotion are to be distinguished rather sharply from the overt behavior which occurs in response to an emotive situation. While these expressions may be similar to or the same as those which occur in an emotive situation, they are not true emotional responses, because the simulated emotion is not present. They have been lifted, so to speak, from the emotions and are now being used purposely and voluntarily to convey the idea that an emotion is being experienced when it is not. The same idea applies when one experiences one emotion but uses the overt responses which customarily go with another in an effort to convey the impression that he is experiencing the latter emotion and not the former. Quite obviously the person may not be successful in his attempt to do this, because the real emotion involves some responses which he cannot control. Though society teaches us, almost from birth, to conceal our emotional responses, our success in doing so is poor at best. The narrowing pupil of the eye, the change in color of the cheeks, the tense, white lips, the quivering of the body, the unconscious blink, the strained breathing — all these give the lie to protestations of friendship when two hated rivals greet one another with a "genial" handshake.

The language of emotion includes, therefore, those expressions which customarily go with emotions but which become divorced from the emotions to be used at will to convey to other people the idea that an emotion is present when it is not. But the language of emotion contains expressions derived in another way. We are taught from early childhood to make certain expressive movements (gestures, facial expressions, and the like) which have been agreed upon as methods of conveying ideas about emotions in social situations. These expressions do not customarily occur as parts of any emotion, but we are taught that different expressions belong to different emotions. Thus we are taught to express the idea of sadness by making a "long face." These conventionalized expressions together with the expressions which become divorced from their emotions constitute our language of emotion.

The Use and Interpretation of the Language of Emotion

Success in using this language depends upon two things. First, there must be a common language. It must be generally agreed and understood that particular responses or expressions go with and are indicators of a particular emotion. Second, the person using the language must have such voluntary control of the expressions that he can turn them on or off as the occasion demands. In short, he must be reasonably skilled in using the language. Take, for example, the facial expressions represented in Figure 58. Most people understand or know that the expression in the top picture goes with surprise and that laughter goes with happiness or joy. There are other facial expressions which we have learned to recognize and to use as indicators of certain feelings and emotions. In a similar way we learn to recognize certain vocal and bodily expressions and to use them as indicators of emotion. Such overt responses as crying, laughing, trembling, shouting, screaming, and swearing are identified with different emotions and are used as indicators of these emotions. Thus crying is identified with grief and sorrow just as laughter is identified with joy and happiness. That we have learned to associate certain expressions with certain emotions is indicated in a study by Fairbanks and Pronovost (9). These investigators showed that the emotions of contempt, anger, fear, grief, and indifference, as simulated by actors, are correctly identified from the voice alone in from 66 to 88 per cent of the trials, when mere chance would account under the same conditions for only 8 per cent of correct judgments. In a subsequent report by Fairbanks and Hoaglin (8) objective measurements of the duration aspects of the voice changes of the five simulated emotions were made by means of sound-wave photography. An analysis of these sound waves revealed that anger, fear, and indifference differed from contempt and grief but did not differ in any significant way from one another. All three involved rapid rate and duration of phonations and pauses.

It should be recognized, of course, that these social expressions or

Figure 58

Surprise and Laughter Are Indicated by Simple Facial Lines

(Acme Photos.)

313

conventionalized responses may occur as parts of the adjustive responses in a particular emotive situation. In fact they may be the dominant aspects of one's overt behavior in those emotive situations which involve social stimulations. As one grows older and learns to use the language of emotion, there is an increased tendency for him to use this language in responding to emotive situations, especially when he wishes to conceal his real feelings. The more or less spontaneous expressions made in an emotive situation become overlaid or mingled with these conventionalized expressions. Awareness of this fact together with practice in looking beneath the surface of conventionalized behavior would increase one's skill in recognizing emotions in other people.

EMOTIONAL DEVELOPMENT

Emotion, like any other kind of behavior, changes as one develops from infancy to maturity. These changes are dependent upon the original nature of the organism (heredity), and upon the processes of maturation and learning. In describing the development of emotions it is customary to start with a description of the emotional behavior of the infant and then proceed to describe the changes in emotional behavior which appear as a consequence of maturation and learning. Studies of emotional development reveal that (1) there is an increase in the number of emotions; (2) there is at first an increase, ordinarily followed in later life by a decrease, in the number of situations which will arouse any given emotion; (3) there is a change in any given emotional reaction in the direction of mature, adultlike behavior and away from immature, childlike behavior; and (4) there is, in general, an integration of all emotional behavior and an incorporation of this behavior into one's habitual modes of adjustment. The way in which these changes come about can be seen in the discussion which follows.

Emotional Responses Present at Birth

One of the earliest investigators to study the emotional responses of newborn infants was John B. Watson. Watson's work on the emotions carefully followed principles of his general behavioristic viewpoint (see p. 309). He observed many infants in many situations, controlling external conditions as carefully as possible and noting changes in the infants' behavior as factors in the environment were varied one at a time. Briefly, Watson's conclusions were that the newborn infant shows only three emotions. These are *fear* (aroused by pain, injury, loud noises, or sudden loss of support), *rage* or *anger* (aroused by restriction of movement), and *love* (aroused by soft noises or gentle stroking of the skin). Watson (32) asserted that all emotions found later in life are the result of conditioning these three primary responses to more complex stimuli.

Watson's conclusions have been modified in several ways as a result of later experiments, but one conclusion which he reached and emphasized seems now to be thoroughly established. This is that infants at birth do have very few emotions, and that only a very few stimuli or situations will arouse emotional behavior. Among stimuli which do *not* cause emotional reactions in infants and young children are furry objects, toads, lizards, snakes, and similar things which adults often dislike. At birth, we have no innate fear of them. If they are fearful or repulsive to us as adults, it is only because we were *taught* in infancy to respond to them with fear reactions, though the teaching may have been quite unplanned and, at the time, unrecognized. The child shown in Figure 59 is a normal little girl whose parents did not teach her to fear snakes.

Watson's conclusion, however, that fear responses may be conditioned with equal ease to any type of stimulus has not been substantiated by later research. Work reported by Valentine (31) and others shows that it is much easier to condition children to show fear responses to *living* than to *nonliving* objects. It is also felt by many psychologists today that definite identification of *three* specific emotions in infants is not supported by research findings. Dashiell (6), after studying and summarizing a great deal of this research, concludes that man is not born with definite patterns of visceral responses worthy of being called emotions. Sherman (29) also states that an observer is unable to judge an infant's emotional states at birth. Though psychologists are not in complete agreement on this matter, most of them agree that in the newborn infant the only clearly recognizable emotional response is one of random movement and crying, which for want of a better name may be called excitement.

Maturation

Development of the primary emotional response of excitement into the complex emotional life of the adult may be due to maturation, to learning, or to a complicated interaction of maturation and learning. Maturation, discussed on pages 64–71, means development which naturally accompanies growth and which thus takes place largely without reference to the training which the child receives. As human beings, we pass from infancy through childhood, adolescence, maturity, and

Figure 59

Natural Reactions

Annette Avers's early fondness for snakes is an example of how most children might feel if not taught otherwise. The study of very early reactions in children is basic to an understanding of the more complicated, and often reorganized, reactions in adults. (Courtesy of Franklin H. Avers.)

316

old age, to death. This cycle of growth and decay is largely determined by our heredity and is, therefore, thought of as the process of maturing. The developmental period is regarded especially as a period of maturing.

Emotional development due to maturation occurs most rapidly in infancy. Though activity similar to excitement is about all that can be observed at birth, in the course of a few months infants show remarkable emotional development. They may sulk or laugh, show anger or love, jealousy or contentment. Bridges (3) has set forth in considerable detail the emotional development of an infant from birth to two years. Figure 60 is a convenient summary of her findings. That this development is to be attributed largely to maturation is the opinion of Goodenough, another investigator of emotional development during infancy. She writes (14, p. 192):

> If crying as a form of emotional behavior can occur without training, there seems to be no logical reason why frowning, kicking, striking, running away, smiling, sneering, stamping, and so on throughout the long list of reactions that appear one after another may not also be the unlearned results of maturation, although . . . their occurrence under particular circumstances may be determined by experience. As age advances, imitation and social custom undoubtedly play an increasingly important part in fixing their exact pattern. An important sign of emotional maturation is to be found in the bringing of these unlearned emotional reactions under voluntary control.

A striking instance of emotional development due to maturation is the development of sex behavior and interest during adolescence. Of course, interest in the opposite sex is aided and abetted by many aspects of the environment, but it depends to a large extent upon inner growth, which thus serves, biologically, the very practical purpose of keeping the race alive.

Maternal tenderness is also undoubtedly due at least in part to physiological changes which occur automatically and are not dependent on learning or social custom. When young male rats are treated either by implanting a bovine pituitary gland or by removing the thyroid gland, they develop maternal behavior which normal male rats never develop. They will make nests, care for the young, lick them in a maternal way, etc. Control male rats, that is, rats subjected to the same environmental influences but not operated on, develop no maternal behavior (22). Such experiments suggest that many kinds of emotional behavior may be dependent upon physiological and maturational factors.

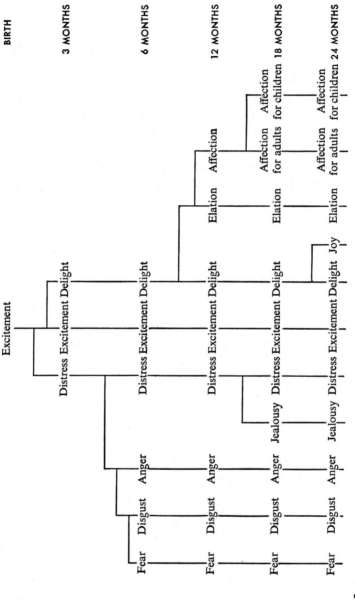

Figure 60

The Development of Emotional Expression from Birth to Two Years

Notice how the single undifferentiated emotion of excitement develops in various channels. (From K. M. B. Bridges, "Emotional Development in Early Infancy," *Child Devel.,* 1932, 3, 324-341.)

Learning

Another important factor in emotional development is experience. As a result of experience, we respond emotionally to new objects and become indifferent to others that once aroused an emotional response. A footstep or a voice that formerly awakened no feeling may now do so. Perhaps we were once afraid of thunder, though it disturbs us no longer. After responding to a complex whole, we tend to respond to a part of the whole as we did to the whole. For example, the infant reacts to the appearance, voice, and movements of its mother with signs of pleasure. Later, merely the voice of its mother may arouse similar activity. Or an infant may respond with fear to the simultaneous occurrence of a loud noise and the approach of a dog. The dog alone would not have caused the fear; but after the fear situation, with the dog figuring prominently in it, has occurred, the sight of the dog becomes sufficient to arouse fear. Throughout life, our emotional development is thus influenced. A dangerous experience on a high place may give rise to fear of high places. After experiencing repeatedly in a particular church such religious emotions as reverence, awe, and trust, a person entering any similar place is likely to have the same feelings aroused. A boy who has repeatedly been made to fear his father on account of his sternness may fear to be in the presence of his father; he may even be vaguely ill at ease in the presence of men who resemble his father; or, in extreme cases, he may be afraid of all men. Psychologists speak of such modifications of our emotions as *conditioned emotional responses* and have studied them in the laboratory. Conditioning is one of the methods of learning described in Chapter 6.

If conditioning emotions only increased the number of objects that are emotionally charged, we should live in a state of perpetual emotional excitement. Conditioning, however, operates to eliminate the emotional charge of objects as well as to endow them with such changes. This can be done by the method of *reconditioning* described in Chapter 6. This is the method which was employed by Jones (17) in eliminating a child's fear of rabbits.

To the credit of learning must also be placed the enrichment of emotion that comes from the development of such sentiments as patriotism, love of truth, and hatred of injustice. The evolution of fear often shows clearly the effect that such sentiments can have on emotions. A person who, as a young child, feared corporal punishment may, as he grows older, learn to fear physical pain or even injury less and less, and to fear more and more the disapproval of his group, until eventually patriotism or the love of country overcomes almost entirely his fear of physical suffering. This is seen frequently enough in the readiness of men to expose themselves to every danger in order to defend the group. And similarly, many men become so imbued with the love of justice that they are willing to risk life and fortune in striving for human welfare.

Emotional development results also from improvement (or changes) in the expression of emotion. In infancy and early childhood the improvement is due largely to maturation. One of the most important improvements of expression comes with language. Goodenough (13) has found that as we pass from infancy to adulthood, we tend more and more to substitute verbal responses for other types of response to anger-provoking situations. This change is shown graphically in Figure 61. The frequency of anger outbursts also varies with age, reaching a peak at around eighteen months. This is shown in Figure 62. During childhood, there is no particular effort to improve or change our emotional behavior, but as we grow older we consciously seek to control and refine our emotional adjustments. And it is important that we do so, for in the life of an adult there is little place for the emotional expressions of the child or the adolescent. Illuminating questions to ask about anyone are: What is the level of his emotional development? Does he periodically have temper tantrums and outbursts of anger (childish expressions)? Does he easily become embarrassed, annoyed, offended, and "hurt," particularly in social situations (adolescent expression)? Or does he carefully evaluate situations and cope with them in a realistic way, using his resources and energy to *solve* the problem rather than merely to "let off steam" (adult expression)? Of course, *any* adult may at times revert to an immature form of emotional expression, but some adults are *typically* adolescent or childish in their emotional life.

Emotional Maturity

Emotional maturity, in the fullest sense, is reserved for those who are fortunate enough to have had wise parents and teachers who themselves enjoyed a high degree of inner peace and harmony. If you are a person who has been humored and petted during childhood, who has been permitted to gain his desires through emotional outbursts or an assumption of weakness and appeals to sympathy, you are unlikely to develop the confidence, self-reliance, and strength necessary for full emotional maturity. Yet you may take some steps toward it. It is true that some do not want to change. "Why should I improve? I am now famous

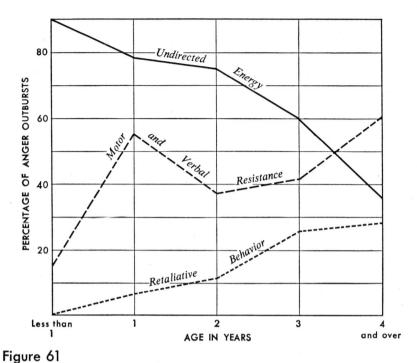

Figure 61

Changes, with Age, in Behavior in Anger Outbursts

(From F. L. Goodenough, *Anger in Young Children*, 1931, p. 72. By permission of the publisher, the University of Minnesota Press, Minneapolis, Minnesota.)

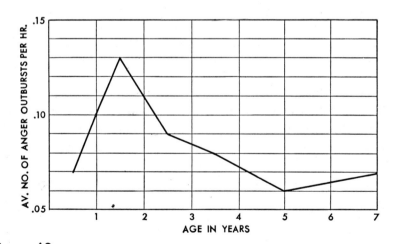

Figure 62

Variation, with Age, of Frequency of Anger Outbursts

(From F. L. Goodenough, *Anger in Young Children*, p. 107.)

for my temper. If I learn to control it, I shall not be famous for any-thing; for I know — do not tell anyone — that I am just a common, average, everyday fellow anyway." If you do want to increase your emotional maturity, you may find the following suggestions of some value.

(1) Avoid situations that are known to produce excessive emotion. If a person knows that certain situations arouse an undesirable response, he should seek to avoid them. Through such insight and prudence many mentally unstable people have been able to live a reasonably satisfactory life. It should be remembered that imagined situations as well as real ones produce emotions. Therefore, the individual who wishes to control his emotions needs to discipline his thoughts. If he finds himself thinking of subjects that arouse undesirable emotions, he should develop other interests and engage in other activities which will direct his thinking along other channels. There are stories of Malays who, after sitting for days nursing their grievances, suddenly arm them-selves and run amuck, killing all in their path. Such tragedies could be avoided if the moody and sulky people were distracted by outside interference, or if they should voluntarily direct their thoughts away from their wrongs, real or imagined, to happier subjects. In general, a person can avoid much unhappiness by not allowing himself to dwell on thoughts that embitter.

(2) Understand the nature of emotions and view them objectively. By holding an emotion off and surveying it, one can reduce its intensity. For example, if an angry person fixes his attention on his anger and removes it from the situation that caused the anger, he becomes less angry. Likewise, the nervous speaker by viewing his excitement as a preparatory adjustment may do much to keep his nervousness within reasonable bounds.

(3) Achieve understanding and mastery of the situation. A child may be afraid of shadows on the wall. But when he has been made to understand their nature, he no longer fears them. Likewise, a child's fear of thunder is not wholly a fear of noise. It is rather fear of a noise *not understood*. When he comprehends its nature, his fear diminishes and may finally disappear. Subjected to many new experiences, some of which are dangerous, he will naturally experience fear if there is no insight. An understanding of the world reduces fear. This has been one of the most valuable contributions of science to human welfare. Mastery also reduces fear. The unpracticed skier learning to jump experiences considerable fear; but as he masters the art, the fear be-comes less and less. So it is with all dangerous occupations. Through

mastery we conquer, if we do not completely eliminate, the fear involved in them.

THE MEASUREMENT OF EMOTION

If we are to attain even a reasonably high degree of success in the important task of predicting and controlling human behavior, we must have precise, accurate measures of behavior. Indeed, the progress of psychology as a science has been intimately tied up with the development of measuring instruments which yield results that can be expressed in numerical terms. The advantages of numerical descriptions of behavior are obvious. Before the advent of the intelligence test one could talk only in the vaguest terms about intelligence. He had no very accurate means of investigating the role of intelligent behavior in school adjustments, vocational adjustments, or elsewhere. The intelligence test with its mental ages, intelligence quotients, centile and standard scores has made it possible for educators, personnel directors, and others to make reasonably accurate measurements of intelligence and, on the basis of known relationships, to predict future success or failure in a wide variety of life situations.

The effort to devise instruments and methods for measuring emotion has met with only a moderate degree of success. A number of techniques and methods are available for measuring one or another of the five aspects of an emotion, but no one of these measures alone can be regarded as an adequate measure of the total emotional process. The simultaneous measurement of two or more facets of the total process leaves much to be desired as far as an adequate picture of emotion is concerned, because of the difficulty involved in combining these separate measures so as to approximate the total process. In addition to the measurement of emotion as such we are confronted with the problem of measuring such dimensions of one's total emotional behavior as maturity-immaturity and stability-instability. The first of these dimensions arises out of the fact that one grows emotionally very much as he grows physically or mentally.

One would expect emotional maturity to vary with intellectual and physiological maturity, and in general it does. Yet the number of bright children who are not as emotionally mature as less intelligent children of the same age, and the number of children who are accelerated in their physiological development but retarded in their emotional development, indicate that emotional development depends upon other factors as well as upon mental and physical growth. Weber (33) reports that the correlation of emotional maturity and mental age is .42

and that that of emotional maturity and school grades is only .18.   This study indicates that many children who are succeeding in their school work are not doing so well in developing emotionally.

Some measure of the stage or level of emotional maturity would most certainly be of value in understanding, predicting, and controlling behavior.   The stability-instability concept grows out of the intimate relation which exists between emotional adjustment and general adjustment, the idea being that emotionally unstable individuals are maladjusted or are likely to be, whereas well-adjusted individuals are regarded as emotionally stable.   Let us examine some of the methods and procedures which have been used for measuring various aspects and dimensions of emotional behavior.

The Verbal Report Method

One approach to the measurement of emotion is to have subjects report the feelings which are aroused by emotive situations.   Emotional stimuli are presented systematically and under controlled conditions.   The subject is asked to report the emotion aroused.   He may also be asked to indicate on a prepared rating form the intensity of the emotion.   In the study by Landis (18) reported above (p. 303), the subjects were asked to report the emotions aroused by such emotional stimulations as picking up a live rat, electric shock, pictures of loathsome diseases, and reading bits of embarrassing personal history.

As pointed out earlier in this chapter (see p. 305), this method cannot be used with animals, small children, and abnormal people, since these subjects cannot make verbal reports or cannot give adequate ones. Another difficulty with the verbal report method arises out of the fact that emotional stimuli cannot be presented in the controlled fashion needed for careful checks and rechecks of the verbal reports.   In using this method to measure visual or auditory acuity, techniques are available for varying the visual and auditory stimuli systematically and for presenting them in such a fashion that errors in the verbal reports, either intentional or otherwise, can be reduced to a point where the reports are highly reliable.   Some techniques for the controlled presentation of stimuli have been used in studying the affective or feeling value of such stimuli as colors, odors, lines, forms, and pictures.   A series of pictures may be presented to a subject one at a time with instructions to indicate that each is pleasant, unpleasant, or neutral, or to indicate whether he likes or dislikes each.   In a method known as the *method of paired comparisons*, two stimuli are presented at a time with the instruction to indicate which of the pair is more pleasant or which is preferred. By presenting every stimulus with every other stimulus, it is possible to obtain a measure of the number of times each stimulus is preferred over every other stimulus. Here, however, one is not dealing with emotions, but with the elemental feelings of pleasantness and unpleasantness. Finally, in using the verbal report method in studying emotion one must recognize that only one component of an emotion is being investigated. For this reason, if for no other, this method does not give a completely adequate measure of emotion. However, when it is used in conjunction with methods which measure other components of an emotion, it adds to the over-all measure information about that component of an emotion which differentiates one emotion from another.

The Questionnaire Method

This method attempts to measure emotion by asking a subject to answer a list of questions about his emotional life. In its usual form the emotional questionnaire — which is sometimes referred to as an inventory, schedule, or personal data sheet — consists of a list of yes-no questions in printed form which the subject is instructed to answer by checking the *yes* or *no*. Following is a sample of the kinds of questions which might go into an emotional questionnaire:

1. Are you afraid to be alone?   Yes No
2. Do you feel that your parents do not love you?   Yes No
3. Did you ever get so angry that you wanted to kill somebody?   Yes No
4. Are you afraid of high places?   Yes No
5. Are you afraid of the dark?   Yes No
6. Do you have temper tantrums?   Yes No
7. Are you afraid of thunder or lightning?   Yes No
8. Do you feel that you worry over small things more than other people do?   Yes No

In such a questionnaire the total number of unfavorable responses is taken as an over-all indication of emotional adjustment or emotional stability-instability. The actual interpretation of the score on a questionnaire of this sort requires the use of a table of norms which is set up by giving the questionnaire to a representative sample of people.

Since one's emotional life is intricately interwoven into his over-all adjustment, it is a common practice to prepare questionnaires which contain questions of the sort listed above and in addition questions which have to do with other aspects of total adjustment. These questionnaires are commonly called *personality inventories*. Most of them are designed to measure a number of aspects of personality, one of which is emotion. A further discussion of personality inventories will be presented in Chapter 14.

The Word-Association Test Technique

In this method a subject is given a number of stimulus words one at a time, generally orally, with instructions (1) to respond to each word with the first word that comes to mind (free association), or (2) to respond to each word with a word which bears some specified relation (such as opposition) to the stimulus word (controlled association). In another form of the word-association test a subject is given a single word with instructions to respond with one word after another, letting each response word be a stimulus for the next response. The free-association form of this technique is the one ordinarily employed in studying emotion. Its use in measuring emotion rests on the fact that emotional experiences become connected with words. These words serve as substitute stimuli to reinstate the experience or remind the subject of the experience. Such words are called emotionally loaded words. It is assumed that in responding to an emotionally loaded word, a subject will "give himself away," so to speak, or reveal in some way that the word is an emotionally loaded word. He may hesitate, thus increasing his reaction time to the word. He may repeat the stimulus word and thus give himself time to think of a response word that will be less embarrassing than the one that first occurred to him. He may respond with more than one word, use the same response word several times, use a previous stimulus word as a response word, or respond very quickly. These indications of emotion in a word-association test are called *complex indicators* because the test is commonly used to study *complexes*. The free associations of a depressed person contemplating suicide are given in Table XIV. How many complex indicators can you find in this table?

Complexes. A *complex* is a group of related interests and activities organized around an emotional core. A complex may be beneficial, worthless, or harmful to the well-being of the total personality. For an example of a beneficial complex take the information and interests organized around the subject of chemistry by a research chemist who, while he makes his living from his research, is truly "in love with" his work. He has a complex for chemistry. His thinking, his life outside *long delay on odd answer denotes complex*

Table XIV

Reaction Times in Free-Association Test to Indifferent Words
and Emotionally Loaded Words (15)

STIMULUS WORDS		REACTION WORDS	REACTION TIME IN SECONDS
1.	Head	Hair	1.4
2.	Green	Meadow	1.6
3.	*Water*	*Deep*	5.0
4.	Stick	Knife	1.6
5.	Long	Table	1.2
6.	*Ship*	*Sink*	3.4
7.	Ask	Answer	1.6
8.	Wool	Knit	1.6
9.	Spiteful	Friendly	1.4
10.	*Lake*	*Water*	4.0
11.	Sick	Well	1.8
12.	Ink	Black	1.2
13.	*Swim*	*Can swim*	3.8

shows emotional toward water

the laboratory, and his interests are all extensively influenced by this dominant activity. When he sees a new plastic material, his thinking immediately turns to the chemistry which made the new material possible. A complex of this type is of value to the individual and to society. For the individual it relates a wide variety of things to his dominant interest, and thus broadens his whole horizon of enjoyable mental activity. Society profits because the individual concentrates his abilities and training in a direction which makes for new developments and discoveries. The person whose daily work has become a complex is in the fortunate position of Professor George Herbert Palmer, who said he had the best job in the world because "Harvard College pays me for doing that which I should gladly do whether Harvard College paid me or not."

Other complexes may be somewhat less general in their effect upon a personality. One's hobbies, for example, are complexes which are relaxing, stimulating, or entertaining, but which influence one's thoughts or activities only "after business hours." Photography, stamp collecting, and sports may become complexes which, practiced in moderation, are wholesome and contribute greatly to general happiness and satisfactory adjustment to life. Link (21) has pointed out that the feelings of unhappiness, restlessness, and insecurity which sometimes develop during middle age can be largely eliminated by deliberately taking up again some of the hobbies which were an important part of our childhood life. With the increasing amount of leisure time resulting from modern industrial methods, the importance, if not the actual necessity, of complexes around which to weave the activities of our leisure time is becoming greater and greater. Perhaps a part of our modern restlessness and of our tendency to be "on the go" we can explain by the fact that leisure time has increased during the past twenty years more rapidly than interests, in the form of complexes, have developed.

Not all complexes, however, are desirable. Indeed, the term was first used to describe those constellations of ideas which are injurious to the individual. Many complexes are of this type. Best known in popular thinking is the so-called "inferiority complex" — the possession of an ill-recognized feeling of inferiority, which may bring about many undesirable consequences. It may cause one man to assume an air of bravado, another to become a downright bully, another to become a silent recluse or a bashful and timid soul. It is very serious when it causes a person to feel himself beaten at the outset of any project which he undertakes. The particular form which an inferiority complex takes depends upon many factors, including the native ability of the person involved. It has recently been said that an inferiority complex is usually an asset to the sufferer because it prompts him to greater efforts to overcome his handicap. In a person who is endowed with some rare ability, this is no doubt true — for instance, Steinmetz was a hunchback, Demosthenes a stutterer — but in the absence of a very high level of ability the effects of a marked inferiority complex are usually detrimental. One should not, however, feel at all unusual if he is afflicted occasionally with feelings of inferiority. Anyone with an ounce of ability to appraise his own powers must, at times, feel quite insufficient. To experience a *moderate* amount of annoyance because of inferiority feelings is doubtless more of an asset than a liability. These feelings are usually quite justified by the facts of the matter and arouse us to action.

Measures of Bodily Changes

A number of instruments are available for measuring many of the internal and external bodily changes which constitute components two and three of an emotion. It has been pointed out that an emotive situation produces changes in breathing, heart rate, blood pressure, electrical resistance of the skin (the psychogalvanic reflex), digestive processes, dilation of the pupils of the eyes, the amount of sugar in the blood, and the amount of adrenalin in the blood. In addition, a number of overt changes may be measured or at least recorded by motion picture cameras.

Changes in the rate of breathing or alterations of depth of breathing are recorded by a *pneumograph*. Pulse rate is measured by a *sphygmograph*, which is commonly attached over the wrist. Changes in blood pressure level, which are frequently regarded as the most reliable indications of emotion, are measured by the instrument commonly used in medical examinations, the *sphygmomanometer*. Changes in blood volume are measured by a *plethysmograph*. Changes in the electrical resistance of the skin, the psychogalvanic reflex, are measured by a *galvanometer*. It is a rather common practice to use two or more of these instruments at a time and to record the measured changes with an apparatus known as a *polygraph*. Let us examine some of the studies in which these instruments have been used in order to see the kinds of bodily changes which are involved in emotion.

Breathing and blood pressure changes. Pneumographic records taken while subjects are responding to emotional stimuli reveal a change in the ratio of the time spent in inspiration to the time spent in expiration. This ratio, known as the I/E ratio, is approximately .70 under normal conditions. Gaskill (12) has found that the ratio falls in responses to disgusting situations and that it rises in response to situations that provoke noble sentiments.

In speech, the ratio greatly decreases — in fact, it is reduced to .20 or .25 — because the breath is drawn in quickly and allowed to escape slowly to form the stream of words. This reduction carries over to sub-vocal speech, that is, to the forming of words which are not actually vocalized. Thus, the increased sub-vocal activity characteristic of lying is accompanied by a reduction of the inspiration-expiration ratio.

Changes in blood pressure also usually occur in emotional activity. Although, as Scott (28) has pointed out, there is no definite correlation between the amount of systolic blood pressure change and the degree of the emotion, as introspectively reported, nevertheless there is some increase of blood pressure in nearly all emotional activity. Probably this is simply one of the many physiological processes which are speeded up because of the heightened state of the activity of the organism.

The psychogalvanic reflex. One of the most interesting of the many physiological changes which accompany emotional activity, and probably the most serviceable to students of emotions, is the change in the resistance of the skin to an electric current. By placing properly constructed electrodes on the surface of the body, we can demonstrate that resistance of the skin to an electric current (the psychogalvanic reflex) decreases during an emotion (25).

By recording this change in electrical resistance, one may determine when an emotion is present and approximately how intense it is. So far no one has discovered a means of determining from the record *what* emotion is being experienced, but in spite of this limitation many interesting investigations on the emotions have been made possible by this technique. Some of the investigations of the effect of movies on children already referred to (see p. 124) have used the psychogalvanic reflex. Other studies have shown that it is possible to condition an emotion, that is, to cause a stimulus which originally had no emotional effect to arouse an emotion. Freeman (10) found that persons responded with an emotional reaction to an electric shock but gave no response at all to a clicking sound. After shocks and clicks had been given a number of times simultaneously, the click alone produced an emotional response. The records from a typical subject are shown in Figure 63.

Eye movements. Asher and Ort (2) have shown that involuntary eye movements as measured by an ophthalmograph occur when subjects are responding to emotionally loaded words in a word-association test. Eye movements were of three kinds: eye-closure, jerk movements away from a fixation point, and a series of blinks. These movements occurred three times more often in response to presumably loaded words than to non-loaded words, and more frequently than any of the complex indicators which occur in word-association tests. This finding is in line with the results of other experiments which indicate that involuntary muscular movement is related to emotional stimulation. French (11), for example, concludes that finger tremor is a more sensitive indication of emotional states than either pulse or the psychogalvanic reflex.

Lie detection. The "lie-detectors" which have recently been given considerable newspaper publicity consist of a polygraph which shows heart beat, blood pressure, breathing rate, and the psychogalvanic reflex. The theory is that lying involves more emotional tension than telling the truth, and that the apparatus, by revealing the emotional condition of the subject, will indicate his degree of veracity. Much headway has been made in this direction, and this instrument, no doubt, will become valuable to detectives in inducing criminals to make confessions and in getting clues leading to evidence admissible in court.

Attempts have been made to apply the free-association test method to criminal detection by requiring the suspect to respond to a number

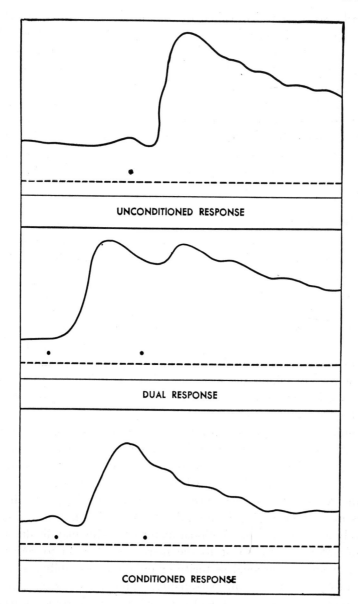

UNCONDITIONED RESPONSE

DUAL RESPONSE

CONDITIONED RESPONSE

Figure 63

A Conditioned Emotional Response Measured by
the Psychogalvanic Reflex

(From G. L. Freeman, "The Galvanic Phenomenon and Conditioned Responses," *J. Gen. Psychol.*, 1930, 3, 529–539.)

of words, some of which, called the key or critical words, are closely connected with the crime and the rest of which are padding. It is assumed that the critical words will cause the subject to think of the crime, and the emotional state so caused will influence his response in some significant way. Perhaps he will hesitate; perhaps he will become confused. As a means of detecting criminals, however, the method of word-association alone has not been very successful. Measures of blood pressure, breathing, eye movements, or the psychogalvanic reflex, taken by means of the "lie-detector" during the association test, may be expected to provide additional "indicators" and thereby increase the value of the word-association test technique.

Other Measures of Emotion

Tests. A few attempts have been made to devise psychological tests for measuring emotion. For example, Willoughby (35) constructed an emotional maturity scale designed to give the highest scores to those whose emotional expression is habitually characterized by self-reliance and an objective attitude toward personal problems. Pressey (27) published a group scale for investigating the emotions which included four tests composed of lists of words designed to diagnose abnormal fears, disgusts, abnormal sex tendencies, and abnormal self-regard. In taking the test, the subject is instructed to cross out words which are unpleasant to him. For this reason the test is referred to as the Pressey X–O test.

Chambers (5) used this test to measure emotional maturity. He found that certain words differentiated between fourth grade, sixth grade, and college students. Scores for these words decreased with increasing maturity, a finding which Chambers interpreted to mean that the X–O test was a measure of emotional development. In spite of this initially promising finding, the X–O test has not been used extensively as a measure of emotional maturity. This may be due to the lack of follow-up studies or to the more recent trend to regard the measurement of emotional maturity or emotional instability as a facet of the problem of measuring personality. This trend is seen in the fact that a number of the measures of personality provide some measure of emotion or yield some information about it. For example, the projective techniques, which will be described in Chapter 14, reveal information regarding anxiety, hostility, inferiority feelings, feelings of insecurity, worries, and emotional conflicts.

Indirect indicators. Slips of the tongue and other mistakes in action that are made in spite of the individual's being on guard also give evidence of emotional difficulties, often hidden from their owner. "I had a very ice time at your party. Pardon me, I meant *nice* time," was said by a girl attending the coming-out party of a successful social rival. If you are becoming a psychologist rather than just taking another course for credit, make it a point to study the next half-dozen slips of the tongue that you hear (or make).

Another everyday indicator of emotional tension which often betrays one unwittingly is very rapid conversation and overactive behavior. The over-hearty laugh, the unduly strong handshake, gay chatter in excessive amounts, all indicate lack of ease. Your dinner partner may brag, "I have been to four teas this week; and, oh dear, next week there are five teas and three dinner parties. I never get any time to myself." Be polite and interested, but also be sympathetic; for the speaker is, in all probability, under an emotional tension so severe that to be alone with herself is intolerable. She finds that the imps that whisper to her the truth of an unsatisfactory emotional life cannot be heard above the din of dinner-party chatter.

MEMORY FOR EMOTIONAL EXPERIENCES

Of the numerous factors which determine whether or not we shall remember an experience, the emotional quality of the experience has unique importance. It is a basic principle of psychoanalysis that we tend to remember events which are pleasant and to forget experiences which are unpleasant. While there are many exceptions to this principle, its general truth seems to be fairly well established from numerous case histories. Some thirty-five experimental studies also indicate that experiences which were originally pleasant tend to be recalled more readily than those which were originally unpleasant (30).

Meltzer (23), who has given a convenient summary of the experimental work in this field, has himself conducted one of the most significant investigations. On the day following a Christmas vacation, Meltzer asked 132 college students to list briefly all their experiences during the vacation. Of the 2,231 experiences reported, 62 per cent were pleasant and 37 per cent unpleasant. Six weeks later the students were again asked to recall their Christmas experiences. Fifty-three per cent of the pleasant experiences were again recalled, but only 40 per cent of the unpleasant ones. There were, however, some individuals who recalled a greater proportion of unpleasant experiences than pleasant ones.

Results somewhat contradictory to these findings were reported by Anderson and Bolton (1), who believe that pleasantness and unpleasantness show no decided difference in their effect on memories, but that both show an advantage over indifference. Lanier (19), studying incidental memory for words differing in affective value, found no general relationship between memory and pleasantness or unpleasantness. In discussing such contradictory results, White and Ratliff (34) suggest that more experiments should be performed in order to establish the facts and, if possible, to explain the divergent conclusions in previous experiments. In three separate experiments these investigators showed that the recall of pleasant and unpleasant materials varied with the method of measuring recall and with the time interval between learning and recall. They suggest that such factors as differences in the intensity of pleasantness and unpleasantness, differences in the familiarity with various pleasant and unpleasant stimuli, and differences in the instructions to the subjects in the experiments might be responsible for the inconsistencies in the results of the various experiments on this topic.

The great majority of experimental studies, however, shows that pleasant experiences are, in general, remembered longer and more accurately than unpleasant ones. This does not mean that the unpleasant experiences have no effect on one's personality once they have been driven from consciousness. They may continue for a very long while to exert a profound and unhealthy effect upon one. But the conscious aspect of unpleasant experiences seems to disappear fairly rapidly in most cases.

We can all make very practical use of the foregoing discussion of memory for emotional experiences. It is economical for a person to forget what tends to deflate him. If we had to carry on our shoulders memories of all our defeats and humiliations, we should have little energy left for the work of the day. It is useful to remember what was successful and pleasant, because the memories of success give us courage with which to meet the contests of the present. "How dear to my heart are the scenes of my childhood." We find this true because we have forgotten most of the scenes that were not dear. Listen to an old graduate tell of the wonderful teachers and brilliant lecturers he used to have when "you really learned something in college." You will be talking that way too in thirty years. The old oaken bucket deludes only those who have forgotten how it really worked on a cold morning or who have never had any manual contact with it. In appraising reports of what really happened, made by witnesses that were emotionally involved, the experienced student of human nature always makes allowances for emotional distortion. Resolutions made during a period of severe depression or remorse usually last little longer than the memory of the remorse, which is soon forgotten. Every convalescent is going to take excellent care of his health just as soon as he gets well.

SUMMARY

An emotion is a complex unit of behavior made up of five major components. These components are: (1) the perception of an emotive situation, (2) internal muscular and glandular changes, (3) immediate overt behavior, (4) feeling, and (5) an adjustment to the emotive situation. Components 2 and 3 follow immediately upon the perception of the emotive situation and in turn serve as sources of stimulation for the arousal of one's feelings and his emotional adjustment. The expressions we use to convey ideas about feelings when no feelings are present are considered under the heading of the "language of emotion." These are not regarded as emotional responses.

Emotions develop through learning and maturation from the generalized emotional reaction of excitement of the newborn to the varied and complex feelings and emotions found in older children and adults. This development is characterized by (1) an increase in the number of emotions, (2) an increase, generally followed in later life by a decrease, in the number of situations which will arouse a given emotion, (3) an increase in the adequacy of emotional reactions, and (4) an integration of emotion with all adjustive reactions. In developing emotional maturity it is important (1) to avoid situations that are known to produce excessive emotions, (2) to understand the nature of emotions, and (3) to achieve understanding and mastery of emotive situations.

A number of techniques and methods are available for measuring one or another of the five components of an emotion. The most widely used methods include: (1) the verbal report method, (2) the questionnaire method, (3) the word-association test, (4) instrumental measures of bodily changes, and (5) tests. The first two methods measure the feeling component of an emotion. The word-association method is useful in uncovering forgotten emotional experiences. The pneumograph, sphygmomanometer, galvanometer, and plethysmograph measure breathing changes, blood pressure changes, electrical resistance of the skin, and blood volume changes respectively. These changes are the most important of the bodily changes involved in the second component of an emotion. Measures of involuntary muscular movements such as finger tremor and eye movements provide data regarding the third.

Emotion is a unique factor in recall.   In general, pleasant experiences are remembered longer and more accurately than unpleasant ones.

QUESTIONS

on the Chapter

1. What is an emotion?
2. Describe each of the five components of an emotion. *(P9 299 [perceptual type overt act logical ch... physical estimat ... feeling])*
3. Distinguish between components 3 and 5.
4. How does the James-Lange view of emotion fit into the diagram on page 299? *2 & 3 being about 4 rather than perception*
5. How does the behavioristic view differ from the five-component view?
6. What is meant by the language of emotion? -
7. What are the principal changes which occur in emotional development?
8. Give an example of a conditioned emotional reaction.
9. What is emotional maturity?
10. Criticize the verbal report method as a way of measuring emotion. *best.*
11. What is the method of paired comparisons? *what do you like best.*
12. What is a complex? *figurative* / Make a list of "complex indicators."
13. List the various instruments which are used in studying emotions and indicate what is measured by each.
14. What is a "lie-detector"?   An ophthalmograph?
15. What can you conclude from the experiments on the relation of emotion to memory? *indifferent thing - forgotten first / bad - / good - remembered longest / next*

for Discussion

1. Does the "language of emotion" fit into our five-component scheme? Explain.
2. In what way is an emotion a motivating condition?
3. What is your reaction to the statement: What we do in any situation is the best we can do under the existing circumstances.
4. In the light of what is measured by a "lie-detector," do you feel that "lie-detectors" should be used by the police?
5. Which is the better measure of emotion, an individual's verbal report of his feelings or a measure of physiological changes?
6. Do all emotions fit into Cannon's notion that an emotion is an emergency reaction?
7. Are inferiority complexes necessarily undesirable?
8. Make a list of the characteristics which you associate with "emotional maturity."

REFERENCES

1 ANDERSON, A. C., and BOLTON, F. J., "Inhibition of the Unpleasant," *J. Abnor. Soc. Psychol.*, 1925, 20, 300.

2 ASHER, E. J., and ORT, ROBERT S., "Eye Movement as a Complex Indicator," *J. Gener. Psychol.*, 1951, 45, 209–217.

3 BRIDGES, K. M. B., "Emotional Development in Early Infancy," *Child Development*, 1932, 3, 324–341.

4 CANNON, W. B., *Bodily Changes in Pain, Hunger, Fear, and Rage*. New York: D. Appleton-Century Company, 1915.

5 CHAMBERS, O. R., "A Method of Measuring the Emotional Maturity of Children," *Ped. Sem.*, 1925, 32, 637–647.

6 DASHIELL, J. F., *Fundamentals of Objective Psychology*. Boston: Houghton Mifflin Company, 1928, Chapter 8.

7 DOCHERAY, FLOYD C., *Psychology*. New York: Prentice-Hall, 1942.

8 FAIRBANKS, H., and HOAGLIN, L. W., "An Experimental Study of the Durational Characteristics of the Voice during the Expression of Emotion," *Speech Monographs*, 1941, 8, 85–90.

9 FAIRBANKS, H., and PRONOVOST, W., "Vocal Pitch during Simulated Emotion," *Science*, 1938, 88, 382–383.

10 FREEMAN, G. L., "The Galvanic Phenomenon and Conditioned Responses," *J. Gener. Psychol.*, 1930, 3, 529–539.

11 FRENCH, J. W., "A Comparison of Finger Tremor with the Galvanic Skin Reflex and Pulse," *J. Exp. Psychol.*, 1944, 34, 494–505.

12 GASKILL, H. V., "The Objective Measurement of Emotional Reactions," *Genet. Psychol. Monogr.*, 1927, 2, 196–233.

13 GOODENOUGH, FLORENCE L., *Anger in Young Children*. Minneapolis: University of Minnesota Press, 1931.

14 GOODENOUGH, FLORENCE L., *Developmental Psychology*. New York: D. Appleton-Century Company, 1934. Quoted by permission of the publishers.

15 HART, BERNARD, *The Psychology of Insanity*, 4th edition. New York: The Macmillan Company, 1935, p. 85. Quoted by permission of the publisher.

16 JAMES, WILLIAM, *Principles of Psychology*. New York: Henry Holt and Company, 1913. (See Volume II, Chapter 25 on the emotions.)

17 JONES, MARY C., "Conditioning and Unconditioning Emotions in Infants," *Childhood Education*, 1925, 1, 317–322.

18 LANDIS, CARNEY, "Studies of Emotional Reactions. II. General Behavior and Facial Expressions," *J. Comp. Psychol.*, 1924, 4, 447–509.

19 LANIER, L. H., "Incidental Memory for Words Differing in Affective Value," *J. Psychol.*, 1941, 11, 219–228.

20 LEEPER, ROBERT W., "A Motivational Theory of Emotion to Replace Emotion as Disorganized Response," *Psychol. Rev.*, 1948, 55, 5–21.

21 LINK, HENRY C., *The Return to Religion*. New York: The Macmillan Company, 1936.

22 MCQUEEN-WILLIAMS, M., "Maternal Behavior in Male Rats," *Science*, 1935, 82, 67–68.

23 MELTZER, H., "The Present Status of Experimental Studies on the Relationship of Feeling to Memory," *Psychol. Rev.*, 1930, 37, 124–139; also, "Individual Differences in Forgetting Pleasant and Unpleasant Experiences," *J. Educ. Psychol.*, 1930, 21, 399–409.

24 MITTELMANN, B., WOLFF, H. G., and SCHARF, M. P., "Emotions and Gastro-duodenal Function; Experimental Studies of Patients with Gastritis, Duodenitis and Peptic Ulcer," *Psychosomatic Med.*, 1942, 4, 5–61.

25 MUENZINGER, KARL F., and BROXON, J. W., "The Changes in Skin Potentials during the Psychogalvanic Reflex," *J. Genet. Psychol.*, 1931, 5, 94–98.

26 MUNN, NORMAN L., *Psychology*. Boston: Houghton Mifflin Company, 1946.

27 PRESSEY, S. L., "A Group Scale for Investigating the Emotions," *J. Abnor. Soc. Psychol.*, 1921, 16, 55–64.

28 SCOTT, J. C., "Systolic Blood Pressure Fluctuates with Sex, Anger, and Fear," *J. Comp. Psychol.*, 1930, 10, 97–114.

29 SHERMAN, M., "The Differentiation of Emotional Responses in Infants," *J. Comp. Psychol.*, 1927, 7, 265–284.

30 THOMSON, RUTH HAINES, "An Experimental Study of Memory as Influenced by Feeling Tone," *J. Exp. Psychol.*, 1930, 13, 462–468.

31 VALENTINE, C. W., "The Innate Bases of Fear," *J. Genet. Psychol.*, 1930, 37, 394–420.

32 WATSON, JOHN B., *Psychology from the Standpoint of a Behaviorist*. Philadelphia: J. B. Lippincott Company, 1924. Quoted by permission of the publisher.

33 WEBER, C. O., "The Concept of 'Emotional Age' and Its Measurement," *J. Abnor. Soc. Psychol.*, 1930, 24, 466–471.

34 WHITE, M. M., and RATLIFF, MARGARET, "The Relation of Affective Tone to the Learning and Recall of Words." *Amer. J. Psychol.*, 1934, 46, 92–98.

35 WILLOUGHBY, R. R., *Emotional Maturity Scale and Manual*. Stanford: Stanford University Press, 1931.

THINKING

10

Thinking is the capstone of man's intellectual activities. It may be regarded as the most complex of all of man's ways of acting, and the one activity that, more perhaps than any other, differentiates man from lower animals. As Woodworth and Marquis (19, p. 588) point out,

> man is distinctively a thinker. Hunched over his desk with only a pencil and a scrap of paper to work with, or even lost in thought with his feet on the desk, he may be alive with inner activity and perhaps taking the crucial steps toward some great achievement. Man is notably a doer as well as a thinker. He loves to manipulate and change his environment. He engages in large enterprises and accomplishes far-reaching results. But these large enterprises depend on previous thinking.

KINDS OF THINKING ACTIVITY

Free Association

The term *thinking* is applied to a variety of activities. It is used to refer to simple thought sequences in which one thought or idea calls up another, which calls up a third, and so on in a more or less free or uncontrolled fashion. Indulgence in such aimless thought sequences or mind-wandering is called *reverie*. This is the type of thinking called for in the free-association test in which a subject is asked to respond to a stimulus word with the first word that comes to mind. It is significant that this test has been used not only to study emotion (see p. 326) but also to discover the nature of one's thought processes, i.e., the extent to which free associations tend to run in a particular direction. There is some evidence to indicate that the free associations of scientists differ from those of literary students. Murphy (14) found that free-association responses which could be classified as coordinates or contrasts (of the stimulus words) occurred more frequently among scientists, while contiguity associations, responses which were classified as completions or predications (of the stimulus words) were more common with literary students.

Daydreams

The thought sequences which occur in daydreaming may be regarded as another type of thinking activity. Here the thoughts follow one another very much as thoughts do in reverie except that they are usually directed toward some goal. The daydreamer wants something. In his imagining, thought sequences lead him to this something. To be sure, the daydream is a process of imagination (see the next chapter), but it is also a kind of thinking, a sequence of ideas which has continuity and which is goal-directed.

Autistic Thinking

When thought sequences are determined entirely by the desires of the thinker, with complete disregard of logical principles, facts, reality, or social confirmation, we have a kind of thinking known as *autistic thinking.* It might be called wishful thinking. It may go on as fantasy-thinking which serves directly or obscurely the imaginary gratification of unfulfilled desires. In this form it is not unlike the daydream. On the other hand, it may occur on a reality level. Here, however, it is so strongly motivated by deep-seated desires that the desires are represented as already fulfilled. Incompatibilities with reality are ignored. This type of thinking is more prevalent in childhood than in adulthood, partly because of the immaturity and lack of experience of children and partly because of the treatment accorded them. The household is regulated to meet the infant's every need. Hardly does he cry for food before it is brought to him. If he drops something on the floor, a willing attendant replaces it. When sleepy, he is made comfortable in bed. If he shows interest in an object, it is given him. His every desire is satisfied through no effort of his own. The infant has reason to believe that thought is omnipotent. It takes time for him to learn differently.

Around Christmas-time little children fight hard to believe that Santa Claus is a wonderful old man who gives presents to all boys and girls. Their thinking is not determined by what they know, but by what they desire to believe. Here is a conversation between a father and his four-year-old son:

> *Father:* How can Santa Claus get down the chimney?
> *Son:* He is not so fat as we think.
> *Father:* How can he get to California and New York during the same night?

Son: Go by train or a big bus.
Father: What is Santa Claus like?
Son: A man.
Father: Who is Santa Claus?
Son: Not you and Mamma.

The little fellow was fighting hard to preserve his belief in Santa Claus as a mysterious creature. Like many adults when placed in similar situations he gave reasons and explanations that did not measure his logical comprehension or ability to think straight. That ability was more truly reflected in his last reply, "Not you and Mamma."

Though many things combine to help bring about the needed discipline, autistic thinking is seldom completely outgrown. Many adults do not see a thing as it is because of their desire that it should be different. A man who wishes to become governor of a state may convince himself that he has numerous friends throughout the state who are anxious to make him governor, when, as a matter of fact, he may be poorly qualified for the office and have only a few supporters. Or a woman may seriously argue that she needs a new dress when she already has more dresses than she can afford.

Reasoning

Think for a moment of a two-volume history as it is situated on a bookshelf. Each volume is two inches thick between the covers. Each cover is an eighth of an inch thick. A bookworm eats his way from the first page of volume one to the last page of volume two. How far does the bookworm travel? If one attempts to think through this problem to a solution, he is engaging in a type of thinking known as reasoning. In thinking or reasoning through this problem to a solution, one recalls how books are ordinarily arranged on a bookshelf. A set of two volumes is generally arranged with the first volume on the left and the second to the right. Next, one tries to recall or "think" where the first page of volume one would be in relation to the last page of volume two. He may have to imagine himself taking the two volumes from the shelf, holding them in position while he tries to "figure out" the relation of the first and last pages of the two volumes. Somewhere in the processes of recall and imagination he sees or realizes that the two pages are separated only by two covers. Adding the thickness of the two covers to get the final answer is not only a simple task, but is in a sense a kind of afterthought, because the important part of the solution consisted in "thinking" of where the first page of volume one was in relation to the last page of volume two. The thinking or reasoning in this example can be described as problem-solving activity. In fact, all reasoning is problem-solving activity.

How does this problem-solving activity differ from the problem solving described in the chapter on learning, where it was seen that lower animals solve problems by overt trial and error behavior, or by doing something to, or in, or with the objects and things in the problem situation? The rat which threads his way through a maze, the cat which manipulates the things in a problem box until he hits upon a method of escape, and even human subjects who stumble on to the solution of a puzzle by manipulating the parts of the puzzle are all solving problems, but not by reasoning.

Reasoning and overt trial and error. In contrast to this type of problem solving, reasoning is distinctly "mental" activity. The reasoning is a sort of mental trial and error process. The problem brings to mind certain previous experiences. These are tried out mentally and discarded. Other experiences are recalled, broken up and rearranged, tried out, and discarded. The process continues until a likely solution is fashioned out of the person's fund of information. If the information needed for solving the problem is not available in the individual's experience, the solution of the problem may be postponed until additional information can be acquired, as in the case of Arrowsmith, who postponed work on an experiment until he could acquire certain mathematical knowledge which he found necessary for the completion of his scientific work. During the process of mental trial and error involved in reasoning, the individual may engage in little or no overt behavior, although an outside observer may judge that the person is thinking by the fact that he is motionless, or that from time to time during the reasoning he raises an eyebrow, gazes fixedly at something which seems not to be the object of his attention, or sits with chin in hand as if supporting a head which is busily engaged with weighty matters.

Both kinds of problem solving involve trial and error behavior. In one case the trial and error activity is open to view; in the other it is not. In one case the trials are direct responses to objects and relations in the problem situation; in the other they are indirect responses, indirect in the sense that they may go on when the objects of the thinking are not present, or in the sense that even though the objects are actually present, there is no direct manipulation of them. This is seen in the case of an individual who, when given a puzzle box to open, proceeds without any direct manipulation of the box itself to "figure out" how it can be opened. His "figuring out" of the solution is very likely to involve a considerable amount of "talking to himself" and a great many implicit movements of fingers and hands, which are abbreviations of the direct manipulatory responses which might be made in overt trial and error.

Let us suppose that an individual is given the bookworm problem as he stands facing a bookcase which has a two-volume work in it. Let us suppose further that this individual attacks the problem by actually taking the two volumes from the shelf, examining them to find the two pages in question, and measuring the distance between the two pages. In this case the problem is solved by the direct manipulation of the objects in the situation. No reasoning is required. In contrast to this procedure, the solution of the problem by reasoning required a number of indirect responses. There was no manipulation of physical objects in a situation. The books and bookshelf were not present, or, if present, were ignored. The solution was reached by manipulating the symbols which represent the objects in the situation. The reasoning in this case is problem solving with symbols. Reasoning, daydreaming, autistic thinking, or any other kind of thinking is characterized by the fact that it involves symbolic processes. In thinking, one is reacting to symbols which represent objects, rather than to the objects themselves.

Solving problems by the direct manipulation of the objects in the problem situation, i.e., by overt trial and error, and solving them by reasoning represent the lowest and highest forms psychologically of problem-solving behavior. Between these two extremes, problem-solving behavior consists of some mixture or combination of the two. Some problem-solving behavior is largely of the overt trial and error variety but shows evidence of some of the indirect reactions or symbolic processes characteristic of thinking. Other problem-solving behavior may give evidence of a considerable amount of thinking but may not be completely free of overt trial and error.

Detour experiments. An example of problem-solving behavior which gives evidence of an elementary kind of ideation is found in Köhler's (11) experiments on "detour" behavior. In one case a dog was released into an alley formed by a wall and a shed (see Figure 64). On entering the alley and discovering that food was on the outside of the bars at the end of the alley, the dog hesitated only a moment, did an about-face, and ran around the shed to get the food. Hens placed in a similar kind of situation made a variety of trial and error responses, running back and forth, rushing against the bars, and craning their necks through the bars. They did not give evidence of the "detour" behavior found in the dog. The dog's about-face and running away from the food are not direct attacks on the objects in the situation. The fact that the dog ran when he could not see the food is suggestive of an elementary kind of symbolic process. It appears that the dog was not responding directly to the food while running away from it.

Delayed reaction experiments. Hunter's (8) delayed reaction experiments provide further evidence of a kind of ideation in animals. An animal is taught that he can get food at one of three boxes, the correct one being distinguishable by being lighted. After the animal learns to go to the lighted box for food, he is placed in a position where he can see all three boxes but cannot go to them. One of the boxes is lighted. The light is then turned off. After an interval of time the animal is released. The object of the experiment is to see if the animal can, after the prescribed delay, go to the box that was lighted. To make a correct response in this situation is interpreted to mean that the animal has some internal process, such as a muscle set or body posture, which serves as a cue or symbol to represent the previously lighted box. In Hunter's experiment, rats, cats, and dogs could go to the correct box after a few seconds' delay if they maintained a definite posture, such as holding the head pointed toward the box, during the

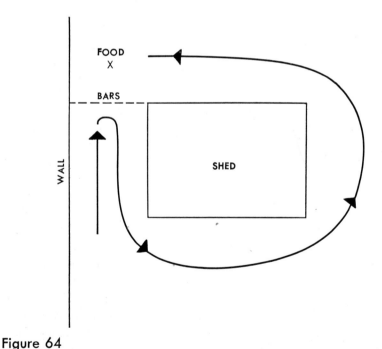

Figure 64

Diagram Showing the "Detour" Behavior of a Dog

(Modified from W. Kohler, *The Mentality of Apes*, Harcourt, Brace and Co., 1925.)

delay.   Raccoons made correct responses after a longer delay and even
when their postures were shifted during the interval.   In another experiment, Hunter (9) found that, during the period from 13 to 16 months
of age, a little girl made correct responses after delays of 10 to 24
seconds in a delayed reaction situation similar to the one described
above.

    Combining past experiences.   Since combining past experiences is
one feature of the reasoning process, one approach to the problem of
whether animals can reason or the problem of how early children can
reason is to teach subjects two separate tasks and then give them a new
problem which can be solved by combining the two previously learned
tasks.   This was done by Maier (12) in an experiment with rats.   Food
was placed on a table behind a screen.   A rat was placed on the table
but could get to the food only by means of an indirect route which required him to run away from the food.   The table and the pathway were
elevated about two feet from the floor.   After the rat had learned to
get to the food by this roundabout route (see Figure 65), he was placed
on the floor.   He now had to learn to climb a post situated at the point

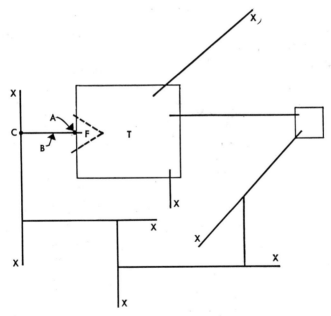

Figure 65

Maier's Elevated Maze

(From N. R. F. Maier, "Intelligence of White Rats," motion picture film.   By permission
of N. R. F. Maier.)

marked A in the diagram in order to get the food at F. Once this task had been learned, the pathway from point C to the food was removed. The rat was then placed on the table. Since he knew how to get to the food by the indirect route, he proceeded to point C only to discover that the "bridge was out" from point C to the food. What to do? He climbed down the post at point C, a new task, and promptly ran across the floor to the post at A, which he climbed to get to the food. In this case the rat combined his past experiences almost immediately upon being placed in a problem situation which could not be solved by either of the previously learned tasks.

In another experiment, Maier (13) gave children two separate kinds of training. After these two unconnected experiences the children were given a new and rather difficult task to see if they could fashion a solution out of the two past experiences. Most of the children under six years of age could not solve the problem. Older children were successful, the number of successes increasing with an increase in age. This cannot be construed to mean that children under six years of age cannot reason or combine past experiences. It must be recognized that success in problem solving is at all times a function of the difficulty of the problem in relation to the age, experience, and ability of the subject. Adults of high ability encounter problems which they are unable to solve.

The foregoing experiments indicate that some problem solving in lower animals and children gives evidence of ideation and symbolic processes. It should not be inferred, however, that problem solving in adults is always the result of reasoning. That adults resort to overt trial and error in attempting to solve problems is seen in Ruger's (16) classic experiments with mechanical puzzles. In these experiments subjects were given mechanical puzzles which they were required to take apart. After each solution the puzzle was put together by the experimenter and given back to the subject for another trial. Careful records were kept of the methods used by the subjects, the time required for each solution, and the comments made by the subjects. In general the subjects attacked the puzzles in an overt trial and error fashion. After a number of trials in which the solutions seemed to come quite accidentally, the subjects would quite suddenly "see" the solution. After this there was virtually no further trial and error. This sudden "seeing the solution" will be recognized as the phenomenon of "insight" which was discussed in Chapter 6. It is a basic characteristic of reasoning. While insight frequently occurs in problem solving which involves the overt manipulation of objects in the learning situation, it is itself regarded as a kind of ideational or symbolic process, and as an alternative to overt trial and error. In reasoning one may make some direct reactions to objects in the problem situation, but reasoning is basically a process in which past experiences, acquired at different times and in different contexts, are brought together, tried out in various combinations, and broken up and rearranged until a solution emerges. The reasoner brings these past experiences or the elements thereof together in a certain relationship. Almost immediately, so it appears, he sees in this relationship a solution to his problem. It is this ability to see relationships that Spearman (17) regards as a fundamental characteristic of intelligent behavior.

STEPS IN THE ACT OF REASONING

A complete act of reasoning according to Dewey (2) can be broken into five steps as follows: (1) a problem or felt difficulty; (2) definition of the difficulty; (3) the suggestion of possible solutions; (4) an examination of the suggested solutions and the bearing of the suggestions on the problem; and (5) observations and experiments leading to the acceptance or rejection of each suggestion. Every act of reasoning does not necessarily involve all of these steps. An individual confronted with a problem may not take time to define it or state it in the form of an answerable question. If he does, he may take the first suggestion as a solution without testing it mentally (step 4) to see how it bears on the problem. Quite obviously the individual is not engaging in a complete act of reasoning though he insists that he is reasoning. Let us examine the steps in more detail.

Step 1 — The Problem

What is a problem and how do problems arise? A problem may be thought of as a felt difficulty. The individual is in a predicament. Such predicaments arise when an individual's desires or wants are thwarted, when for any reason he is unable to get what he wants. Making a passing grade in a course is a problem to the extent that the student wants to make a passing grade and to the extent that this want is thwarted by lack of ability, lack of application, or other conditions.

One's desires or wants may be thwarted in a great many ways. In general it is possible to classify these thwarting conditions into four groups. First, desires may be thwarted by obstacles in the environment. Such environmental conditions as cold, heat, drought, mountains, rivers, and oceans have always been serious obstacles standing in the

way of man's desire for comfort, security, and survival.   The solutions
to the problems created by these conditions comprise an important
chapter in the history of man's development.   On a smaller scale, the
infant's urges to "go places and do things" are repeatedly blocked by
doors, chairs, steps, and the prison bars of his playpen.   Second,
desires may be thwarted by one's own inadequate physical and mental
equipment.   The high school boy's desire to be a football star is
thwarted by the fact that he does not have the physical build and stamina
needed for football competition.   Third, desires may be thwarted by
other desires.   The saying "you can't have your cake and eat it too"
illustrates a conflict between desires.   Finally, desires may be thwarted
by acquired modes of thinking, moral principles, social conventions,
and taboos.   The child's desire to carry off an attractive toy from the
toy shop is thwarted by his ideal of honesty.   The team's desire to win
at any cost may run counter to acquired ideals of sportsmanship, fair
play, and honesty.

Step 2 — Definition of the Difficulty

It has been stated that a clear statement of a problem is half the battle.
Indeed, in some cases it is the whole battle.   This is seen in reports
made by clinical counselors of clients who, in the process of trying to
tell about their difficulties, actually define their problems for the first
time and are able to see the solutions to them without further assistance.
It goes without saying that one cannot hope to solve a problem if he
does not know precisely what it is.   A felt difficulty is ordinarily a vague,
poorly defined predicament.   A good reasoner reduces this vague feeling to a specific statement of the nature and source of the difficulty.
He is able to "put his finger on the precise difficulty."   But how does
one do this?   First, one must recognize that felt difficulties need to be
defined precisely.   Second, one may need to make additional observations before he can define the difficulty.   Once the results of these
observations are in, they should be examined and compared with the
facts which were originally available.   Third, one should attempt to
formulate a statement of the problem.   This may be done by trying to
describe the problem to someone else or by trying to describe the
problem in writing.   Such verbal or written formulations force one to
concentrate more carefully, to spend more time on the problem, and
thus increase his chances of discriminating between relevant and irrelevant details.   The reader may be able to think of other ways by which
a reasoner can reduce a felt difficulty to a precise statement of the
nature of the difficulty.

Step 3 — Suggestion of Solutions

A concise statement of the problem suggests almost immediately a number of possible solutions or answers; these in turn may suggest others. Entertaining all the possibilities may sometimes appear to lead one far afield; but one should avoid sticking too rigidly to some assumption or point of view, since it may exclude suggestions which, though they appear at first blush to have no relation to the problem, may eventually lead to a solution. At this stage one may do well to let his thinking wander somewhat as in reverie, at least to the extent of being spontaneous and not holding to a strict thought sequence dictated by logical considerations. There will be time enough later (in step 4) to examine each suggestion and test it logically. In this phase of reasoning one is making guesses, having hunches, collecting suggestions, and from these formulating tentative solutions in the form of hypotheses. It is here that imagination plays a prominent role in the reasoning process. Past experiences are combined in novel ways to produce new ideas or suggestions. It is in step 3, perhaps more than in any other phase of reasoning, that new discoveries, inventions, and creations have their origin.

Steps 4 and 5 — Examining and Testing Suggestions

Here we have elected to consider steps 4 and 5 together. In step 4 a suggestion is examined carefully and tested subjectively. One deduces that if the suggestion is correct certain other things must be true. In step 5 the suggestion is tested objectively by observation and experiment to provide the final proof of the validity of the suggestion as a solution to the problem.

Induction and deduction. All reasoning involves two movements: one from the particular phenomena observed to a generalization, hypothesis, or theory; the other from the generalization to its consequences. The former is called the inductive movement of thought; the latter, the deductive movement. For example, Pasteur advanced the generalization that hydrophobia is caused by the saliva of dogs suffering from that disease. This was an induction. He then deduced that, if hydrophobia were so caused, the inoculation of other animals with the saliva of a diseased animal should cause the disease. This was the deductive movement of his thought. It suggested a test which failed to verify his hypothesis. Hence the rise of a second hypothesis and its final verification.

Sometimes we speak of inductive thinkers and deductive thinkers.

This is probably due to the fact that some people accept the generalizations of others and seek to guide their lives by making deductions from them, while others tend to lean on their own experience in formulating principles of conduct. The distinction has even been extended to whole periods of history. The Middle Ages were outstandingly a period of authority. The present age has been interested in extending knowledge. It has, therefore, greatly emphasized induction. In reality, however, this difference can be only a matter of emphasis; for induction and deduction are but the different directions of our mental activity when we are confronted with a puzzling situation. To understand the situation we must advance new hypotheses or pick one already advanced. Unless we did one thing or the other, we should be completely bewildered. We must also test our hypotheses in the light of their implications. Otherwise, we should act impulsively instead of rationally.

The mental trial and error most characteristic of reasoning occurs in step 4, in which the hypotheses are tried out subjectively one after another and examined critically and carefully. Here each suggestion must be followed through to its logical conclusion. If this is true, then so and so must be true. A check will serve to establish the validity of the conclusion. This process of checking hypotheses is illustrated in the following account of Pasteur's discovery of the cause and the means of prevention of hydrophobia. Pasteur, having seen a child die of hydrophobia, became interested in its cause and prevention. His first hypothesis as to its cause grew out of the common fear of being bitten by a dog suffering from hydrophobia; it was that the disease is transmitted by the saliva of the diseased animal. If this hypothesis were true, then hydrophobia should follow upon an inoculation of animals with the saliva of diseased animals. Inoculation with such saliva failed to produce the disease in a majority of instances. The first hypothesis was therefore rejected. Pasteur's second hypothesis grew out of the observation that animals dying of hydrophobia suffer many muscular contortions. This suggested that the disease involved the medulla, the seat in the brain of control over involuntary muscular action. If this hypothesis were true, then animals inoculated with an emulsion of the medulla from a diseased animal should develop hydrophobia. This implication of his hypothesis was tested, and it was found that all animals so inoculated, without exception, died of the disease. Having discovered the cause, he was faced with the next problem — to find a way of protecting those who had been exposed to the disease. Working on the theory that the living organism will build up immunity to a disease if it is exposed first to a weak charge of the virus that carries the disease and then to more virulent forms, he was able so to immunize dogs that no injection of diseased medulla gave them the disease. Shortly afterwards he had an opportunity to test his method on a boy who had been badly bitten by a mad dog. It proved as effective on the boy as on dogs (15).

CONDITIONS FAVORABLE FOR EFFECTIVE THINKING

Freedom from Fixed Assumptions

As pointed out above, a problem brings to mind certain past experiences. In many cases there is some similarity between the problem and previous ones. This similarity may lead the reasoner to make unwarranted or false assumptions which keep him from solving the problem. In the bookworm problem, for example, the statement that "a bookworm eats his way from the first page of volume one to the last page of volume two" leads some people to assume that the bookworm travels all the way through both volumes. The problem cannot be solved until one rids himself of this assumption. The tendency to make unwarranted assumptions is seen in many problem-solving situations. Ruger (16) found that some subjects when given a mechanical puzzle to solve would assume incorrectly from a first glance at the puzzle that it could be taken apart in a given way. Many subjects had difficulty in ridding themselves of the false assumption. It was found that the question "What are your assumptions?" or "Do you see any other possible assumptions?" was sufficient to get the subject to abandon his initial assumption.

Some so-called difficult problems are difficult largely because of the pronounced tendency to derive from the statement of the problem an incorrect idea as to how it should be solved. This is illustrated by the problem in which a subject is given six matches and asked to make four equilateral triangles. All of the matches are to be used and none of them are to be broken. Since the matches are placed on a table the subject makes the assumption immediately that the triangles must be in one plane. The problem cannot be solved as long as the subject operates with this assumption. Another factor which operates against the abandonment of the false assumption in this problem is the tendency of some subjects to continue to manipulate the matches. This is a problem that can be solved more readily by reasoning than by manipulation.

The tendency to make unwarranted assumptions and to persist in trying to solve a problem by methods dictated by these assumptions is one of the most common causes of failure in problem solving. One characteristic of any kind of problem solving is variability of attack on the problem. This was pointed out in the description of step 3 in the reasoning process. The reasoner entertains many suggestions, and many different ones. These represent the trial solutions or hypotheses that are to be tried out later on. It is clear that fixed ideas will tend to limit the number and the kinds of suggestions which will occur to the reasoner. In solving problems, one needs to remind himself repeatedly of this fact. He would do well to develop (1) a willingness to change his assumptions and modes of attack on a problem, and (2) a habit of asking himself from time to time "What are my assumptions?" and "Are there other possible assumptions?"

In the foregoing illustrations the unwarranted assumptions or fixed ideas were suggested by or grew out of the problem itself. There is another source of fixed assumptions. An individual brings to a problem certain fixed ideas or preconceptions which have the same effect upon his attacks on a problem as the unwarranted assumptions suggested by the problem. These personal preconceptions tend to limit the kinds of suggestions which will occur to one in reasoning. They tend to force one to look for a particular kind of solution or to make incorrect deductions from the suggested solutions. Such fixed ideas make objective thinking difficult or impossible. Freedom from such fixed ideas, which may be regarded as openmindedness, favors effective thinking.

Environmental Conditions That Stimulate Effective Thinking

Social contacts. Reasoning must be motivated. People do not reason for nothing. Social contacts create a need or an urge to reason. The desire to win social approval and to communicate with others makes thinking almost a necessity. Young children do not, as a rule, feel the importance of making their thoughts explicit, and many university students on examinations seem to assume that a mere suggestion of their thought processes is enough to enable the instructor to understand them. As we learn that understanding is not so easily imparted, we become more and more careful to express ourselves clearly. With this effort we become more conscious of our thinking and make more explicit the grounds of our conclusions. We wish, however, not only to be understood but also to convince. Hence we support our statements by connecting them with more generally accepted propositions. This necessarily involves deduction and the use of causal relations. Moreover, when others do not agree with us and we finally appreciate the fact that they may really see things differently, we become more careful in thinking through our problems to a rational conclusion. In this way we make our thought processes more explicit and more accurate.

Change. Social habits and traditions are sufficient to guide behavior when social change is slow, for then there is little need to think. But in a rapidly changing environment, new paths must be made. At such times we are driven to think. In this respect our own culture is one of the most stimulating the world has ever known. The invention of machinery has provided us with the means of creating enough material things to satisfy the legitimate wants of every family. Yet we seem unable to take advantage of our opportunities. Indeed, machines, instead of ushering in an era of plenty, have apparently produced scarcity and suffering for millions. One need only turn the pages of our best magazines to see how these economic changes have stimulated thought. Many problems in the fields of religion, science, and politics have also arisen during our era and are compelling us to think.

Contacts with other cultures. When members of one cultural group are thrown into contact with those of another, thought is stimulated. An important cause of the fact that Greek philosophy arose among the colonists instead of in Greece itself was that the colonists came into contact with cultures different from their own; the discovery that men might have beliefs and values different from their own stimulated them to reflect. Ordinarily we become set in our favored ways of doing things and cease to think of new possibilities. Today knowledge of widely different cultures, both past and present, is stimulating social thinking. Though some of us may believe that our society is so perfect that we can learn nothing from others, the large majority have become experimental in their attitude and are willing to consider the possibility that social change may mean social progress.

Environments conducive to reflection. There are some environments that place a premium upon thought and some that regard thinking with suspicion. As has been pointed out, our own culture is especially conducive to reflective thinking by virtue of the many changes that are taking place. Yet even here, in spite of these changes and of our wide contacts with other peoples, there are communities that fear thought. They feel that reasoning is apt to uproot custom and tradition, leaving in its wake a chaos of uncertainty and bewilderment. And their anxiety is not unreasonable; for it is easy to confuse the reasoner and the revolutionist. Indeed, the revolutionist has encouraged this confusion; for if he can show that the change he advocates has been dictated by "reason," who can say that he is wrong? We should bear in mind that the new is not necessarily reasonable and that the reasonable is by no

means always new.   A reasonable solution to any problem is one which
is based upon an impartial consideration of all facts pertaining to that
problem.   Habits, customs, and traditions that have been considered
satisfactory by many former generations as well as our own are often,
but not always, more reasonable than untried theories.   Bearing this
in mind, we should be quite willing to subject current social practices
to a logical analysis.   Reason will probably dictate quite as much con-
tinuance of present practice as change.

CONCEPT FORMATION

What Is a Concept?

Earlier in this chapter it was pointed out that thinking involves the
manipulation of symbols or the reaction to symbols which represent
specific objects or things.   But everyone knows that some of our symbols stand, not for a single object, but for any one of a large group of
objects or for certain relationships among objects.   Thus the word
"pencil," instead of representing some specific pencil, stands for the
entire class of objects.   At the same time the word "pencil" comes to
stand for or symbolize the feature or features which these objects have
in common.   The process by which we discover the feature or features
which are common to a large number of objects and associate these
with a symbol which thereafter may be applied to other similar objects
is called concept formation.   A *concept* is a symbol which stands for the
quality or characteristic that is common to a number of objects, situations, or events.   Such words as "pencil," "chair," "table," and in fact
most of the words in a language stand for the elements possessed in
common by a large number of things which are in other respects quite
different from one another.

Development of Concepts

Abstraction.   The formation or development of a concept involves
two processes: *abstraction* and *generalization*.   The first is the process
of discovering the common element in a large number of situations.
One observes that two or more objects are alike or similar in some one
respect while being different in other respects.   For example, in acquiring the concept "dog," a child may hear the word *dog* while he is
playing with a rag dog.   Later he hears the same word while playing
with a wooden dog, and while looking at the picture of a dog.   Still
later he hears the word when he is playing with a pet poodle dog.   He
hears the word *dog* over and over in different situations and learns to

apply the word to any object that has the same general characteristics as a dog. Thus in the early stages of the development of the concept, the child may apply the word to cats, or horses seen at a distance, or other four-legged animals, because up to this time he has observed one common element in his experiences, namely, four-leggedness. Additional observations and finer discriminations will refine the concept to the point where the word will be applied only to dogs.

Generalization. The process of generalization is the process of extending the concept to include objects which possess a quality in common with other objects but which have not been experienced as any of the objects in the abstracting process. Let us suppose that the child has acquired the concept dog, and that he now sees a dachshund for the first time. If he calls the dachshund a dog, he is evidently seeing in this particular dog the qualities which a dachshund has in common with other dogs. He is extending the concept to include other objects which have the features common to the class of objects covered by the symbol *dog*. To do this the child must put his present experience together with his past experience and, in a sense, reason that since the new object has some features like the old ones, it must belong to the same class. Quite obviously, a concept is learned through trial and error reactions to objects, situations, or events. The refinement and enrichment of the concept are functions of the number and the variety of the trial and error reactions or experiences involved in the development of the concept. If one's experiences with dogs have included playing with dogs, pulling a dog's tail, wrestling with a dog, running after and away from dogs, feeding dogs, being hurt by dogs, being jumped on by dogs, throwing things for dogs to retrieve, whistling to dogs, watching dogs chasing cats, and observing dogs barking and biting, his concept of *dog* will be richer and carry more meaning than it would if his experiences were limited to only a few of these situations.

Since the development of concepts is dependent upon experience, it should be clear that concepts are in a continuous process of change, refinement, and enrichment. The child who abstracts from his experiences with dogs the common element of four-leggedness has developed a concept of *dog*, but not an adequate one. Subsequent experiences will refine the concept. But at every stage of the development the symbol *dog* will be used to refer to or stand for the feature which the child has abstracted out of his experiences up to that time. The symbol is the same at all levels but the meanings are different. This introduces a difficulty in communicating with others and in thinking. A number of children hear the word *dog*. To one it means four-legged animals;

to another it means something that barks; to still another it means something that bites. The latter child would be confused, to say the least, by the statement "Man's best friend is his dog." Yet this statement is another experience that may be associated with *dog* and may contribute to the eventual revision of the child's present concept.

Experimental Studies of Concept Formation

It is difficult to discover the precise nature of concept formation as it takes place under the complexity of everyday living. In the area of concept formation, as in many other kinds of behavior, we must isolate the phenomenon by experimental procedures if we are to obtain the kind of information needed for directing the development of concepts. Experimental studies of concept formation attempt to set up controlled conditions in which (1) concepts can be formed, (2) quantitative measurements of the concepts can be made, and (3) the stages in their development can be studied.

Hull's study. One of the early studies in this field was made by Hull (7). He used twelve series of drawings, composed of twelve drawings each, the drawings being adaptations of Chinese characters. Each drawing in each series was presented along with its name. The subject was asked to learn to name each drawing. In the different series the same name was applied to different drawings, but it was possible for the subjects to discover that the different drawings with the same name had some element or characteristic in common. Once this discovery was made it was possible for the subject to name a new drawing correctly on its very first appearance. The subjects discovered that drawings having the same name all had a common characteristic. The common characteristic was associated with the name. The name was then applied to new drawings which had the characteristic common to other drawings of the same name. This will be recognized as the processes of abstraction and generalization described above. Here, however, the concept formation occurs under controlled conditions which make possible a step-by-step analysis and measurement of the process and the eventual discovery of the factors which are essential to the process.

Hanfmann and Kasanin's study. Another approach to the experimental study of concept formation is illustrated in a study by Hanfmann and Kasanin (5). These investigators used a test developed by Vigotsky. The test material consists of twenty-two blocks of two sizes, large and small, two heights, tall and short, five colors, and six shapes (see Figure 66). On the under side of each block is printed one of four nonsense syllables, *lag*, *mur*, *hik*, and *cev*. *Lag* appears on all of the tall, large blocks; *cev* on all of the small, flat blocks; *mur* on all of the small, tall blocks; and *hik* on all of the large, flat blocks. The blocks are arranged in front of the subject as shown in Figure 66. The subject's task is to group the blocks into four groups. The experimenter turns over a block, reads its name and asks the subject to pick out all of the blocks that belong with it. The subject proceeds to pick out blocks, being told only that a response is correct or incorrect, until he eventually discovers the basis for properly classifying the blocks into four groups. The test requires the subject to classify or group the blocks, not according to one common characteristic, but two common features, the two features in this case being size and height. The test is set up in such a way that a classification according to one common feature, or according to two common features other than size and height, is incorrect.

What does one look for in the reactions to this test and how are these reactions scored or interpreted? The answer is provided in a quotation from Heidbreder (6, p. 114).

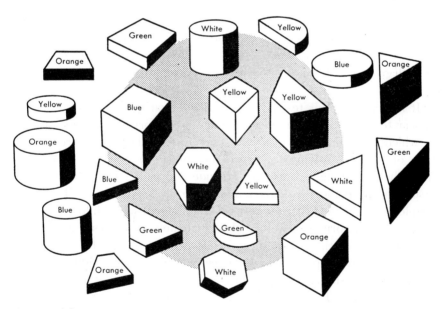

Figure 66

The Materials Used in the Study of Concept Formation
by Hanfmann and Kasanin

(From E. Hanfmann and J. Kasanin, "A Method of Studying Concept Formation," *J. Psychol.*, 1937, 3, 521–540. By permission of the Journal Press, Provincetown, Mass.)

The primary concern in this kind of inquiry is not with test scores and quantitative measures; it is with a *qualitative* analysis of the subject's procedure. Although two quantitative measures are available and are actually used — the time of the total performance and the number of "corrections" or blocks turned up — these are regarded as constituting in themselves neither reliable nor significant measures of the subject's proficiency. The quality of the performance is far better indicated by the manner in which the subject arranges and rearranges the blocks and by his accompanying comments. Such reactions are used as evidence of the course of his thinking from moment to moment; in particular, of his interpretation of the instructions, of the kinds of groupings he attempts, of the hypotheses he employs, of the use he makes of the nonsense words and of the "corrections," and above all, of whether he treats the blocks simply as concrete, individual objects or as representatives of the general qualities on the basis of which he makes his classification—in other words whether the level on which he is operating is concrete or abstract, whether he is working with "things" or with "categories." By observing the subject's behavior, the examiner tries to discover whether he realizes that the material affords many possible bases of classification, whether he has insight into the structure of the classification as a whole, and whether, if he has failed to make the classification himself, he is able to grasp the principle when the experimenter demonstrates the correct classification. Thus the subject's reactions are interpreted as indicating degrees of concreteness and degrees of abstractness, i.e., degrees of proficiency within each of the two levels.

It is clear that this test calls forth a wide variety of reactions which appear to range from the overt trial and error sort of problem solving, in which the subject reacts to the concrete materials, to the reasoning type of problem solving, in which the subject assumes, more or less from the beginning, an abstract attitude and proceeds to "think out" a solution even though the concrete materials are present. This fact, coupled with the fact that the test is suitable for testing children as well as adults, and normal as well as abnormal subjects, makes it a valuable test for investigating thinking and concept formation. The results of its use with schizophrenics (seriously maladjusted individuals) seem to indicate, as shown by Kasanin and Hanfmann (10), that these patients have difficulty in thinking abstractly. The "concrete" attitude is dominant over the "abstract" attitude. Goldstein (3) has found that this is true of brain-injured cases.

It should not be concluded, however, that any person who has difficulty in thinking abstractly is a schizophrenic or a brain-injured case. If conceptual ability as measured by concept-formation tests is positively related to intelligence, one might expect normal or schizophrenic individuals of low intelligence to display a lack of the "abstract" attitude or of conceptual thinking on the Vigotsky test. Schizophrenics and normal subjects of equal intelligence may perform essentially alike on tests of concept formation.

In a recent study by Wright (20), it was found that a group of schizophrenics who were matched with a group of normal subjects on the basis of intelligence and age performed as well as the normals on a group of concept-formation tests. If brain-injured persons and schizophrenics are functioning at a low intellectual level because of a loss or lack of intellectual powers, they would be expected to show a loss or lack of ability to think abstractly. Any person of low intelligence would be expected to show a similar deficiency.

CREATIVE THINKING — involves imagination

It has been customary in psychology to characterize some thinking as creative and then attempt to analyze this thinking and describe the stages involved in it. Thinking that results in strikingly new or original solutions to old problems or in the solution of problems which have heretofore been unsolved is commonly designated as creative thinking. There can be little doubt that some of man's thinking is creative. Think for a moment of the inventions and discoveries in the field of transportation, or the creations in the fields of music and art, or the discoveries and creations in the various sciences, or the new insights in law, economics, and government, or the inventions and discoveries in industry and agriculture. These products of man's thinking are among his highest achievements.

Efforts have been made to examine, analyze, and describe the stages in the process by which such products evolve. If we review the five steps in a complete act of reasoning, we note that the final solution to a problem has its inception in step 3 of the process. It is at this stage that possible solutions occur to the reasoner. It is here that he can exercise his ingenuity, originality, and creative abilities. It is here that he turns the problem over and over in his thinking, letting it call up whatever suggestions it will. It is here that he gives free rein to his imagination. Past experiences are recalled. These are combined and recombined with one another and with facts obtained from the problem situation itself. It is out of this imagining process that the happy idea emerges, the idea that may be a new discovery, an invention, a creation. Every idea, of course, is not a happy one. When the idea is examined and tested, it may prove to be a "dud," but every idea has its origin in this imagining process. This is the crucial stage in any thinking, creative or otherwise.

Wallas's Analysis of Creative Thinking

Wallas (18) has analyzed the process of creative thinking into four stages as follows: (1) preparation, (2) incubation, (3) inspiration, and (4) verification. The stage of preparation is the period preceding the presentation of a problem, during which one acquires the knowledge and skills out of which he must fashion a solution to the problem. It is not a period of special preparation except in those rare instances in which an individual takes time out after a problem arises to search for facts which might bear on the problem. One may, of course, spend a considerable period of time acquiring knowledge in a particular field, not for solving some particular problem, but in order to deal with any of the problems that might arise in the field of his specialization. The atomic physicist is better prepared to deal with problems that might arise in connection with the development and utilization of atomic energy than individuals who have prepared themselves to deal with problems in the general area of music, or medicine, or psychology.

The stages of incubation and inspiration correspond approximately to step 3 of the reasoning process. Ideas emerge following a period of incubation in which they have their inception, growth, and eventual birth. During this period the germinating idea must be nourished and allowed to develop. This nourishment and protection must be provided by the thinker, who is at this stage still unaware of the existence of the embryonic idea. Writers have emphasized the importance of sleep, relaxation, and freedom from tension or outside interference as factors favoring the incubation of ideas. The growth of the idea cannot be rushed. It appears that conscious efforts to hurry it are as likely to impede the growth as to facilitate it. The food necessary for its growth is not something that is provided from the outside. It is already present in the reservoir of knowledge built up during the period of preparation.

The idea, once it has developed or matured sufficiently, emerges into full recognition or awareness. The emergence or birth may occur suddenly and at any time and place. It may occur while the individual is busy at some other task. It may, so it is reported, occur in a dream. It may occur following a period of restlessness during which the thinker has paced the floor, smoked one cigarette after another, and finally given up thinking about the problem. The fact that, in many cases, the idea emerges quite suddenly even when one is not at the moment trying to "think up" a solution has given rise to the notion of inspiration. It should be recognized, however, that there is nothing mysterious about the fact that a suggested solution may come suddenly. Even in solving puzzles it was found that some subjects seemed to "see" the solution quite suddenly. But in every case a considerable amount of fumbling with the puzzle and some "accidental" solutions had preceded the sudden insight. The same thing is true in thinking. Happy ideas do not occur to reasoners who have had little or no preparation, or who do not have a problem, or who have not entertained one suggestion after another in their search for a solution to the problem. As Dashiell (1, p. 566) points out, "Coleridge's dream-delivered *Kubla Khan* came to Coleridge, not to Newton or Wagner or Whitman."

The stage of verification is the one in which the suggested solution, the new idea, is evaluated and subjectively tested, and eventually tried out in actual practice. It corresponds to steps 4 and 5 of the reasoning process and needs no further comment here.

What has been said above about creative thinking as a process could be said about thinking that does not lead to the kinds of products that are commonly regarded as creations. Step 3 of the reasoning process is in no way peculiar to creative thinking. It is involved in any act of reasoning whether the act leads to strikingly original solutions or not. We have seen also that the steps involved in creative thinking as described by Wallas can be identified with Dewey's steps in the reasoning process except for the stage of preparation. This stage is implicit in any act of reasoning. It follows, therefore, that creative thinking as a process cannot be distinguished from thinking that is not regarded as creative. The distinction between creative and noncreative thinking must be, as seen in our definition of creative thinking, in terms of the products of thinking, not in terms of the thinking process as such. This means that an analysis of the thinking process, such as that made by Wallas, or any anecdotal accounts by distinguished persons of their creative thinking, does not throw much light on the problem of creation. It fails, for example, to tell us why some thinking leads to strikingly new or original products while other thinking does not. It fails to tell us how to train people to do creative work, or what factors or conditions are prerequisites for creative thinking. If the answers to these and other questions that might be asked about creative thinking are not to be found in an analysis of the thinking process, where are we to look for the answers?

Creativity

Guilford (4) has suggested that we study the abilities and personality traits which determine the extent to which individuals exhibit creative behavior. Such a study may reveal that there are patterns of traits characteristic of people who produce results of a creative nature. It may provide us with the answers to the questions raised in the preceding paragraph. At the very least, it provides us with another approach to the problem of creative thinking. To date no study of this sort has been made, but Guilford has outlined a design for such a study and has suggested a number of hypotheses concerning creative abilities.

The central problem in this proposed investigation is *creativity*. In a general way, creativity refers to the abilities of individuals to create or to produce results of a creative nature. "In its narrow sense," as Guilford (4, p. 444) points out, "creativity refers to the abilities that are most characteristic of creative people." But all individuals, except for the occurrence of pathologies, can be regarded as having these abilities in some degree. "Creative acts can therefore be expected, no matter how feeble or how infrequent, of almost all individuals" (4, p. 446). The important point is that individuals can be arranged on a continuous scale from low to high amounts of these abilities. The individuals at the high end of the scale, those with the highest amount of creativity, can be regarded as having more of what all of us have, and creativity can be investigated in all individuals, not just in the few whose creative efforts are particularly spectacular.

In setting up hypotheses regarding creative abilities, Guilford describes eight variables or possible primary abilities that may contribute to or be involved in creative behavior, and suggests a number of tests or other devices for measuring some of them. These variables are regarded as descriptive of the behavior of such creative people as scientists, technologists, and inventors. The first variable is *sensitivity to problems*. One earmark of creative people is their ability to see problems which other people do not see. The second variable is *fluency*, or the number of ideas produced in a given unit of time. The third variable is *novelty*, or the number of unusual or uncommon associations or responses. The fourth variable is *flexibility*, or the ease with which one can change sets or shift from one set of assumptions to another. The fifth variable is described as a *synthesizing ability*. This ability and its counterpart, *analyzing ability*, refer to one's ability to take ideas apart and build new ones. The sixth variable has to do with the *reorganization* or redefinition of organized wholes. This would be involved in redesigning or transforming objects or concepts. The seventh variable "has to do with the degree of *complexity* or intricacy of conceptual structure of which the individual is capable" (4, p. 453). Individuals who can handle or keep in mind a number of ideas at one time would stand high on tests designed to measure this variable. The eighth variable is *evaluation*. In reasoning, ideas are tested mentally and then tried out experimentally. Such testing can be done with different criteria of excellence in mind. The testing is in part an evaluation of the ideas in terms of some set of criteria.

These hypothetical variables, presumably involved in the creative behavior of scientists, technologists, and inventors, are amenable to experimental investigation. Investigations designed to test these and/or other hypotheses in different types of creative people or in people in general may be expected to provide us with the kinds of knowledge needed for understanding, predicting, and controlling creative behavior. This approach to the problem of creative thinking may prove to be far more fruitful than the traditional analysis of the thinking process approach.

SUMMARY

The kinds of thinking activity are: (1) free association, (2) daydreaming, (3) autistic thinking, and (4) reasoning. Reasoning, the most important of these, is a kind of problem-solving activity which involves the manipulation of symbols in a trial and error fashion. Evidence of an elementary kind of reasoning is found in the ability of animals to solve "detour" problems, to make delayed reactions, and to combine past experiences.

The steps in reasoning are: (1) a felt difficulty, (2) definition of the difficulty, (3) the suggestion of possible solutions, (4) an examination of the bearing of the suggestion on the problem, and (5) experimental test of suggested solutions. Two major movements in reasoning are induction (from the specific to the general) and deduction (from the general to the specific). Conditions which are favorable for effective thinking are: (1) freedom from fixed assumptions and (2) such environmental conditions as social contacts and contacts with other cultures.

A concept is a symbol which stands for the quality that is common to a number of objects, situations, or events. Concept formation involves two processes: abstraction and generalization. The first is a process of discovering the common element in a large number of stimulations. The second is one of extending the concept to include objects which possess the common quality.

Creative thinking has been analyzed into four stages: (1) preparation, (2) incubation, (3) inspiration, and (4) verification. Stages 2 and 3 correspond to step 3 of the reasoning process. Another approach to an understanding of creative thinking is to make a study of *creativity*, the ability to create or produce results of a creative nature. All individuals are regarded as having this ability in some degree.

QUESTIONS
on the Chapter

1. What is reverie? Autistic thinking?
2. What is reasoning?
3. Distinguish between reasoning and overt trial and error.
4. What is the significance of Köhler's "detour" experiments?
5. Describe Hunter's delayed reaction experiment.
6. What are Dewey's five steps in the reasoning process?
7. Why do we regard reasoning as made up of both induction and deduction?
8. What environmental conditions are favorable to effective thinking?
9. Give some examples to show how fixed assumptions interfere with reasoning.
10. What is a concept?
11. Distinguish between the process of abstraction and the process of generalization.
12. Describe Hanfmann and Kasanin's study of concept formation.
13. Distinguish between the "concrete" and the "abstract" attitude.
14. What is creative thinking?
15. What are the stages of creative thinking according to Wallas?
16. What is meant by creativity?

for Discussion

1. To what extent is man's thinking dependent upon his use of language?
2. In what way does the delayed reaction throw light on "ideation" in animals?
3. Do animals think?
4. Why is the ability to combine past experiences an indication of reasoning?
5. Does a discussion of insight belong more properly under reasoning or under learning?
6. Is the process of generalization in concept formation the same process as generalization in conditioning?
7. Does everyone do creative thinking? Does everyone have some amount of creative ability?

REFERENCES

1 DASHIELL, J. F., *Fundamentals of General Psychology*, 3rd edition. Boston: Houghton Mifflin Company, 1949.

2 DEWEY, J., *How We Think*. Boston: D. C. Heath and Company, 1910.

3 GOLDSTEIN, K., "Frontal Lobotomy and Impairment of Abstract Attitudes," *J. Nerv. Ment. Dis.*, 1949, 110, 93–111.

4 GUILFORD, J. P., "Creativity," *Amer. Psychol.*, 1950, 5, 444–454.

5 HANFMANN, E., and KASANIN, J., "A Method for the Study of Concept Formation," *J. Psychol.*, 1937, 3, 521–540.

6 HEIDBREDER, EDNA, "Studying Human Thinking." In Andrews, T. G., ed., *Methods of Psychology*. New York: John Wiley and Sons, 1948. Reprinted by permission of the publishers.

7 HULL, C. L., "Quantitative Aspects of the Evaluation of Concepts," *Psychol. Monogr.*, 1920, 28, No. 123.

8 HUNTER, W. S., "Delayed Reactions in Animals and Children," *Behav. Monogr.*, 1913, 2, No. 6.

9 HUNTER, W. S., "The Delayed Reactions of a Child," *Psychol. Rev.*, 1917, 24, 74–87.

10 KASANIN, J., and HANFMANN, E., "Disturbances in Concept Formation in Schizophrenia," *Arch. Neuro. and Psychiat.*, 1938, 40, 1276–1282.

11 KÖHLER, W., *The Mentality of Apes*. New York: Harcourt, Brace and Company, 1925.

12 MAIER, N. R. F., "Reasoning in White Rats," *Comp. Psychol. Monogr.*, 1926, 6, No. 3.

13 MAIER, N. R. F., "Reasoning in Children," *J. Comp. Psychol.*, 1936, 21, 357–366.

14 MURPHY, G., "An Experimental Study of Literary vs. Scientific Types," *Amer. J. Psychol.*, 1917, 28, 238–262.

15 PATTERSON, C. H., *Principles of Correct Thinking*. New York: Burgess Publishing Company, 1936.

16 RUGER, H. A., "The Psychology of Efficiency," *Arch. Psychol.*, 1910, No. 15.

17 SPEARMAN, C., *The Nature of Intelligence and the Principles of Cognition*. New York: The Macmillan Company, 1927.

18 WALLAS, G., *The Art of Thought*. New York: Harcourt, Brace and Company, 1926.

19 WOODWORTH, R. S., and MARQUIS, D. G., *Psychology*, 5th edition. New York: Henry Holt and Company, 1947. Reprinted by permission of the publishers.

20 WRIGHT, GLEN E., *An Investigation of the Relationship between Concept Formation and Intelligence in Schizophrenics and Normals*. Unpublished M.S. thesis, Purdue University Library, 1951.

IMAGINATION

11

When we are hungry we think of food; when lonely we think of friends. In such instances we become conscious of what would satisfy us, though the desired object is not present. These are instances of imagination (23). The significance of this capacity is evident. There are organisms which, when dissatisfied or in a state of disequilibrium, must wait for a stimulus to aid them in discovering what they need. And the same thing, too, happens with human beings. We may be discontented and ill at ease without knowing what is the matter. Then if we luckily meet an old friend, our unrest gives place to a state of satisfaction. In such a case our need is defined with the aid of a stimulus. Frequently, however, we are able to imagine what would satisfy us, that is, to discover without a stimulus what would restore our equilibrium.

Sometimes imagination is a guide to action, at other times it is a source of enjoyment, and at still other times it is an outgrowth of anxiety. When we sit before our fire and idly dream of what we should like to do, or recall the pleasant events of the past, we make of imagination a source of enjoyment. When a small boy imagines that he is a fireman and acts the part as best he can, imagination is a guide to action and, at the same time, a source of enjoyment. Similarly, at a higher level, imagination may guide action. Artists, scientists, and social philosophers imagine what would be desirable or what would work, and attempt to embody their ideals in practice. But we do not always imagine the useful and desirable. Placed in a world of uncertainty and sorrow, we at times imagine the death of loved ones, or other possible sources of sorrow. Such acts of imagination are outgrowths of our anxieties and fears.

IMAGINATION AND PERCEPTION

Imagination occurs when no external stimulus corresponds specifically to our conscious ideas; perception, when there is an obvious correspondence between sensory stimulation and consciousness. Though it is easy to distinguish imagination from perception in definition, it is not always easy in real life to tell whether we are imagining or perceiving, as an occasional mistake reminds us. Ordinarily we are able to distinguish images from perceptions by the following differences: (1) The perceived object is usually more realistic and stands out in greater detail than the imagined one. (2) We can examine a perceived object in such a way as to get more knowledge about it. Images are too unsteady and fleeting to serve as sources of new information. (3) By stopping the functioning of our senses, that is, by closing our eyes or by putting our hands over our ears, we can cause perceptions to disappear. Images are, if anything, made more vivid by so doing. (4) Finally, perceptions fit in with our general understanding of reality; images frequently do not.

Eidetic Images *vivid type of imagery*

Because children have not learned these differences, they sometimes confuse images and perceptions. If a ghost were to appear to an adult, the latter would know he was imagining; but a child, having no clear conception of reality and fantasy, might well take the "ghost" to be a perception. The images of children are also more vivid than those of adults. They frequently experience a very vivid type of imagery called *eidetic images*. In an eidetic image one can see details, such as the number of windows in a house, that do not usually appear in ordinary imaginings (1).

An experiment reported by Titchener (24, pp. 198, 199) shows how strong images may be confused with weak sensations:

> If, for instance, the observer is seated in a well-lighted room facing a sheet of ground glass, behind which is a screened projection lantern, it is often impossible for him to decide whether the faint colours that he sees on the glass are due to the lantern or to his own imagination. You say to him: Imagine that there is a picture of a banana on the glass! . . . and in many cases it makes no difference at all whether you show a strip of very faint yellow light from the lantern or whether you shut off the objective light altogether. The strip of seen yellow is confused with a yellow image. The experimenter, who regulates the course of the observations by signalling to a third person when the lantern is to be turned on, is sometimes greatly surprised at the gross errors made by the observer. What seems to him obviously sensory may be reported, without hesitation, as imaginative.

Again, we are frequently in doubt, in everyday life, whether we hear

a particular sound or merely imagine it.   And if, in the laboratory, the
observer is required to listen intently to a continuous faint noise, such
as is produced by the falling of a stream of fine sand, the same confusion
will be noted.   The experimenter may reduce the stream to a mere
trickle, and may finally stop it; the observer will still, in many cases,
believe that he hears the hiss.

Lastly, a similar confusion is found in experiments upon pressure and
tickling.   If, for example, in the course of a series of stimulations of a
pressure spot, the experimenter says Now! but omits to touch the skin,
the observer may, nevertheless, report the arousal of a pressure sensation.

In everyday situations similar confusion results.   Mothers are not
always able to tell whether they hear or only imagine that they hear a
baby crying.   Violin players are said to take advantage of our inability
to distinguish images from perceptions when they wish to produce an
extremely *pianissimo* effect by pretending to bow, though actually they
do not touch the strings (13).

Adults can help children to distinguish between imagination and
perception by teaching them to distinguish between the real and the
unreal.   An effective means of doing this is to tell a child fantastic
stories, which forces him to understand that we can talk about unreal
as well as about real things.   At the same time, the child should be
taught a reasonable view of the world in order that he may have a background to distinguish the perceptual from the imaginary.

Relation to Experience

However bizarre imaginary objects may be, the elements of which they
are composed are all drawn from previous experience.   The person
born blind cannot imagine color any more than we can imagine life
without a body.   From this point of view, imagination may be defined
as the recalling and recombining of experience.   This definition marks
imagination off from memory and at the same time indicates the essential
role of experience in imagination.   Conscious recall, we have learned,
is the consciousness of the past, or the reliving of the past in idea.   Error
arises when the past as recalled differs from what it really was.   Imagination, on the contrary, though based on the past, involves a new
combination of past experience, and there is no pretense of recalling
the past accurately.

But how can memory images be distinguished from imagined ones?
Let the reader think of some object.   Is the image a recollection or a
product of fancy?   How can we tell?   For one thing, we judge by our

manner of responding.   One mental image seems familiar, the other strange.   If we were asked to justify the feeling of familiarity, we should proceed to tie the memory image to other memories; that is, we should find for it a place in our organized mental life.   In brief, we recognize images in the same way that we recognize physical objects.   Both feel familiar.   When we are able to place the image or perception in our organized experience, we complete the act of recognition.

Reproductive and Creative Imagination

Imaginings are divided into two groups, depending on how closely the organization and structure of the past are preserved.   If the product of the imagination differs little from an earlier experience, it is spoken of as a product of *reproductive imagination*.   The recalling of an experience of last summer and the weaving it with slight changes into a story would be an instance of this.   When the past provides the elements of the imaginative product but little of its structure and organization, we speak of creative imagination.   Fairy stories, novels that are not biographical, and scientific hypotheses are instances of creative imagination.   For example, the hypothesis of ether as an invisible, imponderable, and perfectly elastic body which transmits wave motion was created from these separate concepts to make intelligible certain phenomena not to be understood otherwise: the action of distant bodies upon each other and the passage of light from the sun to the earth. The nebular and the atomic hypotheses are also products of creative imagination designed to make our world more understandable.   Similarly, the creations of musicians, poets, and novelists are also products of creative imagination.

DREAMS

According to psychoanalysis, sleep is a means of escaping from the boredom of waking life to the more exciting and satisfying world of dreams.   In support of this theory the psychoanalysts claim that people in quiet, uninteresting communities sleep more and appear less alert than people in progressive ones.   They also call attention to the fact that people in the frigid and torrid zones sleep more than those in temperate climates, and to the fact that men engaged in interesting work need less sleep than those not so fortunate in their vocations.   Further support of this theory is found in the fact that in dreams we derive a sort of satisfaction for many unsatisfied desires.

If this theory of sleep is true, it should follow that we dream continually while asleep.   This inference, however, cannot be satisfactorily tested. Suppose a person should decide to determine how much he dreams during sleep. With that purpose he sets an alarm clock so that he will be awakened at intervals throughout the night. If he recalls a dream whenever he is awakened, there is the possibility that the alarm and his unusual mental set caused his dreams. On the other hand, if he recalls a dream only occasionally, there is the possibility that the alarm caused him to forget the dreams. Since no way of eliminating these difficulties has been found, it cannot be stated what proportion of sleep is passed in dreaming.

Since dreams do not always appear, on superficial observation at least, to be an outgrowth of desire, psychoanalysts insist that the desire is frequently disguised and that dreams therefore must be interpreted. Their interpretation of dreams can only be understood in terms of their general psychology. According to their theories, there are three levels of mind: the unconscious, the foreconscious, and the conscious. The unconscious is the source of our psychic energy; in it are the roots of our instincts, and into it are repressed painful memories or desires. The foreconscious consists of all our mental life that can be brought easily into consciousness, such as the memory of what we had for breakfast, our knowledge of history, and our engagements for the day. Consciousness consists of that small part of our mental life of which we happen at the moment to be conscious. Mind may be likened to the earth. The inside of the sphere corresponds to the unconscious; the surface, to the foreconscious; and the illuminated part of the surface, to the conscious.

Desires or memories that are painful to us are driven into the unconscious. Our ideals are regarded as maintaining a close censorship over what is admitted into consciousness. However, in spite of the alertness of the "censor," the contents of the unconscious at times slip into consciousness. To do this they make use of all sorts of disguises, so that their genuine nature cannot be recognized.

Dreams offer an ideal opportunity for repressed desires of all sorts to enter consciousness, though even in dreams it is frequently necessary that they be disguised. The use of symbols is a favorite device. For example, one person dreamed of himself as a hunter armed with a rifle and surrounded by a group of savages armed with spears. In this dream, the rifle symbolized the dreamer's feeling of superiority over his ignorant neighbors, whom he symbolized as savages armed with spears. All this becomes clear when we learn that the dreamer was a young man contemplating an adventure in marriage not approved by his neighbors and friends (22).

Psychoanalysts assert that certain images or pictures in dreams usually mean the same thing for all dreamers. For example, they claim that a snake usually has sexual significance; the failure to catch a train frequently means the fear of missing something of great importance; having to take an examination repeatedly means the fear of facing some ordeal which the dreamer fears he will not meet successfully. It is this uniformity that provides a measure of justification for dream books. However, the same symbol may mean different things, and, conversely, the same things may be symbolized in many different ways (10, 22). Since symbols have no fixed meaning it is necessary that an interpretation be made in each instance.

The method of free association is frequently used by psychoanalysts for the purpose of interpretation. The dreamer is asked to think of a certain picture which appeared in his dream and then to tell the analyst whatever comes into mind. Several pictures of the dream may be treated in this way before the dreamer or the analyst is satisfied that the meaning of the dream has been reached. The difficulties of making a true interpretation of a dream are so great that any particular interpretation should, at best, be accepted with considerable reserve. In spite of this, however, the analysis frequently proves helpful. The dreamer, at least, believes that the true meaning of the dream has been discovered and that the roots of his trouble have been brought from the unconscious into consciousness, where its power for harm is greatly reduced.

Evaluation of the Psychoanalytic Theory of Dreams

The psychoanalysts have added much to our knowledge of dreams and of mental life in general. To them should be given credit for stressing the purposive nature of dreams and for making many dreams intelligible. On the other hand, they have probably erred in maintaining that all dreams are significant or even motivated by a definite purpose. In the second place, some of the psychoanalysts, particularly Freud, have exaggerated the place of sex in dreams. Sex wishes are not the only wishes that may be repressed or that may serve to motivate dreams. The study of the dreams of soldiers just before a battle, in which fear rather than sex is the dominating motive, has convinced most students that Freud's theory of motivation is too narrow. Freud himself seems to have recognized this before he died. In the third place, the psychoanalytic theory does not attach sufficient importance to the physiological condition of the dreamer or to the exciting stimuli.

Some interesting facts regarding the importance of the latter factors have been discovered. Retiring with a clove in the mouth has been found to cause more taste imagery in dreams than is usually experienced; gazing at colored objects causes more imagery of color. Gummed paper stuck on the body also influences dreams (5). The smell of smoke may result in a dream of fire. Dreams may also result from such factors as the moon shining in the face, a cramped position of the body, unusual noises, bad odors, and extreme temperatures.

The importance of physiological conditions has also been shown. When pituitary extract is given to subjects, dreams become more frequent and pleasurable. When suprarenal extract is administered, dreams become highly disagreeable (7). Bad air or lack of oxygen may cause disagreeable dreams. One writer reports that a whole company of soldiers sleeping in a poorly ventilated barn which had a tradition of visits from ghosts dreamed much the same dream of demons jumping on their chests (16).

The psychoanalytic view might be reconciled with the fact that sensory stimulation plays an important part in dreams. It could be argued that the elaboration or interpretation of the sensory process is the important thing to consider, and that to understand either of these we must look into the mental life of the dreamer. Undoubtedly this is true. But desires should not be regarded as little entities within the personality. They are outgrowths of changing circumstances. Kimmins (14), in a study of many thousands of dreams, has found that both dreams and desires change with maturity, and that the content of our dreams varies as social conditions and domestic problems create various desires within us.

In other words, the psychoanalytic view of dreams is based on too narrow a view of the psychological whole. It thinks of behavior as issuing from the personality in some mysterious manner, whereas all behavior should be regarded as due to the whole situation in which exciting stimuli as well as purposes play an important part.

Kinds of Dreams

Some dreams seem to point to dangers ahead and are called *premonitory dreams;* others appear to the dreamer as *prophetic;* still others, apparently caused by some bodily disorder or incipient disease, are called *prodromic.* An instance of the last kind occurred in a person who frequently dreamed of a cat gnawing at his throat. Upon examination, it was found that he had a cancer of the throat. Dreams of flying through the air are called *dreams of levitation.* Such dreams have been regarded as outgrowths of the mastery motive. Another interpretation is that they are caused by the dreamer's becoming conscious before the cutaneous sensations make their usual contribution to the stream of consciousness. This explanation is supported by the fact that when the cutaneous senses are slowly anaesthetized a feeling of levitation results. Dreams of paralysis, with their consequent terror, are probably caused by the dreamer's awakening before he is able to move as he wishes. The dreamer evidently requires more time than usual to pull himself together sufficiently to perform the muscular coordinations involved in overt activity.

Nightmares are frequently caused by cramped positions; at other times, they may be due to a degree of disintegration which allows one's fears to run riot. As we have previously pointed out, when integrated, our emotional states are modified by our understanding of conditions and by other interests. But as the integration breaks down, there is an opportunity for a single interest or emotion to dominate our behavior. In nightmares, fear assumes such a role. This view is substantiated by the experience of soldiers. On account of exhaustion they often find it difficult to hold themselves together even when awake. When, thus exhausted, they fall asleep, their integration breaks down and they experience again the scenes of terror through which they have passed.

Influence of Dreams on Personality and Behavior

Popular thought has always been inclined to attach considerable value to dreams. The reader will recall how Joseph's interpretation of Pharaoh's dream saved Egypt from famine by causing that country to store the surplus grain during years of plenty for the years of drought. Brutus seems to have been disturbed and unnerved by a dream before the fatal battle of Philippi. One effect of enlightenment in our culture has been a decrease of interest in dreams and their interpretation. However, in recent years, largely as a result of the influence of the psychoanalysts, more significance has been attached to them. Dreams are no longer regarded as prophetic, but rather as a source of information about certain aspects of the dreamer's personality of which he himself may be quite unaware.

Dreams may influence behavior, especially that of children, by introducing a possible source of confusion. To discriminate between dream and waking experience is not always easy. A boy of three was greatly concerned one morning about his mother's falling down stairs. He urged her not to fall again. Evidently he had dreamed of his mother's falling. Doctors, in seeking to get a full account of the history of their patients, find they must guard against this possible source of error. Even delusions may be based on dream experiences.

The prolongation of the emotional or affective states of dreams into the waking life of the dreamer may influence his behavior either by encouraging or by discouraging him.   That pleasant dreams should induce pleasant affective states should be no more a mystery than that pleasant waking experiences should make us feel better.   Thinking of cheerful things makes us brighter and happier, whereas thinking of sad events makes us unhappy and depressed.   The influence of imagery on our affective states, even after the imagery has been forgotten, may be the explanation of the fact that on some mornings we awake feeling unusually fit and optimistic without any apparent reason, while on other mornings we awake feeling depressed with equally little cause.

Dreams may influence the behavior of superstitious people indirectly through their interpretations of them.   This is apparently what happened to Brutus.   A man may be depressed by "learning" through a dream book that some misfortune is in store for him.   He may modify his behavior in a way that he thinks will protect him from the impending disaster.   A dream may cause worry, and this may lead to other effects. For example, a person may dream of going insane, and the worry so caused may subject his mental health to additional strain.   On the other hand, a person may be incited by a dream of poverty to work hard to provide himself with a comfortable living.

DAYDREAMS

Daydreams afford an easy way of obtaining satisfaction.   The stories of "Cinderella," "The Ugly Duckling," and "The Milkmaid" are excellent illustrations of the tendency to weave a world of fantasy in which our desires are fully realized.   The milkmaid, evidently an unpopular girl, dreams, as she carries the milk on her head, of the eggs she will be able to buy after selling the milk, of the chickens that she will raise, of the new dress she will wear, of the fine appearance she will make, of the rush of young men to ask her for a dance and of how she will scorn them.   Unfortunately, she acts her scorn too soon; for, in tossing her head, she spills the milk, and all her dreams perish.

The pleasure we get from novels of adventure or from motion pictures depends largely on the help they give us in weaving daydreams that appeal to us.   We identify ourselves with the hero, suffer and conquer with him, and with him enjoy the applause of the admiring crowd.   In this way the book or picture carries us away from the world of our limitations into a world patterned after our desires, where we live richly, if only for a short time.

Sometimes we daydream because of indolence; sometimes, because of discouragement; sometimes, in order to compensate for a life of monotony; and sometimes, because it is a pleasant way to pass the time when we have nothing else to do. That indolence should be a cause of daydreaming is easily seen. For a lazy person, in fact, is one who finds it more to his liking to find satisfaction through fantasy than through more strenuous exertion. Likewise, when we are discouraged we frequently "let ourselves down easy" by imagining that the next time we shall be more successful or by dreaming of success in another field.

In the stories mentioned above, the compensatory nature of daydreams can be clearly seen. People who are excessively ugly, or people who are very conscious of their lack of sociability or money, may compensate for their misfortunes by imagining themselves enjoying the adulation of crowds on account of their beauty, or the envy of neighbors on account of their social prestige or wealth. Sometimes daydreams are taken so seriously that they are embodied in the overt activity of the dreamer, as a little girl may so vividly imagine herself playing with little friends that she talks and acts as though other children were actually present.

Some daydreams, instead of being dreams of success and honor, are dreams of suffering and persecution. Why should such daydreams be a source of satisfaction? One reason is that they cater to the desire to be significant, a desire so powerful that many are ready to endure pains and dangers of all kinds to satisfy it. We should not be surprised that this need lies behind many daydreams of suffering. Such dreams give us satisfaction in much the same way as boasting of our sufferings and misfortunes does. The person who boasts of his painful operations is making a bid for the attention and the concern of others. If successful, he holds the center of the stage for the time being. His craving for significance and importance is satisfied. In the same way, the individual who dreams of being the object of persecution or of being scorned and neglected by others raises his importance in his own eyes. Knut Hamsun (11) in *Hunger* illustrates this motive excellently. The hero of that story finds satisfaction in the thought that he is important enough to be noticed by God, if only to be persecuted.

Daydreams thus motivated have many ramifications. When a person believes that he is being persecuted, he feels a need of explaining the situation. If he were an ordinary person, he thinks, there would be no sense in the persecution which people inflict upon him. The fact that he has been made the object of persecution proves (to him) that he is important. Perhaps he is a prince who is being deprived of his rights.   Perhaps he is a man of such limitless possibilities as an inventor or reformer that, out of jealousy, people have decided to ignore or persecute him or even to confine him in an asylum.   Thus arises a whole set of false beliefs regarding himself and the attitude of others toward him.   Such false beliefs are called *delusions*.   Since an effort is made to defend these beliefs by arguments, they are commonly regarded as disorders of reasoning.   In passing, we should note the close relation between delusions of persecution and delusions of grandeur.

Finally, daydreams of persecution, like any other daydreams, may serve as convenient excuses for lack of effort.   Why should we put forth effort when everyone is against us?   Thus the lazy or indolent man protects his self-regard while doing nothing.

To daydream is a perfectly normal activity.   All people daydream, children perhaps more than adults, the introverted more than the extroverted.   Unless we substitute daydreaming for action, it is an innocent and perhaps a desirable pastime; for daydreams not only enrich life, but they also help an individual find himself by revealing to him his most powerful desires and ambitions.   Daydreams become dangerous and pathological only when engaged in excessively and when they are substituted for action.   Extravagant daydreaming may lead, as we have seen, to a retreat from reality.   This danger is especially great, according to McDougall (15), during adolescence.   Too much indulgence in daydreaming may also cause confusion between fantasy and reality, as will be seen below in our account of the disorders of imagination. Finally, certain types of fantasy may influence one toward crime.

As an instance of crime produced by daydreaming we may cite the case of two wealthy Chicago boys who murdered a younger boy for the thrill of being talked about.   Writing about that case, McDougall (15, p. 214) says:

> The medical experts . . . brought out clearly the fact that one of the murderers, a youth of good intellectual capacity and education, had indulged in daydreams of great crimes by means of which he would startle the world and enjoy the secret knowledge that he was the person of whom all the world was talking.   In this case the daydreaming went so far that, as he walked the streets, he would be occupied with imagining the details of his fantasied crimes, and even hallucinate, it would seem, some such detail.

HALLUCINATIONS

An imaginary object mistaken for a perceptual one is an *hallucination*. Some drugs cause hallucinations by making our images so vivid that we mistake them for perceptions. The alcoholic, for example, is apt to see snakes and other terrifying objects. Other drugs, such as hashish, opium, and pyote, have a similar influence. Hallucinations are also caused by powerful emotional states. A person who has recently lost a close relative may experience a sense of his presence. In rare instances he may even "see" him or "hear" his voice. A person dying of thirst may project so vividly into the external world what would satisfy him that he "sees" a beautiful stream of water. That such hallucinations may be experienced by a group of individuals is indicated in a recent report (2) of the experiences of shipwrecked men isolated on the sea. These men experienced hallucinations of ships, often vivid enough to permit "identification" of the ship. The average duration of the hallucinations was about twenty minutes.

Hallucinations may also result from repressing the memory of some painful event. The following is an example. An officer on board a torpodoed transport was greatly agitated by the suffering of so many dying men. He stayed on deck until the last. Just before the ship went down, another officer already in the water called to him asking for his life belt. Since the man in the water already had a life belt, the officer refused. That event he tried to forget, but he did not succeed and he had frequent hallucinations of it (15). Soldiers often suffered hallucinations of the cries of enemy soldiers who had been run through with the bayonet. Others, hundreds of miles from active warfare, had hallucinations of gunfire and exploding shells.

Hallucinations may result also from a feeling of unworthiness. Within many people there is a struggle between different interests of the total person. Sometimes this struggle is dramatized. For example, before making an important decision, a certain girl made a practice of inquiring what an imaginary companion would do. This "companion" was, in reality, a part of herself. This girl, fortunately, had insight into what she was doing, but some lack this insight. Consequently, there is for them no conscious bridge between their personality as known and the projections of imagination. To such persons desires which they do not wish to recognize may seem to come from without, thus giving rise to hallucinations. Such hallucinations save an individual from recognizing frankly certain aspects of his nature, and thus bolster up temporarily his feeling of self-respect; but they do so at the price of self-deception and stunted development (12).

In a recent experiment (6) it is suggested that hallucinations may be the result of sensory conditioning. In this experiment a tone with a gradual onset and decline was paired for sixty trials with a light. The light was the conditioned stimulus.   Thirty-two of forty subjects reported hearing the tone when the light was presented alone.   Control experiments seemed to indicate that the effect was not due to suggestion.

Hallucinations vs. Illusions

Hallucinations result from mistaking imaginary objects for perceptual ones; illusions are erroneous perceptions.   In spite of such concisely defined terms, it is sometimes difficult to distinguish one phenomenon from the other.   The difficulty lies in the fact that all mental life arises from a complex whole involving the personality and the environment. Since we are constantly played upon by stimuli, how can we say that any experience is merely the projection of our inner states?   May it not, in some way, have been aroused by a sensation?   When a person claims to hear voices which no one else can hear, we are tempted to say he is experiencing an hallucination; but can we be sure that his experience is due to the projection of his inner states?   Perhaps it is due to an erroneous judgment of some actual sound, such as the creaking of the stairs.   Or suppose a person passing outside a closed window in which flowers are placed should enjoy their fragrance.   Would he experience an hallucination or an illusion?

A good working principle is to hold that an experience is an hallucination when it is highly individual and can be made intelligible only by viewing it in terms of the inner states of the subject, and that it is an illusion when knowledge of the external world makes the experience intelligible.   We should say that the person who hears voices experiences an hallucination even though creaking stairs accompany the experience, since the noise does little, if anything, to make the experience intelligible.   To understand the experience, we must study the individual.   On the other hand, we should say that enjoying the fragrance of flowers behind a closed window is an illusion, because the presence of the flowers does much to make that experience intelligible, even though there is no olfactory stimulation.   Illusions are not pathological; but hallucinations, unless caused by a drug or by some acute crisis, are symptomatic of a seriously deranged personality.   Such disorders of imagination, if persistent, may indicate the existence of a more general mental disorder, one involving the disorganization of the whole personality structure.

DEVELOPMENT OF IMAGINATION

The development of the imagination depends on the maturation of the nervous centers, especially of the higher areas, and on experience.

Little need be said of maturation except to point out that imagining, as we experience it, is as truly beyond the range of the possible activities of an infant as is walking. The fertility of imagination depends upon maturity. Moreover, as we mature, new interests give direction to our imagination.

The Role of Experience

More important from the psychological point of view is the influence of experience on imagination. As previously stated, all the elements of imagination come from experience. It therefore follows that a rich and varied life of the imagination depends upon a rich and varied experience. The individual who understands people and is familiar with the world about him, who is acquainted with the world of fairy stories, who has read widely in history and in the best literature, who has a knowledge of the different scientific and philosophical systems, and, above all, who has the habit of playing with ideas, has a background and an attitude that are well calculated to increase the fertility of his imagination and to invest all things with deeper meaning and significance. The development of imagination may also be stimulated by varied motor experiences. The active person, one who has danced, hiked, fished, hunted, and tended a garden, has a background for reverie which adds much to his enjoyment of music, painting, and aesthetic dancing. Imagination is also stimulated when desires are thwarted. For example, children who have no real playmates create for themselves imaginary ones with whom they talk and play. When real companions are provided, the imaginary ones tend to fade away. Similarly, out of thwarted romance arises much of romantic literature and music, productions that have done a great deal to enrich human life by idealizing a primitive impulse.

Valentinier's study. An interesting study of the development of imagination has been made by Valentinier (25), who gave to almost 5,000 boys and girls between the ages of nine and eighteen the following story to complete in one of the ways indicated:

> This is the beginning of a story about the moon.
> "On a recent night," narrated the moon, "I was sliding through heavy clouds of snow. My beams tried to pierce them in order to see what was happening on earth. Finally, the clouds parted before me and . . ."
> 1. The moon saw a shipwreck.
> 2. The moon had a conversation with the giant, Roland, at the town hall of Bremen.

3. The moon comforts a sick man who is lying in bed.
4. The moon tells about a camp of hikers in the neighborhood of Bremen.
5. The moon talks with a pupil who cannot prepare his lessons.

There were three outstanding differences between the themes of child and adolescent. The children represented the moon primarily as an acting being, while the adolescents described the moon's thoughts and emotions. The older pupils enlivened their stories with various minor episodes, droll happenings, and artistic touches. The children's style was bald, but that of the adolescents showed numerous embellishments. The girls showed evidences of maturity earlier than the boys (4, p. 209).

A typical composition by a child, Cole (4) continues, "shows certain elementary imaginative touches — the spyglass, the glowworms, the moonbeams used as messengers. But on the whole, the story is prosaic; the tale would not have varied essentially if the boy had been helped by his uncle." The adolescent shows greater imaginative power, a finer sense of humor, and more genuine psychological insight. Greater maturation and a wider range of experience yield a bountiful harvest of imaginative embellishments and of appreciation.

Individual Differences in Imagination

There are other factors than those just discussed which create individual differences in imagination. Variations in age and in ability to define problems at the abstract level are two factors. People also vary considerably regarding the type and vividness of their imaginations. Some are able to bring before their mind's eye images which they claim are as vivid as perceptions. Others have only faint images. In some individuals, visual imagery is the most vivid; in others, auditory or kinaesthetic. These differences have led to a theory of types of imagination. This theory, however, has been generally abandoned. For only a few people belong to one type or another; that is, few experience one mode of imagery that is consistently more vivid than the others.

Generally speaking, the imagery of children is more vivid than that of adults; that of women is more vivid than that of men; that of men in general more vivid than that of men of science (8). Differences in the strength of imagery seem to go hand in hand with preoccupation with concrete things. The child's interests are almost wholly centered around the concrete; the scientist's are centered to a considerable degree about ideas and principles which cannot be imaged. He cannot, for example, form an image of gravitation, evolution, or the law of diminishing returns.

IMAGINATION AND ADJUSTMENTS

The important place of imagination in adjustments was indicated in the opening paragraph of this chapter. The person who can tell without the aid of a stimulus what would satisfy him obviously has an advantage over one who cannot. Take two men who are restless and worried. One man cannot tell what the trouble is. His energy is spent in unhealthy bodily tension and anxiety. Perhaps in time his difficulty will drive him to consult a psychiatrist or a friend, or to commit some impulsive and foolish act. The other man proceeds deliberately to discover the cause of his worry and tension. He considers the various possible causes of his condition. Is there some physiological disorder? Is the tension due to lack of opportunity for professional advancement, to the coldness and indifference of friends, or to financial difficulties? Let us assume that it is due to the last of these. Having defined his difficulty, he is able to proceed more intelligently to discover the best way of meeting it. Shall he cut out some unnecessary expenditure? Shall he try to increase his earnings through additional work? Shall he postpone paying some of his bills? Or shall he borrow money? If he should decide to borrow money, he would continue the same rational procedure. Should he borrow it from a bank, or from an individual who makes a business of lending money, or from a friend? If from a friend, from which one? Shall he ask the friend for the loan when he happens to meet him, or shall he make a call at his home or at his office, or shall he invite him to lunch and there make known his needs?

Through this procedure he rationally decides his course of action. By so doing he moves from an abstract definition of his need to concrete action. There is thus opportunity to consider possible alternatives and objections before committing himself to the consequences of an overt act.

Relation to Thinking

As pointed out in the preceding chapter, imagination is one of the kinds of activity involved in thinking. In thinking, one attacks a problem by recalling the various facts which may have some bearing on the problem. One may then imagine what would happen if these facts, and any others that might be provided by the situation itself, were put together in various ways as possible solutions to the problem. All rational guidance of behavior involves imagination in the foregoing way. Suppose, for example, a committee is appointed to deal with the problem of an increasing number of accidents in a factory. The valuable men on the committee are those who can see in advance the situations that are likely to arise and can plan to meet them. Someone makes the statement that the workmen must be educated and warned of the danger. So far, so good; but how is this to be done? The course of action is then defined a bit more by the suggestion that signs with proper warnings printed on them be placed at all dangerous places. It then occurs to another member of the committee that some of the employees cannot read, and the suggestion is made that pictures be painted on the signs to represent possible accidents.

To be able to define one's problem in abstract terms and then to proceed to a definite course of action after examining all the possibilities is, as Thurstone (23) says, a mark of genius. Yet there are times when quick thinking that issues into action is also a mark of genius. One of the most essential qualities of leadership is the ability to imagine quickly what will meet the needs and desires of the group. Perhaps it is for this reason that some people boast of being "concrete-minded," and enjoy showing their contempt for those who think in abstract terms. Apparently, they have not paused to consider that the development of science, government, and philosophy depends upon the ability to think imaginatively and abstractly. They do not realize that the lower animals are even more concrete-minded than those who boast of their inability to think in abstract terms.

Relation to Worry

Imagination may sometimes make adjustments more difficult. It does so when we create imaginatively a world of fearful objects. For example, the child who has peopled the world imaginatively with witches and goblins which torment his sleep and make him afraid of the dark has created for himself a heavy handicap. Similarly, adults, by imagining fearful dangers and by magnifying slight ones, may undermine their confidence and capacity for action. Such persons do not take an opportunity when it is offered, but imagine so many dangers that they prefer to hold to what seems to them a safe course. In these cases, imagination, instead of being a spur and director of activity, becomes a source of timidity and an inhibitor of action.

On the other hand, imagination may become a source of courage. For example, one boy who knew that he was unusually fearful was able to gain courage by going to the radiator and letting out a little steam.

This served, he said, to release the friendly servants of the Three Kings who lived behind the radiator. The thought that these servants were rushing to aid him inspired him with courage. Later, by a mere gesture of turning a valve, he was able to tap this source of courage (26).

When we are confronted with a crisis, as when a close friend or anything we value is in danger and there is nothing that we can do about it, we worry. Worrying under such circumstances is a normal process. Some people, however, worry excessively. Sometimes this is merely a way of fighting against boredom and monotony or, as Woodworth (27) says, a form of "indoor sport." Consider, for example, the worries of a mother regarding her child out coasting. Her love for him and her fear that something may happen to him, even though she does not doubt his safety, may cause her to imagine him involved in all sorts of accidents. Such mild worries, like mild forms of fear, seem pleasant. Being thrown in the air and caught again is a source of mild fear that is a delight to the small child. Older people get pleasure in sports that arouse mild fear. Perhaps this is due to the fact that anything, unless it is too disagreeable, that raises consciousness to a higher level is pleasurable. Whatever the explanation, mild states of fear are frequently enjoyable. The mother would rather be worried than bored. Her worries give excitement to an otherwise monotonous day. In addition, the relief experienced on the return of the child does much to compensate for the element of unpleasantness that was contained in the worry.

Excessive worry is more serious. It may be symptomatic of excessive timidity, of lack of confidence, or of mental conflict. Persons who as children have been too carefully protected and who have been prevented from making decisions for themselves are apt to be excessively timid and lacking in confidence. In a situation which requires them to make decisions and to act on their own responsibility, they are likely to worry excessively. The same is true of those who have a haunting fear of making a mistake or who attach excessive importance to the opinion of others.

The following is an account of excessive worry due to mental conflict. An oversolicitous mother worried unduly about the health of her child. She shielded the child from every danger and gave her the best of care, and yet she was in constant fear of the child's dying. When she finally consulted a psychologist, he was able to discover the real source of the worry very quickly. The mother had never been able to reconcile herself to the restrictions imposed upon her by bearing and caring for the child. If the child were to die, she would regain her liberty. Her lavish attention and excessive worry were a means of driving from consciousness a thought which was shocking to her moral nature. This type of response is frequently resorted to in repressing something unpleasant.

In the case just mentioned, the attitude of the mother toward her daughter also illustrates what the psychoanalysts call the *ambivalence of desires and emotions.* To live we must assume obligations and duties. We bind ourselves to one another with bonds of affection. But however much we may seek such bonds and however great the satisfaction derived from them, they impose some more or less irksome restrictions upon us. In the foregoing case, the young mother's life was doubtless enriched by the bonds that bound her to her child; but at the same time, those bonds deprived her of many other desirable contacts. As a result, there was much in her that protested against the mother-child relationship and that longed to escape from it.

When thoughts that are felt to be disloyal occupy consciousness, they may become the cause of excessive grief. For example, a girl who was devotedly caring for her invalid mother occasionally thought of the pleasures she was missing by being tied to her mother's bedside. This was almost inevitable in the circumstances. It could have deserved no censure unless the girl had dwelt upon these thoughts and permitted them to influence her behavior. This, however, did not happen, for the daughter was most dutiful. But when the mother died, the girl, feeling that she had been disloyal, mourned excessively and refused to take advantage of the freedom that she had previously regretted was not hers. When, however, she was helped to understand the causes of her excessive grief, she made a normal adjustment.

Excessive worry about one's health is called *hypochondria.* Like the mother's worry about her child, this may be due to an internal struggle. Hypochondria is frequently a way of escaping something disagreeable. To be strong and vigorous would necessitate the assumption of a more active role in life, and the worrier finds this prospect unpleasant. Yet it would be a severe blow to his self-regarding sentiment to recognize that he was refusing to play his part. An excuse to shirk is found in magnifying any physical disability and developing an excessive concern over his health. To be sure, the hypochondriac does not think the matter through in this manner. We should consider, rather, that his anxiety is congenial and satisfying to him because it saves him from facing a disagreeable fact and enables him to attain an agreeable objective. It may serve as an excuse for failure or as a means of gaining attention and power. Hence it is given free indulgence.

Relation to Play

It is generally recognized that the fantasy with which children fill their play is responsible for much of its zest. The little boy picks up a stick, places it across his shoulder, and marches away a soldier; the next instant he bestrides it and dashes away on a fiery steed; a little later he puts an arrow to the stick, and it becomes a bow. The stick is only a means of focusing his imaginative activities, without which his overt activities would have been lacking in zest and interest. Likewise, the little girl, as she plays with her dolls, caring for them as a mother, scolding them, dressing them, making their beds, and preparing their food, is living in a world of fantasy from which much happiness is drawn.

Occasionally a child will assume a particular role for a whole day, and will assume for himself a new and appropriate name. A boy may enjoy playing for a day that he is a coal-heaver; the next day he may be an iceman or a street-car conductor. Many lonely children create for themselves imaginary companions with whom they play and talk as with real children. Though such play lacks the needed give-and-take of reality, yet it does create imaginative social situations useful for the cultivation of various attributes, such as politeness, consideration, and friendly conversation.

In the foregoing illustrations of play, imagination is almost unhampered. They are genuine as-if attitudes. Play that takes the form of games is not so completely an activity of the imagination. Games involving imagination may be regarded as an intermediate step between play and the more serious concerns of professional and social life. Compare the boy who plays that he is Bob Feller with a boy a little older who takes part in a real game of baseball. The former takes his ball and bat and, in imagination, becomes the greatest pitcher in the baseball world; the latter is forced constantly to compare the products of his imagination with his actual performance. Games thus compel the abandonment of the world of pure fantasy for the world of real accomplishment (17).

In the games of adults, the as-if attitude persists in an attenuated form. We play *as if* our games were serious. We attach considerably more importance to winning and losing than an objective consideration of the situation would warrant. In a somewhat similar class of activity should be placed the loves of adolescents. As viewed by the adolescent such loves are extremely serious; nothing could be more so. But the extravagance of the love and the fact that it is usually of short duration and leaves little impression other than bewilderment upon the lover show that such love does not deeply involve the personality. These experiences have been appropriately labeled "Ernstspiel" by Stern (21). Youthful lovers play at being in earnest; but really serious things, such as family relations, professional success, or religious beliefs, involve more deeply their personalities and their careers.

In emphasizing the role of imagination in play, there is no intention of implying that play is entirely an expression of the imaginative activities. Play, particularly that of children, is an act of self-expression. Not all the activities of an individual are motivated by a concern for the practical or useful. There are, it is true, some writers who have regarded play as an offshoot of work. Patrick (19), holding that play is a relic of the serious pursuits of our primitive ancestors, contends that children like to paddle around in water because wading in streams to catch fish was an important source of food for our ancestors. Groos (9), regarding play as preparatory to the work of adulthood, maintains that the little girl plays with her doll in order to prepare herself for motherhood. No doubt play has such values, but to regard these values as the chief function of play is to misunderstand life. Play is a simpler and more elementary response than work. When an organism develops the capacity to perform an activity, it seems to experience an impulse to exercise the capacity; from such exercise it apparently derives satisfaction — witness the playful flying of birds, the activities of pups, the gurgling and cooing of infants, the young child's constant climbing in and out of chairs, and the laughter and good fun of older children. These activities are expressions of the life of these creatures as truly as the more directed and highly organized activities of an adult are expressions of his life (20). Play is activity engaged in spontaneously because it is intrinsically pleasant. Only when there is sufficient development of imagination and self-control do we engage in activities because they are useful. For this reason we do not expect the young child to work. We know that he will have to learn that he can attain certain desired objects only by sticking to the task of getting them, and by persisting in spite of uninteresting activities and of the loss of more immediate satisfactions. If an activity is engaged in for the sheer joy in the activity itself and not because it is a means of attaining some other desired object, it is play. Play is spontaneous activity engaged in because it is pleasant; yet, when such activity is invested with the magic of imagination, it becomes doubly enjoyable. The activity remains pleasant; the pretense that it is of some great significance adds another measure of enjoyment. The more meaningful and significant our behavior, the more enjoyable it becomes.

Relation to Enjoyment

In addition to its value as an aid in making adjustments, imagination, like memory and perception, adds much to the joy of living. Life would be relatively drab were we limited to what is actually before us. By recalling the past and projecting our ideals into the future, we are able to contemplate a world made rich by the interweaving of many incompatible desires and freed of all annoyances. Moreover, to enjoy the future we do not have to give up equally satisfying courses of action (3). In anticipating a picnic we seldom think of gnats and flies. The old oaken bucket in our memories is an object of quiet pleasure and joy. We do not recall how heavy it was, nor the splinters that used to get in our fingers.

Because the future, on becoming the present, frequently does not bring the joys anticipated, many people become disappointed and pride themselves on their disillusionment. Here lies an evil of romanticism. The girl who dreams of a perfect lover who will bring her complete happiness is setting the stage for a severe disappointment. So do all those who imagine that the satisfaction of a particular desire or group of desires will bring them perfect happiness. They fail to realize that life is a continuous process of adjustment and an endless series of changing interests, and that the zest and joy of life lie not so much in the satisfaction of ends accomplished as in the act of attaining them. Lacking this understanding, they fondly look forward to the day when their desires shall be satisfied, little realizing that new desires must take the place of the old unless they are to sink into apathy and indifference.

The story is told of a distinguished artist who deeply realized this truth. In the midst of his admiring friends he began to weep. When asked why he wept in the hour of success, he replied, "I weep because I have attained my ideal; there is nothing more to work for." He realized that satisfaction meant the end of progress and that he should never again know the joy of achievement; he realized that he was spiritually dead.

Though imagination may be a source of disappointment and of unhappiness when dreams are not realized, yet the dreams themselves are sources of enjoyment. An individual may obtain satisfaction either through mastery and positive accomplishment or through make-believe. The former we shall call the realistic way; the latter, the "as-if" way. The difference between these two ways may be briefly illustrated. An individual who becomes a great financier through hard work follows the realistic way. He finds his satisfaction or happiness in accomplishment.   Another person may wish to become a great financier, but, instead of working to become one, he only dreams of success.   He may even imagine that he is already a great financier, and enjoy in his dreams his make-believe success.

The satisfaction gained through the as-if way seems closely akin to that enjoyed by hypnotized subjects who, when told that they have inherited a fortune, apparently experience the affective states that they might be expected to experience were they in fact suddenly to become wealthy.   Similarly, people who cannot follow the realistic way of objective success or who do not put forth the effort necessary to do so create for themselves a world of fantasy which ministers to their desires. They may do this when awake or when asleep.   The more vigorous of them give objective expression to their dreams in works of art, or use them to enrich their play.   Of the various ways of gaining pleasure or enjoyment through imagination, four are particularly important: play, daydreams, dreams, and art.

Aesthetic Enjoyment

Aesthetic enjoyment is the enjoyment that comes from any form of art. Aesthetic enjoyment may accompany all modes of sensory experience. The appreciation of visual and auditory objects is the most common form of aesthetic experience.   To such objects we apply the term *beautiful* — a "beautiful" picture, a "beautiful" symphony.   For other aesthetic experiences we do not have equally convenient terms.   Yet a person may appreciate, as a work of art, the taste of a cake as well as its appearance.   He may also get deep aesthetic satisfaction from an odor, or a clear-cut logical or mathematical demonstration.   Again, he may enjoy a home that is filled with peace, love, and mutual consideration.   As human beings we have broken the bonds that bind us to exclusive concern with the practical; we aspire to and enjoy the beautiful wherever it is found.   Such enjoyment lies in the fact that we by nature appreciate some things, not because they are useful or practical or elevating, but because they appeal to us.   We enjoy muscular activity and marching and dancing.   We enjoy colors, tones, and odors.   The breathing of cool, fresh air gives us pleasure.   At a higher level, we find much satisfaction in peace, companionship, harmony, successful effort, security, and love.   The source of all aesthetic appreciation is in these kinds of enjoyment.

Aesthetic enjoyment is greatly enriched by contrast.   It is worth being cold to enjoy the warmth of the fire; it is worth being tired to enjoy the comfort of an easy-chair.   Harsh, rasping noises serve to bring out smooth, melodious ones. Turmoil and disorder increase our appreciation of peace and order.

Imagination, by investing all experiences with deeper meaning and by enabling us to enter sympathetically into the sorrows and joys of others, adds greatly to the depth and range of all enjoyment. Much of the pleasure of watching a gifted dancer is thus caused. The dancer engages in an act of self-expression. Unless we identify ourselves with her, we cannot enjoy her dance to the fullest. We appreciate not only the grace of her movements but her success in self-expression as well. With music it is the same. There is no vehicle of emotional expression more effective or more generally used than music. When we listen with maximum enjoyment to music, we enter into the emotional life not only of the performer but of the composer as well. Were it not for man's ability to enter imaginatively into the life of another and to share his emotions, music would lose much of its charm.

In the enjoyment of paintings, it is not so much color as color or form as form that counts. We enjoy paintings when they have high suggestive value, when they enable us to relive our past in an idealized fashion, or when they present our unfulfilled desires in an attractive form. A woodland scene may enable us to relive a picnic without such uninvited guests as flies and mosquitoes. The picture of a man bearing bravely his suffering may enable us to be, if only vicariously and for a short time, the hero we aspire to become.

Perfection in art consists largely in the ability of the artist to make the observer feel and live with him. To do that he must be a master of his craft. But we do not find enjoyment in living over all events. The successful artist is the one who has an interesting theme. Since this must grow out of his interests, there must be a close kinship between him and his patrons. Through his art the artist attempts to realize his longings and hopes so as to permit all who will to live them with him. In this way many of the highest aspirations of man have been made articulate, and many of his desires have found an idealized realization.

Works of art resemble dreams in an important respect. The dreamer weaves a world of imagery in accordance with his longings and wishes. However whimsical they may seem, his dreams are acts of self-expression. But there is also an important difference between the creative fancy of the dreamer and that of an artist. The former is individual and subjective; there is no pretense of universalizing or communicating to others the impulse behind the dream. In the case of the artist, on the other hand, there is no less creative fancy, but there is, in addition, a serious effort to universalize the motive or feeling behind the fancy. The wishes of the dreamer find adequate expression in an idle imagery that defies all limitations of logic and causal relations, whereas the wishes of the artist are embodied to the best of his ability in the available medium, with the result that the artist communicates his feelings to others. Great works of art thus give a particular and concrete expression to universal sentiments.

The artist, like the conceptual thinker, rises above the particular to the universal, but his procedure is radically different. The conceptual thinker expresses in abstract terms what is true of a class of particulars; the artist expresses an abstract conception in a concrete and definite form. The abstract thinker universalizes the concrete and particular; the artist individualizes the universal (18).

Not all artistic productions, any more than all dreams, are wish fulfillments. At times art is used to show the ugliness of vice, or to ridicule sham and hypocrisy or any value which is distasteful to the artist. This is perhaps the sole motive in showing cruelty and suffering ignobly borne. At other times, art represents sorrows, misfortunes, and disappointments in an idealized form, nobly endured. Such works of art give us a better perspective. By lifting us above our individual sorrows, they enable us to see sorrow as the common lot of man. By showing us disaster faced courageously, they half-convince us that misfortune nobly borne is not wholly misfortune.

Works of art, by symbolizing and expressing in an ideal form the longings of man, increase our belief that these longings are essentially sound and that they will find their fulfillment. Hence they help keep alive our courage. For example, Michelangelo's *Pieta*, representing the crucified Christ in the arms of his mother, acts as a sort of confirmation that our longing for protection and heavenly support is well founded. There is no argument; but the calm assurance of the artist and the beauty that clothes his theme none the less deepen our faith. Such faith is no mean asset in keeping alive our zest and joy in life and in maintaining a healthy-minded attitude toward it. Works of art serve not only to entertain, to elevate, and to inspire; in addition, they help us to maintain mental health (18).

SUMMARY

Imagination refers to mental activity that is not directly related to or dependent upon external stimuli. Imagination is an adjustment which may be a guide to action, a source of enjoyment, or an outgrowth of anxiety. Imagination differs from perception in that (1) imagined objects are not so realistic as perceived ones, (2) we can examine perceived objects in more detail than imagined ones, (3) we can close off perceptions by blocking our sensory organs, and (4) perceptions fit into the general pattern of reality in a more logical way than do the products of our imagination.

Eidetic images are a particularly vivid form of imagery often experienced by children. Very vivid images, such as those of the eidetic variety, are sometimes confused with perceptions.

The content of imagination is always made up of combinations (though often strange and bizarre combinations) of impressions taken from past experience. Creative thinking is largely a product of our power to imagine.

Dreams are one of the least understood forms of imagination. According to the psychoanalysts, they are disguised wish fulfillments, giving to us the things which we cannot (or will not) attain during working hours. Dreams are known to influence, and to be influenced by, physiological conditions and events which have recently taken place.

Daydreams are a form of adjustment in which we create for ourselves a world of fantasy which caters exclusively to our desires. In a mild form, daydreams, like play, are not only a source of enjoyment but an aid to development. If carried too far, however, they are a serious menace to one's ability to meet the world as it is.

Hallucinations are images which are mistakenly interpreted as perceptions. Hallucinations differ from illusions in that the former are not directly related to external stimuli, whereas the latter are caused by misinterpreting sensory stimuli.

Investigations show that the content of one's imaginative experiences is definitely influenced by his other experiences, his desires, and his wishes. As in other traits of a personality, there are great individual differences among people as to kind and amount of imagined experiences.

Imagination enables one to adjust his behavior and guide his actions with intelligence and foresight, because he can try out various lines of action in the ideational stage before actually making a behavior adjustment. In this way imagination definitely aids successful adjustment. It can, however, make adjustments more difficult if it departs too far from reality.

Worry is an attempt to meet on the imagination level a situation that cannot be coped with successfully on the behavior, or action, level.

When carried to excess, worry is symptomatic of a deep-seated personality maladjustment.

Aesthetic enjoyment is very largely dependent upon the imagination. By investing a picture or a symphony with meanings brought from our own experience, we attain a breadth of meaning and understanding which goes far beyond the perception of the colors or sounds.

QUESTIONS
on the Chapter

1. What is imagination? Why do we consider imagination as a form of adjustment?
2. In what ways are imagined objects and perceptions alike? In what ways are they different?
3. What are eidetic images?
4. Under what conditions are images and perceptions sometimes confused?
5. What are hallucinations? How do they differ from illusions?
6. Discuss the relation between experience and imagination.
7. How does imagination function in creative thinking or invention?
8. What facts about imagination are shown by Valentinier's study?
9. In what ways does imagination differ from one person to another?
10. How may imagination aid in adjustment? How may it make adjustments more difficult?
11. Define worry from the psychological viewpoint.
12. What is the relation between imagination and play?
13. Under what conditions are daydreams desirable? Under what conditions are they harmful?
14. What are dreams, according to the psychoanalysts?
15. Are dreams ever affected by external stimuli? Give examples.
16. How is imagination related to aesthetic enjoyment?

for Discussion

1. Can you think of a simple test to determine whether one's images are eidetic?
2. Could imagination be thought of as both an adjustment and an aid in adjustment? Explain.
3. What do you see in the ink blot in Figure 87 (page 481)? Compare your reports with those of the other members of your class. What does the comparison show concerning the relation between imagination and experience?
4. Give some instances from your own experience in which daydreams have been a beneficial and helpful influence.
5. Give some instance where they have been a harmful influence.

6. Why do we consider excessive worry a symptom of personality maladjustment?
7. What is the main psychological distinction between play and work?
8. What significance have past generations mistakenly attributed to dreams?
9. What significance does scientific thought today attribute to dreams?

REFERENCES

1 ALLPORT, G. W., "Eidetic Imagery," *British J. of Psychol.*, 1924, 15, 99–120.
2 ANDERSON, E. W., "Abnormal Mental States in Survivors, with Special Reference to Collective Hallucinations," *J. R. Nav. Med. Serv.*, 1942, 28, 361–377.
3 BERGSON, HENRI, *Time and Free Will.* New York: The Macmillan Company, 1913, pp. 9, 10.
4 COLE, LUELLA, *Psychology of Adolescence.* New York: Farrar and Rinehart, 1936. Reprinted by permission of the publishers.
5 CUBBERLY, A. J., "The Effects of Tensions of the Body Surface upon the Normal Dream," *British J. of Psychol.*, 1923, 13, 245–265.
6 ELLSON, D. G., "Hallucinations Produced by Sensory Conditioning," *J. of Exp. Psychol.*, 1941, 28, 1–20.
7 FINLEY, C. S., "Endocrine Stimulation as Affecting Dream Content," *Arch. Neuro. and Psychiat.*, 1921, 5, 177–181.
8 GALTON, F., *Inquiries into Human Faculty and Its Development.* New York: E. P. Dutton and Company, 1911.
9 GROOS, KARL, *The Play of Man* (translated by Elizabeth L. Baldwin). New York: D. Appleton and Company, 1901.
10 GUTHEIL, E. A., *The Language of the Dream.* New York: The Macmillan Company, 1939, Chapter 4.
11 HAMSUN, KNUT, *Hunger* (translated by George Egerton). New York: Alfred A. Knopf, 1920.
12 HART, B., *The Psychology of Insanity.* Cambridge University Press, 1923, pp. 123–125.
13 JAMES, WILLIAM, *Psychology.* New York: Henry Holt and Company, 1908, p. 311.
14 KIMMINS, C. W., *Children's Dreams.* New York: Longmans, Green and Company, 1920.
15 MCDOUGALL, WILLIAM, *Outline of Abnormal Psychology.* New York: Charles Scribner's Sons, 1926. Reprinted by permission of the publishers.
16 MANACEINE, M. DE, *Sleep: Its Physiology, Pathology, Hygiene and Psychology.* New York: Walter Scott Publishing Company, 1908.
17 OGDEN, C. K., *The Meaning of Psychology.* New York: Harper and Brothers, 1926, p. 145.
18 PARKER, DE WITT, *The Analysis of Art.* New Haven: Yale University Press, 1926.
19 PATRICK, G. T. W., *Psychology of Relaxation.* Boston: Houghton Mifflin Company, 1916.

20 ROGERS, JAMES E., *The Child and Play*. New York: The Century Company, 1932.

21 STERN, W., "'Ernstspiel' and the Affective Life: A Contribution to the Psychology of Personality," *The Wittenburg Symposium*. Worcester: Clark University Press, 1928, pp. 324–331.

22 TANSLEY, A. G., *The New Psychology and Its Relation to Life*. New York: Dodd, Mead and Company, 1921, p. 144.

23 THURSTONE, L. L., *The Nature of Intelligence*. New York: Harcourt, Brace and Company, 1927.

24 TITCHENER, E. B., *A Textbook of Psychology*. New York: The Macmillan Company, 1909. Reprinted by permission of the publisher.

25 VALENTINIER, T., "Die Phantasie im freien Aufsatze der Kinder und Jugend-lichen," *Beihefte zur Zeitschrift für angewandte Psychologie*, 1916, 13, 1–168.

26 WICKES, FRANCES, *The Inner World of Childhood*. New York: D. Appleton and Company, 1927, p. 205.

27 WOODWORTH, R. S., *Psychology*, 2nd edition. New York: Henry Holt and Company, 1929, pp. 478–479.

INTELLIGENCE

12

Like many other concepts in psychology (and some concepts in physics and chemistry), intelligence is more easily measured than defined. Various definitions have been attempted, as: the ability to learn; or the ability to solve problems; or the ability to carry on abstract thinking; or the ability to use one's experience in analyzing and solving problems; or the ability to carry out the tasks of everyday life. Some psychologists, wishing to avoid any possible conflict between what is referred to in a definition and what is measured by intelligence tests, have elected to define intelligence as the ability or abilities measured by intelligence tests.

Regardless of the precise words which we use in defining intelligence or the degree of completeness attained in any definition, we can at least agree that whatever else may be said of intelligence, it has its basis in the behavior of the individual. Intelligence is not a thing, not a substance, not some inherent power that makes us do things. The word refers to that behavior of the organism which is best designated as *intelligent behavior*. This behavior has certain characteristics which can best be observed by comparing an individual who acts very intelligently with one who acts very stupidly. Watch the person who learns easily and quickly and compare him with one who learns with difficulty or not at all. What can you discover that throws light on this difference in ability to profit by experience? Or better yet, make a careful study of the biography of some great artist, physician, scientist, economist, or inventor. What characteristics distinguish these men from individuals found in an institution for the feeble-minded? Some of these differences will be discussed in the following section.

INTELLIGENT BEHAVIOR

Characteristics

Alertness. The highly intelligent person is alert, wide awake, sensitive and attentive to what goes on around him. He is sensitive to stimuli which do not arouse the ordinary person. He goes about any task in a "heads up" fashion. He has normal sensory equipment (ears, eyes, etc.) and this seems to be integrated with his high level of nervous energy and of general bodily activity. The importance of alertness as a characteristic of intelligent behavior is attested by the fact that the early intelligence tests were frequently called "mental alertness" tests. The dependence of alertness upon normal sensory equipment is seen in the fact that children with defective sense organs who appear dull or stupid show marked shifts toward alertness and normal intelligence when their defects are corrected.

Assimilation and retention. It is obvious that we cannot profit fully from our impressions, no matter how clear they are, unless they are *assimilated* and *retained*. Some individuals, apparently without effort, retain all of their experiences as memories whether they are important or not. Some are able to repeat eight digits on hearing them once, while others can repeat only five. This matter of retention is such an important factor in intelligence that nearly all intelligence tests include a memory span test. The importance attached to this test has been shown to be well justified by an investigation by Brotemarkle (5), which indicates that the memory span test is highly diagnostic of general intelligence. A similar conclusion was reached by Louttit (9), who found that students who made superior grades also excelled in ability to learn and recall experiences. Buckingham (6) also reports a relation between ability to reason and ability to remember.

Active manipulation of ideas. A fertile imagination is an important element of intelligence. Some people do very well as long as things move in the usual way, but are completely at sea when a novel situation arises. They are very likely to plod along day after day doing the same thing in the same old way. It never occurs to them that a short cut might increase their efficiency. In contrast, there are those who imagine a number of ways of meeting new situations. They are able to see a new situation as a combination of familiar elements, and to apply what they have learned to it. When performing a task, they are likely to try various methods; thus they have a good chance of learning to perform the task more efficiently. These are the mentally alert, who, no matter how they are turned, always land with their feet on the ground and their heads up.

Insight. The intelligent person does not sit for hours trying to force a square peg into a round hole. He has an amazing ability to see into a situation, to see the solution to a problem with relatively little trying and erring. He has a marked ability for keeping many factors in mind in solving a problem, and an equal ability to see in these factors a solution to the problem. He is very unlikely to make blind, stereo-typed trials against frustrating conditions.

Self-criticism. An intelligent man sees what is required and com-pares his performance with it. The importance of this comes out clearly when we give an intelligence test to a dull child. An outstanding char-acteristic of such children is their self-satisfied complacency, no matter how complete may be their failure. If such a child is given the task of making a rectangle out of two triangles, he is apt to put them together so as merely to make a large triangle, and then turn to you for approval. The intelligent child, on the other hand, has a clearer understanding of what is required and is able to judge whether or not he has succeeded.

Confidence. The intelligent man has met successfully problem after problem; he has thus developed confidence in his capacity to meet new situations, and this confidence in turn helps him to continue to do so. "Nothing succeeds like success." On the other hand, lack of confidence gives rise to worry and so to distraction, and it thus makes success more difficult. Furthermore, lack of confidence may result in lack of effort. When this happens, the discouraged individual deprives himself of the means necessary for further growth and development. "Failure breeds failure."

Strong motivation. Finally, the intelligent person is interested or strongly motivated. As was stated above, alertness seems to be de-pendent upon high levels of nervous energy and bodily activity. This is another way of saying that the alert person is highly motivated; for motivation is unquestionably tied up in some way with the general level of bodily energy. It is interesting to note in this connection that Spear-man (13) in his two-factor theory of mental abilities regards his uni-versal or common factor "g" (which has frequently been identified as general intelligence) as a measure of a person's "mental energy."

Energy as a characteristic of intelligent behavior is not fully appre-ciated in most of our thinking. It is a common misconception that an individual who is manifestly low in ability could rise to a much higher level if his interest could be aroused, if he could be properly motivated. This notion fails to recognize that ability and interest are symptomatic each of the other, that motivation varies with levels of intelligence. One very striking characteristic of gifted children is this very factor of motivation. They seem to have an almost insatiable desire to know things and to do things. And interestingly enough this strong motiva-tion does not come from stimulating conditions in the environment, as is seen in the fact that other children in the same situations seem never to find anything to do and seem never to be aroused by the conditions around them. That the motivation is somehow internal and tied up with bodily energy is well illustrated in the case of Helen Keller. She was able to achieve a life of distinction with a lack of normal sensory equipment which precluded the possibility of being aroused by many outside stimulating conditions.

Our analysis of the factors involved in intelligent behavior is confirmed by an experimental study made by Alpert (1) of the reasons young children fail to solve simple problems. She found one important factor to be self-consciousness, or the inability to lose oneself in the task. She also discovered that other significant factors were lack of confidence, lack of interest, discouragement, excitability, lack of observation, and emotional immaturity or failure to respond to the situation.

THE MEASUREMENT OF INTELLIGENCE

Only in recent years have qualitative estimates of intelligence been converted into quantitative measurements. This is a great scientific advance, for one of the aims of science is to substitute quantitative judgments for qualitative ones. Instead of saying a man is tall or heavy, it is more definite and therefore more scientific to say that he is six feet tall or that he weighs two hundred pounds. We then have information that enables us to compare accurately the size of the man in question with that of others, provided a large number of other men have been measured in height and weight. Likewise, when we consider intelligence, it is an advance in definite and precise knowledge and statement to say that a given person is as intelligent as the highest 10 per cent of his group rather than merely that he is bright.

Value of Measuring Intelligence

Such quantitative measures of intelligence are important in a number of ways. They enable us to choose a career more wisely; for obviously, we ought not to choose a profession which demands for success a greater degree of intelligence than we possess. Parents should also know the intelligence of their children. Perhaps, if they did, fewer would attempt to make professional men and women out of children who lack the necessary ability. Knowledge of the intelligence of their children would also enable them to tell more reliably whether their children are working to their full capacity. That teachers should know the learning capacity of pupils in their care is obvious. Children frequently show behavior problems in school because they are not given enough work to keep them busy. Other children give up their school work because they cannot do what they are required to do. When the ability of each child is known, the teacher can do much to adapt requirements to meet the needs of each.

Knowledge of how an individual's mental ability compares with that of others is also of help to judges of juvenile courts. A bright boy who has broken the law needs different treatment from that needed by a dull boy. Placement bureaus also need similar knowledge. To place an exceptionally bright boy with dull foster parents is to invite trouble. The quick-witted child is likely to be a jump ahead of the parents, with the result that he is denied needed discipline, guidance, and mental stimulation. On the other hand, to place a dull child with superior foster parents is to invite hardships and disappointment for both parents and child. Exact knowledge of intelligence is also of value to employers. Some types of work can be done only by those who have superior intelligence. Other types of work are done better by those who have inferior intelligence.

Binet's Pioneer Work

The first successful attempt to measure intelligence was made in France by Alfred Binet. Early in the twentieth century the school authorities of Paris became interested in the problems of individual differences in intelligence and of the bearing of intelligence on school work and conduct. Binet was asked to devise a way of separating the bright and dull pupils. He was guided in his efforts by the very simple observation that older children are, on the average, more intelligent than younger children: that is, five-year-olds are more intelligent than four-year-olds, six-year-olds are more intelligent than five-year-olds, and so on. In these differences Binet saw a natural yardstick. With this simple observation as his guiding idea, he proceeded to calibrate the measuring stick provided by nature. He set out to discover the abilities of children of different ages to perform various tasks requiring intelligence, such as repeating short sentences and digits, solving simple problems, and learning from experiences common to all children of a given culture. In the first investigation about 200 children were studied. Each child was asked to do a number of tasks, in order to get an approximate idea of what children of a given age level can do. On the basis of this preliminary survey, Binet arranged the tests tentatively and gave them to a larger number of children between the ages of three and twelve. He was then able to state with assurance what the average child of Paris of any age could do. From a knowledge of the average, it was simple to determine how far any particular child rose above or fell below that point (4). This process of obtaining average scores from a large group of subjects tested on experimentally selected material is called *test standardization.*

Almost immediately Binet's work was heralded as a great scientific advance, and psychologists all over the world began to adapt his test to meet the needs of children in different cultural groups. Some of the men who quickly recognized the value of Binet's approach and began to use it in America were H. H. Goddard, F. Kuhlman, and L. M. Terman. The most recent and probably the best American revision of Binet's scale is the Terman-Merrill (17) revision, which was made available for use in 1937. This revision is based upon extensive experiments, which have revealed many tasks that children of different age levels can perform and that younger children cannot execute successfully. For example, it was found that children between 3 and $3\frac{1}{2}$ years can string beads on a shoestring, repeat three digits, and locate familiar animals in a picture. The average child between $3\frac{1}{2}$ and 4 can, in addition, obey such simple commands as "Put the spoon in the cup"; he can select the longer of two sticks which are two and two-and-a-half inches long; and he can reply correctly to simple questions, such as "What must you do when you are thirsty?" Still older children can, on the average, perform these tasks just as well, and many other more difficult ones besides. Difficulty advances steadily with age. Since the test is scored in terms of years, the average child of a given age will score on the scale the number of years equal to his own age. The score on the test is called *mental age.* It is not expected that an average child will pass all the tests in the group corresponding to his age. In fact, he will probably fail to pass some tests in that group, but he will pass, besides, enough tests in the groups above his chronological age to give him a mental age score equal to his chronological age. For example, an average child of 10 may pass all tests in year 8; this will bring his score to 96 months. He may fail one of the tests for year 9; of tests for year 10, he may fail on two. Therefore, to make the average score for his years, reckoned chronologically, he must pass enough tests above 10 to make up for the points lost on tests in his own age group and below.

The Concept of Mental Age

Mental age, often expressed as M.A., represents the level of mental development attained by a child (or adult), stated in terms of the average mental development of children of a given age. If the mental development of a child of 6 is equal to that of the average six-year-old, we should say that his mental age is also 6. If his mental development equals that of the average child of 8, we should say that his mental age is 8 and should class him as a superior child. If he should score less than 6, his mental development would be below average. Since mental age indicates the level of intelligence attained, it is a measure of what the child can actually do. Hence, in selecting a child for a given task, or in classifying children in terms of their learning ability, it is important to know their mental ages.

If, however, we should be more interested in the future of a child, it would be more important to know his rate of mental growth than the level that has been attained at any particular time. Two boys may have the mental age of 8. But one may have attained it in six years, and the other may have required ten. In that case, the former would be developing one and a third times as rapidly as the average, whereas the latter would be developing only eight tenths as rapidly as the average. Since both will develop for approximately the same number of years, it is evident that the rate is important in order to determine the level of mental development each can be expected to attain eventually. It is also frequently desired to compare the intelligence of individuals of different ages. To do this the rate of mental development, or of the degree of brightness or dullness, provides a common denominator that makes possible such comparison.

The Intelligence Quotient, or I.Q.

The rate of mental development is found by dividing the level of mental development (M.A.) by the time taken to attain the level, that is, by the chronological age (C.A.). The quotient thus obtained is multiplied by 100, and the product is called the intelligence quotient, or I.Q. For example, if a child whose chronological age is 6 has a mental age of 9, his rate of mental development would be 9 divided by 6, or 1.50. This means that he is developing mentally one and a half times as rapidly as the average child. Since the quotient 1.50 is multiplied by 100, which eliminates the decimal point, this gives his intelligence quotient as 150. The intelligence quotient of the average child is, of course, 100. If a child's mental age is less than his chronological age, his I.Q. is less than 100. The smaller the I.Q., the greater the retardation of development indicated. The concept of the intelligence quotient was devised by Stern, a German psychologist. Its popularity in this country is due in no small measure to Terman.

$$IQ = \frac{MA}{CA} \times 100$$

Since the I.Q. is used as a measure of rate of mental growth, one meets a serious difficulty in using it with adults or after mental maturity has been reached. Take, for example, an individual who at the age of 16 earns an M.A. of 16. At this time he has an I.Q. of 100. Now let us suppose that at the age of 20 this individual still has an M.A. of 16 because mental maturity as measured by this particular test is regarded as being reached at the age of 16. We obtain by the customary procedure an I.Q. of 80. With advancing age the individual's I.Q. would continue to drop if we continued to calculate the I.Q. in the customary way. It is obvious, of course, that some adjustment should be made to take care of the fact that mental maturity *as indicated by M.A.* does not increase after age 16. This adjustment is made by dividing the M.A. earned at any time after maturity by the C.A. at which the particular test in question regards mental maturity as being reached. Terman and Merrill (17) set 15 as the average age of maturity for the 1937 revision of the Stanford-Binet Scale, but psychologists are not in agreement on the matter. The average age used differs from one test to another. This is due to the fact that all tests do not measure exactly the same functions. Different mental functions, of course, develop at different rates and reach their maxima at different times. The ability to discriminate between lifted weights, for example, may reach its maximum level at about the age of 10, whereas the ability to repeat digits (memory span for digits) may reach its maximum level at the age of 18.

Since the I.Q. concept is designed primarily for the purpose of describing the rate of mental growth of children, its use with adults, except those mentally retarded, is questionable even when adjustments are made. The common practice in testing adults, therefore, is to use other types of tests (these will be described in a subsequent section). There is one notable exception to this practice, however. The Bellevue Scale, an individual intelligence test devised by Wechsler (20), makes use of M.A. and I.Q. in testing both adults and adolescents. The I.Q. used with this test, however, is not defined in exactly the same way as the I.Q. which has been defined above. In the usual formula, I.Q. equals M.A. divided by C.A. In Wechsler's definition, I.Q. equals the score earned on the Bellevue Scale divided by the expected mean score for individuals who have the same C.A. as the person being tested. For example, let us suppose that a 43-year-old person earns a raw score of 40 on the Bellevue Scale and that the average score made by a typical group of 43-year-olds on this test is 40. The earned score of 40 divided by the expected score of 40 for persons of this age gives an I.Q. of 100.

Intelligence is native ability + environment

In this way the concept of I.Q. is refashioned to make it comparable for all age groups from 10 to 60 years.

There are several limitations which apply both to the original Binet scale and to its revised forms. First, the test is an individual test — it must be given to one person at a time, and its administration requires approximately an hour. Obviously, this greatly limits the number of persons who can be tested by a single examiner. Second, it can be administered reliably only by a trained examiner, usually called a psychometrist. The examiner must have memorized thoroughly every detail of the test, and must also have a thorough knowledge of how to score the innumerable responses which a child may make in the test situation. Finally, a number of the items in the scale are so-called "language" items. They presuppose at least an average ability to understand, speak, and read the English language. The test may penalize severely a child who is for any reason retarded in language development, as, for instance, children are apt to be who are brought up in homes where a foreign language is spoken.

Performance Tests of Intelligence

In order to overcome the language difficulty of tests of the Binet type, psychologists very early turned to the development of what has come to be known as a *performance test*. This type of test generally requires the subject to manipulate materials with his hands; for instance, to place blocks of different geometrical designs into their appropriate places in a board, to put together parts of a picture very much as in a jig-saw puzzle, or to complete a picture by placing cut-out pieces into the proper holes. The earliest test of this kind was devised by Seguin and later modified by Goddard. In 1917, Pintner and Paterson (11) assembled into one scale and standardized a series of fifteen performance tests. In 1930, Arthur (2) published a restandardization of ten of the fifteen tests in this scale. The Arthur Performance Scale is now used extensively in psychological clinics when there is evidence of a language handicap or when it is desirable to check or to supplement the results which have been obtained by other tests.

Most performance tests are individual tests. The descriptive term "performance" is widely applied, however, to any kind of test, either individual or group, which makes little or no demand upon language. It is even used to describe paper-and-pencil tests without true language items. An example of a group non-language or performance test is the Visual Classification Test used at Army Induction Stations to test all non-English-speaking and illiterate inductees. Another non-language test, known as Test "2abc," was given in Replacement Training Centers in pantomime to Grade V men (i.e., very slow learners) and to men who could read little or no English. It might be stated, however, that these tests are not, strictly speaking, intelligence tests, having been devised to determine the inductee's ability to profit from army training (19).

Group Tests of Intelligence

Many group tests of intelligence, tests which may be given to many persons at the same time, have been devised. These tests are clearly more suitable than the Binet tests for measuring large groups of persons, such as the children in public school systems or applicants for industrial jobs.

Among the group tests most widely used with school children are the Kuhlman-Anderson Intelligence Tests, designed for grades one through twelve, and the Otis Quick-Scoring Mental Ability Tests, designed for grades one through sixteen. The California Tests of Mental Maturity are designed for individuals from kindergarten age to adulthood. The American Council Psychological Examination, prepared by L. L. Thurstone and T. G. Thurstone, is used extensively in high schools and colleges. A group test designed for use in industrial situations is the Wonderlic Personnel Test. This is an adaptation of the higher form of the Otis Self-Administering Test of Mental Ability. The word *personnel* rather than *mental ability* or *intelligence* is used in the title to avoid the negative reaction of many applicants and employees to a test dealing with mental ability. Another test of this type adapted to the needs of business and industry is the Purdue Adaptability Test. The Army General Classification Test, which was given to all enlisted men during World War II, resembles the ordinary group intelligence test in many respects although it was not called an intelligence test. It was designed to measure the enlisted man's ability to learn. Five levels of learning ability were designated: Grade I, very rapid learners; Grade II, rapid learners; Grade III, average learners; Grade IV, slow learners; and Grade V, very slow learners. Men were assigned to these grades according to the army standard scores (not I.Q.'s) earned on the test (19).

As already indicated, most of the group tests, especially those designed for testing adults, do not measure intelligence in terms of M.A. or I.Q. In such tests it is customary to give the testee a raw score based upon the number of test items answered correctly, and then to convert this raw score into a derived score, such as a *percentile score*.

The percentile score corresponding to a given raw score indicates the per cent of individuals in some standard group that earns this score or a lower one. For example, suppose that the American Council Psychological Examination has been given to all the freshmen at Purdue University. John Doe, who is a freshman at Purdue, takes this test and makes a score of 107. Having calculated the per cent of the Purdue freshmen who have scores of 95 and less, 96 and less, 97 and less, and so on, we are able to tell John Doe that he has a percentile score on this test of 40, since 40 per cent of the Purdue freshmen have been found to score 107 or less on this test. If this test had been given to a representative sample of the entire population, assuming that it had been designed to measure the entire population, we could by the same procedure tell John Doe what per cent of the general population have scores of 107 or less on the test.

An examination of various group tests of intelligence reveals that these tests contain a wide variety of materials or test items which measure a variety of mental functions. The more common kinds of test items found include: vocabulary items, arithmetic reasoning items, number series completion items, disarranged sentences, verbal and spatial analogies, general information items, and reading comprehension items. Like the Binet tests, these tests place a great deal of emphasis upon language ability. In fact, the ability most commonly measured by the ordinary group intelligence test is verbal ability. It is not surprising, therefore, that group tests of intelligence show very high correlations with achievement tests — those tests designed to cover achievement in specific school subjects — and with success in school as indicated by school grades. Indeed, many of the present group tests were constructed for use in school situations. This is true of several of those listed above. Another is the Ohio State University Psychological Test, which was devised by H. A. Toops for use in testing high school and college students. A trend toward the construction of group intelligence tests for specific purposes or for particular groups can be seen not only in these tests designed for school use but also in the tests designed for use in army placement, vocational guidance, and industrial situations.

INDIVIDUAL DIFFERENCES IN INTELLIGENCE

Differences in intelligence are normally distributed; that is, there are more people of average ability than there are very bright or very dull ones. This is shown in Figure 67 by the distribution of the I.Q.'s of 2,904 children between the ages of 2 and 18. On this curve, the base line represents I.Q., and the height of the curve represents the

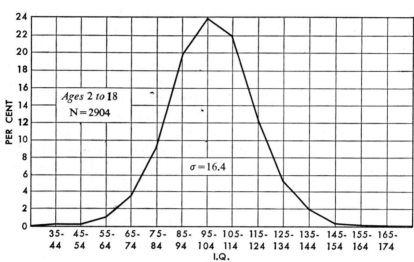

Figure 67

Distribution of I.Q.'s of 2904 Children on the 1937 Stanford Revision
of the Binet Test

(From L. M. Terman and M. A. Merrill, *Measuring Intelligence*, Houghton Mifflin, 1937, p. 37.)

per cent of children. More persons have I.Q.'s between 95 and 104 than at any other point on the scale. As we go above or below this average, numbers decrease. This graph is based on the composite results of the two forms of the 1937 Stanford revision of the Binet Test. Data obtained from other standardized tests confirm the findings summarized in this curve. On the basis of these results, Table XV was constructed to show the percentage of persons in a "randomly" selected group with I.Q.'s above a certain point.

It is clear from this table that the great bulk of people, in fact 80 per cent of the total, have I.Q.'s between 85 and 115. One conclusion that may immediately be drawn from the facts is that when we classify a person as dull or bright — as we are apt to do all too frequently — the chances are about eight out of ten that we are wrong; that is, he is probably neither stupid nor bright, but of average intelligence. The statement that God must have loved the common people because he made so many of them is entirely in accord with the measurements of intelligence which have been obtained.

In recent years, excessive emphasis has been placed on intelligence as a condition for successful living. But for a person to achieve vocational success, to be a good citizen and neighbor, to win the love, con-

adult I.Q = *your grade now*
              ───────────
            average grade score

INTELLIGENCE   407

Table XV

Per Cent of Persons in a Randomly Selected Group Having I.Q.'s above a Certain Point (10)

Ten per cent		115
Twenty per cent		110
Thirty per cent		106
Forty per cent		103
Fifty per cent ▶ of persons have an I.Q. of ◀	100	▶ or above
Sixty per cent		97
Seventy per cent		94
Eighty per cent		90
Ninety per cent		85

fidence, and respect of his family, to enjoy beauty in nature, in art, and in social relations, it is not important that he excel in intelligence. If we leave aside the extreme lower end of humanity and the extreme upper end, the 80 or 90 per cent that remain do not differ greatly in the fundamental human traits. The great bulk of them experience the same joys and sorrows; they have similar ideas of right and wrong; they think about the same things. The fact that some can solve problems in algebra or can read Greek is, after all, a matter of little importance when seen against the background of their common characteristics. Neither a man's humanity nor his success in living depends upon excelling his neighbor in intelligence.

At the extremes of the distribution, however, there are persons who do need special treatment. This is especially true of those at the lower extreme. The definitions of such terms as *genius, feeble-minded,* and *moron* in terms of the I.Q. are given in Table XVI.

The feeble-minded group, that is, those with I.Q.'s of 70 or below, need special treatment or observation. Many of those in the upper division of this group, those with I.Q.'s of about 50 to 70, can and do lead fairly independent lives as long as no emergency or need of original thinking arises. A person with an I.Q. below 50 almost invariably calls for institutional care, since such an individual is unable to avoid the common dangers of everyday living without constant supervision.

The adjustments of individuals at either extreme of the intelligence range, however, are not entirely a matter of their I.Q.'s. The term *genius* may be applied to an individual with an I.Q. below 140, or it may be withheld from an individual who has an I.Q. above 140. In short, there are other criteria upon which we normally base our judg-

Know how to get I Q of
children + adults

Table XVI

I.Q. Level of Different Classifications of Intelligence

CLASSIFICATION	I.Q.	% OF ALL CHILDREN INCLUDED
Genius or near genius	*above* 140	.25
Very superior	120–140	6.75
Superior	110–120	13.00
Average	90–110	60.00
Dull normal (backward)	80–90	13.00
Dull (borderline)	70–80	6.00
Feeble-minded	*below* 70	1.00
Morons (mental age of 8–10 years)	50–70	.75
Imbeciles (mental age of 3–7 years)	25–50	.19
Idiots (mental age of 2 or below)	*below* 25	.06

(Adapted from L. M. Terman, *The Measurement of Intelligence*, Houghton Mifflin, by permission.)

ments of genius. An individual with a very high degree of some special ability may be labeled a genius although his tested intelligence is only slightly above normal. Some individuals who have very high I.Q.'s may never impress the general public with their accomplishments. At the other extreme, several factors in addition to I.Q. are taken into account in the diagnosis of feeble-mindedness. The individual's I.Q. must be viewed against a background composed of such elements as his medical history, his family history, his school history, and his adjustment to his present social environment. The lines of demarcation between "normal" and "feeble-minded" and between the various grades of the feeble-minded are not fixed but subject to change or variation in particular cases.

THE VALIDITY AND RELIABILITY OF INTELLIGENCE TESTS

Psychological tests are customarily evaluated in terms of a number of criteria, chief among which are the criteria of *validity* and *reliability*.

Validity — *is it measuring what you are trying to measure*

Validity is the degree to which a test measures what it is supposed to measure. Or stated in terms of the methods of determining it, validity refers to the relationship between the scores of a test and some recognized index or criterion of the thing which the test reputedly measures.

I q valid test to predict success in college

Remmers and Gage (12) have pointed out that validity is a specific concept. That is, it must always refer to a specific purpose (what is reputedly measured) and a specific group of individuals. If a test is supposed to measure the intelligence of preschool children and does so, it is a valid intelligence test for preschool children. It would not be a valid measure of musical ability; neither would it be a valid measure of the intelligence of high school pupils.

The general validity of present-day intelligence tests is indicated by the fact that the results obtained correlate with those of other indicators of intelligence, such as success in school, educational level, occupational level, social competency, and previously validated tests or measures.

Almost any intelligence test, and especially one designed for use in school situations, shows a significant correlation with success in school as measured by grades. Correlation coefficients between college grades and intelligence test scores range from around .35 to .65. These are useful degrees of validity. The higher coefficients, at least, make it possible to pick out with great accuracy those who will leave college on account of poor grades and those who are most likely to win scholastic honors. The same picture is obtained when test scores are compared with educational level, as seen in Table XVII. Here the results agree

Table XVII

Average Scores on Personnel Test Attained by Education
and Sex Groups (24)

EDUCATIONAL LEVEL	SEX	NO. OF CASES	AVERAGE SCORE
Eighth grade and under	Male	2249	10.96
	Female	1601	10.87
First, second year high school	Male	1845	19.69
	Female	2533	21.00
Third, fourth year high school	Male	5361	24.40
	Female	8981	22.48
First year college or equivalent	Male	2302	28.92
	Female	2714	24.75
Second, third year college	Male	2827	28.38
	Female	1560	26.04
Four years college (graduate)	Male	3227	30.84
	Female	1042	29.12
Beyond fourth year college	Male	478	31.50
	Female	144	30.65

quite well with what we should expect. The higher the educational attainment, the higher the average intelligence score. It was found in using the General Classification Test with enlisted men in the Army that men who made high scores usually did best in various Army training courses, and that those who made low scores were likely to learn slowly and be less alert in their army work (19). The relation of scores in this test to certain occupations is shown in Figure 68. As we go from the occupations which require high degrees of ability to those which require low degrees of ability, the median scores decrease.

From these facts we can conclude that intelligence tests enable us to predict with considerable accuracy the likely success of individuals in situations where intelligence is recognized as a large and an important factor.

Reliability — *Consistency*

The second criterion used in evaluating a test is *reliability*. The term refers to the self-consistency of a test; that is, the extent to which a test yields the same result when one part of it is compared with another, when one form of it is compared with another form, or when the test is repeated. To determine the reliability of a test, it is necessary to obtain two sets of scores from the same population. This can be done by giving the test twice, by giving two comparable forms of the test, or by dividing the test into two parts (for example, odd items and even items). The two sets of scores are then correlated. If the resulting coefficient, known as a *reliability coefficient*, is high, the test is said to be reliable. Most intelligence tests yield coefficients of reliability between .85 and .95. For example, the correlation between Form L and Form M of the 1937 Stanford revision of the Binet-Simon tests as reported by Terman and Merrill (17) was .93 for children above six years of age. The reliability coefficient for the Bellevue Scale determined by the test-retest method was .94 for adults (20). Group tests yield correspondingly high reliability coefficients. The reliability coefficients for the four batteries of the California Tests of Mental Maturity range from .90 to .96 (15).

One of the persistent problems in the use of intelligence tests is the prediction of intelligence at one age from measurements made at an earlier age. The problem is only indirectly related to reliability, since the test-retest method of determining reliability, while it involves comparison of scores earned at different times, is a very specialized case of retesting. The problem is basically one of validity; for one of the specific purposes of intelligence tests is the prediction of intelligence.

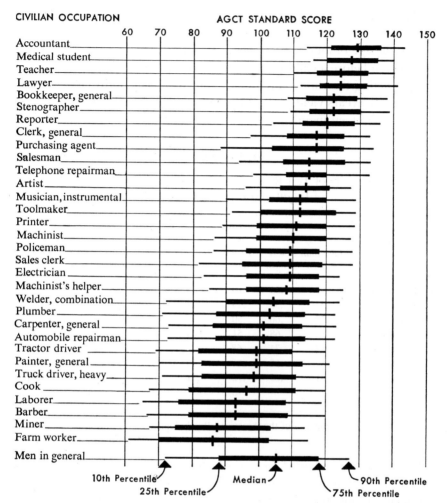

CIVILIAN OCCUPATION   AGCT STANDARD SCORE

Figure 68

Army General Classification Test Scores for Various
Occupational Groups

For each occupation the small vertical dash represents the median and the length of the
heavy horizontal bar the middle fifty per cent. (From Lee J. Cronbach, *Essentials of Psychological Testing*, Harper, 1949. After Naomi Stewart, "AGCT Scores of Army Personnel
Grouped by Occupation," *Occupations*, 1947, 26, 5–41. By permission of *Occupations*
and Harper & Brothers.)

An examination of the literature reveals that intelligence cannot be predicted with a very high degree of accuracy on the basis of tests given before the age of four or five years. It can be seen in Table XVIII that tests given before a child is four months old have practically no validity for predicting the child's intelligence four to nine months later. A test given at four years yields a validity coefficient of about .70 for an interval of about eighteen months.

Table XVIII

Composite of Test-Retest Correlations from Several Studies of Infant and Preschool Groups (18)

AGE AT EARLIER TEST	INTERVAL BETWEEN TEST AND RETEST							
	Less than 4 mos.	4–9 mos.	★ 10–15 mos.	★ 16–21 mos.	★ 22–29 mos.	30–41 mos.	42–53 mos.	Over 53 mos.
Under 4 months	.57	.33	.10	−.03	−.09			
4–9 months	.77	.53	.49	.23	.16	.46	.00	
10–15 months	.78	.66	.50	.45	.33			.55
16–21 months	.76	.68	.51	.44	.38	.41	.25	.33
22–29 months	.82	.74	.68					.43
30–41 months	.87	.68	.66	.49	.57	.57	.56	.66
42–53 months	.81	.65	.72	.71	.66	.63	.63	.41
54–65 months			.76		.73			

(By permission of the American Psychological Association.)

There are a number of factors which contribute to this lack of consistency. The immaturity of such a mental function as attention makes it difficult to obtain an accurate initial record of the few mental functions which can be tested. The rapidity of growth during early infancy, the appearance of new modes of behavior, the unreliability of the tests, and the relatively large increment of growth represented by an interval of a month or three months during infancy all contribute to the inconsistency. Then, too, there is the possibility, if not the fact, that the tests measure different kinds of behavior at different age levels. This factor affects the predictive value of tests at all ages, but it undoubtedly plays a larger part in preschool tests than it does in the tests for older children.

Regarding the predictive value of tests for school-age children and adults the situation is quite different. The facts seem to indicate that it is possible to predict intelligence at one age from measurements at an earlier age with a high degree of accuracy. If the tests are properly administered and the individuals examined remain in fairly stable surroundings, predictions can apparently be made with a range of accuracy which varies between a correlation of around .90 for immediate or short-time predictions and one of around .60 to .70 for long-time predictions (from six to ten years). Putting together data from various studies bearing upon the interval between test and retest of school-age children, Thorndike (18) worked out a curve for all of the data. From the curve he estimated that the correlation for an immediate retest was about .90 and the correlation for a test given after a five-year interval was about .70.

The high correlation for an immediate retest agrees with what has been said above regarding reliability. It means that if the tests have been well administered, shifts or changes in test-retest results are likely to be relatively small in the majority of cases of immediate retest. With a correlation of .93, Terman (16) found that for 6 per cent of a group of 435 children the I.Q. remained the same, for 37.2 per cent it varied three points or less, and for 81.2 per cent it varied nine points or less. In only 18.2 per cent was there a variation of as much as ten points.

The correlation of .70 for a retest after a five-year interval indicates that we can predict intelligence over a five-year period with as much accuracy as we can predict success in school or the occupational level likely to be attained. Even if the accuracy of prediction drops still further with an increase in the interval between test and retest, it will remain in the neighborhood of the validity coefficients reported for various intelligence tests. It is important, however, to note that the accuracy of prediction decreases as the interval for which the prediction is made increases, at least up to a certain point.

Changes in Tested Intelligence

To summarize, shifts in tested intelligence do occur from one testing to another, and these shifts tend to increase as the interval between the test and retest increases. Now the question is, Why do such shifts occur?

First of all, it should be pointed out that we are talking about tested intelligence, that is, performance on an intelligence test, not some hypothetical potentiality which underlies such performance. Keeping this point in mind, we can see that there are several factors which might be responsible for the shifts in results from one testing to another. For one thing, shifts may occur because of inaccuracies in the administration and scoring of the tests. Or they may result from the fact that the subject has had increased practice in taking tests. The practice may be a larger factor in one case than in another. Or shifts may be due to changes in the subject's attitude toward the tests. Or the tests may not measure exactly the same mental functions at different age levels. This is very likely to be the case when the test-retest interval is large, necessitating the use of a different test or a different form of the same test at the later testing date. Finally, a shift may result from differential rates of mental growth due to the favorable or unfavorable opportunities for development. In view of the fact that intelligence tests are measuring certain kinds of behavior, we can expect an individual's tested intelligence to increase, decrease, or remain relatively constant depending upon the favorableness, unfavorableness, or constancy of the developmental conditions affecting his growth over a period of time. If a child, during a given period of time, is subjected to extremely unfavorable environmental conditions, it is entirely possible that his rate of growth will be slower than that of other children who have remained in fairly stable surroundings. In relation to these children, he would show a drop in I.Q. from the beginning to the end of the stated period.

A large number of studies have dealt with the changes or shifts in the intelligence level of children over a period of time or from one testing date to another. Some of these studies have attempted to investigate the effect of the favorableness or unfavorableness of the developmental conditions affecting growth over a period of time. Typical of this group of studies is a number of studies by Wellman and her associates at the University of Iowa. In one study Wellman (21) shows the decrease in I.Q. of seven children who were in a very unfavorable type of orphanage (see Table XIX). Table XX gives the results for four children who were in a very favorable preschool environment, later followed by what is described as an unusually stimulating elementary school experience.

One of the first studies to bring out the retarding effect of an impoverished environment upon intelligence-test performance was conducted by Gordon (8) with a group of canal-boat children in England. The canal-boat children had an average I.Q. of 69.6 which, taken at face value, would indicate a low normal or borderline group. Gordon points out, however, that the correlation between age and I.Q. for this group was −.755. In other words, there was a marked tendency for the I.Q. to drop as the children grew older, a natural result if the children lived in an environment which did not provide opportunity for the kind of mental growth measured by the tests.

In a study of mountain schoolchildren in southeastern Kentucky,

Asher (3) found that the average I.Q. of these children dropped gradu- ally from 83.5 at the age of 7 to 60.6 at the age of 15. He points out the serious deficiency in the material environment of these children and suggests that it fails to provide opportunities for acquiring the kind of knowledge measured by the tests. Essentially the same results were obtained by Wheeler (22) in a study of mountain children in Tennessee. In a follow-up study made ten years later, however, Wheeler (23) re- ports a marked improvement in the intelligence-test performance of children living in the same areas and coming largely from the same families studied ten years earlier. He suggests that this improvement is related to an improvement in the general economic, social, and educa- tional status of the people in the area.

Table XIX

Decrease in I.Q. in Unfavorable Type of Environment (21)

AGE AT TEST (MONTHS)	INTELLIGENCE QUOTIENT ★						
	Child 1	Child 2	Child 3	Child 4	Child 5	Child 6	Child 7
17–19	103	98	86				
20–22			73	83			
23–25		93			85	80	
26–28	72	83		83			
29–31		80	63	75	85	80	
32–34						74	79
35–37			58			74	
38–40	63	61		63	70		72
41–43							
44–46					71	67	70
47–49			64				67
50–52	60	61		60			69
53–55			62				
56–58						70	
59–61							69

In evaluating these and similar studies, several points should be kept in mind. First, it is necessary, as Stoddard (14) points out, to differentiate between potentiality and delivered power in connection with intelligence testing; it is only the latter that can be measured by intelligence tests. Second, as was pointed out in discussing shifts in tested intelligence (p. 414), one cannot definitely attribute a shift

Table XX

Increase in I.Q. in Favorable Type of Environment (21)

AGE AT TEST	INTELLIGENCE QUOTIENT ★			
	Child 1	Child 2	Child 3	Child 4
Three years	89			
Three and one-half	118	98	98	124
Four years	128	120		135
Four and one-half	129	145	109	137
Five years	119	167		146
Five and one-half			126	144
Six years	117		125	143
Seven years	140		134	
Eight and one-half	135			
Nine years		155		148
Nine and one-half				160
Ten years		143	153	
Ten and one-half	149			165
Eleven years	130	152		
Twelve years	139	143		154
Thirteen years		(100C)*		
Thirteen and one-half	132			
Fourteen years				(99C)*
Fifteen years	(99C)*		(99C)*	
Seventeen years			(93U)*	
Eighteen years	(99U)*			

* Figures followed by a C or U in parentheses represent percentage of randomly selected persons (of the same age and education as the person tested) falling *below* the subject on an intelligence test which does not directly yield the I.Q. These figures are called *percentiles*, or percentile ranks. An intelligence score percentile of 99 corresponds roughly to an I.Q. of at least 130, probably higher.

to environmental influences unless he is reasonably sure that other factors are held constant or are ruled out experimentally. This has been the basis of Goodenough's (7) criticism of the recent studies of environmental influences and their effect upon mental growth. Finally, it must be recognized that the development of any trait, and any real shift in the rate of development of that trait, is dependent upon both heredity and environment. It is as much a mistake to suppose that the hereditary factors exert a constant influence in development as it is to suppose that any shift in rate of growth is due wholly to environment.

It is not a question as to whether environment plays a part in such shifts, but rather one of finding out what particular factors in the environment will, when combined with given hereditary factors, change the rate of mental growth.

The fact that appreciable changes or shifts in intelligence occur in certain cases under certain circumstances does not invalidate or change the reliability of the intelligence test. The data on validity which we have presented indicate that these tests possess high predictive value for a variety of purposes. The fact that the predictive value is not perfect does not mean that the tests should be discarded. A more thorough knowledge of intelligence tests, what they are related to, and how well we can predict from them, should make it possible to predict the kinds of shifts needed for adequate adjustments. Perhaps we could actually control such shifts. Facts are needed for the prediction and control of human behavior. Intelligence tests provide some of the facts and frequently lead to the discovery of other facts.

SUMMARY

Intelligence, or intelligent behavior, depends upon (1) alertness, (2) ability to assimilate and retain, (3) fertile imagination, (4) insight, (5) self-criticism, (6) confidence, and (7) strong motivation.

Beginning with the work of Binet, many tests for the measurement of intelligence have been constructed. Some are scored in terms of the I.Q. (intelligence quotient), a measure of the rate of mental growth or development. The I.Q. is obtained by multiplying by 100 the mental age divided by the chronological age. Some intelligence tests must be given individually; some may be given to groups. Each type of test has its uses, advantages, and limitations. The validity of an intelligence test is indicated by its correlation with such criteria as success in school, educational level, occupational level, and other previously validated tests. The reliability of intelligence tests refers to the consistency with which they yield the same results when they are repeated, when one part is compared with another, or when one form of the test is compared with another.

Studies reveal that shifts or changes in tested intelligence occur from one testing date to another. As the interval between test and retest increases, the differences between the original scores and the later scores become larger. Some studies indicate that the direction of the changes in tested intelligence, i.e., increases or decreases over a period of time, is related to the increase or decrease in the favorableness of the conditions which affect mental growth.

QUESTIONS
on the Chapter

1. What are the main characteristics of intelligent behavior?
2. State the evidence which shows that memory is an important aspect of intelligence.
3. What was Binet's contribution to psychology?
4. Describe the general theory of the Binet method of measuring intelligence.
5. Define the I.Q. and describe its computation.
6. How does Wechsler's definition of the I.Q. differ from Terman's definition?
7. How do we know that intelligence tests are reliable?
8. How do we know that they are valid?
9. How accurately can one predict intelligence at one age from tests given at an earlier age?
10. Why doesn't intelligence as measured by tests remain constant from one testing date to another?
11. What is the effect of environment on tested intelligence?

for Discussion

1. What are the main difficulties in defining intelligence? Is it necessary that a completely satisfactory definition be arrived at before any measurements of intelligence can be made?
2. How might our list of the characteristics of intelligent behavior be expanded or reduced?
3. What problems had to be met in adapting Binet's test in the United States?
4. Discuss the major advantages and limitations of the Binet scale.
5. Compare and discuss the uses, advantages, and disadvantages of (a) individual vs. group tests; (b) language vs. performance tests.
6. Of what social significance is the fact that intelligence is "normally" distributed?

REFERENCES

1 ALPERT, A., *The Solving of Problem-Situations by Preschool Children.* New York: Teachers College, Columbia University, 1928 (*Contributions to Education*, No. 323).
2 ARTHUR, GRACE, "A Point Scale of Performance Tests," *Clinical Manual*, 2nd edition. Commonwealth Fund, 1943.
3 ASHER, E. J., "The Inadequacy of Current Intelligence Tests for Testing Kentucky Mountain Children," *J. Genet. Psychol.*, 1935, 47, 480–486.
4 BINET, A., and SIMON, T., "La mesure du développement de l'intelligence

chez les jeunes enfants," *Bul. de la Société libre pour l'Étude psychologique de l'Enfant*, 1911, 11, 187–248.

5 BROTEMARKLE, R. A., "Some Memory Span Test Problems — An Analytical Study at the College Adult Level," *Psychol. Clinic*, 1924, 15, 229.

6 BUCKINGHAM, B. R., "Correlation between Ability to Think and Ability to Remember, with Special Reference to United States History," *School and Society*, 1917, 5, 443.

7 GOODENOUGH, FLORENCE L., "Can We Influence Mental Growth? A Critique of Recent Experiments," *Educational Record*, Supplement 13, 1940, 21, 120–143.

8 GORDON, H., "Mental and Scholastic Tests among Retarded Children," *Educational Pamphlet No. 44*, Board of Education, London, 1943.

9 LOUTTIT, C. M., "Racial Comparisons of Ability in Immediate Recall of Logical and Nonsense Material," *J. Soc. Psychol.*, 1931, 2, 205.

10 OTIS, A. S., *Manual of Directions and Key (Revised) for Otis Self-Administering Tests of Mental Ability*. New York: World Book Company, 1922 and 1928.

11 PINTNER, R., and PATERSON, D. G., *A Scale of Performance Tests*. New York: D. Appleton and Company, 1917.

12 REMMERS, H. H., and GAGE, N. L., *Educational Measurement and Evaluation*. New York: Harper and Brothers, 1943.

13 SPEARMAN, CARL, *The Abilities of Man*. New York: The Macmillan Company, 1927.

14 STODDARD, G. D., "New Light on Intelligence," *Proceedings of the Iowa Academy of Science*, 1942, 69, 51–60.

15 SULLIVAN, E. T., CLARK, W. W., and TIEGS, E. W., *California Test of Mental Maturity*. Southern California Book Depository, 1937.

16 TERMAN, L. M., *The Intelligence of School Children*. Boston: Houghton Mifflin Company, 1919, p. 141.

17 TERMAN, L. M., and MERRILL, M. A., *Measuring Intelligence*. Boston: Houghton Mifflin Company, 1937.

18 THORNDIKE, R. L., "Constancy of the I.Q.," *Psychol. Bull.*, 1940, 37, 167–187.

19 WAR DEPARTMENT, *Technical Manual*, 12–260, Personnel Classification Tests, December, 1942.

20 WECHSLER, DAVID, *The Measurement of Adult Intelligence*. New York: Williams and Wilkins, 1944.

21 WELLMAN, B. L., "Our Changing Concept of Intelligence," *J. Consult. Psychol.*, 1938, 2, 98.

22 WHEELER, L. R., "The Intelligence of East Tennessee Mountain Children," *J. Educ. Psychol.*, 1932, 23, 351–370.

23 WHEELER, L. R., "A Composite Study of the Intelligence of East Tennessee Mountain Children," *J. Educ. Psychol.*, 1942, 33, 321–334.

24 WONDERLIC, E. F., *Personnel Test Manual*, 1945, p. 7. Reprinted by permission.

ABILITIES AND APTITUDES
13

While intelligence plays a prominent part in adjustment and personality, it is by no means the only kind of behavior involved. In many instances an adjustment is dependent primarily upon some specific skill, knowledge, interest, or sensory equipment. For example, in many simple and routine jobs, individuals testing at the very bottom on standardized tests of intelligence are at least as well adapted to the work as persons testing at average or above, because the special skills which they possess are more important for the jobs than a high level of intelligence. Anyone can think of numerous jobs in which success is more dependent upon a specific skill or kind of knowledge than it is upon intelligence. In educational and vocational guidance and in personnel selection and placement, it is important to know what specific skills and kinds of knowledge are needed for successful adjustments, and even more important to be able to determine the extent to which particular individuals possess these skills and knowledge.

ACHIEVEMENT AND TRADE TESTS

Many psychological tests have been devised for measuring the specific skills and the knowledge which individuals have already acquired and which they can bring to bear on a particular task, job, or situation. The tests used for measuring what an individual has learned as a consequence of a period of training in a particular school subject, course of study, or school grade are called *educational achievement tests*. Such tests are ordinarily used to determine the achievement status of each pupil in each school subject, the achievement status of a class or grade, or the achievement status of the school. The knowledge thus provided may be used for a variety of purposes, but the purpose of the test itself is to provide information about what pupils know about a subject or subjects at the time the test is administered.

Achievement Tests

Table XXI shows the scores and the achievement levels expressed in
school grade units of a 13.5-year-old eighth-grade pupil on the nine
parts of the Metropolitan Achievement Test (1). It will be noted that
this pupil's over-all achievement represented by the total score on the
entire test gives him an average achievement level of 8.9 grades. The
test was given near the end of the school year or just at the completion
of the eighth grade; hence the achievement level is about what would
be expected of pupils in a typical eighth grade. It should be noted,
however, that the pupil in our example was 13.5 years of age at the
time the test was taken. The average grade placement of pupils of this
age is 8.0. This means that the pupil in our example is accelerated .9
of a grade in comparison with pupils of his age.

Table XXI

Scores and Grade-Placement Levels of an Eighth-Grade Pupil
on Parts of the Metropolitan Achievement Test

SUBJECTS	SCORES	GRADE LEVEL
Reading comprehension	72	9.2
Reading vocabulary	65	8.5
Arithmetic fundamentals	84	10.4
Arithmetic reasoning	78	9.8
English *fundamentals*	68	8.8
Literature *- understanding*	60	8.0
History	72	9.2
Geography	66	8.6
Spelling *- knowledge*	57	7.7
Total Score	622	8.9

Another significant point to be noted in Table XXI is the fact that
the pupil is quite uneven in his achievement in the various school subjects. He varies from a grade placement of 10.4 in arithmetic fundamentals to 7.7 in spelling. He is not 8.9 grades in any of the nine
subjects. This kind of variation in achievement may be regarded as
typical of individuals in general. Indeed it would be unusual to find
an individual who was at exactly the same level in all school subjects.
The same result is obtained when one measures several abilities or
traits. A single individual will be found to stand relatively high in
one ability, relatively low in another, and at points scattered between
these two extremes in others. The variation in a single person between

the highest-ranking ability or trait and the lowest has been found to be equal on the average to about 80 per cent of the variation found between the best and worst individuals in a large group in a single trait (14).

Achievement tests like the Metropolitan and the Stanford Achievement Tests (15) are essentially test batteries. A number of separate tests are assembled into one test and administered at one time. Each of the areas of achievement measured by the parts of such a test can be measured separately by tests especially designed to measure knowledge and skill in that area. In fact, tests are available for measuring achievement in any school subject. Let us examine some of the work that has been done in developing tests for measuring two of the basic skills ordinarily acquired in school, namely, reading and writing. Some of the problems and difficulties involved in acquiring these skills will also be discussed.

Reading tests. There are two general aspects of reading ability: rate and comprehension. They may be measured together or separately. A program of remedial reading must consider both factors, since it is of little value to increase the speed of reading by sacrificing comprehension of what is read, and it is unsatisfactory to increase comprehension by making an undue sacrifice of speed.

The most serviceable reading tests, from the diagnostic point of view, are those which measure rate and comprehension separately. A typical test designed to measure rate, while holding comprehension constant, is Test 6 of Advanced Form A of the *Iowa Silent Reading Tests*, prepared by H. A. Greene, A. N. Jorgensen, and V. H. Kelley. A part of this test is illustrated in Figure 69. In this test the subject reads as far as he can in a specified period of time. He follows the directions as he reads. Reading rate is measured by the amount of material covered. The tasks which must be executed are inserted to keep comprehension constant for all persons taking the test.

Comprehension is measured by tests in which the pupil is allotted a specified period of time to study a paragraph, and is then asked to answer several objective questions which determine how well he has understood the material. The length of the paragraph is sufficiently short to allow even very slow readers to finish in the time allotted. The 1939 edition of the *Iowa Silent Reading Tests* covers the various phases of comprehension in reading, by including separate tests to measure such factors as word meaning, sentence meaning, paragraph comprehension, and location of information. The test also includes a measure of rate of reading.

ATTEMPTS TO PREVENT ABUSES AND TO INCREASE CITIZEN CONTROL

The government of the United States is merely the agency by which and through which 1
the people protect their own rights and liberties. Our government may be said to be the 2
organized will of all the people. The people govern in this country, and the men and the 3
means by which they govern, all combined, may be said to be the government. But do 4
not ever forget this fact: The President is not a master, but a servant. Does the para- 5
graph state that the source of governmental authority is in the people? Yes No. 6
The President, Senators, Congressmen, and judges in the nation, the governors, senators, 7
and members of the legislatures in the states, are only agents or servants of the people to 8
carry out the people's will. Also do not forget that the power of government does not 9
rest in Washington, the capital of the nation, nor at the capitals of the different states. 10
The power of government exists all over these United States. Is it correct to conclude 11
from this paragraph that the control of government is centralized in Congress? Yes No. 12
The power of government exists right in the homes and hearts of the people. 13

Figure 69

Part of a Rate-of-Reading Test

The student reads as far as possible in a given period of time. Certain tasks are inserted
from time to time to insure comprehension. (From H. A. Greene, A. N. Jorgensen, and
V. H. Kelley, *Iowa Silent Reading Tests*, World Book Company, 1933 edition.)

Tests of this kind have considerable value in locating the poor reader's
disability. They reveal great differences in ability, not only among
children in the same school grade but also among children of the same
mental ability. An indication that the differences in reading ability
are not entirely due to differences in intelligence is found in the correlation between Stanford-Binet mental age and composite scores on the
four Gates Silent Reading Tests. For sixty fourth-grade pupils this
correlation was found to be only .66 (12). Low intelligence is a common cause of poor reading, but there are many pupils of average or
even superior intelligence who are definitely below average in reading
ability. Investigations of such cases have revealed a number of causes
which can frequently be eliminated.

Reading disabilities. In spite of the great progress made in teaching children to read, all children do not learn to read equally well. The
great differences in reading ability revealed by a standardized test are
shown graphically in Figure 70. This distribution, constructed from
a random sample of sixth-grade children, shows some who read no
better than the average child of the third grade, while, at the other
extreme, a few read as well as the average eleventh-grade child. If a

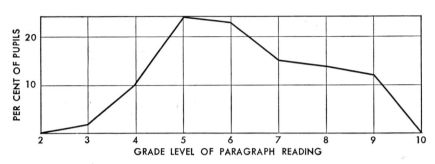

Figure 70

Distribution of Sixth-Grade Pupils According to Achievement in Paragraph Comprehension

(This distribution was constructed from data obtained with the Nelson Silent Reading Test for Grades 3 to 9, constructed by M. F. Nelson and published by Houghton Mifflin.)

child is 30 per cent retarded in reading for his age and is twice as backward in reading as in other school subjects or in general intelligence, he is regarded as having a special reading disability (33, p. 406). Reading disabilities and the less serious variations in reading accomplishment among pupils who have been given essentially the same training have been the subject of extensive study among educators and psychologists.　One of the results of their investigations is the emphasis that modern school systems are now placing upon remedial instruction in reading, that is, upon individual instruction adapted to those children who, for a variety of reasons, do not learn to read in a satisfactory manner by ordinary instruction or who, because of special sensory or perceptual characteristics, require individualized instruction.　The identification of such pupils is made possible by means of standardized reading tests, and every progressive school system makes use of these tests at all grade levels.

Many factors operate to cause reading disabilities.　One factor which will cause inefficient reading, no matter how intelligent the pupils may be, is inadequate vision.　We read with our eyes, and good vision is a necessity for normal reading.　The need for measures of visual skills is, therefore, obvious.　Betts (5) has made available a battery of tests for measuring certain aspects of vision which are related to reading ability.　Another factor often resulting in poor reading is incorrect initial instruction.　Another is seen in the relation between defective reading and defective speech.　About 10 per cent of the children who are retarded in reading also stutter, while only 1 per cent of the children who read normally have this defect in their speech. Likewise, approximately 18 per cent of defective readers have a minor articulatory speech disorder, such as baby speech, lisping, or mispronunciation, while these defects are found in only 7 per cent of normal readers.

Another factor which has received much attention in experimental studies of reading is the movements of the eyes. In reading a line of printed material, the eyes do not move gradually across the page, but proceed by jumps from one stopping point, or *fixation*, to another. Each fixation lasts about a quarter of a second, and the time occupied by the movement is about a twenty-fifth of a second. Comparison of the eye movements of good and poor readers indicates that the former have fewer and shorter fixations, fewer regressions (a return to a point already passed) and that in general they exhibit more even and regular progressive movements (7, 40, 45). Some clinicians, impressed by these differences, have proposed that poor readers should be trained in pacing their eye movements to make them more closely parallel to the movements found in good readers (31). Such training does result in improved reading ability in certain cases. However, more recent work indicates that the eye movements are determined not so much by fixed motor habits as by (a) the difficulty of the material for the particular reader, (b) the purpose of the reader at the moment (whether it be scanning, reading for detail, and so on) (2), and (c) the central aspects of the reader's perceptual ability (10). The poor reader ponders at each fixation, looks back frequently, and moves forward in a halting and jerky manner because he is not assimilating the material. Fairbanks has shown that the great majority of regressive movements follow a misunderstanding of the material. The regressive movement, apparently, is resorted to in order to remedy an error in reading that has already been made. A typical case of this type is shown in Figure 71, which is a record of the eye movements and the sound wave from the voice in oral reading. The downward trend of the lines labeled *Eyes* indicates the progressive movements across the page. The words read orally are identified below, in the line labeled *Voice*. At *B* the reader made a mistake in his oral reading, saying "rai . . ." (the beginning of *rain*, a word not in the test) instead of the correct word, *snow*. Immediately afterward, the eyes show a regressive movement indicated at *A*, and, following this regression, the correct word, *snow*, is spoken. Training a poor reader to eliminate such regressions without first improving his reading ability so that he does not need to look back is likely to do more harm than good.

Reading disabilities, like disabilities in speech, cannot be reduced to

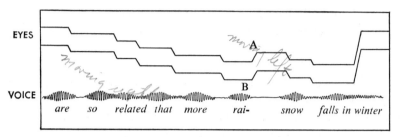

Figure 71

Simultaneous Record of Movements of the Eyes and of Sound Waves from the Voice in Oral Reading

A. Regression of eyes to point where mistake was made. B. Mistake in oral reading. (From J. Tiffin and G. Fairbanks, "An Eye-Voice Camera for Clinical and Research Studies," *Psychol. Monogr.*, 1937, 48, 70–77.)

a single cause nor treated in terms of a stereotyped therapy. Two cases seldom present the same clinical picture. Each is, in a sense, a unique problem and must be treated in the light of the particular combination of circumstances that seems to be operative.

Handwriting scales. Corresponding to tests of reading, scales for the measurement of handwriting have been carefully constructed that enable one to determine how the progress of a child compares with that of other children or with a predetermined standard. One of the most widely used scales of this type is the Ayres Handwriting Scale, a sample of which is reproduced in Figure 72. This scale provides eight qualities of handwriting, numbered from 20 to 90 in steps of ten. Figure 72 shows samples of qualities 20, 50, and 90. Measurement with this scale shows that both rate and quality of handwriting improve together from the second to the eighth grade. This is shown graphically in Figure 73.

Trade Tests

The tests used for determining a person's knowledge of a specific job or trade are called *trade tests*. The trade test is a kind of achievement test, but it is more aptly called "trade test" because its object is to measure an applicant's information about a trade or his skill in the performance of standard tasks. For example, suppose that the use of a micrometer is necessary for the successful performance of a certain job. A man's fitness for the job could be determined, in part at least, by administering the Purdue Vocational Test, Can You Read a Micrometer? (19) The tests in the Purdue Vocational Series are paper-and-pencil tests that measure achievement in technical information related to

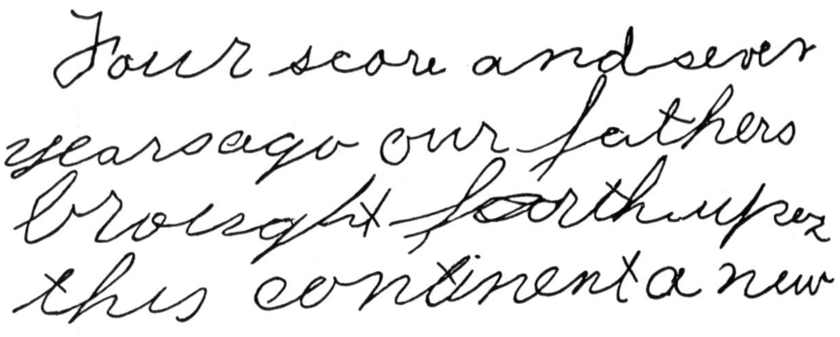

QUALITY 20

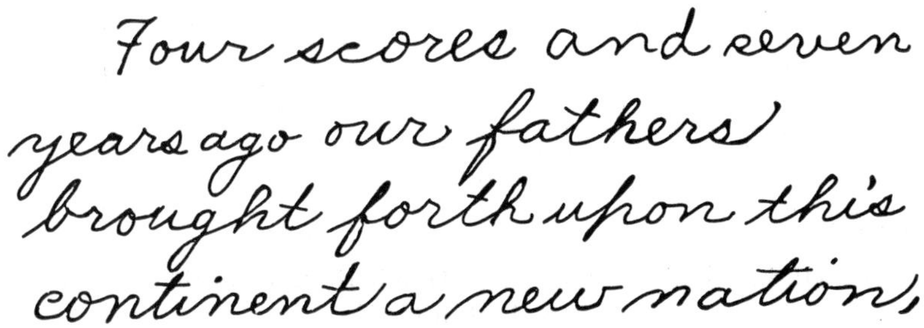

QUALITY 50

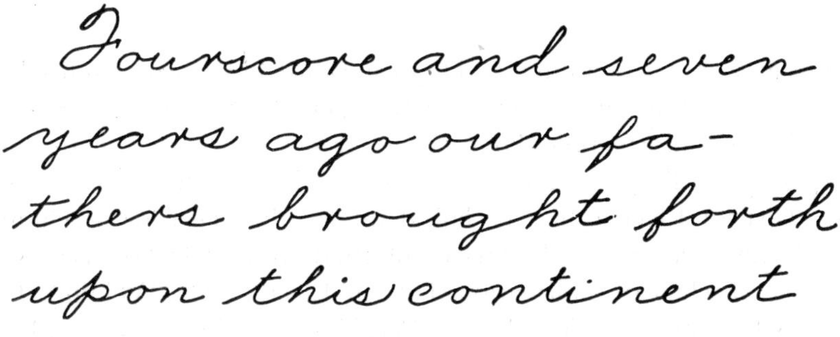

QUALITY 90

Figure 72

Samples from the Ayres Handwriting Scale — Used to Rate
the Quality of Handwriting

(Courtesy of the Russell Sage Foundation.)

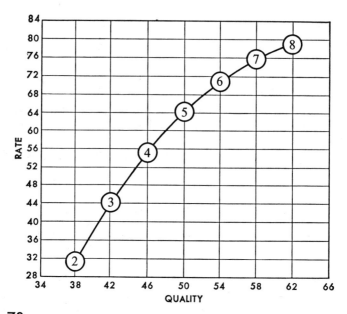

Figure 73

Growth in Speed and Quality of Handwriting from the Second
to the Eighth Grade

Rate is in letters per minute; quality is indicated according to scale shown in Figure 72.
(Courtesy of the Russell Sage Foundation.)

various areas of trade training. They can be used by vocational teachers
in public school systems or by industrial personnel men for measuring
an applicant's information about various trades. There are eight tests
in this series at the present time. They are: Purdue Blueprint Reading
Test, Test for Electricians, Technical Information Test for Machinists
and Machine Operators, Technical Information Test in Oxy-acetylene
Welding, Technical Information Test in Electric Arc Welding, Can
You Read a Scale? Can You Read a Working Drawing? Can You Read
a Micrometer? (43)

Some trade testing is accomplished by the use of performance tests.
In these tests the applicant is given certain tasks to perform or certain
materials to be manipulated in the way in which they will have to be
handled on the job. The job may be set up in miniature. For example,
Tiffin and Greenly (44) reported a study in which a miniature punch
press was constructed and used for measuring the eye-hand-foot coordination of industrial punch press operators. Trade skills and information may also be measured by the use of standardized *oral trade*

questions (36). Such questions have been prepared for most of the standard trades and are in use in many state employment offices.

SPECIAL ABILITY TESTS

There are some complex coordinated skills or restricted groups of performances which are not measured by achievement or trade tests. For example, the motor skills involved in a wide variety of locomotor and manipulative performances and the mechanical skills and knowledge involved in shop work or in other kinds of mechanical activity are measured by motor ability and mechanical ability tests. Tests of this kind are called *special ability tests*. It is common to refer to any particular one of such tests as a test of motor ability, or musical ability, or mechanical ability. These tests, like achievement and trade tests, measure what the individual has learned, what he knows or what he can do in rather restricted areas of activity — areas defined by the titles, musical ability, mechanical ability, clerical ability, etc. In a sense they are achievement tests, but since the word achievement is ordinarily reserved for knowledge acquired as a result of a specific course of training, generally that provided in a school situation, it is not a common practice to call the tests achievement tests.

Motor Abilities

From infancy into adult years, such motor or muscular activities as those involved in standing, walking, running, grasping, throwing, and the many complex, coordinated skills involved in finger, hand, and arm manipulations play a very prominent role in everyday living. One need think only of the earning capacity and the social prestige enjoyed by the professional athlete, or of the high degree of manipulative skill needed by loopers in a hosiery mill, by watch repairmen, or by coil winders, to realize that motor skills not only are important but in many cases are the basic framework of personality and adjustment. One of the recognized techniques for overcoming timidity and shyness in children is to teach the child some skill — it need only be dressing a doll or skating — so that he can perform as well as other children or better and then to place him in a social situation where the skill can be utilized. Motor skills like those involved in cutting with scissors, buttoning clothes, tying shoestrings, and walking play such an important part in the total activity of the infant that most of the preschool tests of intelligence or mental growth make extensive use of motor test items (41).

Prominent among the various motor skills are a number of so-called simpler motor processes. These include speed of movement, steadiness, strength, and accuracy of movement. Speed of movement is most frequently measured by recording the number of taps made in a given time on a metal plate. The subject holds a metal stylus in his hand and taps the metal plate as rapidly as possible. Each tap closes an electric contact which operates a counter. The number of taps per unit of time, usually one minute, constitutes the subject's score. Speed of tapping increases from the age of six to adulthood, with a tendency toward greater speed with the preferred hand at all ages but with no significant differences due to sex (30).

Speed of movement as measured by the tapping test should not be confused with such kinds of speed as those involved in adding numbers, canceling letters in lines of pied type, or making dots in small squares. These performances involve, in addition to speed, the factors of discrimination and accuracy, which are not involved in any appreciable way in the tapping test. They also involve a series of stimulations, each one of which requires a separate response, in contrast to the simple,

Figure 74

Steadiness Test

The number of times the metal stylus touches the side of the hole in fifteen seconds is a measure of steadiness. (From Purdue Psychological Laboratory.)

Figure 75

Tracing Test

repetitive muscular movement involved in tapping. The speed with which an individual can solve problems, answer quiz questions, read a paragraph, or decipher a code is a still more complicated matter, since there is still more mental activity between the stimulus (problem or question) and the final response. Mere speed of movement is a negligible factor in such performances.

The equipment most frequently used for measuring steadiness (see Figure 74) consists of a metal plate containing a graded series of holes which vary in diameter from one half to seven sixty-fourths of an inch. The subject is required to hold a metal stylus in each hole for a given period of time, usually fifteen seconds, while attempting to keep it from touching the side. The test is scored in terms of the number of contacts per hole, or in terms of the smallest hole in which the subject can make less than some standard number of contacts in fifteen seconds. Steadiness as measured in this way increases with age, although there are wide individual differences at each age level. An individual's performance fluctuates from time to time according to the presence of such conditions as fatigue, lack of sleep, illness, and emotional states.

Muscular strength is measured by an instrument known as a dynamometer. Strength of hand grip is measured by a hand dynamometer, leg and back strength by a leg and back dynamometer. Studies indicate, as one would expect, that boys are uniformly stronger than

girls, and men than women. The difference cannot be attributed entirely to differences in size. Other factors are women's poorer muscular development and the fact that they have less inclination to exert full
muscular strength in taking the test (48).

Accuracy or precision of movement is customarily measured by the
tracing test shown in Figure 75 or by some kind of aiming test. In
the tracing test the subject is required to move a metal stylus along
the graduated groove formed by two metal strips. Each contact of the
stylus with the metal strips is recorded on a counter which is attached
to the apparatus. The test may be scored in terms of the distance traced
without touching either strip or the number of errors made while tracing the entire distance. Another test for measuring precision of hand
movement is illustrated in Figure 76. The apparatus consists of a
metal disk with three holes located on the corners of an equilateral
triangle. Each hole is .5 of an inch in diameter. The plate is covered
by a rotating shutter which exposes the holes at the rate of 126 per
minute. The subject is required to punch a metal stylus successively
into the holes as they are uncovered. The subject is given a thirty-
second practice trial followed without interruption by a two-minute
period of punching. The number of contacts outside of the holes is
recorded in a counter which is attached to the apparatus. This record
is the subject's error score (42).

A number of tests have been devised for measuring simple motor
coordination. One such test measures the coordination of the hands
by having a subject trace the grooves of a three-sided figure with his
right hand while at the same time he is tracing the grooves of a four-
sided figure with his left hand. Metal styli are used in tracing and
the number of contacts with the sides of the grooves is recorded on a
counter which is attached to the metal board in which the figures are
cut.

The simpler motor processes measured by these tests, taken singly
or in combinations, may be important in determining a worker's qualifications for simple, routine jobs. For example, a study of tin-plate
inspectors resulted in setting up four qualifications that a girl must
meet before being trained as a tin-plate inspector. These requirements
were that she must (1) pass the near and far visual discrimination tests
and the vertical balance test, (2) be at least 5 feet 2 inches tall, (3) weigh
at least 118 pounds, and (4) score not over 2.00 (low scores are indicative of high proficiency) on the Purdue Hand Precision Test. It is interesting to note that a measure of hand precision proved to be valid
for this job. Tests of speed of reaction, strength of grip, and rate of

Figure 76

Purdue Hand Precision Test

The subject punches the stylus successively into three holes as they are exposed by the rotation of the disc on top of the apparatus. The number of misses is recorded in the counter on the front of the apparatus. (From Purdue Psychological Laboratory.)

manipulation were also tried but were not included in the final qualifications because they did not yield useful degrees of validity (42, p. 300).

Motor skills of a somewhat higher order, in which the simpler motor processes are combined or integrated in various ways, can also be measured. Tests have been devised for measuring finger and hand dexterity. These manipulative skills are involved in a wide variety of industrial jobs, household tasks, and office work and in some kinds of professional work. Their measurement is of particular importance in the selection of workers for such jobs as assembly, packing, and the operation of certain machines — jobs in which success is largely dependent upon rapid, precise, and coordinated movements of the hands and fingers.

Prominent among the tests of finger dexterity are the O'Connor Finger Dexterity Test and the O'Connor Tweezer Dexterity Test. In the Finger Dexterity Test, which is shown in Figure 77, the subject is required to take cylindrical brass pins one inch in length and .072 inch in diameter from a shallow tray and place them in the holes of a metal plate. There are one hundred holes in the plate arranged in ten rows of ten holes each. The holes are .196 inch in diameter and are spaced one half inch apart. The subject is instructed to fill the board — three pins to a hole — as quickly as possible. The Tweezer Dexterity Test is a similar test in which a pair of tweezers instead of the fingers is used in placing the pins (13.).

Another test of manipulative dexterity is the Purdue Pegboard (29). This test provides separate measurements of the right hand, the left hand, and both hands together. It measures dexterity for two types of activity: one involving gross movements of hand, fingers, and arms, and the other involving what might be called "tip of the finger" dexterity. The test (see Figure 78) consists of a board with a series of four trays across the top and two parallel columns of holes near the center of the board. The right- and left-hand trays contain metal pins. One of the two middle trays contains small washers which fit over the pins; the other contains small metal collars which fit around the pins. Separate thirty-second trials provide a test of the subject's speed in placing pins with the right hand, left hand, and both hands together. Finer dexterity is measured in a one-minute trial in which the subject must assemble a pin, a washer, a collar, and a washer, using right hand, left hand, right hand, and left hand in order. Norms are available for one, two, and three trials. The test can be given as a group test by providing a board for each subject.

The importance of measures of dexterity and coordination is sig-

Figure 77

O'Connor Finger Dexterity Test

For measuring a skill required in many industrial jobs, such as radio assembly, electrical fixture assembly, and "looping" in a hosiery mill. (Described in M. Hines and J. O'Connor, "A Measure of Finger Dexterity," *Personnel Journal*, 1926, 4, 379–382.)

Figure 78

The Purdue Pegboard

This is a test of manipulative dexterity designed to assist in the selection of employees in industrial jobs such as assembly, packing, operation of certain machines, and other routine manual jobs. (From Purdue Psychological Laboratory.)

nificantly illustrated by the use of such measures in the selection and classification of air-crew personnel in the Army Air Forces. Six of the battery of twenty tests used as a basis for making recommendations for classification of air-crew personnel were apparatus tests. These included measures of coordination, finger dexterity, and discrimination reaction time. In an article regarding the use of these tests, Flanagan (11) points out that these apparatus tests made a significant contribution to the over-all prediction of ability in the various air-crew specialties, and that the aptitudes measured by these tests were not measurable by any of the printed tests which were available at the time. The significance of the kinds of tests under consideration in this chapter is further indicated by the fact that the selection and placement of air-crew personnel was made on the basis of a composite measure of aptitudes, abilities, interests, and personal characteristics rather than on measures of general intelligence or educational attainment.

Mechanical Ability Tests

A vast amount of everyday activity as well as a great number of occupations and industrial jobs involves a group of special skills and knowledge commonly referred to as mechanical ability or, as some psychologists prefer to call it, mechanical intelligence. The importance of mechanical ability in occupational adjustments is so obvious that we need not enumerate the hundreds of situations in which it is involved. It is significant to note that in World War II the War Department considered the measurement of mechanical ability of such importance that a Mechanical Aptitude Test was administered at reception centers to all enlisted men who could read and write (46).

Mechanical ability tests can be classified into two main groups: tests of mechanical knowledge or comprehension, and mechanical assembly tests. The tests of mechanical knowledge are group tests of the paper-and-pencil variety. For the most part, they consist of pictures and diagrams of machines or situations which test the subject's information about mechanical devices or his comprehension of mechanical relationships. Mechanical assembly tests are, for the most part, individual tests which provide a number of commonplace mechanical devices, such as a mouse trap, an electrical plug fixture, or a wrench which may be easily taken apart and reassembled.

In these two kinds of mechanical ability tests there is a clear distinction between knowledge or information and manipulative skills. Individuals who have little mechanical skill may earn fairly high ratings on tests of mechanical information. This is especially true in the case of paper-and-pencil tests which may be answered on the basis of the subject's comprehension of relationships given in the materials and do not call for previous experience with mechanical devices themselves. On the other hand, the mechanical assembly test should not be looked upon as just another dexterity test, since some comprehension and discrimination are essential for the manipulative performances called for.

The Bennett Test of Mechanical Comprehension (4), which may be considered fairly typical of tests of mechanical comprehension, is made of a large number of diagrams and pictures about which the subject is to form a judgment and answer certain questions. For example, two kinds of shears are pictured with the question, "Which would be the better shears for cutting metal?" The pictures cover a wide range of materials and situations connected with practical mechanical experiences. One of the oldest mechanical comprehension tests is the Stenquist Mechanical Aptitude Test (39). Two other tests which are of the same type but which place a greater emphasis upon familiarity with tools, machines, and operations involved in shop work are the O'Rourke Mechanical Aptitude Test (26) and the Detroit Mechanical Aptitudes Examination (9).

An interesting variation of this type of group test of mechanical ability is the Purdue Mechanical Adaptability Test (20). It is composed of one hundred "yes, no, don't know" items which deal with simple information of a mechanical, electrical, or related nature. To be included in the test, an item had to discriminate between individuals who had high mechanical information scores and those who had low scores, and, in addition, the item had to show little or no correlation with intelligence test scores.

The Minnesota Assembly Test (27) is a typical example of the manipulative type of mechanical ability test. This test is prepared in two forms: a long form which consists of three metal boxes referred to as Box A, Box B, and Box C, each of which contains a number of mechanical devices; and a short form which is made up from the materials found in the long form. Such devices as a monkey wrench, a bottle stopper, a bicycle bell, a clothespin, a spark plug, a mouse trap, and a radio switch are separated and placed outside a metal tray. The subject is supposed to assemble the parts of each device and place the device in its proper compartment in the box. Scoring is in terms of a number of connections to be made or parts to be assembled. Percentile norms for each age group from 11 to 21 are provided.

That mechanical tests of the assembly type do not depend to any appreciable extent upon intelligence is indicated by the low correlations which have been reported. The quality criterion used in the selection and standardization of the Minnesota Mechanical Ability tests showed a correlation of .21 with intelligence quotients. The correlation between this criterion and the complete battery of tests making up the Minnesota test was .73, while the correlation with the apparatus tests alone was .65 (27). These correlations are indicative of very satisfactory validity.

Stenquist reports correlations of .80 between his Mechanical Assembly Test (37) and ranks in shop work, and some correlations going as high as .87 and .90. In one place he found that of a group of 275 seventh- and eighth-grade boys scoring below average on general intelligence, 20 per cent scored above average on the Stenquist Mechanical Assembly Tests (38). Essentially the same result is shown graphically in Figure 79, in which Stenquist scores and Binet I.Q.'s of a group of reform school boys are plotted in comparable units in such a way that the relation between mechanical ability and intelligence can be seen in comparison with the scores for a normal population. All of the boys in this group are in the lowest quarter of the general population in intelligence, but 65 per cent of them are above the average of normal boys in mechanical ability. This is a very significant fact to consider in arranging a training program for the reform school boys.

The relation of mechanical ability as measured by the paper-and-pencil group tests and intelligence is generally higher than that found for the assembly tests. Bennett (4) reports correlations ranging from .25 to .54 between his test and various intelligence tests. Conover (8) found a correlation of .81 between the General Classification Test and the Mechanical Aptitude Test in testing a group of 1,100 enlisted men at Fort Snelling and Fort Riley. This relationship between the G. C. T. and the M. A. T. for various occupational groups can be seen very clearly in Figure 80. It is significant to note that the mean score on the M. A. T. is larger than the G. C. T. score for just those occupational groups that one would expect to score high on mechanical ability. The closeness of the relationship between the G. C. T. and the M. A. T. scores for this group is not surprising in view of the fact that the G. C. T. was designed to measure a man's ability to absorb army training while the M. A. T. was designed to measure aptitude in learning mechanical duties in the Army.

Clerical Ability

Such skills as typing, taking dictation, alphabetizing, together with knowledge of office practice and business organization, make up another relatively restricted area of knowledge, which is called *clerical ability*.

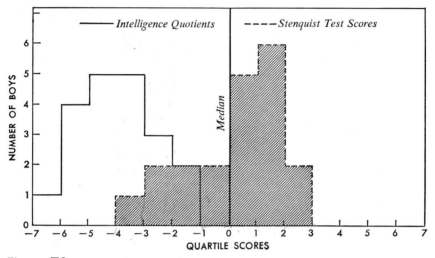

Figure 79

I.Q.'s and Stenquist Mechanical Assembly Test Scores of Twenty
Fourteen-Year-Old Reform School Boys

The intelligence quotients and mechanical assembly test scores are expressed as quartile
deviations from the median score of a normal population on each test. (From E. J. Asher,
"The Training Needs of Reform School Boys Experimentally Determined," *Journal of
Delinquency*, 1927, 11, 151–158.)

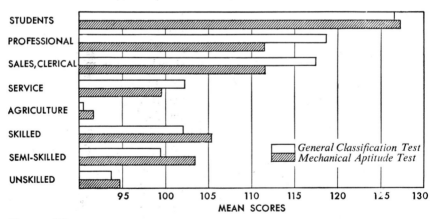

Figure 80

Mean Army General Classification Test and Mechanical Aptitude Test
Scores in Major Occupations (Main Occupation)

(From D. M. Conover, "Some Relationships Obtaining between the Army Classification
Test and the Mechanical Aptitude Test and Other Variables." M.S. thesis, Purdue University Library, 1944.)

The skills and knowledge are involved in one degree or another in such jobs as stenography, typing, mimeographing, bookkeeping, accounting, multigraphing, and filing and in the use of a variety of office equipment and machines. It is important here, as in other areas, to be able to measure the knowledge and skills necessary for success in various types of office work. Such is the aim of clerical ability tests. For example, the Purdue Clerical Adaptability Test (21) measures several of the abilities required in clerical and stenographic work, namely: spelling, memory for oral instructions, arithmetical computation, checking of names and numbers, word meaning, accuracy in copying, and arithmetical reasoning. The Blackstone Stenographic Proficiency Test (6) attempts to measure several of the essential abilities involved in stenographic work. Seven parts of the test measure knowledge of English, syllabification, office practice, alphabetizing, abbreviations, business organization, and transcription. The Minnesota Vocational Test for Clerical Workers (3) consists of two parts: a name-checking test and a number-checking test. The test does not attempt to measure specific proficiencies or skills in specific activities but yields an over-all indication of ability in various kinds of clerical work. That it does so is indicated by the fact that it differentiates employed clerical workers from workers in general, that it shows a higher correlation with grades in accounting than does an academic ability test, and that it differentiates employed clerical workers from unemployed clerical workers. Other tests in this general area attempt to measure such specific skills as typing, taking dictation, and transcribing.

Musical Ability

Musical ability is composed of a group of skills and knowledge more clearly restricted and more unrelated to other abilities than any other group of performances. It is our most typical special ability. No other ability is so completely dependent upon one field of sensory stimulation as musical ability is upon audition. Musical ability is special also in that it is not dependent to any appreciable degree upon intelligence and in that measures of motor ability, intelligence, mechanical ability, or any other group of abilities do not afford much indication of an individual's capacities in music. There is also one other way in which musical ability is unique. So far we have been interested in the measurement of ability as an indication of a person's present condition and the likelihood of his success or failure in an immediate job or situation. Measurement of musical ability, on the other hand, has been more often concerned with predicting future success or potentiality for absorbing training than with selection and placement of trained musicians.

Musical talent, according to Seashore (34), is composed of five major elements: musical sensitivity, musical action, musical memory and imagination, musical intelligence, and musical feeling. Under musical sensitivity he lists eight capacities: sense of pitch, of intensity, of time, of extensity, of timbre, of rhythm, of consonance, and of volume. Seashore, Lewis, and Saetveit (35) have designed tests to measure six of these sensory capacities. In the *sense of pitch* test the subject is required to discriminate between the frequencies of two tones with intensity and duration held constant. In the *sense of intensity* test the subject is to indicate which of two tones is louder. The test of *timbre* measures ability to discriminate between the quality of two complex tones. *Tonal memory* is measured by having the subject indicate which note in a short series has been changed when the series is repeated. In the *sense of rhythm* test the subject hears two rhythmic patterns of tones. He is to indicate whether the two are the same or different. *Sense of time* is measured by presenting two tones which differ in length and having the subject indicate whether the second is longer or shorter than the first. From thirty to fifty pairs of tones or series of tones are used in each test. Each test appears in two series: Series A, which is used for unselected groups, and Series B, which is used for musical groups. Each series is recorded on three phonograph records with a complete test on each side of each record. Percentile norms are available for adults on Series B, and for fifth-sixth grades and seventh-eighth grades and adults on Series A. Somewhat similar tests have been prepared by Kwalwasser and Dykema (17).

It should be recognized that these tests do not attempt to measure all of the factors that comprise what Seashore calls musical talent. Failure to do so has led to the criticism that the tests are invalid or fail to get at the kernel of musical talent (28). They are, strictly speaking, measures of musical discrimination or musical sensitivity. Such measures of sensitivity can be thought of as basic factors in musical talent only in so far as the lack of them so handicaps an individual that he cannot go far in certain types of musical training. The possession of them does not mean that a person will necessarily succeed in music or that he has all of the abilities needed for absorbing musical training. One could not expect these tests to yield high correlations with success in a school of music where the curriculum was made up of a wide range of subjects, many of them straight academic subjects. The information provided by these tests should be of greatest value for guidance in musical education and for appraising individuals at various stages during musical training.

Other aspects of musical ability, such as the ability to read music, knowledge of composers, instruments, and compositions, and appreciation of music, have been measured. Kwalwasser (16) has devised a paper-and-pencil test to measure information about composers, compositions, and instruments. Another test by Kwalwasser and Ruch (18) was designed to measure the ability of school children to recognize the names of notes in a scale, note values, rest values, and other items involved in reading music.

Artistic Ability

Closely related to musical ability is an area of activity which is commonly referred to as artistic ability. In a broad sense, music might be included under this heading since some form of aesthetic sensitivity — the ability to distinguish between degrees of beauty or artistic excellence — is needed both by the composer and the musical performer. Artistic ability is undoubtedly present in some degree in almost all individuals, but the high degree to which it is developed in the musician, sculptor, painter, designer, and other artists tends to set it apart as a special ability.

The appraisal of artistic ability in such individuals is still largely a matter of the subjective estimate of instructors and recognized masters. One attempt at objective measurement of certain components of artistic ability has been made by Meier and Seashore (23). The Meier-Seashore Art Judgment Test (later superseded by the Art Judgment Test of the Meier Art Tests [22]) attempts to measure ability to discriminate between the aesthetic merit of pairs of pictures which are identical except in one respect. The subject is to select from each of 125 pairs of pictures the one that is better. Each pair consists of a reproduction of a painting and the same picture altered so as to lower its artistic merit. High scores on the test are supposed to be good indicators of artistic aptitude.

APTITUDES

Aptitude is defined as "a condition or set of characteristics regarded as symptomatic of an individual's ability to acquire with training some (usually specified) knowledge, skill, or set of responses such as the ability to speak a language, to produce music, etc." (47). The condition referred to in this definition is some measurable behavior of the individual, some knowledge or skill which he now possesses. Such knowledge and skill is an aptitude if it is symptomatic of ability to acquire knowledge and skill which the individual does not now possess. Thus a knowledge of mathematics may be symptomatic of an individual's ability to learn chemistry, or a knowledge of physiology may be a good indication of a student's ability to profit from medical school training. An individual's present knowledge and skill is an aptitude to the extent that present knowledge is indicative of future knowledge. The difference, therefore, between the ability tests which have been described and aptitude tests is fundamentally one of purpose. If the ability test is used to predict future knowledge and skill, it becomes an aptitude test.

Ability tests may be classified according to the purposes for which they are used, as follows: (1) A test may be used to find out what an individual is like at the moment — how much intelligence he has, or how much he knows about arithmetic, or how he compares with others in motor ability. (2) A measure of one kind of behavior may be used as an indication of the individual's present status with respect to another kind of behavior. Thus knowledge of mathematics may serve as an index of knowledge of physics or chemistry, or knowledge of English fundamentals may serve as an index of present achievement in other school subjects. (3) A measure of one kind of behavior may be used as an indication of the individual's future status with respect to the same kind of behavior. Thus knowledge of arithmetic at twelve years may be an excellent index of a child's knowledge of arithmetic at fifteen years. (4) A measure of one kind of behavior may serve as an indication of an individual's future status with respect to a different kind of behavior. One might find that vocabulary and knowledge of mathematics are indications of what an individual will know about chemistry after a period of training.

The aptitude test falls in either of the last two classifications. For example, the Seashore Test of Musical Talent, while it may be used as an instrument of appraisal, is intended primarily to measure ability or readiness to acquire proficiency in music. If it were a complete enough measure of readiness to acquire, it could be used to indicate the likelihood of one's profiting from a musical education. Since it is a measure of only a limited portion of the complex of musical ability, it should be used for this purpose with caution.

The reason for calling some mechanical tests mechanical aptitude tests should now be obvious. Some mechanical tests are used primarily as instruments to reveal an individual's present condition with reference to mechanical ability. These fall in the first class mentioned above.

Others, however, are used primarily (or any of them may be so used) as measures of ability to acquire mechanical knowledge and skill. Present knowledge is then used as an indication of future knowledge of the same kind after training.

One of the difficult problems in aptitude testing arises in connection with tests of the fourth class. Suppose that a high school graduate enlists in the Army Air Forces. He wants to be a pilot. He does not possess the skills and knowledge possessed by qualified pilots. His present ability as a pilot, which is presumably zero, cannot be used as a measure of his ability or readiness to acquire the requisite skills and knowledge. However, he does have other kinds of knowledge and various kinds of skills which may be used as indications of his ability to acquire with training the specific skills and knowledge necessary for an airplane pilot. An aptitude test for pilots would therefore use a measure of one kind of behavior as an indication of the student's future status in another kind of behavior. It should be recognized, of course, that in talking about different kinds of behavior we are speaking in relative terms. Piloting an airplane and driving an automobile are different kinds of skills not because many of the same elementary responses are different, but primarily because the combinations or patterns of these responses are different. Thus it is possible to find a number of responses or characteristics in an individual which are indicative of skills and habits which he will eventually possess but which are present at the moment only in the form of the raw materials out of which the skills may be developed.

This situation is nicely illustrated in the case of the Medical Aptitude Test developed by Moss (24) for the Association of American Medical Colleges. The test is designed to serve as a measure of ability to succeed in medical school and is used as one of the aids in selecting medical students. Since applicants to medical schools do not possess the technical knowledge and skills which are ordinarily acquired only in medical training, it is necessary to measure knowledge of other kinds known to be related to subsequent knowledge of medicine or to subsequent performances in medical school. That the test does not measure knowledge of medicine is seen in the following list of subtests which comprise one form of the medical aptitude test: comprehension and retention, visual memory, memory for content, logical reasoning, command of scientific vocabulary, and understanding of printed materials. That the knowledge represented in these subtests is related to performance in medical schools is indicated in another study by Moss (25). A comparison of the scores on Form 13 of the Medical Aptitude Test with medical school performance in the freshman year shows a progressive increase in failures as one goes from the high to the low scores on the aptitude test. Failures in the top 10 per cent of aptitude scores was 1 per cent, as contrasted with 18 per cent in the lowest 10 per cent. The average freshman grades decreased progressively from 85.5 for the top 10 per cent to 77.7 for the lowest 10 per cent.

Any test — achievement, ability, or even intelligence — is an aptitude test when it is used to predict success in acquiring a specified knowledge, skill, or habit system; but generally speaking, tests are most valid if used for the purposes for which they are intended. If a test is designed as an instrument of appraisal in selecting industrial workers, it should not be used as an aptitude test unless experimentation reveals that it is valid for such a purpose.

A great many tests have been developed specifically for use as aptitude tests. In addition to those already described, aptitude tests have been developed for law, engineering, dentistry, science, aeronautics, nursing, machine bookkeeping, and business administration, and for clerical workers, truck drivers, and other kinds of workers.

THE INTERPRETATION OF TEST RESULTS

One psychologist, in describing a series of experiments, stated that upon the completion of one experiment he found it necessary to conduct two others in order to find out what the first one meant. This is another way of saying that a fact derives its meaning from other facts and must be interpreted in terms of other information. A particular fact of human behavior is meaningless when it is viewed in isolation from other behavior or when it is lifted from the behavior situation in which it was obtained.

It is particularly important to keep this fact in mind in dealing with the results of psychological tests. The very act of measurement makes the interpretation of the result difficult because in testing we seek to isolate and measure a specific part of an individual's behavior. The score or rating of a test is supposed to tell us what we want to know. Actually, however, it is only the beginning of our understanding of the individual. We must have a great deal of additional information in order to interpret the score and evaluate the individual.

There are a number of general facts that are important in interpreting test scores. First, a test measures a particular portion of an individual's total behavior. It may be a very specific portion, such as auditory reaction time, finger dexterity, or knowledge of algebra. It may be a relatively complex portion, such as mechanical ability, intelligence, or interests. It may be a larger portion of the total in one case than in another, but in no case is it a satisfactory index of all of one's behavior.

Second, a test is based on a sample of all of the responses that go to make up the particular portion of behavior under consideration. A test of mechanical ability is made up of a number of items which are samples of all of the kinds of responses that go to make up mechanical ability. This is true of any kind of testing. If one wished to determine the ash content of coal from a certain mine, he would run a test on a sample of the coal from this mine, not wait until all the coal has been mined and burned.

Third, a test provides us with a cross-section picture of the behavior which it measures, a picture of behavior at the moment of testing. This picture is in contrast to a longitudinal picture, which can be obtained only from a complete record of every act (of the sort under consideration) of the individual, or which might be approximated by means of a case-history record or a succession of cross-section pictures. Any kind of behavior which we attempt to measure by means of tests has had a developmental history, a beginning and a period of development. A view of this behavior from its beginning to the present is a longitudinal view. A test, however, provides a picture of the behavior only at a particular stage in its development.

These facts are part of the background of information that a trained mental examiner or psychometrist brings to bear upon the problem of administering and interpreting psychological tests. The examiner knows that the behavior measured is part of a dynamic whole, that the cross-section picture represented by a test score is what it is because the behavior in question has had a developmental history, that many factors have contributed to its development, and that its true significance is to be found in its relation to these factors and to other portions of the individual's total behavior.

In addition to these general facts, one must have in mind a number of more specific facts properly to evaluate and interpret the results of psychological tests. First, one must know the test which is being used. He must know what the test measures, the evidence in favor of its measuring what it claims to measure, how it was constructed, its reliability, and what purposes it is supposed to serve. Here it is extremely important to go beyond the title of the test itself to see what the test actually measures and what it is good for.

Second, one must know on what group the test was standardized. When an individual is tested, his raw score is compared with the scores of some standard group of individuals. The scores of the group are so scaled as to represent a sort of human measuring stick. The measure of the individual is a statement, in numerical terms, of the individual's position in the group. It is adequate just so far as one obtains an accurate description of the group as well as an accurate record of the individual's performance on the test itself.

Third, one must know to what extent an individual's performance on a test is determined by other aspects of his total behavior. Rust (32) has shown how the performance of children on intelligence tests may be affected by negativism; 58 per cent of the items initially refused were answered correctly when presented to the children again within a few days.

Fourth, one must know what developmental factors have conspired to make the test performance what it is. Two twelve-year-old children are given the Stanford-Binet intelligence test. Each earns an I.Q. of 80. A case history reveals that one child lives with his grandmother in the slums. His father is dead and his mother works in another city. He has attended school irregularly and can scarcely read. The other child's father is a physician. The child has had the very best educational opportunities, including tutoring during three summers. It is clear, in the light of these facts, that the I.Q.'s of the two children do not mean the same thing. The prognosis for the first child is much better than for the second because we can see possibilities in his case that are not apparent in the other.

A problem which arises frequently in vocational and educational guidance and in industrial selection and placement is the over-all evaluation of an individual's behavior or of some relatively large portion of it. The problem has been met by the use of test batteries, groups of tests which together provide a picture of the individual's behavior which appears to be the key to his success. This practice is illustrated in the psychological testing in the Army Air Forces, where test batteries were used in testing air-crew men (see p. 437).

In using test batteries we try to obtain a single unified picture of an individual from a group of tests each of which measures a limited portion of the total behavior pattern and each of which overlaps the others in varying degrees. It is true that the scores of the several tests may be combined by statistical procedures to yield an over-all prediction of success or failure in some specific life situations, as was done in the Army Air Forces; but the picture of how the parts work together, the pattern of behavior represented by the several scores, is likely to be lost in the process. Several different patterns may yield essentially the same over-all statistical result. For example, suppose that individual A earns scores of 40, 50, and 60 on three different tests, while individual B earns scores of 60, 40, and 20 on these tests. A statistical analysis reveals that these tests should be weighted 3, 2, and 1 respectively for predicting the individual's success in college. The combined score of individual A and individual B is the same, yet the patterns of behavior represented by the three tests are quite different. Some device is needed for bringing the several scores together in such a way as to reveal the pattern or profile of the behavior represented by the several scores, and in such a way that each score can be seen and interpreted in relation to all of the others.

The *psychological profile* or *psychograph* is just such a device. It consists of a list of behavior traits (or names of psychological tests) each of which is accompanied by a scale on which an individual's rating is represented. The traits may be listed along the vertical axis of the graph, with a horizontal scale after each, as in Figure 81; or the traits may be listed along the horizontal axis, with a vertical scale. In the former case the horizontal line for each trait represents the percentile scores, or other derived scores, of some standard group of individuals. Ideally the same group should be used as a standard for each trait. Under no circumstances should the scales represent the scores of different groups unless it is known that the groups are equivalent. Such a practice would give an individual a very distorted picture of himself. For example, suppose that John Doe's percentile position in his freshman class in college on three tests is 52, 37, and 81. In each case he is being compared with college freshmen. But suppose that on the first test we compare him with college freshmen, where he receives a percentile score of 52, and on the second we compare him with a sample of men from the general population. In this group he has a percentile score of 76 instead of 37. On the third test we compare him with still a third group, and here his percentile score is 69 instead of 81. Since the standard of measurement in psychology is the behavior of a selected group of individuals, it is clear that the same group or equivalent groups should be used throughout in comparing an individual's performance on one test with his performance on another, or in combining scores on several tests to obtain a profile.

A psychograph of John Doe is shown in Figure 81. The raw score and percentile score on each test are listed after the name of the test. In constructing this psychograph, the percentile score for each trait was plotted on the horizontal scale at the right of the trait. The plotted points were then connected by straight lines to form the profile. This psychograph gives us a picture of John Doe that does not show up in

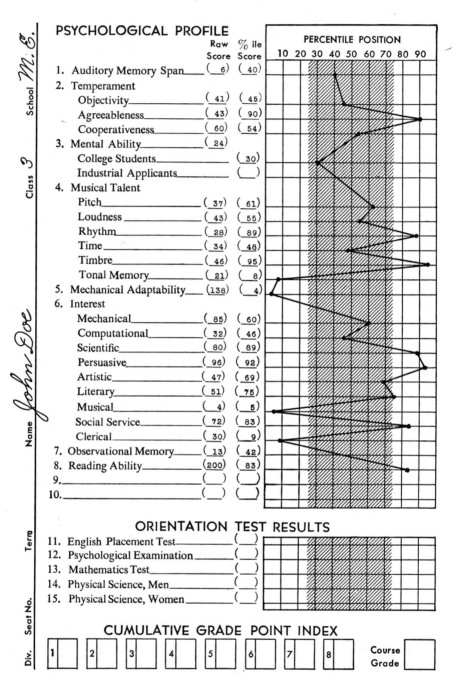

PSYCHOLOGICAL PROFILE

School _M. E._ Class _3_ Name _John Doe_ Term Seat No. Div.

	Raw Score	% ile Score
1. Auditory Memory Span	(6)	(40)
2. Temperament		
Objectivity	(41)	(45)
Agreeableness	(43)	(90)
Cooperativeness	(60)	(54)
3. Mental Ability	(24)	
College Students		(30)
Industrial Applicants		( )
4. Musical Talent		
Pitch	(37)	(61)
Loudness	(43)	(55)
Rhythm	(28)	(89)
Time	(34)	(48)
Timbre	(46)	(95)
Tonal Memory	(21)	(8)
5. Mechanical Adaptability	(138)	(4)
6. Interest		
Mechanical	(85)	(60)
Computational	(32)	(46)
Scientific	(80)	(89)
Persuasive	(96)	(92)
Artistic	(47)	(69)
Literary	(51)	(75)
Musical	(4)	(5)
Social Service	(72)	(83)
Clerical	(30)	(9)
7. Observational Memory	(13)	(42)
8. Reading Ability	(200)	(83)
9.	( )	( )
10.	( )	( )

PERCENTILE POSITION

10 20 30 40 50 60 70 80 90

ORIENTATION TEST RESULTS

11. English Placement Test	( )
12. Psychological Examination	( )
13. Mathematics Test	( )
14. Physical Science, Men	( )
15. Physical Science, Women	( )

CUMULATIVE GRADE POINT INDEX

1	2	3	4	5	6	7	8	Course Grade

Figure 81

Scores in Several Psychological Tests Given to One Person,
Plotted to Show His Psychological Profile

450

the test scores themselves. It is easy to see his relative strengths and weaknesses not only by noting the high and low points in the profile, but by noting the position of the profile with reference to the 50 percentile line, which represents the averages of the standard group, or with reference to the shaded portion of the graph, which represents the middle 50 per cent of the standard group.

SUMMARY

Various tests have been devised for measuring specific abilities and aptitudes. Tests which measure knowledge of school subjects are called achievement tests. Trade tests measure knowledge of some specific job or trade. Such special ability tests as tests of motor ability, mechanical ability, clerical ability, and musical ability measure the knowledge and skills involved in the rather restricted areas represented by the titles of the tests. Motor abilities include the simpler motor processes of steadiness, strength, speed, and accuracy, and the more complex skills involved in finger and hand dexterity.

An aptitude test measures an individual's ability to acquire with training some specified knowledge or skill. The ability measured is some present condition of the individual which is symptomatic of some future condition. Any ability test is an aptitude test to the extent that the ability measured by it is indicative of ability to acquire additional skill and knowledge of a specified kind. Aptitude tests have been developed for law, engineering, dentistry, music, art, science, aeronautics, nursing, and other fields of endeavor.

The interpretation of test results requires a knowledge of the tests used, of the groups used in standardizing the tests, of the relation between the test performances and other kinds of behavior and between the test performances and such developmental factors as family background and educational opportunities. The test performances of an individual may be plotted on a psychograph as an aid in understanding the interrelation of the various performances, and as a means of evaluating a relatively large portion of an individual's total behavior.

QUESTIONS
on the Chapter

1. What is an achievement test? A trade test?
2. What is the difference between an achievement test and a special ability test?

3. Are differences in reading ability due to differences in intelligence?
4. List some causes of reading disability.
5. What is the difference between the eye movements of good and poor readers?
6. Do the rate and quality of handwriting develop together? Explain.
7. Describe the instruments used in measuring speed of movement, steadiness, accuracy, and strength.
8. How is finger dexterity measured?
9. What is the difference between mechanical ability tests of the paper-and-pencil type and the assembly type?
10. What are the five major elements of musical talent according to Seashore?
11. What is measured by the Seashore Test of Musical Talent?
12. What is the relation between mechanical ability and intelligence?
13. What is an aptitude test? How does it differ from a special ability test?
14. For what purposes may ability tests be used?
15. List as many different kinds of aptitude tests as you can.
16. What general factors should be considered in interpreting a test score?
17. What specific facts are needed for interpreting a test score?
18. What is a psychograph?

for Discussion

1. Defend the notion that all special ability tests are in reality achievement tests.
2. Are aptitudes learned?
3. Should an individual who makes low scores on the Seashore Test of Musical Talent be given musical training?
4. What does a psychograph tell about an individual that cannot be determined from test scores themselves?
5. Does the correlation between reading rate and reading comprehension mean that slow readers will comprehend better if they are forced to read faster?
6. Can one obtain a longitudinal picture of an individual by the use of tests?

REFERENCES

1 ALLEN, RICHARD, and others, *Metropolitan Achievement Tests, Advanced Battery.* New York: World Book Company, 1933.
2 ANDERSON, I. H., "Studies in the Eye-Movements of Good and Poor Readers," *Psychol. Monogr.*, 1937, 68, 1–35.
3 ANDREW, DOROTHY M., *Minnesota Vocational Test for Clerical Workers.* New York: Psychological Corporation, 1933.
4 BENNETT, GEORGE K., *Test of Mechanical Comprehension, Form AA.* Psychological Corporation, New York, 1940.
5 BETTS, E. A., "A Psychological Approach to the Analysis of Reading Dis-

abilities," *Educ. Research Bull.*, Ohio State University, 1934, 13, Parts 6 and 7. The apparatus described in this article is distributed by the Keystone View Company.

6 BLACKSTONE, E. G., and MCLOUGHLIN, MARY W., *Blackstone Stenographic Proficiency Tests.* New York: World Book Company, 1931.

7 BUSWELL, G. T., *Fundamental Reading Habits: A Study of Their Development.* Chicago: University of Chicago Press, 1922.

8 CONOVER, D. M., *Some Relationships Obtaining between the Army General Classification Test and the Mechanical Aptitude Test and Other Variables.* M.S. thesis, Purdue University, 1944.

9 *Detroit Mechanical Aptitudes Examination for Boys.* Bloomington: Public School Publishing Company, 1928.

10 FAIRBANKS, GRANT, "The Relation between Eye-Movements and Voice in the Oral Reading of Good and Poor Silent Readers," *Psychol. Monogr.*, 1937, 68, 78–108.

11 FLANAGAN, JOHN C., "Personnel Research in the AAF," *Public Personnel Review*, 1945, 6, 33–40.

12 GATES, ARTHUR I., *The Improvement of Reading.* New York: The Macmillan Company, 1935, p. 372.

13 HINES, MILDRED, and O'CONNOR, JOHNSON, "A Measure of Finger Dexterity," *Personnel Journal*, 1926, 4, 379–382.

14 HULL, CLARK L., "Variability in Amount of Different Traits Possessed by the Individual," *J. Educ. Psychol.*, 1927, 18, 97–106.

15 KELLEY, T. L., et al., *The New Stanford Achievement Tests.* New York: World Book Company, 1929.

16 KWALWASSER, J., *Tests and Measurements in Music.* New York: C. C. Birchard and Company, 1927.

17 KWALWASSER, J., *Kwalwasser-Dykema Music Tests.* Carl Fisher, 1930.

18 KWALWASSER, J., and RUCH, G. M., *Tests of Musical Accomplishment.* Iowa City: Extension Division, State University of Iowa, 1924.

19 LAWSHE, C. H., *Can You Read a Micrometer?* Chicago: Science Research Associates, 1943.

20 LAWSHE, C. H., and TIFFIN, JOSEPH, *Purdue Mechanical Adaptability Test.* Technical Extension Division, Purdue University, 1945.

21 LAWSHE, C. H., TIFFIN, JOSEPH, and MOORE, H., *Purdue Clerical Adaptability Test*, Purdue Research Foundation, Purdue University.

22 MEIER, N. C., *The Meier Art Tests. I. Art Judgment: Examiners Manual.* Iowa City: Bureau of Educational Research, University of Iowa, 1942.

23 MEIER, N. C., and SEASHORE, C. E., *The Meier-Seashore Art Judgment Test, Examiners Manual.* Iowa City: Bureau of Education Research and Service, University of Iowa, 1930.

24 MOSS, F. A., "Report of the Committee on Aptitude Tests for Medical Schools," *J. of the Assoc. of Medical Colleges*, 1935, 10.

25 MOSS, F. A., "Report of the Committee on Aptitude Tests for Medical Schools," *J. of the Assoc. of Medical Colleges*, 1942, 17, 312–315.

26 O'ROURKE, L. J., *O'Rourke Mechanical Aptitude Test.* The Psychological Institute, 1937.

27 PATERSON, D. G., ELLIOTT, R. M., ANDERSON, L. D., TOPPS, H. A., and HEID-

BREDER, E., *Minnesota Mechanical Ability Tests.* Minneapolis: University of Minnesota Press, 1930.

28 PRATT, C. C., *The Meaning of Music.* New York: McGraw-Hill Book Company, 1931.

29 PURDUE RESEARCH FOUNDATION, *Purdue Pegboard.* Chicago: Science Research Associates, 1943.

30 PYLE, W. H., *A Manual for the Mental and Physical Examination of School Children.* University of Missouri Bulletin, 1920.

31 ROBINSON, F. P., "The Role of Eye-Movement in Reading, with an Evaluation of Techniques for Their Improvement," *University of Iowa Series on Research,* 1933, No. 39.

32 RUST, M. M., *The Effect of Resistance on Intelligence Test Scores of Young Children.* New York: Teachers College, Columbia University, 1931 (Child Development Monographs).

33 SCHEIDEMANN, NORMA V., *The Psychology of Exceptional Children.* New York: Houghton Mifflin Company, 1931.

34 SEASHORE, CARL E., *The Psychology of Musical Talent.* New York: Silver, Burdett and Company, 1919.

35 SEASHORE, CARL E., LEWIS, D., and SAETVEIT, J. G., *Measures of Musical Talents.* Camden: R.C.A. Manufacturing Company, 1939.

36 STEAD, W. H., SHARTLE, C. L., and associates, *Occupational Counseling Techniques.* New York: American Book Company, 1940.

37 STENQUIST, J. L., *Stenquist Mechanical Assembly Tests of General Mechanical Ability, Manual.* Chicago: C. H. Stoelting Company.

38 STENQUIST, J. L., "The Case of the Low I.Q.," *J. Educ. Research,* 1923, 4, 241–254.

39 STENQUIST, J. L., *Mechanical Aptitude Test.* New York: World Book Company, 1921.

40 STROMBERG, E. L., "Binocular Movements of the Eyes in Reading," *J. Gener. Psychol.,* 1938, 18, 349–355.

41 STUTSMAN, RACHEL, *Mental Measurement of Pre-School Children.* New York: World Book Company, 1931.

42 TIFFIN, JOSEPH, *Industrial Psychology,* 3rd edition. New York: Prentice-Hall, 1952.

43 TIFFIN, JOSEPH, editor, *Purdue Vocational Tests.* Chicago: Science Research Associates, 1940.

44 TIFFIN, JOSEPH, and GREENLY, R. J., "Experiments in the Operation of a Punch Press," *J. Appl. Psychol.,* 1939, 23, 450–460.

45 WALKER, ROBERT Y., "The Eye-Movements of Good Readers," *Psychol. Monogr.,* 1933, 64, 95–117.

46 WAR DEPARTMENT, *Technical Manual,* 12–260, Personnel Classification Tests, December 31, 1942.

47 WARREN, H. C., *Dictionary of Psychology.* New York: Houghton Mifflin Company, 1934.

48 WHIPPLE, GUY M., *Manual of Mental and Physical Tests, Part I.* Baltimore: Warwick and York, 1914.

PERSONALITY AND ADJUSTMENT

14

PERSONALITY — *How a Person Appears to others*

If you were called upon to describe a person whom you have known for some time and with whom you are very well acquainted, you would probably tell what you know about his family background, his education and experience, his intelligence, his ability and interests, and his special skills and attainments. You would not stop here, however. You would insist on telling what you know about his *personality*. Depending upon what you know about the person, you would find yourself using such words as cheerful, generous, aggressive, honest, realistic, optimistic, hard-boiled, irresponsible, energetic, impulsive, hostile, shy, kind, sociable, talkative, phlegmatic, and pessimistic. We all recognize that these words do not refer to specific responses. Walking and talking are responses, but kindness and shyness are not. Neither is hostility nor aggressiveness. Fighting is a specific response, but impulsiveness is not. When we say that a person is impulsive, we mean that impulsiveness is a characteristic of his general behavior, a characteristic which is manifested in virtually everything he does, whether it be thinking, learning, talking, playing, or working. We say "virtually everything" because one need not be impulsive in everything that he does in order to be characterized as impulsive. He must, however, manifest this characteristic in most situations or with a reasonably high degree of consistency. Such a characteristic is called a *personality trait*.

Definition of Personality

In interacting with his environment over a considerable period of time, an individual manifests many personality traits, each of which is deduced from his total behavior. Each is characteristic of the individual as a whole. These traits are interrelated in such a way that they fuse into a single integrated unit or whole. It is this organization or fusion of personality traits that constitutes one's personality. Personality, therefore, may be defined as the organization of all of the characteristics manifested in one's total behavior, or in one's interactions with his environment. It should be emphasized that personality is concerned with and deduced from all of one's behavior (5). Yet it is not in itself a way of acting. It is the organization of the characteristics which one manifests in all of his activities. Being an organization of traits, it is only partially characterized by naming the traits. It is not enough to know that one is impulsive and generous and self-reliant and hostile and energetic. One must know how these traits (assuming that each trait name represents a separate trait) are interrelated and integrated into an organized unit.

Distribution of personality traits. Each personality trait exists in varying degrees from a low amount of the trait to a high amount. One individual may manifest a high degree of a trait, another a low degree, and still another an average amount. The probable distribution of trait scores (cheerfulness, for example) for a large random sample of the population is shown in Figure 82. This distribution of scores is continuous from small amounts of the trait to high amounts. Most people cluster around the average, very few being extremely high or extremely low. Since many personality traits come in pairs of opposites, such as submissive-aggressive, reliable-unreliable, and cheerful-gloomy, it is customary to place one of the pair at one end of a continuous scale, such as the base line of the graph in Figure 82, and the other one of the pair at the other end. With aggressiveness at one extreme of the distribution in Figure 82, and submissiveness at the other extreme, it can be seen that very few people are extremely aggressive or extremely submissive, and that most people, being between the two extremes, are about equally aggressive and submissive.

In this connection it should be noted that people in general commonly think of everybody as being either submissive or aggressive, reliable or unreliable, stingy or generous. They do not recognize that an individual may be both generous and stingy in many degrees from one extreme to the other, or that the population distributes itself in the manner shown in Figure 82 with respect to this pair of traits. This incorrect view of the distribution of the population with respect to pairs of personality traits, degrees of intelligence, or physical traits is shown in Figure 83.

Trait names. In considering the problem of personality organization it is important to recognize that each separate trait name does not represent a separate personality trait. A trait may be partially described by each of several words. To put it another way, several words may

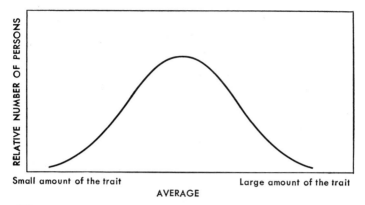

Small amount of the trait   Large amount of the trait

AVERAGE

Figure 82

Showing the Distribution of a Psychological Trait among
a Large Group of People

Many are mediocre — few very high or very low.

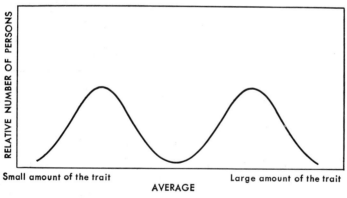

Small amount of the trait   Large amount of the trait

AVERAGE

Figure 83

Showing the Distribution We Assume (Incorrectly) When We Classify
Persons as "Stupid" or "Smart," "Blonde" or "Brunette,"
"Generous" or "Stingy"

be used to refer to a single trait. For example, the words *impetuous, excitable, impulsive, fiery,* and *hasty* all refer to essentially the same characteristic. Some idea of the duplication and overlap in trait names can be obtained from the fact that Cattell (5) in his research work on personality organization was able to reduce a list of 4,500 personality trait names to about 160 to form a "kind of basic English for the description of personality." This does not mean that there are 160 personality traits. It means only that this very long list of trait names can be reduced to approximately 160 groups or clusters that appear to refer to different characteristics. Whether they do or not is a matter to be determined by experimental studies of personality organization. There is still another problem related to the use of trait names. A trait name may actually refer to a segment of one's personality which includes two or more separate traits. For example, it appears that the pair of opposite trait names, introversion-extroversion, instead of representing a single dimension or trait of personality, actually includes several independent traits (5, 14).

The interrelation of traits. The procedure used in recent studies of personality organization involves the measurement of traits or facets of personality, the correlation of these measurements, and an analysis of the intercorrelations by a statistical technique known as factor analysis. The purpose of these studies has been to discover how personality traits are interrelated, and then to see whether or not these interrelations are due to the existence of a relatively small number of basic or primary personality factors. The first step in this procedure is to measure as many separate traits or segments of personality as possible in a large group of individuals. This is done by the use of one or another of the methods of measuring personality to be described later in this chapter. The scores on each trait are correlated with the scores on each of the other traits. This yields a group of intercorrelations. These correlation coefficients are then subjected to a statistical analysis, the purpose of which is to discover the factors which are responsible for the interrelations represented by the coefficients. A factor is the thing which a number of measured traits or segments of personality have in common. In an extensive investigation of personality organization, Cattell (5) has obtained evidence of the existence of twelve primary personality factors. These factors are listed below. The factors are arranged in order of their importance and are designated simply as factors A, B, C, etc. The titles for these factors are given in terms of pairs of opposites. Some of the common trait names associated with each factor are listed in the parentheses after the factor titles.

A   CYCLOTHYMIA *versus* SCHIZOTHYMIA (easygoing, genial adaptability, trustfulness *versus* inflexibility, coldness, suspicion)

B   INTELLIGENCE, GENERAL MENTAL CAPACITY *versus* MENTAL DEFECT (intelligent, thoughtful, wise *versus* stupid, unreflective, silly)

C   EMOTIONALLY MATURE, STABLE CHARACTER *versus* DEMORALIZED, GENERAL EMOTIONALITY (emotional stability, steadfastness, perseverance *versus* emotional changeability, evasiveness)

D   HYPERSENSITIVE, INFANTILE, STHENIC EMOTIONALITY *versus* PHLEGMATIC FRUSTRATION TOLERANCE (excitability, unrestrained emotionality *versus* emotionally stable, tolerant, phlegmatic)

E   DOMINANCE *versus* SUBMISSIVENESS (ascendant, adventurous, self-assertive *versus* submissive, mild, meek, self-effacing)

F   SURGENCY *versus* AGITATED, MELANCHOLIC DESURGENCY (placid, unemotional, realistic cheerfulness *versus* sorrowful, pessimistic depression)

G   POSITIVE CHARACTER INTEGRATION *versus* IMMATURE, DEPENDENT CHARACTER (mature, strong-willed, facing life *versus* dependent, demoralized, infantile)

H   CHARITABLE, ADVENTUROUS CYCLOTHYMIA *versus* OBSTRUCTIVE, WITHDRAWN SCHIZOTHYMIA (adventurous, carefree, kind *versus* inhibited, fearful, withdrawn)

I   SENSITIVE, IMAGINATIVE, ANXIOUS EMOTIONALITY *versus* RIGID, TOUGH, POISE (tenderhearted, sympathetic emotionality *versus* hard-boiled, mature, unemotional)

J   NEURASTHENIA *versus* VIGOROUS "OBSESSIONAL DETERMINED" CHARACTER (indolent, retiring, languid *versus* nervous vigor, energy, perseverance)

K   TRAINED, SOCIALIZED, CULTURED MIND *versus* BOORISHNESS

L   SURGENT CYCLOTHYMIA *versus* PARANOIA (friendly, trustful, adaptable *versus* suspicious, withdrawn, hostile, rigid)

It should be noted that this approach to the study of personality has not yielded unequivocal results. Other investigators (8, 12, 13), using different methods of measuring personality traits in different populations, have obtained somewhat different or very different sets of personality factors. Subsequent investigations designed to explain these differences may be expected to further our understanding of personality and its organization. In the meantime a list of primary traits such as Cattell's may be regarded as descriptive of the measurements and analyses which he has made and illustrative of the results obtained in factor studies of personality.

JUDGING AND MEASURING PERSONALITY

The problem of judging or measuring personality is not a new one. Man has been interested in this problem for thousands of years. As might be expected, he has used a wide variety of methods and techniques in judging personality and in making decisions about other men and women. In most of the early methods, judgments of personality were based upon horoscopes, bumps on the head, physical characteristics, shape and size of the hand, and characteristics of handwriting. These methods are commonly called pseudoscientific methods because at one time or another it was claimed that they were scientific when they were not. None of them makes any pretense of observing or measuring man's behavior, in spite of the fact that personality is concerned with and deduced from man's total behavior. Other methods of judging personality are based upon such indirect appraisals of behavior as can be obtained in letters of recommendation, personal interviews, letters of application, and reports of associates. These methods may be designated as common-sense methods. While they are widely used and may be useful in judging personality, they lay no claim to being scientific. Scientific methods of measuring personality are based upon behavior ratings, questionnaires, clinical observations, and tests, all of which attempt to obtain direct, first-hand information about adequate samples of an individual's total behavior. Let us examine each of these groups of methods.

Pseudoscientific Methods of Judging Personality

Astrology. According to the ancient "science of astrology," to be born under a certain star indicates health; under another, cheerfulness; under another, masterfulness; and under another, cowardice. The reading of horoscopes by astrologers has fascinated not only the giddy, but at times the serious-minded. The position of the stars is supposed to indicate both one's personality traits and also one's future. This so-called "science" was based originally on the belief that gods, inhabiting the planets and the stars, exercise an influence upon human affairs. At first, efforts were made to foretell the fate of large groups or of empires. Since the fate of a nation depended then, as it still often does, to a great extent on the personality of its ruler, special efforts were made to tell his character and predict his fortune. Later, perhaps partly as a result of a deep yearning in the masses to know their future, and partly as a result of the desire of astrologers to acquire easy money, fortune telling from the stars became widespread. Today one need not listen long to radio programs to realize that astrology is still an easy method of extracting money from the superstitious.   Needless to say, the predictions of astrologers have nothing but a guess and a hope behind them.   The best use which we, as psychologists, can make of astrology is to see in it an impressive illustration of the fact that man's wishes may seriously distort his judgment.

Phrenology.   When the motor and sensory areas of the brain were discovered, it occurred to some that an examination of the shape of the skull would reveal the shape of the brain and, consequently, the character traits of the person.   Without pausing to test this hypothesis, they claimed that well-developed bumps above the ears indicated destructiveness, that bumps a little farther back indicated combativeness, and that

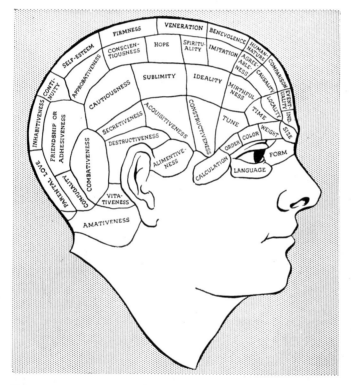

Figure 84

The Measurement of Personality According to the Phrenologist

The bumps on your head have different meanings for different locations, according to this pseudoscience. Compare Figure 85, which shows what is really known of localization in the brain. There is no basis for the phrenologist's scheme.

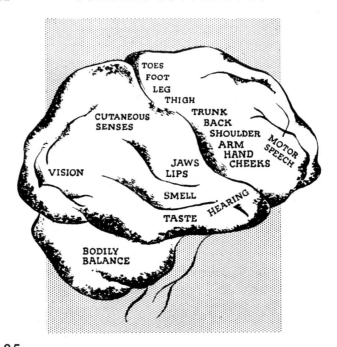

Figure 85

The Actual Locations of Functions in the Brain

Notice that locations have to do with movement of different parts of the body and with the senses — not with personality traits such as hope or cautiousness.

bumps in various other locations had different meanings. Figure 84 shows the departmentalized head which they conceived. In all, some thirty-five or more "organs of the brain" were thought to have corresponding bumps, and it was believed that the degree of development attained by the bumps indicated the strength of definite character traits. These claims were embodied in the scientific language of the day and were called the "science of phrenology." The *actual* location of functions in the brain is shown in Figure 85. The arrangement is much less spectacular than the claims of the phrenologist and it is not revealed by bumps on the head.

As frequently happens with those who propose a new theory, phrenologists disregarded negative cases — that is, instances of bumps which, by their system, should have indicated a certain trait, but failed to do so. An examination of the anatomy of the head and brain, which could readily have been made, would have shown that the outer shape of the skull does not correspond to the surface of the brain.

Moreover, a serious effort on their part to learn the basis of such personality traits as kindliness, ambition, and jealousy would have shown that these traits depend too much upon training and experience to be determined by some bump on the head which cannot change. Such traits are outgrowths of present and past psychological situations. No single cause can be held responsible for them.   Assume some conceivable single cause, such as a physical defect or home training, and you will find so many negative instances that the assumption is rendered untenable.   Much less can we relate these traits to such superficial things as bumps on the head.   Within the variations in head formations found among normal people there have been no adequate demonstrations of the validity of phrenology.   It is not taken seriously by any competent student of human nature.   One would be hard pressed to find a better example of a psychological "gold brick" than this pseudo-science.

Physiognomy.   The belief that character is revealed in the face is persistent and widespread.   The following paragraph from Blackford and Newcomb (3, pp. 154–157) is an extreme instance:

> The significance of the pure convex type [of face] is energy, both mental and physical.   Superabundance of energy makes the extreme convex keen, alert, quick, eager, aggressive, impatient, positive, and penetrating. . . . The tendencies indicated by his convex mouth will cause him to speak frankly and at times even sharply and fiercely without much regard for tact or diplomacy. . . .   The pure concave, as might be expected, is the exact opposite, so far as the indications of form are concerned, of the pure convex.   The keynote of his character is *mildness*. . . .   He is slow of thought, slow of action, patient in disposition, plodding. . . . The convex is also, in the majority of cases, a blonde.   The combination of hopeful, optimistic, restless, organizing, creating, domineering characteristics of the blonde with the quick, alert, practical, aggressive qualities of the convex make this type distinctly the type of action. . . .

In the paragraph quoted, considerable importance is attached to complexion.   In general, blondes are supposed to be more active, energetic, and aggressive than brunettes.   When, however, Paterson and Ludgate (34) asked 187 people to rate their brunette and blonde friends on these and many other traits, no significant differences were found.   The physiognomist, confronted with such facts, might acknowledge that complexion alone does not enable us to judge personality, but still insist that the character of the face as a whole reveals a great deal.   If this were true, judgments of personality based on photographs should have some value.   However, when such judgments are compared with the pooled judgments of intimate associates, they are found to correlate very poorly, though exceptions must be made for judgments of beauty, intelligence, and snobbishness (20). It might be thought that judgments based on inspection of an actual person would be more reliable than judgments based on photographs. However, there is no significant difference. Table XXII, which sets forth the findings of Cleeton and Knight (6), indicates that little can be inferred regarding personality merely from an opportunity to see a person, even when the judges, as in this case, are experienced businessmen, school principals, and employment managers.

Table XXII

Correlation Existing between the Ratings of 20 Close Associates
and the Ratings of 70 Casual Observers (6)

TRAIT	CORRELATION	TRAIT	CORRELATION
Judgment	.32	Ability to make friends	.18
Intelligence	.02	Leadership	.31
Frankness	.21	Originality	.32
Will power	.26	Impulsiveness	.20

An "expert physiognomist," confronted with the diversity of individual judgments based on photographs and on actual observation of the person to be judged, would no doubt retort that physiognomy is a science that must be mastered through long study; that we should not expect untrained persons to make accurate judgments. In that case physiognomists ought to be willing to demonstrate their ability themselves. Yet they do not seem willing to do so. Hull asked a leading physiognomist to judge a group of girls on the basis of their photographs. (The girls had already been judged by their sorority sisters.) Though the physiognomist was assured that if he failed his name would be kept secret, he refused to cooperate in the experiment. As Hull (20) points out, this is typical of physiognomists in general. They will not venture to test their ability. Under such conditions we must be skeptical of their claims.

This attitude of skepticism is further confirmed by examining the claims of physiognomists regarding the relation between profile and personality traits. In order to test the validity of the claims of Blackford and Newcomb quoted above, Evans (7), working under Hull, asked twenty-five members of a sorority to rank one another (no one ranked herself) in respect to a number of characteristics. When this had been done, the judgments of thirteen of the judges were compared with those of the remaining twelve. The high correlations between the ratings by the groups show that this method of rating personality traits gives consistent results from one group of raters to another. These correlations are shown in Table XXIII. They are highest for ambition and domination, and lowest for popularity. This means that a person judged ambitious or dominating by a few close acquaintances will be judged ambitious or dominating by nearly everyone who knows him, but that a person may quite probably be judged popular by some acquaintances and unpopular by others. Ambition and domination are more *consistent* traits than popularity.

Table XXIII

Correlation between the Pooled Judgments of the Group of 12 Raters and the Group of 13 Raters for the Various Traits (7)

TRAIT	CORRELATION	TRAIT	CORRELATION
Optimism	.75	Domination	.87
Activity	.80	Popularity	.44
Ambition	.90	Blondeness	.93
Will power	.82		

Turning now to the relationships between these personality ratings and the degree of convexity of the profile, we find the correlations shown in Table XXIV. The only correlations that are far enough from zero to indicate any possibility of significant relationship are those, in the fourth row, showing the relation between the chosen traits and the convexity of the part of the face between the chin and eyebrows, not including the nose. Even these correlations are by no means high enough to afford proof of anything.

Other investigations of physiognomy, several of which were directed and reported by Hull, show in general that, while there may be a small degree of relationship between personality traits and physiognomy, the relationships are slight, often doubtful, and of little practical importance.

Physique. Regarding general physique it has been found that there is a small but reliable positive relation between size and intelligence. The large well-developed person is on the average slightly more intelligent than the small one. The physique of a person, however, seems to throw more light on his emotional nature or temperament

Table XXIV

Correlation between Various Physiognomic Traits and a Number
of Character Traits (20)

PHYSIOGNOMIC TRAITS	CHARACTER TRAITS ★					
	Optimism	Activity	Ambition	Will power	Domi- nation	Popu- larity
Convexity, whole face with nose	+.10	−.05	−.17	−.13	−.11	−.03
Convexity, chin to eye-brow, with nose	+.13	+.01	−.13	+.13	−.08	−.11
Convexity, whole face without nose	+.02	−.24	−.17	−.11	−.13	−.27
Convexity, chin to eye-brow, without nose	+.37	+.39	+.33	+.34	+.24	+.17
Convexity of upper face, with nose	−.06	−.08	+.04	+.06	+.08	−.17
Height of forehead from eyebrow to hairline	−.17	−.29	−.23	−.39	−.22	−.10
Blondeness	−.26	−.02	+.05	+.28	+.14	+.03

than on his intelligence. Kretschmer (27) found that certain body types are associated with certain personality traits. He reports that there are three physical types: the short-round, the thin-long, and an intermediate type. The first he calls the pyknic type; the second, the asthenic; and the third, the athletic. The pyknic individual, he claims, tends to be an extrovert. When a person of the pyknic type becomes mentally ill, he is likely to develop manic-depressive insanity (characterized by alternating periods of intense excitement and depression). The asthenic individual is introverted and differs sharply from the pyknic. He lives within himself and is a poor mixer. Instead of experiencing the emotions of those around him he remains a spectator. If he becomes mentally ill, he often develops schizophrenia (characterized by extreme indifference to all that goes on around him). The athletic type tends toward the personality traits of the asthenic.

Supported as these conclusions are by years of clinical experience, they have attracted much attention and have been the subject of several careful investigations. Most of these studies have dealt with patients in mental hospitals. One study, made by Wertheimer and Hesketh (41), determined the average morphological index of 11 manic-depressive cases and 23 schizophrenes. (The morphological index is a convenient way of quantifying "body-build." It is the ratio between length of the limbs and volume of the trunk. A tall, thin person would accordingly have a high morphological index and a short, fat one a low index.) Wertheimer found the manic-depressives to have an average morphological index of 233, while the corresponding index for the schizophrenes was 281. These findings tend to support the theory advanced by Kretschmer. Another study has been made by Shaw (36) with similar results. He found that all patients with a morphological index between 250 and 340 were manic-depressives, whereas all having an index above 680 were schizophrenes.

In a recent study, Fay and Middleton (10) had an audience judge the physical build of nine speakers heard over a public address system according to Kretschmer's three physical types. The judges scored 20 per cent, 22 per cent, and 1 per cent above chance in identifying the men of asthenic, pyknic, and athletic build respectively. There were three men of each type.

A new approach to the study of physique and its relation to human behavior has been made by Sheldon, Stevens, and Tucker (37). In the first of two volumes these authors present a three-dimensional system for the description of human physique. Three components of bodily constitution are identified as endomorphy, mesomorphy, and ecto-morphy. The endomorph shows a predominance of soft roundness throughout the various regions of the body. The mesomorph is heavy, hard, and rectangular, showing a predominance of muscles, bone, and connective tissue. The ectomorph is linear and fragile, having in proportion to body mass the greatest sensory exposure to the outside world. Each of these components is rated on a seven-point scale according to the degree of the component involved, a rating of 1 indicating the lowest degree of the component. Thus a "7–1–1" physique shows an extreme amount of endomorphy and a minimum amount of the other two components.

In a second volume Sheldon and Stevens (38) have presented a three-way temperament scale for three temperamental components, viscero-tonia, somatotonia, and cerebrotonia, and point out the relation of these components to the three components of physique. Since the three components of temperament are extreme variations from "average," most people combine in their temperaments various mixtures of the three components. The extreme viscerotonic loves comfort, is greatly interested in food, likes social gatherings, and expresses his feelings easily. The extreme somatotonic is an active, energetic person who behaves aggressively. The extreme cerebrotonic shrinks away from sociality, avoids attracting attention, is inhibited and restrained. A scale for temperament composed of 60 traits, 20 for each of these three primary components, is used for assessing the individual's temperament.

It should be noted, however, that most people cannot be sharply classified at all into such types as the long-thin and the short-round. Very few people belong to these definite types; the great bulk of people fall in between. It is not surprising, therefore, that studies to determine the relation between the physique and temperament of normal people have not yielded clear-cut, positive results (24). Even for pathological cases, physique should, according to Farr (9), be suggestive rather than diagnostic. In this, Paterson (33), whose survey of the studies in this field is the most comprehensive, fully agrees.

Graphology. The claim has been made frequently that handwriting reveals character and personality traits, and there is some evidence that expert graphologists are able to tell something about the personality of a person by studying his writing. For example, Binet (2) gave to several graphologists specimens of the writing of pairs of men, one member of each pair being famous and the other not. The members of each pair were from the same cultural level and had enjoyed the same educational advantages. The graphologists were asked to say which specimens were written by the famous men. This they were able to do in more cases than could be accounted for by chance. Other graphologists have demonstrated their ability to tell with considerable accuracy the sex of a person by his or her handwriting.

Graphologists claim to have a reliable system. However, a careful check of their system by Hull and Montgomery (21) yielded results which were not related to personality ratings. In another study by Super (39) the vocational recommendations of a professional graphologist showed no more than a chance relationship with the personality traits of 24 college students as measured by intelligence, interest, and personality tests. The occupations recommended by the graphologist were quite different from those revealed by an interest inventory. This may mean merely that the graphologists did not describe all the clues which they really use. That they are able to derive from a person's handwriting at least some indication of his neatness and individuality seems, from the experimental evidence, quite possible; and it would not be necessary that they should also be able to describe how they do it so that a novice could get the same results (20). The explanation of the popularity and uncritical acceptance of graphology as a system of personality analysis may lie not so much in anything it reveals as in the fact that graphologists usually provide highly flattering analyses. Do not be afraid to submit your handwriting to a graphologist. The chances are that no serious weakness will be exposed and that such a venture will prove an excellent test of your ability to withstand flattery.

Common-Sense Methods of Judging Personality

The "hunch," or intuition. These words refer to judgments based on vague feelings for which no explicit grounds can be given. The following lines offer a good illustration:

> I do not like thee, Doctor Fell,
> The reason why I can not tell;
> But this alone I know full well,
> I do not like thee, Doctor Fell.

In such judgments it is frankly admitted that definite grounds for the judgment are lacking. If, however, the person making the judgment is pressed, he may say that the man he dislikes "gives him a creepy feeling," that he does not like his expression, that his eyes are shifty, or that he has the bearing and appearance of a man who cannot be trusted. Sometimes we form aversions toward individuals who have certain mannerisms or toward members of certain races and classes. Occasionally these judgments are based on unpleasant experiences, occasionally upon group suggestion, but the inadequate grounds of such judgments always become apparent when an effort is made to justify them. Obviously, the accuracy of "hunches" cannot be much greater than chance. But if a man's hunches have seemed to serve him well, his faith in his own special ability to judge men is often unshakable. No "scientific heresy" disturbs him. He refuses to ask himself the question: How much better might my judgments have been if I had used other methods?

Personal interview. The personal interview is a method, highly prized by common sense, of sizing up the personality of another. It is used especially in the appraisal of applicants for a position. Obviously, face-to-face talks are of some value. After talking with a person, we know more about him than we did before, and probably we have learned whether or not we shall like him, which may be very important. But how well a person conducting an interview can, in this way, pick the person really best suited to a position the reader may infer from the following account of an investigation made by Hollingworth.

Twelve experienced sales managers were asked by Hollingworth (19) to interview fifty-seven applicants for a job as salesman and to rate them in order of merit. The managers were permitted to ask the applicants any question and to assign them to any task they wished. The only requirement was that they rate the applicants in terms of their probable success as salesmen. The lack of agreement among the managers was enlightening. One applicant was rated one by one judge, fifty-seven by another, two by another, and fifty-three by another; in general, the applicant was given positions all along the scale. His case was by no means exceptional. Only occasionally did the judges agree in their estimates of a man. In some instances there was a decided tendency to rate certain applicants low and others high, but even here there was a wide diversity of ratings.

Two questions of interest are suggested by Hollingworth's study. In the first place, if personal interviews lead to no more reliable results than this investigation indicates, why do employers attach such importance to them? In the second place, what can be done to increase the value of personal interviews?

The answer to the first question is probably found in the fact that employers have no adequate check on their judgments. Each picks the man that he believes to be best, and if the man selected does fairly well, the employer is satisfied, even though he may have rejected a number of men who were better qualified for the work or who would have been, in other ways, more valuable members of his organization. In the absence of a check, a personnel manager may continue to make mistake after mistake and still maintain confidence in his ability to pick the right man. Employers, furthermore, are interested, to a certain extent, in selecting men who are likable and congenial, and these are qualities that can be determined fairly well by an interview. In the matter of congeniality there are obviously individual preferences. One person likes chocolate cake; another does not. One person likes a certain personality ensemble; another does not. The personal interview serves at least to give the employer a chance of learning whether he is likely to find the applicant congenial.

As to how the personal interview can be made more reliable, Hollingworth (19, p. 123) makes the following suggestions: (1) Frame questions so as to require a definite reply, and make a random reply impossible. (2) Establish favorable *rapport*. (3) Distinguish between relevant and irrelevant questions and replies. (4) Keep a careful record of facts obtained, in addition to any inferences drawn therefrom. (5) Use a standardized form of report. (6) Carefully weave together all information gained. (7) Make a clear statement of personal reaction.

To the sound advice given by Hollingworth, two considerations must be added. The personal interview is of limited value because first impressions may be deceiving. During an interview a candidate puts his best foot forward, unless he is so embarrassed that his panic makes it impossible. One must recognize that the relation between being a good candidate and a good performer may vary all the way from zero to one hundred per cent correspondence. Furthermore, we should care little, if at all, about "candidacy performance" in a research chemist, whereas we should care a great deal about the first impression made by a prospective salesman.

A second consideration is that the *interviewer* as well as the *one interviewed* is on parade. If the interviewer is without benefit of psychological insight, he may not realize that his judgments are often connected with his own traits as these are contrasted to those of the candidate. It is well known that interviewers usually find some excuse for turning down men if they find themselves feeling vaguely uncomfortable because they are in the presence of ability superior to their own. The employment manager is working for a living and he might lose his job to someone he employs. The degree to which he is conscious of this ultimate consideration may vary greatly.

Letters of recommendation. The reliability of a personal interview may be further increased by pooling the judgments of several persons. Since it is generally not feasible to have an applicant interviewed by several men, letters of recommendation are frequently resorted to.

The reliability of letters of recommendation depends on the judgment of the persons writing the letters and on their willingness to give accurate reports. Investigation has shown that the opinions of friends regarding one another are none too reliable. For example, twenty-five people well acquainted agreed to rate one another and themselves with respect to a number of traits. The person who stood highest in respect to any trait was to be rated one; the person who was second, two; and so on to the lowest, who was to be rated twenty-five. In regard to some traits the disagreement was approximately as great as chance would have yielded, and even where there was closest agreement there was considerable variation (19, pp. 103 f.).

Similar investigations show that there is greater agreement in judging some traits than others. There is greater agreement, for example, in rating efficiency, quickness, and energy than there is in rating cheerfulness and kindliness (19, p. 105). The reason for this is that the first traits are more objective and depend much less than the others on the social situation. When, however, the persons who do the rating all stand in the same relation to the person rated, as with students and an instructor, there is closer agreement regarding kindliness and cheerfulness than regarding efficiency and energy (19). This indicates that one reason a person may impress different people differently is that with different people he acts differently. Though this is true to some extent, real *split personalities* are not found among normal people. A man who is a lamb at home deceives only himself and other stupid people by making believe he is a lion at the office. Still, it is possible to stress one fraction of one's personality at the office, another at home, and still another at the club; and this brings into clear relief the importance of obtaining letters of recommendation from men who know something about the complexity of human nature and who possess a genuinely judicial temperament. It is given to few men to write letters of recommendation that are worth reading, and many letters of recommendation tell far more about the writer than about the candidate being considered.

Opinions of those who have seen the person to be judged from the same angle can be pooled to secure a counterbalance to personal bias. Pooled ratings attain a high degree of reliability, even though the ratings made by any two individuals may differ greatly. An investigation showing this has been made by McCabe (28). She selected from the forty members of a certain sorority the twenty who were best acquainted with the other girls. Each of the twenty rated all the thirty-nine other members of the sorority with respect to ten traits. The raters were then divided into two groups of ten each and the average of their judgments compared. The correlations ranged from .80 for crudeness to .96 for beauty. The correlation for intelligence was .92. The average correlation for the ten traits considered was .88.

Other investigations also have shown the importance of pooling the judgments of a number of acquaintances. The bearing of this on the use of letters of recommendation is obvious. Friends, in spite of intimate association, form different judgments of each other; and a letter of recommendation written with every effort to be honest may reflect a different impression from another letter written by an equally honest and capable person. Hence in using letters of recommendation, an effort should be made to get several and to pool the judgments expressed. Eight or ten are usually sufficient for ordinary purposes.

There are other reasons why a number of letters should be secured. We cannot be certain that all letters of recommendation are written with the sole purpose of conveying correct information. The writer may be biased for or against the person about whom he is writing. An employer may feel that it would be well for the individual in question to move on and make room for someone more promising. Many an undesirable employee has been "sold" in this way by a good letter of recommendation. These additional sources of error should be considered in evaluating testimonials.

In order to increase the value of letters of recommendation, it has been suggested that printed forms, listing numerous personality traits, be used. The advantage claimed for such forms is that by providing a ready-made list of both good and bad qualities for a person to check, they lessen the chance of the writer's neglecting the weaker traits because of his goodwill toward the person under consideration (32). It should be remembered, however, that no aid, printed or otherwise, will enable a man to write an accurate letter of recommendation if he is careless, ill informed, or seriously biased.

Letters of application. Having the applicant write a letter of application is another common-sense method of judging personality that has much to commend it. Apart from any revelation of personality that may be made by the handwriting and neatness of the letter, something regarding the applicant's command of language, his attitudes, and his judgment can frequently be learned in this way. The inability of many college students to write a convincing letter of application is a severe handicap. The letter of application is the first contact with a possible job and, unfortunately, often the last. It is the applicant's full-page advertisement, his crucial sales talk. Good intentions will not produce good letters. Letter writing is a difficult art, which cannot be acquired over night. The reader can probably well afford to take this hint.

Pitfalls in Judging Personality

The methods of judging personality discussed in the foregoing paragraphs, alluring as they are, possess little if any dependability for the serious student of normal people. But before considering some of the more useful methods of judging personality, we must mention certain pitfalls to be found even here.

Halo effect. The first pitfall is the tendency to think that a person is superior, or inferior, in a number of ways because we know (or think) that he is so in some particular way. This transfer of impressions is known as the *halo effect* (40). To give an example, if we know a person to be kind, we are apt to rate him high in other traits as well, courage and industriousness, perhaps. If a boy is noisy and uninterested in his studies, his teacher will be likely to suspect him of being generally unintelligent and a congenital bully. Such judgments are obviously unwarranted; for though desirable traits do tend to be associated with other desirable ones, and undesirable traits to go together, the correlations are far too low for making specific judgments. A recognition of this fallacy can prevent us from extending a general estimate to particular characteristics, or from turning an accurate estimate of one trait into a false estimate of an unrelated trait. This caution should lead us to seek for definite and positive grounds for any judgment which we may form about an individual.

Long acquaintance with a person is apt to increase for us the halo effect. Thus, transfer of judgments to unrelated traits increases with the length of time that the judge has known the individual whose personality he is analyzing. If we approve, on the whole, of someone, we tend to forgive his weaknesses more and more the longer we know him. On the other hand, if we have found a man dishonest, we underrate his other traits in spite of ourselves. Judgments based upon long acquaintance are almost certain to suffer from a psychological near- or farsightedness. Friends who have worked together for many years lose the ability to judge each other critically. A person may have known another *too long* to be the best judge of him.

Unconscious bias. Our judgments of a man are often greatly reduced in accuracy because of the influence of our unconscious prejudices and biases. It is very difficult to allow for these factors because they *are* unconscious. Thus, just as one may dislike salmon without knowing why, or similarly prefer Baptists to Methodists, or a man from Harvard to a man from Yale, so also our casual estimates of people are affected by unrecognized influences and in unknown degrees. The more expert the judge, the more willing he is to admit the possibility of error. Only the quack or the novice is sure.

An example of this source of error is the tendency to apply to an individual the judgments we have previously formed of his group. For example, we have probably formed a type-judgment of communists; and if we should meet a communist, we should consequently expect him to be "true to type" — to have a certain appearance and to act in certain ways. Such type-judgments are called *stereotypes*. A common experience which reveals the influence of stereotypes is the surprise we experience on discovering that a person from another nation is not at all queer but a likable human being. Forewarned is forearmed. Knowledge of the fact that we tend to crowd individuals into the molds of our preconceptions should put us on our guard against doing so and make us fairer in our judgments of those who belong to groups other than our own.

The error of the pigeonhole. Another pitfall is our tendency to divide people into two groups. We say that a girl is *blonde* or *brunette*,

that she is *tall* or *short*, that she has a *pleasant* or an *unpleasant* personality. We know now from repeated measurements that most people are about average in the various psychological traits — that only the exceptional individual is at one extreme or the other. If a trait is measured in a large number of people and the results are graphed so that the amount of the trait is laid off horizontally and the percentage of persons having each amount is laid off vertically, we obtain a curve of the general form shown in Figure 82. The curve is highest over the point marked *average*, and lowest over the points representing very great and very small amounts of the trait. From the high point in the center the curve drops, not abruptly, but gradually toward either end. Such distribution of a trait is known as *normal distribution*. Most psychological traits approximate normal distribution. This is illustrated by the distribution of intelligence (see p. 406) and the distribution of reading ability (see p. 424). When we use simple, unmodified categories, such as *smart* and *stupid*, we are assuming that the distribution is like that in Figure 83. Such a distribution almost never exists.

Scientific Efforts to Measure Personality

Personality is so complicated and involves so many characteristics that we can construct no personality scale comparable in accuracy to weight scales or temperature scales. Much often depends, however, upon our judgments of others and their judgments of us, and we must judge as accurately as we can. Following are brief discussions of some of the more promising, though far from perfect, methods of judging and measuring personality.

Rating scales. Rating scales are devices for making more definite and explicit the personality trait to be rated and for making the judgment more quantitative in character than it could otherwise be. If you are asked whether a certain person is generous, or honest, or ambitious, you perhaps feel the need of standards of judgment. How generous must a person be before we can call him a generous person? Even with such objective characteristics as height and weight, we feel the same need. How high must a person be before we call him a tall man? How much must he weigh before we say he is a heavy man? Standards are needed in making all such judgments. In some instances, also, we do not have a clear understanding of the traits to be judged. Hence an adequate description of the personality traits in question is also helpful.

Figure 86 shows part of a rating scale of the type in common use. This particular scale was developed by the American Council on Education. It has the merit of describing in explicit terms the kind of

Part of "The Personality Rating Scale" of the American Council on Education

Question						No opportunity to observe
How do his appearance and manner affect others?	Avoided by others	Tolerated by others	Unnoticed by others	Well liked by others	Sought by others	
Does he need constant prodding or does he go ahead with his work without being told?	Needs much prodding in doing ordinary assignments	Needs occasional prodding	Does ordinary assignments of his own accord	Completes suggested supplementary work	Seeks and sets for himself additional tasks	
Does he get others to do what he wishes?	Probably unable to lead his fellows	Satisfied to have others take lead	Sometimes leads in minor affairs	Sometimes leads in important affairs	Displays marked ability to lead his fellows; makes things go	
How does he control his emotions?	Too easily moved to anger or fits of depression, etc. / Unresponsive, apathetic	Tends to be over-emotional / Tends to be un-responsive	Usually well balanced	Well balanced	Unusual balance of responsiveness and control	
Has he a program with definite purposes in terms of which he distributes his time and energy?	Aimless trifler	Aims just to "get by"	Has vaguely formed objectives	Directs energies effectively with fairly definite program	Engrossed in realizing well-formulated objectives	

(Reprinted by permission of the Council)

Figure 86

476

behavior meant when a certain trait is to be rated. It also provides the rater with a convenient way of giving his judgment without the confusion of requiring an excessively large number of small measures.

Self-rating. Rating scales are sometimes used to learn what an individual thinks of himself. Estimates a student makes of himself are obviously of value to the educational adviser. Many people have too low an opinion of themselves — that is, they rate themselves lower than others rate them. More people, however, rate themselves higher than others rate them. This is perhaps due to the fact that, when a person rates himself, he does so on the basis of what he "knows" he could do, if he only tried, whereas others rate him on the basis of what they have seen him do (23). To a skillful counselor, the fact that one rates himself very differently from the way others rate him is of significance. A man may rate himself low in courage while others rate him high. Such differences have meaning, although their true significance is not always immediately evident. To be overmodest, to be egotistical, or to agree with the ratings of others — all these things are in themselves personality traits and, interpreted in the light of the other factors in the total situation, they throw light on personality. The unreliability of self-ratings clusters around two poles: we are quite willing to underrate ourselves on traits which we consider unimportant and, on the other hand, we find it excessively difficult to rate ourselves low on important traits. If you want to know how a person feels about the relative importance of various personality traits, study his self-ratings. A would-be colonel might rate himself low in table manners but never in courage.

Questionnaires. Closely related to the method of self-ratings is the questionnaire or inventory method which seeks to measure personality by obtaining the individual's opinion of himself (see p. 325). In its usual form the personality inventory — which is variously referred to as an inventory, a scale, a schedule, or a test — consists of a list of "yes–?–no" questions in printed form which the subject is instructed to answer by checking the *yes*, the question mark (if he cannot answer the question as yes or no), or the *no*. An example of this type of questionnaire is the inventory devised by Bernreuter which combines in a single test measures of neurotic tendency or emotional stability; of introversion-extroversion; of self-sufficiency (absence of need for companionship, encouragement, and sympathy); of dominance-submission; of confidence in oneself; and of sociability. Since this questionnaire can be answered in twenty to twenty-five minutes, can be administered as a group test, and measures a number of personality traits at once, it saves considerable time in administration. Scoring has been simplified by convenient keys. Below are some sample questions (1):

1. Does it make you uncomfortable to be "different" or unconventional?
2. Do you daydream frequently?
3. Do you find it difficult to get rid of a salesman?
4. Do you lack self-confidence?
5. Are you willing to take a chance alone in a situation of doubtful outcome?
6. Do you prefer a play to a dance?

An interesting variation of the questionnaire type of inventory is found in the Minnesota Multiphasic Personality Schedule. This test consists of a box of 550 small cards, each containing a simply worded statement to be assigned by the subject to one of three sections of the box, "true," "false," or "cannot say." The statements cover a wide variety of subjects, such as general health; sexual, religious, social, and political attitudes; affective states; phobias; and honesty. The inventory yields eleven scores, eight of which represent different phases of personality. The other three scores indicate whether or not the responses of the subject yield a valid set of scores. The eight phases of personality covered by the scale are as follows: hypochondriasis (abnormal concern about body functions), depression, hysteria, psychopathic personality (absence of deep emotional response), masculinity-femininity, paranoia (characterized by suspiciousness, oversensitivity, and delusions of persecution), psychasthenia (troubled by phobias or compulsive behavior), and schizophrenia. The scores for these characteristics are translated into comparable units and are plotted on a prepared profile chart which reveals the relative strength of the various phases and at the same time provides a personality pattern which is often more important than the score on any one phase. The schedule is designed for individuals over sixteen years of age. Sample items are given below (18):

1. I find it hard to make talk when I meet new people.
2. I do many things which I regret afterwards (I regret things more or more often than others seem to).
3. I cannot keep my mind on one thing.
4. I have numbness in one or more regions of my skin.
5. I have been told that I walk during sleep.
6. My hardest battles are with myself.
7. I am greatly bothered by forgetting where I put things.

A personality inventory devised specifically for use in the field of industrial personnel has been developed by Humm and Wadsworth. This scale, known as the Humm-Wadsworth Temperament Scale (22) is based upon the assumption that an individual's behavior tendencies or temperamental traits tend to occur in groups called components. The 318 items of the scale yield measures of seven components which are listed in Table XXV together with some associated traits.

One interesting feature of the scale is the fact that it does not call for nor expect complete honesty in answering the questions. Methods are provided in scoring for measuring and compensating for overreporting or underreporting in answering the questions. For purposes of interpretation the scores for the seven components are plotted on a profile chart. An individual's profile is then compared with typical profiles of individuals of known personality characteristics.

The Guilford-Martin Personnel Inventory (15) is another personality scale designed specifically for use in industry. The traits measured are objectivity, agreeableness, and cooperativeness. A subsequent scale, the Guilford-Martin Inventory of Factors G A M I N, measures five additional traits as follows: G, general pressure for overt activity; A, ascendancy in social situations; M, masculinity of attitudes; I, lack of inferiority; and N, lack of nervous tenseness and irritability.

Table XXV

The Components of Temperament Measured by the Humm-Wadsworth
Temperament Scale

COMPONENT	SYMBOL	CONSTITUTED OF TRAITS ASSOCIATED WITH
"Normal"	N	Self-control, self-improvement, inhibition
Hysteroid	H	Self-preservation, selfishness, crime
Manic cycloid	M	Elation, excitement, sociability
Depressive cycloid	D	Sadness, retardation, caution, worry
Autistic schizoid	A	Daydreams, shyness, sensitiveness
Paranoid schizoid	P	Fixed ideas, restiveness, conceit
Epileptoid	E	Ecstasy, meticulousness, inspiration

Questionnaires of the sort listed here yield the kind of knowledge that a trained clinical psychologist could obtain by talking at length with the person to be rated, but they yield this knowledge in far less time and with greater ease than a personal interview could do. They have the additional value of enabling the investigator to determine the significance of the answers by comparing those of one person with those of thousands of others, some of whom are known to have certain personalities, perhaps defective or perhaps especially fitted for certain types of work. In this way it can be learned how a particular person compares with others, which is frequently very important and the very essence of measurement. For example, a person may want to become a salesman, but his answers to a questionnaire may reveal that he lacks the degree of aggressiveness possessed by most of those who have succeeded as salesmen. Obviously, with this knowledge that person could choose his vocation more wisely than he could without it.

Projective techniques. The term "projective technique" is applied to any one of several methods in which personality is measured or diagnosed by analyzing a person's interpretation of, or his responses to, such materials as cloud pictures, ink blots, finger paintings, puppet shows, drawings, pictures, and music. In telling what a picture means to him or what he sees in an ink blot, or in drawing a picture, or in finger painting, an individual reveals facts regarding his feelings, habits of thinking, moods, concepts, and attitudes. In short, he projects his inner world of meanings and feelings into the materials and situations, and does so without being aware of the fact that he is revealing his personality.

The best known and most widely used of the projective techniques is the Rorschach ink blot test (35). This test owes its origin to the Swiss psychiatrist Rorschach, who made extensive use of ink blots in an attempt to classify individuals into imagery types and also to define types of insanity. An ink blot (not one of the Rorschach series) typical of those used is shown in Figure 87. The Rorschach test consists of a standard set of ten ink blots, five in various shades of gray and five partly or entirely colored, printed on cards.

The procedure of administration presented by Klopfer and Kelley (26) may be briefly described. The cards are presented to the subject in a specified order, each card in a given position. No time limit is set. Instructions are given at the same time, as follows: "People see all sorts of things in these ink blot pictures; now tell me what you see, what it might be for you, what it makes you think of." The subject is allowed to turn the card as he pleases, but not to look at it from any greater distance than his own arm's length. Any part of the instructions may be repeated. The examiner records everything the subject says in response to each card. In a second phase of the administration each card is presented to the subject a second time. The subject is questioned about where on the card the concept was seen and how it was formed. Any additional spontaneous responses are also recorded.

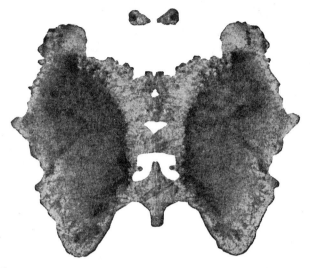

Figure 87

What Do You See in This Figure?

The scoring is in terms of the location (the area on each card which forms the basis of the concept), the qualities of the stimulus which determine the characteristics of the subject's concepts, the content of the responses, and the popularity or originality of the responses. A variety of symbols is used for scoring each of these categories. For example, the location symbols include "W" for whole blot area, "D" for large usual detail, "d" for small usual detail, "S" for space, "Dd" for unusual detail, and "dr" for rare detail. The quality symbols include "M" for movement, "F" for form, and "C" for color. The content symbols include "H" for human figures, "A" for animal figures, "Pl" for plant figures, and "At" for figures from anatomy.

The interpretation and even the scoring of a Rorschach record is a highly technical task which presupposes a very considerable amount of specialized training. According to Klopfer (25), who has described the development of Rorschach training in America, the technique of instruction of fellows of the Rorschach Institute recognizes three skills: administration, which can be acquired easily; structural interpretation, which takes from one to five years to master; and clinical diagnosis, which cannot be taught.

In general, a complete Rorschach record is supposed to reveal the interplay between various intellectual and emotional factors in the subject's personality. These factors include the degree of security or anxiety, and specific imbalances; the degree of personality maturity; creative and imaginative capacities; and a general estimate of intellectual level (26). Such mental disorders as schizophrenia and epilepsy have been diagnosed from Rorschach records, as have such conditions as feelings of inferiority, negativism, and neuroticism. For example, Miale and Harrower-Erickson (29) compared the Rorschach records of forty-three psychoneurotics with the records of twenty normal individuals of comparable intellectual and age levels. A number of Rorschach "signs," such as the number of "M" responses, the proportion of pure form responses, and the percentage of animal content responses, seemed to differentiate the two groups. The average number of such signs was 6.5 for the psychoneurotic group in contrast to an average of 1.5 for the normal group.

It has been difficult to evaluate the Rorschach technique in terms of the ordinary measures of reliability and validity because the scores of the test do not lend themselves to statistical treatment. In one study Fosberg (11) gave the Rorschach test to the same group four times with different instructions. The subjects were tested once under standard instructions, once under instructions to make the worst possible impression, once under instructions to make the best possible impression, and once under instructions to look for various things indicated by the examiner. The results seem to indicate that the same fundamental pattern obtained for all four conditions. Validity has been studied principally by the technique of "blind analysis," in which cases are diagnosed from the test records alone and these diagnoses later compared with the diagnoses based upon clinical examinations.

A modification of the Rorschach method for use as a group test has been made by Harrower-Erickson. The ink blots have been mounted on slides, and the test can be administered to a number of individuals at one time. A multiple-choice form of this group Rorschach test is now available (16).

Tests. Another method which psychologists have devised to measure personality traits is the provision of test situations. Efforts to measure by test situations such personality traits as aggressiveness, persistence, and honesty have been made. Moore and Gilliland (30) devised an interesting test for the measurement of aggressiveness. These investigators asked the students and faculty of Dartmouth to select the thirteen most aggressive and the thirteen least aggressive men among the students. The men selected were then drilled in adding numbers until they showed no further improvement. They were then given various tests.   One was the requirement of performing addition under the distraction of returning the stare of a member of the faculty without looking away; another was that of adding while expecting a painful electric shock.   The men who had been picked by their fellow students and by the faculty as aggressive were much less disturbed than the others by these distractions and were better able to control the movements of their eyes.

As another part of the test the subjects were asked to respond to six stimulus words with the first word which came to mind — a *free-association* test.   Here again there was a marked difference between the two groups.   For example, to the words *enterprise* and *success* the aggressive group responded much more frequently than the other with such words as *initiative, push, money, activity, scheme, undertake, ambition, power, gain, win, wealth,* and *advance.*   The probability of a definite, forward-looking response to *enterprise* and *success* from an aggressive person was four times as great as from an unaggressive one.   The aggressive men were also only one fourth as likely to give a negative response, such as *failure.*

When the scores on the different parts of the test were combined and the two groups compared, it was found that only two men in the least aggressive group made as high scores as the lowest score in the aggressive group.   The average score for the most aggressive group was 93, and for the least aggressive, 59.   Though this test has not yet been generally used as a measure of aggressiveness, it is a good illustration of the possibilities which this type of instrument offers.

A number of tests of honesty have been devised and used in studying children.   Some of them, containing devices to detect dishonesty, give children an opportunity to cheat, lie, and steal on the playground, in the schoolroom, and at home.   The underlying principle of several of these tests of honesty is to find out what children can do on a test without cheating, and then to note whether a particular child greatly exceeds this when given an opportunity to cheat.   If, under these conditions, a child greatly exceeds the best regular score, there is a strong probability he has cheated.   For example, one test used is a puzzle peg test, consisting of a board with thirty-three holes and a peg in every hole except the center one.   The object of the game is to jump every peg until only one is left.   This test is of such difficulty that no one of any age has been known to solve it in less than five minutes.   If, therefore, a child claims to have solved it in the five minutes allowed, it is almost certain he has cheated.

One of the most striking conclusions reported by Hartshorne and May (17) after extensive investigation is that honesty is not a single personality trait. A person cannot be said to be "honest" or "fairly honest" or "dishonest." He may be scrupulously honest in one situation and quite dishonest in another. He may not pay his monthly bills and at the same time he may be meticulous in paying his gambling debts. An executive may abhor the notion of robbing a bank while he is actually speculating with stockholders' money.

A new kind of personality test has been devised by Cattell (4). The subject is required to perform certain tasks with a pencil on lines and figures printed on a roll of paper. The paper moves beneath a small opening in the top of a box in such a way that the figures are presented one after another at a certain rate of speed. The test is designed to measure such traits as excitability, quickness of decision, restraint, and resourcefulness. The results so far obtained with this test indicate that the traits measured show low correlations with age and intelligence. The scores of psychotics are markedly different from those of normal subjects.

These tests are samples of the many facets of personality measurement. The above discussion serves only to call attention to a very important area of psychological theory and application which deserves far more consideration than can be allotted to it here. In evaluating results of this type it is important to remember, in the first place, that a trait such as aggressiveness is not a thing in itself, like white hair or web toes, but is a general name given to a *resultant* of many variables working together in certain ways. Thus, two persons who are equally aggressive may be, and often are, aggressive for diametrically opposite reasons. In the field of personality testing, identical scores hardly ever mean identical personalities, just as, in medicine, two severe stomachaches may mean quite different physiological conditions. A second caution is to guard against easy, unanalyzed judgments, which are little better than sheer name-calling. To label a child dishonest — with all the insinuations of this judgment — because he cheated on an honesty test, and to evaluate another child as honest because he did not cheat on an honesty test would be unwise. It would be equivalent to expecting adult values of a child. It would be a misleading and harmful interpretation of activity that might be quite innocent from the child's point of view. One should remind himself that a person's behavior, whether it be in a test situation or any other situation, must always be interpreted in the light of the question: What was the person really trying to do?

ADJUSTMENTS

Units of behavior in which several separate acts or responses are joined or integrated are called *adjustments* (see p. 3). An individual's adjustment to any situation, simple or complex, is the combination of his reaction to the situation. The adjustments which we make vary from relatively simple physiological responses to extremely complex activities embracing a large number of responses covering a long period of time. To remain alive we must draw from our environment sufficient food, water, and oxygen, and maintain a reasonably constant temperature. Deprived of any of these things, we die. The efforts of man to insure for himself a plentiful supply of food and water, and of clothing and shelter as means of keeping a constant body temperature have given rise to complicated economic systems.

Air is so abundant that it has no economic value, and yet the physiological adjustments a person makes to meet the need for oxygen are worthy of notice. Under ordinary circumstances, our breathing is regular and easy. But in a room where the amount of carbon dioxide is great, we unconsciously breathe more rapidly because more air must be taken in for the same amount of oxygen. The same is true when the air is rarefied, as on a high mountain. The rate of breathing is, then, a variable of the amount of available oxygen in a given volume of air. We also breathe faster when we are strenuously exerting ourselves. Exertion requires more energy; and conversion of latent energy into available forms is a process of oxidation, for which we require an adequate supply of oxygen. When oxygen itself is scarce, therefore, or when the organism needs extra oxygen for a special purpose, breathing is faster. In other words, the organism, by breathing more rapidly, adjusts itself to the changed circumstances.

Physiological adjustments of this kind are of interest to us because they show that even such simple behavior of an organism as rapid breathing is an outgrowth of the whole situation in which the behavior occurs. Given organic needs on the one hand and an ever-changing environment on the other, we see the organism always struggling to adjust its needs to the fluctuations outside itself. Thus the muscles will shiver to keep up body temperature. But there is another kind of adjustment besides the physiological. A person will quite unconsciously become involved in psychological shivering to keep up social temperature, even to the point of buying what he does not need and can ill afford. For the human being is an organism that adjusts to a threat of losing face about as surely as to a threat of losing body heat. Some adjustments are good — they *pay* as long-term "habit investments"; some are bad — they do not pay; many are between these two extremes. An adjustment good at one age or in one situation is not good at another age or in another situation. It is well to be able to report: "When I was a child, I spake as a child. . . . When I became a man, I put away childish things."

An individual does not wait, however, until he is of age to begin making adjustments. The infant that is hungry cries. Food is brought; he eats, and shortly afterwards falls asleep. He has made an adjustment. The infant cries when he is frightened. His mother picks him up, and in her arms he is reassured and soon falls asleep again. Another adjustment has been made. The happy ending of a struggle to adjust is the relief in the organism of stresses and strains — the bringing, as it were, of the organism into peace with itself and its environment.

As a person matures, he becomes less dependent on others in making adjustments. The lonely child craves companions and would be delighted to have playmates. But if these are denied, he creates for himself imaginary companions and plays contentedly with them. A boy may wish to have a bicycle, which his parents do not have the money to buy, and he adjusts the conflict by earning and saving money until he is able to buy one himself. If a man's wife complains that he is so absorbed in his work that he does not give enough time and attention to his home, he agrees to rearrange his habits.

The adjustments of politicians, though more complex, are of the same order. Different constituents make different demands. The interest of one section of the country conflicts with the interest of another. To plot a course that does justice to the conflicting demands and the conflicting interests is an adjustment of an extremely high order. It is complicated by the private need of doing also those things which will lead to reëlection, since personal defeat is a maladjustment few human beings are tough enough to contemplate. Much of the confused and exhausting action of public officers is due to the fact that they have to adjust to too many opposing factors. A politician must keep his ear to the ground and his feet on the ground at the same time. Try the adjustment and see what it looks like.

Criteria of Satisfactory Adjustments

For an adjustment to be intelligent and satisfactory, it must relieve the organism of tension without involving it in another maladjustment of equal or greater severity. Note that here there are two requirements: first, it must remove immediate tension, and second, it must not make more difficult the future attainment of fundamental needs and purposes. That some sense of satisfaction, relief, or attainment must accompany adjustment is implied by the very meaning of the word. If adjustment, which is a goal-seeking activity, takes place, pleasure accompanies our success in attaining our goal. If we remain dissatisfied, no adjustment has been made. Pleasure alone, however, does not insure a *satisfactory* adjustment. If pleasure were the only criterion, drunkards and mental patients with grandiose delusions would be regarded as making satisfactory adjustments. For an adjustment to be satisfactory, it must not make more difficult the attaining of fundamental human ends, such as development, race preservation, and social approval. *Adjustments must be evaluated in view of one's whole life as well as in view of momentary release from tension.* The crucial question to ask of an adjustment is: Does it pay, all things considered, as a permanent long-term habit investment?

As long as a process runs smoothly we pay very little attention; but when something happens to upset it, we are compelled to observe more carefully, and, as a result, we are likely to learn more about it. This is strikingly true of our adjustments. When they are made smoothly, their mechanism is not revealed; but when we fail in various ways to attain our goals, our behavior lends itself more easily to analysis. Partly for this reason we shall describe a number of maladjustments, and our account should have some guidance value since it deals with some of the more common pitfalls into which we may stumble.

Some Futile Adjustments

When a person acts in a way that makes more difficult the attaining of his fundamental ends, he makes a maladjustment. Maladjustments may accordingly be divided roughly into two classes, those that fail to provide satisfaction, and those that provide satisfaction at the cost of future good. The first class we shall call *futile adjustments*. The phrase *blind alley* aptly describes them. The second class are "spendthrift" adjustments, too costly to be satisfactory. Since they generally stunt or thwart development, we may call them *thwarting adjustments*.

In futile adjustments, the individual seeks to resolve a state of tension and disequilibrium, but instead of doing so he performs useless acts, which perhaps get him into more trouble. Like a person in quicksands, he sinks deeper with each effort to extricate himself. Thwarting adjustments, on the other hand, may resolve the original tension; instead, however, of making for the full realization of one's potentialities by providing this relief, they only make such development more difficult.

They afford a certain satisfaction, but the satisfaction is gained at the cost of social usefulness and of the great objectives that give worth and significance to life.

Bragging. Bragging is an effort to gain the favorable regard of one's fellows — perhaps by hiding some defect or by bidding for leadership. The psychologist understands the forces that produce the braggart, but the chances are excellent that the poor fellow himself understands neither his compulsion to brag nor the relative futility of such action. Instead of attaining its objective, bragging is more likely to be taken as a defect in the personality of the braggart, who not only fails to win admiration, but is probably humiliated and ridiculed into the bargain. Even if he should succeed in gaining favorable notice, the ultimate effect would be bad; for, instead of being incited to real accomplishment, he would be encouraged to substitute permanently appearances for accomplishment and thus to deceive not only others but himself as well.

Fortunately, as people mature, the tendency to brag is curbed by expansion of interests and by social pressure. The mature person identifies himself with various groups; and because of his interest and pride in the success of any group, he finds satisfaction similar to that of individual accomplishment. Group pressure tends to bring about the same result. The group does not countenance bragging about oneself, but it delights in the person who brags of the group. Bragging is further checked by a man's positive accomplishments, for the person who has proved his worth to himself and to others is not impelled to conspicuous boasting.

Teasing and cruelty. Teasing is frequently an effort to gain attention. Nothing is so unendurable as being ignored. The child who cannot get attention otherwise is sure of it if he mistreats or teases another. The child whose feelings of worth are lowered by failure or lack of appreciation in the classroom may, on the playground, seek to regain his feeling of worth by bullying. Similarly, the child neglected in the nursery may seek to gain his mother's attention by hurting his younger brother or sister. In such cases, the kind of attention received in return is not the kind sought, but at least the satisfaction is gained of being an object of some kind of attention and of showing power by arousing others to action.

The desire for mastery and power is one of our most powerful interests, and the possession of it is valuable to the adult. We should, therefore, not be too severe in our censure of teasing. It is better for a child to attempt in this way to keep up his spirit and confidence than to accept defeat and cease to struggle. Since, however, we are compelled to stand up for the child that is being mistreated, the aggressor frequently feels that his victim and the adult are in league against him. This tends to produce resentment and new acts of cruelty or teasing. Thus the child continues to cut himself off from the favorable notice and the companionship he craves. In such cases the child should be helped to find constructive ways of gaining attention. When this is done, the motive back of the teasing and cruelty finds an outlet in acts that gain not merely attention, but favorable attention. Teasing and bullying in their many forms are, to the psychologist, symptoms of deeper trouble, as sore throats and earaches are symptoms to the physician.

Timidity and bashfulness. Sometimes the desire for favorable attention produces behavior the opposite of that we have described. Just as fear may either incite to energetic action or paralyze action completely, so the desire for attention may cause a person to become unduly aggressive or unduly retiring. The excessively bashful person is apt to be egocentric (that is, concerned chiefly with self) and to have a great desire for favorable attention. Less concern over the opinion of others and more genuine interest in what he is doing would cause him to lose some of his self-consciousness and help him to act without the tormenting anxiety that others may not admire what he is doing. Excessive desire to win approval diminishes efficiency in much the same way that fear of falling makes it difficult to walk a plank fifty feet in the air which we could easily walk on the ground.

Bashfulness, perhaps more than any of the maladjustments we have so far considered, indicates a serious personality defect. The person suffering from it needs outside help. He needs to take part in social situations that merge the individual with the group. Games, which mix people rapidly, costume parties, which create a festive and carefree atmosphere, special training in graceful movement, and public appearances in which action rather than speech predominates are all helpful. Adults can help bashful children by paying less attention to them and by treating their actions and work in an objective manner. The bashful child does not need to be the center of attention. He must rather be helped to cease regarding himself as the center of things.

Pouting and temper tantrums. Children and the emotionally immature frequently pout or fly into a rage when denied what they desire. Both methods are poor adjustments. Pouting is completely ineffective; tension cannot be resolved by withdrawing from the field of action, by thinking harshly of others, or by dreaming of revenge. Such behavior is bad enough in a child; it is inexcusable in adults. It should, therefore, be nipped in the bud. Temper tantrums are habits that thrive on the success they achieve. If the child gains nothing — not even attention — by a tantrum, he will soon learn to contain himself. On the first display of rage the parent should pay no attention at all to the child. If guests happen to be present, this is difficult, but it is by far the best means of meeting the situation. If attention is *lost*, rather than gained, by a tantrum, the child will quickly eliminate this response from his repertoire of adjustments. Adults who have tantrums (and unfortunately there are still too many of them) are simply persons whose parents did not recognize this simple principle. In most of us there is still potent a large fraction of our childhood. In a sense, our maturity has not taken the place of our childhood but has been placed on top of it, and childish anger will break through the upper crust under sufficient provocation in the absence of restraining factors.

Lying. An individual may lie in order to gain the regard of others. He may misstate what he has done, or make promises that he cannot fulfill, or give false reports of others.

Delinquents avoid punishment by lying about what they have or have not done. Unfortunately, when the lie is not discovered, a satisfactory adjustment is the temporary result. But just to the extent that lying is *not* discovered, and hence becomes a fixed pattern of adjustment, the future is being built on a precarious basis. Any adjustment is poor which, to be successful, must be kept unknown to others; sooner or later the liar will be found out and the whole structure of his adjustments will be undermined. Whatever one's moral views are, there is much truth in the saying that "Honesty is the best policy." But furthermore, lying, involving as it does the violation of one's moral ideals, results in a feeling of lowered worth, no matter how successful it may be in gaining the immediate object.

The young psychologist must free himself from the childhood notion that lying is solely a matter of *saying* something that is not so. Lying uses many other instruments besides words. Lying is a special form of the more general device of deception. In the affairs of life many forms of deception are in good standing. The basis of much excellent football offense is good honest deception. For a doctor to tell the truth is under some circumstances to inflict needless pain. And not every guest need tell the truth to his week-end host. But lying and other forms of deception for most of us are usually sure signs of weakness. The world clearly tells us that if we lie, we must also take the risk of punishment. Forgery of checks is only one form of lying; many other forms can turn a free citizen into a hunted man.

Stealing. Stealing may be employed as a method of gaining the esteem of one's fellows. For example, a certain schoolboy who craved more popularity stole five dollars from his mother's purse in order to treat his playmates. The theft was detected, and the boy, instead of gaining the esteem and friendship he hoped for, was looked down on as a thief. If the theft had not been detected, he would have held his new high pitch of popularity only while his money lasted. He would probably have felt it necessary to steal again. Thus, he would have again purchased satisfaction at the cost of feeling disloyal to his mother and of violating his moral sense, and thereby he would have generated a feeling of lowered self-esteem.

Some Adjustments Which Thwart Development

Because the maladjustments so far considered do not relieve tensions or result in satisfactory adjustments on a long-time basis, we have called them futile adjustments. The maladjustments we are about to consider may succeed in relieving the particular tension, but they do so at the cost of development and future satisfaction. We have, therefore, called them *thwarting adjustments*. They are evidence of weakness or even stupidity.

Capitalizing a defect. Some people use their defects to gain sympathy and to escape the ordinary responsibilities of life. A person may avoid many disagreeable tasks and establish himself as a tyrant in a household by persistently pleading a headache. A crippled boy may cherish his weakness as a means of escaping competition with other boys in rough sports. In contrast to such weaklings are individuals who, in spite of handicaps, succeed by hard work in making themselves valuable and respected members of society. Demosthenes is said to have struggled for years to overcome a speech defect. Helen Keller, though deaf and blind, has enriched her mind far beyond the average person who suffers no handicap. In spite of blindness men have become members of the United States Senate. Crippled boys have been known to take an active part in athletics; men without arms have become good marksmen or have learned to write with their feet or mouths.

Why some people use their handicaps to escape an active life (some even create imaginary difficulties for the same purpose) while others rise above them must be explained in terms of the interaction of P and E variables. Of undoubted importance is environment. If a handicapped child is permitted to gain satisfaction by using his handicap as an excuse, we need not be surprised that he develops the art. On the other hand, if the child is stimulated to live up to the full measure of his capacity, he

experiences the satisfaction of positive achievement and learns to overcome obstacles.   The experience of success is especially important for
handicapped children, for out of such experience confidence and the will
to succeed are born and nourished.   Since handicaps are not always
insuperable, confidence and determination may win the day.   Demosthenes, a stutterer, became a famous orator.   Glenn Cunningham, whose
legs were so badly burned when he was a child that it was thought he
would be a cripple for life, became the master miler of his day.   After
all, one *can* compensate for handicaps; and on the other hand, too great
dependence on his strength often actually creates weak spots for a man.
Life is a fight to be met with courage; and if he is not abnormally stupid
or cowardly, no one who reads this book need be very sorry for himself
in the competition in which he continually has to engage with his fellows.

Rationalization, or excuse-making.   When a person makes a mistake
or acts in a manner of which he is ashamed, he may look facts in the
face, try to understand his failure, and resolve to do better in the future.
On the other hand, an individual who has made a mistake, instead of
looking at his conduct squarely in order to improve it, may attempt to
convince himself that he acted rightly.   He searches for reasons to
justify his conduct.   Since he is at once the lawyer, judge, and jury and
is exceedingly anxious to save his pride, he readily succeeds in his
search.   Having justified himself for acting as he did, he is, of course,
encouraged to make similar mistakes in the future.   Deception is always
bad; self-deception stunts one's growth and development.

It has become common to accuse others of rationalizing, or "finding
reasons," when they do not agree with us.   No doubt much that formerly
passed for logical thinking or reasoning is rationalizing.   Yet we should
hesitate a long while before accusing an antagonist of rationalization,
for so to accuse him puts an insurmountable obstacle in the path of social
thinking.   For example, if two men discuss our economic order and
one says, "You feel as you do because you are wealthy," and the other
retorts, "You condemn this order because you are poor," all possibility
of critically examining the merits of the case is at once destroyed.   A
series of personal remarks shedding no light on the economic situation
and of doubtful value as psychological analyses would be the only result.
Everyone's thought is much affected by rationalization but no one enjoys having this fact pointed out.   In fact, it is difficult even for one
determined to be honest with himself to decide just how much his
wishes and blind spots affect his reasoning.   It is far easier to detect
rationalization in another's words than in one's own thinking.   After

listening to your roommate explain the long and involved reasons why he "ought" to carry out his plan, it is easy enough to say, "Now that I have listened politely to your rationalization, tell me the *real* reasons." It is more difficult and more important to insist upon knowing the *real* reasons for one's own decisions and actions.

In abnormal psychology there is frequent use for the concept of rationalization, but even there it is profitless to accuse a person of rationalizing. Although a psychiatrist may be sure that everything his patient says is rationalization, yet, instead of attending to the arguments as such, he more wisely examines them as symptoms, to gain understanding of the patient's underlying disorder. When that is discovered, he is in a position to help the patient make a more satisfactory adjustment. For example, if he finds a man in the depths of despair, accusing himself of many sins and expressing fear of eternal damnation, and upon investigation discovers that the sufferer has been a good citizen and father, he knows that the patient is merely trying to find reasons for his state of depression. The psychiatrist needs to learn the real cause of the depression if he is to help the patient take a brighter attitude. It would be futile to show the sufferer that his statements are wrong. That would only cause him to make other statements equally wrong. The depression must be attacked at its roots. If it can be uprooted, the rationalizing will take care of itself (31).

Apathy and self-absorption. When a person has suffered defeat after defeat, he may cease trying and lose interest in his undertakings. This happens to the schoolboy who is unable to master his subjects. If a person's failures are spread in many fields, or if he feels that they are, he may develop a permanent attitude of indifference. In the end, failure in his work or profession, failure to make friends, failure in love, failure to attain physical vigor will lose their power to disturb, because he has become indifferent to everything. Such states of apathy are frequently accompanied by persistent daydreaming. In his dreams a man gains satisfaction otherwise denied. This method of relieving tension reaches a pathological extreme in schizophrenia, one of the most common of mental disorders. Overdosing oneself with daydreams, as a substitute for satisfaction and zest in real life, leads to a personality debility which renders one progressively unable to extract from the world enough interest to make the game worth the candle. Daydreams may be used sparingly when the edges of reality are too sharp; but, at best, they should be analogous to the frosting on a cake after a well-balanced meal of the roast beef, potatoes, and vegetables. It is better to play ball on the sand lot than to dream away the afternoon fancying oneself a hero of the

World Series. It is better actually to own and run a "collegiate flivver" than to dream of foreign travel in a Rolls Royce with chauffeur and footman.

So acceptable are daydreams as a psychological aspirin that they have been highly commercialized. Many moving pictures, magazines, and novels are but daydreams offered for those who are too lazy to create their own flights of fancy. It is easy to identify oneself with either the hero or the heroine and, for a time, literally lose oneself in fantasy.

Teachers and future teachers of literature may use the foregoing paragraph as a caution, lest their teaching actually harm students who are too quiet and submissive. The student who is earning a high grade by reading one "good novel" after another may be learning to feed on fantasy under the plausible rationalization that he is learning to love good literature.

Expressionism.   Children are by nature creatures of impulse. Experience, insight, and discipline are needed to convert a life of impulse into one of rational control. In few of us, perhaps, is this conversion so complete that we do not at times feel urged to throw off all restraint and to live again the life of impulse. Regression to childhood has its uses, but here again moderation is recommended. Civilization itself is still in its infancy; all of us have so much of our babyhood and childhood still in us that life is full of tension. To unbend the bow on occasion is good management. In a perfect world, perfectly mature people might require no vacations from adult duties; but at present, for most of us, vacations are psychologically wise. The old job looks good to us upon our return. Fourth of July celebrations and Christmas festivities with the children are probably even better for the parents than the children. The enormous crowds at football games show that child's play gives adults something that they need. Undue interest, however, in athletics on the part of adults, or undue absorption in young people's affairs may be symptoms of lack of development.

The fundamental defect of expressionism as an adjustment lies in the very nature of personality. Whether we will or not, the gratification of one impulse affects the gratification of others. Choices must be made. The artistry of a writer does not consist in describing everything within range. What should we think of an author who attempted to describe everything in view at a crowded beach? A person wins distinction as a descriptive writer by his choices, as well as by the handling of the selected material. Similarly in living, a person's success depends upon his choices, as well as upon his subsequent method of handling himself in the situations which he chooses for himself.

Flight into reality. When life becomes too difficult, some people, instead of withdrawing into the world of fantasy, pursue the opposite course of losing themselves in a round of activity. Those who do this find moments of reflection unbearable. They cannot endure an hour of thinking things over or an afternoon of being alone. They must be constantly "on the go." Pleasure seekers are typically of this sort. The pathological extreme of this is manic excitement, the antithesis of the self-absorption of schizophrenia, which we mentioned above. The normal person is one whose mind is occupied with the external world, but who, at the same time, is not averse to thinking matters through in the hope of deepening his understanding of himself and of the world in general. To deviate far from the normal in either direction is unhealthy. The behavior of those who complain that their engagements at clubs, dances, and committee meetings never allow them to have a quiet evening at home often shouts to an understanding psychologist that they are really running away from something or other.

In the foregoing sections we have described briefly a number of maladjustments. The reader will do well to add as many maladjustments to the list as he is able, and attempt to classify them as thwarting or futile adjustments. He will find it profitable to note how frequently, in his own life, he acts in a way that either fails to resolve the tension or does so at the price of future development. Among adjustments which usually do not pay are: gossip, some forms of nervous breakdown, "sour-graping," attempting to keep up with the Joneses (which we may call the "Jones complex"), hating, seeking revenge, and bearing grudges. These warrant the careful study of the serious student of psychology. Do not expect to understand human nature unless you understand how people make adjustments to internal tension and external difficulty.

SUMMARY

Personality may be defined as the organization of all of the characteristics manifested in one's total behavior, or in one's interactions with his environment. A personality trait is a single characteristic of one's total behavior. A personality trait exists in varying degrees from a low amount of the trait to a high amount. Separate trait names do not necessarily represent separate personality traits. A single trait may have several names. The organization of personality traits has been studied by the methods of correlation and factor analysis.

Methods of judging personality are of three general types: pseudo-scientific methods; naïve, or common-sense, methods; and scientific methods. Pseudoscientific methods include: (1) astrology, (2) phrenology, (3) physiognomy, (4) physique, and (5) graphology. The common-sense methods make use of: (1) "hunches," (2) personal interviews, (3) letters of recommendation, and (4) letters of application. Three sources of error, or pitfalls, inherent in our judgments of others are: (1) the halo effect, (2) unconscious bias, and (3) the error of the pigeonhole. Scientific methods of judging personality, which attempt to eliminate these sources of error, are: (1) the use of rating scales, (2) rating oneself, (3) the use of questionnaires, (4) projective techniques, and (5) the use of tests.

Behavior is essentially and always an adjustment, whether it be breathing or rescuing a child from a fire. Adjustments are not textbook trivialities. They are being made ceaselessly in the fundamental wants and needs of *living organisms.* Man is forever wanting, and doing something about his wants. Much of our task in studying psychology is to learn how adjustments must change from time to time, how best to make these changes, and how to avoid maladjustments. Some futile adjustments are: (1) bragging, (2) teasing and cruelty, (3) timidity and bashfulness, (4) pouting and temper tantrums, (5) lying, and (6) stealing. Some adjustments which thwart development are: (1) capitalizing a defect, (2) rationalizing, (3) self-absorption and daydreaming, (4) expressionism, and (5) flight into reality.

QUESTIONS
on the Chapter

1. What is personality and what is its relation to behavior?
2. What is the probable distribution of trait scores in the general population?
3. Describe the procedure used in studying personality organization.
4. What is a personality factor?
5. Describe astrology and evaluate it as a method of judging personality.
6. Do the same for phrenology; for physiognomy; for graphology.
7. What are Sheldon's components of bodily constitution?
8. Distinguish between visceratonia, somatotonia, and cerebrotonia.
9. How can the personal interview be improved?
10. How can letters of recommendation and letters of application be improved?
11. What are the pitfalls in judging personality?
12. What is the purpose and make-up of a rating scale?
13. What is a projective technique?
14. What facts were revealed in the investigation of honesty?
15. What is a successful adjustment?

16. What are the chief kinds of futile adjustments?
17. What are the chief kinds of thwarting adjustments?

for Discussion

1. To what extent is one's personality a matter of what other people judge it to be?
2. Is everyone either honest or dishonest?
3. Does one have to be dishonest in all of his behavior to be labeled as dishonest? Explain.
4. Why do such methods as astrology, phrenology, and physiognomy persist?
5. Does rationalizing always thwart adjustment? Explain.
6. How can one's physique affect his personality?
7. Would you place greater dependence upon one's rating of himself than on ratings by acquaintances? Why?
8. If you could use only one method of measuring personality, which one would you use? Why?

REFERENCES

1 BERNREUTER, R. G., *The Personality Inventory and Manual.* Stanford: Stanford University Press, 1931.

2 BINET, ALFRED, *Les Révélations de l'écriture d'après un contrôle scientifique.* Paris: F. Alcan, 1906.

3 BLACKFORD, M. H., and NEWCOMB, A., *The Job, the Man, and the Boss.* New York: Doubleday, Doran and Company, 1914. Reprinted by permission.

4 CATTELL, R. B., "An Objective Test of Character-Temperament: I," *J. Gener. Psychol.*, 1941, 25, 59–73.

5 CATTELL, R. B., *Description and Measurement of Personality.* New York: World Book Company, 1946.

6 CLEETON, G. U., and KNIGHT, F. B., "Validity of Character Judgments Based on External Criteria," *J. Appl. Psychol.*, 1924, 8, 215–229.

7 EVANS, ALICE L., *The Alleged Relations between the Face and the Character.* Unpublished thesis, University of Wisconsin Library, 1921.

8 EYSENCK, H. J., *Dimensions of Personality.* London: Kegan, Paul, Trench, Trubner and Company, 1947.

9 FARR, C. B., "Bodily Structure, Personality and Reaction Types," *Amer. J. Psychiatry*, 1927–28, 7, 231–244.

10 FAY, P. J., and MIDDLETON, W. C., "Judgment of Kretschmerian Body Types from the Voice as Transmitted over a Public Address System," *J. Soc. Psychol.*, 1940, 12, 151–162.

11 FOSBERG, I. A., "Rorschach Reactions under Varied Instructions," *Rorschach Res. Exch.*, 1938, 3, 12–31.

12 GUILFORD, J. P., "Personality Factors S, E, and M," *J. Psychol.*, 1936, 2, 109–127.

13 GUILFORD, J. P., "Personality Factors D, R, T, and A," *J. Abnor. Soc. Psychol.*, 1939, 34, 21–36.

14 GUILFORD, J. P., and GUILFORD, R. B., "An Analysis of the Factors in a Typical

Test of Extroversion-Introversion," *J. Abnor. Soc. Psychol.*, 1934, 28, 377–399.

15 GUILFORD, J. P., and MARTIN, H. G., *The Guilford-Martin Personnel Inventory and the Guilford-Martin Inventory of Factors GAMIN.* Beverly Hills: Sheridan Supply Company, 1943.

16 HARROWER-ERICKSON, M. R., and STEINER, M. E., *Large Scale Rorschach Techniques; A Manual for the Group Rorschach and Multiple Choice Test.* Chicago: C. C. Thomas, 1945.

17 HARTSHORNE, H., and MAY, M. A., *Studies in Deceit*, Vol. I, Book I. New York: The Macmillan Company, 1928.

18 HATHAWAY, S. R., and MCKINLEY, J. C., *The Minnesota Multiphasic Personality Inventory and Manual.* Minneapolis: University of Minnesota Press, 1942. Items quoted by permission of the publishers.

19 HOLLINGWORTH, H. L., *Vocational Psychology and Character Analysis.* New York: D. Appleton and Company, 1930.

20 HULL, CLARK L., *Aptitude Testing.* New York: World Book Company, 1928.

21 HULL, CLARK L., and MONTGOMERY, R. E., "An Experimental Investigation of Certain Alleged Relations between Character and Handwriting," *Psychol. Rev.*, 1919, 26, 63–74.

22 HUMM, D. G., and WADSWORTH, G. W., *The Humm-Wadsworth Temperament Scale, Manual of Directions, 1940 Revision.* Los Angeles: Humm-Wadsworth Personnel Service, 1940.

23 JONES, ARTHUR J., *Principles of Guidance*, 2nd edition. New York: McGraw-Hill Book Company, 1934.

24 KLINEBERG, O., ASCH, S. E., and BLOCK, H., "An Experimental Study of Constitutional Types," *Genet. Psychol. Monogr.*, 1934, 16, 141–221.

25 KLOPFER, B., "Instruction in the Rorschach Method," *J. Consult. Psychol.*, 1943, 7, 110–112.

26 KLOPFER, B., and KELLEY, D. M., *The Rorschach Technique.* New York: World Book Company, 1942. Quoted by permission of the publisher.

27 KRETSCHMER, E., *Physique and Character.* New York: Harcourt, Brace and Company, 1925.

28 MCCABE, FLORENCE E., *The Relation between Character Traits and Judgments of Character Based on Photographs.* Unpublished thesis, University of Wisconsin Library, 1926.

29 MIALE, F. R., and HARROWER-ERICKSON, M. R., "Personality Structure in the Psychoneuroses," *Rorschach Res. Exch.*, 1940, 4, 71–74.

30 MOORE, H. T., and GILLILAND, A. R., "The Measurement of Aggressiveness," *J. Appl. Psychol.*, 1921, 5, 97–118.

31 MORGAN, J. J. B., *The Psychology of Abnormal People*, 2nd edition. New York: Longmans, Green and Company, 1936.

32 MORRIS, E. H., *Personal Traits and Success in Teaching.* New York: Teachers College, Columbia University (*Contributions to Education*, No. 342).

33 PATERSON, D. G., *Physique and Intellect.* New York: The Century Company, 1930.

34 PATERSON, D. G., and LUDGATE, K. E., "Blonde and Brunette Traits: A Quantitative Study," *J. Person. Res.*, 1922, 1, 122–127.

35 RORSCHACH, H., *Psychodiagnostik*. Berne: Hans Huber, 1932.
36 SHAW, F. C., "A Morphologic Study of the Functional Psychoses," *State Hospital Quarterly*, 1924–25, 10, 413.
37 SHELDON, W. H., and others, *The Varieties of Human Physique*. New York: Harper and Brothers, 1940.
38 SHELDON, W. H., and STEVENS, S. S., *The Varieties of Temperament*. New York: Harper and Brothers, 1942.
39 SUPER, D. E., "A Comparison of the Diagnoses of a Graphologist with Results of Psychological Tests," *J. Consult. Psychol.*, 1941, 5, 127–133.
40 THORNDIKE, E. L., "A Constant Error in Psychological Ratings," *J. Appl. Psychol.*, 1920, 4, 25–29.
41 WERTHEIMER, F. I., and HESKETH, F. E., "The Significance of the Physical Constitution of Mental Disease," *Medicine*, 1926, 5, 375–451.

INDEX

INDEX